Correspondence

Theodor W. Adorno and
Siegfried Kracauer

Correspondence

1923–1966

Edited by
Wolfgang Schopf

Translated by
Susan Reynolds and Michael Winkler

polity

The translation of this work was supported by a grant from the Goethe-Institut which is funded by the German Ministry of Foreign Affairs.

GOETHE
INSTITUT

Polity Press
65 Bridge Street
Cambridge CB2 1UR, UK

Polity Press
101 Station Landing
Suite 300
Medford, MA 02155, USA

ISBN-13: 978-0-7456-4923-8

A catalogue record for this book is available from the British Library.

Typeset in 10 on 11 pt Times New Roman MT by
Servis Filmsetting Ltd, Stockport, Cheshire
Printed and bound in Great Britain by TJ International Limited

Contents

1 Kracauer to Adorno

Frankfurt am Main, 5.4.1923

Warmest greetings to your aunt and mother, and many, many thanks!

FRANKFURTER ZEITUNG
UND HANDELSBLATT.
REDAKTION
TELEGRAMM-ADRESSE
ZEITUNG FRANKFURTMAIN

FRANKFURT A.M., 5 April 1923

Please read when *alone*!

My dear Teddie, my dear friend,

I arrived at noon today, all torn up, all in a fog. Now I am going to write without delay. These past two days I have again been feeling such a tormenting love for you that it now seems to me as if I could quite simply not exist on my own. Existence had become stale for me, apart from you; I don't see how it can continue like this. I must tell you, too, that your account of your relationship with Gretel did hurt me deeply – not the fact that you were having it, but that you walked alongside me for so long without my knowing anything about it. Of course, this is not meant as a reproach – after all, discretion has its value – but the simple fact that it was so is hard to bear.

I am in a terrible state. I am so fearful about the transience of what is dearest to me – what to me is the meaning or the fulfilment of my existence. Do you believe in the everlasting nature of our friendship? It would always need to be a presence – a living presence – and yet how could that be? I tremble as I fear for its continuation. You are 19 and I am 34 – you are going your own way, you must strike out into the world – and at 19 nobody can provide any guarantees – not even you. In short, things between us are falling apart, and I am left crushed. Are you not much more resolute than I am? I am an abyss – and as insecure as a boy. I shall never be a mature man – I don't know what to do. If I were to be offered a position which was to all intents and purposes a good one, far away from here, I wouldn't accept it because I should have to get along without your presence. But you are going away! Yes – how am I ever to endure that? I should need a guarantee that the bond will last until death and that we should both continue to exist, equally great and good – until death. You tell me that you experience our relationship as profoundly as I do (in my case it is surely a sin, a burning sin, born equally of loneliness and suffering the sense of transience), you *do* say this to me – but, can it be possible? I should dearly like to believe so – sometimes it even seems like that to me, sometimes not. Believe me, you may perhaps be more sensible than I am, more grounded in yourself – that is fortunate for you – you have more stability – I am a caricature of a human being, an abyss, a gaping abyss – and if I did not have another soul to call my own, someone like you, what should I do? See, my dear, dear Teddie, I am completely serious when I say to you that philosophy and all that stuff isn't worth a damn to me compared with a *present* where loneliness is suspended and love reigns, and we find 'simplicity, stability and meaning' in our existence. For me, our state of being, transient as it is, would suffice to serve as a religion; I would ask for nothing more than for my work to emanate from our fellowship and for us to go on 'walking side by side'. Do you have this fire within you too? You *must* have it, or how could we ever be destined for each other as human beings – for it *is* destiny, is it not, that we came to know each other, sometime and somewhere? And now the terrible thing is: I don't know whether one *may* love like that. We die alone, after all, and we almost devalue the world if we love like this – one turns into no more than a helpless part. Today, and often, I feel like a part – of 'us'. And if that breaks – I shouldn't want to be forever dying and forever being born anew – it is beyond my strength. Do you understand me? Or how do you feel? Of course, you still expect more from the world than I do, and quite rightly, which is why in the end you don't need me as much as I need you. Forgive me for writing in such a state of confusion and for longing so much for us to be together, but that is how I feel in my heart – inwardly I am all at sea, the weight of the merest feather causes me to collapse, and sweeps me away – so how much more does the fear of our parting do so – the fear that you might not regard our relationship as being as exclusive and eternal as I do.

Dear Teddie – destroy this letter if at all possible, and, in any case, not a word about it – it's a secret; who would be allowed to see me so closely, as I truly am? I spoke briefly with Herrigel today; Simon is said to be back; Forell is taking his doctoral examination in a fortnight and then will probably join the Voss as a full-blown editor – a real career. Just imagine – there had arrived a card from Rosenzweig in which he expresses his pleasure at my 'fine essay'. Isn't that kind and generous of him? No sign of anything other than that. Herrigel understands the work on history, the critique of the times, the facts before principles, and finds these subjects worth writing about. Leo is in the Taunus today, and Erich with him. I am completely lost, like a child which has just had its umbilical cord snipped off. What am I going to do in life? Are you my friend? Oh, I could weep, Teddie – I have wept very often; the rift running through the world is also running through me – especially through me. I shall write something for your aunt – perhaps in the form of a dialogue following on from the end of *Das Lied von der Erde*.

Farewell, Teddie, my dear Teddie,
Friedel

Nobody is to see this letter – be careful, Teddie. You are 19 – I am 34 – may it work out, after all?

Original: manuscript with printed letterhead; Theodor W. Adorno Archiv, Frankfurt am Main.

aunt: Agathe Calvelli-Adorno (1868–1935), singer and pianist, living with Adorno's family in Frankfurt am Main.

mother: Maria Wiesengrund, née Calvelli-Adorno (1864–1952), singer, married to Oscar Wiesengrund (1870–1946) from 1898.

I arrived at noon today: Kracauer returned to Frankfurt am Main on 5 April 1923 after meeting Adorno in Amorbach the previous day on the way back from Nuremberg (see *Marbacher Magazin* 47, p. 39).

account of your relationship with Gretel: probably Margarete ('Gretel') Karplus (1902–1993), chemist and physicist, married to Adorno from 1937. Kracauer returns to the constellation described in the letter in a scene in his novel *Georg*: the eponymous protagonist travels with his friend 'Fred' (also known as 'Freddie') to the Black Forest, where one night the former makes a confession to him about his relationship with a woman named Margot (see Kracauer, W 7, pp. 348–59, esp. p. 358).

'*simplicity, stability and meaning*': 'and everything, even scientific effort, possesses simplicity, stability and meaning' (see Adalbert Stifter, *Der Nachsommer*, trans. Wendell Frye. New York, Peter Lang, 1985); Kracauer is quoting the final words of the novel.

'*walking side by side*': the letter inaccurately quotes from the final line ('noch ein rundgang zu zwein') of a poem by Stefan George, 'Es lacht in dem steigenden jahr dir'; third verse: 'So let us conceal what we miss, then, / And vow to be happy again, / Though no more be granted but this, then: / A round to be gone by us twain': Stefan George, *Poems*, trans. Carol North Valhope and Ernst Morwitz. London, Kegan Paul, 1944. Adorno composed a setting of this poem (see *Vier Gedichte von Stefan George für Singstimme und Klavier*, op. 1, in Adorno, *Kompositionen* 1, pp. 8–23, esp. 19–23); an early edition of compositions to words by George was dedicated to Kracauer (Theodor W. Adorno Archiv). Adorno, for his part, used a quotation from the poem to sum up Kracauer's character in 1964 (see letter no. 250).

Herrigel: Hermann Herrigel (1888–1973), journalist and philosopher, from 1912 archivist and editor of the *Frankfurter Zeitung*; he had been known to Kracauer, who joined the editorial team in 1921, since 1920 (see *Marbacher Magazin* 47, p. 34).

Ernst Simon: Ernst Simon (1899–1988), teacher of German and history, working for the Freies Jüdisches Lehrhaus in Frankfurt am Main; emigrated to Palestine in 1928; from 1935 professor of pedagogics at the University of Jerusalem.

Forell: Siegmund Forell (1896–1972) studied law from 1919 to 1922 at the Johann Wolfgang Goethe-Universität; there is no record there of his having gained a doctorate, and his dissertation has not survived. Kracauer had previously mentioned his 'friend Forell' in a letter of 30 June 1921 to Gottfried Salomon-Delatour (Internationaal Instituut voor Sociale Geschiedenis, Amsterdam); he was on the staff of the *Frankfurter Zeitung*, with responsibility for regional economic questions, before joining the city magistrates' press office for Frankfurt am Main. He was dismissed in 1933 and presumably went into exile in Australia in the late 1930s.

a card from Rosenzweig: Franz Rosenzweig (1886–1929), theologian and philosopher, co-founder of the Freies Jüdisches Lehrhaus in Frankfurt am Main.

Rosenzweig's undated postcard is postmarked 31 March 1923; he wrote: 'I should not wish to omit to express my pleasure to you at the fine essay in today's F.Z.' (Kracauer archive, Deutsches Literaturarchiv, Marbach). It refers to 'Das zeugende Gespräch' [the generative conversation] in *Frankfurter Zeitung*, 30 March 1923 (see Kracauer, W 5, no. 121).

work on history: In a letter to Leo Löwenthal of 1 March 1922, Kracauer had mentioned plans for a piece of work 'against constructions relating to the philosophy of history' (see Kracauer/Löwenthal, *Briefwechsel*, p. 38); the 'work on history' which he mentions is not preserved among Kracauer's papers.

Leo: Leo Löwenthal (1900–1993), friends with Adorno and Kracauer; completed his dissertation in 1923 at the Johann Wolfgang Goethe-Universität on 'Franz von Baader's philosophy of society: examples and problems of a religious philosophy'. Three letters from this year written jointly by Adorno and Kracauer to Löwenthal survive (see Kracauer/Löwenthal, *Briefwechsel*, letters no. 11, 12, 14).

in the Taunus: Kracauer's family also appreciated the restorative qualities of the central mountains to the north of Frankfurt am Main: his uncle, the teacher and historiographer of the Jews in Frankfurt Isidor Kracauer (1853–1923), published the brochure *Feldbergtouren in älterer und neuerer Zeit* [Mountain rambles, then and now] in 1912.

Erich: Erich Fromm (1900–1980) was, like Leo Löwenthal and Ernst Simon, one of Kracauer's friends from the Freies Jüdisches Lehrhaus circle.

the rift running through the world is also running through me: Kracauer is paraphrasing Heinrich Heine: 'Ah, dear reader – if you are disposed to complain about this state of laceration, you should rather lament the fact that the world itself is torn apart down the middle. For as the poet's heart is the centre of the world, it cannot help being terribly lacerated at the present time. Whoever boasts that his heart has remained whole merely admits that he has a hole-and-corner, prosaic kind of heart, remote from everything. But the great rift in the world tore through my heart, and precisely for this reason I know that the great gods have favoured me highly above many others and considered me worthy of a poet's martyrdom.' (See Heinrich Heine, *Reisebilder* III, 'Die Bäder von Lucca', chap. V, in his *Sämtliche Schriften* 2, ed. Klaus Briegleb. Munich: Carl Hanser, 1976, p. 405f.)

I shall write something for your aunt: not preserved among Adorno and Kracauer's papers.

Das Lied von der Erde: This composition by Gustav Mahler (1860–1911), shifting between a symphony and an orchestral song cycle, received its first performance under Bruno Walter six months after Mahler's death. In the sixth and last movement, 'Der Abschied' [Farewell], we read: 'I stand here waiting for my friend; I wait to bid him a last farewell. I long to enjoy the beauty of this evening by your side, my friend. Where do you linger? You have left me alone so long! [If only you would come! Oh, if only you would come, my faithless friend!]' He dismounted and proffered him the cup in token of farewell. He asked where he was going and why it had to be. He said, and his voice trembled: 'O my friend, in this world fortune did not smile on me. Where am I going? I go into the mountains. I seek peace for my lonely heart. I am making for home, for my resting-place. I will never roam into strange lands. My heart is still and bides its time. Everywhere the dear earth blossoms in spring and grows green again. Everywhere, for ever, the distant horizon shines blue and bright. Ever, ever, ever, ever, ever, ever, ever.' (*The Penguin Book of Lieder*, ed. and trans. S. S. Prawer. Harmondsworth: Penguin, 1964, pp. 149–150)

2 Kracauer to Adorno

Frankfurt am Main, 22.9.1924

FRANKFURTER ZEITUNG
UND HANDELSBLATT.
REDAKTION
TELEGRAMM-ADRESSE
ZEITUNG FRANKFURTMAIN

FRANKFURT A. M.,
22 September 1924

My dear Teddie,

Last evening, I took another letter to you to the Munich train, which I would have liked to board again, and this morning there comes a letter from you – of a threatening nature. So Lila wrote to you, saying that you should write to me? And you are afraid that I discussed our relationship with her? And she – or so you imply – feels herself called upon to 'mediate' between us? Teddie, child, how excessive you too are at bottom, and how false are the superficial appearances of our true and essential natures! I naturally told Lila when I saw her the last time that I had not yet had a letter from you, and of course not everything that relates to us could remain unspoken, as talking about you was the main point of our spending time together. I hope that I don't have to assure you that the crucial aspects – spiritual as well as empirical – remained unmentioned; and Lila is as blameless as I am, and I shall emphatically take her under my protection to defend her against your accusation. She probably only gave you the advice because she feels – and how could she do otherwise? – that I am bound to you with every fibre, and she simply feels in herself a vocation for bearing others' suffering – both yours and mine. This is not overstepping the mark as far as she is concerned, and much less is it an improper intrusion into our relationship – what a fantastically unjust assumption on your part! It is a trait in her nature which she is following, and you – yes, you of all people, who wants to be assured that the boundaries of your way of existing are treated with respect – have no right to misjudge the very different nature of someone who loves you, as you are now doing in calling something crude tactlessness and human brutishness which is the expression of a genuine and unquestionable sentiment (though the form of expression may not seem wholly appropriate to you). That awareness of a limit which you call for in relation to yourself, please apply it in this case too, and offer the same trust which you yourself demand instead of reacting, all by yourself, with indignation when some remark or other seems to you to be questionable. No, Teddie, I have no intention of rebuking Lila, and I think that this means acting more in your sense than you do by flaring up. Leave outrage to the outraged. And as for you – try to be a little more understanding and affectionate and love as you would be loved.

However, the actual reason for your excitation is that you feel abandoned because of my alleged indiscretions. Is this the trust that you demand for yourself? Even assuming that I had said more about us than I could have answered for (which I did not) – even then, it would not have been admissible for you to fall into a frenzy of reproaches and register a vote of no confidence against me. Even then you should still have been mindful of the differences in our natures, and first should have attempted to derive from them the possibility that I could perhaps, while speaking, be here, without, however, abandoning you. You may take issue with me on specific points, but not readily in a general sense. For the sake of our love I am compelled to understand you, but please don't set yourself up as a judge without taking me into account. But, as I have already said, all this is immaterial; I was not upset by your silence, and Lila has committed no offence against you – against *us*. Don't write anything foolish to her, and – believe me – I am entitled to demand that of you. I beg you to do so.

In addition, if you think that I am only consoling Lila, you are mistaken; Kilia, whose soul-mate (soon, we hope, to be her husband) is away just now, has also chosen me as a comforter in her loneliness. I fulfil the vocation of a *soter* [Greek: 'saviour'] only with an *inner* inclination, and in my few hours of leisure I eye up the prostitutes in the Kaiserstrasse, contemplating acts of my own with which I am just toying.

I know nothing about your mother's indisposition. I visited her immediately after my return and speak to her on the phone quite frequently. We shall probably see each other this week. I shall write to Agathe.

On 1 October I may be with the sociologists in Heidelberg. It will be splendid when we are together.

Please have my letter of yesterday sent on from the Hotel Helvetia, Florence. The final sentence has been confusing, I think (because of tiredness); it ought to read: You are the only person to whom I am afraid to confess my love – or something like that.

Benjamin, from whom I had a card, sends warmest greetings to you.

It is very bad that you can only write to me secretly and not at such length as you would like. After all, we are not having a relationship.

So, Teddie, you too must have faith. Yours, Friedel.

Original: manuscript with printed letterhead; Theodor W. Adorno Archiv, Frankfurt am Main.

another letter: neither of these survives.

Munich train: Munich was one of the stops on the journey to the Dolomites which Kracauer and Adorno began on 28 July 1924 after the end of the latter's defence of his doctoral thesis on 'The transcendence of the objective and noematic in Husserl's phenomenology' (see Adorno, GS 1, pp. 7–77). The last stop was Lake Garda, from which Kracauer began the return journey to Frankfurt am Main alone on 5 September 1924 (see Adorno, *Bildmonographie*, p. 82). He converted his travel impressions into feuilletons: 'Aus den Grödner Dolomiten', *Frankfurter Zeitung*, 31 August 1924 (see Kracauer, W 5, no. 202); 'Empfang in den Dolomiten', *Frankfurter Zeitung*, 11 September 1924 (see Kracauer, W 5, no. 203); 'Station', *Frankfurter Zeitung*, 14 September 1924 (see Kracauer, W 5, no. 205); 'Jenseits des Brenners', *Frankfurter Zeitung*, 10 September 1924 (see Kracauer, W 5, no. 207).

Lila wrote to you: a woman named Lila is repeatedly mentioned in letters from the Viennese period; this probably refers to the journalist and author Lili Körber (1897–1982). Indications suggesting this include a copy in Adorno's library of Franz Werfel's *Der Weltfreund: Erste Gedichte (1908–1910)* bearing the handwritten dedication 'For Teddie from Lila; 18 Nov. 1924, before the examination'. Körber concluded her studies at the Johann Wolfgang Goethe-Universität in February 1925 with a dissertation on 'The Lyric Poetry of Franz Werfel'; she then moved to Vienna (see Lili Körber, 'Meine Biographie', typescript, Lili Körber papers, Deutsches Exilarchiv Frankfurt am Main). A comparison of the dedication with her handwritten curriculum vitae of 27 January 1925 (in Ute Lemke, *Lili Körber: Von Moskau nach Wien: Eine österreichische Autorin in den Wirren der Zeit, 1915–1938*, Siegen: Carl Böschen, 1999, p. 191) shows distinct similarities. The letter from Kracauer to Adorno which the latter mentions has not survived.

Kilia … her husband: MS difficult to decipher; nothing further is known about the individuals mentioned here.

I shall write to Agathe: not preserved.

sociologists in Heidelberg: Kracauer reported on the fourth Deutsche Soziologentag congress which was held in Heidelberg on 28–30 September in the *Frankfurter Zeitung*, 3 October 1924 (see Kracauer, W 5, no. 211); the conference focused on social policy and social structures.

Benjamin, from whom I had a card: the card from Walter Benjamin (1892–1940) has not survived.

my letter of yesterday: after Kracauer's return home, Adorno continued his stay in Italy until the end of September 1924 in the company of his aunt Agathe Calvelli-Adorno.

3 Adorno to Kracauer

[Frankfurt am Main, probably 27.9.1924]

Saturday afternoon

Dear Friedel,

It seems that we have had a misunderstanding: because I had things to do at the university I could not go back to the transcript then, but only this morning – and so I can only now return the manuscript to you (which, by the way, has only gained in transcription).

It is not good that we shall not be seeing each other for another two days – and the very days on which I should have had most time.

I wish you plenty of sensational experiences in Heidelberg, and Professor Gundolf a certain degree of enlightenment.

This evening I am at Herr Sekles', and in the afternoon I am going in search of a room, which will take me deep into the Cameroon district.

Original: manuscript; Siegfried Kracauer papers, Deutsches Literaturarchiv, Marbach am Neckar; date and place conjectural, based on the possible context suggested by the notes.

the manuscript: not preserved.

Heidelberg: a reference to Kracauer's visit to the fourth Deutsche Soziologentag (29–30 September 1924 (see the preceding letter); these dates fell on a Monday and Tuesday.

Professor Gundolf a certain degree of enlightenment: Friedrich Gundolf, born Gundelfinger (1880–1931), literary scholar, member of the Stefan George circle, and from 1920 a professor at the University of Heidelberg. Adorno gives specific details of his aversion later, among others in his *Jargon der Eigentlichkeit*: 'Neo-romantic poets who drank their fill of the precious, like George and Hofmannsthal, by no means wrote their prose in the jargon. However, some of their intermediaries – like Gundolf – did so. Their words become terms of the jargon only through the constellation that they negate, through each one's gesture of uniqueness. The degree of magic that the singular word has lost is being provided nonetheless as if by dictated measures, as a directive. [It is a secondary magic, one that is delivered ready from the factory, a transcendence which is a changeling said to be the lost original.]' See *The Jargon of Authenticity*, trans. Knut Tarnowski and Frederic Will (London: Routledge & Kegan Paul, 1973), p. 7.

Sekles: The composer Bernhard Sekles (1872–1934) taught composition from 1896 to 1933 at Dr Hoch's Conservatory in Frankfurt am Main; Adorno took private lessons from him from 1919 to 1924/5.

in search of a room: possibly Adorno's attempt to escape from the parental home on attaining his majority on 11 September 1924; no evidence survives for his renting a room.

Cameroon district: 'Kamerun' was a colloquial name for the Gallus district of Frankfurt, where reasonably priced lodgings could be found on account of the fumes and coal dust from local industry.

4 Adorno to Kracauer
Vienna, 8.3.1925

8 March 1925 Vienna IX, Eisengasse 2, Pension Luisenheim.

My dear Friedel,

I am writing to you only today because the days up to now have been too chaotic for me to have been able to say anything to you that would make sense, and even now I am not writing you a proper letter but just want to give you some kind of sign so that you will see how things stand with us – if you will believe me. The main thing is: I consider it *out of the question* for Vienna to maintain any lasting hold on me, let alone that any person or business here could ever keep me away from you. Not so much because I was feeling unhappy in Vienna; on the contrary, I am relatively well-off here. I am in comfortable lodgings, believe that I will be able to work profitably, have been cordially welcomed by the friendly people, and even admit the necessity of staying here for educational purposes – but the reason for staying goes no further than that educational necessity. I feel wholly typical as a young man who must see something of the world and provide for himself; however, the various levels of my nature are not substantially affected by this but remain enclosed in their obstinate privacy. Everything that I see and experience happens to me as if a long way away, and remains curiously unreal. The city and its people seem to me like an imaginary province invented to demonstrate the questionable nature of a purely aesthetic attitude more vividly than a description by an aesthetic person might. Vienna is more Kraus-like than Kraus, more Schnitzler-like than Schnitzler – an astronomically exaggerated Seldwyla whose culture – already worth questioning – has now been cast into a barbarous civilization. With hindsight I must wholly accept your pronouncement on Kraus: he understands himself only in terms of polemics against this milieu and is diminished by that very milieu. More irritating to me was the realization that something similar is also going on here around Schoenberg. Berg is indeed a proper human being, a true heir through and through, and of a naivety which borders on greatness – but a bitterness going back over decades (he has shared Schoenberg's existence for over twenty years, experienced all the attacks with him, and seems to be spiritually dependent on him) has narrowed his horizons to polemics; everything to do with Schoenberg is sacred. Otherwise, of his contemporaries only Mahler is of any account; anyone who opposes him is crushed – in short, he constitutes a 'circle' in the true conclusive George sense, and one cannot challenge the basis of all this because he himself adopts an absolutist stance. However, I had the pleasure of discovering that Berg understood my pieces at once; he acknowledged my talents and skill and (I played him things from the most diverse periods) noted an unusually serious and intense process of development, even harbouring doubts as to whether I could continue this development at such a pace along those same lines. So at last I have both a response to and a criticism of my music; admittedly, Berg left me in no doubt that I now have to learn everything decisive from myself. But he is too rigidly fixed, located somewhere between Mahler, Kokoschka, Webern and Schoenberg, for any complete rapport to be possible – especially as the way in which his purblind certainty expresses itself actually repels me as a human being. Anyway, he knows Kraus and has written a polemic against Pfitzner *in modo Krausico* (with stylistic analysis!) which is the most striking and intellectually brilliant work that I know of in the whole realm of music. I shall see about getting it sent to you – the only thing is that there is rather too much specialist musical knowledge in it.

Otherwise, the people here are: a curious woman, a Viennese super-Bobi, with whom I travelled here; Willi Zahn, a friend of Lila's, the son of Ernst Zahn, a bookseller à la Niederlechner and in addition a drinker à la Dostoevsky, a despairing, albeit profound man of refined nuances who communicates with such difficulty that one cannot get to know him – the subtle facets are entirely lacking; then Frau von Dolnay, 50, a Hungarian, very lachrymose but very cultured, living in the boarding-house, who acts like a mother to me; her only son, a communist, is a close friend of Lukács, who is said to be lurking somewhere in Berlin at present; it is said that he only carries on philosophical discussions with young people. I am going to meet the son, and probably Lukács too, perhaps through Balabanova, about whom the Russians here are talking a lot: she is a friend of Lenin and was in charge of the 'Avanti' for many years. But I am not in any hurry and am not bothered about anything; at present I am far away though actually living in the present, and for the last six months have been feeling like a general pause with a fermata on top of it. That is *true*, not just meant as consolation. See? Do you understand?! So, faithfulness is not an empty delusion, 'so let me appear, until I shall be …' coming back to Frankfurt

as yours alone – Teddie.

Original: MS, Siegfried Kracauer papers, Deutsches Literaturarchiv, Marbach am Neckar. Handwritten note by Kracauer: '1. Brief von T. aus Wien; beantwortet 13. März' ['First letter from T. from Vienna; answered on 13 March']; the reply has not been preserved.

Eisengasse: now Wilhelm-Exner-Gasse (see Heinz Steinert, *Adorno in Wien*, Vienna: Verlag für Gesellschaftskritik, 1989, p. 15).

writing to you only today because the days up to now have been too chaotic: Adorno wrote this letter three days after his arrival in Vienna, on 5 March 1925 (see Adorno/Berg, *Correspondence*, p. 5).

Schnitzler: Arthur Schnitzler (1862–1931); the novelist, dramatist and lyric poet was born and died in Vienna.

Seldwyla: Seldwyla means, in the language of former times, a blissful, sunny place – and, indeed, that is just what the little town of that name, somewhere in Switzerland, is. It is still tucked away among the same encircling walls and towers as it was three hundred years ago, and so it is still the same provincial backwater. (See Gottfried Keller, *Die Leute von Seldwyla*, ed. Thomas Böning, Frankfurt am Main: Deutscher Klassiker Verlag, 1989, p. 11.)

your pronouncement on Kraus: not preserved in a review or anywhere else.

with Schoenberg: Adorno describes his problems with the circle around Arnold Schoenberg in a letter to Alban Berg of 23 November 1925: 'Attempt to draw a clear line between the work and Schönberg, in a manner to which Schönberg himself must consent; namely by deducing the impossibility of forming a "school" from his own stance (my aim: this prattling on about the "Schönberg pupil" must stop)' (*Correspondence*, p. 28).

Berg is indeed a proper human being: Adorno in his 'Memoir' of the composer Alban Berg (1885–1935): 'I made his acquaintance at the festival of the Allgemeine Deutsche Musikverein in Frankfurt in 1924, in spring or early summer, on the evening of the première of the *Three Fragments from Wozzeck*. Captivated by this work, I asked Scherchen, with whom I was in touch, to introduce me to Berg. In a few minutes it was agreed that I should come to Vienna as his pupil; I had to wait for my graduation in July. The move to Vienna dragged on until the beginning of January 1925. My first impression of Berg, on that occasion in Frankfurt, was one of the greatest kindness, but also of his shyness, which in its turn dispelled the anxiety which this man whom I admired immensely would otherwise have aroused in me.' See Adorno, GS 13, p. 340.

A polemic against Pfitzner: Hans Pfitzner (1869–1949), composer and conductor; Berg's 'polemic': 'The Musical Impotence of the "New Aesthetic" of Hans Pfitzner', in Willi Reich, *Alban Berg: Leben und Werk* (Munich: Piper 1985), pp. 194–206.

Bobi: also Bobbi, nickname of Maria Proelss (1892–1962), pianist, founder of the Frankfurter Kammermusikgemeinde (see Adorno's obituary of her, Adorno, GS 19, pp. 465–7).

bookseller à la Niederlechner: not attested in Vienna; possibly Emil Niederlechner, originally from southern Germany, who in 1922 took over his wife's parents' bookshop in Fehmarn; however, to date only journeys by the Wiesengrund family to Sylt and Rügen have been recorded.

Willi Zahn: (1899–?); no further information is available about the son of Ernst Zahn.

Ernst Zahn: (1867–1952), an author from Zurich, previously a restaurateur and local politician.

Frau von Dolnay: Adorno wrote 'Dolnay', but the information about her son which follows confirms that this refers to Anna von Tolnay (no dates available).

a son … friend of Lukács: Karl von Tolnay (1899–1981), known after emigrating as Charles de Tolnay, an art historian from Budapest, where he was a member of Georg Lukács's circle. From 1929 to 1933 he was a lecturer at the University of Hamburg; then an exile in France and from 1939 in the USA.

Balabanova: Angelica Balabanova (1878–1965), Russian revolutionary. In the early 1920s she distanced herself from the Bolsheviks and emigrated to Vienna, fled to Paris from the National Socialists, and went into exile in the USA.

Avanti: the journal of the Partito Socialista Italiano which appeared from 1896 to 1993.

companion of Lenin: Angelica Balabanoff (this is the spelling of the author's name) knew Lenin (1870–1924) 'at first hand' (according to the blurb) from his period of exile in Switzerland – to such an extent that she recorded her experiences in *Lenin: Psychologische Beobachtungen und Betrachtungen* [Lenin: psychological observations and reflections] (Hanover: Verlag für Literatur und Zeitgeschehen, 1961).

faithfulness: 'Und die Treue, sie ist doch kein leerer Wahn' ['Yet faithfulness is no empty delusion']; see Friedrich Schiller, 'Die Bürgschaft', in *Gedichte*, ed. Georg Kurscheidt (Frankfurt am Main: Deutscher Klassiker Verlag, 1992), p. 30.

So let me appear...: 'Let me appear an angel till I become one! / Do not take my white robe from me. / I am hurrying from the lovely earth / to the solid dwelling you know of.' Mignon's song, first verse, from Goethe's *Wilhelm Meisters Lehrjahre*; the song was set to music by Franz Schubert. See *The Penguin Book of Lieder*, ed. and trans. S. S. Prawer (Harmondsworth: Penguin, 1974), p. 115.

5 Adorno to Kracauer

Vienna, 14.3.1925

Vienna IX, Eisengasse 2, Pension Luisenheim
14 March 1925.

My dear Friedel,

If, in Bloch's words, the one who leaves is like an arrow and the one who stays behind like an egg, it follows, neo-logically, that *you* must have left, for indeed your letter is more like a sharpened arrow than mine, shot from the stretched bow by irony and its tip poisoned with the toxin, so to speak, of definitive hopelessness, unless one impolitely and deliberately overlooks the metaphysical determinacy of that irony and feels as if one had simply been pelted with rotten eggs, which might just about restore the relationship that I originally expected. I don't mean that that was exactly what happened to me, especially since I groped my way through the layers of irony and penetrated to the basic tenderness underlying it; but I didn't feel happy on reading this letter – not happy about what it contained, and still less so about what it failed to say. To take the first point first and attempt an apology: the reproach of excessive haste, which you are constantly levelling at me – overtly, covertly and masochistically – makes no sense to me. The astoundingly sure judgement for which you so punitively blame me, as if you had just read the *Wanderjahre* and wanted to drum the category of tact into me (that category, indeed!), is not some dubious merit of mine, but the essence of Viennese life assails one with such monstrous and yet grim vehemence, everywhere, every step of the way, that while registering the *soi-disant* facts one falls, through no fault of one's own, into the attitude of the paraenetic, while in reality it is nothing but the facts themselves – and the louder these speak, the less they can be called facts. If I, being more obliging than Else (the Hamburg one, not the Viennese), were prepared to concede this point either to you or to myself, and let myself become a mouthpiece for these facts, you would certainly attribute this willingness to my creative imagination, for which Vienna can never be Viennese enough, although it is even more Viennese than that. I also have the liveliest doubts as to whether you would adopt a very different attitude in my situation and not add something of your own. However, your correction was not aimed at Vienna in itself, which you might have wanted to protect from my subjectivistic distortion. Rather, you feared that my vehement and, in your eyes, frosty rejection of this city, which Berg alleges is nothing more nor less than a printer's error – that my rejection of this printer's error was based on illusion, that I had had no experiences here – not even of myself, as yet – and was at present heartily cursing Vienna to comfort you, to reassure you, and to make the phenomenon of absence as innocuous as possible. *N'est-ce pas*? Your letter betrays a deep mistrust: you believe that I am lost and interpret every remark I make to you as a sentimental masquerade. Even the tone of wisdom, in which only the uncertainty with which it constantly teeters between the old Goethe and Polonius affords me any pleasure, is part of this (apart from the deliberate accentuations!). Or do you think – so far away and all too near – I would not have noticed the reproach, couched in such masculine terms, in the introductory words: 'I hardly expected news from you any earlier, as I believed to some degree (!) that you would have preferred to write something that made sense' (! a polemical quotation from my letter!). In the background there are those Gröden disjunctions which forget, in communication by letter, how false they are. O Friedelein, o Friedelein, how green they are, your branches!

For I really don't feel at home here; I really am full of longing, and I was quite serious in what I said about the *grande pause*. It isn't external things that depress me; I have settled in well here, found my bearings, and am in good accommodation, so good that I should like to find some way of staying in the boarding-house permanently. But the atmosphere – I don't want to say any more to you about it just now, because you simply wouldn't believe me! I am still getting on very well with Berg; yesterday I went with him to a workers' concert which Webern was conducting – he conducted excellently, with a grim fanaticism that I know of in no other conductor, and with incredible musicality. Schoenberg was also there; it was the first time that I saw him, but I didn't speak to him; he does indeed have a powerful countenance. Today I am going with Berg to Universal Edition for a rehearsal by the Kolisch Quartet; they are playing Rathaus, Szymanowski, Casella and Wellesz, so we shall be among friends, though not in the best company. As for the other people whom I have seen: Lila's parents, the mother very pleasant, the father quite meshuggah; Frau Berg, an archetypal eccentric – beautiful, an intimate friend of Alma Mahler, from whom she had just had a card from Jerusalem; her Kokoschka legends alone could fill volumes. On Monday my travelling companion invited me to a nightclub where she was a habituée; she is very witty but goes around with two revolvers and cocaine, something which naturally arouses concern. I am still not quite sure whether she is a literary lady, the madam of a brothel, or simply has a talent for hysterics – perhaps a synthesis. Anyway, she claims to be married and to go by the name of Lu.

My life goes something like this: I get up at eight or eight-thirty and spend the morning composing, work on my trio, whose first movement is developing slowly but well, and on a difficult set of variations for string quartet, something like a school exercise for Berg, which, however, I can shape to my own liking (I no longer have to write tonally, as I did with Herr Sekles). The afternoon is for other things; first and foremost, I have polished off all the outstanding discussions of scores – a longish essay on the Bartók pieces, one on the folksongs which Holl gave me, and a little one on a trio by Jemnitz. Now I am sticking with Bloch, and also find time to compose in the afternoons. I spend the evenings with Lila and read Kierkegaard with her; at least I don't get bored doing this, whereas there are plenty of opportunities to do so in other ways. Yesterday we went out to Schönbrunn, which is on the way to Hi[e]tzing (to Berg). I drink lots of coffee with whipped cream and study the creations of the expert Viennese confectioners.

Why are you writing nothing about yourself? I know that you scorn to discuss your intellectual projects in letters, but there are other things of a Marianne-like nature which find their way even to Vienna in the local newspaper; a new way of life (Parisian, I hope), new cafés, new ways of being bored – new people too, perhaps? You will see Walter [Benjamin] with mixed feelings; I expect, too, that you will be going to Kronberg; give the people there my best wishes. Leo, too, will make the most of my absence and have the opportunity to carry the holy flame (of the apocalypse) in the church candelabra through the corridors of the F.Z., which is his transcendental location; I shall write to him. Even Salomon would be glad of a telephone call from you. Are you still implacable as regards your aunt? Or are you back on good terms again? *Tant pis pour moi.* I am not Papa Krull, but I do speak a lot of French. Ah, well.

I didn't care for Fred's essay; he is pretty enough when he is being playful, but when he tries to make some positive pronouncement he becomes crassly banal. How can one *continually* go on speaking of 'exemplariness'? I am always open to enlightenment. Teddie.

Original: MS; Siegfried Kracauer papers, Deutsches Literaturarchiv, Marbach am Neckar. Handwritten note by Kracauer: '2. Brief. Beantwortet 17.–18. März.' ['Second letter. Answered on 17–18 March.'] The reply has not been preserved.

in Bloch's words, the one who leaves is like an arrow and the one who stays behind like an egg: this motif from Ernst Bloch (1885–1977), compressed by Adorno, comes from the essay 'Eine hellere Symbolintention' [A clearer symbolic idea], in *Der neue Merkur*, 1921/2. Bloch included it under the title 'Kleine Ausfahrt' [A little excursion] in *Spuren*, published in 1930: 'Already the obvious inability of all human beings, including the friendliest and inwardly richest persons, to converse from the car down to the platform on leaving, or the other way around, is due to the fact that the one staying back looks like an egg, the one leaving on the other hand like an arrow; that both already inhabit different spaces.' (See *Traces*, trans. Anthony A. Nassar. Stanford, CA: Stanford University Press, 2006, p. 99.)

Wanderjahre … the category of tact: 'Here we have to be tactful, otherwise we are in danger of losing quite unexpectedly the goodwill we may already have gained from people. This is something we take for granted as life goes on, but not until we have paid dearly for the experience; unfortunately, we cannot pay in advance on behalf of our successors.' See Goethe, *Wilhelm Meister*, trans. H. M. Waidson. Richmond, Surrey: Alma Classics, 2013, p. 695.

Else: Probably Else Herzberger (1877–1962), a friend of the Wiesengrund family; she met Adorno and Kracauer during their travels in the Dolomites in 1924.

Gröden disjunctions: This location in the Dolomites was one of the stages on the journey which they undertook together in 1924 and the subject of a travel feuilleton by Kracauer (see letter no. 2, note).

workers' concert: The Workers' Symphony Concerts were founded in 1904 by David Josef Bach (1874–1947), later the director of the Social Democratic *Kunststelle* [art centre]; the event attended by Adorno and conducted by Anton Webern was the 'Märzfeier' [March festival] at the Großer Konzerthaussaal on 13 and 14 March 1925, with performances of Beethoven, Brahms, Liszt, Weber and Mendelssohn (according to its billboard; see Henriette Kotlan-Werner, 'Sinfonie für Arbeiter', *AZ Journal*, 19 March 1977).

Universal Edition: music publishing company, founded in 1901 and since 1914 headquartered on Karlsplatz. Its catalogue lists works written by the most important composers of New Music.

Kolisch Quartet: The 'Viennese String Quartet' around the violinist Rudolf Kolisch (1896–1978), from 1939 in exile in the USA. Adorno dedicated to him both 'Der getreue Korrepetitor' ('Rudolf Kolisch / Eduard Steuermann / den Freunden seit der Jugend'; see Adorno, GS 15, p. 158) and 'Die Funktion des Kontrapunkts in der neuen Musik' ('Für Rudolf Kolisch / in treuer Freundschaft'; see Adorno, GS 16, p. 145).

Rathaus … Wellesz: Karol Rathaus (1895–1954), from 1921, Karol Szymanowski (1882–1937), from 1912, Alfredo Casella (1883–1947), from 1910, and Egon Wellesz (1885–1974), from 1915, were all exclusively represented by Universal Edition.

Lila's parents: Lili Körber's parents: Ignaz Körber (1864–?) and Jeanette Körber, née Schanzer (1875–?); see letter no. 2, note: Lemke, pp. 24f.

Frau Berg: Helene Berg, née Nahowski (1885–1976), married to Alban Berg since 1911.

Alma Mahler: Alma Mahler-Werfel, née Schindler (1879–1964), musician and writer, married Gustav Mahler (in 1902), Walter Gropius (in 1915) and Franz Werfel (in 1929); 1938 exiled in France, 1940 in the USA.

a card: Alma Mahler and Franz Werfel travelled in Egypt and Palestine from the end of 1924 until the beginning of 1925.

Kokoschka legends: the visual testimony of the relationship between Alma Mahler and the painter and writer Oskar Kokoschka (1886–1980) is his oil painting *Die Windsbraut* [The bride of the wind] of 1913/14.

travelling companion: unidentified.

my trio: probably his 'Satz für Streichtrio' (see Adorno, *Kompositionen* 3, pp. 174–89), which was written at that time.

variations for string quartet: opus 2, the second part: 'Variations' (see Adorno, *Kompositionen* 2, pp. 5–28).

Bartók pieces: 'Über einige Werke von Béla Bartók', *Zeitschrift für Musik*, nos. 7/8, 1925 (see Adorno, GS 18, pp. 282–6; GS 19, p. 643); 'Béla Bartóks Tanzsuite', *Pult und Taktstock*, no. 6, 1926 (see Adorno, GS 18, pp. 279–81; GS 19, p. 643).

folk songs: 'Volksliedsammlungen', *Die Musik*, May 1925 (see Adorno, GS 19, pp. 287–90, 650).

Holl: Karl Holl (1892–1975), music scholar and music editor, from 1922 until 1934 at the *Frankfurter Zeitung*.

trio by Jemnitz: 'Alexander Jemnitz, trio for flute, violin and viola, op. 19', *Zeitschrift für Musik*, no. 1, 1926 (see Adorno, GS 19, pp 291f., 650).

Bloch: could be the philosopher Ernst Bloch or the Swiss composer Ernest Bloch (1880–1959).

Leo: no letter relevant to this context has been found among Leo Löwenthal's papers (Archivzentrum der Universitätsbibliothek Johann Christian Senckenberg) or in the Theodor W. Adorno Archiv.

Salomon: Gottfried Salomon-Delatour (1892–1964), sociologist, in 1921 Privatdozent at the Johann Wolfgang Goethe-Universität; 1933 exiled in France, 1941 in the USA.

aunt: Hedwig Kracauer (1862–1942), sister of Kracauer's mother Rosette Kracauer, married to Isidor Kracauer. Until 1941, her letters informed Siegfried Kracauer about the events in Frankfurt am Main. She was deported to Theresienstadt in 1941. (Kracauer papers, Deutsches Literaturarchiv, Marbach.)

tant pis pour moi: too bad for me.

Papa Krull: see the description, including his fondness for sprinkling his individualistic style of speaking with French phrases, of a character in Thomas Mann's novel *The Confessions of Felix Krull, Confidence Man* (London: Secker & Warburg, 1955). The first part appeared in 1922 as *Buch der Kindheit* [The early years].

Fred's essay: presumably Frederick Goldbeck (1902–1981), writer about music and music teacher, schoolmate of Adorno and, like him, a student of composition under Bernhard Sekles, from 1925 active mostly in Paris. The essay has not been identified.

6 Adorno, Agathe Calvelli-Adorno and Maria Wiesengrund-Adorno to Kracauer
Vienna, 19.3.1925

Vienna, 19 March 1925

Dear Friedel,
So here we are! We had a very good journey and arrived safely, and Teddie took excellent care of us. He looks well – better than at home. Vienna is still beautiful – but, nevertheless, 'Poor father – how changed you are!' Many cordial greetings from your Agathe. Dear Friedel, I too send you many cordial greetings. Vienna is still Vienna, though greatly changed. As always, Your old Maria.

Did you not receive my letter? Or what is the matter? Teddie.

Original: MS, postcard: Vienna, Stephansplatz. Siegfried Kracauer papers, Deutsches Literaturarchiv, Marbach am Neckar. Handwritten note by Kracauer: '3. With card to Agathe' (the rest is obscured by the postmark).

'Poor father …': The punchline of an anecdote originating from Hungary, in which 'Mikos commissioned a portrait of his late father from a painter of note. The painter took on the task without having access to a picture of the subject of the portrait, as, according to the son, he could "paint a likeness of anyone!" The painter took note of the situation, finally accepted the commission, and told the bereaved man to come back in about a month. So that was what our Mikos did. The painter received him respectfully and unveiled the picture in his studio. Mikos stood in front of the portrait, deeply moved, and then declared, in a typical Hungarian accent, 'Poor father – how you have changed!' (After Alexander Scheiber, 'Alte Geschichten in neuem Gewand' [Old stories in new clothes], in *Studies in Aggadah and Jewish Folklore*, ed. Issachar Ben-Ami and Joseph Dan. Jerusalem: Magnes Press/Hebrew University, 1983, pp. 106f.)

7 Adorno to Kracauer
Vienna, 26.3.1925

My dear Friedel, just for now, please accept something intellectual as a hasty greeting; the mothers have just left for Salzburg; now I am sitting alone in Café Westend, which is even dirtier than ours, and feeling sad. As I have to go to Alban for my lesson, and tomorrow to search for a piano, to Steuermann, and to practise the piano, I shall have to wait another two days to write a proper letter – so you will have to wait too.

The fragments here are appearing in the conductors' journal *Pult und Taktstock*, edited by Erwin Stein, which is very good. Stein, who heard about me through Berg (he too is a pupil of Schoenberg's, and you may perhaps recall that Erika Wagner praised his conducting of *Pierrot Lunaire*), kept on tormenting me about it, and I wrote them for him. They made a great impression on him; we discussed them for hours, and now he is publishing them with a preface and giving his own opinions about them in a second essay. The alterations in pencil are his; in the course of the discussion, when he understood my stylistic ideas, he abandoned them all. He really does know, in fact, what it entails. Query: is the Wilhelmine quality of the essay broken up by its loose programmatic form and qualifications? That was my intention, which should also become clear from the style, although, on the other hand, it did require scrupulous accuracy to be comprehensible at all.

Within certain limits I can get on intellectually with Stein. Berg is much more, a truly profound human being, but already very set in his ways and with a cramped, ingrown artist's horizon (he was very much to the mothers' liking). The others do not count, perhaps excepting Eisler. I have spent a lot of time in close proximity to Schoenberg, and have studied him but asked not to be introduced to him, although the Bergs and Rathaus were very keen on it. I feel a sense of both tolerance and bashfulness towards him. Facially he reminds me of you, around the forehead and eyes, at least. I shall write to you soon about all my impressions of him as a person. My relationship with Lila is in the process of completely disintegrating; the spitefully deprecatory, venomously normal manner in which she relayed to me a hateful remark that Balabanova made about me (a Marxist monster! You would fly into a rage!) led to a catastrophe. She is leaving for Italy on Wednesday. Ghastly, ghastly in moral terms for me, and sad for her that she is having problems with her lungs just now.

Be patient for two days!

Teddie. Vienna, 26.III.25.

Original: MS; Siegfried Kracauer papers, Deutsches Literaturarchiv, Marbach am Neckar. Enclosed: 'Zum Problem der Reproduktion: Fragmente von Theodor Wiesengrund-Adorno' [On the problem of reproduction: fragments by Theodor Wiesengrund-Adorno], MS (see below). Handwritten note by Kracauer on the envelope: '4. Received on 30th; answered by postcard on 30th.' The reply has not been preserved.

Café Westend: coffee-house on the Mariahilfer Strasse in Vienna. It was in the Café Westend in Frankfurt, on the Opernplatz, that Adorno met Walter Benjamin in 1923 as a result of an introduction by Kracauer (see *Erinnerungen* [Memoirs], Adorno, GS 20.1, pp. 173–8).

Steuermann: Eduard Steuermann (1892–1962), composer and pianist. Adorno writes in his obituary of him: 'Through Berg I made Steuermann's acquaintance in 1925 and took piano lessons with him; the friendship lasted, largely without interruption, until the present. Words are inadequate to express what I have to thank him for.' (See Adorno, GS 17, p. 313; in addition to 'Der getreue Korrepetitor' (see letter no. 5, note), Adorno dedicated his 'Kriterien der neuen Musik' [Criteria of New Music] to Steuermann (see Adorno, GS 16, p. 170).

the fragments: 'Zum Problem der Reproduktion: Fragmente von Theodor Wiesengrund-Adorno', *Pult und Taktstock*, April 1925 (see Adorno, GS 19, pp. 440–4, 652). The manuscript of the essay is stored with this letter among Kracauer's papers.

Stein: Erwin Stein (1885–1958), conductor; he received his musical training under Arnold Schoenberg, among others, and edited the journal at Universal Edition, whose orchestral department he headed (see Adorno's obituary, Adorno, GS 19, pp. 453f.).

Wagner: Erika Stiedry, née von Wagner (1890–1974), singer and actress at various theatres in Vienna.

his conducting of Pierrot Lunaire: according to a study by the musicologist Andreas Meyer, in 1922 Alma Mahler-Werfel organized a salon concert in Vienna in the course of which Erwin Stein directed his version (approved by the composer) of Arnold Schoenberg's *Dreimal Sieben Gedichte aus Albert Girauds 'Pierrot lunaire'* [Three times seven poems from Albert Giraud's *Pierrot Lunaire*], op. 21, with Erika Wagner as the speaker (see Andreas Meyer, 'Schönbergs *Pierrot* in Paris: Rezeption, Projektion und Einfluß' [Schönberg's *Pierrot Lunaire* in Paris: reception, projection and influence], in *Pierrot Lunaire: Albert Giraud – Otto Erich Hartleben – Arnold Schönberg: A Collection of Musicological and Literary Studies*, ed. Mark Delaere and Jan Herman. Dudley, MA: Peeters, 2004, pp. 173–192, esp. p. 187).

a preface: 'The present essay examines the problem of reproduction less from the practical than from the theoretical point of view. For this reason, it was open to question whether it was appropriate for inclusion in this journal. Nevertheless, the reader will soon realize that it is a *musician* who is speaking here – and, indeed, one of extraordinary importance in terms of abstract thought. His examination of the connections between the style of a work and freedom in interpreting it gives rise to stimulating suggestions for performance. The Editor.' (See *Pult und Taktstock*, no. 4, 1924.)

giving his own opinions about them in a second essay: the editor's next essay appears in the following issue (see Erwin Stein, 'Einiges über Dirigiertechnik' [A few words on the technique of conducting], *Pult und Taktstock*, no. 5, 1925).

the alterations in pencil: handwritten additions or alternative formulations in the manuscript (Siegfried Kracauer papers, Deutsches Literaturarchiv, Marbach); as Erwin Stein 'abandoned' these, it was decided not to reproduce them.

Eisler: in exile in America, Adorno was to write *Composing for the Films* in collaboration with the composer Hanns Eisler (1898–1962), who likewise studied with Arnold Schoenberg (see letter no. 138).

remark that Balabanova made about me: not preserved.

8 **Kracauer to Adorno**

(no address given; 2.4.1925)

2 April

Draft of a letter to Teddie.

D.T. Before you come to Frankfurt I should like to write you a letter which is a genuine response to everything I have heard from you during your absence; for my previous letters were masks – easily recognizable as such.

At the risk of appearing petty, I am going to confront you with the following reproach. When you were leaving, you said to me that your letters would represent something special. Judge for yourself whether they did so – both in content and in nature. You allowed this break to come

Original: MS; Siegfried Kracauer papers, Deutsches Literaturarchiv, Marbach am Neckar. Dating: year inserted from the context and its place in Kracauer's papers.

Draft: based on a sketch from the previous day:

1 April

To: Teddie

1) The first letter completely unimportant.
2) It was said by Teddie that he would prove to me, as it were, by the form of his letters how faithful he was to me (he must have recalled the conversation about Bobbi and Hanni's correspondence).
3) Break lasting from 14 March until after 1 April, and in between only the commission, with the few lines in which he asked for two days' patience. These two days were exceeded, of course.

Recognition: there is no excuse for this – not the presence of the 'mothers', nor work, not even pleasure (I always answered immediately, as silent evidence).

4) Not only were the two days exceeded, but it was reported to me by *Agathe* that he had not yet had the time to write but would get round to it in the next few days. Oh, how this disgusts me

Bobbi: Maria Proelss (see letter no. 4).

Hanni: Hanni Rocco (1896–1990), violinist, Maria Proelss's friend; co-founder of the Frankfurter Kammermusikgemeinde. For Adorno's friendly relations with Rocco and Proelss, see the published extracts from their correspondence (Adorno, *Bildmonographie*, pp. 70–4).

9 Adorno to Kracauer
Vienna, 10.4.1925

Vienna, 10 April 25.

My dear Friedel,

Today I can finally manage to write a letter; after several very hectic weeks I am back within my own four walls – seeing not a soul apart from my teachers, working, and getting on with my existence. A piano, old but serviceable – a grand – stands in my room; the bookcase has been there for some time with plenty of Kierkegaard; Lila is away for an indefinite period (at least six weeks!), and so it is possible to live, if one so wishes. I am constantly sad, lonely, lacking in *l'enthousiasme* in the Victorine sense as well as the purely immanent psychological one, and longing for you, to whom I am bound in life and death now, no matter how it all turns out. The only thing that props me up is work, or, more precisely, composition, which is making slow but serious progress: a few days ago I completed the variations for string quartet, and today a little piece for orchestra (the first of a cycle) for which I in fact needed only two days – very quick, for the way I work. The main item, too – the big trio – is making progress: I hope to finish the first movement next week, although by then I shall have been working on it for three months and still have a lot of changes to make. I know that you are averse to any kind of faith in work and even to any hint of a tendency towards that, even as slight as the claim that 'work is a prop', but it is available to fulfil that function, and usually I cannot help myself on account of this melancholy about the imperfect life.

Well, about that imperfect life: I have made the acquaintance of two important people – Schoenberg and Frau Mahler; Schoenberg at a private performance of chamber music by the Kolisch Quartet (Kolisch is Schoenberg's brother-in-law now – the brother of his second wife). Berg took me along and introduced me in his warm and kindly way; Schoenberg immediately remembered, when my name was mentioned, that I had once sent him something (little pieces for string quartet), and he then talked to me – rather as Napoleon might have conversed with a young adjutant newly arrived from a distant theatre of war in which he naturally had to show an interest, but whose details he had long since forgotten – about musical life in Frankfurt and asked me to show him my compositions. These are the facts – few enough; but I have been so long and so often in his presence that I have already formed an impression of him. His face is the face of a dark – perhaps an evil – man, with something low – even vulgar – about it, with a natural talent for anything base and even mean, with a twitching, busy, greedy mouth and an uncanny mobility about his features, which adapt themselves to whatever is going on around him; Benjamin would say: a *petit esprit*, but one from the Café Goldschmidt – the restless, harassed face of a Jewish gambler, with nothing 'mellow' about it (he is ageless, too), but an obsessive personality through and through. Above it there are two powerful – almost staring – eyes and a mighty forehead. All in all, the fellow has something creepy and oppressive about him, and, the more conciliatory he tries to be, the stronger this impression becomes. If, in addition to this, we look at his handwriting, of which Berg gave me a sample and which I declined to analyse – without knowing whose it was – because it was amazingly similar to mine, but in which I found something hectic and yet at the same time collected, then it is possible to get an accurate impression of him. I think that he would make as strong an impression on you as he did on me. When he has returned from Spain, where he is conducting *Pierrot Lunaire*, I shall probably get to know him better, as far as that is actually possible; since he suffers from paranoia (not wholly without reason – just recently he was spat on in a café yet again!), he can barely tolerate being contradicted, which of course excludes the active principle of any sort of discussion. Moreover, he is obsessed with a passionate love of pedagogics and offers advice to everyone, and to composers in particular.

And now to Frau Mahler: first I met her step-sister, the daughter of the painter Carl Moll, at Alban Berg's (even at her age an exquisite creature – outrageous in a discreet way!). Then Berg (who plays the piano without sufficient technical skill) asked me to perform his *Wozzeck* for Barbara Kemp (Frau von Schillings) – or, rather, to study with her the role of Marie, which she is to create at the première in Berlin. (I had to practise it like mad for a whole week!) The meeting took place at Alma Mahler's; she was leaving for Venice at 8.30 that night, and we were at her place until eight o'clock – Kemp full of sweet liqueur and constantly spouting nothing but her own praises – Alma Maria goes at a pace that leaves Else absolutely nowhere – completely off the map – by comparison, the only difference being that here everything runs along with considerably less friction. She is a phenomenon in every respect: still beautiful, entirely without pretensions, any tendency to be excessively emphatic, or the smug complacency which her position might suggest; intelligent, a gifted talker, and equipped with the latest theological tips from Prague (here, by the way, is a good joke which the poet Morgenstern – of whom more anon – made yesterday: when a man from Prague sees snow and three people standing in it, he thinks it's Dostoevsky!); with plenty of secrets, but quite aware about herself and displaying remarkable objectivity towards herself. At the same time she is an astonishing diplomat – the way she handled Kemp's unbearable delusions of grandeur – fêting her, but with a touch of covert irony at the same time – and how she helped to get a fair deal for *Wozzeck* – that truly significant *Wozzeck* – for Berg, who is so unbelievably modest (or at least ostensibly modest!), never mentions his works at all and would prefer to creep away and hide when they come up in conversation, and is without the least aptitude for doing anything for himself – how she suggested to Kemp, who scarcely understood the opera at all, that it was indeed – *sit venia verbo sine ullo principio* – a work of genius! The whole thing achieved the best possible effect, and Kemp is going to sing the role – I resented the fact that Frau Mahler was continually talking about Werfel and Koko, Beer-Hofmann and other literary lions less than you might perhaps have done, half-accustomed as I am, in a passive fashion, to these Viennese ways. The only amusing thing was how amazed she was (or affected to be) that I didn't know the whole crew personally. We got on very well and parted on cordial terms. On the 20th she is coming here for the première of Werfel's *Juarez*, and I shall probably get to see her then.

Otherwise I am living very quietly; the only new face that I see from time to time is this Morgenstern, a clever Polish Jew, who is very good-looking and relatively free from despair – an intense character, it's true, with a gift for dialectic, but of a quite modest stature. It is possible (up to a point) to have a conversation with him. He is as thick as thieves with the composer Rathaus (who has also been performed in Frankfurt) – a very talented but unpleasantly arrogant youth, whom I am avoiding.

The thing that surprises me about the whole Viennoiserie is its relative naivety. With all their refinement within the limits of whatever they are doing, all the people I have met here are, beyond any doubt at all, fixated on their own demands and assumptions; they regard the whole sphere of psychology as their private domain, treating it as if it were self-evident or had been created by the Good Lord exclusively for them. Their slog-trotting attitude towards empiricism glides along without a hitch, smoothly slipping into a theoretical and aesthetic individualism which, despite all the so-called problems which it entails, nevertheless has *toto genere* something very agreeable about it, because it never overreaches itself and knows nothing of the misery of existence – or only in a distorted sense. This is an agreeable quality, which when seen from outside amounts to its true problematical nature. They are all the same in this respect – even the enemies Karl Kraus and Werfel (who now, as a follower of *Sachlichkeit*, no longer knows a word of Russian but is lit up by the glow of the South – he will be building skyscrapers any day now!), and I am inclined to believe that this Seldwyla-like naivety towards their own kind contains, when turning towards its own kind, a part of something that is basically good at heart; but in fact it seems to me that a crisis is being played out here – that of a bourgeoisie which, subjected to Marxist examination (Marxism is a response to Vienna!), lies beyond the realms of dialectic – a cultural island, to some extent, which has become soft in the head in its attitudes as a result of inbreeding and, objectively speaking, falls deeper and deeper into oblivion with its increasingly monomaniac obsession with itself. The external image of a city in a state of complete economic stagnation, left behind by the business of the world, laboriously raising its temperature by means of sensations, is entirely consistent with the fact that, fundamentally, it is reactionary both in artistic and (as far as I can see) in philosophical terms. The fact that all radicalism is nothing but an illusion (Koko!) – nothing but the exaggerated or externally projected psychology of the individual – can be understood as an exact reflection of that false bourgeoisie in concrete form within which piano companies which wish to – and have to – export their goods are going bankrupt because, being culturally befuddled and out of touch, they have no machines – not even telephones. Kraus's phrase 'I'm quite cosy myself' is in fact true, in a polemical sense, of the whole city. It would be useful to shed some light in metaphysical terms on the connection or structural relationship between the economically backward petite bourgeoisie and psychological individualism: how the 'persona' of the existential community here, as there, dissolves its links with sense and community; for, in economic terms too, the attitude of the eccentric loner, which romantically adheres to 'immediacy' and thus leaves production, is a phenomenon of detachment. Topics that have long since been passé among us, such as those of Strindberg and Péladan, are still held in high esteem here; Shaw, with his philistine peasant cunning (I saw his *St Joan* – repellent – not only stupid but also essentially mendacious), is viewed as the apogee of consummate Western civilization. Even Berg, who is more advanced in his music and entirely capable of criticism of a material nature, doesn't understand that something has turned putrid about *Tristan*, or, rather, that the rottenness is plainly visible.

But that's enough of that. Grotesquely enough, I feel as if I have been banished to the provinces like Ovid in his old age, although I – nebbich that I am! – haven't seduced any emperor's ladies with my poems, and haven't even been capable of managing anything worth mentioning with a willing girl from the cabaret. I am trying to learn as much as possible and have already learnt a great deal, especially as regards the orchestra, of which I have always had a certain wariness and which I can now handle without ever having studied 'instrumentation'; Sekles was quite right there. A few tips of Berg's have been amazingly helpful to me. I am even thinking of making myself into a competent repetiteur and shall learn a lot in pianistic terms from Steuermann, who plays splendidly – just as long as he is not too phlegmatic to pay attention to me during our lessons. I have not yet been to the university; all kinds of threads are being spun in the direction of Lukács but have not yet reached this far; he is very exclusive – very 'upper crust' in his attitude to the proletariat. I have seen Alois Hofmann; he is as gifted as ever, and as hard to bear.

How did you find the essays which you corrected (God knows what an act of masochism that was)? The other one is for you, of course; there is also a note in it – a symbol that must have escaped your notice. What's the news at home? Has der Waltende [Benjamin] passed his habilitation?

Lila is sicker than was thought – a pulmonary embolism; she is writing letters full of complaints and has not received a single line from me so far. I'm sorry for her, but the relationship has run its course – and she thinks it is only just beginning.

I think that I shall return from Vienna less changed than you imagine. Perhaps a little more independent as regards external things, about which, however, I trouble myself no more than I did at home – and a little sadder, too. I wonder whether the people in Frankfurt whom I couldn't get away from fast enough – i.e. Hanni, and everyone involved with that business – wished me well at all? I am living no differently here from how I did there – it is just that I am all too free in the things that matter. So why withdraw from me that empirical warmth without which it is absolutely impossible to live a life like mine? Why take away from me what I have – my people? Perhaps I was too approachable – to some extent, without admitting it – towards those who don't love me. But that must remain between us – *any* third person would completely misunderstand it!

In faithful passion,

Your Teddie.

'Greetings may be taken as read.'

Original: MS; Siegfried Kracauer papers, Deutsches Literaturarchiv, Marbach am Neckar. Handwritten note by Kracauer on the envelope: '5. Received *14 April* 25 … answered on 16 April.'

a little piece for orchestra (the first of a cycle): *Sechs kurze Orchesterstücke* [Six Short Orchestral Pieces], op. 4 (see Adorno, *Kompositionen* 2, pp. 29–54); the second piece is dated 1925 and the first 1929.

the variations for string quartet … the big trio: see letter no. 5.

l'enthousiasme *in the Victorine sense*: no information survives.

his second wife: Gertrud Schoenberg, née Kolisch (1898–1967); the marriage took place in 1924. Mathilde Schoenberg, née Zemlinsky, Arnold Schoenberg's first wife, had died the previous year.

little pieces for string quartet: *Sechs Studien für Streichquartett* [Six Studies for String Quartet], 1920 (see Adorno, *Kompositionen* 3, pp. 67–83, and *Bildmonographie*, pp. 64–6).

Café Goldschmidt: relocated to the Allerheiligenstrasse in Frankfurt am Main.

the daughter of the painter Carl Moll: after the death of Alma Mahler's father, the painter Emil Jacob Schindler (1842–1892), Carl Moll (1861–1945), also a painter and graphic artist, married her mother, Anna Sofie Bergen (1857–1938), an actress; Alma Mahler-Werfel's half-sister Maria Eberstaller-Moll (1899–1945) was the offspring of this marriage.

Kemp: Barbara Kemp (1881–1959), opera singer; engagements at major European theatres, especially the Staatsoper in Berlin and at Bayreuth; Sigrid Johanson actually sang the role of Marie.

Schillings: Max von Schillings (1868–1933), composer; intendant at the Staatsoper in Berlin (1919–1925).

the première in Berlin: the première of Alban Berg's opera *Wozzeck* took place on 14 December 1925 at the Berlin Staatsoper, conducted by Erich Kleiber.

Alma Maria: Berg's *Wozzeck* is 'Alma Maria Mahler zugeeignet' [dedicated to Alma Maria Mahler]; (see Alban Berg, *Wozzeck*. Vienna: Universal Edition, 1952, p. 3).

Morgenstern: Soma Morgenstern (1890–1976), author and journalist for (among others) the *Frankfurter Zeitung*; a friend of Alban Berg.

Koko: Oskar Kokoschka.

Beer-Hofmann: Richard Beer-Hofmann (1866–1945), author.

première of Werfel's Juarez: Franz Werfel, *Juarez und Maximilian*, first performed in Magdeburg on 20 April 1925; Viennese première directed by Max Reinhardt on 26 May 1925 at the Theater in der Josefstadt. In 1929 Franz Werfel (1890–1945) became Alma Mahler's third husband after an affair which had been going on for more than ten years.

even the enemies Karl Kraus and Werfel: the conflict was sparked off by Franz Werfel's *Spiegelmensch: Magische Trilogie* (Munich: Kurt Wolff, 1920); Karl Kraus responded in 1921 to this drama, which was in the nature of a parody and partly directed at him, with a travesty directed at Werfel (see Karl Kraus's *Literatur oder Man wird doch da sehn*, ed. Martin Leubner. Göttingen: Wallstein, 1996).

'I'm quite cosy myself': 'What I ask of a city in which I am to live is asphalt, street-cleaning, front-door keys, hot-air heating, running hot water. I'm quite cosy myself' (see Karl Kraus, *Aphorismen*, ed. Christian Wagenknecht. Frankfurt am Main: Suhrkamp, 1986, p. 209).

Strindberg: the complete works of the Swedish author August Strindberg (1849–1912) were published between 1902 and 1930 by Georg Müller.

Péladan: Georg Müller published a selection of plays by the French author Joséphin Péladan (1859–1918) in 1914 and his novels between 1911 and 1925.

Shaw … St Joan: The Viennese première of *Die heilige Johanna*, by George Bernard Shaw (1856–1959), took place at the Deutsche Volkstheater on 24 October 1924; no information is available as to which of the 58 further performances Adorno attended (see *Bernard Shaw's Letters to Siegfried Trebitsch*, ed. Samuel A. Weiss. Stanford, CA: Stanford University Press, 1986, p. 252n.).

Hofmann: Alois Hofmann (1859–1927), operatic conductor and director; in 1923 he was appointed to a professorship at the Staatsakademie für Musik und darstellende Kunst in Vienna.

the essays… a note: at least 'Zum Problem der Reproduktion' [On the problem of reproduction] (see letter no. 7), and possibly also 'Béla Bartóks Tanzsuite' [Bela Bartók's *Dance Suite*] (see letter no. 5); the 'note' has not been preserved.

Der Waltende: Walter Benjamin set in motion his attempt to qualify as a lecturer by submitting his habilitation to the faculty of philosophy at the Johann Wolfgang Goethe-Universität on 12 May 1925. Hans Cornelius pronounced a negative verdict on his postdoctoral thesis *Ursprung des deutschen Trauerspiels* [Origin of German tragic drama]; (see Benjamin, GS 1.1, pp. 203–430), and the enterprise came to nothing (see Benjamin, *Gesammelte Briefe* III, p. 35; Burckhardt Lindner, 'Habilitationsakte Benjamin' [Benjamin's postgraduate thesis] in Lindner, ed., *Walter Benjamin in Kontext*. 2nd edn, Königstein: Athenäum, 1985, pp. 324–41).

'Greetings may be taken as read': these were the words with which the dramatist Friedrich Hebbel ended a letter of 29 June 1858 to Christine Hebbel (see *Friedrich*

Hebbels Briefe, ed. Richard Maria Werner and Fritz Lemmermayers, 2 vols. Berlin, 1900. Vol II: *1853–1863*, p. 98). This edition is not to be found in the library left behind by Adorno; however, the library does contain seven volumes of Hebbel's works, some of them with markings and marginal notes.

10 Kracauer to Adorno

Frankfurt am Main, 16.4.1925

FRANKFURTER ZEITUNG
REDAKTION.
Telegr. - Adr.: ZEITUNG FRANKFURTMAIN.

16 April 1925

1.

Dear Teddie, I did get a rather strong sense of Schoenberg and Alma Maria from reading your letter. The former, set against the background of his works, could not help creating the demonic effect that you describe. The fact that his handwriting is so like yours might be construed as an omen, as could your mutual aptitude for linking theory and practice. I had no idea that he had married for a second time. Your Aunt Agathe had already told me that you were going to rehearse the role with Kemp, so I was not surprised to learn that you were with her at Circe's – because that is exactly what she seems to be, from what Holl also tells me. It seems a very good thing to me that you get on well with her and will certainly be able to come and go freely in that circle; this will allow you to know all kinds of odd creatures and gain a thorough insight into Koko and other notables. I'm sure that I wouldn't have held that bit of vanity about the half- and full sizes against her. As a woman who plays that kind of game, she can afford it; it might even suit her – and indeed it does. If serious love would set in there would have to be a place for comedy in it. The *grande dame* with spirit and a capacity for adventure is in any case one of the finest inventions of the civilized world, and is something she may be forgiven much more than spinning webs with the threads of her *connaissances*. The poet Morgenstern bears a compelling name. By the way, it has just occurred to me that Rudolf Steiner died recently; how quickly that hobgoblin fell into oblivion. You must be uncommonly industrious from what *la tante* reported in the Café Hauptwache. In musical terms you really had been in exile here, as you had nobody except for Sekles, and later you no longer had even him. In matters of creative productivity – not only of a musical kind – solitude is as much of an evil as in morality – as a state of mind, at least. One gets tangled up in gloominess, and a single conversation or touch of sympathy from the outside world would be enough to provide stimulation. After all, everything is inside ourselves, but I often sense that what lies deepest does have to rely to a great extent on superficial expression – or else it is lost in silence. You think that I am opposed to the idea that work offers a support. Alas, no – in the end it does just that, but colliery explosions do occur. I shall have more to say about your melancholy and sadness. I found your sociological interpretation of Vienna persuasive; I agree unreservedly with it, and can well understand that at times you feel as if you were in the provinces. It was like that with me in Berlin; my goodness – with all the spectacles that dominated everything there, one lived on quite a different level. The provinces in close-up – that's how Berlin seemed to me. Are you going over there in May as you intended? If I were you, I would immerse myself in the whole business from A to Z – you will find out what it is all about, and why harbour unnecessary illusions? Once again, about Vienna – I am ready to believe in the link between naivety and the psychology of the individual – the fundamental verities may extend all the way to *Fräulein Else* – otherwise none of the characters in Schnitzler's novels or Kassirer's chimeras could sustain their pseudo-existence. Going on to Lukács, the reality of his unreality is like being trapped in jelly. By the way, your dismissal of *St Joan* delighted me; we are alone in our opinions, as the others feel like Western Europeans. You ask what I thought of your music reviews. Clever and to the point. Your hint about masochism – what is that supposed to mean? I hope I corrected it properly. You did not write anything about my comments on your essay about [musical] reproduction. May I have an offprint of it? I did notice that your letter was connected with the essay; I just thought that you needed it back to make a copy. Alban Berg must be a fine and profound person indeed with no pretensions about him; your people were enchanted with him too. Anyway, I squeezed your aunt very hard to extract some information to flesh out the picture.

As far as your melancholy is concerned, I find a certain lack of consonance between the surface of your letter and its undertones – assuming that this is not a matter of a general groundless melancholy which never subsides as long as one is predisposed to it, as the sense of incompleteness appears to be constitutional. I know of no remedy for this, either in your case or in mine. This kind of melancholy, frankly, is simply how you are. But the other kind – the one which is perhaps indicated by the words that you may come back 'a little sadder' than you went – at least no longer echoes from the surface tone of your letter – or, rather, I had the feeling that you were swimming in a wider river over there, and many worries had subsided. Not that I thought that you were vanishing into a new environment and the sense of continuity was blotted out, but everything that you wrote had a positive note, and your mothers also said something of the kind – they were even satisfied with your physical state, which says a lot. Well, then – those are my impressions. The last sentences of your letter must have emanated from the sadness of which you write; I don't understand them. First: why are you bothered about whether Hanni & co. wished you any good when they wanted you out of Frankfurt? That's [x];

I go so far as to believe that they actually did. You then ask, 'Why take away from me what I have – my people?' There are two things I don't understand here. First: do you think I would take anyone away from you? You can't believe that. Second: the logic of the matter. How can anyone in fact take away from someone those whom he has? In an external sense it might be possible (perhaps?), but that isn't what we are talking about. In any real sense: never. The relationships which exist here – this is my firm conviction (just as much as yours) – are reciprocal ones. In the case of human relationships, nobody can take away from another an iota of what he has. Think of 'equilibrium': the principle of the scales is valid – in a negative sense, at least. One love may always be greater. But if it appears to have been withdrawn, we may presume that it no longer shines forth, and so it is just as if one had never had it. A curious point here: Susman wrote to me yesterday to break off our friendship, addressing me as 'Dear Herr Kr.' She had read some essay or other of mine, found it contrary to her opinions (or whatever), declared a state of estrangement between us, and, so to speak, officially ended the relationship as it stood. She did not take, because I did not have. If I had been her friend this could not have happened 'by the very nature of things'. Anyway, I couldn't care less about it; what is one supposed to write in reply to such inanities? While we are on the subject of people: you told me about Lila, her illness, and about not writing to her. Let me suggest something about this. Of course, I don't know the details of your quarrel, but I do in fact find it rather *brutto* of you not to write a line to her – the poor ailing creature. You yourself are always saying that she is still a human being no matter what, and you stick to that – at whatever distance. But I don't know about the last sentence: 'Perhaps I was too approachable – to some extent, without admitting it – to those who don't love me' – that's a mystery to me, and that's how it should remain between us. Please tell me what this means, if you would, as I am blind in this respect, I am ashamed to say. You haven't sent any reply to my last letter (of 18 March – an answer to yours of the 14th) – did it reach you?

2.

You want to know about things 'at home'. Der Waltende is in Berlin, as far as I know; the proceedings for his habilitation will probably not go ahead until next semester. Horkheimer gave me a call after drifting in from Paris; I may possibly visit him this week or next. I haven't seen Zickel at all since you left – but why the devil hasn't he been in touch even once? I had a short, indecipherable letter from Fred. He was asking after you most fervently without knowing anything at all about you. I'll let him have your address shortly (or not? Or shall I – it's such an extrinsic matter?), but do write to the fellow. Leo pesters me from time to time; I feel a kind of impassioned faithlessness towards him but am too much of a coward to draw the necessary inferences. Fräulein Kamnitzer isn't even sailing past on the horizon, as I believe she is on the Riviera just now; the girl will soon be engaged to be married. No new faces to speak of; the painting is quite monotonous. Some people have been asking after you very warmly, such as Dr Frankenberger and some of the other regulars. I have no idea where Hanni and Bobbie have got to; I never heard any more from them and besides – solidarity!

Over Easter I was in Würzburg and Bamberg, on my own. There were plenty of visual sensations. The basalt with the perspective it offers of a general review of the whole cosmos is quite a thing. The artist plays with the pantheon and conjures up redemption; *tutto il mondo* is reduced to a cultivated society, which is still capable of feeling fear and a connection with nature, to a formula drawn from its own assets – the last positive entity. The rococo period still preserves this world, collected at the time when Philippe d'Orléans was regent, and grins cheerfully above it in timorous farewell, with the transcendental homelessness of glorious memory already fixed in its spinal marrow. Rocailles over ancient cornices – what a symbol! The steps leading to the Käppele – a masterpiece of religious attitudinizing; the park of Veitshöchheim, an unprecedented cosmogony of Christian eschatology, a supreme play of extreme fears – weeping in its form – the lamentation of objects (like the lamentation of the subject in Mozart). Bamberg: I was overwhelmed. The horseman was a vision from another realm (the unicorn is a nebbich next to it). Then Hohenlohe with his nervous narrow-cheeked spirituality from the 13th century. The Sibyl: her gaze seemed to be resting on centuries, and her wrinkles like incantations. And so on. Catholicism in its living state is partly incredulous Middle Ages (women, elderly, with stony faces full of objective piety; examples of ceremonial with a high degree of *joie de vivre*) and partly theatre in a chapel in the Michaelskirche – an alabaster Christ laid out in white linen trimmed with red pleats [?] with candles all around and electricity behind evergreen twigs – Good Friday spell. The mocha, of course, is bad in these worn-out enclaves, and the cinemas show films that are hard to shift. At least, I know that they are – and Fräulein Emerantia can study the customs and practices of five o'clock tea here or shrink from them in horror. Lastly I saw Vierzehnheiligen and Banz. That outrageous-sounding rococo with a dangerously sociable worldly quality; the Middle Ages, a saucy pleasure-house, leap into the loosely curving forms, and the allegorical figures blend silently into the splendour. Opposite is Banz, a good solid point in the landscape, with a Trappist colony. The area is Old German with horrible little villages, planned to create a fussy effect – you know the painting = background kind of thing. Now I am back here again.

Now that the photographs have finally arrived I am enclosing these for you. I can't exactly say 'I'm quite cosy' with them. I hate pictures of myself – these, and every single one.

Ah, well. There we are.

Yours, Friedel.

Original: MS with printed letterhead; Theodor W. Adorno Archiv, Frankfurt am Main.

Kemp: Kracauer wrote 'Kempp'.

Rudolf Steiner: the founder of anthroposophy (1861–1925). Kracauer wrote an obituary, 'Zum Tode Rudolf Steiners', in *Frankfurter Zeitung*, 18 April 1925 (see Kracauer, W 5, no. 238).

Café Hauptwache: an establishment on the square of the same name in central Frankfurt.

Berlin ... as you intended: The Berlin première of Alban Berg's *Wozzeck*, postponed to December, was planned for May 1925.

Fräulein Else ... Schnitzler: Arthur Schnitzler, *Fräulein Else* (Berlin, 1924).

Kassirer's chimeras: no information survives.

an offprint: not preserved among Kracauer's extensive collection of offprints of Adorno's essays (Kracauer papers, Deutsches Literaturarchiv, Marbach).

'equilibrium': 'The equilibrium between the aesthetic and the ethical in the explication of the personality' is the title of the second section of the second part of Søren Kierkegaard's *Either/Or*.

Susman wrote to me yesterday: Margarete Susman (married name Bendemann; 1872–1966), author and literary scholar, a friend of Kracauer's since the early 1920s. The letter cited is not preserved among Kracauer's papers.

brutto: (Italian): ugly, bad.

my last letter: not preserved.

Horkheimer ... from Paris: Max Horkheimer (1895–1973), philosopher and social scientist, a friend of Adorno's since the early 1920s; professor at the Johann Wolfgang-Goethe-Universität from 1930; co-founder of the Institut für Sozialforschung [Institute for Social Research] and its director from 1931; went into exile in Switzerland in 1933 and the USA in 1934; returned to Frankfurt am Main to resume his academic activities in 1949; rector of the university 1951–1953. No information survives about his visit to Paris.

Zickel: Reinhold Zickel (1885–1953), Adorno's German teacher at the Kaiser-Wilhelms-Gymnasium in Frankfurt am Main (see 'Reinhold Zickel', Adorno, GS 20.2, pp. 756–67, and also Horst Stemmler, 'Rückblicke auf eine Freundschaft: Theodor W. Adorno und sein Lehrer Reinhold Zickel 1913–1965' [Looking back on a friendship: Theodor W. Adorno and his teacher Reinhold Zickel 1913–1965], in *Adorno-Portraits: Erinnerungen von Zeitgenossen* [Portraits of Adorno: memoirs by his contemporaries], ed. Stefan Müller-Doohm (Frankfurt am Main: Suhrkamp, 2007), pp. 175–210.

letter from Fred: two undated letters from Frederick Goldbeck are preserved among Kracauer's papers.

Fräulein Kamnitzer: probably Marianne Kamnitzer (1901–1993), a journalist and lecturer; married name Marschak.

Dr Frankenberger: possibly Dr Julius Frankenberger, who according to the Frankfurt directory for 1925 was a secondary-school teacher whose home was Im Trutz.

Hanni and Bobbie: see letters no. 4 and 8.

Easter ... in Würzburg and Bamberg: Kracauer described this in 'Der Reisevorschlag: Eine Viertage-Reise nach Würzburg und Bamberg' [Suggestions for a journey: a four-day trip to Würzburg and Bamberg], *Frankfurter Zeitung*, 17 May 1925 (see Kracauer, W 5, no. 240).

park of Veitshöchheim: rococo gardens surrounding the summer residence of the prince-bishops of Würzburg.

The horseman was a vision from another realm: Adorno and Kracauer also knew the equestrian statue in Bamberg Cathedral and its iconographical context from Stefan George's poem 'Bamberg' (in *Der Siebente Ring*, 1907) v. 2 [Then in the Kemenate you lie in chains / bodily – neither Ghibelline nor Guelph / only a silent artist, taking pains / pensive, awaiting help from heaven itself.] (Quotation from Stefan George, *Werke*, Vol. I, pp. 336f.)

Hohenlohe: sculpture on the tomb of Friedrich von Hohenlohe (prince-bishop of Bamberg from 1344 to 1352) in Bamberg Cathedral.

Sibyl: together with the statue of the Virgin Mary and the 'laughing angel', part of the group of figures in the east choir of Bamberg Cathedral.

Michaelskirche: the monastery church of the former Benedictine abbey of St Michael in Bamberg.

Vierzehnheiligen and Banz: a pilgrimage church dating from the 18th century and a former Benedictine monastery founded in the 11th century, both situated to the north of Bamberg.

photographs: no photograph of Kracauer which can be matched to this description survives among Adorno's papers; however, there is a portrait with a handwritten dedication from 1923: 'for Teddie. Friedel. March 1923' (see Adorno, *Bildmonographie*, p. 80). A similar one of Adorno from 1924 is preserved among Kracauer's papers: 'For my Friedel, this sad likeness in memory of our journey to the Dolomites. 2 September 1924, on the way to Lake Garda' (Deutsches Literaturarchiv, Marbach).

11 Adorno to Kracauer
Vienna, 19.5.1925

Vienna, 19 May 1925.

My dear Friedel,

I hardly need to tell you that it was a series of quite extraordinary events which struck me dumb towards you for so long; my silence was too radical for you to have taken it for forgetfulness, and I am most surprised that I didn't receive a few lines from you in the very weeks when I needed you most of all. This surprise is wholly un-Leonine and genuine; I feel that you lack trust in me if you could think that I didn't write to you because it is so lovely and interesting in Vienna and because existential characters are sitting waiting for me in the corner of every café. But in the final analysis I am so profoundly unhappy that I can even understand this mistrust; when it is already so difficult to exist with each other, how much more difficult is it to vegetate without each other and still maintain the belief that one does exist. And so this is being done not in the hope of conjuring up a present but only for the sake of biographical accuracy, and because I should like to sense your smile as I tell you that a very intelligent young lady, when we met for the second time – and without knowing *anything* about me – declared to me most decidedly that I was homosexual and absent-mindedly with a far-away friend at the very minute when I was thinking quite intensely about you. In short, I believe that I am fanatically faithful to you – much more faithful that I myself could have thought when I was wholly in the grip of your intimation that it was all over. But more of that later.

I can't tell you in a letter what happened to me, although it stemmed from very simple external circumstances and sounds on the surface like an absurd novel in which living and dead people, some of whom are quite close to me and others whom I only know from books, newspapers, are entangled in the most bizarre way. I can't write to you about it because a certain sense of shame prevents me from turning terrible, incomprehensible chains of events – the fates of others, into which I just happened to be blindly drawn – into a proper novel, distinguishable from one by Perutz only by the fact that it lacks a key. I have an overwhelming feeling that everything would have come out aesthetically *malgré moi*, and that could not be allowed to happen. You will learn everything (perhaps I may soon know more than I do today, although I forbid myself any attempts at investigative interference), but only when you see me and my voice can vouch for the fact that I am not lying. That's all for now; it relates to something which befell me in the past, not the present – to poor Gretel, the responsibility for whose illness suddenly seems to have fallen on me. Don't think that I am mad or suffering from paranoia, although I did think myself that I was until I came to my senses weeks later. Now that I can breathe, you are the first person I have talked to; I am alive, and I am going to go on living, and hungering for a sign from you.

During the worst days Alban Berg took care of me in a truly magnificent and humane way, as hardly anyone else could have done. Otherwise I was entirely alone; Lila, who would have been out of the question in any case, was in Italy and is only returning this evening; Morgenstern is far from being close enough to me, and the musicians notice nothing about me except counterpoint, as I have completely drawn in my feelers as regards personal matters. My sense of musical continuity, of course, was entirely destroyed; on the very day of the decisive encounter I had just completed the first movement of the new trio, which seems as if it might actually be some good. Afterwards I could do nothing at all, and only squeezed out a few songs as I felt myself drifting into a hazy state of mind (one of them is a completely new version of one which is three years old, and of which I am especially fond). Nor have I practised the piano as regularly as I should have done under Steuermann. Now I am working my way with infinite difficulty into the second movement of the trio. I have arranged a few French folksongs which Agathe is sure to sing.

A little more from the outside world: early tomorrow morning I shall be going to Prague – not to the music festival itself (that is over and would only have bored me) but for its after-pains – Dukas' *Ariane et Barbe-Bleue* and Berg's *Wozzeck* fragments which Zemlinsky is doing to round things off. For my own part I'm not keen to go, but am doing so for Berg's sake and because, on account of the story which I mentioned, I am very eager to get to know Zemlinsky and the Werfel family (I'll probably see the man himself in Vienna). I don't, of course, expect a hack writer's box [*Schmockkästlein*] to turn into the jewel casket [*Schmuckkästchen*] in the *Wanderjahre*. I shall probably stay only until Friday, or Saturday at the latest, so write to me in Vienna. The *Wozzeck* première has been postponed until the winter, so I shall not be coming to Berlin for the time being, but I should like to take a look at that curious place Budapest, whose dirt and pathos have reached even as far as here. My plans for the summer are still quite uncertain; I may possibly (for those same reasons again) be in Aussee for two weeks – might the two of us (as I should like) go to Italy? In late summer?! What do you think of that? What are your plans? Do you think I could contrive to pull it off with the folks at home? Do write to me so that I can prepare an offensive.

As to your letter: the mysterious sentences in my last one (the one written *before* my experience, whose sadness had no acute and specific cause) referred only to the fact that I was under the impression that my distance from you in terms of space – something which I feel ever and always – had not arisen freely, or that it was timely – or even for our good – but would, as if under the pressure of the evil emanating from and around Hanni, separate me from you to destroy me. Of course, I know just as well as you that nobody can take the essence of another person away from someone else, but you know as well as I do, or even better, that I could never really be sure of that – that even the uttermost kind of love is still bound up with the basic facts and the conditions in which one is trapped – otherwise no hatred could ever be possible, and the world would be a rosy place. As surely as I believe in the supremacy of intimacy in interpersonal relations, I believe in the constant tragedy which underlies that intimacy. For that reason, I could feel myself to be under threat – alienated – without slipping from our way of thinking into Strindberg's.

Your report about Susmann shook me with hindsight, as I know that you had contrived to love this very unusual woman despite every argument against it, and that because of this the downright disappointment that she became must have hurt you greatly – all the more because of the tone in which you reported it, and which actually resembles that picture which I am carrying with me now, and which produced a similarly ambivalent effect on me, delighted me in aesthetic terms, while I should like to transport myself from myself to you, be with you and melt you, if I can still do so. Your contempt for humanity (which, symbolically enough, calls itself by that name) touches me more than any open confession could, just as the pain of rigidity and dumbness moves me altogether more profoundly than tears, which, however, are still shed in this world. Don't think me any more sentimental than you yourself claim to be; for us *âmes désordonnées* are both only correlative in so far as the one On can, to some extent, exorcise the other or reduce it to the fundamentals of existence. But perhaps one day you will look different from the way you do there and I shall, perhaps, no longer have any need of those awkward words that come straight from the soul when I am with you.

The reason for Susmann's behaviour is Bloch – and her own vanity. As she has no intellectual essence, she thinks with her empirical equivalent, which is not suited to the absolute dimension of her thoughts and constantly disavows them with its pettiness. In theological terms she stubbornly persists in living beyond her means, goes luxuriously bankrupt on a grandiose scale, confuses you with the bailiff, locks the door and empties her chamber-pot over your head. What a pity about her and her messianic waste of calories!

Your criticisms of the [musical] reproductions essay are indeed accurate except for the accusation of Benjaminism, which was evoked solely by the pointed differentness of the fragments (conducted quite anti-systematically), which in general – even within the structure of the language itself – are equipped with teeth to deal with specious ontologism. The essay has brought me respect but has had no consequences whatsoever, although Stein is pressing me earnestly for a continuation and says that it may possibly be published in pamphlet form. Of all the conductors that I know here, not a single one has said anything *to any purpose* about it to me; neither, of course, has that dimwit Klenau. The only person to understand it properly was Morgenstern, and even he did so more *à la lettre* – not the background, although he is a disciple of Buber – and yet he was *not* hard on it. The approach you took in your Steiner essay did not wholly please me in Vienna; I found its humanity a bit pointed, and I would almost have found it more human if it had been inhuman – simply the tone of a blunt polemic, with the absolution, based on the logic of the spheres, implied only in an undertone, not pinning out the dead like butterflies in a display case complete with instructive blanket descriptions. The case is, however, different from that of Holzapfel. I found everything just a bit too correct, without the honorific injustice with which one should address even minor demons as devils in order to force them to yield. For my own part I would have placed a slightly stronger emphasis on the idea of theological materialism – the skipping over the relationship by which the *it*-categories are boldly carried into the *you*-world, and by which the *you*-world is also falsified in accordance with the *what* that it contains – in other words, I would not merely have noted the natural scientist's involuntary acts of fraud but would have interpreted them. That would certainly have produced data serving to facilitate a delimitation from gnosis. But perhaps that would not have been feasible out of consideration for the newspaper, and it is certainly not important. Intellectually Diebold seems to have gone completely to the dogs; he now only works on posters and puts them on display. I had no idea at all that he was in Vienna, and he took no notice of me, as is only right.

As for me, the sphere in which I live has now become established and taken on a definitely sociological character. The Russians are in the background; Berg figures in it, together with his wife (in the Schoenberg book that I have at home – the old one – there is the portrait of a woman by Sch. which depicts her; get them to show it to you, and also his picture in the Allg. Musikztg. or the 'Kunstschau'). I frequent the Café Museum (I haven't been there in the last few weeks), and see Eisler quite often, Schoenberg's most gifted pupil (more gifted than Křenek and Hindemith), and also a man named Ratz, who is very serious, and Morgenstern. In general, I can find a sympathetic response to my music there, especially with Eisler. And that may be a good thing, even if it doesn't affect me.

The only person here about whom I have anything of importance to tell you is that clever lady. Her name is Ellen Delp; she is an actress and lives in my boarding-house. She is beautiful (not my type, actually – womanly, the line of her shoulders a sweeping curve), with a splendid, quite narrow mouth and large dark eyes, and blonde in a very unusual way – wheat-blonde. She is talented, knowledgeable *a priori*, cultured and childish; not a trace of the world behind the scenes about her, doesn't talk about the theatre; I have never seen her on stage, and she doesn't know a single note or line that I have written – a tacit understanding. She has a precious way of talking in a manner that is all ready to go straight to print, which touches me; she is a girl of the most audacious (but genuine) innocence; she has the whole of Freud's psychology and so on at her fingertips and knows, along with us, that it is nothing but a joke. You can talk to her properly and play with her, and she is kind-hearted enough for me not to have to be afraid that she will suddenly rise up in front of me with an air of feigned sincerity and accuse me of insincerity. She has a specific type of feeling for me and makes, in a mature fashion, amazing remarks of which she is as proud as a girl in her teens. We parade our emotions around the environs of Vienna, make secret assignations which the whole boarding-house notices, feel like a pair of lovers in the presence of third parties, and are nothing of the kind when it's just the two of us; I don't pester her, and she takes it as read that I have ties – something about which, of course, she is right. I desire (in poetic terms) no other situation than my present one, and I am perverse enough to prefer the kindly illusion I have here to a reality which cannot be. If I have come to my senses in the last few days, it is thanks to her more than anything else. For me it is your Marianne Kamnitzer all over again, and of course

Maschtenka [?] will never die as long as one 'believes'. More about Ellen Delp soon. My hand is aching now, my head is growing befuddled, and I am fretting about your reply.

Teddie.

Please: send me the 'Romantische Suite von der Bergstrasse'. I have inexplicably mislaid it, and I have a hankering for it. I know that you will object – but please do it for my sake.

Original: MS; Siegfried Kracauer papers, Deutches Literaturarchiv, Marbach am Neckar. Handwritten note by Kracauer on the envelope: '6) arrived 22 May 1925 (Friday) morning. Answered: *24 May*'. The reply has not survived.

un-Leonine: probably a dig at Leo Löwenthal, perhaps suggesting: not at all spurious/artificial.

what happened to me: Adorno was a witness to Alban Berg's passion for Franz Werfel's sister Hanna (1894–1964), who was married to the Prague entrepreneur Herbert Fuchs-Robettin (1886–1949), and in whose house Berg, like Adorno, was a guest during his forthcoming visit to Prague (see Adorno/Berg, *Briefwechsel*, p. 13).

Perutz: The writer Leopold ('Leo') Perutz (1882–1956) came from Prague; the family moved to Vienna in 1899. Perutz's novels, which appeared in part in the Austrian press before publication in book form, ran into extensive print runs. Adorno and Kracauer had a particularly high regard for *Der Meister des jüngsten Tages* (1923); Kracauer reviewed the book (the review appears, without a title, in *Frankfurter Zeitung*, 4 October 1923; see Kracauer, W5, no. 135).

Gretel: Gretel Herzberger, a member of the Herzberger family, friends of the Wiesengrunds; in a letter to his parents of 4 March 1948 (see Adorno, *Letters to his Parents*, p. 317), Adorno specifies her illness, which he vaguely mentioned to Alban Berg (see Adorno/Berg, *Correspondence*, pp. 25, 44–6, 53–5) as 'schizophrenia'.

squeezed out a few songs: *Vier Gedichte von Stefan George für Singstimme und Klavier* [Four Poems by Stefan George for voice and piano], op. 1 (see letter no. 1, note), written between 1925 and 1928.

to Prague – not to the music festival itself: the International Society for Contemporary Music, 2nd Music Festival in Prague, 15–20 May 1925 (see also the programme in *Musikblätter des Anbruch*, special issue, May 1925).

a few French folksongs: *Sept chansons populaires françaises arrangés pour une voix et piano* (see Adorno, *Kompositionen* I, pp. 92–100).

Dukas: Paul Dukas (1865–1935), composer; his opera *Ariane et Barbe-Bleue* received its première in Paris; the performance in the Neue Deutsche Theater concluded the Prague music festival (see *Musikblätter des Anbruch*, special issue, May 1925).

Wozzeck *fragments*: the composer and conductor Alexander von Zemlinsky (1871–1942) performed *Drei Bruchstücke aus Wozzeck* in Prague on 20 May 1925 (see Adorno/Berg, *Correspondence*, p. 13, note 1).

the casket in the Wanderjahre: see the episode of the casket and the key in the letters of Hersilie to Wilhelm in Johann Wolfgang Goethe, *Wilhelm Meister*, trans. H. M. Waidson. Richmond, Surrey: Alma Classics, 2013, pp. 720–2.

one On: 'that which is' (Greek).

The reason for Susmann's behaviour is Bloch: the relationship between Margarete Susmann and Ernst Bloch was full of tensions (see Bloch's descriptions to Georg Lukács in Bloch, *Briefe* I, pp. 25–208). They were reconciled in 1921.

Klenau: Paul August von Klenau (1883–1946), a composer and conductor from Copenhagen; choral conductor and concert manager of the Wiener Konzertgesellschaft.

Steiner essay: Kracauer's obituary (see letter no. 10).

The case is, however, different from that of Holzapfel: Rudolf Maria Holzapfel (1874–1930), cultural philosopher: Kracauer reviewed his *Panideal: Psychologie der sozialen Gefühle* [Panideal: psychology of social emotions] ([1901] 1923; i.e. the new edition): 'Holzapfels "Panideal": Zur Kritik der Kulturgläubigkeit' [Panideal: on the critique of cultural devoutness], *Frankfurter Zeitung*, 7 February 1924 (see Kracauer, W 5, no. 175). The review sparked off an extended debate in the *Frankfurter Zeitung*.

Diebold: Bernhard Diebold (1886–1945); from 1917 to 1936 editor of the features supplement and drama critic at the *Frankfurter Zeitung*.

Schoenberg book … portrait of a woman: in the library left behind by Adorno: *Arnold Schönberg, mit Beiträgen von Alban Berg u. a.*, Munich: Piper, 1912; Schoenberg's *Damenporträt* (Portrait of a Lady) is reproduced between pp. 64 and 65.

Café Museum: a café built by Adolf Loos on the Friedrichstrasse.

Křenek: Ernst Krenek [spelt thus after he emigrated] (1900–1991), composer; as described by Adorno, 'Ernst Krenek became famous at a very early age, around 1920, at the time of the Donaueschingen music festivals and those events in Salzburg where the city, as much as the Internationale Gesellschaft für Neue Musik, was identified with the avant-garde. Next to Hindemith, Krenek was at that time the most striking exponent of the second generation of radical composers' ('Zur Physiognomik Kreneks' [On Krenek's physiognomy], *Theaterzeitschrift der Deutschen Oper am Rhein*, no. 13, 1957–8; see Adorno, GS 17, pp. 109–13, 348; here, p. 109).

Hindemith: Paul Hindemith (1885–1963), composer; taught, like Adorno, by Bernhard Sekles at Dr Hoch's Conservatory in Frankfurt am Main.

Ratz: Erwin Ratz (1898–1973), musical theorist; in 1955 founder and president of the Internationale Gustav Mahler Gesellschaft and from 1960 editor of the Mahler-Werkausgabe edition of Mahler's works. Adorno dedicated to him his article 'Zur einer imaginären Auswahl von Liedern Gustav Mahlers' [On an imaginary selection of songs by Gustav Mahler] (published for the first time in Adorno, GS 17, pp. 189–97).

Delp: Ellen Delp, née Schachian (1890–1990), actress and author. A resumption of contact between them is documented in the correspondence from the years 1960–3 preserved in the Theodor W. Adorno Archiv.

Romantische Suite von der Bergstrasse: 'Empfindsame Suite aus der Bergstrasse', *Frankfurter Zeitung*, 26 May 1923 (see Kracauer, W 5, no. 129); in it Kracauer idealized an excursion which the friends had made together.

12 Adorno to Kracauer

Prague, 21.5.1925

Prague, 21 May

Just think – in the midst of the hustle and bustle of the music festival I met Herr Grab, who, full of the wisdom of Solomon, heard you reading 'Hotelhalle' in a café. I cannot tell you how much the symbolic intention delighted me. I have been accepted in Werfelia and elsewhere with a hospitality straight from the realms of fantasy which would have sent you into philosophical convulsions. The music was nothing except *Wozzeck*, but what a city! I had a good look at it and spent a long time in front of the grave of Rabbi Löw, which the Orthodox Jews still decorate with pebbles even nowadays. You will have had my letter from Vienna now. Write soon. If only you were here – everything here is made for us to be together, and I feel even more incomplete than ever without you.

Teddie.

Best wishes

Hermann Grab

Original: manuscript, postcard; Siegfried Kracauer papers, Deutsches Literaturarchiv, Marbach am Neckar. Handwritten note by Kracauer: '7) answered: 24 May, arr. 23 May from *Prague*.' The reply has not been preserved.

Grab: Adorno had been acquainted with the Prague-born musician and author Hermann Grab (1903–1949) since Grab's student days in Heidelberg around 1924 (see Adorno, *Bildmonographie*, pp. 93–7). Adorno made a posthumous dedication to him of 'Valéry Proust Museum', *Die Neue Rundschau*, no. 4, 1953 (see Adorno, GS 10.1, pp. 181–94; GS 10.2, p. 839) and 'Richard Strauss', *Die Neue Rundschau*, no. 4, 1964 (see GS 16, pp. 565–606, 679); see the obituary (Adorno, GS 20.2, pp. 464f.).

heard you reading 'Hotelhalle': no information survives about the time and place of Kracauer's coffee-house reading from 'Hotelhalle' in the presence of Hermann Grab (see Kracauer, W 1, pp. 130–9, 378f., 389f.); the text was first published in *Das Ornament der Masse*, Frankfurt am Main, Suhrkamp, 1963, pp. 157–70.

Werfelia: Hanna Fuchs-Robettin, née Werfel, and Herbert Fuchs-Robettin.

The grave of Rabbi Löw: the grave of Rabbi Löw (Juda Löwe ben Bezalel, c. 1525–1609), according to legend the creator of the Golem, in Prague's Jewish cemetery.

13 Adorno to Kracauer
Vienna, 26.5.1925

Vienna, 26 May, Tuesday morning.

My dear Friedel,

Your letter delivered a terrible blow, it struck me to my core, and although your tone would actually forbid me to answer – even though you have used not a single word to provoke this kind of reaction – I am replying at once – half an hour after receiving it – without giving us time to reflect. The sentence, 'The time for that may come, if indeed it comes at all' might on its own be enough to do that, if it were not far outdone by later ones. You are giving up on our relationship – or, even worse, you are making preparations for it with all those deliberate 'virtues' of admonitory cleverness and distanced humaneness which you so thoroughly despise that the tone of your contempt discolours all your well-meant phrases. Your letter is worse than an open attack – even worse than the silence that it doesn't merely break but flogs to death with words, as that very silence seems so final that your letter picks it up and, taking it for granted, continues it – something which loses all reality when it is a sequel to silence. At the same time your letter is silence itself, but in a much cruder sense, because it cloaks in silence whatever happened to you in Frankfurt – and if that was the break with Marianne Kamnitzer, you are, if nothing else, covering up the fact that this is the case by stubbornly saying that you cannot assume that I appreciate the true importance of this relationship, about which you have continually been unburdening yourself to me. But let me, first of all, consider your letter in some detail. Your attack on my astonished reaction seems unjustified to me. That I wrote home in a contented tone proves nothing – there would have been no sense in conveying anxiety to people who are unable to offer me any help, and, besides, an official optimism prevails in Seeheimer Strasse – among the women, at least – which cannot possibly put you under any kind of obligation. Whatever you may think, I did not write my letter to them in a 'contented' tone at all, but in a matter-of-fact, reassuring one. The cruel sentence stating that 'the only difference between this break and the previous one is its greater length' is not only cruel but wrong, because if you were to suppose that my life here would come to a standstill after the crisis of moving to a new environment, it would be equally incomprehensible to you that even the rhythm of my life had also acquired some degree of stability. If, though, you did not believe that my life is running at a more tranquil pace, you might have asked yourself (and perhaps even me) what was standing in the way of that. I am not saying this, like Herr Csokor in the Café Museum, in order to declare that I – the one at fault – was right yet again, but to defend myself against the reproach (I hope that it is still only a reproach!) of having forgotten you when I was under the delusion that *I* had been forgotten; moreover, I was under no such delusion about myself, but only thought that stubbornness had got a grip on you. I never, of course, took Frankfurt for a Magic Mountain where time was suspended, or supposed you to be in the arms of a purely philosophical Venus, and, if I didn't write, this really was solely the result of the pressure of a paralysing encounter – that experience which I alluded to in veiled terms in my last letter to you, and which I am explaining to you now because, in these terrible days in which all the demons have been unleashed on me (your letter is the last of them, the Vij), something much worse has happened about which I must remain completely silent, as I was not the only one affected. The content of your sentence saying that it didn't seem wholly impossible to you that 'for one reason or another' I 'wanted to let the correspondence become dormant' is completely incomprehensible to me, and I take it as evidence of your wounded heart, but not as something which you meant objectively.

As to the real 'correspondence' (with the others): as soon as I have got myself a little more under control I shall meet my responsibilities; Fred has written me an even more insulting, snarling letter based on a premise which has become an *idée fixe* with him – namely, that I am a cheat; but, assuredly, he too is one of God's creatures and must have his say.

Now, about my experience: no, it is not an affair, neither with Alma Maria (our relationship is confined to one afternoon, a letter from me and two from her – she wrote the second because she had forgotten the first!) nor with anyone else; on the contrary, I am breaking off my relationship with Lila with all the energy which this requires because she has really got her teeth deep into me. Your second assumption is nearer the truth – just that I *haven't* been given the key. To make it clear to you what happened, I must remind you that Gretel had a friend, a girl from Vienna, whom she loved passionately. This friend was in Aussee in the summer of 1921, while I was staying in Sölden; Gretel asked me to visit her there, but that didn't come about as Alfons didn't want to go. Two weeks later – in that place – Adrienne killed herself, and her death was the final trigger for the outbreak of Gretel's illness. On the one hand, she laid the blame for the suicide on me because I didn't get to her in time; on the other, she convinced herself (as early as the autumn of 1921) that Adrienne was not dead at all but living somewhere in secret, and was involved in a conspiracy with me. The fate of that girl has given me no peace ever since, and you know that it had a literary aftermath. After her name – that unusual French name – had been staring out at me from all the posters for a whole fortnight, the following event occurred. Dead tired after working and dreadfully sad, I was wandering aimlessly into town late one night without any definite plan in mind. As I was finally making my way home, I looked into the Grabencafé again, and sat down by a girl who took my fancy – one of those Viennese creatures who is something between a boy and a girl, but one thing rather than the other. As we were leaving the hotel, I took her along to the café again to talk to her because I was feeling so lonely. In the course of the conversation it emerged after three minutes that this girl had not only been staying in Aussee in the summer of 1921 but had witnessed Adrienne's death at first hand – she knew her name and gave me a precise description of her – and also of Gretel. The next day I heard from Berg that Adrienne had had an affair with Werfel; he knew about this from the jealousy which Alma Mahler still felt. I don't need to tell you what this chain of romantic entanglements meant to me; of course, this was the reason for the plan of going to Aussee. For weeks I felt – quite literally – persecuted. Perhaps you will no longer consider it a mere excuse that I resisted writing to you about these incomprehensible and fateful external matters which, taken out of their spiritual continuum, sound like the plot of a film – it is impossible, just from a recital of the facts and without being physically present, to sense anything of the significance which it inevitably acquires; and it was only a fear of the inevitable understanding that explains my reticence. As I am speaking now I am running the risk that you may regard me either as mad myself or as a theological traitor, although – believe me – I am neither. You doubt that I ever genuinely needed you and pin me down to the contradiction between this and my silence. No – I *should* have needed you if you had been there, I shouldn't have needed to keep quiet – and it is only the terrible uncertainty of our relationship, which has become quite simply intolerable to me – only this constant anxiety about losing you here and everywhere constrains me. You doubt, too, that I am 'vegetating' and imagine that, for the sake of an inconceivable fidelity, I am painting the lovely days here grey! Oh, if only I *were* vegetating! Instead of that, though, I am being smitten by one disaster after another. Scarcely had I calmed down a little after this business than that other thing happened about which I *must* not speak because it relates to the fate of a third party, not my own – but which, in its turn, is mine too, as I bore a great weight of the responsibility for it. If there is any hope of saving that person I am the only one who may possibly be able to avert the worst – if I make a mistake, all is lost. I am not getting any work done; all practical matters are of utter indifference to me – more than anything else I want to sleep, I'm so dreadfully tired. The only good thing that I can say at this point is that I do have the prospect of being of some genuine help.

Ellen Delp, now, is in Munich and asked me as we parted to find her the kind of husband she yearns for – tall, slim, strong, kind-hearted, fatherly – a brilliant doctor. As a husband I am as much out of the question for her as you are for that Marianne Kamnitzer, whom I always mistrusted – it was just that at the same time I mistrusted my distrust and took it for jealousy, which, however, it could not possibly be. This is how proudly I still think of you and me even at this time: two people who cannot be divided by any third person if we don't break up of our own volition. Ellen Delp doesn't love me in the slightest, and I no longer believe that I have any ability left at all to feel love for a woman. It never was more than a beautiful illusion, sadly and artificially cultivated, and it has come to an end. Your belief that I am lucky with women, which, like everything in your letter, was intended to create a distance between us, can only be viewed as 'objective irony'.

Summer: I shall not be going to Aussee, after all. I shall still be here throughout July. By August, though, I shall be free. As I *literally* did not understand how you feel about the plan of our travelling together, I am asking you urgently for information – above all for an explanation of page 4. The fact that I mean the world to my people persuades you to conclude that 'for *this very* reason I shall say nothing else about the future'. Why?! And then: 'One day the future will arrive – better, much better, not to anticipate it prematurely' (does that mean by travelling together?!) 'After what happened, it will not be a good thing.' (Now? Or forever? And what if I need you?) 'It would be cut off as if with an axe!' Who or what? The future? Or were you thinking of the past? But all this is full of contradictions which you will have to explain.

Once again, may I ask you for the Bergstraße essay? I had long since forgotten the folksong review and was surprised that you liked it. As with all my literary stuff I still have a feeling that the framework is not adequate for the concrete material.

I find your acknowledgement of my card from Prague – 'many thanks' – undeserved and needlessly hurtful. Are you really trying to make it impossible for me to get through to you? The card, certainly, couldn't accomplish that, but it came to me so immediately that it might at least have lit up the impossible way for me like a sharp spotlight – and you extinguished it. All this leaves me in complete despair, and I beg you, once again and imploringly, for a proper word. I have nothing else to anchor me; I am absolutely bound to you – nothing but evil has befallen me here, but nothing that could tear me away from you; in fact I am waiting only for you and actually see everything else as merely temporary – but if I don't hear from you once more in words – no matter how ambivalent – that you believe me, that you feel, beneath all that burdens me, the willingness to be there and are there for me yourself – if you continue to look in despair at this shy, hesitant creature, then it may be – it *will* be – that I shall turn to stone, and that we, who loved each other more than anything and yet are enemies, will be lonely for lack of each other. Just bear in mind that I scarcely have the strength to make the least effort any more. I am thinking of you too, and know everything about you, just as I always did – only I cannot know our external fate, and *you* must tell me what it will be. What has happened to you? Not just my silence – I sense that – and not just M. K., but something primitive, something deadly, proceeding from another world, surely something very bad which is causing you to shy away. Despite my anxiety about you and me, I have said what I could to you. Now force yourself to say the same to me. We must not be dumb and inarticulate towards each other.

I *really do* want the Bergstraße essay – although I think it must be in Frankfurt. I shall stop now, although I am only just beginning, but the letter must be off. This evening I have to go to the theatre, and then meet up with Werfel.

Your Teddie.

Two more things: *first*: while suffering the effects of the latest catastrophe I carelessly wrote a letter home which will sound ominous. Do look in there and say that all will be well and that things are already better. (Of course, they don't know either what it's all about – otherwise you would know.)

Next: Morgenstern gave me a short essay yesterday about the decline of the confidence trickster – good as an idea, not fully developed, but publishable despite its literary stance, for me to send you for the F.Z. I am telling you but not sending it, as in our situation every kind of mud, even the mere appearance of it, seems inadmissible.

Original: MS: Siegfried Kracauer papers, Deutsches Literaturarchiv, Marbach am Neckar. Handwritten note by Kracauer on the envelope: '(8.) arr. 28 *May* answered in Harzburg 31 *May*.' The reply has not been preserved.

Your letter: not preserved.

wrote … Seeheimer Strasse: not preserved.

Csokor: Franz Theodor Csokor (1885–1969), dramatist and novelist.

the last of them, the Vij: in the story 'The Vij', by Nikolai Gogol (1809–1852), the appearance of a demon of the same name forms the climax of a series of persecutions over the course of several days which lead to the death of the protagonist Choma Brut. In the library left behind by Adorno there is a 1923 edition of Gogol's works.

Fred has written: the oldest letter from Frederick Goldbeck which is preserved in the Theodor W. Adorno Archiv dates from 1927.

a letter from me and two from her: in a letter of 3 April 1923 Adorno thanked Alma Mahler for the meeting in her house (Mahler-Werfel Papers, Rare Book & Manuscript Library, University of Pennsylvania, Philadelphia; details from information provided there); only letters from Alma Mahler from 1942 onwards are preserved among Adorno's papers.

Gretel: Gretel Herzberger.

a friend … Adrienne: Adrienne Sachs (1893–1921), 'painter, granddaughter of Marianne Benedict' (see Arthur Schnitzler, *Tagebuch 1920–1922*, ed. Peter Michael Braunwarth, Susanne Pertlik and Reinhard Urbach. Vienna: Österreichische Akademie der Wissenschaften, 1993). From Schnitzler's entry for 11/12 August 1921: 'in the afternoon (during a thunderstorm) Adrienne Sachs threw herself out of a boat into the lake' (see ibid., p. 215).

staying in Sölden: not documented in Adorno's papers.

Alfons: Alfons Herzberger (1879–?), brother of Else Herzberger.

literary aftermath: the basic motif of a young woman from Vienna taking her own life in a holiday resort recurs in Arthur Schnitzler, *Fräulein Else* (see Kracauer's allusion to the book in letter no. 10).

French name … from all the posters: no information survives about performances of the opera *Adriana Lecouvreur* by Francesco Cilea or the play of the same name by Eugène Scribe to which this might refer; on the other hand, *Ariadne auf Naxos* by Hugo von Hofmannsthal and Richard Strauss was performed on 25 May 1925 at the Operntheater (*Neue Freie Presse*, 25 May 1925).

Grabencafé: Graben-Kaffee in Vienna, Graben 29.

that other thing … about which I must not speak: Alban Berg's involvement with Hanna Fuchs-Robettin (see letter no. 11).

the folksong review: see letter no. 5.

M.K.: presumably Marianne Kamnitzer.

a letter home: the letter as well as the reaction of the 'mothers' has not been preserved.

a short essay: probably Soma Morgenstern, 'Casan', in the same author's *Dramen, Feuilletons, Fragmente*, ed. Ingolf Schulte. Lüneburg: zu Klampen, 2000, pp. 369f., previously unpublished.

14 Adorno to Kracauer
Vienna, 31.5.1925

Vienna, Pentecost, 31 May 1925.

My dear Friedel,

I received your card, the sign, and it did me good, even though it could not remotely reassure me. Once again, I beg you *urgently* to tell me what happened to you; late last night it came into my head that it might be Hanni who was approaching you, and I believed her capable of giving herself to you in order to drive us apart. But that is most likely paranoia, even though it also strikes me that, even after I enquired, in my last letter but one, about how things were going in the Kettenhofweg, you didn't mention the unfortunate woman's name.

I have now radically accomplished the break with Lila (who, as I know, wrote a card to you *even before that* about Bedya-Beata Hinzburg-Tanya, whom I also know, albeit superficially) after my attempt to carry on the relationship without the erotic element had led to nothing but senseless torments. I insisted that we should no longer see each other at all; she clung to me in despair, but in the end brutality was the gentlest way, as *laisser faire* would have only bound her to me with even heavier chains, and because it would have been impossible for me – estranged from her as I truly am – to support her in the way that she had a right to demand. I hope, as I think of our many conversations, that she will think of my conduct as moral – it was certainly not irresponsible and, if not purely altruistic, did show great consideration for others. I myself am genuinely sorry for Lila, and how I acted felt objectionable enough to me, but curiously I have no sense at all of the great wrong (a public one, to some extent) that one inflicts on an abandoned mistress – either because I never really loved her or because (as I believe) the solemn, pompous events in life are beyond the sphere of moral dialectic, so to speak. In their rigidly fixed symbolic nature they are wholly detached from the ego, and the more important they make themselves out to be, the more incidental they are in personal terms: signs of how little the external is in accord with the internal in this, while little haphazard things – a harsh or a kind word that one says, or even a gesture – are often quite transparent, reveal the true essence and relate to the conscience. So much is obvious: I am feeling the same way when I am in a positive frame of mind – that is, when I take upon myself an objectively 'great' sacrifice, I don't feel in the least exalted – in fact I didn't feel that I myself was involved in it at all, but only my transcendental subject – not even the one to be understood in Kantian terms as intelligible, about whose existence I am thoroughly sceptical.

My Whit Sunday is *un peu gris*: yesterday afternoon I went with Alban Berg, his wife and Morgenstern on the Cobenzl, which has a splendid view and lots of prettily dressed girls from Viennese Jewish families; and now there are strawberries with whipped cream, and it is the time when at home one sits in the Café Hanselmann on warm evenings and then takes refuge in the dark Miquelstrasse when acquaintances turn up. I spent the evening with Morgenstern and his very odd (married) girlfriend – a Romanian princess called Renée. I slept in and dozed the morning away. Now, early in the afternoon, I am going into town, to the Stadtpark, to the Südbahnhof, thinking of you and waiting for a sensation.

I read the Seeheim essay with 'oh, such emotion', and its past is very much in tune with my sad present.

I am gradually forcing myself back into the trio. How is the detective novel going? Sometimes I fancied that you would surprise me with a printed copy, but no – you won't do that, probably for fear of creating a symbol of something that doesn't quite exist, and because you hate any kind of lasting symbol for us if at the same time we don't live spontaneously. You are probably right about that, but, for me, disoriented as I am at present, even the symbol without the idea behind it would be precious – which doesn't mean, by the way, that I want to encourage you to do anything – no, I'm not that sentimental. Are you writing about the philosophy of history?

Morgenstern is really being kind to me here, and I am grateful to him. The structure of the relationship will become clear to you when I tell you that I call him Morgenstern – formally but without the Herr – and he calls me Wiesengrund. A relationship between men – based on trust, intellect, and a sense of spiritual desolation, without passion and restrained.

Did I tell you that the composer Eisler, with whom I go about a lot, is the brother of Ruth Fischer?

Gütersloh, regrettably, has turned up here. Berg, who used to be a friend of his, can't introduce me to him because he has quarrelled with him via Karl Kraus. Incidentally, he is a goy and is really called Alois (but according to other sources only Alfred or Albert) Kuhtreiber. As a substitute for

him the Bergs want to pair me off with Franz Blei's daughter, but I won't take the bait and she, a sporty Catholic girl, is even less likely to do so. Because of all kinds of twists and turns of fate I still haven't seen Werfel (who, as I am sure I wrote to you, knew Gretel's friend well – perhaps *extremely* well). Just a word about my relations with the world of famous names and men of letters: I regard it all in a suitably comical spirit. I am waiting eagerly for your letter.
Teddie.
Good luck with surviving that place called Saxony – even when you brush against it while passing through in the train, it is terrible.

Original: MS; Siegfried Kracauer papers, Deutsches Literaturarchiv, Marbach am Neckar. Handwritten note by Kracauer: '(9) rec. 2 June in Halle answered 5 June a.m. in Halle ... written for no reason, on *11 June* (Frankf.).' The letter has not survived.

your card: not preserved.

Hanni: see letter no. 8.

Bedya-Beata Hinzburg-Tanya: no information survives.

Cobenzl: Vienna's own mountain.

Hanselmann: a café on the Opernplatz in Frankfurt.

Miquelstrasse: the present-day Siesmayerstrasse.

Renée: Irene Maria Caroline Nossal, née Loewenthal (1893–1962), a musician from Vienna and friend of Soma Morgenstern since 1915; she went into exile in Australia in 1939. On her role for Morgenstern as a transmitter of Viennese musical culture, see Soma Morgenstern, *Alban Berg und seine Idole: Erinnerungen und Briefe* [Alban Berg and his idols: memoirs and letters], ed. Ingolf Schulte. Lüneburg: zu Klampen, 1995, pp. 44f.

'*oh, such emotion*': a parallel can be found in Goethe's *Italienische Reise*: 'This morning the letters which Winckelmann wrote from Italy came into my hands. With what emotion did I begin to read them! Thirty-one years ago, at the same age, he came here, even more of a poor fool than I; he too was full of just such German earnestness about the fundamental and unchanging nature of antiquities and of art' (see Johann Wolfgang Goethe, *Briefe, Tagebücher und Gespräche*, I, ed. Christoph Michel and Hans-Georg Dewitz. Frankfurt am Main: Deutscher Klassiker Verlag, 1993, p. 159).

detective novel: *Der Detektiv-Roman: Ein philosophischer Traktat* [The detective novel: a philosophical treatise]; unpublished apart from 'Hotelhalle' until its inclusion in Kracauer, *Schriften* (1971). The study bears the dedication 'To Theodor Wiesengrund-Adorno, my friend' (see Kracauer, W 1, pp. 103–209).

Ruth Fischer: i.e. Elfriede Eisler (1885–1961), who participated in the founding of the Communist Party of Austria in 1918. She changed her name after moving to Berlin in 1919; from 1924 she represented the KPD in the Reichstag. A supporter of Leon Trotsky, she was expelled from the party in 1926 at Stalin's instigation and was exiled in 1933.

Gütersloh: Albert Paris von Gütersloh, originally Albert Kiehtreiber (1887–1973); painter and writer.

Franz Blei's daughter: Sibylla Blei (1906–?) [*Deutsche Biographie* gives her dates as 1897–1962], an actress; the information about her profession comes from a fictitious dialogue with Hamlet into which she was written by her friend Hermann Broch: 'Well, now; I am Ophelia – that is, I play her part; In real life, though, I am Sibylla Blei, / The actress' (see Hermann Broch, 'Kommentar zu Hamlet' in *Novellen, Prosa, Fragmente*, ed. Paul Michael Lützeler. Frankfurt am Main: Suhrkamp, 1980, p. 279); Franz Blei (1871–1942), author, critic and translator; in exile in Italy and France, and in the USA from 1941.

Saxony: Adorno's warning refers to an official mission of Kracauer's on which he reported from Halle: 'Philosophen-Kongress: Zur Tagung der Kant-Gesellschaft: Halle, Anfang Juni' [Philosophers' congress: on the Kant Society conference: Halle, early June], *Frankfurter Zeitung*, 13 June 1925 (see Kracauer, W 5, no. 244).

15 Adorno to Kracauer
Marienbad, 10.6.1925

Marianské Lazné, 10 June 25.
(Marienbad)

Dear Friedel,
You must be patient for a few days until I get round to answering your letter. This dark, questing, difficult life has once again brought me, not to my liking and, as it seems, not to any purpose, to Czechoslovakia – Karlsbad and Marienbad; tomorrow I have to go on to Prague. But as I am not seventy yet and you are no longer seventeen, I shall spare you a Marienbad Elegy, especially as, compared with my virtual one, that melancholy of Goethe's might be described as hopeful. Melancholy in general, and a specific kind in particular, is getting me more and more tightly in its clutches, and I can sense the hour coming when I shall silently succumb to it. Your letter hurt me very much – that was the final result, at any rate – quite apart from the fact that one passage was calculated to wound me deeply. I have a sense of having been pushed away by you – by *you*, the one person who could hold me and will not do so, because he disdains to offer support even when someone is drowning and does not believe that this one is drowning, but thinks that he is just trying to swim away. For me, this is a very serious matter; I am telling you this all over again. It is up to *you* now to do something. I can no longer do anything. It is all a matter of such indifference to me that I can even write about it on a postcard. Not that I am planning to kill myself; in crude terms, don't worry about that. But in mental and spiritual ones, that is how it is, and you must make up your mind to accept it.

Your Teddie.

Original: MS, postcard; Siegfried Kracauer papers, Deutsches Literaturarchiv, Marbach am Neckar. Handwritten note by Kracauer: '(10) received *12th June*; replied 12th June'. The reply has not been preserved.

on to Prague: Adorno was travelling in the company of Anna von Tolnay, who jointly signed a picture postcard addressed to Alban Berg in which Adorno assured Berg that he was 'truly relaxing for a few days' (see Adorno/Berg, *Correspondence*, p. 6).

Marienbad Elegy: see Johann Wolfgang Goethe, *Trilogie der Leidenschaft, Elegie*, in *Gedichte 1800–1832*, ed. Karl Eibl. Frankfurt am Main: Deutscher Klassiker Verlag, 1988, pp. 457–62.

16 Adorno to Kracauer
Vienna, 17/18.6.1925

Vienna, 17 June 25.

Dear Friedel,

My life, my outer life has assumed such a turbulent tempo in the last week that, while I have no shortage of unrest, I do lack the rest necessary to maintain an inner life. So once again the reply has been postponed. Just this much: the passage which wounded me so deeply was the 'scattered assurances', a mocking, patronizing expression which in no way corresponds to the truth and unkindly brushes aside my fear, my constant fear of losing you, which often breaks through quite suddenly in a clumsy, insecure fashion – yes, that very fear. That word 'unkindly' applies merely to specific instances and describes the effect – for who could know better than I that the reason which causes you to detest casual remarks (and all remarks which describe themselves as such without simply emerging from existence are casual) is love.

I get the feeling from all your letters, just to touch on one more point, that it does hurt you that I say nothing about the 'second' matter. On the one hand you are curious – I can understand that fundamentally and lovingly – but then you see in this – well, not a lack of trust, for trust is too meagre and moderate an *óv* to have any validity between us; it belongs to precisely the same sphere as 'solidarity' – but with a lack of shared existence in it. Just one more word on this subject: it concerns not my own existence but solely that of others, over which I have no control, as I am neither subject nor object but merely an attribute which has sadly become attached to it. Inasmuch as all this is also *mea res*, it entails nothing but the agonizing torment of having to witness a terrible accident and stumbling on iron or an even harsher coincidence whenever I try to help – and a certain, merely external personal risk. *C'est tout*. Imagine that I was the inspector of that lake in Goethe's *Elective Affinities* and had the task of pulling the child, which was doomed not to live anyway, out of the water. That is the easiest way for you to understand my situation.

My trip to Czechoslovakia was undertaken in the midst of this 'drowned corpse' situation and was a complete failure, despite the fact that I expended an improbable and childish amount of energy on it. Terribly depressed at the outset, I took refuge in indifference; however, the days (it would be sentimental to deny it) did have a certain beauty, especially in Prague with young Grab, with whom I philosophized (he is a Schelerian – luxuriously ontological – is writing a book about Max Weber in friendly terms, and feels as comfortable in his approach to *universalitas ante rem* as only a multimillionaire's son *post rem* can be!), makes music (he is a pupil of Zemlinsky's, and, what is more, plays the piano splendidly!), and, most of all, I enjoyed his charm and his human and cultural virtue[s] – a warm summer evening in the open air up on Hradčany was especially splendid.

Immediately after my return there was a sensation: Morgenstern rang me up and invited me to meet Lukács, whom he knows through Balasz, a dreadful Hungarian literary fellow. On Sunday I was out at his home, quite alone, in Hütteldorf (Istarygasse 12), where he lives on the ground floor in a decidedly scruffy little room. My first impression was a great and profound one; a small, delicate, awkward fair-haired Ashkenazic Jew with a Talmudic nose and marvellous, unfathomable eyes; dressed in a linen sports suit, with a very scholarly air, but with a quite unconventional, deadly clear and gentle air about him, through which the only personal quality which subtly penetrated was shyness. He is the personification of the ideal of unobtrusiveness and also, of course, the idea of intangibility. I sensed at once that he was beyond any kind of possible human relationship, and so I too behaved accordingly and maintained a certain reserve during our conversation, which lasted over three hours. Our exchange, therefore, assumed the form of an interview rather than a conversation. I am writing up the conversation at present and shall send you the document. Just a couple of tips for now, as I am writing in a great hurry: first of all, he roundly disavowed the theory of the novel, saying that it was 'idealistic and mythological'. He contrasted it with the 'conversion into content' of history by means of Marxist dialectics. To my objection that this too was idealism (a criticism which he did not understand properly), he retorted that 1) it was precisely by means of dialectics that the object was 'included and created in its nature of being in and for itself' (something which I shall never comprehend); 2) Nature would only be perceptible in a 'classless society'. He energetically rejected Bloch's interpretation of his 'agnosticism[']; what was a 'shell' in Bloch's eyes was his whole world. He declared himself in favour of Feuerbach's anthropomorphism, which left only Hegel's 'logic of appearances' out of consideration – i.e. his claim that because God had operated as a historical entity, he was real (terrible!). Finally, he embarked on a violent polemic against Kierkegaard, against whom, he said, he had written a book which had gone missing in Hungary. He said that Kierkegaard's criticism of Hegel was directed against the 'Hegel who misunderstood himself in pan-logistical terms', but not the one purified by Marxism. He had no idea of objectivity, and history did not extend into the realm of the concrete; his Calvinistic God was nothing but a 'black abyss of despair', and he was (here he became mocking in his usual fashion) an ideological representative of the bourgeoisie in decline. In his Kierkegaard polemic he also turned on you (I at once affirmed that we were in complete intellectual agreement) because of the Bloch review, which annoyed him very much. Later, though, surprisingly, he attacked us both: Kierkegaard's 'personality', he claimed, was made up of 'private problems' which 'were not part of history'.

He did shock me at one point when he declared to me that, in his conflict with the Third International, his opponents were in the right, in actual terms, and in dialectical ones all that was required of him was an absolute approach to dialectics. His human greatness and the tragedy of his reversal of fortune are rooted in this nonsensical error. Sadly, he said some unpleasant things about Tolstoy, perhaps thinking of himself.

18.

Friedel, I am almost harried to death, and just want to get this letter on its way so that you will finally have something from me. I hardly know what I am writing, though.

I have been busy all day negotiating with Universal Edition, which has offered me the post of editor in chief on *Anbruch* (in place of Stefan), but baulked in the end, or, rather, made a disclaimer; and I didn't take the bait either. So matters are still up in the air.

Now I have been offered a leading position with the Internationale Gesellschaft für neue Musik – all without my having had to lift a finger. This is strictly between us (that includes Holl); you can talk about it to my people.

More soon – *ça ne va plus.*

I too should like to be 'included' 'as a creature'. But first I should like to sleep for 48 hours.

Your Teddie.

Original: MS; Siegfried Kracauer papers, Deutsches Literaturarchiv, Marbach am Neckar. Handwritten note by Kracauer: '(11) rec. *22 June 1925* – answered 24 June.' The reply has not been preserved.

that lake in Goethe's Elective Affinities: a child loses its life in a boating accident (see Goethe, *Elective Affinities*, trans. R. J. Hollingdale. Harmondsworth: Penguin, 1971).

book about Max Weber: Hermann Grab, *Der Begriff des Rationalen in der Soziologie Max Webers: Ein Beitrag zu den Problemen der philosophischen Grundlegung der Sozialwissenschaft* [The concept of the rational in the sociology of Max Weber: a contribution to the problems of establishing a philosophical basis for social science], Karlsruhe: G. Braun, 1927.

Balasz: probably Béla Balász, originally Herbert Bauer (1884–1949); Hungarian writer and film theorist.

writing up the conversation at present: not preserved.

Bloch's interpretation: Ernst Bloch, 'Aktualität und Utopie: Zu Lukács' Philosophie des Marxismus' [Actuality and utopia: on Lukács's philosophy of Marxism], *Der neue Merkur*, Vol. 1, October 1923 – March 1924, pp. 457–77, i.e. the review of Georg Lukács, *Geschichte und Klassenbewußtsein* [History and class consciousness] (see 'Aktualität und Utopie: Zu Lukács' "Geschichte und Klassenbewußtsein"' [Actuality and utopia: on Lukács's *History and class consciousness*], in Bloch, *Philosophische Aufsätze zur objektiven Phantasie*, Frankfurt am Main: Suhrkamp, 1985, pp. 598–621).

Kierkegaard, against whom, he said, he had written a book: an essay on Søren Kierkegaard survives: Georg Lukács, 'Das Zerschellen der Form am Leben: Sören Kierkegaard und Regine Olsen', in *Die Seele und die Formen*, Berlin: Luchterhand, 1971, pp. 44–63).

Bloch review: probably Kracauer's lacerating attack on Ernst Bloch's *Thomas Münzer als Theologe der Revolution* [Thomas Münzer as a theologian of revolution], Munich: Kurt Wolff, 1921: 'Prophetentum' [Prophethood], *Frankfurter Zeitung*, 27 August 1922 (see Kracauer, W 5, no. 87); on Bloch's reaction to this, see letter no. 47.

Lukács ... conflict with the Third International: at the 5th World Congress of the Communist International (June–July 1924 in Moscow) Georg Lukács was accused of 'deviation from the left'.

the post of editor in chief on Anbruch: The *Musikblätter des Anbruch* appeared from 1919 to 1937, published by Universal Edition. The head of the opera section there, Hans Heinsheimer (1900–1993), suggested to Adorno that he should take over the post held since 1922 by Paul Stefan (1879–1943). According to Adorno's letter to Alban Berg of 21 June 1925, Heinsheimer withdrew the offer, as Emil Hertzka (1871–1932), the head of Universal Edition, could not make the decision to dismiss Stefan (see Adorno/Berg, *Correspondence*, pp. 9–12).

position with the Internationale Gesellschaft für neue Musik: The International Society for New Music was founded by 24 composers in Salzburg in August 1922 during the festival; no information survives about any plan to involve Adorno in a professional capacity.

17 Adorno to Kracauer
Vienna, 29.6.1925

Vienna, 29 June 25.

Dear Friedel,

First of all, listen to my plan; in the *middle of August* (probably beginning on the 11th) there is going to be a big Zionist congress here, attended by many international delegates; and, as I am reliably informed, the movement will be represented across its entire spectrum. Now, the *Frankfurter Zeitung* will hardly be able to manage on this occasion with Herr Weichardt's journalistic skills alone, but even more, as a cultural and political organ, it will also see the need to cover this representative event with an equally representative delegation. In other words, it shouldn't be difficult for you to make a case to convince H. S. that you should be sent there as a delegate on a special mission. There is no need for you or even Herr Simon to worry about excessive costs, either; you could get full board and lodging at the guest-house here for about 6.50 Reichsmarks, and the rest would be cafés and confectioners (which are, however, a great temptation here) – that said, my finances are, after all, and will most likely still be, in quite good shape, and my annoyance with Lukács is not great enough to rob me of my pleasure in communism at the private level. What is more, on 9 September the music festival in Venice begins, which I should very much like to attend, although I don't care much for its actual content. So I would suggest to you that we might stroll about Vienna for a day or two after the Zionist palaver [*gediwwer*], then leave to spend a few days in the high mountains – the Dolomites (I would be particularly tempted to stay with you under friendlier atmospheric conditions – as a returning prodigal in every sense – in that hotel on the Karersee, and to make amends – as is only fitting in such a theological context. But naturally the decision rests with you!), and then travel slowly southwards along the valley, perhaps stopping in Vicenza and Padua. We don't need to stay long in Venice. You wouldn't have to listen to *any* music, except perhaps Schoenberg's Serenade, which you will understand instinctively anyway; we could watch all the local creatures without any kind of obligation, maybe enter into a conversational exchange with Werfel and Alma on occasion, and then hurry off – either go somewhere nearby, take in Siena and Assisi, and have a rest in Rimini, or, which I should like even better but which might be too much of an adventure for you, travel directly to Sicily with just a stop in Naples – or on Capri, as long as things don't look all too allegorical there. Then at the end of September we would travel back to *Frankfurt* together (just imagine – a return from Sicily right up to Frankfurt) where I absolutely have to be for 1 October, my mother's sixtieth birthday.

Of course, the plan admits of so many variations that next to nothing remains of its 'basic form' (this is what they call something musical in the latest Schoenberg jargon). If you can, you could simply pick me up in Vienna without hearing the Zionists' ideological mumblings; it would be nice, of course, to have some leeway here. If the idea of Venice horrifies you, I'd be happy to give it up without a second thought; there are only practical reasons (those of a critic) for me to go there, and they would be immaterial in the face of your reluctance. If you are in agreement about Venice, which itself does, of course, harbour beings other than musicians from Podolia, even in September, it would please me very much if I could get the commission for reporting on Venice for the F.Z., as a major critical article would later on count a lot in the eyes of Hertzka. You can talk it over with Holl (whom, by the way, I oddly missed in Prague); if (as I can well understand) mixing our relationship up with journalistic business, no matter how peripherally, is not to your liking, but you still find the plan of visiting Venice together agreeable, let me know in good time so that I can write to Holl or whoever. But, once again, Venice is not important for me, and it would be wrong – wrong, first and foremost, in the sense of our relationship, which can only renew itself and grow old without making concessions to incidental matters – if, that is, you felt it necessary in this situation to assume an attitude of feigned willingness. Above all it would be very bad (and I should see through it at once) if you let yourself be persuaded to go to Venice by a feeling that the relationship is lost, dictating an external mildness and sociability to you. This cannot and must not be the case.

In any case I am expecting an answer from you soon. I shall meet with no difficulties from home, but don't talk about the plan there before I have your fundamental agreement and can tell them about it myself.

Now let me return from possibilities to reality, only hoping that the possibility will soon become more real than the reality is possible.

Now at last, after many horrendously turbulent weeks, I have a bit of peace and can state that, in spite of everything, I am still alive, and that it is even good still to be alive, though not always beautiful. I am, so to speak, busy with the work of reconstruction; I practise the piano diligently, compose a little and see people selectively. I can now see ahead as far as the end of my time in Vienna, which sometimes appears to me like a desolate dream, and that alone gives it a different rhythm – spending eight weeks in a strange city no longer has that threateningly definitive character that six months had, and now I once again believe with some justification that I may speak about our relationship without arousing in you the sad suspicion that I am scattering comforting phrases into an empirical reality which lacks all signs, as Hansel in the fairy-tale scatters breadcrumbs in the wild woods to find his way home with his sister, while the birds swoop down on them straight away. I don't believe that the Internationale Gesellschaft will persuade me to stay any longer in Vienna; my people don't like the idea of my taking over the editorship of the *Anbruch*, and anyhow the prospect is vague enough, and so the Normaluhr will soon be able to set itself by me once more. As the question of my habilitation is also becoming topical, it cannot be assumed that I shall be staying away from there again any time soon – a few weeks in Berlin and Paris won't create too heavy a cloud on the horizons of the imagination.

So: will things work out for us?

I must return to your letter of 31 May, to which I still owe you a reply anyway. What remains unacceptable to me in this letter is the assumption which is constantly in operation that I have actually separated myself off from you, and that all that is left is illusions or hope or remnants which have to be wiped out for the sake of the whole. I certainly don't underestimate the differences between us in important areas, or the power of separation by distance. But what counters your presupposition is the fact that our relationship was wholly present every day and every hour, apart from the catastrophic points, and – believe it or not – in the final instance it decided the course of my life. It was present for me in the way that was appropriate to me – not as longing earlier on (though that, too, unrestrained and melancholy, is constantly seizing me – it's just that I can't exist in a state of longing and out of longing alone, any more than you will be able to do so either, in the end!) but instead as fidelity and – yes indeed – as an *ongoing* feeling of commitment which not only determines external arrangements (that was why I imposed the condition on *Anbruch* that I must be able to do my work in Frankfurt, only occasionally cruising over to Vienna like a guest conductor!) but also governs human relationships – whether because, like a compass, you lead me in the choice of people, or whether in that choice I am guided by my clear awareness of the supremacy of our relationship, or whether in the end it is that our relationship, the one and only, forms, moderates, tempers or allots a place to all the others that have ever been begun. Not to speak of the relativization of everything objective that takes place in me through you. Is all this, then – the weight of a life with a definite direction – not strong enough to overcome even the divergence inherent in a different kind of love, as it itself – I cannot give way on this – is nothing but love? Enough has happened to me here that could have abducted and scattered me to the four winds, and I would have been too real not to let myself be abducted if it had had any power over me. But as for forgetfulness, in the gravest sense that we attach to it, I have never experienced it. You must take that into account as well before you start on the dialectics of loving estrangement which, however deeply you mean it and live it out, must, if it genuinely claims to consist of love, meet its paradoxical limits in my kind of existence. I understand now – and only now! – fully what urges you towards it. However, I also know – and only now! – that there is no need of this in view of my feelings for you, which are so little confused by empirical reality that they could probably even overcome the empirical where the latter is blind and dark. It cannot be blinder and darker than here in this *Magic Flute* sort of trial by fire and water, and with no Pamina it cannot be even in the Café Goldschmidt, where we did in fact go after Mozart's *Entführung*.

I have already told you how things stand with myself and the people here. The most emotionally charged relationship is the one with Berg (who is returning today from Klenau's estate in Bavaria) – but the age difference, many mental qualities, and, despite all his great openness towards me, a strange muteness of the essential core around which this incomprehensible man lives, nevertheless make for a division here; of course, the relationship had to extend to the deepest and most serious levels for its limited nature to become manifest (to me; not, perhaps, to him). That Lukács must be ruled out is self-evident in view of the weight, in personal terms, of our material differences. Morgenstern is nice, a fine person, clever (he sees through not only the Karl Kraus phenomenon but also the Lukács phenomenon with perfect acuity and in agreement with us), and accepts the boundaries himself. He accepted the rejection of his little article, on which he did not set too much store, with splendid openness, although it caused him some financial embarrassment, and accepted your arguments. He is 32 years old, but speaks Polish and/or Yiddish as his mother tongue and has difficulties with all aspects of Western cultural formation; his tendency to affect the manners of the literati, his present danger, springs from his being drawn towards precisely that way of being formed, which he did not have from the outset and against which he bangs his little Talmudic head at a crooked angle. He has no lack of experiences in any respect, and his genuineness and reality in all human matters (a barbaric reality, and yet that of a delicate and fragile being) is the best thing about him. I am reluctant to engage in psychological gossip in such hints; but I just want to give you some pointers now, as I should like to see him as a pupil of yours.

There remains Ellen Delp. The relationship with her is, it seems to me, the only frank and open one that I have here – the only one which is not predestined from beginning to end, with many possibilities and dangers. Our innocent and yet not formless novel goes on; since her return from Munich the relationship has become still more intense, and it is not out of the question that it might turn into a love story, as I am sufficiently in love, and when she declared to me yesterday that she didn't love me at all it didn't sound very convincing – at least, not to my ears, familiar as they are with Hanni's voice. Even this relationship is quite problematic, as she is the most literary of all the girls of the literati class that I have ever had anything to do with, egocentric to the point of autoeroticism and self-reflecting through and through; at the same time she is childish and, yet again, full of a goodness and simplicity that impose obligations where there ought to be fun. Aestheticism as a moral problem, which seems to constitute a central motif in my life, has, in the case of this girl, assumed the form of the most fantastic masquerade. I myself do not quite have an overview of this relationship but take it very seriously, and therefore am mentioning it to you too, although in all probability we shall rapidly be blown away from each other before getting together – for I employ a mannish brutality of approach here as little as you did in the case of Marianne Kamnitzer – not only for good reasons, but even more because the intermediate stage has the greatest appeal for me. I will keep you constantly and precisely informed. About us and my commitment, she knows what, as a woman, she can know – it is unavoidable, then, that she stubbornly subsumes me under §175.

I had a shameless letter from Fred in which he asked me to find a place for an article – which I did. I let him go, and yet I'm still fond of him. Strange, and probably explicable only by Hanni, who is, after all, a caesura in my existence.

I feel an inexplicable inhibition – fear, in fact – which keeps me from writing to Reinhold Z. However, I must bring myself to do so – also in the case of the Horkheimers, where it is certainly much less dangerous.

Warmest greetings to Leo; give me his address – I owe him a letter most of all!

Fare thee well – I'm dead tired and know that the last two pages of my letter have been going nowhere. Don't be angry with me about this, and don't see anything behind it but the fact that all creatures are subject to empirical conditions, something which you must allow me, no matter what. And do travel with me. All will be well, all will be well, etc. Teddie.

Original: MS; Siegfried Kracauer papers, Deutsches Literaturarchiv, Marbach am Neckar. Handwritten note by Kracauer: '(12) received: 1 July answ. 3 July.' The reply has not been preserved.

Zionist congress: the 14th International Zionist Congress, accompanied by a Palestine exhibition in the Konzerthaus, took place from 18 to 31 August 1925. On the day before the opening, violent anti-Semitic riots occurred.

Weichardt: Carl H. Weichardt (1878–?), journalist and author; editor and correspondent on the *Frankfurter Zeitung* (1912–1932), then on the *Berliner Tageblatt*.

H. S.: Heinrich Simon (1880–1941); joined the *Frankfurter Zeitung* in 1906; co-heir to the publishing house (1909); publisher of the newspaper until 1934; exiled in France, Palestine and the USA.

a special mission: Kracauer did not write about the Zionist congress; 15 reports about the conference appeared between 17 August and 1 September under the abbreviation 'dt', together with an unsigned leading article on 29 August 1925.

the music festival in Venice: the festival was organized by the Internationale Gesellschaft für neue Musik. Arnold Schoenberg presented his Serenade, op. 24, which Adorno discussed under the title of the composition in *Pult und Taktstock* 125/7 (see Adorno, GS 18, pp. 324–30, GS 19, p. 643).

gediwwer: from *Gedibber*, derived from the Hebrew *dibbuv* (talk).

hotel on the Karersee: a stop on the Dolomites journey of 1924.

Normaluhr: the clock next to the Café Hauptwache in central Frankfurt.

Café Goldschmidt: see letter no. 9.

Mozart's Entführung: Wolfgang A. Mozart, *Die Entführung aus dem Serail*, last performed before this letter at the Frankfurter Oper on 4 February 1924.

from Klenau's estate in Bavaria: Annemarie von Klenau, née Simon (1878–1977), and Paul von Klenau owned the estate of Keilhof in Beuerberg (see Soma Morgenstern, *Alban Berg und seine Idole: Erinnerungen und Briefe*, ed. Ingolf Schulte. Lüneburg: zu Klampen, 1995, p. 19).

the rejection of his little article: see letter no. 13.

§175: this paragraph of the penal code, in force from 1872, made homosexual practices punishable by law. Adorno wrote of this in 1963: 'The heinous paragraph on homosexuality took refuge and survived in a liberated Germany. The mitigation which at least allows minors who are inculpated to go unpunished easily becomes a gift to blackmailers. In fact, no argument can be levelled at the paragraph on homosexuality; we can only remember the shame' ('Sexualtabus und Recht heute',

in *Sexualität und Verbrechen: Beiträge zur Strafrechtsreform*, ed. Fritz Bauer, Frankfurt am Main, 1963; see Adorno, GS 10.2, pp. 533–54, 841, here p. 543).

a shameless letter from Fred: probably Fred Goldbeck (see letter no. 13).

Reinhold Z: Reinhold Zickel; the correspondence from the years 1920 to 1923 and 1950 is preserved in the Theodor W. Adorno Archiv.

in the case of the Horkheimers: Max and Rosa Christine ('Maidon') Horkheimer, née Riekher (1887–1969), married to Max Horkheimer since 1926; in the context of this letter 'Horkheimers' also includes Friedrich Pollock (1894–1970), a national economist and Max Horkheimer's closest collaborator, especially on the organization of the Institut für Sozialforschung. The first surviving letter from Adorno to Horkheimer dates from 1934 (see Adorno/Horkheimer, *Briefwechsel* I, pp. 22–8).

I owe him a letter: no corresponding letter to Leo Löwenstein survives.

18 Adorno to Kracauer
Vienna, 3.7.1925

Vienna, 3 July

Dear Friedel,

I have given you a couple of wrong dates. The Zionists don't begin until the *18th* of August (instead of the 11th), but on the other hand Venice begins on 2nd September (instead of the 9th), so we would have to travel direct from here to Venice, and I don't know whether that would be all right with you – but you decide.

I'm quite well; a bit slack at present, but the work is still getting done. Nothing new has been happening to me. Berg is here again, and I spend a lot of time with him, sometimes making music and sometimes talking.

I have heard Karl Kraus: as a prophetic figure he is a nebbich, but all the more a great comedian (a clown and a priest rolled into one) for that. You can't imagine a more extreme example of 'aesthetic' behaviour than his way of making an entrance on the stage as a moralist – and his wit is too forced for me not to have grown bored with it.

Write to me soon. Teddie.

Original: MS, postcard; Siegfried Kracauer papers, Deutsches Literaturarchiv, Marbach am Neckar. Handwritten note by Kracauer: '(13) received 6th July.'

I have heard Karl Kraus: Karl Kraus's earlier 'lectures' in Vienna had taken place on 18–19 May 1925 in the Kleiner Konzerthaussaal. The programme included 'Shakespeare', 'Words in Verses', 'Inscriptions' and 'Dream Pieces'; see *Die Fackel*, July 1925, pp. 27f. (photocopy, ed. Heinrich Fischer, vol. 31, 1972).

19 Adorno to Kracauer
Vienna, 6.7.1925

Vienna, Monday morning.

Dear Friedel,

Your letter is not kind. Every sentence directs its ironic point more against me than against itself, and the deliberation with which all the recent emotional events here are transplanted into an aesthetic medium is wholly calculated to devalue them all too quickly – and, like all irony which is much too sure of itself, this too misses the real point often enough. I can draw something instructive from the fact that you don't think that anything has escaped me. I used the quotation from Stifter, 'all will be well' about our relationship with a certain sadness, which lies precisely in the fact that the prophecy expressed in these words actually only evoked the mere memory of that time when we, still living in the present, were toying with the sadness of that prophecy, while now, when we really are in a state of sadness, we treat the phrase as if it were joyful – not some kind of Wilhelmine optimism, though (it is, incidentally, light and not of a sublime nature, but a baseless irony of the Thomas Mann kind, with the overbearing tendency which Nietzsche has to jeer at any form of optimism, and also a functionalistic irony which tries subjectively to break up the consolidation of being which is essential to all optimism). For me, optimism, and precisely the shallow kind – for in fact there is only the shallow kind, where the word has any validity! – has something very touching about it, and in the paradoxical affirmation of existence which it constantly suggests it seems deeper to me than pessimism with a belief in identity. The paradox of shallow optimism lies, of course, in the fact that it affirms on its own behalf entities which have no objective existence, and that at the same time it rightly affirms (rightly, of course, in objective not subjective terms) that meaning still persists in the objective as hope and what remains. Enough of that; we will be in fundamental agreement about it, especially as you too regard it as a confirmation that Goethe, before his return home, had carried with him so much shallow optimism. In Mittler this is also present in a correspondingly simpler and more paradigmatic form!). And what do you do? First, you act as if I had used the phrase in a naive way (and indeed in a sentimental tone!). And then you use it polemically with reference to my relationship with Ellen Delp, where it does not apply at all, not this way and not the other, and where for purposes of revenge it actually assumes a clumsy naivety which in the end will be disproved quite simply by empirical experience, as all has gone far from well in this relationship. In short, I might have reason to be really angry about the clownish *quid pro quo* if I did not also take that odious quotation *à la lettre* and think that it was all the more certain that all would go well with us because they were not going well with the blonde but tending towards a peaceful end, as if it were my transcendentally purified relationship (transcendental, alas!

and not Ottilie-like!) with that Hanni, who was the only person who could represent a greater external danger to our relationship, and whom I shall never forget.

Quite simply, I see the reason for your stubborn irony (for in no way did it ever seriously occur to me that it is baseless in the sense of Thomas Mann's!) in the fact that I failed to answer that letter which came in reply to my card from Marienbad and *qui paraclites dicitur*. But, steady on – this time I was more inclined to make peace than you, Friedel – you, whose name means 'peace'! Deeply as the confession which was so difficult for you moved me in that letter, it seemed all too obvious to me that you had written it when you were driven into a corner by the situation, and by my acute distress, for me to have dared to use it to draw conclusions from it for our life. Rather, the fact is that I did not disguise my words metaphorically and that I *consciously* refrained from answering; and you will concede that, in comparison, the reality of our time together was not bad, even in your sense of the word. But it is naturally a profound mistake on your part, which only proves the insecurity of all our points of contact, if you think that I ignored this letter and did not take it in the same emotionally fraught spirit in which it was sent by you. Indeed, perhaps the shallow optimism of my last letter might not have been possible at all without this better reason. How matters really stand is something which we shall have to decide soon.

As far as my chiliastic Baedeker is concerned, I did at least have a laugh about the word – and then even about the matter itself– even though I'm not happy about it. To retain this image: the legendary Hassidic joke certainly proved valid in your case. The Messiah really did pass you by without being recognized, and you and I will just have to watch out to be sure that it wasn't Zarathustra, who is passionate about passing by incognito and, so to speak, has local jurisdiction in Venice. In this special instance, though, one must not become two, but two must become one in order for the kingdom to come to fulfilment. However, it is a matter of indifference whether the journey has a symbolic purpose (of the 'journey into the interior' kind) or is an allegory of life (so rightly popular) – running its course in time, empty of meaning (with purple sails) – it must happen. Perhaps things can be sorted out about the Zionist congress in spite of Weichardt. What is required here, first and foremost, is the will, and perhaps the atmosphere of Vienna will lose its demonic power over our shared future if you take a look at the nature of the new empirical reality. Incidentally, I can get away from here as early as the second half of August (i.e. in six weeks – that is not an eternity, and allows us to think it over so that we can make arrangements) and travel south together, if it is not too hot for you then. In that case I shall let Venice go. It won't matter anyway, as I don't have a newspaper for which I could report back on it.

The only problem which remains is my appointment on 1 October, which I can't get out of. On the other hand, I am by no means keen on going back to Frankfurt on my own – not at any price. That was why I thought about starting the journey earlier, as you, dear creature, mustn't cut your holiday short. But, if halfway through August doesn't suit you, I am prepared (just about) to meet you in Genoa on 1 September. In this case, too, nothing will come of Venice. That would only come into question as an *ultima ratio* and without Ellen Delp, if you couldn't make up your mind to travel with me.

Please let me know *by return post*: I should like to present the folks at home with a finished plan.

The idea of Paris and Berlin isn't as dangerous as you might think. I shall have to go to Berlin for about two weeks – four weeks at most – for the première of *Wozzeck*, in mid-October at the earliest and probably in December at the latest. I should like to look around Paris in about February or March. But that is still quite vague and is at best only a matter of a few weeks.

You ask me about my work. I'm reluctant to talk about it, although I am assured of your sympathy, because I know that it is dangerous – and the tone in which you ask me reminds me curiously of the one in which Gretel questioned me when we were living in a state of conflict. But I shall give you an answer. I am working on the trio, writing songs, sketching out a piano sonata, and occasionally working on my little pieces for orchestra. Berg is exerting a looser control over me and wants to see my things in print. I am putting serious efforts into some of the songs. My identity as a composer has become firmly established over the last few months, and Berg speaks of my things in a tone that would have made me happy three years ago. Nowadays I feel – *sit venia verbo* – too shattered for that. Writings on music: two essays on Bartók, one published in *Pult und Taktstock* (I won't send it to you; I find it too boring), and the other with the printer in Leipzig. I have a batch of reviews to write up: Schoenberg, Hindemith, Křenek, Eisler – a lot of work of minor importance. For the Venice Festival I have to write about Schoenberg's Serenade at greater length for *Pult und Taktstock*, and that might be something important.

My own stuff: I have in mind a book about psychology (a parallel to yours on sociology or the projected one on history). At the same time, I am writing a lot of fragments on psychological-material topics, which strike me as quite innovative and remarkable and which I would like to discuss with you. They are only notes on various experiences – entirely without any definite purpose at present, but with a common intention which I sense in a quite obscure way. In any case, whether it is objectively valid or not, it is entirely my own original idea and has no relation to any existing categories. I shall leave it to grow.

I have no idea where the Paradise Garden is. There were fireworks on the Hohe Warte on one occasion, but I didn't see those either. I am tense, reclusive, not happy and not sad. That particular evil is by no means averted, and something bad could happen at any minute – but I am indifferent even about that. By the way, Ellen Delp has a friend who is a privy councillor and a worthy and serious man, with whom I recently had a conversation about sociology. The weather is fine, and yesterday the freethinkers organized an impressive rally with music. In the bars they are singing a song which begins with the words 'Vienna, Vienna, Vienna, dying fairy-tale city'.

It all comes down to one's spirit and attitude. That all will be well, all will be well, you know anyway.

Teddie.

Original: MS: Siegfried Kracauer papers, Deutsches Literaturarchiv, Marbach am Neckar. Dated by the postmark and Kracauer's handwritten note next to the location: '6. Juli 25', and also on the envelope: '(14) This letter and card (13) rec. 7 July; answ.: 9 July'. The reply has not been preserved.

Your letter: not preserved.

the quotation from Stifter, 'all will be well': from a dialogue between Heinrich and Natalie in Adalbert Stifter, *Der Nachsommer*: 'And I shall strive never to annoy you,' she replied. 'All will be well,' I said. 'Everything will be well, as our second father said,' she replied. (See the allusion to Stifter in letter no. 1, note; ibid., p. 664.).

the overbearing tendency which Nietzsche ... irony: 'Irony has its place only as a pedagogical technique to be used by a teacher when interacting with any sort of pupil: its aim is to arouse humiliation and shame, but only of the salutary sort that awakens good intentions and enjoins us to offer respect and gratitude to the person who treated us in this way, as we would to a physician' [*Human, All Too Human*, I, trans. Gary Handwerk. Stanford, CA: Stanford University Press, 1997, p. 214.

baseless irony of the Thomas Mann kind: possibly an allusion to the parallels between conservatism and irony in Thomas Mann, *Reflections of a Nonpolitical Man*, New York: Ungar, 1983.

Mittler: a character in *Elective Affinities*; a former clergyman, who is constantly striving to mediate: 'Unflagging in his office, he had distinguished himself by his ability for settling and silencing all disputes, domestic and communal; first between individual people, then between landowners, and then between whole parishes' (see Goethe, *Elective Affinities*, trans. R. J. Hollingdale, Harmondsworth: Penguin, 1971).

the legendary Hassidic joke: the variant alluded here of the legend about the Messiah who remains unrecognized on his arrival has not been identified.

'journey into the interior': 'This is as far as the *internal* path can at first go, namely toward what we call a self-encounter, the preparation of the inner word, without which every gaze outward remains empty, instead of being the magnet, the force that draws forth the inner word and helps it break through the falseness of this world.' See Ernst Bloch, *The Spirit of Utopia*, trans. Anthony A. Nassar. Stanford, CA: Stanford University Press, 2000, p. 3.

première of Wozzeck: on 14 December 1925 at the Staatsoper.

Paris: the journey never took place.

two essays about Bartók: see letter no. 5.

Hindemith: probably 'Kammermusik von Paul Hindemith' [Chamber music by Paul Hindemith], *Die Musik*, no. 1, October (i.e. part 2 of 'Ad vocem Hindemith: Eine Dokumentation' [On the voice of Hindemith: a documentation]; see Adorno, GS 17, pp. 217–22, 348).

Křenek: no review corresponding to this has survived.

Eisler: 'Hanns Eisler, 'Duo für Violone und Violoncello, op. 7, no. 1', *Musikblätter des Anbruch*, no. 7, 1925 (see Adorno, GS 18, pp. 519–21, GS 19, p. 645).

Schoenberg's Serenade: see letter no. 17.

a book about psychology ... fragments on psychological-material topics: it cannot be proved with any degree of certainty whether Adorno developed this into his first attempt at a postdoctoral dissertation, 'Der Begriff des Unbewußten in der transzendentalen Seelenlehre' [The concept of the unconscious in transcendental psychology] (1927).

yours on sociology: *Soziologie als Wissenschaft: Eine erkenntnistheoretische Untersuchung* [Sociology as science: an examination based on the theory of perception], Dresden: Sibyllen-Verlag, 1922 (see Kracauer, W 1, pp. 7–101, 375–8).

projected one about history: see letter no. 1.

Paradise Garden: in the local idiom, 'Paradeisgartel', a pleasure-garden laid out for the Habsburg emperor Albrecht II (1298–1358), close to the site of the old Burgtheater on the Michaeler Platz.

Hohe Warte: a hill and a street of the same name in the Viennese district of Döbling.

a friend who is a privy councillor: there is no information as to whether this refers to Ellen Delp's future husband Friedrich Wilhelm Krafft (see letter no. 52).

the freethinkers: a splinter movement that broke away from the Catholic Church which originated in 1848 and organized itself in 1887 into the Viennese Verein der Confessionslosen (association of those belonging to no church) and gradually expanded into the Freidenkerbund Österreichs (Austrian League of Freethinkers).

Vienna, dying fairy-tale city: a song by the Austrian composer and cabaret artist Hermann Leopoldi (originally Hermann Kohn, 1888–1959).

20 Adorno to Kracauer
Vienna, 18.7.1925

Vienna, 18 July.

Dear Friedel,

Excuse the card – I shall answer your letter at length in the next few days. Just this for now: I agree with your plan, and after careful consideration of your concerns I think that I can assume the responsibility towards you and myself of travelling with you. I certainly don't underestimate these concerns; nor do I regard the situation with an embarrassing broken sort of optimism, let alone with one of the shallow and well-meaning kind, but I believe that we do have to take the risk of making a fresh start. I wrote home some time ago. What Latin word do you mean? – at any rate, it didn't imply anything serious, and even the Zarathustra quotation has more of a funny sound to it than a sad connotation. Before Monday I have to finish two essays which I have been putting off for a long time, and because of this I am under a lot of pressure. One question: might not the last days of August in southern Italy be too hot, after all? If so, we could stop off in a more temperate clime first. Vienna is trickling away from me now; hardly any of the people I know are still here. I live like a hermit, sleep a lot, work with a certain degree of consistency but without the minimum of illusion necessary to sustain life, and wait to see whether something might still change. Occasionally I write cheerful songs – playful trifles of the kind so dear to you. Can you send me your Angerstein articles – even if only out of respect? And would it be a nuisance for you to hunt out the little piece called 'We need it' and my Meyer-Eckhardt critique? I should like to show them both to Alban Berg.

Please send me – as quickly and precisely as you can – the date of your departure, and also the day and the place that we can meet in Genoa. With the crush in Vienna at present you will need to book a sleeper *now*. Above all, do let me have all the practical details that I need to know – four weeks are not as long as your mistrustful nature might be inclined to believe. A letter from me will follow soon. Teddie.

Original: MS; postcard; Siegfried Kracauer papers, Deutsches Literaturarchiv, Marbach am Neckar. Handwritten note by Kracauer: '(15) arr. 22 July, answ. 22.'

your letter: not preserved.

your Angerstein articles: from 6 to 13 July 1925 Kracauer reported on the trial of the serial murderer Fritz Angerstein. The final article was 'Die Tat ohne Täter: Zum Fall Fritz Angerstein' [The act without an agent: on the Fritz Angerstein case], *Frankfurter Zeitung*, 13 July 1925 (see Kracauer, W 5, no. 247).

the little piece 'We need it': by Adorno, published in the *Frankfurter Zeitung* on 26 February 1925 (see Adorno, *Bildmonographie*, pp. 83f).

Meyer-Eckhardt critique: 'Ein Bildungsroman', i.e. Adorno's review of Victor Meyer-Eckhardt, *Die Möbel des Herrn Berthélemy* [The furniture of Mr Berthélemy], Jena: Eugen Diederichs, 1924 (see Adorno, *Bildmonographie*, pp. 82f.).

21 Adorno to Kracauer
Vienna, 28 July 1925

TRAVEL WITH YOU IN ANY CIRCUMSTANCES = TEDDIE.

Original: telegram, Siegfried Kracauer papers, Deutsches Literaturarchiv, Marbach am Neckar. Dating in accordance with Kracauer's handwritten note on the back: '(16) rec. 28th July. Letter in reply … 29th July.' The reply has not been preserved.

22 Adorno to Kracauer
Vienna, before 6.8.1925

Wednesday morning

Dear Friedel,
You are mistaken; it isn't illness, indifference, work or a profound structural difference at the core of our being in our ways of relating to empirical reality which renders me dumb but, on the contrary, a deliberate plan and design. You have wounded me severely – without intending to do so, I am sure – in the most sensitive layers of my innermost self, and it was clear to me from the outset that the quarrel would inevitably bring up everything that had happened and not happened over the last six months, that the letter would have nothing but a distorting and inhibiting effect on our forthcoming meeting, which I had become accustomed to thinking of as a return, and that if our journey together should become impossible – and during the caesura, until the telegram, I was convinced of its *im*possibility – it would be superfluous. During this period of waiting I intended to speak to you only about practical arrangements, but I couldn't even do that, as for the time being they were not at all clear to me. Then a message came from you which, with just a few words, moved me so much that once again I resolved that we should make the journey. The telegram – the answer to that message – contained many intentions that you completely misunderstood or did not even see, and which I should like to mention to you. First, as a 'sensation' and an exceptional occurrence in terms of mail, the telegram was meant to draw your attention to the emotionally fraught and exceptional nature of that decision and to show you that I was ready to make it; the phrase 'in any circumstances' was meant in a highly symbolic sense, and you obviously related it solely to the things about the newspaper – which is, however, only the historical background to our tragedy, badly drawn like all historical backgrounds by all bad dramatists. In addition, though, the telegram – reduced in American fashion to the crudely factual – was meant to convey to you something of the spiritual agnosticism which had me in its clutches, so that I would rather have

confined our correspondence to express timetables, names of ships, hotels and passport offices. (The fact that at that time I was even thinking of meeting you as early in the journey as Innsbruck may in any case still be of interest to you.) Your letter now makes my agnosticism as impossible as Bloch's breakthrough makes Lukács's – though he now insists that he is not an agnosticist at all – or, to put it more Blochishly, an agnostic [Agnostiker] – well, yes ... Anyway, your letter produced the effect of a breakthrough on me, and, the longer I go on living in its thrall, the more I find the sad irony of it intolerable.

Of course it is not the postponement of our travelling plans as such which has hurt me so much, although I am Friedelish enough to take it as part and parcel of the whole complex of suffering. But the manner in which you handled it was wrong, most of all, because of the way in which, in making the arrangements, you attributed to me from the outset a minus quantity of love and an empirical equanimity which I don't possess. I said nothing to you about the fact that, for the sake of our journey together, I had put off all kinds of plans which had come up for August – a meeting with Morgenstern, Else's invitations, and one from Ellen Delp to join her and possibly also her friend Regina Ullmann in Munich (Ellen Delp has since left Munich for the North Sea with a sick friend, but that could not have been foreseen). I don't take any credit for this, as I consider that it goes without saying, and because I had to do it. But how did you behave? Not only did you dismiss my plan for the journey with an air of irony, by making *me* look foolish, though I was not actually waiting for you to arrange for God Himself to appear in Capri; when Herr Simon came on the scene you assumed – and not even openly, but in a roundabout way – that I should go home earlier and on my own – for you must admit that your questions admitted of no other answer from the very way in which they were phrased. Two things hurt me about that: first, that it didn't occur to you at all to suggest *of your own volition* that we might settle for a four-weeks holiday (if *I* mention it, I actually make it quite impossible for both you and me) and, if you still needed some rest, to settle down in the Taunus for another ten days or so (Weilnau: how gladly I should have gone there in autumn to join you). No; the insistence on five weeks for your stay in Italy was the stubborn *a priori* which you refused even to discuss by offering me a way out of the lack of time, knowing perfectly well that the solution I was talking about could not come from me – and at the same time you refused to recognize this *a priori* as an *a priori* at all. What is more, you completely dismissed the possibility of travelling back from this expedition in a way that indicated that your love and your urgent desire for the present moment were much too great, of course, for you to tolerate such a humiliation yet again – how often had we not discussed it? Now, though, you were building nothing less than a golden bridge for me to provide this solution, so that I could not help thinking that you were convinced that it wouldn't be such a humiliation for me as it would for you, as I, of course, in empirical reality ... but you know the gramophone record I'm putting on. However, you weren't willing to take the responsibility for that either, but manipulated the situation in such a way that the suggestion that I might make the journey home alone had to come from me, in accordance with your idea (which you were careful to leave vague), and also as a convincing proof for you yourself that I was in fact not so bound up in an empirical reality with you as you were with me, since I was actually agreeing, without objecting, to a way of travelling which I had previously regarded with such disdain. You ought to have understood that I would turn stubborn, and the only legitimate means of breaking that stubbornness would have been if *you* had presented me with a concrete plan for the journey, with definite dates.

You didn't – and in spite of that I still clung firmly and fixedly to the journey – only starting to doubt when you wrote to me that you were not well – and I am saying so now. The inconsistency lies, first and foremost, in the insight that your mental condition is such that I have no right to take offence; in my belief, which persists at the deepest level of my being, that this journey is necessary; and, finally, in considerations which confronted me for the first time during my stay in Vienna as a result of my experiences there of harsh external facts – i.e. that a relationship like ours which suffers from a hypertrophy of its spiritual elements can only survive when no room remains to give unethical and overpowering psychological pressure the right to dictate all practical decisions, but when external reality is granted a space in which its own weight, and many *raisons* of lesser dignity, prevail. And so, for the sake of the lower and unenlightened element which does still harbour the elemental within it too, I beg you, my Friedel, to go ahead with the journey anyway – you whom I shall never abandon, and because of whom I suffer as much as you do because of me. (I am by no means well; I'm lonely and have headaches, and anything that I do is no good and doesn't even interest me.)

Else has sent me another invitation – to Madonna, from 20 August. I may go there as you can't get away on the 20th anyway. In any case, let's meet on 1 September or – if this is still too early for you – on the 2nd in Genoa. If you don't feel like looking round Genoa, as you know it, I would arrive there a day earlier – for family reasons, as the Corsican lady can't bear me not to see the Palazzo Adorno. I leave the choice of hotel to you – and also the way in which we shall travel home. Yes, I am abject enough to accept it if you are willing to travel home with me earlier and sensible enough to travel alone if that has to be.

One more question: do you have any inhibitions about staying in the place in Capri where Ellen Delp stayed? They say it is splendid – with a view of the sea, and not expensive. In that case I'll ask for the address – but I can assure you that I shall respect any quirks and scruples. You will find me no less quirky than you yourself are – but all the more relaxed and talkative for that.

It is already six o' clock (your letter came at nine; I had to break off writing and only return to it in the afternoon), and because of the post, which is about to go, I must go too.

Teddie.

I shall report back to you about Lukács.

Original: MS; Siegfried Kracauer papers, Deutsches Literaturarchiv, Marbach am Neckar. Dated by the postmark of the express service in Frankfurt am Main on the envelope and Kracauer's handwritten note there: '(17) rec. 6 August answ. 8 August'; location from the sender's details given by Adorno on the envelope.

Ullmann: Regina Ullmann (1884–1961), writer of verse and stories and friend of Ellen Delp; they carried on a correspondence, parts of which they wrote jointly, with Rainer Maria Rilke (see letter no. 52, note).

Weilnau: second to Amorbach in the Odenwald, this resort in the Taunus Mountains was a favourite destination with the Adorno-Wiesengrund family for excursions and holidays (see Adorno/Pabst, *Amorbach*, pp. 126f.).

the Corsican lady can't bear me not to see the Palazzo Adorno: Adorno's maternal grandfather, Jean-François Calvelli (1820–1879), came from Corsica. During a stay in Genoa he was said to have been a guest at the 'Villa Adorno' and to have borrowed the name from it. The Palazzo Cattaneo Adorno is located in the Via Garibaldi.

your letter: not preserved.

23 Kracauer to Adorno
Frankfurt am Main, [8.8.1925]

FRANKFURTER ZEITUNG
UND HANDELSBLATT
REDAKTION
TELEGRAMM-ADRESSE
ZEITUNG FRANKFURTMAIN

FRANKFURT A.M., 192

2.

… didn't mean what you call my stubborn *a priori.* But the weight of that letter lay much more in the passage demonstrating the impossibility of the journey; the *a priori* was meant to make you see that it would be better for us not to travel together. You understood it, though, as meaning that I did want to make the journey and also wanted to stay for five weeks; my veiled outburst, in your view, was only provoked by the fact that I had to put the blame for what was upsetting me onto you. No – I didn't actually want to travel with you, but on my own. And if, now, you are asking why, my answer is: out of an instinct for self-preservation – a wholly unconcealed urge towards that wretched self-preservation. To explain this to you in a letter is something that I really cannot do; I would have to unfold the story of the last few years – it can only be done face to face. This is not to say anything against you – *au contraire*, at the profoundest level of my being I trust in your nature, and your love and faithfulness towards me which springs from it; it is directed only against myself, against the impossibility of my cross-grained feelings and my exag[g]erations, which I must control, and which I can only control when I am alone. But this is unimportant – I am only mentioning it to explain the meaning of that ominous letter. Now, though, when the journey has to be made – now that I could scarcely acknowledge the possibility of not making it any more; it is too late – I will, naturally, correct the *a priori*: we shall certainly be *coming home together*. Of course I didn't want to write that in response to that one solitary telegram from you, as the very fact that it *was* solitary seemed to me to be grounds for abandoning the journey. A journey with a stranger – how could that be? But you did write – a letter by express post – from which I was unable to cut myself off, coming as it did by return of post – something wholly unprecedented.

However, I do want to break off the dialectic of our positions; as those positions are now, there would be no end to it. Enough: *now we shall travel together, then*. More honest, or shall we say, more resolute, would have been the alternative: you to Else, Morgenstern or E. D., I on my own – but now we shall travel together – with just one essential condition, of course: that you don't agree to this because I am not well or my mental condition could not tolerate your being offended. Not on these terms – because if I were to draw the conclusion that I was not well, the only possibility would be for us *not* to travel together. For heaven's sake, no act of charity which would become yet a further act of cruelty, as I would indeed feel better if I were alone. If you don't accept this condition, then let us meet on 1 or 2 September in *Genoa* – perhaps even as early as the first. Until now I haven't bothered about this whole business, and it is only now that I am able to do so; my sparrow-brain refuses to consider plans for the distant future. But ad hoc it will go on as always. Just let me know that that condition does not apply and send your address for …

Original: MS with printed letterhead, fragment; Theodor W. Adorno Archiv, Frankfurt am Main. Dated in accordance with Kracauer's annotation on the envelope of the preceding letter.

Else: Else Herzberger.

E. D.: Ellen Delp.

24 Adorno to Kracauer
Vienna, 15.8.1925

Saturday.

Dear Friedel,

I am leaving here on *Wednesday* (address: Madonna di Campiglio, Hotel Campo di Carlo Magno, Trento, Italy). About the shipping line, a suitable hotel in Genoa and the lodgings in Capri I shall make inquiries – as far as it is actually possible in the state of chaos at the Vienna travel agency – to secure reliable information. In any event, you may expect more activity on my part in technical matters than before. I shall keep you up to date about everything of any importance.

Otherwise I am making preparations for the journey, tearing myself free in all quarters from the milieu here, and hoping that the ontological fact of my return will assert itself somehow despite all the nominalistic obstacles.

This evening I am saying goodbye to Berg at a choice restaurant out in Speising; he is coming there from Schoenberg's, and there will be a great fuss about Strindberg, Karl Kraus and all the local notables.

In my imagination I am now, so to speak, up in the air; Vienna is already completely passé and I still have not yet regained any sense of being at home. I wonder whether this is even possible? –

Give my regards to Michel – and also, if you think fit, to our acquaintances from Ulm.

Teddie.

Original: MS, postcard: Siegfried Kracauer papers, Deutsches Literaturarchiv, Marbach am Neckar. Date in accordance with postmark; location from the details of the sender as given by Adorno. Addressed to Kracauer, Innsbruck, Hotel Arlbergerhof. Handwritten note by Kracauer: '(18) 18. … Rep. 20 Aug.' The reply has not been preserved.

Speising: district of Vienna to the south-west of the centre.

Michel: presumably Ernst Michel (1889–1964), left-wing Catholic social scientist and psychologist; lecturer at the Akademie der Arbeit, Frankfurt am Main (1921–1933); associate lecturer at the Johann Wolfgang Goethe-Universität (1931–1933), where he resumed teaching in 1946.

Acquaintances from Ulm: Kracauer was travelling as a correspondent to Innsbruck, to report on a conference of Catholic academics ('Das Religiöse und das Profane: Zur Tagung der katholischen Akademiker' [The religious and the profane: on the Catholic academics' conference], *Frankfurter Zeitung*, 25 August 1925; see Kracauer, W 5, no. 252); in August/September 1923 Ulm had been the location for the Tagung der katholischen Akademiker, and Kracauer also sent a report from there (among others, 'Die Tagung der katholischen Akademiker' [The Catholic academics' conference], *Frankfurter Zeitung*, 24 August 1923; see Kracauer, W 5, no. 144). Adorno and Kracauer combined the conference with an excursion; on 22nd August 1923 they sent greetings to Leo Löwenthal in a letter from Bad Überkingen (see Kracauer/Löwenthal, *Briefwechsel*, pp. 44–6). Among the 'acquaintances' attending the conference may have been the theologian and philosopher of religion Romano Guardini (1885–1968), Bishop Paul Wilhelm von Keppler (1852–1926) and Hermann Platz (1880–1945), an expert on Romance languages and literature.

25 Adorno to Kracauer

Vienna, 19.8.1925

ARRIVING INNSBRUCK WEDNESDAY EVENING AROUND TEN = TEDDIE =

Original: telegram; Siegfried Kracauer papers, Deutsches Literaturarchiv, Marbach am Neckar. Date in accordance with postmark. Addressed to Kracauer, Innsbruck, Arlbergerhof.

26 Adorno to Kracauer

Madonna di Campiglio, 26.8.1925

MADONNA DI CAMPIGLIO, 26 August.
TRENTINO (ITALIA) Wednesday.
Hotel Campo di Carlo Magno.

Dear Friedel,
Your letter doesn't surprise me; from observation and gossip it was already obvious to me that there is still something wrong between us: I know from Else that Lila, who was in Madonna, rushed over to her one day, asking whether I loved someone else, claiming she had heard it from you. So, you betrayed my relationship with Ellen to her. I am cruel enough to be able to understand your behaviour, and there would have been no need for an explanation any longer. Less comprehensible to me is the tangled plot of a novel which is allegedly set on Capri and titled 'From Tiberius to Krupp'; I wouldn't have believed it of the author – or, rather, the gap between the introduction to your letter and its true core could be effortlessly closed by the hypothesis of such a concoction conceived in a similar, somewhat playful way. Be that as it may, I am no longer surprised by anything; I am entirely devoid of optimism, whether shallow or profound – and yet I still believe that the journey must take place, as I love you too much, and at a different level, for any impossible situation (that I know of!) to end up getting a grip on me. Perhaps you, rather than I (whom you thought changed and lost to you) can still take some comfort from Innsbruck; I almost wrote *Parakleton ti* – the Greek translation – but then you might scold me for being forgetful!

All this is still in store for our stay in Italy, as *soi-disant* happiness at first hand. For now, just a few words about practicalities. You mustn't miss Simon, and the arrangements at the newspaper are important enough to be taken into account even in the case of the most complicated internal affairs. Those few days don't matter; on the contrary, as my exhaustion (for I haven't had a holiday at all this year!) is only really making itself felt now, it will be good for me to relax in the mountains, and then I'll be in quite a different shape from what I am at present. So let us meet on 8 September in Genoa. I shall hunt up a hotel and order the *stanze* by telegram. As I can well understand that you need more time for recuperation, I shall travel home alone without any ulterior motives – nothing really depends on that any longer. Send me the details by telegram; I shall fall in with your plans.

As far as the Sorrento–Castellamare plan is concerned, I shall accept it at the risk of hurting you by doing so and showing you that I take nothing – *nothing* – too lightly, and that I myself am prepared to risk and endure the most painful intrusions. It is surely permissible to suppose that your sudden distaste for Capri is connected with the Krupp affair. As Else says that Castellamare is not very tempting, we might have to modify our plan by writing to two hotels in Sorrento, which it would still be possible to do in Genoa. I would prepare to do so at once, but must have your consent, and am also rather short of information.

It is beautiful here, and the beauty has an effect on me – it is painful to an almost fatal degree, full of danger, and harshly lights up all the dark places in my life. I am extraordinarily susceptible to the landscape, in a yearning, rambling way that fundamentally cannot be satisfied – no, I am not happy either, Friedel, and there is no need for you to contradict me by saying that my longing does not have to mean unhappiness. Else is kind and gentle and doesn't organize things; she too is suffering, and I feel like Frau Susmann's Dostoevsky. The hotel, not a mammoth one as in Karersee, is exquisite, the company refined in a somewhat affected way; there is a fabulous Hungarian cocotte, Baroness Villányi, who is kept by a consortium – even this is wonderful.

Another piece of gossip away from the centre: Benjamin's Naples essay is extraordinary, Borchardt couldn't do it better – and who is Asja Lacis? The sister of Theodor Däubler or a cabbalistic ibbur conjured up by Walter's schizophrenia? I found the obituary for poor Uhl very bad – all too true, and tactless and, for this reason, insulting. I should like to assume that you think otherwise for very deep-seated reasons, and I am writing this on that account.

Oh, Friedel, why don't things go well with us when they really ought to do so? I am constantly racking my brains over it, just like you – only I do so over the impossibility of what is possible, and you over the possibility of what is impossible.

I have no news at all of Ellen. Perhaps she has become engaged.

Will you cable me?

Always – your Teddie.

Original: MS with printed letterhead; Siegfried Kracauer papers, Deutsches Literaturarchiv, Marbach am Neckar.

your letter: not preserved.

'From Tiberius to Krupp': Tiberius Julius Caesar Augustus (42 BC – 37 AD), Roman emperor; retired to Capri in 26 AD; Friedrich Alfred Krupp (1854–1902), a steel magnate and honorary citizen of Capri, built a memorial to himself there through the landscape architecture of 'Via Krupp'. The novel has not been identified.

Parakleton ti: as Adorno wrote: some consolation.

Krupp affair: in 1902 Alfred Krupp reacted to allegations in the German press about his love-life with an action for slander.

Susmann's Dostoevsky: 'Zusammengefasst: Margarete Susmann, Dostojewski' [Summary: Margarete Susmann, *Dostoevsky*], in *Gestalten und Kreise* [Figures and circles], Stuttgart: Diana, 1954, pp. 88–109.

Baroness Villányi: no information survives as to whether this refers to a member of that Hungarian family.

Benjamin's Naples essay … Lacis: 'Walter Benjamin und Asja Lacis, Neapel' [Walter Benjamin and Asja Lacis, Naples], *Frankfurter Zeitung*, 19 August 1925 (see Benjamin, GS 4.1, pp. 307–16, GS 4.2, p. 987). Asja Lacis (1891–1979), a director and actress from Latvia, was a friend of Walter Benjamin's from 1924 onwards.

Borchardt: Rudolf Borchardt (1877–1945), a philologist, moved to Tuscany in 1903; he was a versatile writer of poetry, dramas, narrative prose and translations. The essay was one of his favoured genres.

Däubler: Theodor Däubler (1876–1934), an author and critic, grew up in Italy. Adorno made a setting of *Drei Gedichte von Theodor Däubler für vierstimmigen Frauenchor a capella* (see Adorno, *Kompositionen* 2, pp. 55–62).

ibbur: the positive equivalent of the dybbuk.

obituary for poor Uhl: Wilhelm 'Willo' Uhl (1890–1925), a contributor to the *Frankfurter Zeitung*, appraised in the obituary as a 'jack of all trades', 'critic of the lighter Muses' and 'irreplaceable factotum' (see 'Willo Uhl †', *Frankfurter Zeitung*, 20 August 1925).

27 Adorno to Kracauer

Campo Carlo Magno, 28.8.1925

URGENTLY ADVISE AWAIT SYMON WE WILL MEET SEPTEMBER EIGHTH GENOA LETTER FOLLOWING = TEDDIE =

Original: Telegram; Siegfried Kracauer papers, Deutsches Literaturarchiv, Marbach am Neckar. Dating in accordance with postmark.

Symon: presumably an error in transmission; this must refer to Heinrich Simon (see letter no. 17).

28 Adorno to Kracauer
Campo Carlo Magno, 30.8.1925

UNTIL WEDNESDAY EVENING GENOA MIRAMARE – TEDDIE –

Original: Telegram; Siegfried Kracauer archive, Deutsches Literaturarchiv, Marbach am Neckar. Dated in accordance with a handwritten notice of delivery.

Genoa: Further stages on the journey were Naples, Positano and Capri. Adorno and Kracauer reported on the journey to third parties – for example, Adorno to Alban Berg in a letter of 12th September 1925: 'Being with my friend is stimulating and significant in every way; in human terms it demands complete attention, and in practical ones it compels me to reconsider the basis of our friendship. Still, we have developed along the same lines over the six months of separation – in a way that would also be gratifying to you' (see Adorno/Berg, *Correspondence*, p. 14; translation modified). Again, to Berg on 15th October 1925: 'In addition to this, there was the ongoing confrontation with my friend, which was in every respect a difficult matter, and which gave me no opportunity at all for repose. In Naples we met with Benjamin shortly before our return, and engaged in a philosophical battle with him in which we were able to control the field, albeit not without finding it most necessary to regroup our forces' (see Adorno/Berg, *Correspondence*, p. 20). Kracauer converted his travel experiences into an article, 'Felsenwahn in Positano' [Madness on the cliffs of Positano], *Frankfurter Zeitung*, 20 October 1925 (see Kracauer, W 5, no. 253).

29 Kracauer to Adorno
Frankfurt am Main, 9.2.1926

FRANKFURTER ZEITUNG
UND HANDELSBLATT
REDAKTION
TELEGRAMM-ADRESSE
ZEITUNG FRANKFURTMAIN

FRANKFURT A.M.,
9 February 1926

Dear Teddie,
About the empirical reason for your letter: Diebold was to have gone to Holl; he was prevented, and I was appointed to take over from him only at the last minute. A refusal, as matters stand within the newspaper, was impossible. Incidentally, if you had told me on the telephone that you could have asked your friend not to come, I would have come alone, and we might have spent some time together. Now I do anything to evade a situation where she and I may run into each other.

The business with Leo still needs clearing up face to face (the three of us *should talk it over* together).

In making your attacks you forget that, in my case, the clear view of our relationship which you insinuate that I have does not exist. This means that it would be an act not of purgation but of annihilation if I agreed now to your suggestion that we should no longer see each other – an annihilation even from an objective point of view. I promise you, though, to make a full break drastically once this becomes inevitable. If that is to happen, it will only take place after a heart-to-heart talk which strikes directly at the very foundations of who we are – not necessarily just now, when we are going about things under the influence of mere skin irritations. Your letter indeed does just that; it mixes peripheral matters with essentials in a way that, explicable as it may be, lays a burden of guilt on you yourself no less than on me – that is not how I want to break with you. I have no intention of denying my peccadilloes and acts of malice or cloaking the cowardice of which you reproach me – at least in part – but I do require of you not to shrink from the responsibility which you share with me for the present state of our relationship. Your letter continues in this vein, as if you were the sole aggrieved party in this – and even today you are not the only victim in this mess.

I beg you for a chance to discuss things, when I shall give you a succinct answer to any questions you may have (relevant matters, etc.) and which need to be answered. I shall telephone you tomorrow morning between 12 and 1 (earlier, if I can) to fix a time when we could meet. If it suits you, as early as tomorrow or the day after – no procrastination. Your absence of hope as regards us may perhaps have other meanings besides the one you assume.

Friedel.

Original: MS with printed letterhead; Theodor W. Adorno Archiv, Frankfurt am Main.

your letter: not preserved.

the business with Leo: there is also a gap at this point in the correspondence between Kracauer and Leo Löwenthal; this probably had something to do with the competitive situation at the University of Frankfurt.

30 Adorno to Kracauer
Büdingen, 1.4.1926

Büdingen, 1 April 1926.

My dear Friedel,
I am sitting in the café which exists here, and thinking of you, who also exist. Over my bed there hangs a portrait of Kaiser Wilhelm, and beneath

him the master Albrecht Dürer as he saw himself. It is possible to be radical even here. But from my room a path leads at street level to the top of the tower of a fortress from the era so full of meaning. That presents certain difficulties. Incidentally, it is spring – the season in which a Jungdo boy of 15¾ shot himself for unknown reasons. Your Teddie.

Original: MS; postcard: Büdingen Rathaus (The Town Hall, Büdingen); Siegfried Kracauer papers, Deutsches Literaturarchiv, Marbach am Neckar.

Büdingen: Adorno was visiting his restaurateur friends Helene Eckstein, née Otto (1878–?) and Adam Eckstein (1865–?) here; until 1911 they ran the Kurhaus Schöne Aussicht in Neuweilnau (see letter no. 22).

era so full of meaning: 'In an "era full of meaning" everything relates to a divine purpose. In it there is neither empty space nor empty time, in the sense that both are presupposed by science … Life is free from the painful infinity and the whole dubious nature of an era which lacks meaning; everywhere it is filled with God as far as it extends, and the very stones are evidence of a divine being' (*Soziologie als Wissenschaft*; see Kracauer, W 1, p. 12.) The castle and fortress complex in Büdingen, which has undergone many changes over the centuries, bears a Gothic stamp.

Jungdo: Jungdeutscher Orden, a national-conservative pressure group founded in 1920. After initial opposition to the 'party system', the Volksnationale Reichsvereinigung which developed out of the 'Young German Order' fused with the Deutsche Demokratische Partei in 1930 to become the Deutsche Staatspartei.

shot himself for unknown reasons: 'Our beloved son and loyal brother Felix Wilhelm Wichert passed away suddenly and unexpectedly tonight at the age of 15¾' (family death announcement, *Büdinger Allgemeiner Anzeiger*, 16 March 1926). Felix Wichert was 'found dead on the road between Büdingen and Hof Thiergarten' on 12 March 1926 (Archiv der Stadt Büdingen; Büdinger Geschichtsverein e.V.).

31 Adorno to Kracauer
Prague, 17.4.1926

Prague, 17 April 26.

My dear Friedel,
Here is a card from Prague just for now – tomorrow I am going to Vienna, and from there I shall be able to send a letter. The days here are pleasant and set me free: my passion for joint sessions of philosophizing has revived in the company of Hermann Grab; the city shows me what is genuine and continues to exist – which, precisely in view of other ways of thinking, is something which one cannot recall often enough. The people are knowledgeable, cultivated and urbane; conversation flits between Hradčany and

Lenin, Heidegger and the Astoria Bar, and we both surrender to all the intellectual seductions one could wish for. A feature of the picture is that the chandelier in the dining-room in Grab's apartment trembles whenever a tram drives past the famous Café Arco. More to follow soon – just this note for today.

Please send the Buber essay, if it has appeared, to my old address in Vienna.

Your Teddie.

Dear Herr Kracauer,
As a great many of your ideas have reached me in fragmentary form through my discussions with Teddy, I am very eager to make your acquaintance *in toto*, although I am even more hostile than you to the concept of totality.

Warmest greetings
Yours, Hermann Grab

Original: MS, postcard; Siegfried Kracauer papers, Deutsches Literaturarchiv, Marbach am Neckar.

Prague: Adorno was taking up an invitation from Hermann Grab; he announced his journey to Prague 'around April 10th' to Alban Berg in a letter of 30th March 1926 (see Adorno/Berg, *Correspondence*, p. 49).

Astoria Bar: a bar by this name ('Astoria') existed in Ovocný trh in Prague's first district.

That famous Café Arco: Prague café on Hybernská, a centre of the city's literary life.

Buber essay: 'Die Bibel auf Deutsch: Zur Übersetzung von Martin Buber und Franz Rosenzweig' [The Bible in German: on the translation by Martin Buber and Franz Rosenzweig], *Frankfurter Zeitung*, 27 and 28 April 1926 (see Kracauer, W5, no. 282), a review to which the translators responded in the issue of 18 May 1925. Kracauer, in turn, replied with a 'Duplik' (see Kracauer, W 5, no. 282a).

concept of totality: presumably referring to the rumours about Adorno's and Kracauer's dispute with Georg Lukács; in a letter to Ernst Bloch of 27 May 1927, Kracauer, citing conversations with Adorno, disassociated himself from Lukács 'in the interest of his own formality's desperate concept of totality' (see Bloch, *Briefe* 1, pp. 272–80).

32 Adorno to Kracauer
Vienna, 4.5.1926

FREMDEN- UND FAMILIENPENSION
"LOUISENHEIM"
INH.: ELSA GLASER
WIEN, IX., EISENGASSE 2 (ECKE GIESSERGASSE)
TELEFON 22132.

Vienna, 4 May 1926.

My dear Friedel,

I am only writing to you today now that I can look back over what has happened to me during these days in Vienna. A good number of things have been decided, which has a considerable bearing on our relationship and about which I would rather not have spoken before I was able to see clearly – which, in the misty atmosphere of the enchanted city, was not as easy as the purpose of breaking the enchantment requires. In the first instance, this applies to my relationship to this city itself. The last remaining possibility of living here permanently, or even just temporarily for a longish time, has vanished – internally and externally. First of all, the latter: my essays for *Anbruch*, especially the one about Berg, met with such opposition that the position of editor in chief is no longer feasible – even if I wanted to take it on; closer acquaintance with the individuals concerned has robbed me of any enthusiasm for it. The opposition – and this throws some light on the situation here – came from Schoenberg, who declared my essays to be incomprehensible, because he understood them and drew from them the inference that I was dismissing any possibility of his forming a 'school' and, what was more, that I was emphasizing Berg's independence of him, something which is intolerable to him and his despotic nature as a teacher – and, for full measure, he really begrudges Berg his success with *Wozzeck*. There is, moreover, the fact that he is annoyed with me because I lived in close sympathy with Berg and did not enrol as a student with him. He is said to have a real Wiesengrund complex and once got into a furious argument with Berg on my account. It is difficult to understand Schoenberg's psychology, and I am only mentioning it to you to give you an idea of how matters stand with me in a milieu where the person on whom I was counting to the highest possible degree is hostile to me. The fact that he is not here at the moment just makes things harder. Eisler and Rathaus are also away (both in Berlin); the Kolisch Quartet broke up out of pure Viennese hysteria during the very period when they were studying my pieces; Berg is not going to be staying here much longer either – he has not a *single student* here! – and Soma Morgenstern is planning to flee to Frankfurt – and, what is more, to you, as he has no confidence in anyone else – so this means a *défaite* in every respect. And the city, the Café Museum with its crazy literati from the day before yesterday, the disgraceful music industry – all this is such torture for me that I don't want to stay here a day longer than I have to. The only reason that I am still here is that I was waiting for the private performance by the Kolisch Quartet, which has vanished into the realms of fancy because of the break-up of the quartet itself. Tomorrow I still have some business with the U. E., where I can at least find a home for my things. I am going home on Friday and shall not be leaving Frankfurt in the near future.

You may regard me as a prodigal son who has returned home once and for all, and so the argument that our relationship was of a temporary nature is no longer true in empirical terms. As my need to live outside the country was brought to an end by the atmosphere of the Vienna in which I lived, there are no more difficulties from that quarter, and everything depends on an initiative on your part, which I am now awaiting with bated breath, stripped bare of all dignity. I feel lonelier and more forlorn than I can say, in spite of being on closer terms with two new people (Morgenstern and Grab). I am overwhelmed by a sense of disillusionment, and the thought has become unbearable that the bond between us, which I thought could never be lost, might only be a deceptive illusion. Because you had come to know Gretel Karplus, who has something about her of the reckless daredevil who is up for anything, I don't need so much as merely to mention the limitation of that relationship to you. That of the friendship with Gabi is obvious in any case. Berg is a great artist and a genuine human being, but inarticulate when it comes to relationships. Morgenstern doesn't go deep enough. In short, my loneliness is real; in addition, I have lost the inner ties with home which always used to be a help to me, without there being anyone to blame for it – it was just that the process of my development took me away.

After all this, I hardly need to tell you how matters stand with Ellen Delp. We have become completely estranged. I kept her at a distance from the outset, as I had become distrustful all at once and bitterly disappointed after Frankfurt, and also completely occupied with Berg. At first she showed dignity, then initiative; I did try to maintain a relationship with her simply as one human being to another, but she could not tolerate my lack of passion, made a foolish assault on me – and now we have reached the stage of calling in the undertakers. With all her paraphernalia, self-important egotism and a soul decked with furnishings from Rilke towers, she has become completely stale and even repulsive in my eyes, as every least idea of hers stands there preening itself in front of the truth and at the same time even lays claim to the pathos of subjective authenticity. I am as little inclined to dispute this with her as I am to deny her personal purity, which only piques me because she herself lays claim to this epithet, and she bores me because I don't love her. In short, I can no longer stand the stupid wisdom of her belief in things à la Buber and her mystic confusion. It has become *vieux jeu*; I see her once a day for lunch, send her no flowers, sit at the piano with Berg or in a café at night with Morgenstern, and am glad that she is not there. I appointed her as Susmann's successor;

she may perhaps attract admiration, but only from a distance. I feel old, at the risk of being regarded as young by you – which would not, in the end, be the worst thing that could happen to me.

Otherwise: two conversations with Lukács, from whom I wrung a lot, which does not take much effort, however. Conversation without brilliance – how bored you would have been! Isn't it sad that I can have a better conversation with my adversary Grab than with the author of the theory of the novel, although he is a comrade of mine? I met up with Rutra from Munich – a minor literary figure who doesn't leave you feeling any cleaner. At a reading one evening he gave us titbits from short stories, ironic in exactly the same way as Thomas Mann's, preceded by poems as drunken as Trakl's – my God! I heard Jeritza as Salome – like a cook preparing the head of John the Baptist *en tortue*. In Bohemia, Herr Klenau conducted Bach as if it were Heinrich Anton; in the Volkstheater Erika Wagner sent me to sleep – a completely broken nebbich in a play by that cretin Roman Rolland – and Moissi was so noble in it, too. Mahler's Eighth under Webern was a plus, but it is worth goofing your way through it, especially because the *Lied von der Erde* is in there somewhere. Berg showed me some very fine songs from his youth which have not been published, and Steuermann a quite exceptional piano sonata. With Kolisch, apart from my own stuff, I played Schoenberg with the authentic approach – in short, something did come out of it, but *dégout* outweighs everything: I am glad to be coming home, although I could imagine no train leaving Vienna before Friday, which would spoil the time that is left.

Friedel – do give a sign to Your Teddie.

Original: MS with printed letterhead; Siegfried Kracauer papers, Deutsches Literaturarchiv, Marbach am Neckar.

the one about Berg: 'Alban Berg: Zur Uraufführung des "Wozzeck"' [Alban Berg: on the première of *Wozzeck*], *Musikblätter des Anbruch*, no. 10, 1925 (see Adorno, GS 18, pp. 456–64, GS 19, p. 645). In addition: 'Anton Webern: Zur Aufführung der Fünf Orchesterstücke, op. 10, in Zürich' [Anton Webern: on the performance of Five Pieces for Orchestra, op. 10], *Musikblätter des Anbruch*, no. 6, 1926 (see Adorno, GS 18, pp. 513–16, GS 19, p. 645); an essay entitled 'Notizen über Zwölftontechnik' [Notes on twelve-tone technique] was announced for publication in the same volume but did not appear (it was eventually published as 'Warum Zwölftonmusik?' [Why twelve-tone music?]; see Adorno, GS 18, pp. 114–17, and Adorno/Berg, *Correspondence*, *Briefwechsel*, p. 82, note).

forming a 'school': 'To speak of Arnold Schoenberg's school means wilfully misunderstanding the truth that nothing came out of the composer's teaching other than what followed on from his works' (see 'Alban Berg: Zur Uraufführung des "Wozzeck"' [Alban Berg: on the première of Wozzeck], Adorno, GS 18, p. 456; see also letter no. 4).

The Kolisch Quartet broke up: the 'Viennese String Quartet' survived the rehearsals and performed Adorno's Two Pieces for String Quartet on 10 December 1926 (see Adorno, *Bildmonographie*, p. 91).

you had come to know Gretel Karplus: Gretel Karplus 'worked as an unpaid trainee ... from October 1925 to December 1926 at I. G. Farbwerke in Frankfurt am Main' (see her curriculum vitae from 1956 in Adorno, *Bildmonographie*, p. 114).

friendship with Gabi: presumably Gabriele Oppenheim-Errera (1896–?), who together with her husband, the chemist Paul Oppenheim (1885–1977), headed 'the definitive intellectual salon' (see Adorno/Horkheimer, *Briefwechsel* I, p. 80n.); the Oppenheims went into exile in Belgium in 1933, and to the USA in 1939.

Rutra: Arthur Ernst Rutra, previously Samuely (1892–1942), an author and translator from Vienna; after the First World War he lived in Munich.

Jeritza as Salome: Maria Jeritza (1887–1982), a soprano, had already been engaged at this time by the Metropolitan Opera in New York; Richard Strauss's Salome was among her major roles.

Klenau conducted Bach: on 27 April 1926, Paul von Klenau conducted Johann Sebastian Bach's cantatas *Sehet, wir gehen hinauf nach Jerusalem*, *Wachet auf, ruft uns die Stimme* and *Der zufriedengestellte Aeolus* in the Grosser Saal of the Konzerthaus.

Heinrich Anton: this may refer to the composer Heinrich Anton Hoffmann (1770–1842) or Heinrich Simon, who used this pseudonym.

Rolland: the author Romain Rolland (1866–1944); his play *A Game of Death and Love* was performed at the Volkstheater in March and April 1926.

Moissi: the actor Alexander Moissi (1879–1935), who fulfilled major engagements in Berlin, Prague and Vienna.

Mahler's Eighth under Webern: Alban Berg drew Adorno's attention to the concert conducted by Anton Webern on 19 April 1926 in a letter of 6 April 1926 (see Adorno/Berg, *Correspondence*, p. 53).

Berg ... very fine songs: Alban Berg, Seven Early Songs.

Steuermann ... piano sonata: the Piano Sonata of 1924.

played Schoenberg with the authentic approach: no more detailed information is available.

33 Adorno to Kracauer
Rottach-Staudach, 14.8.1926

14 August
1926

Rottach-Staudach 109
c/o Schwab.
(Upper Bavaria).

Dear Friedel,
I greet you in the era of decay, which is a positive definition. It is really beautiful here, with no yodelling; the people are all from Berlin, and the mountains are all around. I am lodging with a woman who claims to be

eighty-five, and who has been supplied by the tourist agency. I am reading French kitsch as I always do – Marcel Proust and Franz Brentano. I am not giving up the ghost because it doesn't exist, but I do pig imitations for the three-year-old baby, Marion, who has taken me to her heart. The friend (who says she has definitely met you several times at Gabi's and talked to you!) has in reality an *impassibilité* about her which other ladies might envy her, if she were to be envied at all. We speak in cultured tones about dissociation, and about the breakdown of private life, wandering along by the lake or under the fleeting moon itself. The mother is an American Céline. You have some idea what *that* means. I am sad to the depths of my soul, but quite calm and relaxed.

Please give Dr *Holl* my address.

Give Leo my regards for now. Your Teddie.

Original: MS, postcard: Kracauer papers, Deutsches Literaturarchiv, Marbach am Neckar.

Marcel Proust: at this time Adorno had at his disposal not only the original but also the first German translation of *Du côté de chez Swann*; it was published in 1926 by Rudolf Schottlaender under the title *Der Weg zu Swann* [The way to Swann] by the Berlin publishing house Die Schmiede.

Brentano: Franz Brentano (1838–1917); philosopher, ordained to the Catholic priesthood in 1864; professor of philosophy in Würzburg (1872) and Vienna (1874); left the Church in 1879.

The friend: Ellen Dreyfuss-Herz (1897–?), actress; divorced at this period from her husband Carl Dreyfuss, a friend of Adorno's (see letter no. 42), took part in the holiday excursion to the Tegernsee; Adorno explains the unhappy constellation in a letter to Alban Berg of 19 August 1926 (see Adorno/Berg, *Correspondence*, pp. 70–3).

Gabi: Gabriele Oppenheim.

an American Céline: no information survives.

34 Kracauer to Adorno

Frankfurt am Main, 19.8.1926

FRANKFURTER ZEITUNG
TELEGRAMM-ADRESSE:
ZEITUNG FRANKFURTMAIN
FERNSPRECHER:
AMT HANSA 9160 BIS HANSA 9175

FRANKFURT A. M.,
19. August 26

Dear Teddie,

I would have answered your letter at once if Herr Henses had not suddenly fallen ill on the day of your departure, so that I had to stand in for him until yesterday, make up the Bäderblatt, etc. – it was no small matter. Your card sounded glum – not that you said as much. Depression is apparent in the way the lines of writing droop – you might be tired, too. In the meantime, perhaps you may have absorbed the family characteristics of your surroundings. Your friend must be mistaken; she didn't meet me at Frau O's. I did once have a conversation with a Frau Dreyfuss there, but it was a different one. Their features are sufficiently present in my memory. I should like to preserve this illusion, which is nothing of the kind. In your place I should just leave work alone for now, recuperate properly and take everything just as it comes. Forgive these suggestions, but I detect a strong feeling of malaise in your lines which ultimately extends to the whole situation in which you have ended up. In any case, I can sense something of the kind behind what you say. I completely understand its deliberately guarded tone. As you were writing on the basis of your initial impressions I shall postpone any further discussion of your card. Unless I am very much mistaken, your pedantic mode of expression was also determined by the combination of alienation + distance. Over the last few weeks this complex has had no less of an effect on me. You know that I regard absence in the case of a passionate relationship as quite simply totally destructive (the limitations of 'quite simply' are self-evident); in our case I feel that a brief separation is an opportunity for self-reflection which makes regeneration possible. In any case I still feel whenever I think of you – which is by no means such a rare occurrence – that our relationship is indestructible; I feel that it is very pure, and I am more intent than ever on overcoming the empirical kinds of resistance which are greater in my case than you may be able even to sense. Whether I shall succeed, *ça dépend*; but unfortunately, we will probably not come unstuck.

Do go on somewhere else after the weeks at Tegernsee – with books and music, if you don't mind. You are missing nothing here, and you would be better off in Aussee or the Dolomites. Before your card arrived, I thought that you would not write for reasons which seemed very sensible to me. Because of the prognosis, I fought shy of making any appointment to discuss our correspondence – but it is all right like that. I have passed on your address to Holl and your good wishes to Leo. At present I have a skin eruption of a nervous kind which is making me less than happy. Perhaps you may still be having some good days now, with your little girlfriend and afterwards. Yours, Friedel.

Original: MS with printed letterhead; Theodor W. Adorno Archiv, Frankfurt am Main.

Henses: detailed information unavailable.

Frau O: probably Gabriele Oppenheim.

35 Adorno to Kracauer
Rottach-Staudach, 19.8.1926

Staudach-Rottach 109,
Haus Schwab
19 August 1926.

Dear Friedel,

First of all, a request; Hermann Grab, during his last stay in Frankfurt, was in a bar whose name he can no longer recall but which can only have been the Clou (opposite Barfüßereck). There, in the cloakroom, he left behind the manuscript of a lecture of his about Lukács's history book and also the typescript of a work by a Russian entitled 'The Economic Potential of Siberia'. He has only just discovered the loss and is particularly concerned about getting the thing by the poor Russian back. Would you just have a look in the Clou – and send it to him in Prague if you should find it? The address is: Dr Hermann Grab, Prague VIII, Villa Koschinka. I would be most grateful to you.

As for me, I am well apart from a quite severe case of sunburn which I got while out boating, but which is getting better now. Please don't say anything about it in Seeheimer Strasse. We lie around on the water all morning in our bathing costumes; I have learnt to row and enjoyed it. In the early afternoons I work: Franz Brentano – a most confused philosophy, but one which is interesting enough in hermeneutic terms as it reveals a very abstruse and very well-hidden connection (but one which goes back to contemporary criticism of Kant and the battle against the Enlightenment) between positivism, which looks at the 'facts themselves' in a way 'far removed from theory', and the phenomenological reaction which hypostasizes these givens as 'objects' in ontological terms and attempts to conceal their actual theoretical–abstract character. Protestant theology played off Hume against Kant in exactly the same way. The downward dissociation deceptively positions itself in the place of configuration, in truth so as to keep the explosive anti-mythological power of theory at a distance. This seems to me to be the centre of all phenomenological fraud today. And in Brentano's writings one gazes into the swamp of nature itself.

As to personal matters: the relationship with Ellen is difficult as only one of this kind could be. I have upset her without being able to comprehend her nature – which I am less inclined to do through letters than ever – she clings to me, and yet wants to put a distance between us. The phenomenon of boundaries plays a threatening part in this. She is greatly endangered by that schizophrenic tendency of hers – a very strange being, strange even to herself, silent and beautiful, and yet very obvious at the same time (she once remarked sadly that she seemed like such a mythical being to herself). There is as little possibility of finding a way of surmounting the difficulty here as at any other place. I no longer believe that it is possible to realize a relationship as such. Only a few intentions growing out of this can be realized, and even those one can only hit upon without attaining fulfilment.

The more valid I find my knowledge of other people, the more uninteresting I become to myself. It is the only possible way of existing, and painful simply because I have to see this so clearly before I am really mature enough for it.

Did you ever receive my card? I fear that you might have misunderstood it. It was not meant to irritate you; what I said about your friend was intended much more to show you that even this is no different or more complete. But perhaps I used the wrong tone of voice. I am probably coming back to Frankfurt at the end of next week. Teddie.

Please tell Holl to send *Nachtmusik* to me along with the twelve-tone manuscript which I still don't have. I need it.

Original: Siegfried Kracauer papers, Deutsches Literaturarchiv, Marbach am Neckar.

Clou: the bar opposite the Barfüßereck restaurant in the historic centre of Frankfurt (Großer Kornmarkt 10).

Lukács's history book: Georg Lukács, *Geschichte und Klassenbewußtsein*, Berlin: Malik, 1923.

send it to him in Prague: no evidence survives of any item being sent that corresponds to this description.

entitled 'The Economic Potential of Siberia': no information is available.

Nachtmusik ... twelve-tone manuscript: Adorno to Alban Berg (22 November 1926: 'I enclose the essay on twelve-tone technique, which, together with the one about you and "Nachtmusik", represents my present theoretical stance. The F. Z. rejected it as too musically specialized, but now it looks to appear in Anbruch after all' (see Adorno/Berg, *Correspondence*, p. 86.) The collection of aphorisms entitled *Nachtmusik* [Night music] appeared in *Anbruch*, no. 1, 1929 (see Adorno, GS 17, pp. 52–9); for the 'twelve-tone manuscript' see letter no. 32.

36 Adorno to Kracauer

Rottach-Staudach, 23/24.8.1926

Monday: noon.

Friedel – just this. There is a fate overshadowing our relationship which seems to me stronger than we are. I wrote my letter when I was without news from you after sending my card – in despair. I know that the letter is terrible, and there are sombre reasons behind the trenchant nature of my insistent pleas. Then there came your first card, which gave me hope. The first *immediate* word from you for an unimaginably long time, and one which went straight to my heart. In the meantime, my letter reached you and ruined everything. Your card now confirms with hindsight the tone which your first denied.

Do at least understand this one thing – that precisely this *normal* tone – which, by the way, leads you to the mistaken assumption of an accommodation which has not occurred – came about on the basis of despair – that anything 'natural' is wholly alien to it. Remember that I recently said to you – I think it was in the Hanselmann – 'now I can talk to you calmly about philosophy and women'.

And yet – how little am I able to do so! Should nothing of that have found its way into that wretched letter?

Do I really have to spell it out to you that all the Holl business and the like are a matter of utter indifference to me – that the unrestrained nature of my pleading only resulted from my being genuinely confused about my emotions? That the importance which I gave the sunburn and all the things in my letter which dissolve into relations were only markers of the loss which I felt was a final one. Is it really final, then? It would be a terrible thing for me if I had blocked the way between you and me!

To answer your question, I have not gone on any major excursions; but yesterday evening, with my friend, I ate some partridges in a restaurant – they had to be ordered specially. I live, but do not quite know how. Work a little, as a discipline; for otherwise living would simply not be possible, especially as what is going on here isn't exactly anyone's ideal way to relax.

In terms of new acquaintances here I have only got to know Leo Slezak's son Walter – a pretty film star of a boy with a horrifyingly right and false knowledge of the world and yet with a comedian's vacuous imagination which might reconcile one to him. His stories about Lya de Putti, especially her prayer in the church, would have moved even you very much. When the moon shines he tells dirty jokes, without this being dire; it is not his true self at all! Otherwise, he swishes around on the lake in a motor-boat.

Apart from that, I only met up with him on one occasion (through Ellen, who has known him from childhood and whom he kisses). He actually doesn't interest me at all; I don't even know why I'm telling you about him. That would be a question for Leo; but he does not know it either.

Do write me another word or two and tell me whether you are holding fast to the conviction that we are not going to get rid of each other. I haven't the words to tell you what I should like to say. Perhaps you know them for me.

Teddie.

Original: MS; Siegfried Kracauer papers, Deutsches Literaturarchiv, Marbach am Neckar; date taken from a handwritten note of indeterminate origin.

your card: not preserved.

Leo Slezak's son Walter: Leo Slezak (1873–1946), a tenor and actor who appeared with great success at the Vienna Staatsoper from 1901 onwards; he maintained a holiday home on the Tegernsee. Walter Slezak (1902–1983) made his debut as an actor in Michael Curtiz's *Sodom und Gomorra* (1922).

de Putti: Lya de Putti (1897–1931), an actress; in 1926 she appeared with Walter Slezak in Manfred Noa's film *Junges Blut*.

37 Adorno to Kracauer
[Rottach-Egern], 2.9.1926

2 September 1926.

My dear Friedel,

I am sitting alone in the café in Rottach, which is going downhill – since the 1st even the musicians have left – and feeling sad. My friend is holding a family council at home with her mother and relatives about some kind of financial matter. It is very cool here, with a pronounced evening atmosphere; the day after tomorrow I am travelling home too – wholly restored physically, but as a human being as needy as ever and wholly unsatisfied, that is, as far as I am at all. But my private life has been much reduced during this time, and I feel altogether apart from the life which I led so intensely here. It feels as if it had not been me at all but another person in my place, and that, indeed, is probably how it must be.

I shall try to answer your letters, which is difficult as they allude to many things in veiled terms rather than stating them explicitly. This is not meant as a reproach; I do understand you, but what is missing is entry-points to seize upon. As far as the erotic situation is concerned, however, I have had an experience that makes things clear to me; in fact, it is always the same experience, and Hanni has already articulated it, but now that experience has been confirmed to me in more concrete terms – i.e. that I cannot accommodate myself in the kind of relationships with women who actually exist. Hanni says I am wholly incapable of loving. My female friend – to say at least that much and because it concerns *us* – finds my kind of intensity unbearable; saying that I do not love a woman as she really is but the idea of her, that I dissolve her connection with nature through my kind of existence – just by my way of behaving – even without any need for words. She says this entirely without reproaches and not for banal feminine reasons, but very perceptively and gently, as our relationship, as a whole, plays itself out in a tone of quiet friendliness which does have its awful side; she too is in truth quite untouchable, and she knows it. Her remarks certainly bear some objective significance; I will not claim that it is complete, but she does see a lot, and the particular situation in which these remarks were made to me should enhance their value. I also believe about myself now that I am so steeped in spirituality that – I am being very careful here, Friedel, and certainly thinking more than I write – I cannot find fulfilment in the kind of relations with women as they are.

You will object: yes, indeed, you knew that too, and didn't confuse me with Herr Ziegler either, but that alone is not sufficient. I am not lacking in the other respect, either – far from it – and aberrations are constantly to be feared. I don't take this argument lightly, and I know the danger that I carry with me and that you – here and now – also represent. But I believe that all my natural tendencies have been slightly transformed (with regard to their intentions, at least) and do not dominate. Yes – today it almost seems to me as if the restless erotic activity of my last few years originated more from the fear of losing nature altogether than from nature itself. However, that may just be psychology, and you have a factual basis for your mistrust, although I cannot believe the real reason for it. I don't attach any concrete hope to all this – now less than ever – because never was I in greater despair about our relationship than in those last weeks in Frankfurt, and your remark that you didn't ask my opinion about your friend taught me a more drastic lesson about its decline – and above all the change in it, which, however, took place after all in *you* – than any theoretical discussion could have done which remained open to correction by existence breaking in on it. Forgive this inconsequential talk, but in private life, so long as my reserves hold out, I am still private, and I stick with Kierkegaard. That remark of yours, then, remains unexpunged, even if – given the initiative in your letters which can be perceived all the more clearly as it is disguised – I could not allow myself to fall into despair, at the lowest point of which, I thought, I would be on peaceful social terms with you – something, incidentally, which I would never have been able to do anyway. As long as our empirical natures remain remote from each other, I don't believe that our relationship can be revived. However, neither do I believe that the way you stubbornly distance yourself from me is grounded solely in the erotic difference. It involves all kinds of psychological pressures between us that one could get a grasp of. Even if that succeeded, of course, I would not feel optimistic. Too much is blocked between us, and the memory of our past relationship is too great to be skipped over at the outset – and also too great to forget. The only motif of hope for our friendship that I allow myself is the definite experience of my indissolubility in mere relations. And our relationship is the only one that is not a mere 'relation', the only one that means something, and at the same time has its basis in it. I don't know whether you accept that, but it is worth thinking about – and, under certain theoretical conditions that are no longer alien to either of us, it means quite a lot. It isn't good to anticipate too much, but we should certainly consider what falls within the realm of knowledge, which here means moral knowledge in a pre-eminent sense.

In Frankfurt I shall be very much alone now – thrown back on Leo and Carl Dreyfuss (Leo, by the way, hasn't replied to a card from me!). Ilona Karolevna, Carl Dreyfuss's girlfriend, has gone mad. It came as a great shock to me; we were together once and felt each other strongly, without a word; I clammed up – you may remember my account of it – and now the muteness is final. I would never have thought that what I said to you in

Frankfurt am Main recently about the sadness of beauty – I was thinking of that girl – would be proved true in such a terrible way. A lot is blocked after all. In September I am going with the mothers to Amorbach for eight or nine days, because, feeling as I do, I couldn't bear being alone in Seeheimer Strasse. Gretel Karplus is coming back in October; I must break with her at all costs, hard as the effort of making the decision will be for me and the fact of the break itself for her. She wants to go to the K. P. now, and I shall have to make her get rid of everything she learnt from me and that she understood in entirely the wrong way. I must tell you about Ellen Delp and the strange thing that happened to us, as it is a sign. But I am waiting for that – and to hear your decision – until you are here. I shall write without delay to Sohn-Rethel at home. Greet the one who is in unreal despair. Now I have (first) to write a major review of Bloch's philosophy of music. Don't tell me too much about the journey, for which I wish you all the very best – because I shall not be with you. To say this is superfluous, but that is just how I feel. Goodbye. Teddie.

Original: MS; Siegfried Kracauer papers, Deutsches Literaturarchiv, Marbach am Neckar. The place can be deduced from the postmark; Adorno, as the sender, wrote his Frankfurt address on the envelope; addressed to Kracauer, poste restante, Marseilles (Kracauer and Lili Ehrenreich travelled to France in September 1926).

Ziegler: Heinz Otto Ziegler (1903–1944), sociologist; friend of Hermann Grab (see Adorno/Berg, *Correspondence*, p. 126, note).

your friend: Elisabeth ('Lilli') Ehrenreich (1893–1971) was at this time a librarian at the Institute for Social Research; her marriage to Kracauer took place on 5 March 1930.

Leo … a card from me: no card corresponding to this description has survived among Leo Löwenthal's papers in the Archivzentrum der Universitätsbibliothek Johann Christian Senckenberg, Frankfurt am Main.

Karolevna: Ilona Karolevna, actress and dancer; no further information is available (see Adorno/Berg, *Correspondence*, pp. 133, 135).

Write … to Sohn-Rethel: the social scientist and philosopher Alfred Sohn-Rethel (1899–1990) was living in Naples in the mid–1920s, where he was a witness to the 'philosophical battle' between Adorno, Walter Benjamin and Kracauer (see letter no. 28, note, and also Sohn-Rethel to Adorno, 18 December 1966, in Adorno/Sohn-Rethel, *Briefwechsel*, p. 151); the correspondence from the years up to 1936 is currently presumed lost.

review of Bloch's philosophy of music: Ernst Bloch, 'Philosophie der Musik', in the latter's *Geist der Utopie*, Berlin: Paul Cassirer, 1923, pp. 45–193; the plan was never realized.

K. P.: Kommunistische Partei.

38 Adorno to Kracauer

Frankfurt am Main, 17.9.1926

Frankfurt, 17 September 26

My dear Friedel, you are indeed right – in many instances we miss the point of our correspondence, and you did not understand my last letter either in the way that it was meant, but construed it as a kind of ideology which I constructed for myself or from the reality of our relationship, whereas it in no way originated from any intention to conceal its dark side – in any case, this was not the time for that. And, of course, the fact that we have so little ability to say to each other what we mean, this seems to indicate that all paths between us are blocked rather than that this is something to be viewed as innocuous and incidental. However, I still believe – quite apart from the warmth traditional on a birthday, to which I am actually more receptive than you would be – yes, I believe that behind the note of ideology-dissolution in your letter, which does not relate merely to ideology, I can sense something good and even hopeful, always assuming that hope is rooted in truth, which I am convinced is the case with you. I also recognize many points on which you are right in your psychological interpretations, and the fact that my inability to love is at present a matter of conscious will is something which has actually been obvious to me for a long time. When I once said to you that I was much more patient than appearances might suggest, that was exactly what I was driving at. However, I must stick to that sentence in which I said that I had changed a little in my relationship towards women. You have obviously taken it the wrong way (which may be the fault of the way I expressed it!); I had no intention at all of sounding a fanfare to announce a new beginning of an era in our friendship. The basis of that sentence is much more concrete and is grounded in the specific experience of my relationship with Ellen Dreyfuss. Perhaps this might indicate to you that (as this friend is not at all my 'type', in the usual sense, but has a beauty which creates an alienating effect) I encountered her as the first woman in whom I did not meet myself or my own image, but *someone who is quite different* in quality and nature. It is a kind of recapitulation of puberty, or the process of becoming a man, which supports this realization and brings with it another firm point of attachment to life, while until now in erotic matters I was more inclined to reproduce my own image and was therefore 'untouchable'.

Perhaps this will make it clearer to you how I have changed. Nothing of the difficulties in my relationship with E. was expunged by this, and I left Egern in a state of great sadness. My life here is going on in the old way, but with only a few people, mainly Leo and Carl Dreyfuss. I am working a lot (the finale of the quartet, which I am finding very difficult indeed); I am also doing plenty of piano practice to fire myself up for music again. My postdoctoral thesis is sketched out in general terms; I won't bore you with that. In addition, I am reading Freud at the moment. I must ask you for some practical advice here – it's to do with Leo, whose wolfish side has once again surfaced recently. You know that after me – and inspired by my preparing for the Cornelius exam – he conceived the plan of studying for his habilitation with Cornelius. This, however, is only possible for one of us, and Leo is now intent on becoming that one rather than me. The very way in which he launched the initiative made me extremely sceptical. Now he is acting as if we had both started at the same time and under the same conditions, and fortune, or Cornelius's own inclination alone, would decide the outcome. All his talk of 'qualifying after me' has completely vanished; he said to me that we would have to 'toss a coin' for the place. He is now planning to use the work on Helvetius that he snatched from you to snatch my prospects of qualifying away from me. He has already worked quite openly with Horkheimer in a similar way, and in any event has achieved the result – probably through his commitments to world revolution, which I cannot enter into to such an extent! – that the Hero of Cronberg has announced to me that he doesn't mind which of us qualifies first and we had to sort it out between ourselves. This – after he himself had suggested my doing the thesis and set things in motion! Leo, of course, already has an ideology, according to which the habilitation is much more important for him than for me – he knows that only one of us will succeed, and is plainly trying to impose a moral obligation on me to step down in favour of him.

I really have had enough of this now. Repellent as it is to me to have to tear myself to pieces in a fight with a friend over a miserable little position, I am equally unenthusiastic about finding myself in the role of an utter dupe. However, the matter is no joke for me because, if the plan to qualify as a lecturer goes wrong, there are threats at home to 'safeguard' me by making me study law and take the state exams, something for which I have no inclination whatsoever. I haven't spoken to Leo yet – first, because I am still overwhelmed by disgust, but also because I don't feel up to confrontations of that kind with him and would be sure to go off deeply aggrieved and with a bad conscience. This matter needs a penetrating view of the situation, and above all a person who has no personal interest in it to put an end to the whole business. I am just asking you for your advice now, but at the same time I would ask you to consider the fact that a conversation about Leo and me is very much a two-edged affair. I would never have entered into competition with Leo over the matter of Cornelius; he (Leo) wishes that I had too obviously for me not to assume that he is well covered in that respect. I must ask you to intervene, and am not even as reluctant to do so as circumstances might require. Only after your return, of course – not at a distance – not even without your hearing Leo first. For the time being, I am just asking for your advice and a basic statement about whether you might be prepared to step in.

As for Sohn-Rethel, his letters are very decent, but *plutôt* Alfred Seidel; your replies are completely clear to me, nothing else would have been possible. I have not yet finished the book; there is a good knowledge of detail in it, but the framework, like the basis, is completely inadequate, it is a messianic Oppenheimer. How can a *ratio* which only differs from Hegel in being more neo-Kantian, *even more* lacking in a sense of history and less concrete, aim to construe nothing less than the Marxist concept of history! And what a murky Bloch-like confusion he stirs up with his concept of the transcendental! And how wrong – at least like Benjaminian ideas – and how unbroken are the metaphysics perching on top of it! He misses the entire content of Marxism in Heidelberg fashion and gives it the spuriously profound quality of a dilettante. Even the *a priori* approach to theory, which might have won the reader over, is no more than academically abstract – not even abstract – with an eye to university circles, from which it differs only in its pretentiousness. The rationality of the work is bourgeois through and through in its reliance on bad, logically abstract entities as opposed to any kind of genuine clarification. History cannot be deduced from transcendental unity, or only in a faulty way; sparkle as it may, it produces only material, static and formal categories whose disintegration has its simply ontological boundaries delimited precisely by unity itself. The image of man which would have to stand up for it might perhaps be more abstract, but it could never establish an abstract totality. Its abstract quality would consist of the disintegration of the natural structure into the dissociated lower reality which Marx aptly defines, while Sohn's abstractions take up the dissociated units of empiricism, which he poorly despises, and attempts to fit them into a totality which is only natural and therefore adopts the mask of a literary/theological superstructure. The banal rejection by every communist would affect Sohn, who, not without cause, aims to revise Marx, with greater justification than Lukács, of whom he is a goyish-pastoral incarnation minus the mask. No, this book is no use, despite his gift for structure – which, by the way, can only be attributed to a lack of philosophical experience – and a capacity for individual imagination in which I have a great deal of confidence. In this I am not forgetting the human side of the case, and I shall handle him with care even when writing outspokenly on these matters – and only when I know whether you accept my judgement. I can't act as an advocate for the book with Pollock; his stupidity is justified as far as it is concerned, but perhaps they can manage to get something else for Sohn-Rethel in the Institute. The hope which he places in Ryazanov, of course, is merely touching.

I was especially pleased to learn that you have already identified in advance with my criticism of the summary, although I can't rid myself of the suspicion that it was only for that reason.

Fred Goldbeck is here again, as an agent for the community of chamber music [Kammermusikgemeinde] – a stranger and an anachronism.

Many thanks for the Gide – I am going to read it.

Are you alone now, or still with your friend?

I shall be going with my people to Amorbach for 8 days at the beginning of October (the second week).

I was planning to learn to dance, but that was as far as it got. I am not particularly sorry; I feel on a firmer footing than before, but the void in our relationship is still there, and nothing in my life can be decided until that is finally resolved.

Enjoy the bouillabaisse (the embodiment of pleasure!), and in Paris don't miss Ravel's *L'Enfant et les sortilèges* – you will find it interesting. Goodbye!

Yours, Teddie

Original: MS; Siegfried Kracauer papers, Deutsches Literaturarchiv, Marbach am Neckar.

finale of the quartet: see letter no. 5.

thesis: the work which Adorno withdrew in January 1928, 'Der Begriff des Unbewußten in der transzendentalen Seelenlehre' [The concept of the unconscious in transcendental psychology] (see Adorno, GS 1, pp. 79–322, 381f.).

In addition, I am reading Freud: the third part of the work planned as a postgraduate thesis bears the title 'Die Erkenntnis des Unbewußten und die psychoanalytische Methode' (see above).

it's to do with Leo: Leo Löwenthal was likewise pursuing the intention of writing a postgraduate thesis for his habilitation under Hans Cornelius (1863–1947); his work on 'The Philosophy of Helvetius' never materialized. The competition surrounding it is documented in Adorno, *Bildmonographie*, pp. 97–102.

suggested my doing the thesis: see the first surviving letter from Max Horkheimer to Adorno of 2 October 1927, which reveals his role as an intermediary with Hans Cornelius (Adorno/Horkheimer, *Briefwechsel* I, pp. 9f.).

Seidel: Alfred Seidel (1895–1924); Adorno described him in a lecture as a 'friend of his youth' (see Adorno, *Lectures on Negative Dialectics: Fragments of a Lecture Course 1965/1966*, ed. Rolf Tiedemann, trans. Rodney Livingstone (Cambridge: Polity, 2008). He had been a friend of Alfred Sohn-Rethel since the latter's student days in Heidelberg (1917–1923). After writing his book *Bewußtsein als Verhängnis* [Consciousness as fate] (ed. Hans Prinzhorn, Bonn: Friedrich Cohen, 1927) he committed suicide in 1924. Kracauer reviewed the book: 'Ein Dokument der Zeit' [A document of the times], *Frankfurter Zeitung*, 9 January 1927 (see Kracauer, W 5, no. 329).

your replies: not preserved.

messianic Oppenheimer: a possible allusion to Paul Oppenheim, *Die natürliche Ordnung der Wissenschaften: Grundgesetze der vergleichenden Wissenschaftlehre* (Jena: Gustav Fischer, 1926) and Kracauer's review: 'Die Denkfläche: Eine neue Wissenschaftslehre', *Frankfurter Zeitung*, 7 July 1926 (see Kracauer, W 5, no. 293).

He misses the entire content of Marxism in Heidelberg fashion: probably an allusion to the 'south-western school' and Alfred Seidel's 1922 Heidelberg dissertation 'Produktivkräfte und Klassenkampf: Ein Beitrag zur Interpretation des historischen Materialismus von Karl Marx und Friedrich Engels' [Productive forces and class struggle: a contribution to the interpretation of the historical materialism of Karl Marx and Friedrich Engels].

hope which he places in Ryazanov: David Ryazanov (1870–1936); Soviet revolutionary and author, editor of the writings of Karl Marx at the Marx–Engels Institute in Moscow; he also collaborated with Carl Grünberg and the Institute for Social Research in Frankfurt.

Thank you for the Gide: probably André Gide, *Les faux-monnayeurs* (Paris: Gallimard, 1925); the library left behind by Adorno contains five of Gide's books which had appeared before 1926.

Paris: Kracauer and Lili Ehrenreich travelled in Provence and to Paris in September 1926 (see *Marbacher Magazine* 47, p. 44).

L'Enfant et les sortilèges: the opera by Maurice Ravel (1875–1937) received its première in Monte Carlo on 21 March 1925.

39 Adorno to Kracauer

Vienna, 7.12.1926

7 December 26.

Vienna IX, Eisengasse 2,
Pension Luisenheim.

Dear Friedel,

After a thoroughly dreary journey I arrived here and found the city covered in dirty snow, which attractively marks out the vacuum which decay and the dark national powers have blasted in the closed coherence of cultural solidity. Someone told me that numerous canals beneath the city, which have long since been drained and are snug enough to be habitable, have been colonized by the lumpenproletariat, who have arranged to have the entrances guarded by their own doormen.

The performance of my quartet has been definitely set for the tenth, as long as no insuperable difficulties reveal themselves late in the day. We are practising incessantly, sometimes separately and sometimes as an ensemble – with the assistance of Berg and Webern starting tomorrow. The piece is still in a very rough state and is very difficult to survey; I can't say anything definitive about this as yet.

My inner man is feeling better, inasmuch as the strangeness and emptiness of the city and of the objective horizon, which I have recently discovered, and the extinction of the old and the deadness of the new people has liberated me to such an extent that I can be sad with a certain degree of concentration, something which I was never able to achieve before. The performance as such is a matter of complete indifference to me, and all I care about is the rehearsals, which fill the time profitably. The people, especially those in the business, have become almost impossible for me to contact, and treat me accordingly; so does Klenau, and so does Dr Weichardt, who greeted me on the telephone with exquisite discourtesy. Kolisch is pleasant and Berg a genuine person with whom I have kept in contact. We spend a lot of time together. E. D., the Viennese with the fateful initials, has become history – quite a museum-piece [?] in my eyes. Do write a line or two to Your Teddie.

Original: MS, postcard, Siegfried Kracauer papers Deutsches Literaturarchiv, Marbach am Neckar.

performance of my quartet: Adorno's Zwei Stücke für Streichquartett [Two Pieces for String Quartet] were performed on 10 December 1926 by the Wiener Streichquartett headed by Rudolf Kolisch (see Adorno, *Bildmonographie*, p. 91).

Dr Weichardt: Carl Weichardt.

E. D.: Ellen Delp.

fateful initials: Ellen Dreyfuss.

40 Kracauer to Adorno
Paris, 14.1.1927

FRANKFURTER ZEITUNG
FEUILLETON-REDAKTION
TELEGRAMM-ADRESSE:
ZEITUNG FRANKFURTMAIN
FERNSPRECHER:
AMT HANSA 9160 BIS HANSA 9175

~~FRANKFURT A.M.,~~ 14. I. 27
Paris (6e)
29, rue Jacob.
Hotel d'Isby.

Dear Teddie,

You derived a poison from my card which it never contained. I justifiably expected a consolidation from your first big public success, a consolidation which would not, of course, displace that famous inner restlessness of yours, but surely would do so for the other disquiet (or impatience) which is generated by lack of recognition. You were thoroughly obsessed with it up till now, and as the success was, as you write, quite considerable, I have new hope that it might tame this Disquiet No. 2. I should like to know what such an opinion has to do with inner conditions. Moreover, your comments about your time in Vienna don't make sense to me at all. You write that now you no longer know what to do with the long-desired affirmation of your status as an artist; that you left Vienna feeling sad and empty; that real life is what matters, and that you have no respect for any kind of ideology relating to artists and their work. Why is it that you don't know what to do with the affirmation of your status as an artist? Did it not make you happy – or give you any satisfaction? (I, at any rate, was very happy for you.) I almost think that, here (as, of course, also in erotic matters), you are adopting an ambivalent standpoint in order to be able to set your foot down everywhere. Hardly have you had a success than you have to brush it off because successes seen from another perspective are immaterial. I regard this attitude as rooted in an excess of dialectic whose psychological sources I think I recognize. At the same time, neither art nor artists are *de facto* contemptible in your eyes, and even you yourself do not believe that 'real life' excludes artistic achievement. To appreciate artistic accomplishment, as you certainly do through your works, in no way needs to imply worshipping an ideology relating to artists and their work. So you can hardly have left Vienna feeling sad and empty because you derived too little satisfaction from your urge towards 'real life' – at least, as far as I can judge; while, on the other hand, I can well understand that the break with Ellen Dreyfuss must have cast a pall of gloom over your stay there.

Your reflections proceed from an appraisal of the artistic principle for which I, at any rate, should not like to have provided the impetus. It is true that I did question the prevailing practices of art in theoretical terms and opposed exaggerated claims on behalf of the aesthetic, and even accepted the possibility that art might come to an end, but it is only in rather negligible conversations that I denied the legitimate existence of art overall and most of all *in praxi*. It is difficult indeed nowadays to capture reality, but you represent the coincidence as achievable, and your Viennese friends' struggle for the existence of art is not based on principles – or I should be worried about their status as artists. In the intermediate levels into which art does indeed penetrate, work still remains to be done for an unforeseeable time – including through the medium of art – before revolutionary theory will prove true (if, indeed, it can do so at all). In your place, then, I should not, for reasons connected with the revolution, declare a rejection of art as such, and the decay of works of art is only *one* aspect of their fate. As I have said before, there's still a while yet before the dustman comes. Even the poor economic situation of artists which you mention doesn't indicate the immediate appearance of this Messiah with the dustbin. Artists who don't accord with the tastes of the paying public have already been starving for centuries, which (*nota bene*) has never been a strict proof of their greatness. You mustn't wall yourself off from the world in which you are living for the time being, nor would I by any means unconditionally diagnose living in the context of social relationships as a transgression against real life.

I would rather tell you about Paris face to face if you are interested. I should also prefer not to put down anything more in writing about the closing passage of your letter. Just this much, with a touch of the oracular: it might perhaps be better for you to think of me properly – from your perspective – rather than from mine. I shall be back on the 22nd, possibly earlier; it is not certain. I shall make a detour to Chartres. I hope you are well; flu is going the rounds again at present.

Warmest greetings,
Yours,
Friedel.

Original: MS with printed letterhead; Theodor W. Adorno Archiv, Frankfurt am Main.

Paris: the journalistic fruits of Kracauer's stay in Paris in January 1927 were his 'Pariser Beobachtungen' [Parisian Observations] in Frankfurter Zeitung, 13 February 1927 (see *Marbacher Magazin* 47, p. 44, and Kracauer, W 5, no. 338).

from my card ... you write: Kracauer's card and Adorno's letter have not been preserved.

41 Adorno to Kracauer
Kronberg im Taunus, 20.5.1927

Cronberg i. Taunus, Hotel Frankfurter Hof.
20 May 1927.

Dear Friedel,

First of all: the fact that this is a typewritten letter isn't meant as an act of aggression or as neo-realism [Neue Sachlichkeit]. It is, rather, the (proverbial) noise-making clatter that is part of my trade and also one of the modest pleasures that I allow myself. I think that you, being no more sociable than I am, can understand this without holding it against me.

Our telephone conversation yesterday upset me so much that I gave up the projected visit and took to my heels as quickly as possible. It was not only the dry, uninterested tone that betrayed plainly enough how little store you set by my visit – not even a scant inclination to visit me here, while you have enough time for trips to Heidelberg; there was also a factual matter which hurt me, and which I should like to bring up for discussion in the context to which it belongs.

It concerns the business of Leo.

You considered it appropriate, in response to my question about his work, to emphasize your neutrality by refusing to give me an answer. That would certainly have been justified, and fair and decent too, if your whole attitude of neutrality had been justified. But is that the case?

You will recall that, after Cornelius had long since promised that I could work for my habilitation with him, I became aware of Leo's project only long after everyone else, and that I was completely taken by surprise because he was deliberately making it impossible for me to advance my own interests in good time. When I became aware of this – it was during your first visit to France (I wrote to you from Egern about it) – you replied with an indignant letter in which you promised me to use your influence on Leo, whose conduct you found unfair. And so you embarked on your *démarche* – obviously with no success. Leo, who had caught me off my guard, spoke to you of 'open competition', and although, under the conditions in which his plan had originated, you should have seen through the 'competition' as a piece of very fishy ideology (and probably did see through it), his answer was enough not only to put a stop to your efforts on my behalf but, in addition, to cause such a volte-face in your attitude that you declared and maintained your neutrality. This neutrality, objectively speaking, has no business to exist, inasmuch as it leaves the way open to rapacity with no restrictions whatsoever. Moreover, to the outside world (to Horkheimer, for example) it is sure to give the impression that you are taking up a definite position *against* me. As everyone knows the closeness of our relationship and must presume for this reason that you are *a priori* on my side, they therefore must also assume definite objective motives if you refrain from supporting me. What *is* definite, though – and something which you, of course, scarcely register – is the personal element – that in a matter which, in the final analysis, is my affair and of great empirical importance for me, it should all come down to your remaining neutral. You know as well as I do that, in a pragmatic sense, there is a great deal depending on it for me; in contrast to Leo, I have focused my expedient work entirely on my postdoctoral thesis and have not taken any other examinations, as my prospects were secure; if I fail to get my habilitation (and on closer acquaintance with the situation it seems to me *impossible* that we should both get through!), I shall be *vis-à-vis de rien* in professional terms – faced with the compulsion to study law in grim earnest – and then there will be major problems about my even staying in Frankfurt at all. You have known all this for a long time without its upsetting your neutrality – you can't hold it against me if I draw certain conclusions from this. But even if all the factual reasons were left out of the equation, there would be something left which would weigh heavily on me in the future if I had to contemplate the fact that I am of so little relevance to you that it is insufficient, in a case involving conflict, to compel you towards a simple and consistent decision in my favour – especially as the decision here would by no means have to be made in the dark. I have not made claims on you with practical demands so often that you should regard this unique and really extremely important one as of such little importance. I am by no means disregarding the attraction of the view that solidarity is a mere trifle because it can be taken for granted; but, if it *cannot* be taken for granted and is simply lacking, all that remains of anarchic immediacy is unreliability.

The whole business assumes an extremely concrete aspect, by the way, in view of the fact that a word of explanation from you to Horkheimer would have been enough to decide the case in my favour, as in the end Cornelius will accept the candidate whom Horkheimer favours, and Horkheimer is far too dependent not to concur absolutely with your opinion of both the person and the matter. Fortunately, I haven't put your ingenious plan with Gabi Oppenheim into action; it did serious damage, where Cornelius was involved, to another competitor who tried something similar.

I am not foolish enough to stage this matter as an affair of jealousy. I know very well that Leo is no closer to you than I am. Rather, I have the feeling that you are viewing the whole business of my habilitation with a mocking scepticism – despite the fact that not long ago you were advising me so vigorously to pursue it – and that the whole drama is providing you, as a spectator, with a certain amount of pleasure which you don't want to relinquish. I can understand something of that in aesthetic terms, although I can't quite imagine such pleasure as all that complete; it isn't the real thing. As this involves a major part of my future in the outer world and, for you, a demonstration of practical allegiance, I can't leave the decision up to you. In the end the fun has its limits in such things, and the hatred you feel towards the university offers no excuse for lethargy, after you yourself had advised me so vigorously in favour of the university and against journalism.

I wanted to call your attention to these matters, and above all to the question of what effect your 'neutrality' inevitably has on my private life.

Incidentally, I am living entirely on my own here and am composing nonsense, with an empty pleasure in putting things together; perhaps you felt something similar with regard to architecture. At least I am making very energetic progress, and definitely hoping to have finished by the end of June.

On Monday I shall be coming to Frankfurt and shall be available to you in the evening. If it suits you, I shall pick you up at the Café Hauptwache around eight. Please let me know whether this *does* suit you – if necessary by express delivery, or by telephoning here. I can't be reached at home in Frankfurt before then.

Well then: Your Teddie.

Original: typescript with handwritten additions and corrections; Siegfried Kracauer papers, Deutsches Literaturarchiv, Marbach am Neckar.

Cronberg i. Taunus, Hotel Frankfurter Hof: the place to which Adorno withdrew to write his postdoctoral thesis: 'I spent the entire summer – already since May – in Cronberg im Taunus, working on my (hopefully) *Habilitation* thesis' (Adorno/Berg, *Correspondence*, p. 109).

clatter: a pun on the phrase 'Klappern gehört zum Handwerk' [clatter is part of the trade]. At this time, it was still considered impolite to write personal letters on a typewriter.

trips to Heidelberg: there is no record of such a journey on behalf of the *Frankfurter Zeitung* and no evidence of a private one.

I wrote to you from Egern: a letter from Frankfurt am Main which relates to this has been preserved (see letter no. 38), but the description does not fit the one of 2 September 1926 from Rottach-Egern.

you replied with an indignant letter: not preserved.

ingenious plan: no information survives about a corresponding intrigue.

with regard to architecture: from 1912 to 1918 (interrupted by his doctorate in Berlin and military service during the First World War) Kracauer practised as an architect in Frankfurt am Main, Munich and Osnabrück.

42 Adorno to Kracauer

Kronberg im Taunus, 26.5.1927

Cronberg, Ascension Day (afternoon)

Dear Friedel,

The day in Frankfurt was so taken up with the Martha Lehner business that it was impossible for me to make any kind of arrangements with you. There was still a mass of rubbish to clear away – a lot of things to clear up with Carl as well as with Gabi, as new lies kept on emerging, including completely nonsensical ones which seem to me to consign the matter to the realm of pathology. Incidentally, I am surprised that the whole business no longer affects me as it once did. It hardly gets to me any more; I am left with a feeling of indifference and a certain kind of knowledge, but nothing else. My capacity for affection in matters within that sphere of confusion is even more limited than I had estimated.

I am really glad that you didn't forget to send me the two articles for which I asked you. I have read the one about Thomas Mann several times with very close attention, and am naturally in complete agreement with its intention; I also think it is of a considerable standard, and I am delighted with the effect which it is sure to produce this time. There might be a few comments to make about tactical and factual points. Tactically: the evidence of superiority to Thomas Mann at his level of writing seems to me to be too radically presented. That level of writing could not have been pierced linguistically. The form of irony, a negative copy of his, cosies up to his style to such an extent that it even takes on its playful quality – i.e. in such a way that it assumes communication with an imaginary reader (who in Mann's works represents society in its present state) with whom the matter is being discussed – whereas Mann would have to be dissociated in linguistic terms from the validity of his form of society and be confronted with the bald truth. The pleasure gained from the immanent destruction is certainly bought at too high a price for the grace with which the review is delivered – serious as the matter is – to be able to seduce us into believing that understanding may still be possible here, given a greater degree of insight. Going by my polemical sensitivities, there is nobody towards whom grace must be avoided more sedulously than considering the illusion of humane reconciliation which radiates in a kitschy manner from every one of that impostor's sentences.

Factually: the sentence which states that the value of a work of art is not determined by its degree of unpopularity can be accepted in general terms, but not applied to the current situation, in which a work of art, in order to achieve any degree of truth, has to transcend society as it exists and its communicative categories. If we overlook that, we run the risk of what you once rightly accused me of doing in my defence of Kaiser Wilhelm, i.e. confusing what is meant in objective terms of the history of philosophy with the subjective perception of truth. In that case, kitsch would immediately and in every case fare better than great art, even if it really were great in small things, a possibility which – as far as I know – you are, in general, not inclined to dispute. I am not telling you anything new in saying this, but it would certainly be better for it to come out, if only so as not to provide any unnecessary arguments in support of bad high art. Conversely, one might very well have pointed to the overwhelming popularity of *The Magic Mountain* as that of just such a lofty work of art in order to show Thomas Mann that he was supplying the bourgeoisie's need for entertainment so generously that he of all writers does not need to rebut the peddlers of trashy literature, because he himself was fulfilling their role, albeit badly. There, however, you would have run up against the boundaries of the *Frankfurter Zeitung*, which at this point also cut into your article.

We lunched at Else's today; she met up with Benjamin and Scholem in Paris. She said that the Russia expert had spoken of us in quite a distant and condescending way – which I can well believe. He was, she said, very dirty, and she had made her escape from him fairly soon – which, though, was partly her own fault. She was enchanted with Scholem.

Gretel Karplus is coming to be with me for the two days of the Whitsun holiday, hurrying over expressly from Berlin for less than forty-eight hours, straight from Berlin. Quite something.

I shall be in Frankfurt on Wednesday until Thursday. Shall I be seeing you before then?

Yours:
Teddie.

Original: typescript with handwritten corrections; Siegfried Kracauer papers, Deutsches Literaturarchiv, Marbach am Neckar. Dated in accordance with a handwritten addition of unknown origin.

Lehner: Martha Everett-Lehner; she is mentioned by Adorno in 1943 and 1949 in letters to his parents. No further information is available (see Adorno, *Letters to his Parents*, pp. 147, 150, 358).

Carl: Carl Dreyfuss (1898–1969), a friend of Adorno's; he went into exile in England in 1937 and Argentina in 1938 (see letter no. 33).

Gabi: Gabriele Oppenheimer.

the two articles: the second (see below) has not been preserved.

the one about Thomas Mann: 'Thomas Mann geleitet: Zu der Serie "Romane der Welt"', *Frankfurter Zeitung*, 22 May 1927 (see Kracauer, W 5, no. 354).

the value of a work of art: see ibid., 'der Wert eines Kunsterzeugnisses bestimmt sich keineswegs nach dem Grad seiner Unpopularität' [the value of a work of artistic creativity is in no way determined by the degree of its unpopularity].

Else: presumably Else Herzberger.

with Benjamin and Scholem in Paris: Gershom Scholem (1897–1982), a friend of Walter Benjamin's since 1915, had emigrated to Palestine in 1923; he describes his reunion with Benjamin on a six-month research trip in the chapter 'Paris (1927)', in Scholem, *Freundschaft*, pp. 164–78.

the Russia expert: Walter Benjamin visited Moscow from December 1926 to January 1927; his travel impressions appeared under the title 'Moskau' in the journal *Die Kreatur*, no. 1, 1927 (see Benjamin, GS 4.1, pp. 316–48; 4.2, pp. 987f.); see also *Moskauer Tagebuch* [Moscow diary] (Benjamin, GS 6, pp. 292–409).

43 Adorno to Kracauer
Frankfurt am Main, 3.9.1927

Frankfurt, 3 September 1927.

Dear Friedel,

I am thinking of arriving in Basel on Tuesday evening *alone*; Gretel can't travel until Thursday, and I could stay in Basel until then. So please write or wire me to let me know whether you will still be there around Thursday and whether we might be able to hear a few Jews together; and, if so, please book me a room in your hotel if it isn't too expensive – I do not have a very clear view of my financial situation yet and don't want to spend too much money right away.

Apart from all other reasons, a meeting will allow us to consider our African plans; mine have consolidated to a certain extent, especially as my father has reacted very positively to the project. The only thing is that it isn't so easy to get into either Tunis or Algiers. A French visa alone is *not* sufficient; you need to have an entry permit from the Résident générale de France in Tunis or the Governor-General in Algiers and apply for it in writing either from here in advance or from France or Italy on the journey. If I get one I am planning to travel from Tunis to Kairouan, Tozeur, Sfax and Gabes – the distances between them are not too great and the connections good – and, from there, back again to Tunis if needs be, but otherwise direct to Algiers via Biskra and home via Marseilles. I want to leave for Tunis from Palermo or Girgenti – it takes no more than twenty-four hours.

Of course, it isn't entirely out of the question that I might go to Egypt after all, as my father would like me to go there because of my health; the fact is that I am seriously run down.

It would be good to talk all this over in detail; left to myself, as I said, I wouldn't have much enthusiasm for any grand enterprises. As I am hardly likely to be back in Frankfurt before November (Herr Cornelius has given me leave until then), the meeting in Basel would make sense in the event of nothing coming of our rendezvous in the South – but the decision is up to you.

Gretel has only two weeks' leave; we shall be staying on Lake Maggiore for two of them and the rest of the time in Fiesole. I shall be going to Sicily on my own; I don't know yet whether I shall go on travelling around there or settle down in Taormina or Girgenti.

My work is finished according to plan, and is already in Cornelius's hands.

See you in Basel – ?

Yours, Teddie.

Original: typescript with handwritten corrections; Siegfried Kracauer papers, Deutsches Literaturarchiv, Marbach am Neckar.

write or wire me: not preserved.

Basel … hear a few Jews: the 15th Zionist Congress took place in Basel from 30 August to 11 September 1927. Kracauer reported on this in seven assignments for the *Frankfurter Zeitung*, including 'Der Zionistenkongreß: Die Eröffnung' [The Congress of Zionists: the opening], 31 August 1927 (see Kracauer, W 5, no. 372); 'Der Basler Zionistenkongreß: Die Krisis im Zionismus' [The Basel Congress of Zionists: the crisis in Zionism], 9 September 1927 (see Kracauer, W 5, no. 373) and 'Der Stand der zionistischen Bewegung: Eindrücke vom Basler Zionistenkongreß' [The status of the Zionist movement: impressions from the Basel Congress of Zionists], 20 September 1927 (see Kracauer, W 5, no. 376).

African plans: the trip to North Africa came to nothing.

I shall be going to Sicily on my own: the next stage of the journey did not materialize.

44 Adorno to Kracauer

San Remo, 29.9.1927

HOTEL EUROPE ET DE LA PAIX
SAN REMO

29 September 1927.

Dear Friedel,

Our postal communications seem to be causing some difficulty. I hear from my mothers that you still have no news of me – while I had already written you a card during my first days in Florence – posted to Sternstraße, as I knew of no other address. On the other hand, I only received both your letters, reconnaissance cruiser and battleship, here by detour via Fiesole, Florence. Now I am hastening to answer them. In the meantime, you will probably have had the first card too.

Your turning down the meeting in Basel – or, rather, your arrangement which is much the same thing as an apparent acquittal à la Kafka – didn't much upset me, as nothing would have come of it in any case because of my illness. After thinking it over, you must have said to yourself that it would have lost all sense for me as a meeting *à trois* – it would have been different in

Tunis – and I am sure that you did say so to yourself, too, so that the whole proposal represented either an excessively polite refusal or quite simply a snub. This is not to say anything against your friend, who of course is entirely blameless as regards the whole affair, and whom I should be glad to meet. On the contrary, only our relationship is involved, and with this in mind a meeting on the journey would only have made sense if we could have had a heart-to-heart about many things, which can only be achieved with just the two of us there – to say nothing of associations which would certainly be just as embarrassing for me as, vice versa, they would be for you. Nor can I understand why – apart from my illness – the matter couldn't have been sorted out if you had *seriously* wanted to do so – if necessary, by postponing your friend's arrival by one day. This is not empty talk on my part. The proof: in view of our prospective rendezvous, I had, very much to Gretel's disappointment, arranged my meeting with her for a few days later in Switzerland – and so it was only after you declined that I left Frankfurt with her.

The whole situation is part of the same complex of problems as the fact that, for a second time, you have turned down my express request for you to travel with me. I didn't make a great fuss about it, but it hit me very hard. I entreat you not to underestimate that.

In Frankfurt – where I shall probably have to return as early as the middle of October because of the business of the habilitation – I shall be free on any evening you may choose for an exchange of views, and I shall leave the decision up to you. My parting from Dreyfuss *e tutti quanti* leaves me surprisingly cold; I am planning to reorganize my milieu – back to the intellectuals; true, they are indeed just as stupid as the society types, but at least they offer a different kind of irritation.

I was in Florence for a week – not bothering very much about culture, but just tired and glad of the warmth. Living in town was impossible because of the dust (I am constantly coughing), so we moved up to San Gervasio, halfway up in the direction of Fiesole, in a Hotel La Luna, which I might have invented – the proprietors gorged themselves and the guests went hungry. We didn't stay there long, and, as Gretel, who had not much more than two weeks' holiday, did not want to go further south because of the long return journey and I was feeling too fatigued for any adventures, we travelled into Frank Heller's country and lodged for a proper rest and recuperation in this hotel, which is as European as its name implies. The season has not started yet, so the place is empty and somewhat melancholy even in this splendid weather – but we are relaxing, bathing in the sea, walking in the shadowy mountains nearby, and watching the country folk, who are like Virgil's peasant:

Justice smiled on him in parting
Before she abandoned the earth.

Gretel left me the day before yesterday and went back to chemistry, after hardly having unwound at all. It was pleasant being with her – she was good to me, something to which I was very receptive, and for which I was grateful. And – short on charisma as she is – she is one of the few people who are capable of genuine change, have a history, and allow cognition to share a considerable part of their lives. That means a lot, and certainly helps one to overlook many weak points in her natural disposition. Her experience of the Lehner circle (he has gone bankrupt, by the way) and, even more, her break with it have done her a lot of good.

She was very pleased with your good wishes, especially in the way in which they were expressed, and returns them cordially.

I am now enjoying the pleasures of being abroad and alone which you made so tempting to me – albeit with a certain determination. They are, as I can assure you, considerable. I am gathering my strength for all the disgusting and annoying business of my habilitation, reflecting on the concept of actuality, which I do not find satisfactory. It is a bridging concept – a maid of all work – to mask the leap of recognition and politics, and the old *καιρός* is always somewhere in there. On the other hand, it is necessary to assert the primacy of cognition in politics very forcefully against this fact. On the subject of politics, I have become aware of many new points of opposition even to the Keller people. Conversations with Gretel about natural science were a help in this; even there, it is not a question of eliminating all qualitative features arbitrarily.

I have sketched out a thoroughly scurrilous piece of work on the interpretation of the game of chess, in which there lurks a critical delimitation of psychoanalysis.

I am practising the piano a little, very *moderato*.

I am quite close to the French border here, and, as I do not know where you are, I may not be far from you.

Please give Lili many cordial greetings from me.

Yours,
Teddie.

Write to me at this address – I shall probably be spending the rest of my holidays here.

Original: MS with printed letterhead; Siegfried Kracauer papers, Deutsches Literaturarchiv, Marbach am Neckar.

a card: not preserved.

Sternstraße: Sternstraße 29, Kracauer's Frankfurt address from 1919 to 1930.

Frank Heller's country: 'The detective was conceived and honoured as a highgrade practical critic of society only in Frank Heller's novels' ('Der Detektiv-Roman' [The detective novel]; see Kracauer, W 1, p. 177). Heller was the pseudonym of the Swedish-born Martin Gunnar Serner (1886–1947), who in Monte Carlo gambled away a fortune which he had obtained fraudulently and then embarked on a career as a crime novelist.

'Justice smiled on him …': No translation in these precise words has so far been identified; the passage with the closest similarity occurs in Virgil, *Georgics*, book II, lines 472ff.

The Lehner circle: see letter no. 42.

the concept of actuality: 'Die Aktualität der Philosophie' [The actuality of philosophy] was the subject of Adorno's inaugural lecture (see letters no. 80 and 81; Adorno, GS 1, pp. 325–44, 383f.).

καιρός: Kairos, favourable moment for an existential decision, interpreted by Paul Tillich in terms of the philosophy of history.

the Keller people: not clearly identifiable.

piece of work on the interpretation of the game of chess: not preserved among Adorno's papers.

I may not be far from you: Kracauer and Lili Ehrenreich travelled to Paris and Marseilles in September/October 1927 (see *Marbacher Magazin* 47, p. 47).

45 Adorno to Kracauer
Berlin, 15.2.1928

15 February 1928

Berlin W.
Joachimsthaler Str. 17.
Pension Violetta.

Dear Friedel,

This letter's delay results from the fact that, at the beginning, I was so caught up in the bustle of the city day and night that I lost any ability to keep track of things to give you a summary; and then I was labouring for a week under a severe attack of the flu, which I disregarded at first, but which has now retreated so that only traces remain. Today I shall give you just a preliminary report, hoping that I shall be able to manage a fuller letter in due course; otherwise a detailed report, especially on the eschatological nature reserve, will have to wait until we meet. In any case, you may see Herr Bloch before I do, as he is thinking of going to the Rhine and Main at the end of this week, while I, after having been set back by eight days because of the illness, will probably not be home before the middle of next week. In the meantime, I don't want to put off mentioning two private matters until then – one involving a request which I have to put to you, and one in which I will possibly have something to reproach you about. This is how things stand: Soma Morgenstern, who can't bear my friend for reasons which are not wholly intelligible to me, but in which I don't have absolute confidence, was not satisfied with making his dislike clear to Gretel by his pointed and deliberate rudeness but, as a grand finale – i.e. immediately before his departure for Vienna – he launched a major *démarche* with me to persuade me to break up with Gretel. He said a great many shrewd and accurate things against her, and in many respects

I could not contradict him. It transpired that his allegations all came from the same realm as mine against Lili, and, from the accuracy with which they missed their target despite all his sureness of aim, I could gauge how inappropriate my attacks might have been. At the same time the emotion of my heart (which is, as is well known, by no means impassioned) showed me something of what you must have felt during my attacks – though the Soma–Teddie relationship does not correspond even remotely to the Teddie–Friedel one! – and, in a word, the impermissible, irresponsible and indefensible way in which I had behaved became clear to me. I have no defence to offer, although from its psychological pre-history it would nevertheless be more feasible than in the case of Soma; I only want to declare to you my obligatory intention no longer to get involved in the sphere of such dubious undertakings and, in addition, to put right, as far as possible, the existing situation which has been corrupted – in other words, putting myself on reasonable and frank terms with your friend, just so long as she has not completely cut herself off from this. You can speak quite openly with her about everything that I write to you. The other matter: in the course of his action Soma played his trump card by alleging that you too had expressed yourself in the most unfavourable terms against my friend. I only want to ask you now if that is correct; I find that hard to imagine after everything that you said to me (especially vis-à-vis Ellen), but if you should secretly have pronounced a death sentence on her, it would have been fairer to do so directly to me rather than to a third party who is not only such in respect of Gretel and me but also – the decisive point – of you and me, and whom you are justified in attacking precisely because of his erotic inclinations. If, however, Soma was lying, he should be taxed with that directly.

There it is, then. Forgive me for maltreating you from the city of Bert Brecht with intimate personal matters. After three weeks I have had it up to here with the external milieu – the crude revolutionary attitudes straight out of Moscow, and I cannot imagine seriously ever living here. Bloch offers a grand spectacle; he is a human being in the old sense of all things only on the whole; he has stripped you to the bone and is avowedly in the process of doing the same to me. I have done a fair amount of important work, some of it perhaps curious – chiefly an interpretation of Schubert which Bloch wolfed down greedily. This evening Bloch, Gretel, a Fräulein Herzfeld and I will meet up; I do seem to remember that you had said some unpleasant things about her, but as Bloch wants to introduce her to Gretel there is nothing to be done.

Once again Benjamin made a stimulating impression on me, too; I feel all the more up to him as in a roundabout way he refused to answer my two decisive questions – about the approach to the abstract and the limit of mythology – but the Arcades Project seems to be turning into an amazing venture.

Bloch and Benjamin – and of course Gretel – send you their warmest greetings.

Now I must go to Ullstein, where they have something planned for me; I shall tell you about it when it gets as far as a concrete offer.

Write soon to your

Teddie.

Original: MS; Siegfried Kracauer papers, Deutsches Literaturarchiv, Marbach am Neckar.

to the Rhine and Main: Ernst Bloch informed Kracauer on 20 February 1928 that he would be travelling at the end of the current week to Ludwigshafen and then on to Frankfurt am Main (see Bloch, *Briefe* I, pp. 297f.).

an interpretation of Schubert: 'Schubert', *Die Musik*, no. 1, 1928 (see Adorno, GS 17, pp. 18–33, 347).

Fräulein Herzfeld: Franziska Herzfeld (no dates available); a friend of Kracauer and Ernst Bloch who promoted the latter's *Erbschaft dieser Zeit* [Legacy of this time] while in exile in Paris in 1935 (see Bloch, *Briefe* I, pp. 389–92).

Benjamin made a stimulating impression: from the opposite perspective: 'Wiesengrund and I have been meeting frequently and profitably; now he has become acquainted with Ernst Bloch as well' (Walter Benjamin to Kracauer, 15 February 1928; see Benjamin, *Gesammelte Briefe* III, p. 334; trans. Manfred R. Jacobson and Evelyn M. Jacobson, *The Correspondence of Walter Benjamin, 1910–1940*, Chicago: University of Chicago Press, 1994.).

Arcades Project: Walter Benjamin wrote about the status of the project which he had begun in 1927 around the time of this letter: 'For the last two weeks I have once more been getting to grips with this piece of work – without actually writing anything in the strict sense – so closely that it leaves me with no breath to report back to you about it' (Benjamin to Kracauer, 10 March 1928; see Benjamin, *Gesammelte Briefe* III, p. 342).

to Ullstein: Adorno wrote on 14 May 1928 to Alban Berg that the stay in Berlin had also been 'with a view to taking over a critic's post', which foundered when he approached the *Berliner Morgenpost*, which belonged to the Ullstein Verlag (see Adorno/Berg, *Correspondence*, pp. 118–21).

46 Kracauer to Adorno

Frankfurt am Main, 18.2.1928

To *Teddie* in Berlin

18 February 28.
Frankfurt.

Dear Teddie,

I have received your letter. I was pleased to hear that, because of your own experiences, you were able to fathom the effects of what you had inflicted on me. But I don't think that you should try to clear up the relationship with Lili straight away by sheer force of resolution, which accomplishes little in things like these. Sympathies cannot be forced, either on your side or on hers, and goodwill may be demonstrated, first and foremost, by a guarantee of inner and outer courtesy, which, when the opportunity arises, may still develop gradually into a relationship with a stronger basis. Lili is taking a cure at present; she is often tired, and a complex human relationship just like that is not really her thing at the moment. To me it seems most advisable to wait and see – quite apart from the fact that in this area drastic measures don't suit me either.

I naturally had a word with Soma Morgenstern about you, and of course the conversation also touched on erotic matters. If I said something about Gretel Karplus – I can't remember exactly what – it was probably in a restrained fashion, as I hardly know her and have no crucial objections to make about her. If I remember rightly, in the course of the discussion M. did make some passing criticism of her, but I can't reconstruct the facts with any precision. To clear things up I am happy to get in touch with M. – with your consent, of course. In connection with this, by the way, I should like to say to you that, as a first sign of life from you, the postcard demonstration with Gretel K. (and Bloch) did not make a particularly pleasant impression on me.

I am sure you have seen many interesting things; that is very good. I am curious to hear what conclusion you will reach with Ullstein. Something important for you: recently I was talking for a moment to Horkheimer, who told me that, on the basis of a conversation with Scheler, he was convinced that *Scheler* was *very strongly in favour* of you. In H's opinion you will be able to gain your habilitation under him without any great difficulty. I regard this as a great opportunity – better than under Cornelius. Incidentally, it just occurs to me – might you not submit a piece of writing on the *philosophy of music* to Scheler instead of the work you are at present preparing for your habilitation? This doesn't seem a bad plan to me. Actually, how are your composition projects going?

I myself am living in the kind of seclusion which offers little to report, and which I must maintain until my work is complete. No evening engagements – nothing. I am hardly reading anything at all. My physical constitution is not strong enough for me to be able to do two things at the same time. I shall perhaps be able to finish the manuscript in May; until then I shall be staying here without a break, come what may.

Wishing you all the best once again for Berlin (in the meantime the flu is sure to have cleared up once and for all). Please give your friend my best wishes. I am very happy for you that you are now able to gather impressions in the midst of the hubbub and of all those people.

Warmest greetings,

Yours, *Friedel.*

Original: typescript (carbon copy) with handwritten additions; Siegfried Kracauer papers, Deutsches Literaturarchiv, Marbach am Neckar.

had a word with Soma Morgenstern: at this period Soma Morgenstern was also writing for the *Frankfurter Zeitung*. In his memoirs he circulates a conversation with Kracauer which, he writes, occurred during Adorno's stay in Berlin; Gretel Karplus was not mentioned in the course of it (see Soma Morgenstern, *Alban Berg und seine Idole*: *Erinnerungen und Briefe* [Alban Berg and his idols: memoirs and letters], ed. Ingolf Schulte. Lüneburg: zu Klampen, 1995, pp. 121f.).

get in touch with M.: not ascertained.

postcard demonstration with Gretel K. (and Bloch): not preserved in Kracauer's papers.

Scheler … very strongly in favour of you: after the retirement of Hans Cornelius, the philosopher and sociologist Max Scheler (1874–1928) was appointed to his post in Frankfurt am Main; Scheler's death on 19 May 1928 put a stop to the realization of this plan.

finish the manuscript: the manuscript of *Ginster* (see Kracauer, W 7, pp. 9–256).

47 Adorno to Kracauer
Berlin, 20.2.1928

Berlin, 20 February 28.

Dear Friedel,

I don't know what I have done to deserve the cooling in the tone of your letter. The intentions behind mine were good, and you should at least have mentioned that; I didn't want to force anything, and there was no need to admonish me about inner and outer courtesy (and surely for intimate relations there are other categories than, of all things, 'courtesy', and you have always cast external forms of it in my teeth as merely hypertrophic!); I was very far from making an attack on your friend's sympathies; I only wanted to prepare the ground – by a definite resoluteness, it is true, which I am maintaining honestly – for the establishment of a normal relationship. I cannot conceal from you that the way in which you are now using the excess moral weight which I granted you in order to humiliate me by dispensing a *refus* to me in a very deliberate tone – this I find completely inappropriate. If you have any serious intention (as I do!) of smoothing matters out between Lili and me, you will not be able to think solely of her and her problems, but just as much of me and mine as well. For some time, all the initiative in this matter has come from me, without success, and in this relationship I am not, by and large, unattached enough to continue my efforts infinitely. Precisely because this is a serious matter for me, you should reflect on it, instead of granting her and yourself alone a prestigious triumph which I am prepared to concede without resistance.

About the Soma business I am still not quite clear – of course it is all right with me if you sort things out, but perhaps you might wait until we have had a talk in Frankfurt; I shall be there in a week, after all. As for the card I sent with Bloch: I was far from intending it as any kind of demonstration. I even believe that it was he who instigated it, and to exclude Gretel (whose attitude to you is entirely amicable and free from guile!) from signing it would not have been consistent with either inner or outer courtesy. Or ought I to have completely excluded her – living, as she now is, in total isolation here – from my relationships with Bloch and Benjamin? I don't believe, though, that you always kept so strictly to the principle of *taceat mulier* in Lili's case – and so I see no reason for you to be put out. I, however, have much greater reason to be aggrieved because you are sending large portions of your manuscript to Bloch while you have not passed a single page on to me. Why, indeed? Do I have to say pretty please to prove my interest to you?

I see a good deal of Bloch and Benjamin – Bloch almost every day. I can testify to all the goodness in human terms which you attribute to him, and, if he uses Karl May to defend Richard Wagner, there is little that can be said against this, because his wrong-headed views are so sincere and genuine. By the way – as is self-evident, though it does need to be said after your rebuke – during our first conversation I assumed an attitude of solidarity and shared responsibility towards him with regard to your criticism, which still hurts him and on account of which I incurred many reproaches. Incidentally, he gave away everything about his essay on the faces of great men by accepting their 'nondescript' quality. Yesterday we were with Döblin – a very difficult case, but he told us a fine tale about the Salvation Army. This evening Bloch, Gretel and I are going to Chaplin, then meeting up with Bela Balasz afterwards. I haven't had much to do with matters of the fashionable world – not a single ball; just once to Horcher's with Gretel and Ellen and to the Zoo Grill with Gretel; in every other respect I strictly uphold the intellectuals' lifestyle – for economic reasons as well. Benjamin is circulating here in an atmosphere notable for the most repulsive literary types; on Saturday afternoon we went to tea at his place with Hessel and other unpleasant characters. I gave him to understand in no uncertain terms that I wanted to be alone with him and not with the herd. By the way, he is pursuing the project of getting a position for a friend in Gretel's company, and seems to be succeeding.

I haven't reached any kind of conclusion with Ullstein yet, although I was dealing personally with the director of the publishing house. However, I am getting an increasingly strong impression that I wouldn't fit in there. I have not followed up Dora Benjamin's assiduous suggestions.

Thanks for the information about Scheler; I would be *very* pleased (on account of my general and very diffuse impressions of Berlin) to obtain my habilitation in Frankfurt. However, I think that there is a prospect of this only if I succeed in getting accepted by Scheler with Cornelius's agreement or on his recommendation, as Scheler has no interest whatsoever in backing me against Cornelius. In any case I absolutely must avoid being offloaded onto Scheler because Cornelius is busy with Leo and Grebe.

It seems to me that there is little prospect in the plan for a piece of work on the philosophy of music under Scheler, and I think it is completely impossible to recycle a work reflecting my genuine interests as the written part of my habilitation. I would very much prefer to stick to my present project, just so as not to waste yet another six months on utter rubbish. You also said that my project would be adequate as a postdoctoral thesis. I would be grateful if, in case you see Horkheimer, you would emphasize this and the need to proceed with Cornelius's agreement. It isn't necessary to see him or ring him up about this – just if you should happen to meet him. *Entre nous* – i.e. this isn't for Horkheimer's ears, as he mustn't even get accustomed to the idea – if I shouldn't in fact succeed with the work on the unconscious, which I still can't believe, I would write something on Salomon Maimon.

I am full of plans for compositions and philosophical projects; I have already made a detailed sketch for quite a curious piece on Schubert, which has been accepted in advance by *Die Musik*. The Frankfurter Tonkünstlerbund has invited me to give its members courses on modern music, and I have agreed in principle to do this. My first task in Frankfurt, where I shall probably arrive on Sunday, will be a precise and pedantic organization of my working hours and working conditions.

I wish you all the best with your novel. I am tired of Berlin and glad to be getting back to an orderly routine – especially as I am still far from being all right again, with violent twinges of pain all over my body and a very stubborn cough, and can only keep myself fit to work with enormous quantities of aspirin.

I shall return your good wishes to Gretel in advance; I shall not see her – as is almost always the case – until this evening. Please pass on my greetings to Lili and assure her that my desire to be at peace with her remains intact.

Warmest greetings,
Yours, Teddie.

Original: MS; Siegfried Kracauer papers, Deutsches Literaturarchiv, Marbach am Neckar.

to Bloch: Kracauer to Ernst Bloch, 5 January 1928: 'Dear friend, I have just now sent the seven finished chapters of my "Ginster" to you, as printed matter, registered and express mail' (see Bloch, *Briefe* I, p. 289).

Karl May/Richard Wagner: Ernst Bloch to Kracauer, 20 February 1928: 'I had important conversations with Wiesengrund about my new hobbyhorse: Wagner and Karl May, Karl May in Wagner … Wagner's redemption through Karl May' (see Bloch, *Briefe* I, p. 298). Ernst Bloch, 'Rettung Wagners durch Karl May', *Anbruch*, January 1929; repr. with slight changes as 'Rettung Wagners durch surrealistische Kolportage', in Bloch, *Erbschaft dieser Zeit* (see Frankfurt am Main, Suhrkamp, 1962, pp. 372–80); trans. *Heritage of Our Times*, by Neville and Stephen Plaice, Cambridge: Polity, 1991. See also letters no. 88 and 96.

shared responsibility: on Kracauer's critique of Ernst Bloch, *Thomas Münzer als Theologe der Revolution* [1921] (see letter no. 16). In a letter to Kracauer of 28

September 1927, Bloch requested a 'rehabilitation' before assuming his regular activity for the feuilleton of the *Frankfurter Zeitung* (see Bloch, *Briefe* I, p. 286).

essay on the faces of great men: See Ernst Bloch, 'Das Bild bedeutender Männer und die Identität' [The image of significant men and identity], *Der Neue Merkur*, April/September 1924, pp. 926–32.

Döblin: Alfred Döblin (1878–1957), writer and physician. In his report 'Zum *Anbruch*' of 1928, Adorno listed Döblin together with Ernst Bloch and Kracauer as one of the 'non-musicians' among the potential contributors of the journal. Bloch about this encounter: 'Yesterday I was in Döblin's company. Wiesengrund was present, too, and was impressed. It was splendid with a great deal of excitement. Before, we had coffee at Benjamin's' (see Bloch to Kracauer, 20 February 1928; Bloch, *Briefe* I, p. 298).

Chaplin: probably to see the film *Der Zirkus* [The circus, 1928]. Kracauer's review in *Frankfurter Zeitung*, 15 February 1928 (see Kracauer, W 6.2, pp. 32–5).

Ellen: probably Ellen Dreyfuss-Herz.

Horcher: a restaurant in Berlin, founded in 1904 and operated by the Horcher family.

Hessel: Franz Hessel (1881–1941), writer, translator and publishers' reader; a friend of Walter Benjamin, with whom he translated vols 2 and 3 of Marcel Proust, *À la recherche du temps perdu* (vol. 2, *Im Schatten der jungen Mädchen*, Berlin: Die Schmiede, 1926; vol. 3, *Die Herzogin von Guermantes*, Munich: Piper, 1930); 1927 originally shared outline of the Arcades Project (see Benjamin, GS V.2, p. 1081).

a friend in Gretel's company: Benjamin's schoolmate Alfred Cohn (1892–1954) was not given a position in the company despite these efforts (see Adorno/Benjamin, *Briefwechsel*, pp. 10f.).

director of the publishing house: Emil Herz (1877–1971), on the board of directors of Ullstein Verlag from 1921. Dismissed 1934, exiled in Switzerland 1938 and, by way of Cuba, in the USA 1941.

Dora Benjamin: Most likely not Walter Benjamin's sister (1901–1946) but his wife Dora Sophie, née Kellner (1890–1964), translator and journalist. Marriage in 1917; mother of their son Stefan Benjamin (1918–1972). Gershom Scholem dates the 'disintegration of the marriage' to April 1921 (See Scholem, *Freundschaft*, p. 120), which did not for a long time preclude friendly dealings in Berlin. Their divorce followed in 1930.

Grebe: Wilhelm Grebe (1897–1946?), Privatdozent (salaried lecturer) at Johann Wolfgang Goethe-Universität. Adorno later reviewed his book *Der tätige Mensch: Untersuchungen zur Philosophie des Handels*, Berlin, 1937, in *Journal for Social Research*, nos.1/2, 1940 (see Adorno, GS 20.1, pp. 236f.).

Maimon: Solomon Maimon (1753–1800), philosopher, in Berlin; he enjoyed the protection of Moses Mendelssohn.

Tonkünstlerbund ... courses: On 14 May 1928 Adorno wrote to Alban Berg about the progress of this plan. This may indicate that he taught using compositions by Arnold Schoenberg and Berg (see Adorno/Berg, *Correspondence*, p. 120).

48 Adorno to Kracauer
Cortina d'Ampezzo, 29.8.1928

MIRAMONTI-MAJESTIC HOTEL
CORTINA D'AMPEZZO
DOLOMITES-ITALIE

29 August 28.

My dear Friedel,

I hope that these lines will still reach you. We are here until the middle of next week, so if you write to me soon it may still also reach me. I can't give you a further address as yet; we are going to Naples, but where we are staying there and how we are going to organize our enterprises in the South is still quite uncertain.

My Leipzig conference actually began on the express train, which Heinsheimer boarded in Erfurt as arranged. I am very satisfied with the result. From 1 January I shall be taking over the practical management of the new enterprise while still living in Frankfurt and without signing officially for it, but with free rights to accept or decline within the limits established by the actual nature of the publishing house. I regard these limits as acceptable after the *minutest* discussion of all the details. The terms are decent in view of the really very small amount of effort required. Above all, they include the printing of my compositions, something which is necessarily of the greatest concern to me. This is all the more important as U. E. is in the process of generally reducing its list of authors (I know about this from a third party too) and is not taking on new authors *of any description*.

At present I am awaiting the ratification of the conditions discussed by Hertzka, who took a great personal interest in my plan, went through the exposé, and took the initiative in offering the management of the new enterprise to me and not to a group of colleagues.

At an earlier period I would have taken it as a sign that the consolidation of our relations with the publisher was successfully established at the same time. Keep your fingers crossed for me, just as I did with you and S. Fischer once before!

I met Gretel in Leipzig; we travelled by way of Munich and Toblach. It is really as lovely here as it was in Karersee and Madonna – that is, the mountains are not so close and so big, but, because of that, the valley is wider and offers more room to breathe, and the Dolomites, above all Monte Cristallo, still form a finely shaped chain. The hotel is excellent, with the advantages of the Grand Hotel but with moderate dimensions which prevents what you call the 'social gulf' (i.e. between hotel and guests; to one another, of course, the guests are *homo homini lupus*). The guests are of the most exclusive kind, far more so than in Karersee; nothing but Italian aristocrats (with many Neapolitans among them, recognizable by their hordes of children!), wealthy Americans and representatives of the world of German high finance – and all of them in the late summer after their high season, the only one which still rightly exists despite all the talk of 'eternal youth'.

Both of us – tired to death at the beginning – are starting to recover, going for long walks and planning even longer ones – Falloria and even Cristallo, footwear permitting. My hip is equal to all kinds of exertion.

Gretel sends you her warmest regards, and was especially pleased with your greetings.

Please give Lili my love, and also Gretel's.

Will you write to me soon, dear Friedel?

Yours, Teddie.

Original: manuscript with printed letterhead; Siegfried Kracauer papers, Deutsches Literaturarchiv, Marbach am Neckar.

until the middle of next week: on a holiday trip with Gretel Karplus.

Heinsheimer … Hertzka: see letter no. 16.

boarded in Erfurt as arranged: Adorno stopped in Leipzig on the way to his holiday accommodation in Italy (see Adorno/Berg, *Correspondence*, p. 128).

printing of my compositions: not realized.

with you and S. Fischer: after advance publication in the *Frankfurter Zeitung*, *Ginster* was published by S. Fischer Verlag, Berlin, in 1928.

49 Kracauer to Adorno
Chamonix, 6.9.1928

GRAND HOTEL BEAU-RIVAGES
ET DES ANGLAIS
CHAMONIX MONTBLANC

Chamonix-Montblanc
6 September 28.

Dear Teddie,

Your letter was forwarded to me here in Chamonix yesterday; I am writing to you in Frankfurt, as you have probably already left. Heartfelt congratulations on your success with *Anbruch*. It is something splendid, and best of all is the prospect of getting your compositions printed. And, while I am at the business of congratulating you, I must also add best wishes for your birthday. I am planning to hatch something nice for you in France. Up till now I haven't been in very good shape physically; I have been feeling very low and will still need some time to pep myself up again. At the Villars Palace I made some very interesting observations from the periphery, and I also made the acquaintance there of an extraordinary hotel-keeper who comes out with more sceptical judgements about the various nations than does many an essay in the *Europäische Revue*. I was there with Selmar Spier, with whom I got on quite well. I then spent half a day in Montreux, an elegant place with good cinemas and a fine view of the lake's gracious aspects. Switzerland, though, is an expensive place. Since Sunday I have been in Chamonix with Mont Blanc in front of my nose and a blue southern sky. What's more, the confectioners here are not to be sneezed at; nougat is a speciality. There is a lot of traffic passing through, and, for the evenings, a café on the boulevard, among whose regular visitors I have already diagnosed a French general, a German operatic tenor and, as the cream of the crop, Count Keyserling, who does not consider me worthy of his notice. Incidentally, his smoking jacket looked rather crumpled, and not a single trace of the whole spectrum of Europe is visible in him – he looks so monotonously sandy-haired. The P.L.M. carriages excite my imagination to a limited degree. As far as *culture physique* is concerned, I have absolved a few little expeditions into the mountains and some efforts at swimming; apart from that, I am letting myself soak up ultraviolet rays from the sun, which is happy to administer them. I contemplate my inner being and trust that the break will be rewarding in creative terms. Thank goodness that it isn't so luxurious here as at the Palace – I've had it up to the ears with the *grande bourgeoisie* there. Up to now the newspaper commissions entrusted to me have been going tolerably well. As regards political events, Russia's joining the Kellogg Pact annoyed me, as did the World Youth Congress, which I should have liked to see criticized *à la Marx* – but the world goes merrily on its way with little regard for our reflections. For the foreseeable future I shall continue travelling, provided that I don't have to return home. If you write to me again – as I hope you will – please do so c/o the editorial office in Frankfurt. I am somewhat envious of your going to Naples; if you should break the journey in Positano, do think of me; hardly any of the old guard are likely to be still there, of course. Lili cordially returns your greetings and Gretel's. I hope that you are still having a lovely time. Warmest greetings to Gretel too.

Yours, Friedel.

Original: manuscript with printed letterhead; Siegfried Kracauer papers, Deutsches Literaturarchiv, Marbach am Neckar.

Chamonix: See Kracauer's two reports on this journey: 'Im Luxushotel', *Frankfurter Zeitung*, 14 September 1928 (see Kracauer, W 5, no. 410), and 'Ferien in September' [Holidays in September], *Frankfurter Zeitung*, 19 September 1928 (see Kracauer, W 5, no. 412): the subtitles of that article read 'Mer de Glace', 'Montblanc', 'Spezialitäten' [Specialities], 'Café', 'O yes', and 'P.L.M.'.

Villars Palace: The director mentioned here of the Villars Palace, built between 1905 and 1910, is not known to the present management of the hotel; the observations made here by Kracauer were incorporated into 'Im Luxushotel' (see above).

Europäische Revue: periodical, edited by Karl Anton Rohan (1898–1975) and Joachim Moras (1902–1961) (vol. 1, 1925/26 to vol. 20, 1944), which 'aims to raise awareness of the intellectual and spiritual unity of Europe ... it will not save this continent ... it can only collect; it incites contributors and readers to the new kind of Europeanness, in keeping with the times, which history demands' (Karl Anton Rohan: editor's preface, no. 1, 1925). Adorno und Kracauer were to publish their work in the journal; e.g. Adorno, 'Abschied vom Jazz' [Farewell to jazz] (no. 7, 1933; see Adorno, GS 18, pp. 795–99, GS 19, p. 647), 'Notiz über Wagner' [Note on Wagner] (ibid., see Adorno, GS 18, pp. 204–9, GS 19, p. 642); Kracauer, 'Internationaler Tonfilm?' [International sound film?] (no. 3, 1931; see Kracauer, W 6.2, pp. 475–79, W 6.3, p. 551).

Spier: Selmar Spier (1893–1962), lawyer, born in Frankfurt am Main, also wrote for the supplement of the *Frankfurter Zeitung*. He emigrated to Palestine in 1936. For his enduring friendship with Kracauer, see letter no. 94.

Count Keyserling: Hermann Graf Keyserling (1880–1946), philosopher; director of the 'School of Wisdom' which he founded in 1920 in Darmstadt. Between 1921 and 1927 Kracauer repeatedly reports on conferences or lectures by Keyserling: 'Von der Schule der Weisheit', *Frankfurter Zeitung*, 6 October 1921 (see Kracauer, W 5, no. 46); 'Schule der Weisheit: Zu der Tagung in Darmstadt' [School of Wisdom: on the conference in Darmstadt], *Frankfurter Zeitung*, 5 October 1922 (see Kracauer, W 5, no. 90); 'Die "deutsche Zukunft": Vortrag des Grafen Keyserling' [The 'German future': lecture by Count Keyserling], *Frankfurter Zeitung*, 18 October 1923 (see Kracauer, W 5, no. 158); 'Die Schule der Weisheit: Frühjahrstagung' [The School of Wisdom: spring conference], *Frankfurter Zeitung*, 7 May 1927 (see Kracauer, W 5, no. 352).

P.L.M. Autocars: Paris-Lyon-Méditerranée, an independent French railway company until the formation of the SNSEE. In the 'P.L.M.' section of 'Ferien in September' (see above), Kracauer writes: 'The Paris-Lyon-Méditerranée Autocars are a wonderful institution; among other routes, they operate the Route des Alpes from Nice to Chamonix ... As they arrive they resemble modern Trojan Horses, occupied to the last seat with armed men – at least, the occupants are sitting in their seats in such a state of tense excitement as if they could hardly wait to charge into town in full travel gear.'

Kellogg Pact: a treaty developed by the ministers for foreign affairs of France (Aristide Briand (1862–1932), awarded the Nobel Peace Prize jointly with Gustav Stresemann in 1926), and the USA (Frank B. Kellogg (1856–1937, Nobel Peace Prize 1929) which outlawed the solution of conflicts by military means; the first call for membership was issued on 27 August 1928. In the eyes of communist cadres, the pact was viewed as a 'pacifist token action' to put pressure on the Soviet Union (see 'Moskau–Brüssel–Kelloggpakt', *Die Internationale*, 15 August 1928).

World Youth Congress: World Youth Congress for Peace, 17–26 August 1928, held in Ommen in the Netherlands; on the resolutions which were to make 'the League of Nations into a genuinely effective means of ensuring peace', see the full-page report in the section 'Für Hochschule und Jugend', *Frankfurter Zeitung*, 3 September 1928.

50 Adorno to Kracauer
Frankfurt am Main, 1.10.1928

Frankfurt, 1 October 1928.

Dear Friedel,

After endless wanderings your letter finally reached me in Italy, just as I was lying ill in Naples with a very severe case of infectious flu, from which I have now recovered. I then received the card in Amorbach and answered you today after I had ascertained from the paper that it would not be advisable to count on your return in the near future. This saddens me, especially as every stay of yours in Paris appears to me in a particularly sad light. Because of the illness, not too much was left of the health which I had recovered, and as this time in Italy I was actually feeling physically unwell all the time, that completely put an end to it. By the way, it really was curious enough to see our tragic locales again in different constellations. Herr Neumann, who remembers you very well, has in the meantime risen to become the manager of the Hotel Palma, without, incidentally, adding much to his activities by doing so. The Clavel–Hohenlohe circle seems to him to occupy the peak of intellectual perfection – something, though, about which one might entertain a different opinion. Carli Sohn-Rethel is no longer in Capri; the new Mussolini morality on the model island appears to have made things difficult for him, too. I have avoided Positano – quite deliberately.

I have heaps of work here at present. I have to write the orchestral pieces for Walter Herbert and, not to mince words, I feel like a bloody beginner. I fear that all my life it will be like this for me with every single piece of work, and I cannot regard this in any way as an advantage, not even as a guarantee of substance – which in fact one really never should allow oneself. At the same time, I have to write an article to a deadline, commissioned for the Universal Edition yearbook, which I am finding extremely difficult. This is making me painfully aware that I have never worked under pressure, and I am convinced that you owe an extraordinary amount to that very pressure to maintain a presence and discipline as an author. Lastly, on 29 October, at the Composers' Association [Tonkünstlerbund], I have to give a public lecture about the musical situation, which I am dreading, as I feel that the spoken word, when addressed to people in any function outside its political one, is not only inadequate but mendacious, as it assumes that the speaker is actually being listened to – which is by no means the case. All this work is weighing on me so heavily that up to now I have not managed to produce anything sensible – although in this context one has to consider that I spent six days in Amorbach for Agathe's birthday, pre-birthday and post-birthday celebrations. But after the productive period of the summer I have a distinct feeling of being in a state of intellectual crisis, which makes everything that I do seem suspect in my eyes. That wouldn't be so bad if I had not embarked on a series of professional commitments with deadlines which I have to force myself to keep.

I hope that you will at least give me some advice about writing the loathsome lecture.

The negotiations with U. E. have not yet reached a conclusion. After I had declared my basic willingness to undertake the work, the gentlemen began to tinker with the conditions that had already been agreed in Leipzig. I granted them a few concessions – first of all, that, in the eyes of the public, I should not be acting as the official editor, with which I am in agreement, as this way my name will not be compromised should my project not succeed. But now they are making difficulties retroactively as regards the songs and the financial terms (which are very modest in any case), and I have made up my mind not to let myself be put under pressure about this; even Holl, with whom I discussed the matter, urgently advised me not to do so. At the same time, the songs have received a very strong recommendation from the reader at U. E.; even Berg, who wrote to me that the songs were 'masterly' (which, however, was not meant as an insult), stuck out his neck with the publishers on their behalf. In principle they declared that they were prepared to publish them but didn't want to commit themselves to a definite date – something which is naturally of the greatest importance to me, as otherwise something else always pushes itself in first.

So much for business matters. Benjamin acknowledged the Schubert with much ado and announced his intention to me of giving his views on it at length. Up to now he has not done so; instead, he has again committed some atrocious things in the L. W. It seems that in the last issue they even printed a letter from his *son*; but this has so far escaped my notice.

From Bloch, who got a card from Capri, I received a really charming answer.

Frankfurt is quite empty; I don't see a soul, and am feeling sad. Herr Cassirer is speaking on Wednesday – the philosopher, that is.

As for Gretel, I had a really lovely time with her. She has developed a lot – she gave a critique of Benjamin's book on the baroque, quite independently and employing the right categories. His thinking, she says, is 'interested' – a feminine term of reproach, it is true, but still correct – and she also says that he attempts to betray history. She was very pleased to receive your greetings. In spite of all her prosperity she leads a very dreary life in Berlin, about which she alleges that it is as impossible to comprehend its unhappiness by applying Marxist formulas as it is to exhaust the problems of Adrienne Mesurat by referring to the question of topicality and its opposite. (I have still not read the book but am waiting for you to give it to me.) Gretel is also tired of her job and would like to switch to psychology.

I am of course very excited about your revisionary report from Paris. Foreign countries as such have lost all attraction for me, and I believe that I can do my stuff best with a moderate degree of continuity. I have the feeling that everything has failed to undergo a radical change not only in the field of history but also as if everything is much the same everywhere in the world in geographical terms. I can almost believe once more that one has to begin with oneself.

Don't stay too long in the city of Freddie and Kasimir.

Yours,

Teddie.

I am in agreement about the title of *Ginster*. Didn't I suggest something similar?

If Lili should happen to be in Paris too (which isn't clear from your card), give her my regards.

Original: typescript with handwritten additions, corrections and postscript; Siegfried Kracauer papers, Deutsches Literaturarchiv, Marbach am Neckar.

the card: not preserved.

The Clavel–Hohenlohe circle: Fanette 'Fanny' Clavel (1883–1967) and Alexander Prinz zu Hohenlohe (1862–1924); they belonged to the wider circle of Rainer Maria Rilke.

Carli Sohn-Rethel: Karli Sohn-Rethel (1882–1966), painter and uncle of Alfred Sohn-Rethel; he divided his time between Capri and Positano (see Adorno/Sohn-Rethel, *Briefwechsel*, p. 135n.).

orchestral pieces for Walter Herbert: the conductor Walter Herbert (1893–1985), 'disciple of Schoenberg, clear, energetic and very sensitive in his efforts in his efforts in support of figurative sculpting and the pure presentation of works of art' (see 'Frankfurter Opern- und Konzertkritiken', Adorno, GS 19, p. 116), gave the première of Adorno's *Sechs kurze Orchesterstücke* [Six short pieces for orchestra], op. 4, on 16 February 1929 in Berlin (see Adorno/Berg, *Correspondence*, p. 136).

article … Universal Edition yearbook: 'Situation des Liedes' [The situation of the song], in *Gesang: Jahrbuch der Universal Edition*, 1929, ed. Hans Heinsheimer und Paul Stefan (repr. from *Musikblätter des Anbruch*, nos. 9/10, 1928); see Adorno, GS 18, pp. 345–53, GS 19, p. 643).

public lecture about the musical situation: a copy of the manuscript is preserved in the Theodor W. Adorno Archiv.

Agathe's birthday: Agathe Calvelli-Adorno's 60th birthday on 27 September 1928.

conditions … agreed in Leipzig: see letter no. 48.

songs: in a letter of September 1928, Alban Berg referred to Adorno's 'Vier Lieder' as 'masterful' (see Adorno/Berg, *Briefwechsel*, p. 12 and letter no. 52). Stefan George, the poet of these songs, was referred to as 'der Meister' (in letters, as D. M.) by his circle of friends ('der Kreis').

acknowledged the Schubert with much ado: Walter Benjamin responded to the manuscript (see 'Schubert', Adorno, GS 17, pp.18–33) in a letter of 1 September 1928 (see Adorno/Benjamin, *Briefwechsel*, p. 12; English translation, *The*

Complete Correspondence, 1928–1940, Theodor W. Adorno and Walter Benjamin, ed. Henri Lonitz trans. Nicholas Walker. Cambridge: Polity Press, 1999).

atrocious things in the L. W.: in the interval between the preceding letter and this one; this suggests Walter Benjamin, 'Paris als Göttin: Phantasie über den neuen Roman der Fürstin Bibesco' [Paris as a goddess: fantasy on the new novel by Princess Bibesco], *Die Literarische Welt*, 7 September 1928 – i.e. the review of Marthe Bibesco, *Catherine-Paris* (see Benjamin, GS 3, pp. 139–42, 630).

letter from his son: in the issue of *Die Literarische Welt* which preceded this letter (28 September 1928), the family was represented not by Stefan Benjamin but by his mother Dora Sophie Kellner (see letter no. 47) through two reviews of works on cultural anthropology. They appeared under the common heading 'Aus China und über China' [From China and on China] in the section 'Buch-Chronik der Woche' [Book chronicle of the week]. A letter from Stefan Benjamin to Walter Benjamin was published by *Die Literarische Welt* in the issue of 31 August 1928, also as a contribution to the 'Buch-Chronik'. 'Stefan *Benjamin* (aged 10)', as the author was identified by the editors, expressed his views in this about his holiday reading. Its title provides the heading for his contribution: 'Hurrah Ferien! Ein Reisebuch für unsere Jugend' [Hurrah for the holidays! A book of travels for our young people], with the addition of the publisher's details, 'Williams & Co., Berlin-Grunewald'. The volume was compiled by Edith Lotte Schiffer (1891–1935), the original name of Edith Jacobsohn, translator and publisher, married to the editor of *Die Weltbühne*, Siegfried Jacobsohn (1881–1926). In 1928, while continuing to run the magazine, Schiffer founded the children's publishing house mentioned above, for which she acquired Erich Kästner, among others. 'Hurrah – Ferien –!' is the title of the poem with which the collection begins (pp. 7–11); the author signed himself as Theobald Tiger (see Kurt Tucholsky, *Gesamtausgabe*, Vol. 10: *Texte 1928*, ed. Ute Maack, Reinbeck bei Hamburg: Rowohlt, 2001, pp. 287–9, 792). Stefan Benjamin differentiated between his opinions of the concept of the book and of its contents: 'I don't think the way that the individual stories follow one another is very good – just the poem, which is quite fun.' His commentary on *Hannibals Ring* by Ludwig Firneisen reads: 'The story is silly in parts; a boy in the fourth year of high school wouldn't believe in dreams and nightmares. The story of what happens in the family, though, is nicely told.'

from Bloch ... I received ... answer: Adorno's card, like Ernst Bloch's answer, has not been preserved.

Cassirer: Ernst Cassirer (1874–1945) was a candidate to succeed Hans Cornelius (see Hammerstein, p. 114); at this time, he was teaching at the University of Hamburg, whose rector he became in 1929. From 1933 he lived in exile in England, Sweden and the USA.

book on the baroque: Walter Benjamin, *Ursprung des deutschen Trauerspiels*, Berlin: Rowohlt, 1928 (see Benjamin, GS 1.1, pp. 203–430); trans. John Osborne as *The Origin of German Tragic Drama*, London: New Left Books, 1977.

problems of Adrienne Mesurat: Julien Green, *Adrienne Mesurat*, Paris: Librairie Plon, 1927; Kracauer reviewed the German translation of this book in: *Frankfurter Zeitung*, 12 August 1928 (see Kracauer, W 5, no. 48); Walter Benjamin also discussed the book: 'Adrienne Mesurat', in *Internationale Revue*, 2 December 1928 (see Benjamin, GS III, pp. 153–6, 632).

the city of Freddie and Kasimir: an allusion to the affinity with Paris shared by Frederick Goldbeck (see letter no. 5) and Kasimir Edschmid (author; 1890–1966).

51 Adorno to Kracauer
Berne, 6.2.1929

Berne, 6 February 29.

Dear Friedel, Now that we have sailed past each other three times, it is going to work out at last – I am writing to you today to say that I am going home tomorrow and have reserved Friday for you. My pieces are finished – I worked like crazy on them. Here you have an image of Walter Benjamin just as you interpreted him. I haven't seen the mountains even once! I spent a lot of time in a café, though. Yours ever, Teddie.

Original: MS, postcard: Berne, Kindlifresserbrunnen; Siegfried Kracauer papers, Deutsches Literaturarchiv, Marbach am Neckar.

Berne: this was where Adorno, together with Walter Herbert, finished his work on the *Orchestral Pieces* (see letter no. 9; see Adorno/Berg, *Correspondence*, p. 140).

an image of Walter Benjamin just as you interpreted him: the sculpture of the 'Kindlifresser' pictured on the card is in the act of biting the head off the figure of a child; Adorno is probably alluding to a passage from Kracauer's review of *Ursprung des deutschen Trauerspiels* [Origin of German tragic drama] and *Einbahnstraße* [One-way street] (both Berlin: Rowohlt, 1928): 'This is also precisely the reason why Benjamin believes he should not have to pay heed to the dangers of immediacy, that he must tear down the façade and smash the form of things to pieces. In his own sense it is very logical that he hardly ever attacks the structures and phenomena in their heyday … the living ones are confused to him like a dream; they become clearer in their stage of decay' ('Zu den Schriften Walter Benjamins' [On the writings of Walter Benjamin], *Frankfurter Zeitung*, 15 July 1928; see Kracauer, W 5, no. 403).

52 Adorno to Kracauer
Frankfurt am Main, 24.4.1929

Frankfurt, 24 April 1929.

Dear Friedel,

Today Kurt Weill rang me from Berlin on behalf of himself and Klemperer and informed me of the death of Adolf Weißmann. Both want me to take over the position and will set everything in motion for this to happen. I myself am determined to seize the opportunity. The post is the greatest and most independent one in Germany, very highly regarded, leaves time for work, and is an excellent one in financial terms; in every respect I should prefer it to that tiresome business of qualifying as a lecturer, and, moreover, as I am convinced that you will come to Berlin too in the long or short term – to join the Rundschau – it would be doubly welcome for me. I could make a position for myself there of a kind that is very rare today and not to be missed. Of the potential applicants, none, so Weill tells me, has a greater chance *a priori* than I do. But there is a catch: I no longer have any direct links with Ullstein. In the final instance a great deal does depend on that, especially as one shouldn't overestimate the influence that Klemperer and Weill have, above all with Ullstein. My main rival is probably Stuckenschmidt, who is extraordinarily skilled in precisely these tactical matters, and of course far ahead of me in everything that involves protection and wrangling of a sophisticated nature. Can you help me – recommend me to one of the really influential directors of the publishing company, perhaps – and give me some tips? I can't tell you how much that would mean to me. It would be best if you got in touch with Kurt Weill and Gretel about this. Weill's telephone number is Westend 6941.

Forgive me for calling on you for help in a business matter – but its extraordinary importance is obvious, and nobody is better able to help me than you. In spite of everything you won't mistake me for Leo.

There are all kinds of news here. Felix Weil is getting divorced from Käte in order to devote his life entirely to communism, as a result of which the chances of the revolution will obviously suffer. He demanded that she should go to Berlin with him and take a job there; she refused, whereupon he decided on a divorce. They say he is constantly making speeches attacking that accursed money, which he blames for all his troubles, but he is having all the financial dealings with Käte handled by Pollock, who seems to be carrying them out with his usual delicacy.

I have heard in a roundabout way that Ellen Delp has married a Viennese aristocrat and is living in a baroque château.

I am doing a lot of work – critical stuff – and beginning to compose, but things which I regard as finger exercises, rather in the same sense as you regard your grotesques – which, incidentally, implies only a formal correspondence, unless it is simply grotesque to do a few precious and artificial things by the young George. If the business of the post at the B. Z. should actually come to something (this, you see, is what all this is about – the most influential paper in Berlin), I should of course go to Berlin at once, and then we could talk as early as in a few days. Please let me know very soon.

I spoke on the telephone with Horkheimer today. He was noticeably cool and condescending towards me. Obviously Leo has done dreadfully vituperative things again. He asked me for your address in Berlin, as he is going there tonight. I gave it to him; if you want to get rid of him, it should be no trouble.

Thanks for your trouble, and very best wishes from your old

Teddie.

Original: typescript with handwritten additions and corrections; Siegfried Kracauer papers, Deutsches Literaturarchiv, Marbach am Neckar.

Weill: Kurt Weill (1900–1950) had completed the *Threepenny Opera* with Bertolt Brecht in Berlin the year before.

Klemperer: Otto Klemperer (1885–1973), conductor and, at this point, director of the Kroll-Oper; after its closure in 1931 he conducted at the Staatsoper (1931) and in 1933 went into exile in the USA.

Weißmann: Adolf Weißmann (1873–1929), music critic of the *Berliner Zeitung*.

take over the position: Adorno went to Berlin on this mission on 30 April 1929 (see Adorno/Berg, *Correspondence*, pp. 143–4); the attempt came to nothing.

Rundschau: *Die Neue Rundschau*, a magazine published by S. Fischer Verlag, founded in 1904 (preceded by *Freie Bühne* and *Neue deutsche Rundschau*).

Stuckenschmidt: Hans Heinz Stuckenschmidt (1901–1988), music theorist and critic; he became Adolf Weißmann's successor.

Weil: Felix Weil (1898–1975), economist and founder of the Institute for Social Research in Frankfurt am Main (1922/23).

Käte: Katharina (Käthe) von Hirsch (1902–?), née Bachert; married to Felix Weil from 1921 to 1929 (see Horkheimer, GS 18, p. 949).

Ellen Delp has married: Ellen Delp and Friedrich Wilhelm Krafft were married in Vienna on 7 June 1928; the 'baroque château' is Villa Xaipe, Schönbrunnerstrasse 309 (see Rainer Maria Rilke, *Briefwechsel mit Regina Ullmann und Ellen Delp*, ed. Walter Simon, Frankfurt am Main: Insel, 1987, p. 449).

your grotesques: feuilletons in the *Frankfurter Zeitung* by Kracauer in which he practised cultural criticism through ironic observation of everyday objects, e.g. 'Das Klavier' [The piano], 23 February 1926 (see Kracauer, W 5, no. 272); 'Falscher Untergang der Regenschirme' [False decline of umbrellas], 7 April 1926 (see Kracauer, W 5, no. 277); 'Die Hosenträger: Eine historische Studie' [Suspenders: a historical study], 30 October 1926 (see Kracauer, W 5, no. 314); 'Das Monokel: Versuch einer Biographie' [The monocle: an attempt at a biography], 30 November 1926 (see Kracauer, W 5, no. 320).

things by the young George: Adorno's setting of Stefan George: *Vier Gedichte von Stefan George für Singstimme und Klavier* [Four Poems by Stefan George for voice and piano], op. 1 (1921–8; see letter no. 1).

B. Z.: *Berliner Zeitung* (see the remarks about Adolf Weißmann above).

address in Berlin: Kracauer used his research from late April to mid-July 1929 for his then current book (*Die Angestellten: Aus dem neuesten Deutschland*, Frankfurt am Main, 1930; trans. Quintin Hoare as *The Salaried Masses: Duty and Distraction in Weimar Germany*, London: Verso, 1998; see Kracauer, W 1, pp. 211–310) to establish contacts for his later position as Berlin editor of the *Frankfurter Zeitung* (1930–3); the address was Pension Stössinger, Augsburger Strasse 47, Berlin W 50 (see *Marbacher Magazin* 47, p. 50).

53 Kracauer to Adorno
St-Jean-de-Luz, 9.9.1929

St-Jean-de-Luz.
Madison-Hotel.
9 Sept. 29.

Dear Teddie, I am so glad to think that we talked everything over before I left; the more cloudless the horizon, the more I enjoy writing to you. Among the birthday presents already earmarked for you there is a new Cocteau, *Les enfants terribles* – a novel which I have just started to read; I hope that you don't know it yet. Actually, you really are getting quite old, and I find these imperceptible changes quite terrifying. It occurs to me on this occasion – could one not connect Kierkegaard's three stages – the aesthetic, the ethical and the religious – with the process of ageing? The three stages do in fact have different concepts of time, and the aesthetic one perhaps corresponds most closely to the youthful intelligence (or, once again – when broken – to that of advanced age). The ethical stage is that of manhood, and the most immature. Incidentally, it would be very interesting to make a comparison transforming the spheres between Comte's four stages (the fourth comes from Salomon) and those of Kierkegaard. In Wiesbaden I worked like mad for five days, and there I also happily typed two chapters = 18 pages. I still have about 10–12 pages left to do, which I am now planning to write here. Until now I have merely lounged about and watched fatigue crawling up on me like a horrible poisonous snake. I was on my own in Paris for two days; then Lili joined me, and we travelled here overnight. Every morning you could see me in my bathrobe making my pilgrimage to the beach, where I swim diligently and toast myself. (Remembering the sunburn on Capri, I provided myself with some coconut oil this time.) In the afternoons we go for walks (not too long). This place is ideal for me: elegant but quiet, and allowing one to lead a life of one's own. The Bar Basque serves as my regular café; in the evenings life goes on there in a very sophisticated fashion. In the casino all kinds of gala events are constantly being held, but these are too expensive for me. There is nothing but Spanish families here, with little dark children who run around in swimming trunks and little chains with amulets. What annoys me more and more, and what I find repellent to the highest degree, is the *jeunesse dorée* whose animal self-assurance and beauty strikes those of us who lived through 1914–23 as a horror and a mockery. They race about in cars, display their limbs and live extravagantly – the human race is hard to tolerate. I am writing to you from Biarritz at the moment. The Atlantic, over which Geisenheyner flew in a Zeppelin, is mostly covered behind cars, among which Rolls-Royces predominate. The day after tomorrow I plan to go to San Sebastian, and next week to Pamplona, a nearby Spanish town. As regards the people, it will probably be much the same in Bellagio as it is here.

I have just read in a journal today that Glaeser's *Jahrgang 1902* is coming out in instalments in the *Nouvelle revue française*. We ought to be able to write like that.

If you write to me, please do so by letter, sealing the envelope. Lili asks me to send her regards to you and Gretel Karplus, to whom I also send my warmest greetings.

Goodbye for now, Teddie – I'd like to be lazy for a good long time yet. If my tan lasts, I shall come back to Frankfurt looking like a negro.

Your Friedel.

Original: MS; Theodor W. Adorno Archiv, Frankfurt am Main.

St-Jean-de-Luz: a holiday resort visited by Lili Ehrenreich and Kracauer on the French Atlantic coast, close to the border with Spain.

new Cocteau: Jean Cocteau (1889–1963), *Les enfants terribles*, Paris: Grasset, 1929.

three stages: Søren Kierkegaard, *Stadien auf dem Lebensweg*, Jena: Diederichs, 1914.

Comte's four stages (the fourth comes from Salomon): August Comte (1798–1857), philosopher, regarded with his doctrine of the three stages (theological, metaphysical and positivist) as one of the founders of sociology (see Auguste Comte, *The Foundation of Sociology*, ed. Kenneth Thompson, London: Nelson, 1976); possibly 'the fourth' comes from a university seminar on sociology by Gottfried Salomon-Delatour.

typed two chapters: of *Die Angestellten*; the study consists of twelve essays.

Geisenheymer: Max Ernst Louis Geisenheymer (1884–1961), author and journalist, also working for the *Frankfurter Zeitung*; he published, among others, *Mit Graf Zeppelin um die Welt: Ein Bild-Buch*, Frankfurt am Main, 1929.

San Sebastian: Kracauer wrote a report about this destination in 'Baskische Küste' [Basque coast] in *Frankfurter Zeitung*, 2 October 1929 (see Kracauer, W 5, no. 450); the subheadings read 'Saint-Jean-de-Luz', 'Biarritz', 'Bayonne' and 'San Sebastian'.

Glaeser's Jahrgang 1902: Ernst Glaeser (1902–1963), dramaturg, editor and author. The novel, in which Glaeser describes the lack of direction among young people after the First World War, was published in 1928 by Verlag Gustav Kiepenheuer, Potsdam; it was translated into 23 languages (incl. *Class 1902*, Columbia, University of South Carolina Press, 2008). In 1939 Glaeser returned to Germany from exile and fought in the Second World War. Shortly before this letter he had carried on a dialogue with Kracauer: 'Les livres de guerre: jeunesse et rationalisation: une enquête en Allemagne: entrevues avec Ludwig Renn, Ernst Glaeser [et] S. Kracauer', *Le Monde*, 17 August 1929 (see Kracauer, W 5, no. 446).

54 Adorno to Kracauer
Bellagio, 14.9.1929

ANBRUCH
MONATSSCHRIFT
FÜR NEUE MUSIK
KARLSPLATZ 6
WIEN I.

Bellagio, Hotel Genazzini et Metropole.
14 SEPTEMBER 1929.

Dear Friedel,

I was really pleased with your letter, which I received yesterday – not only because you view our last talk as a kind of caesura and have some hopes of it, as I do, but above all because its tone, which I picked up very precisely, actually has something about it which has been missing from your remarks for a long time – something which is difficult to identify, but which I can sense very clearly. It is as if for the first time you had once more relaxed that wretched attitude of humane neutrality which afflicted our relationship for so long, and instead you were at last behaving more openly and spontaneously towards me again. What makes me especially glad about this, and really gives me hope, is that the process is neither programmed nor pointed; it doesn't read as if it were following a resolve but much more as if you were once again taking the risk of using a language in front of yourself and me which is as dear to you as to me, as it is the one appropriate to our relationship. I don't want to go on about it, but just want to tell you that I sensed this with a joy which I have not known to exist between us for years. By the way, there is still something between us that we need to talk about – first and foremost, my actions with Ullstein. You are certainly right in your appraisal of the facts of the matter, and I greeted its failure with the same reaction as you did, but psychologically the situation is quite different from what you think; you were ready to put it down to ambition, whereas quite different motives came into play. Of course, one can retort that it wasn't about psychology but about what actually occurred, but I think that, sceptical as we are, we shouldn't be too ready to discard psychology altogether. In any case I do need to discuss the Ullstein business with you too.

As for your theory about the ages in Kierkegaard, I am very much inclined to accept it; incidentally, Theodor H[a]ecker once wrote something similar – I believe it was in an essay about Newman. The only thing is that this theory is very un-Kierkegaardian – Kierkegaard would have rejected it violently as a 'mediation' of the ethical and as Hegelry. That is not to imply anything in factual terms, but it does indicate yet again that the Kierkegaard–Hegel dispute cannot be settled in such a clear-cut way as we once thought. As for Comte, I believe that I am acting in the same way as you when I bequeath the whole business of the theory of stages to your Daniloff.

Incidentally, I had an especially distinct feeling of growing older on my 26th birthday.

My life here will not be too different from yours. I can't escape from work this time, either; I have to do the *Anbruch* (almost entirely alone this time) and have to reorganize Heinz Simon's studio, etc. We spend every morning on the boat to shelter from the sun and, although the sun here is more moderate than that on the ocean, I am also using io crème and with good results; I too am getting a tan, and I also don't think that it will last. Bellagio, however, is not a sophisticated place; people don't even put on dinner jackets in the evenings. There is little to be seen of the *jeunesse dorée* here – almost nothing but sedate elderly English people, who have something agreeable about them. The mini-car generation here contents itself with racing noisily over the lake in tiny motor-boats that soar high above the water – they are triumphant here too, but at least dust-free. By the way, I must make a formal declaration – i.e. that Hans Lothar, whom I had taken for something better, is one of that type to his very core. His articles on cars in the F. Z. were indescribably disgusting.

We ramble very peacefully around the lake and its environs and sleep a lot; our intellectual exertions are modest. We have done a bit of mathematics together (Gretel knows a lot more than I do) and are now reading Kant together (the *Critique of Pure Reason*), as you and I did eight years ago. It is remarkable in this respect how greatly modern natural science has changed our awareness in real terms; Gretel finds it most difficult to relate to a theory of knowledge which assumes Euclidean geometry and Newton's physics as natural givens. Incidentally, we do it in such a way that I always try to progress from textual exposition to interpretation in terms of the philosophy of history. I am now reading in quite a different way from how I used to do and often find the most remarkable approaches in quite obscure places – even the one to a materialist dialectic in a polemic against Plato whose ideas 'find no support in experience'. It continues to be a mighty business.

I envy you your Spanish enterprises a little – I have long had a hankering in that direction. Is the work on the *Angestellten* finished?

I have a new catchphrase for Benjamin: 'The Heavenly Delusion'. The worst thing about this is that he himself would be sure to be very proud of it.

Reading *The Spanish Farm* by Mottram, very interesting as a documentary, better than Remarque, Renn and Glaeser, in fact, who is now being published by the *Nouvelle Revue* for which Proust once was not good enough. Then the Surrealist Bible: Breton's *Nadja* – he is not an artist but a very poor abstract man. His tendency results from a lack of substance.

Many thanks in advance for the Cocteau. Gabi wrote to me at the same time as you, highly delighted with it.

In the meantime, you will have had a card which I wrote to you. I was crafty enough, though, to send it to your home address, so that you won't be annoyed that it appears without an envelope. Or had you perhaps already received it when you wrote me the letter? That would be an amazing achievement on the part of the Italian, German and French postal services.

Carry on enjoying the chance to relax and come home looking thoroughly negroid. I shall be back in Frankfurt as early as the 22nd.

Give Lili my very best wishes and also Gretel's – she sends her best to you too, of course.

Ever yours.
Teddie.

Original: typescript with printed letterhead, handwritten additions and corrections; Siegfried Kracauer papers, Deutsches Literaturarchiv, Marbach am Neckar.

Bellagio, Hotel Genazzini: holiday residence on Lake Como which Adorno visited with Gretel Karplus.

H[a]ecker… Newman: spelt 'Hecker' in the letter; this refers to Theodor Haecker (1879–1945), an author and cultural critic influenced by Søren Kierkegaard; besides the latter's writings he also translated, in the 1920s, those of the English theologian John Henry Newman (1801–1890). No information is available about what afterword or similar piece of writing Adorno is referring to here.

Kierkegaard–Hegel: Adorno would go on to elaborate on connections and differences between Søren Kierkegaard and Georg Wilhelm Hegel, including those referring to the theory of stages, in the fifth chapter of *Kierkegaard: Konstruktion des Ästhethischen* (see Adorno, GS 2, pp. 124–50).

your Daniloff: no information available.

Heinz Simon's studio: 'The Frankfurter Musikstudio was established several years ago in the context of the local Frankfurt group of the "Verband der konzertierenden Künstler" on the initiative of Dr Heinrich Simon' (see Adorno, 'Musikstudio', *Anbruch*, January 1931, GS 19, pp. 520–4, here pp. 521, 653.)

Lothar: Hans Lothar (1900–1944), editor and member of the board of directors of the *Frankfurter Zeitung*; he went into exile in England in 1936.

his articles on cars: Hans Lothar was among the 'automobilists' on the *Frankfurter Zeitung* whose articles in the main section or supplements such as the *Bäderblatt* and *Reiseblatt* contributed to the idealization of motor vehicles – in Lothar's case, through writings such as 'Fahrt mit dem Frühling' [Travelling with the spring], 'Nach Rom in 3 Tagen' [To Rome in 3 days] or 'Im Auto unterwegs: Von Frankfurt nach Straßburg' [On the road by car: from Frankfurt to Strassburg' (*Frankfurter Zeitung*, 18 April 1926, 5 May 1929 and 26 August 1929; all details from Andrea Wetterauer, *Lust an der Distanz: Die Kunst der Autoreise in der 'Frankfurter Zeitung'*, Tübingen: Verein für Volkskunde, 2007, pp. 205–8).

Plato, whose ideas 'find no support in experience': 'In just such a way did Plato abandon the world of the senses as it imposes such narrow limits on intellect, and dare to venture beyond this on the wings of ideas into the empty space of pure intellect. He did not notice that he was making no progress by his efforts, as at the same time he had no support as a foundation against which he could brace himself and to which he could apply his forces to remove the intellect from its place.' (See Immanuel Kant, *Kritik der reinen Vernunft*. 2nd edn 1787, ed. Königlich Preußischen Akademie der Wissenschaften, Berlin: Georg Reimer, 1911, p. 32).

work on the Angestellten: Kracauer finished the manuscript in October 1929 (see *Marbacher Magazin* 47, p. 51). See *The Salaried Masses: Duty and Distraction in Weimar Germany*, trans. Quintin Hoare, London: Verso, 1998.

'The Heavenly Delusion': Adorno's preceding account of his reading of Immanuel Kant draws the eye towards a possible model for the catchphrase: in Kant it is 'illusion of freedom' (*Blendwerk von Freiheit*; see Immanuel Kant, *Kritik der reinen Vernunft*. 2nd edn 1787, p. 311); Adorno proves his knowledge of this passage by later quoting it in *Negative Dialektik* (see Adorno, GS 6, p. 249); see *Negative Dialectics*, trans. E. B. Ashton, London: Routledge, 1973. Alternatively, a choice of models might be provided by a misappropriation of the title of Karl Kraus's gloss *Blendwerk der Hölle* (*Die Fackel*, January 1913); and finally an adaptation of Don Cesar's exclamation (Act III, scene iv): 'Blendwerk der Hölle! Was? In seinen Armen!' ['Vision of hell! What is this? In his arms!'] in Friedrich Schiller's *Die Braut von Messina* (ed. Matthias Luserke, Frankfurt am Main: Deutscher Klassiker Verlag, 1996, p. 354); see *The Bride of Messina*, trans. F. J. Lamport, Cambridge: Modern Humanities Research Association, 2018.

Mottram: Ralph Hale Mottram (1883–1971), author of *The Spanish Farm*, a trilogy of novels about the First World War.

Remarque: Erich Maria Remarque (1898–1970), author of *All Quiet on the Western Front*, trans. A. W. Wheen, London: G. P. Putnam's Sons, 1929.

Renn: Ludwig Renn (1889–1979), author; he achieved national and international success with *Krieg* [War], published in book form in 1929.

Proust once was not good enough: in 1912 the publisher Gaston Gallimard (1881–1975) had rejected the first volume of *À la recherche du temps perdu*, which was why the book was published in 1913 by Grasset; in 1916, however, Proust received an offer to publish his future works in the *Nouvelle Revue Française*.

Nadja: the story by André Breton (1896–1966) was published in 1928 by Editions Gallimard, Paris.

wrote … highly delighted with it: no letter from Gabriele Oppenheim which corresponds to this description is preserved in the Theodor W. Adorno Archiv.

a card: not preserved.

55 Adorno to Kracauer
Vienna, 4.3.1930

ANBRUCH
MONATSSCHRIFT
FÜR NEUE MUSIK
KARLSPLATZ 6
WIEN I.

4 March 1930.

Dear Friedel,

With all respect for your unceremonious nature, I cannot change mine to the extent that I would consider what comes about as an external decision to be an infinitely small matter in terms of human continuity. I am very much aware of this caesura and what it signifies. Out of simple kindness you will not deny me the chance to say that, on the day when you are getting married, I wish you and Lili, sincerely and unconditionally, all the happiness that can be hoped for between two people who have chosen to share their lives.

Yours faithfully,
Teddie.

Original: typescript with printed letterhead; Siegfried Kracauer papers, Deutsches Literaturarchiv, Marbach am Neckar.

you are getting married: on 5 March 1930, Kracauer and Lili Ehrenreich were married in Frankfurt am Main.

56 Adorno to Kracauer
Kronberg im Taunus, 1.4.1930

ANBRUCH
MONATSSCHRIFT
FÜR NEUE MUSIK
KARLSPLATZ 6
WIEN I.

(at present) *Cronberg* i. Taunus
Hotel Frankfurter Hof.
1 April 1930.

Dear Friedel,

I am answering your letter, for which I thank you, only today and from here, where I have retreated to finish my book and am intending to stay for many weeks in complete isolation – at least throughout the whole of May and into June, should I not have finished it by then. I have left everything behind and am glad of this in more than one respect; only modest waves from the *vie mondaine* roll onto my beach. I can work for ten hours a day on my things with complete concentration (even in the evenings, which is unthinkable in Frankfurt) and am getting real satisfaction from the work itself – even, and precisely, by my own standards. I don't wish to talk to you about this; there is no point in doing so *par distance* and still less without a distance, as you have taught me; nevertheless, I will not keep to it as strictly as you do and will send you a typewritten copy as soon as I have finished it. The book will be dedicated to you; in keeping with its intention, this is self-evident, and officially, again, this corresponds to my incorrigible intention. There is nothing of significance to report from my private sphere – nothing at all. I had a lovely time with Gretel in Weimar, but what really affected me was Goethe's house, with the official, encrusted system of guest-rooms and the completely bare living areas; it demonstrated very drastically what was cheerful, sociable and pleasant in him, and also his self-denial. The tastelessness of the furnishings was splendid, too – no white-collar worker would live like that today; people have blended into their apartments (in an issue of the *Berliner Illustrierte* there was an article called 'At home with young people', which I strongly recommend to you; we couldn't have made it up). The two of you will see Gretel before I do; she is not coming here until Easter and we shall simply stay here, as I don't want to get out of touch with my work by travelling.

The only person in Frankfurt with whom I have better contact than with others – not with my mother – is Erna Pinner, an amazing woman, despite Kasimir and her senseless ladylike drawings of animals. Carl, meanwhile, has returned to society in a state of repentance, probably under pressure from the noble sibyl who tried to snub me at a party at the Andreaes to which I took her in order to do my bit for the divine world order. I saw Herr Gubler briefly once when we met at the station and collected Herr Křenek. He immediately vanished to discuss matters of concern with the young genius (that was what Redlich called him). I did so the following day and once again found the genius very clever and infinitely unsure of himself, which is why Holl takes him for a seeker. That same Holl has torn *Mahagonny* to pieces in a way with which you, with all your criticisms of it, would scarcely identify; believe me, the scandal was justified in many ways. The incriminated criticism of the studio evening also emanated from Holl, but I am not at all annoyed that he didn't mention my name, especially as I wasn't mentioned in the programme and deliberately avoid this – so don't worry about that, either.

The dream about Gabi and me is very beautiful, and if I were still undertaking that kind of analysis I could discover a lot from it. By the way, I never use the expression 'chérie'; it is one of yours, I believe – we are not responsible for our dreams. Paul and Gabi have bought an extraordinarily splendid house, the former De Neufville one on the Schaumainkai, for a good price and will probably be moving in as early as this summer.

How have your relations with Frau Bergner developed in the meantime? I too can come up with a mythical being: Benji, who was here and said many kind things to me about my articles on Berg (I wonder whether Berg himself has read it? In *Anbruch* he thought very poorly of another one instead of pressing me for mine) and *Mahagonny*. On the other hand, when I forced him into a confrontation about the categories of the person and of the self and defended them theologically with the argument that all positive religions rejected the destruction of the self as gnostic or satanic, he retreated to the position of hell, which I did not find very brave despite its warmth, as not much of that warmth remained in his arguments. You know, of course, that he collects his essays and edits them.

I hope that you have had a really good chance to recover in Gastein as regards all the fatigue which you described in allegorical terms, and also the sciatica which is not mentioned but is nonetheless painful. Please write and tell me about it. I hope, too that Lili has recovered from the last lingering after-effects of revolutionary Marxism. Tell her, to reassure her about any consequences of my stay here, that until further notice neither the Horkheimer family nor Herr Dr Pollock will be here; they are sojourning in the South, where things are volcanic.

Everyone in Vienna will be angry with me – Bloch, Berg, Steuermann, Webern – because I owe them all letters. Please cite my work as an excuse; I want to discharge all my debts now, but little by little. I would be grateful to you if you would just look in on Heinsheimer at U. E. and show a bit of initiative there, especially emphasizing my reputation, as I am still having the greatest difficulties with that bunch. I hope that you both had a wonderful time in Vienna. If the weather is as splendid as it is here, you must surely have gone up the Kobenzl with Berg and Soma.

I got the *Angestellten* book today and was delighted with the written dedication. I wonder whether I understood it as well as you did my last letter? I shall write to you about it after reading it several times.

All the best to Lili. Write soon, and send your address to this one of mine.

Always your
Teddie.

Original: typescript with printed letterhead, handwritten additions and corrections; Siegfried Kracauer papers, Deutsches Literaturarchiv, Marbach am Neckar.

your letter: not preserved.

my book: the postgraduate thesis 'Konstruktion des Ästhetischen in Kierkegaards Philosophie' (see the edition in book form: *Kierkegaard: Konstruktion des Ästhetischen* (Adorno, GS 2, pp. 7–213).

dedicated to you: the dedication reads 'To my friend Siegfried Kracauer'.

with Gretel in Weimar: the dates of the journey have not been recorded.

'At home with young people': Viktor Dohna, 'Bei den jungen Leuten', *Berliner Illustrierte Zeitung*, 23 March 1930. The article, illustrated with three motifs drawn from the contemporary idea of connubial bliss, begins: 'Whoever considers the life of young people with close attention to detail will discover that a crisis has been overcome, and that young people have developed new ways of living, and above all a new approach to the form and content of marriage. The stock phrase about "endangering the young" no longer has any validity for this hard-working generation, so sure of its goals.'

Pinner: Erna (Wilhelmine) Pinner (1890–1987), an artist, illustrator and author born in Frankfurt am Main; she went into exile in England in 1935.

Kasimir: Kasimir Edschmidt; he and Erna Pinner were a couple until they emigrated; Edschmidt did not follow her to England but worked for some time in Italy. In 1941 he was officially forbidden to write.

Carl: Carl Dreyfuss.

Andreaes: The Andreae family from Frankfurt; Adorno was especially friendly with Norah Andreae (1888–1949), who later shared his exile in California (see Adorno, *Bildmonographie*, p. 191).

Herr Gubler: in 1930 Friedrich T. Gubler (1900–1965) succeeded Benno Reifenberg, who until 1932 was the paper's Paris correspondent, as editor of the feuilleton of the *Frankfurter Zeitung*.

collected Herr Křenek: Friedrich T. Gubler and Ernst Krenek agreed during the latter's visit to Frankfurt am Main in late March 1930 that he should become a freelance contributor to the feuilleton of the *Frankfurter Zeitung* (see *Der hoffnungslose Radikalismus der Mitte: Der Briefwechsel Ernst Krenek–Friedrich T. Gubler, 1928–1939*, ed. Claudia Maurer Zenck, Vienna: Böhlau, 1989, p. 43n.).

Redlich: Hans Ferdinand Redlich (1903–1968), composer, conductor and musicologist, went into exile in England in 1939. His designation of Ernst Krenek as a 'young genius' was probably verbal.

Holl has torn Mahagonny *to pieces*: Bertolt Brecht and Kurt Weill, *Aufsteig und Fall der Stadt Mahagonny*, first performed on 9 March 1930 at the Neues Theater, Leipzig (director: Walther Brügmann; stage design by Caspar Neher; conducted by Gustav Becher); the opera unleashed a violent debate. A short report (K. H., 'Aufstieg und Fall der Stadt Mahagonny', *Frankfurter Zeitung*, 10 March 1930) was followed by an extended review under the same title (*Frankfurter Zeitung*, 12 March 1930). The thrust of Holl's argument is apparent from the subheadings: 'The Firm' (i.e. Brecht and Weill), 'A way but no goal' and 'Ideology in word and sound'.

criticism of the studio evening: an event organized by the Frankfurter Musikstudio (see letter no. 54). No review relating to this by Karl Holl in the *Frankfurter Zeitung* survives.

dream about Gabi: Adorno for his own part occasionally noted down his dreams; a selection is available: Theodor W. Adorno, *Dream Notes*, ed. Christoph Gödde and Henri Lonitz, trans. Rodney Livingstone (Cambridge: Polity, 2007). The first published record of a dream relates to an experience with 'G.' but dates from January 1934.

Paul and Gabi: Gabriele and Paul Oppenheim.

the former De Neufville one on the Schaumainkai: Carl de Neufville (1849–1938), banker; in the early 1890s, the family built the neo-Renaissance villa at Schaumainkai 53, Frankfurt, which housed the Suhrkamp Verlag from 1951 to 1956. It is now the site of the Museum für Kommunikation.

Bergner: Elisabeth Bergner (1897–1986), actress; engagements in Vienna, Munich, Berlin and overseas; in 1933 she went into exile in England and thence to the USA.

Benji … collects his essays and edits them: a contract was drawn up between Walter Benjamin and Ernst Rowohlt Verlag for the publication of a volume of literary essays (Walter Benjamin Archiv, Berlin); the volume did not materialize.

Gastein: Kracauer reported on the stay: 'Badgastein aus der Märzperspektive', *Frankfurter Zeitung*, 13 April 1930 (see Kracauer, W5, no. 470); during a stay at the spa he attempted to cure his sciatica (see *Marbacher Magazin* 47, p. 58).

Horkheimer … in the South: no information survives about this journey.

a wonderful time in Vienna … up the Kobenzl: Kracauer's return journey from Badgastein took him through Vienna (for 'Kobenzl' or 'Cobenzl', see letter no. 14).

Angestellten: following pre-publication in the *Frankfurter Zeitung* in December 1929/January 1930, this study came out in book form.

written dedication: no copy with a personal dedication to Adorno survives in the library which he left behind; the edition bears the printed dedication 'For Benno Reifenberg as a token of our binding friendship and our work together' (see Kracauer, W 1, p. 212).

57 Kracauer to Adorno
Berlin, 20.4.1930

FRANKFURTER ZEITUNG BERLINER REDAKTION

BERLIN W 9
POTSDAMER STRASSE 133
TELEPHON: SAMMEL-NO. W2
LÜTZOW 3981
20 April 1930.
W 15
Pariser Str. 24., II. St., 1.
Telefon: Oliva 3753

Dear Teddie,

I am taking advantage of Easter Sunday to write to you at last. I received your letter on my last day in Vienna, where it had been forwarded to me from Badgastein. I had had no idea at all that you had moved to Cronberg. However, it has proved its worth several times as a sanctuary in which to work – and now it will once again be shaken to the core by the storms of world revolution. I am all the more excited about your work as you appear to be satisfied with it. I am delighted with the dedication.

To start with Berlin: we have been here exactly two weeks now. The first five days consisted of a hellish wandering through the petty-bourgeois splendours of furnished rooms. Fortunately, our persistence was rewarded. We now have two splendid big rooms (they even have running water) just behind the Kurfürstendamm; the 1 and 2 buses run quite close by. Over the last week I have begun to find my way around the office, talk to a few people who may be potential collaborators, and organize my work – the irregular days of first settling into a new home, which have made me very tired. Nothing flies into one's hands; even the most ridiculous trifle has to be overcome by effort. Mostly I am already in bed by 11; night-life can wait. Apart from the most essential people I have still not spoken to anyone; I haven't even seen Gretel K. I met Benji the day before yesterday. He was very taken with your article on *Mahagonny*, and even more with Brecht himself, on whose *Versuche* (which have just come out) he is going to write a commentary. I only glanced at the book in passing. It contains some formidable aphorisms in dark Führer-speak. That may be very profound, but the following pronouncement by Benji contradicts that: Brecht champions the statement that in a classless society the individual should be poor but the whole of society rich. To my question about who represented the whole and had control of the finances, Benji replied that Brecht would presumably decline to answer this question. But what is the good of a profundity which lies so far down that it doesn't push its way to the surface? I may possibly meet up with Brecht sometime soon; I shall ask him this question then, and some others, too – that is, if it is worth the trouble. In a conversation I'm not one for dialectics. Benji also said that Brecht was the only person who applies his talents in the right place. Perhaps so – but he is certainly not the only one. But Benji, of course, can't help being impressed by that. Have you read the first section of his 'Paris Diary' in the *Literarische Welt*? Of course you know the facts from his verbal narrative. He is milder than he used to be; he isn't well, either – still because of the quarrel with his wife.

My novel is progressing slowly but steadily. I sometimes work on it in the evenings in the Hotel Bristol or the Fürstenhof or simply in Café Hessler, where all the fine bourgeois types sit and men of letters never do. I am enjoying the work enormously. In the Romanisches Café on Good Friday a young man kept giving me a nasty stare and then pulled out the newspaper *Fridericus*. It is no longer very pleasant there.

The *Angestellten* seems to have got off to a good start, although no major reviews have appeared yet. Benji has written a long article about it which the L. W. has rejected because of its excessive length. He has now deposited it with *Gesellschaft*, which unfortunately doesn't penetrate into society, and is just writing a short note on it for the L. W. The fact that the Deutschnationalen Handlungsgehilfen regard me as a dangerous person and the Volksparteiliche Reichsvereinigung (Jungdo) has launched a violent polemic against me will leave you as cold as it does me. Very interesting: all these people are getting annoyed with me for getting rid of the *Angestellten*'s class consciousness and ranking it with the proletariat. This is a sensitive point. The democratic unions of white-collar workers are of course the most furious with me – they are a particularly crummy band of petty-bourgeois types. As far as I know, the German Communist Party is by no means averse to my product. I have the impression at any rate that the work has made some impact – even if only by giving offence.

I still have to give you the news from Vienna. We met up with Bloch and Carola almost every day. Bloch was still stuck in a plaster cast and could hardly move. The girl is a Jewess from the East – there is not much to say about her. I know the type, and the appearance of the individual is somewhat overshadowed for me by the type. At present Bloch is still working on the proofs of his *Spuren*. He will probably stay in Vienna over the summer. Soma is morose, witty and somewhat reserved. I was never really able to get him to unbutton. He joined us for afternoon tea at the Bergs'. I had imagined Berg as much more aristocratic – even degenerate. On the contrary, the effect he produced on me was one of simplicity – very agreeable; I like it when achievements support this. His wife is still beautiful – there's certainly something about her. The two of them must love each other in spite of all the conflicts that such a long-lasting relationship entails. I enjoyed the visit very much; even just being in the apartment with Berg was a pleasure for me. There are two laurel wreaths hanging in the hall from the Vienna première of *Wozzeck*. Vienna, by the way, is entrancing – the beautiful streets, the splendid cafés – at times it reminds one of Paris. I shouldn't like to live there, though.

So little by little I shall be seeing more people, whether I want to or not. Basically, though, I shall be living here in monkish seclusion. This business is not going to gobble me up just yet. I am giving my address to only a very few people, and I have already erected stout barricades against an influx of literary types.

Do write to me soon. I always liked Erna Pinner. When are she and her Ede travelling to South America? Please give your folks my best wishes from Lili and me – she sends you all her best as well.

Yours, Friedel.

Original: typescript with printed letterhead and handwritten corrections: Theodor W. Adorno Archiv, Frankfurt am Main.

article on Mahagonny: 'Mahagonny', *Der Scheinwerfer: Blätter der Städtischen Bühnen Essen*, no. 14, 1930 (see Adorno, GS 17, pp. 114–22, 348).

on whose Versuche … *he is going to write a commentary*: Bertolt Brecht, *Versuche*, vol. 1, Berlin: Gustav Kiepenheuer, 1930; the volume contains the first eleven *Geschichten vom Herrn Keuner*, *Der Ozeanflug*, *Radiotheorie* and *Fatzer 3*. Walter Benjamin took the *Versuche* as his inspiration for the radio lecture 'Bert Brecht' (see Benjamin, GS II.2, pp. 660–7).

'Paris Diary' in the Literarische Welt: 'Walter Benjamin, *Pariser Tagebuch*', *Die Literarische Welt*, 17 April 1930 (see Benjamin, GS IV.1, pp. 567–87, GS IV.2, p. 1044).

quarrel with his wife: the divorce from Dora Sophie Benjamin (see letter no. 47).

my novel: *Georg*; Kracauer finished the novel in Paris in 1934. It remained unpublished until its inclusion in Kracauer, S 7, 1973 (see Kracauer, W 7, pp. 257–516, 664–6).

Bristol: Hotel Bristol, Unter den Linden 5–6, built in 1890–91, destroyed in 1943.

Fürstenhof: Café Fürstenhof, Leipziger Platz; destroyed in 1943.

Café Hessler: Kaffee Hessler, at that time near the Kaiser-Wilhelm-Gedächtnis-Kirche.

Romanisches: Romanisches Café, on the corner of Tauentzienstrasse and Kurfürstendamm, a centre of Berlin's literary and cultural activity; destroyed in 1943.

Fridericus: a nationalist weekly published from 1922 to 1943.

Benji … a long article: Walter Benjamin, 'Ein Aussenseiter macht sich bemerkbar: Zu S. Kracauer, "Die Angestellten"' ['An outsider shows himself: on S. Kracauer, *The Salaried Masses*'], *Die Gesellschaft*, Vol. 1, 1930 (see Benjamin, GS III, pp. 219–25, 638f.); the 'short note': 'S[iegfried] Kracauer, Die Angestellten: Aus dem Neuesten Deutschland, Frankfurt a.M. 1939', *Die Literarische Welt*, 16 May 1930 (see Benjamin, GS III, pp. 226–8, 639).

Deutschnationale Handlungsgehilfen: the Deutschnationale Handlungsgehilfen-Verband financed the journal *Deutsche Handelswacht*, in which Ernst Niekisch wrote, in his article 'Ein Kracauer auf Entdeckungsreisen' [A man from Kraków on journeys of discovery]: 'The country of origin … from which Kracauer penetrates into the dark habitat of the white-collar workers is the preserve of the Jewish liberal democracy with a Frankfurt stamp. In this preserve nothing is regarded with greater abhorrence than the organic structuring of the people' (see *Deutsche Handelswacht*, nos. 3 and 4, 1930; quotation from Kracauer, W 1, p. 388).

Jungdo: see letter no. 30.

democratic unions of white-collar workers: on the book's reception by the trade unions at large, see Kracauer, W 1, pp. 386ff.

with Bloch and Carola … plaster cast: Ernst Bloch confirmed the appointment with Kracauer in Vienna in a letter of 13 March 1930. Bloch and Karola Piotrkowska (1905–1994), a future architect from Łódź, were married in 1934. Bloch reports on an injury to his ankle which he had suffered on a winter sports holiday, and which needed a plaster cast, in the above-mentioned letter and also in a previous one, dated 4 March 1930 (see Bloch, *Briefe* 1, pp. 331ff.).

his Spuren: see letter no. 72.

Wozzeck: spelt 'Wozzek' in the letter.

Ede: Kasimir Edschmidt.

58 Adorno to Kracauer
Kronberg im Taunus, 12.5.1930

ANBRUCH
MONATSSCHRIFT
FÜR NEUE MUSIK
KARLSPLATZ 6
WIEN I.

Cronberg im Taunus
Hotel Frankfurter Hof.
12 May 1930.

Dear Friedel,

I have kept on putting off the answer which I kept planning – first because I was ill (a severe attack of sinusitis), and then because of the huge amount of work which Tillich is urging me to do; he wants me to qualify as early as this semester so that I can lecture as his official assistant next semester. However, it is hardly likely that anything will come of this, as I don't think that I shall have finished before the middle of June – but I am staking everything on it and labouring like a workhorse on Kierkegaard. But today there came the nice joint card from Schwannecke's home turf, and so now I am finally replying.

I was glad to hear that you are feeling comfortable in Berlin, something which I not only gather from your letter but which Benjamin has also reported to me – he spent a week in Frankfurt, where I found lodgings for him with Seligmann, and he visited me here one day. I am delighted with the progress of your novel and am very curious about it. In the meantime, I have read *Die Angestellten* and enjoyed it very much; it is a very solid piece of work, and at the same time has a very good take on real life. In literary terms, too, it is highly respectable in every way, and especially in its grouping of quotations it is astonishing. There would be little I could say in the way of criticism – you know as well as I do that a certain divergence exists between aesthetic intentions which conceive the object as something to be created by means of language and political ones which think of it as a predetermined entity and report on it – and, altogether, there is nothing to be said against this, given the book's overall liberal approach. One might, however, ask whether the author always found the right relationship between the form of *prima vista* improvisation, the *a priori* experience of things, and a way of proceeding based on a documentary approach. This is to ask whether any study which starts out without all the research, hence only from the surface, limits itself by this and could have expressed its message even more coherently, inasmuch as studies of source material are not definitive without a broad economic basis. It almost seems to me as if, with your specific way of viewing things, it really would not be most appropriate for you to stick to what you yourself have experienced at first hand and to go by the impressions formed in close connection with this. However, I regard this not as a criticism, but merely as endeavours that pertain to methodology and your approach to work in that same area. In every respect that matters I am very much taken with it. It is just that I see reality in an even deeper shade of black than you (if that is possible), as I don't believe that any change in humankind is going to come about, or even that there is any serious chance of it.

I am really enjoying my work and have never been so intensely preoccupied with a literary project as I am this time. It does make a definite difference whether one is writing essays or a book; the dimensions also alter the problems connected with the topic. My subject itself stands, in a certain sense, between Lukács and Benjamin and tries to use them to correct each other – not, of course, to undertake a 'synthesis', which is patently ridiculous. The social dialectic, then, which is the basis of the philosophical element in it, must be given concrete form, and conversely the material/ontic definitions must be freed from their mythical rigidity to become dialectical in a particular sense. This is just to provide directions in the specific area in which to locate the issue; of course, it has nothing to do directly with the facts themselves. Within this parameter I develop a theory of the *intérieur* which is interpreted as a model of Kierkegaard's inwardness – in fact, a critical analysis of the concept of existence without, however, abandoning the concept of humanity in a gnostic way – a theory of sacrifice which appears to me to be ever more central to Kierkegaard's thought, the longer I think about it. I am speaking here of the passion of autonomous reason.

I have read an endless amount of material on this – most of it poor; relatively speaking, Haecker and Guardini come off best. The highly praised Przywara is very poor and highly ideological, and the rest is beyond discussion. In addition, I have taken on Lukács, *Die Seele und die Formen*, in which there is a very poor essay about Kierkegaard, and *Geschichte und Klassenbewußtsein*, which leaves a shocking number of loose ends and diffuses a kind of Heidelberg local colour in an unbearable fashion; it is only a step to Mannheim, most of all in the wholly abstract conception of the concept of ideology which cannot be handled in this schematic way of deducing it in idealistic terms. In spite of this there are a few outstanding passages in his work. These days, though, we have advanced a considerable way beyond that. I have also consulted Benjamin on the subject of mythology, and for other reasons. In this respect, the long essay on *Elective Affinities* was remarkably much more to my liking than in the past. No matter how well this piece may serve the purposes of a commentary, there are some very fine ideas behind it, above all the fact that the mythical, that nature itself is conceived in dialectical terms, thereby preserving the 'illusion', something which is very close to my heart. It must be the best of Benjamin's writings. In comparison, the famous introduction to his book on the baroque, despite marvellous things such as the concept of configuration, cannot be sustained because of its stark Platonism – entirely without any sense of history, and in the final analysis downright mythological; it is no accident that on several occasions it has to invoke phenomenology. I have discussed this with him, and he conceded me several points after I had cornered him like St Hubert's luminous stag.

I find his Paris Diary sickening (like everything of that kind) and wasn't even able to bring myself to say anything to him about it, although he clearly thinks that it is 'colossal'.

I can't get the *Frankfurter Zeitung* here, and because of that (as I hardly ever go to Frankfurt) I am completely out of the picture as far as examples of your small-scale production are concerned. It would be very kind of you if you would send me whatever you feel is important; if you should need them, you will get them back.

I often see that pair of friends Lenin and Trotsky to spend some pleasant times with them; incidentally, both of them are furious with you because you haven't sent them a copy of your *Angestellten*, with which, moreover, they feel a strong sympathy. Unless you intended it as an open affront, do send them one – if you have done so, then it doesn't matter, but I really don't see any necessity for it.

The last volume of *Anbruch* dealt with France and was quite pretty, with an article by me about Ravel – perhaps you have seen it.

As far as my health is concerned, at long last things are once again passable now. I am staying here for the time being and shall not be going on holiday before August – probably to the southern Tyrol. Gretel will probably be with me over Whitsun.

Have you any impression about my chances with Berlin? I shall come over immediately after my examination, have a look around, and should be glad to have some inkling in advance of how matters stand. For your information (and only for yours), I heard that, aside from the assistantship, I shall soon be offered a contract to lecture on aesthetics, which may also be of some significance for Berlin. Curjel would be the best person to talk it over with.

How is your sciatica? You don't write about it, so I assume that Gastein has done its duty.

Do send me more details of your existence in Berlin, as well as of Vienna (I have none at present).

Has Lili read my articles, and what did she say? Give her my very best wishes. And write soon to your old

Teddie

I have only very briefly glanced at Brecht's *Versuche* and am not able to say anything about it as yet.

Original: typescript with printed letterhead and handwritten additions, corrections and postscript; Siegfried Kracauer papers, Deutsches Literaturarchiv, Marbach am Neckar.

Tillich: Paul Tillich (1886–1965), philosopher and theologian; from 1929 professor of philosophy and sociology at the Johann Wolfgang Goethe-Universität; the process of Adorno's habilitation came to an end in February of 1931. Tillich emigrated to the USA in 1933.

joint card from Schwannecke's premises: Victor Schwannecke (1880–1931), actor and director; in 1921 he established the 'Stephanie' wine bar in Berlin's Rankestrasse; it was presumably there that Kracauer wrote this card to Adorno which has not survived – perhaps together with Ernst Bloch, and possibly also with Kurt Weill (see letter no. 61). Bloch, who had travelled from Vienna to Berlin, describes the previous evening 'at Schwannecke's' and also a forthcoming appointment for the evening of the same day in a letter of 8 May 1930 to Karola Piotrkowska (see Ernst Bloch, *Das Abenteuer der Treue: Briefe an Karola, 1928–1949*, ed. Anna Czajka, Frankfurt am Main: Suhrkamp, 2005, pp. 44ff.).

Benjamin ... lodgings for him with Seligmann: it was from here that Walter Benjamin wrote to Alfred Cohn on 8 May 1930 about the 'generous hospitality of a gentleman from Frankfurt', who is identified in the note as the lawyer Milton Seligmann (1866–1948); see Benjamin, *Gesammelte Briefe* III, pp. 526ff.).

especially in its grouping of quotations: Kracauer describes his method of proceeding in the preface: 'Quotations, conversations and observations on the spot form the basis of the work. They are intended to serve not as examples of any kind of theory but, rather, as exemplary cases drawn from reality' (see Kracauer, W 1, p. 213).

Haecker ... Guardini ... Przywara: Theodor Haecker (see letter no. 54): Adorno quotes in *Kierkegaard* from Haecker's study *Sören Kierkegaard und die Philosophie der Innerlichkeit*. Munich: Schreiber, 1913), and from the lecture *Der Begriff der Wahrheit bei Sören Kierkegaard* (Innsbruck: Brenner, 1932); from the essay *Der Ausgangspunkt der Denkbewegung Sören Kierkegaards* by the theologian and philosopher Romano Guardini (1885–1968), and also from the book *Das Geheimnis Kierkegaards* (Munich: Oldenburg, 1929) by the theologian and philosopher Erich S. J. Przywara.

poor essay about Kierkegaard: Georg Lukács, 'Das Zerschellen der Form am Leben: Sören Kierkegaard und Regine Olsen' (see letter no. 16).

I have also consulted Benjamin: Adorno does not quote from *Goethes Wahlverwandtschaften* but, rather, four passages from *Ursprung des deutschen Trauerspiels* (see Adorno, GS 2, pp. 202–13).

pair of friends Lenin and Trotsky: this refers to Max Horkheimer and Friedrich Pollock (see letter no. 61).

article by me about Ravel: 'Ravel', *Anbruch*, nos. 4/5, 1930 (see Adorno, GS 17, pp. 60–5, 347).

contract to lecture on aesthetics: see letter no. 81.

Curjel: Hans Curjel (1896–1974), director and dramaturg working at the Kroll-Oper, Berlin, from 1927 to 1931.

59 Adorno to Kracauer
Kronberg im Taunus, 13.5.1930

Cronberg, Hotel Frankfurter Hof.
13 May 1930.

Dear Friedel,

I am sending you here a little thing which I wrote early this morning. It is a by-product of my work which may lead to still more of them. I have something of a soft spot for things like this, since I believe that I somehow managed to hit the mark with it. I am sending it to you hoping that you can contrive to find it a place in the sun, i.e. in the *Frankfurter Zeitung*. Please let me impose on you with this request, as I should like to know your opinion about it, and also because I shouldn't like to run the risk of a refusal from Křenek's admirer Gubler, as it cannot possibly be to his taste. I think that, apart from the literary element, the piece also has a certain curiosity value because of the astonishing quotation.

Please forgive this interested action and attribute it solely to a commitment arising from nothing other than my interest in its subject matter, and accept my thanks in advance.

Warmest greetings to you and Lili from your

Teddie.

Original: typescript with handwritten corrections; Siegfried Kracauer papers, Deutsches Literaturarchiv, Marbach am Neckar.

little thing: 'Kierkegaard prophezeit Chaplin', *Frankfurter Zeitung*, 22 May 1930 (i.e. the first part of 'Zweimal Chaplin'; see Adorno, GS, 10.1, pp. 362f.).

place in the sun: The *Frankfurter Zeitung* was founded in 1856 by Leopold Sonnemann (1831–1909) as the *Frankfurter Handelszeitung*.

astonishing quotation: Adorno quotes Kierkegaard from his 'früheren pseudonymen Schriften, der "Wiederholung"' [his early text *Recovery*, written under a pseudonym]: 'He is not able merely to walk, but to make an entrance walking. This is something quite different – to enter walking – and through this touch of genius he at the same time improvises his entire surroundings on stage and is able not just to portray a wandering journeyman but to enter walking like one, and do it in such a way that one experiences everything with him and sees the welcoming village from the dust of the country road. … He can make an entrance on the stage followed by street urchins whom we cannot see.'

60 Adorno to Kracauer
Kronberg im Taunus, 23.5.1930

Cronberg, 23 May 1930.

Dear Friedel, yesterday I chanced on the Kierkegaard piece in the *Frankfurter Zeitung* and was really delighted by the indirect greeting. From the fact that the little piece appeared so quickly and in such a good setting I think I may conclude that you enjoyed it too. Thank you! By now you will also have had a more detailed letter from me. I did *not* like Benjamin's notice about the *Angestellten*; it has an undertone which is not as friendly as his official stance and actually devalues it. Besides, it is hardly relevant to the issue. What do you think?

My work is now at the stage where the outline is imperceptibly changing into the text – i.e. the last chapters, where I am presently taking a break, are already substantially complete, although not yet edited for precision of language. I only hope that readers will understand it.

Don't forget to send me some of your articles; I have no idea as yet how you will get on with Berlin as a writer. Meanwhile, I have written my Křenek polemic and can send it to you if you are interested. Otherwise I am finessing an older essay which is still unpublished. I see very few people – Margot Sulzbach yesterday, for the first time in years (a friend of Ellen Dreyfuss and your cousin Hanne Kracauer); she asked after you very warmly.

Otherwise there isn't much to report to you, except about my work.
Warmest regards to you and Lili
from your

Teddie.

Original: typescript, postcard; Siegfried Kracauer papers, Deutsches Literaturarchiv, Marbach am Neckar.

Křenek polemic: 'Reaktion und Fortschritt', *Ausbruch*, no. 6, 1930 (see Adorno, GS 17, pp. 133–9, 348).

Margot Sulzbach: also Margot Sulzbach-Rocholl-Loeb (see letter no. 64), a friend from Adorno's youth (see Adorno, *Letters to his Parents*, pp. 270n. 4, 356).

cousin Hanne Kracauer: no information is available about which branch of the family this cousin belonged to; evidence exists among Kracauer's papers of her successful emigration to the USA, dating from 1935 at the latest.

61 Kracauer to Adorno

[Berlin,] 25.5.1930

25 May 30.

Dear Teddie,

I have only today got around to thanking you for your detailed letter. I received your card yesterday. I was very pleased, of course, with your note on Kierkegaard and was glad that it was published so quickly.

I am very excitedly looking forward to your work on Kierkegaard, and most of all on the relationship between inwardness and *intérieur*. If only it were not all so difficult to read. Please do get *Anbruch* to send me the French volume; I should very much like to read your article on Ravel. Lili, by the way, was greatly taken with your articles. She found the Stuckenschmidt controversy especially convincing, as she is interested in that at present – and, of course, the collection of aphorisms.

About the *Angestellten*: one of your locutions seems to me incorrect. It isn't that I had delivered my verdicts *prima vista*, but actually my insight into the purely defensive position of capital developed from a view of empirical reality that is based on theory. Elsewhere, too, I have repeatedly had to revise my original intuitions with hindsight. I regard this work as very important in methodological terms inasmuch as it constitutes a new type of statement – one which does not, as it were, juggle between general theory and specific practice but represents an autonomously structured way of seeing. If you like, it is an example of material dialectics. Analogous instances are the situational analyses conducted by Marx and Lenin, but these rely on Marxism even more than we can do today, and for that reason – and that alone – they conjure up an illusion of greater rigorousness. Dialectics in that case are still the last remnant of the philosophy of totality, whereas I should like to liberate them from this form of reinsurance and regard them as a volley of machine-gun fire from minimal intuitions. You know, of course, that in this I grant the abstract and connective elements validity to a certain degree which cannot be determined theoretically. Benjamin's review: do you mean the long one in *Gesellschaft* or the shorter one drawn from it in L. W.? In the first, at least, I wasn't actually able to detect any subterranean counter-current. But, nevertheless, Benjamin has made an effort, and I really don't care what he thinks in private. He missed the real impetus behind my work, as was inevitable. He has no sense of *élan* for real life. This is the place where a gaping hole in him exists.

Horkheimer and Pollock: I find it absolutely incomprehensible that the two of them see an 'open affront' in my not favouring them with a copy of the *Angestellten*. Not only did they take no notice of the work at the time I was writing it; they didn't give a single sign of life even when it was appearing in F. Z. and after the publication of the book, when a simple telephone call would have sufficed. People completely unknown to me, without even a specialist's interest in the subject, have dropped me a line or spoken to me about the book – so I was forced to assume that, in view of the obvious lack of interest in it on the part of H. and P., it would be superfluous to send them a copy. I am writing to you in such detail about this so that you can have a clear understanding of this business. By the way, you know, of course, that I do have things to do other than concoct open affronts, in which I have no interest at all.

As far as your prospects in Berlin are concerned, I think that the offer of a contract to lecture on aesthetics could only enhance them. When I got together with Weill recently – that was when we sent you the joint postcard – we also talked about your chances, but no concrete suggestion emerged. Weill thought that Curjel had no influence; that aside, I will of course be glad to make an appointment with him (I haven't seen him yet). I think that it will become a matter of immediate importance only once you have got your habilitation behind you. It would be best to wait until then to take any practical steps. What seems to me to go without saying is that you should concentrate your efforts on the Staatliche Hochschule für Musik. You can already make a start on something in this direction on your own initiative.

My life here is, from an outsider's point of view, very uninteresting at present. I don't see many people and don't have the time for it, but I do have to write quite a lot for the paper and perform my editorial duties. Time management on the whole is still a practical problem, and I couldn't claim to have discovered the miraculous elixir which would enable me to make the fullest use of my time in economic terms. (I shall get the secretary's office to send you some of my newspaper articles at the earliest opportunity.) For all that, I have noticeably broadened my practical knowledge of human nature, and I am gradually catching up with my novel and enjoying the combination of poetry and precision. The general standard of things here is appalling, and every day I find it difficult to choke back my disgust. (Of course, it is no better in Frankfurt, but the loathsomeness is more aggressively prominent here.) We went with Diebold once to Schwannecke's, but it is quite unbearable there. I see Benjamin at longish intervals; he is very nice at times. My many official duties, when I am obliged to go out and mix socially, are bad. Sometimes I am so tired that I simply neglect even obligations which are dearer to me – for example, I have not yet been up to getting in contact with Gretel K. The best thing one can do is to move anonymously through the anonymous crowds. Closer human contact is almost invariably a disappointment. Consciously verifying my influence by setting up practical relationships has always been repugnant to me. I don't want to do this, and I hate it. I can manage to achieve anything at all only in the wake of things which I have already accomplished.

In spite of Gastein my sciatica is still very active, which makes me less than happy.

Very best wishes to you, from Lili too. Do write back soon to your …

Please give your people our warmest regards. I hope that they are all well.

Original: typescript (carbon copy); Siegfried Kracauer papers, Deutsches Literaturarchiv, Marbach am Neckar; the location can be presumed from the context to be Berlin.

Stuckenschmidt controversy: Adorno and Hans Heinz Stuckenschmidt engaged in a 'controversy about cheerfulness' in *Anbruch*, no. 1, 1930 (see Adorno, GS 19, pp. 449–52, 652).

collection of aphorisms: the latest series of musical aphorisms, 'Motive IV: Musik von außen' [Motifs IV: music from outside], appeared in *Anbruch*, nos. 9/10, 1929 (see Adorno, GS 18, pp. 18f.; GS 19, p. 241).

Staatliche Hochschule für Musik: until 1931 part of the Akademie der Künste for administrative purposes; Arnold Schoenberg was in charge of the masterclass in composition from 1925 to 1933.

62 Adorno to Kracauer
Kronberg im Taunus, 26.5.1930

Cronberg, 26 May 1930.

Dear Friedel,

Warmest thanks for your letter, which I am able to answer at once on a free evening after an extremely stressful day. I am immersed in Kierkegaard but also heavily burdened with other things, critical commitments, and now on top of that a major article on Schoenberg commissioned by Curjel for the Kroll-Oper's programme for the Schoenberg performance on 7 June – something that I can't get out of. Incidentally, I should *most strongly* urge you and Lili to go. You will get far more out of it than you did from the comic opera with the nocturnal gas-man, and a great deal about it is sure to become clear to you. Yesterday I conferred for a long time with Heinsheimer, with very satisfactory results – all my projects for the rest of the year have been accepted, so that my position is the same as it was last year. I contrived this partly through intransigence and partly by cunning, and it is giving me a certain amount of pleasure. Kierkegaard chapter V concept complete. Working on the theory of sacrifice now.

About the *Angestellten*: first of all, your concept of material dialectics interests me very much because, in my Kierkegaard, something quite similar to it appears under the name of 'intermittent dialectics' – i.e. it is the kind that does not proceed in closed definitions of thought but is interrupted by a reality that does not fit into it and at the same time 'catches its breath' within it (Kierkegaard's expression) and arises refreshed every time. All my debates with Marxism revolve around this, and, like you, I proceed against the closed concept of dialectics with the argument that it is idealistic by virtue of the category of totality as a mere definition of thought. Once again, then, we are *d'accord* without having previously discussed the matter. In this respect I also fully agree with you concerning the method you employ in *Die Angestellten*. My criticism is much less radical than you have obviously understood it to be. I am not reproaching you with having written *prima vista*, but, on the contrary, it would seem to me more appropriate in analyses of this kind to rely to a greater extent on impressions and their construction, as one does not have access to the full economic background (it is all the same whether it is conceived in purely Marxist or empirical terms), and since, moreover, one becomes embroiled in antinomies as soon as one investigates the economy – at that point anyone knows better. Rather than laying ourselves open to attack by the numbskulls, we should stay in our sphere of constructive interpretation, which, to be sure, these people cannot tolerate and in which they feel chronically uncomfortable, but against which they feel all the more powerless when the accuracy of the findings can finally no longer be denied. *C'est tout.* Your interpretation of the H. and P. business is very different from the Cronberg one; they have constantly assured me of the ardent interest with which they have followed your work and also claim that they supplied you with material. What is more, they are very enthusiastic about it. Would you like me to do something about this?

About Berlin I entirely agree with your opinion – not to make a start until after the habilitation. The only thing is that one must know exactly where to deploy one's forces. The Staatliche Hochschule would be the obvious place, only Hindemith is a professor there and would move heaven and earth to stop me.

Your impressions of Berlin, by the way, sound none too cheerful. Perhaps it is partly because you haven't settled in properly yet and, just like me, are putting up every imaginable kind of resistance to a new milieu. However, the literati there are certainly of the worst kind. My impression of Diebold, incidentally, was more favourable than yours; I found him very humane and full of ideas in his own sphere – but perhaps he was putting it on. With Gretel, whatever the circumstances, I should prefer you to behave as you might be inclined to do of your own accord and not, please, to resume a friendly relationship with her for my sake, unless this is really important to you – this for her sake, too.

Yesterday there was the première here of the terrible American opera *Transatlantik* by Antheil. You feel ashamed to be sitting there; one may become culturally conservative as one gets older and, at the same time, completely infantile. Perhaps this is how the sacred early eon and the archaic age look when one is actually part of them – poor prospects for Herr Ranofer.

Don't be alarmed that I am enclosing another trifle for the F. Z. with a request for you to find a place for it. You don't need to worry that this will happen with every letter, but my success has gone to my head after enjoying nothing but disfavour there for years – and, to tell the truth, I have a certain need to write little and (as it seems to me) decent things of this kind. Even with the great expenditure of energy on Kierkegaard there sometimes remains a surplus of vigour which cannot be released in any other way. This time it is something humorous. Obviously, the material corresponds to the truth in all the facts, etc., even in the name Nietsche. Only the interpretation is original with me. In this case it would suit me to let it be published under a pseudonym.

All is well at home. A lot of telephone calls are going back and forth between your mothers and mine. I spoke to your aunt today; she moans a lot, but there's nothing to be done about that. Negotiations are in process for us possibly to take over your Margret, as Annachen is getting married this autumn, and that is irrevocable.

I shall have a copy of the *Anbruch* volume sent to you as I don't have one to hand. I hope that they won't go and lose it in Vienna. The most straightforward source would be Gretel. Please don't forget to have your essays sent to me. Are you interested in my Křenek polemic? If so I'll send it to you.

Give Lili my very best wishes. I am very sorry that your sciatica is still making you suffer. Might it not be advisable to undergo the Munari cure in Treviso or Florence? If you are interested, I can obtain all the details for you from Walter Herbert, who is completely cured now.

Write soon. All the best from your old

Teddie.

Original: typescript with handwritten addition and corrections; Siegfried Kracauer papers, Deutsches Literaturarchiv, Marbach am Neckar.

article on Schoenberg: 'Stilgeschichte in Schönbergs Werk' [History of style in Schoenberg's work], *Blätter der Staatsoper und der Städtischen Oper Berlin*, no. 32, June 1930 (see Adorno, GS 18, pp. 385–93, GS 19, p. 644).

Schoenberg performance on 7 June: the one-act opera *Erwartung* (op. 17) was performed under Alexander von Zemlinsky and *Die glückliche Hand* (op. 18) under Otto Klemperer.

comic opera with the nocturnal gas-man: Arnold Schoenberg, *Von heute auf morgen* (op. 32), libretto by Max Blonda [i.e. Gertrud Schoenberg], includes a passage of dialogue between 'Husband' and 'Wife' after a ring at the front door: 'Darling, the gas-man is out there! Is he coming in the middle of the night now?' (see Arnold Schönberg, *Von heute auf morgen* / Elliot Carter, *What next? Zwei Einakter*, ed. Staatsoper Unter den Linden Berlin, Frankfurt am Main: Insel, 1999, p. 61). The opera received its première on 1 February 1930 in Frankfurt am Main; Adorno discussed it in *Anbruch* and in *Die Musik* (see Adorno, GS 18, pp. 376–84, GS 19, p. 644).

in my Kierkegaard ... 'intermittent dialectics' ... 'catches its breath': The quotation from Kierkegaard ('A sigh which catches its breath slowly and deeply') is followed by 'Instead of the Hegelian "mediation" between freedom and necessity intermittence appears as breath which is drawn, held in and begins afresh; it moves on the spot, not in progress and continuity' (see Adorno, GS 2, p. 144). The section in which Adorno examines the relationship between dialectic and reality begins in the GS under the column title 'Immanente Dialektik' (see Adorno, GS 2, pp. 47–57).

Hindemith is a professor there: Paul Hindemith taught composition at the Berlin Hochschule für Musik from 1927 to 1935.

Transatlantik *by Antheil*: George Antheil (1900–1959), American composer; Adorno's discussion of the opera appeared under 'Juli 1930', *Die Musik*, no. 10, 1929/30 (see Adorno, GS 19, pp. 179–82, 649).

Ranofer: no information is available.

something humorous … even the name Nietsche: In a gloss Adorno points to a passage in Immanuel Kant's will in which his 'cook Louise Nietschin' receives a bequest. Adorno's ironic treatment of the facts continues: 'For it is not far from the Königsberg cook to that Polish aristocracy from whose blood Nietzsche liked to claim descent – but also to resentment … Might it be, then, that the hatred towards Kant meant nothing other than that hatred directed against the cook within himself?' ('Beitrag zur Geistesgeschichte', *Frankfurter Zeitung*, 6 June 1930; see Adorno, GS 20.2, pp. 555f., 817).

your Margret: Margret Diestler, a domestic servant of the Kracauer family; on 1 July 1930 she moved to Paris to join the household of the 'press consultant to the German embassy' there. Previously she had been discussed as a possible successor to Anna (mentioned below) in a conversation carried on by the Kracauer and Wiesengrund-Adorno ladies about questions concerning staff: 'You will be astonished when I tell you that Margret is not going to Oberrad (tomorrow I shall have the pleasure of letting Agathe know about this), but that from 1 July her address will be – Paris' (Hedwig Kracauer to Kracauer, 1 June 1930; Kracauer papers, Deutsches Literaturarchiv, Marbach).

Annachen: a domestic servant of the Wiesengrund-Adorno family, married name Anna Reinhard; after the wedding in spring 1930 she was resident at Friedberger Landstrasse 154. Hedwig Kracauer arranged for a wedding gift from Kracauer: a 'set of salad-servers for 4.50 marks' (Hedwig Kracauer to Kracauer, undated, spring 1930; Kracauer papers, Deutsches Literaturarchiv, Marbach). Her successor, according to a quotation attributed to Agathe Calvelli-Adorno, was a 'girl from Amorbach' (see Adorno/Pabst, *Amorbach*, p. 100). Adorno met 'Annachen' again in Frankfurt am Main immediately after his return from exile (see Adorno, *Bildmonographie*, p. 210).

Munari cure: therapy for joint, muscle and nerve ailments in which a warmed paste of oil, spices and minerals was applied to the affected parts of the body.

63 Adorno to Kracauer

Kronberg im Taunus, 1.6.1930

Cronberg, 1 June 1930.

Dear Friedel,

Many thanks for your letter and the essays, which I have just received and which I read at once all at one go. I am very enthusiastic about them, and, if any proof were needed that it was the right decision to go to Berlin, they would supply it. Everything that you write has become incomparably more liberal and far more self-confident. You have laid aside the last residues of moderate caution and also an inhibiting fear of the 'literary', are much more precise in the polemics and much more trenchant in your use of the grotesque than in your earlier things, and – to sum it up in a word which might be seen as a mockery in itself – sovereign, as the humane mean is still perceptible even in the thick of the attack. I would have nothing whatsoever to say against it (only the sentence attacking the communists in the broadcast essay is somewhat questionable). Many pieces, such as the essay on the Gedächtniskirche, have a measure of profundity which could not have been predicted; here, too, a noticeable element of surrealism comes into play for the first time, also in the essay on Berlin on Sunday with its beautiful evocation of the past, which is so much to my taste. The essay on the Rhineland with the analysis of the film is a model of a polemic which fits the material. It is really magnificent, and the leap forward is all the more perceptible for someone who has not read anything of yours for some time. I am doubly excited about the novel as I hope that all this will be incorporated there, too. It would of course be of great importance for these pieces to be read in Berlin itself. I have just read something by Joseph Roth – it is quite inferior in comparison with yours, and, incidentally, even without that comparison. In every way, Soma's entire output is completely bleak, with its empty irony which stems only from a sense of his own inadequacy and never from outrage over things.

I am sending you the Křenek polemic with this; in the *galley proof* (it will appear in *Anbruch* in a few days) I improved some linguistic points, but nothing of any importance. I had some good ideas, as I was working on it, and am very eager to hear what you have to say. I can't send you the parallel essay by Křenek; I haven't seen it yet and don't have a copy to hand, but I have been told that he is greatly impressed with mine – so overall evidence is mounting that my theoretical works are beginning to make an impact. I likewise arranged for the Ravel to be sent to you a few days ago. I hope this will happen – one can never know, in view of Viennese sloppiness – but if you don't receive it, please let me know.

A few words about your critique of *Kantor* and Cook. First about the *Kantor*. It is an ornament, a bit of fun, dashed off in five minutes; to criticize it does it too much honour – it can be as precious as it likes because it is allowed to be so, and the disproportion in relation to its object is its very point. The Nietzsche is different. I'm not putting too much weight on it (the Kierkegaard, which was intended to be serious, was more important to me and is obviously much better), but there is some substance in it – i.e. dealing an oblique blow at the very centre of something entirely contingent – and I believe that I succeeded, most of all by taking the attack right into the sphere of Nietzsche. A lot of work, then, went into that little piece, because the matter means a lot to me; the immanent unmasking of the doctrines of blood and nobility – and even you will not dispute the fact that the act of discovery as such is a fine thing. You are definitely doing me a wrong here by accusing me of inhumanity – simply because the pathos of language is that of the Nietzschean kind which is open to mockery; and behind it stands something completely different as a positive standard by which to measure it. Of course I am not annoyed by the critique – where would we be if we let ourselves be angry with each other about critiques? You obviously have the right to radical criticism without my ever being sensitive about it, and I claim the same right for myself – but do take another look just for the sake of the matter. I should also be very pleased if it could appear in the paper, but it absolutely must be published under a pseudonym because of the university; the *Wunderkantor* also came out under a pseudonym and appeared without my knowledge under my code-name. By the way, Horkheimer particularly liked it. You may say that in that case he probably didn't understand it, but the absence of humanity should be his speciality. I'm glad that the business with Pollock is all right; that the two of you also had to put up with Sascha Schwabacher, however, is one blessing too many – what a lot of gossip she must have poured into your ears. Over the last few years she has developed to attain an astonishing level of inferiority.

I was very ill for a few days – I had overworked to such a degree that I collapsed; now I have had some sleep and am all right again – and deep in Kierkegaard once more, after all kinds of duties as a critic had held me back.

About Schoenberg: I can arrange with no trouble to reserve two tickets for the première; I can completely understand that you don't want to pay, or to incur any expense – only please let me know on a postcard *by return* so that I can notify Curjel in good time. As I have done these people some considerable favours (as well as the Schoenberg essay, which was written very quickly, I reported back to him at once about the Antheil) – so I really can expect this without making any excuses for you or myself.

I am staying here for Whitsun. Gretel is coming on Saturday – by plane. She is only staying until Tuesday; I couldn't interrupt my work for any longer than that.

What sort of thing are the sophisticated adventures via Benjamin to which you allude? Has he introduced you to his friend Baron Schey – Minka's father? You must tell me all about it. I am seeing very little of such things at the moment – on Ascension Day, though, a few characters of this genre arranged a 'party' for me, but I escaped from them with Horkheimer. Solitude agrees very well with me. Apart from work, all I read is rubbish.

Have you seen the whale on display in the booth near the royal castle? It is a gigantic object. Do you dine at Habel's from time to time? And eat carp done the Jewish way at Berg's near the zoo?

Give Lili my very best wishes.

Much love from your old

Teddie.

Please spare a thought for the lamenting Zillig.

Original: typescript with handwritten additions, corrections and postscript: Theodor W. Adorno Archiv, Frankfurt am Main.

Many thanks for your letter: not preserved.

the sentence attacking the communists in the broadcast essay: 'Apart from two unrelated communist speakers, who designated the broadcasting service in its present form as a weapon of bourgeois society and demanded the proletarian station' ('Aussprache über den Rundfunk: Festsitzung anläßlich des fünfjährigen Bestehens der Reichs-Rundfunk-Gesellschaft' [Discussion about the broadcasting service: session marking the fifth anniversary of the founding of the Reich's Broadcasting Company], *Frankfurter Zeitung*, 17 May 1930 (see Kracauer, W 5, no. 476).

on the Gedächtniskirche: 'Ansichtspostkarte: Kaiser-Wilhelm-Gedächtniskirche bei Nacht' [Picture postcard: Kaiser Wilhelm Memorial Church by night], *Frankfurter Zeitung*, 26 May 1930 (see Kracauer, W 5, no. 474).

Berlin on Sunday: 'Sonntagsausflug' [Sunday excursion], *Frankfurter Zeitung*, 5 May 1930 (see Kracauer, W 5, no. 474).

evocation of the past: e.g. 'No wave of strikes has yet broken on the houses which line the canal, and not the slightest breath troubles the peace of the Ministry of Defence. The streets of the old West are undiscovered landscapes where the foot of the explorer scarcely treads ... And what locality in the nearer or more distant environs could compare with the Tiergarten? It is as silent as the past, and its tree trunks arranged in loose rows, its flower beds and ponds have withdrawn from life together with the bourgeois culture which created them, as soundlessly as old palaces' ('Sonntagsausflug', *Frankfurter Zeitung*, 5 May 1930; see Kracauer, W 5, no. 474.)

The essay on the Rhineland: 'Rheinland-Konjunktur', *Frankfurter Zeitung*, 9 May 1930 (see Kracauer, W 6.2, pp. 354f.) – i.e. the review of the film *Das Rheinlandmädel*, directed by Johannes Meier (1930).

Joseph Roth: Adorno wrote 'Josef'. From June 1929 to October 1930 the *Frankfurter Zeitung* and Joseph Roth suspended their collaboration; in the weeks preceding the letter he published in *Das Tagebuch*, *Münchner Neueste Nachrichten* and *Die Literarische Welt* (see Joseph Roth, *Das journalistische Werk 1929–1939*, ed. Klaus Westermann, Cologne: Kippenheuer & Witsch, 1991).

Soma's entire output: previous articles by Soma Morgenstern: 'Männerrechtler' [Rights for Men!], *Frankfurter Zeitung*, 12 May 1930; 'Wien: Natürlich: Das Kaffeehaus' [Vienna: naturally: the coffee-house], *Frankfurter Zeitung*, 27 April 1930 (see Soma Morgenstern, *Dramen, Feuilletons, Fragmente*, ed. Ingolf Schulte, Lüneburg: zu Klampen, 2000, pp. 248–57, 459).

the parallel essay by Křenek: alongside Adorno's 'Reaktion und Fortschritt' [Reaction and progress], there appeared in the same volume of *Anbruch* Ernst Krenek's reply 'Fortschritt und Reaktion' [Progress and reaction]. The friendly staging of an exchange of 'polemics' is documented in Krenek's letter to Adorno of 16 May 1930 (see Adorno/Krenek, *Briefwechsel*, pp. 18f.; Krenek's contribution is also reprinted there, pp. 181–6).

Kantor: Adorno's gloss, 'Der Wunderkantor', *Frankfurter Zeitung*, 27 May 1930 (see Adorno, GS 18, p. 790).

business with Pollock: no information survives.

Schwabacher: Sascha Schwabacher (1875–1942?), art historian; she was deported in 1942.

Baron Schey … Minka: Philipp Schey von Koromla (1881–1957), married to the patroness of the arts Lili Schey von Koromla, née Goldschmidt-Rothschild (1883–1929), and their daughter Minka Schey von Koromla (1909–?), born in Frankfurt am Main.

the whale on display in the booth: no information survives.

Habel's: restaurant and wine bar in Berlin's Luisenstrasse.

at Berg's near the zoo: the trade directory for 1928 mentions the 'Restauration Berg am Zoo, Helene und Arthur Berg, Charlottenburg, Hardenbergstr. 27'.

Please spare a thought for the lamenting Zillig: Winfried Zillig (1905–1963), composer, pupil of Schoenberg; no information survives about the reason for his lamentations. Adorno mostly wrote about him later (among others, 'Zilligs Verlaine-Lieder' [Zillig's Verlaine songs], *Bayrischer Rundfunk*, July 1961; see Adorno, GS 17, pp. 123–32, 348; 'Winfried Zillig: Möglichkeit und Wirklichkeit' [Winfried Zillig: potential and reality], *Bayrischer Rundfunk*, 10 June 1964; see Adorno, GS 17, pp. 318–26, 349).

64 Adorno to Kracauer
Kronberg im Taunus, 1.7.1930

Cronberg im Taunus.
Hotel Frankfurter Hof.
1 July 1930.

Dear Friedel,

Forgive me for not answering your letter until today – but I am completely tied to my work, without being able to find a single free minute. You can hardly imagine the concentration with which I am writing. Every day I write 3 to 4 pages like the pages of the manuscript of the essay against Křenek, and, as you can imagine, ever denser prose – so my head doesn't produce much else with any sense in it, and even now I must beg you for a certain amount of forbearance. I am now at work on the final version, the fair copy. The first chapter is completely finished; the second will be tomorrow or the day after. In terms of quantity, it is true, I am not yet even half done, but in fact, though in fact it really is, as the first chapters were only in schematic form in the sketch and had to be written in their entirety, while the text of the last ones already exists in substance, needing only the insertion of quotes, which, by the way, do of course mar the text to some extent because they are so extensive, but they have to be included for academic purposes, and besides, they have been selected in such a way that readers will be able to put up with them. I am really very keen to see how you will like the work, which is of course dedicated, officially and unofficially, to you both. Horkheimer, who is familiar with large parts of the first chapter, is quite delighted, which, of course, is not saying very much. The analysis of Kierkegaard's poetry and the 'Aestheticism' from *Either/Or* is finished, as are the methodology (of a somewhat idiosyncratic kind), the analysis of Kierkegaard's aesthetics, the theory of obstructed ontology, that of the subject–object relation as objectless inwardness, the immanent theory of dialectics – a material interpretation of dialectics from the angle of the category of demythologization will follow later – and, today, the interpretation of the philosophy of history. So, all kinds of things – over 60 printed pages. It would be difficult for me to tell you about its content – it would be too cumbersome; but you are sure to be able to fill in the periphery.

I was especially glad about your praise for the Křenek polemic. As I know that you really do take as critical a view as possible of my things – the only proper attitude – I take it in the positive light in which it is offered. I myself think that the essay turned out respectably and that I have somewhat gone beyond myself with the Kierkegaard – but there are many things that one learns only when working on a larger scale. It must surely have been like that for you with your novel. The Křenek polemic has now appeared in *Anbruch*, but I don't have it yet and am worried that they may have botched it out of fear that Křenek might be unable to defend himself against it, though I haven't been shown his response. I shall keep you posted about this odd business. By the way, did you get the Ravel? The publisher wrote to me some time ago to say that it had been sent to you, but I haven't heard anything about it from you and would be very eager to know how matters stand with it and whether you liked it. Everyone here is full of praise for your last articles, which once again I, as an isolated provincial, never got to see. Horkheimer spoke enthusiastically about the 'hiring hall' piece, and Carl Dreyfuss in just the same way about the critique of the fashion for biography – which, though, if I remember rightly, was originally meant for the *Neue Rundschau*. Please do send them to me – and whatever else of importance you have written. I still have to thank you for placing Nietzsche the Cook – about which, though, you haven't continued the discussion. Incidentally, the F. Z. has indeed paid a fee for the Kierkegaard, but not for the *Wunderkantor* or Nietzsche. I wonder whether Simon has deducted my fee because of my work for the studio? That would only make sense. I have written a little piece about names which I will send you sometime for publication if you like. Proust and Fleisser appear in it.

Your life in Berlin must have taken shape by now. Moreover, you have seen Gretel in the meantime, as she wrote to me. I hope that you will get enough time for your novel. I am living in complete isolation. A few weeks ago I also saw Benji, for just a moment in the hotel, without experiencing any great emotion. Sometimes in the evenings I go to Königstein, to Anita or to Margot Sulzbach-Rocholl-Loeb, the friend of your cousin Hanne Kr. Now and then I drink schnapps very late at night with Horkheimer. *C'est tout.* Leo has more or less completely disappeared from my purview, but I don't have any use for sophisticated circles either. I can't say that I am missing anything.

So I am hoping to finish my book at last in July – definitely by the beginning of August. On 9 August I am going to Karersee with Gretel, as she may have told you (although of course it only became certain after a telephone call yesterday). As she has only three weeks, we want to make things as pleasant as possible for ourselves. It is not out of the question that I may be coming to Berlin in September. That depends, of course, on how the matter of the habilitation progresses – i.e. it depends on whether I am needed in Frankfurt, perhaps to explain my work to Tillich. In any event I should like you to write to me with your plans for the summer, as it might still be possible for us to arrange something together.

That's all for now. Once again, forgive me for writing nonsense – but I have been sitting at the typewriter for nine hours now. Goodbye, my friend, and give Lili my very best wishes. Ever your old

Teddie.

Original: typescript with handwritten corrections; Siegfried Kracauer papers, Deutsches Literarturarchiv, Marbach am Neckar.

your last letter: not preserved.

the 'hiring hall' piece: 'Über Arbeitsnachweise: Konstruktion eines Raums', *Frankfurter Zeitung*, 17 June 1930 (see Kracauer, W 5, no. 483).

critique of the fashion for biography: 'Die Biographie als neubürgerliche Kunstform', *Frankfurter Zeitung*, 29 June 1930 (see Kracauer, W 5, no. 486).

work for the studio: see letter no. 54.

piece about names: 'Notiz über Namen', *Frankfurter Zeitung*, 7 August 1930 (see Adorno, GS 20.2, pp. 533f., 817).

Anita: probably Anita Seligmann (1904–?), daughter of Milton Seligmann; she studied philosophy and sociology at the Johann Wolfgang Goethe-Universität (1924–31) and in 1931 married Hans Lothar (see Adorno, *Letters to his Parents*, p. 35n. 3); in 1936 she went into exile in England.

65 Kracauer to Adorno

[Berlin,] 22.7.1930

22 July 30.

Dear Teddie,

I am writing to you only today and probably not at such length as I should like, because my life in Berlin has grown no easier as regards my duties. The only thing is that the work consists more of writing and is more rewarding as a result. This is how it actually is: I have to toil dreadfully to make anything like a decent job of turning out the necessary items for the paper and finish my own work. You are at least in the fortunate position of being able to carry on unhindered with works which are exclusively your own. I, on the other hand, am sacrificing my strength for articles and essays which for the most part will have no life beyond the newspaper – and I can't contrive to pull this sort of thing off with one hand tied behind my back, but write them with the same love as I do my novel, etc. This is also why I send out so few letters and have not seen, let us say, Gretel K. since that more or less chance encounter. Nor, by the way, has she rung us up again as we arranged that time. I assume you are in the very thick of the Kierkegaard business or even at the end of it. You will be very happy when you have finished the work. I am most excited about it – and then everything is sure to go smoothly with the habilitation. What have you been writing on the subject of names? Please send it to me – and indeed all the articles that you think are good. For my own part I am enclosing the biography essay and the one on hiring halls. It is a pity that you don't often look at the papers; I think that most of the things I write are decent. Taken as a whole they produce quite a nice destructive effect. I haven't had any special experiences, though there was an evening in the Eden Bar where I talked to Frau Rosie Gräfenberg-Ullstein. She was there in the company of Fränze Herzfeld, who, by the way, is completely at odds with Bloch. Then a few days ago I was at an interesting general assembly at which Alsberg spoke very clumsily. The meeting, which went on in far too abnormal a way for me to be able to write about it, confirmed many of my theoretical findings and indeed consolidated them. The plan has taken root in me to write a series of 'Political Tales' – a sort of modern version of Hebel's *Schatzkästlein* – 'The Little Treasure-Chest'. The first tale has already appeared in the paper under the title 'Peaceful Solution'. At present I am working on the second, which is going to be called 'The

Inquisitive Reporter'. My novel is naturally making (slow) progress. You can imagine that I have a strong desire for greater autonomy. You are right to be going to the Dolomites again. Where we are going – probably in mid-August – is not yet certain. Please do write to me again before you go on holiday, even if it is only a short letter. Benjamin has already left; he is going to travel north on a freighter – a Viking in reverse. Beautiful writings about the northern lights will come out of it.

Warmest regards from your old

Lili joins me in this.

Original: typescript (carbon copy); Siegfried Kracauer papers, Deutsches Literaturarchiv, Marbach am Neckar; the location can be deduced from the context as Berlin.

Eden Bar: presumably the bar of the hotel of the same name on the Kurfürstendamm; it was destroyed during the Second World War.

Rosie Gräfenberg-Ullstein: Rosa Waldeck, née Goldschmidt (1898–1982); married names Gräfenberg and Ullstein (both marriages ended in divorce); journalist and author. At this time, she was still married to Franz Ullstein.

general assembly … Alsberg: no information survives.

Hebel's Schatzkästlein: Johann Peter Hebel (1760–1826), *Schatzkästlein des Rheinischen Hausfreundes*, Tübingen: J. G. Cotta'sche Buchhandlung, 1811.

'Peaceful Solution': *Frankfurter Zeitung*, 23 June 1930 (see Kracauer, W 1, no. 484).

'The Inquisitive Reporter': not realized.

Benjamin has already left: information about Walter Benjamin's journey to Scandinavia, which he undertook at the end of July 1930, can be found in his *Reisenotizen* (see Benjamin, GS VI, pp. 419–21).

writings about the northern lights: Walter Benjamin, 'Nordische See', *Frankfurter Zeitung*, 18 September 1930, about bright midsummer nights (see Benjamin, GS IV.1, pp. 383–7, GS IV.2, p. 997).

66 Adorno to Kracauer
Kronberg im Taunus, 23.7.1930

Cronberg, 23 July 1930.

Dear Friedel, whatever is the matter? I have gone for weeks without a reply to a very lengthy letter; didn't you receive it? I am submerged in work – four chapters quite finished, and I am deep in the fifth; then there will be two left, so I shall probably not get any more done before the holidays. As I shall be back in Frankfurt as early as 3 September, I may possibly settle here again for another three weeks. The matter of my habilitation has been greatly helped by Horkheimer's appointment, which is now 99% certain. I liked the article against the *Blue Angel* and *most of all* against biographies very much; the categories are perhaps a bit broad for the B. A. Do send me some more! How is the novel going? Have you read the novellas by Green? How is your sciatica? Things aren't at all good with me as regards my health; I have been struggling with neuralgic headaches for weeks without a break. I am more than ready for a holiday. Kierkegaard already comes to about 150 printed pages of text! From 9 August: Carossa al Lago, Hotel Karersee.

Give my very best wishes to Lili and write soon to

Your old

Teddie

Original: MS, postcard; Siegfried Kracauer papers, Deutsches Literaturarchiv, Marbach am Neckar.

Horkheimer's appointment: Max Horkheimer's appointment as professor of social philosophy followed by a decree of 29 July 1930 (Universitätsarchiv Frankfurt am Main).

article against the Blue Angel: 'Der blaue Engel', *Die Neue Rundschau*, June 1930 (see Kracauer, W 6.2, pp. 375–8).

novellas by Green: Julien Green, *Le Voyageur sur la terre*, Paris, 1930. A copy can be found in the library left behind by Adorno.

67 Adorno to Kracauer

Kronberg im Taunus, 25.7.1930

Cronberg, 25 July 1930.

Dear Friedel, thank you for your letter, which crossed with my card, which you will have received in the meantime. I am immersed in work, just as you are, and you are mistaken if you think that I can pick and choose my work, as I am beginning to wish the whole of Kierkegaard would go to hell and the devil whose advocate he played. I am now deep in chapter V, an interpretation of Kierkegaard's logic of the spheres, and the critical discussion of the problems of concretion in S. K. Chapter IV has, I think, turned out particularly well: 'Analysis of the Existential'. Much blood, of course, is being shed over the work. Not much of either Heidegger or 'dialectical theology' should go unchallenged – but that is no more than it deserves. By no means do I deny my own theological motives. On the contrary, I cannot put my head in the sand and rely on its being 'meant in an objective sense' when I clearly and explicitly mean it myself. Horkheimer has read the whole of the fourth chapter and is delighted, but nevertheless finds it tremendously difficult – more difficult than the baroque book. I can't help that; it is intrinsic to the matter – I have revealed the mythical/demonic character of Kierkegaard's concept of existence, and if it can't be translated into Suebo-Marxian I can't do anything about it.

I liked your essay on the hiring halls (I already knew the other) very much indeed. I noticed with amazement and yet with agreement that you accepted Benjamin's catch phrase about the houses as dreams of the collective – but without the word 'collective', which I can't bear either. The piece is really very aggressive and striking, too – one of your best things; it follows up certain ideas from *Ornament der Masse*, but in a more radical way. I am in complete agreement with it.

I am enclosing the little piece about names. I would be amused if you would publish it should you happen to like it. I should appreciate that for a particular reason, too. The day before yesterday, at Schoen's instigation, Carl and I read our little stories together (the ones which I gave the name 'Pieces for Reading' and prefaced with a few words about their approach). I had gone over them once again and, without attaching too much importance to them, I think that they are decent – they fulfil their intention. I am supposed to have read very well, as everyone assures me – but in the F. Z. there appeared the scandalous review which I am enclosing for you. I don't know the man; it might be Herr Weyrauch, who was actually a schoolmate of mine and whom I loathed even then. I know that you don't care for the stories; I myself don't rate them too highly by any means, but this stupidity does not lie within the sphere which deals with that kind of thing. The man didn't understand the intention, and so he is incapable of judging whether it has been realized or whether it deserves to be realized. I should really appreciate a rehabilitation by one means or another. You would surely not allow Benjamin or Bloch to be treated in such a way.

Gretel: I know that she would be very glad to meet up with you, but, as you have hesitated for an exceedingly long time in resuming the relationship with her and have firmly emphasized your lack of time, I can understand that she is holding back. It is equally certain, though, that she would be very glad if you would take the initiative.

As I am hardly now likely to be finished before the journey – there will probably be one chapter left – it is probable that I shall come back here again at the beginning of September for a fortnight or three weeks. However, that will not bother me; I can live alone very well indeed – much better than I should have thought – especially as the solitude is no more profound than I should ever have liked; I can see people whenever I wish. I very much hope to come to Berlin in the autumn; as yet I don't know when – for practical reasons, probably not until after the habilitation – perhaps over Christmas. Have your holiday plans taken shape? Shall we perhaps meet up somehow and somewhere, or will you flit, regardless of Mulackstrasse and Ackerstrasse, to the *ville lumière*?

I am very excited about the novel and the *Treasure-Chest*, which ought to arouse Brecht's envy. I think it a pity that you are absorbed by the newspaper to such a degree. Can you not reorganize matters so that you could do more editorial work without having to write so much yourself? One expends so much of one's resources like that. Some editorial initiative on your part would also be of great benefit to the F. Z. By an unlucky chance I have read a sequel to Herr Hauser's novel; before long I was literally sick. He ought to be put in one of Lampel's reformatories.

The Křenek polemic seems to have gone down very well.

Goodbye, Friedel. What has happened to our Kierkegaard? The longer I work on it, the more uncomfortable I feel; he was an intolerable ideologue even in his own opinion, and in spite of all his tales of woe and acts of penitence, in spite of Regine and the arrow in the flesh, he was fundamentally complacent at every moment – it bears very, very little examination. I even found the expression which fascinated us most, the 'qualitative leap', in Hegel: the preface to the *Phenomenology*. There's nothing to be done about it.

Give Lili my very best wishes, and do get in touch soon.

Ever your old

Teddie.

Original: typescript with handwritten corrections; Siegfried Kracauer papers, Deutsches Literaturarchiv, Marbach am Neckar.

go to hell and the devil: Adorno wrote: '… da ich anfange, den ganzen Kierkegaard zum Teufel zu wünschen, den er an die Wand gemalt hat', using two popular phrases ('zum Teufel wünschen'/wish to be rid of; and 'den Teufel an die Wand malen'/to paint the devil on the wall – i.e. to imagine the worst). He may have had Nietzsche's epigram in mind: 'Erst das Christentum hat den Teufel an die Wand gemalt' [It was Christianity that first spoke of the devil]. See aphorism 78 in *Human, All Too Human II*, trans. Gary Handwerk, Stanford, CA: Stanford University Press, 2013.

Benjamin's catch phrase: this phrase varies and reads, among other versions, 'Dream houses of the collective: arcades, winter gardens, panoramas, factories, waxworks, casinos, railway stations' (see *Das Passagen-Werk*, Benjamin, GS V.1, p. 511).

Schoen: Ernst Schoen (1894–1960), musician and author; from 1929 director of programming at Südwestdeutscher Rundfunk in Frankfurt am Main; a schoolfriend of Walter Benjamin, he went into exile in England in 1933.

'Pieces for Reading': see the published version in Adorno, GS 20.2, pp. 587–97.

scandalous review: the discussion appeared in the 'Kleine Mitteilungen' [Short reports] in the 'Radio' section, signed 'K. Z.' (see the following letter): 'The Südwestdeutscher Rundfunk broadcast "Pieces for Reading" by Theodor Wiesengrund-Adorno and Carl Dreyfuss. The authors read one of their bagatelles after another, back-to-back, alternately, without a break. We have to assume that they aimed to achieve neither a good distraction nor a more profound effect. Both lacked wit as much as they did a penetrating grasp of the subjects they tackled. Granted, here and there one might sense a not wholly unsympathetic care in their choice of words, but the careless rendition robbed them of even this effect – and so many of these little pictures from everyday life had slipped past before they could be noticed' (see *Frankfurter Zeitung*, 24 July 1930).

Weyrauch: Wolfgang Weyrauch (1904–1980), editor, lecturer and author; like Adorno, he attended the Kaiser-Wilhelms-Gymnasium in Frankfurt-Sachsenhausen.

Mulackstraße ... Ackerstraße: synonym for a peculiarity of town planning to be seen in the tenements of Berlin: 'The loathsomeness of the Ackerstraße is the exact complement to the loathsomeness of the Kurfürstendamm. The definitive splitting of society into mutually incompatible classes is reflected in the architecture' (see 'Städtebau und Gesellschaftsordnung' (1949), in Adorno, *Bildmonographie*, pp. 214–28; here, p. 222). In Kracauer's work the combination of the street names appears as a disparaging expression: 'whether it originates from a foreigner or p.p. Mulack' (Der Detektiv-Roman; see Kracauer, W 1, p. 167). Adorno's reference includes an allusion to the notorious restaurant Mulack-Ritze ('die Ritze'). Both Mulack- and Ackerstraße were locales for films about the lives of Berlin's industrial working class (see Kracauer, W 6.2, pp. 329ff.).

Herr Hauser's novel: Heinrich Hauser (1901–1955), journalist and writer. The *Frankfurter Zeitung* was publishing his novel *Die letzten Segelschiffe* (The last sailing-ships, Berlin: S. Fischer, 1930) in serial form. Its fourth instalment appeared in the edition bearing the date of Adorno's letter. It is titled 'Full sail: the log of the *Pamir* (13 February)'.

one of Lampel's reformatories: Peter Martin Lampel (1894–1965), author; in 1930 he found himself involved in a lawsuit as a result of his criticism of contemporary welfare practices which he expressed in his play *Revolte im Erziehungshaus* (Revolt in the reformatory, 1928).

Regine: Regine Olsen, engaged (1840/41) to Søren Kierkegaard; the engagement was broken off. Adorno on 'Regine' as a cipher: 'For this reason, in Kierkegaard's philosophy pure spirit transcends towards the ghostly as its primal image from prehistoric times. It is said of a figure of "modern tragedy" – probably Regine – "Her life unfolds in a different way from that of the Greek Antigone; the movement towards development proceeds inwards, not outwards – it is a scene played out by ghosts"' (see 'Kierkegaard: Konstruktion des Ästhetischen', Adorno, GS 2, pp. 81f.).

arrow in the flesh: Søren Kierkegaard, *Der Pfeil im Fleisch*, Übersetzt und mit einem Vorwort von Theodor Haecker [the cover details appear thus in the copy left behind by Adorno; 2nd edn, 1922], Innsbruck: Brenner, 1914.

'qualitative leap' in Hegel: 'But as, with a child, the first breath after a long, silent period of nourishment breaks off the gradual process of mere increase – a qualitative leap – and now the child is born, the developing spirit matures slowly and silently towards the new form' (see Georg Wilhelm Friedrich Hegel, *Phänomenologie des Geistes*, auf der Grundlage der Werke von 1832–1845 new edn, ed. Eva Moldenhauer and Karl Markus Michel. Frankfurt am Main: Suhrkamp, 1986, p. 18). Adorno quotes the passage in 'Kierkegaard: Konstruktion des Ästhetischen' for the purpose of comparison with the concept of the 'leap' in Kierkegaard (see Adorno, GS 2, pp. 128f.).

68 Kracauer to Adorno
[Berlin,] 1.8.1930

1 August 30.

Dear Teddie,

I sent on your gloss about names, which I liked very much without underestimating the difficulty of writing it, to Frankfurt with a recommendation as soon as I received it. While on the subject of newspapers, the radio review, of which I only learnt from your newspaper cutting, was written, to go by the code letters, by Karl Zimmermann, a young man who contributes to the feuilleton. I am convinced that this young man, who has no feeling for such things, did not understand the ideas underlying the stories at all – but I have the feeling that, even if I complain about this and other reviews, further faux pas of this kind will occur. There are very few people indeed whose opinions are decisive. The criticism is based by no means on malice but probably only on a lack of understanding – and you must have known what you were doing when you took your place in front of the microphone with these stories. In your place I should have refrained in spite of Schoen's invitation. Could these things actually be taken in at all by an unprepared listener who couldn't even see you? They are too subtle for that. But if you risk the experiment you really ought not to complain that it has misfired. Please give this some thought. The fault is more on your side than that of the public, for whom the critic writes as a representative. Give the radio your little finger, and it will take your whole hand.

I should like to correct a comment on my 'hiring halls'. You think that I have accepted Benjamin's phrase about houses as the dreams of the collective. That, however, is not the case. I referred to certain forms of space as the dreams of society because they represent the being of that society which is concealed by the latter's consciousness. On this point, then, I concur with Benjamin, who, by the way, is of the same opinion – only as regards the word 'dream'. It is as if we were meeting at a crossroads and then going off in different directions. The conception of the city as the dream of a collective still seems a romantic one to me.

I am very sorry that you will not have finished your work on Kierkegaard before the holidays. It was just the same with me a year ago with the *Angestellten* book; of course, I then had to finish it during the holidays themselves. Having to go back to something old is not pleasant. I hope to receive a copy soon after you have finished. We shall be going on holiday in mid-August but are not sure yet where – perhaps to the French Alps or Brittany. In spite of all my work for the paper I am not dissatisfied. A considerable number of the newspaper articles are written from uniform viewpoints, so that they don't vanish with the setting sun. And, what is more, I was clear in my mind from the outset that I should have to regard my first days in Berlin as a period of learning. My novel will progress faster on holiday than it is doing at present. I am also continuing to produce the

'Political Tales'; they have little to do with Brecht's ideas, by the way, and are hardly likely to arouse his envy.

I wish you all the best for a lovely holiday with Gretel, to whom I send my warmest regards. Lili sends you her very best wishes.

Your …

Original: typescript (carbon copy); Siegfried Kracauer papers, Deutsches Literaturarchiv, Marbach am Neckar; the place can be deduced to be Berlin from the context.

Zimmermann: Karl Zimmermann, who worked on the *Frankfurter Zeitung* from 1930 to 1943.

certain forms of space: self-quotation from 'Über Arbeitsnachweise': 'Certain "Raumbilder" (constructions inside a space) are the dreams of society' (see Kracauer, W 5, no. 483).

I concur: the original has 'ich begegne mich', which implies 'meeting'.

69 Adorno to Kracauer

Kronberg im Taunus, 6.8.1930

Cronberg, 6 August 1930.

Dear Friedel, I should have finished my work had I not suffered a complete nervous breakdown as a result of the overexertion – of which you can scarcely have any idea. I could no longer sleep at all, lay awake uninterruptedly all day and all night and was thus incapable of thinking or writing anything sensible, and had the most appalling palpitations. For this reason, I took a break for a few days and am now sleeping passably once more; things are generally better. There are just the palpitations still – I am going to the doctor, as I am worried that it may be something organic. The exasperating thing was that it stopped me finishing my work. I finished Chapter VI today; there is still one more left to do – i.e. in the final version; it has existed as a concept for a long time. It would take only a week's work, but I can no longer get to grips with it now. I have still worked up some things for *Anbruch* – new aphorisms, etc. I am glad to be getting away on Saturday. Unfortunately, it is only for three weeks; Gretel can't manage any longer than that, and just now I haven't the nerve to travel on my own.

On to your letter. What you say about the suitability or unsuitability of the *Lesestücke* for broadcasting is certainly right – but I cannot agree that 'the critic has to represent the public'. You don't do that; neither do I; an idiot like K. Z. is a danger to the public; why do you protect him? It is not the question of the suitability of these trifles for broadcasting which is up for discussion but his for writing critiques, and this presupposes that he is even capable of understanding anything at all. I am really curious to hear how you respond to that – for the sake of the basic principle, not the case, which is a matter of indifference to me and can quite happily be left to go no further than the newspaper. By the way – the newspaper. I have suggested giving Heinz a Jungdo uniform for his 50th birthday. Shouldn't we be more tolerant towards, let us say, Tucholsky?

Why do you so often take a defensive attitude in your letters when there is no need at all for it? You did so twice more in your last letter. First in the case of Benjamin. You think that you have to defend yourself by saying that you didn't adopt the dream of the collective from him – it was merely that your paths crossed. *Très bien*, but is that really important? Is that what matters? I didn't mean to accuse you of dependency – on the contrary, I was delighted with the idea, because it proceeds from a certain 'realism' – the same that I sensed and criticized in *Ginster* under its absurd mask because absurdity can, to some degree, be detached from realism – and leads into a less familiar region. Nor did I mean to attack you. Moreover, in practical terms I find even the 'dream' of the collective an excessively romantic formula. But that something is meant objectively by buildings and that this meaning cannot be reduced to the subjective reactions or expressed adequately in psychology – yes, of that I *am* sure, and so are you. Questions of priority are a matter of complete indifference in every genuine instance of expert knowledge of a subject; true knowledge always has its *primeurs*, even when it 'was there' before.

Next: you defend yourself against my comment that it is a pity that much of your work is lost. However: I only regretted this because that was what you wrote to me in your last letter but one: stating that, unfortunately, much of what you write vanishes with the setting sun. Now that I accept that, and am thinking of a way to help, you feel insulted, like Hamlet, who plays the madman but flies into a rage when people believe that he really is one. I think that there is no need for any official optimism in the distance between us – it would ill become Ginster to issue military despatches, and there really is nothing to laugh about. Things as such are a matter of indifference – I say them in the interests of our relationship. It could not survive a correspondence which denies actual difficulties and unerringly takes on the character of an apologia. In this connection I can admit to you that I often feel quite uncomfortable with Kierkegaard – I have gone deeper into theological categories than I wished and am worried that, in attempting to save the situation and, above all, of course, to effect a natural reconciliation, I have burst out laughing too much. Well, then – you will soon see.

That you would end up in France was just what I expected – in spite of your present blind spot as regards bouillabaisse (which, by the way, is feminine, not neuter, and which I also find very tasty, although you will not argue with me for preferring the Marseillaise). I hope that you are relaxing properly – I'm sure that you need it, too. I am becoming anxious about my chances in Berlin. The Social Democrats are certain to leave the government coalition in the autumn, and then there will be even less call for people like me than there is now.

Please be so kind as to write and tell me whether you received the Ravel article from U-E – just for the sake of order, so that otherwise I can put in a complaint there. I see the F. Z. more often now and enjoy reading your reviews – something which I cannot claim of those written by Diebold, but above all of Kircher's and Reifenberg's articles. On the other hand, Brentano has made a more decent start in Moscow than I would have thought possible.

It would be best for you to write to me at the Karersee: Hotel Karersee, Carezza al Lago, Italia, Dolomiti. You mustn't be angry with me if I can't manage to write long letters from there. I am completely exhausted and will be leading as mythical an existence as possible.

I expect, though, that you will be writing again before you leave.

Give Lili my very best wishes. Gretel wrote to me today about your telephone call to say goodbye. By the way, she has *not* been informed about my state of health.

As ever, your old

Teddie.

Original: typescript with handwritten corrections and additions; Siegfried Kracauer papers, Deutsches Literaturarchiv, Marbach am Neckar.

new aphorisms: this refers to 'Motive V: Hermeneutik', *Anbruch*, nos. 7/8, 1930 (see Adorno, GS 18, pp. 19–23; GS 19, p. 641).

Heinz ... for his 50th birthday: Heinrich Simon's fiftieth birthday was on 31 July 1930.

more tolerant towards ... Tucholsky: The year before, Kracauer's report on a reading by Kurt Tucholsky (1890–1935) in Frankfurt am Main ended with the words: 'The packed hall proved that Tucholsky has a considerable public even in Frankfurt. The audience exploded in radical jubilation; it was precisely the cheapest aperçus which received the loudest applause. The public will have deserved them' ('Tucholsky in Frankfurt', *Frankfurter Zeitung*, 26 March 1929; see Kracauer, W 5, no. 442).

blind spot as regards bouillabaisse: 'Why in Marseilles, of all places? Presumably for the many snobs who prefer a bouillabaisse to the Marseillaise' ('Kabarett und Operette', *Frankfurter Zeitung*, 6 August 1930; see Kracauer, W 5, no. 498).

Social Democrats ... the government coalition: after the Reichstag elections of 14 September 1930, the SPD [Sozialdemokratische Partei Deutschlands] did not abandon Heinrich Brüning's minority government.

Brentano ... in Moscow: Bernard von Brentano (1901–1964), journalist and author; Kracauer succeeded him in the Berlin office of the *Frankfurter Zeitung*. In 1933 he went into exile in Switzerland, but returned to the Federal Republic of Germany in 1949. Under the abbreviation 'bB', he reported from Moscow on Russo-German relations: 'Die deutsch-russischen Beziehungen (Von unserem Sonderberichterstatter)', *Frankfurter Zeitung*, 27 July 1930.

Gretel wrote to me: not preserved.

70 Kracauer to Adorno
St Malo, 24.8.1930

St-Malo (Brétagne)
Hôtel de France et
de Chateaubriand.
24 August 30.

Dear Teddie,

I was so busy during my last week in Berlin that I could no longer write to you. Above all I was taken up with questions concerning the staff of the newspaper, about which I had to have endless conversations – then with some politics, and finally with some urgent articles. The last of these, which I wrote attacking Stefan Zweig and the rotten state of German literary criticism, caused quite a stir according to reports that reached me here. On Saturday we travelled directly to Paris, where I had a talk with Reifenberg on Sunday. I shall be there again for another week on the way back. It is only here in St-Malo that I realize for the first time how turbulent the last six months have been. I am dead, reading one French detective story after another and doing only a little work on my novel. Chateaubriand was born in St-Malo, an enchanting place which is entirely to my taste: a harbour for ships from England, a beach, the town, a square with cafés and open-air cinemas, and fashionable Dinard, the perfect place to spend an afternoon, ten minutes away by motor-boat. The whole town is surrounded by walls which make for a most delightful walk. If I ever can and wish to retire to embark on a major work, St-Malo will come in for serious consideration. As for the rest, there are clouds on the horizon: the situation in Germany is more than serious – for the paper as well. We are going to have 3 to 4 million unemployed, and I can see no way out. There is a doom hanging over this country, and I know very well that it is not only that of capitalism. That this system can become so bestial does not come down only to economic factors. (How should I be able to express it? It is just that I observe over and over again in France – where, however, there is also plenty to criticize – everything that has been destroyed back home: fundamental decency, good nature as a whole and, along with this, every kind of trust that people have in one another.) As, however, in our country a revolution would not, as perhaps it did in Russia, stimulate a 'people' full of fresh energy to action, I have no belief either in the healing powers of revolution. I can only perceive a general mess, and I could almost feel that it would be best if everyone could just go on muddling through.

I hope that you have already recovered from the exertions of your work on Kierkegaard! At least more peaceful times are beckoning to you now. What is the weather like? And is that splendid hotel still awash with Italian high aristocracy? I can still remember every detail of it very clearly.

On the way back to Berlin I shall be in Frankfurt for a day and a half. I shall telephone you at once.

Lili sends her very best wishes to both of you. Kindest regards to Gretel,

Your old Friedel.

Original: MS; Theodor W. Adorno Archiv, Frankfurt am Main.

attacking Stefan Zweig: 'Weltjugendstadt? – Brünstiger Zauber! Nebst einer Anmerkung über Literaturkritik', *Frankfurter Zeitung*, 17 August 1930 (see Kracauer, W 5, no. 501) – i.e. the review of Otto Zarek, *Begierde: Roman einer Weltstadtjugend*, Vienna: Zsolnay, 1930, which includes these words: 'And now at last I come to *Stefan Zweig*. It is not the first time that he has indulged in gushing adulation of an unworthy object .... He diminishes his own reputation; he helps pieces of poor hack writing to be taken seriously; and he brings literary criticism into utter disrepute.'

Chateaubriand: François René Vicomte de Chateaubriand (1768–1848), diplomat and author.

71 Adorno to Kracauer
Frankfurt am Main, 17.9.1930

DR TH. WIESENGRUND-ADORNO
FRANKFURT A. M.-OBERRAD
SEEHEIMER STRASSE 19 TEL. SPESSART 62480

17 September 1930.

Dear Friedel,

Here is a little essay which I have written and request you to find a home for in the F. Z. if you like it. As this is a subject dear to my heart, I have taken pains to write as simply as possible. The quotations are great. The *enquête* appeared in Ullstein's *Uhu*.

It is a pity that I saw you only so briefly; there was still so much more to discuss that barely surfaced in an hour. In any event, I shall come to Berlin straight after the examination (fingers crossed).

I hope to hear from you very soon. How do you like the Kierkegaard?

Very best wishes to you and Lili from your old

Teddie.

Original: typescript with stamped letterhead; Siegfried Kracauer papers, Deutsches Literaturarchiv, Marbach am Neckar.

little essay: 'Was lieben Sie eigentlich an Ihrem Mann?' [What is it that you really love about your husband?], *Neue Blätter für den Sozialismus*, January 1931 (see Adorno, GS 20.2, pp. 557–9, 817).

Ullstein's Uhu: at this point Peter Suhrkamp was a member of the *Uhu* editorial board. In the September 1930 issue the periodical published twelve 'anonymous confessions' (pp. 69–71) in which female readers replied to the question 'What do you really love about your husband?'

72 Adorno to Kracauer

Kronberg im Taunus, 27.9.1930

Cronberg im Taunus.
Hotel Frankfurter Hof.
27 September 1930.

Dear Friedel, thanks for the letter and the manuscript. I am very glad that you like the first chapter – first, because it does, after all, set the tone for the whole thing and could scarcely be accepted if there were deep-seated resistance to the conception as a whole, and, second, because I am aware that, as it is actually an 'exposition', it could be outdone in originality and what its thought achieves by any of the following chapters. I hope to be able to give you the whole thing very soon. I have settled down here for eight to ten days to correct the three carbon copies – a very protracted and taxing task, but by no means a completely stupid one, as I can still change and improve many details. While correcting it I really do have the impression that for the first time I have brought something into being in the medium of language which will last. I am still assuming, by the way, that you have bestirred yourself and formed a certain impression of the thing as a whole.

I was especially glad about the Kayser business – almost more because of the energy and readiness with which you championed my cause than because of the business itself. As far as my November plans for Berlin are concerned, they are, it is true, a little uncertain, as Tillich has written to me saying that he will not be back in Frankfurt before 1 November. Because of this we have to reckon with the possibility that the business of the habilitation will drag on until Christmas. Tillich will, of course, have to read the book first, and that is no small task. At any rate, the situation has changed, inasmuch as I shall hardly be likely to lecture in the coming semester and should be relatively free until the beginning of the following one. I am planning to come to Berlin for weeks – perhaps months – after the business is settled (fingers crossed) – possibly in January. Until then the Rundschau business will be somewhat delayed even so, and I should be grateful if you would make another agreement with Kayser, pointing out my situation to him. It would be especially important to me, of course, to write not just 'glosses' but independent essays like the ones the NR also publishes about the visual arts, and, if possible, to build up a music column. It would be good if you would advocate this to Herr Dr K. If you give me his address and a few tips I shall write to him. As to which issues, I shall leave it to Gretel to do what is necessary, but would be very glad if you would make the selection together with her, which is very important, as in the end you are the only one who knows the man and the internal workings of the journal. Thank you very much indeed in advance. By the way, you can make use of the fact that the Frankfurter Rundfunk has invited me to give lectures (on a major scale) about modern music.

Cassirer-Verlag has sent me *Spuren*, what a really terrible disaster. It is shameful – I compared it to the *Lustiger Marcell Salzer-Buch*. If Reifenberg should write about it now – that should be something rather delicious. Incidentally, Bloch has also been picking your pocket and has stolen a Paris story from you which I definitely remember hearing from you (the drunken woman who talks about *pauvreté* and *saleté*). After this book Bloch is a spent force intellectually, and being a teller of fairy-tales is, in the final analysis, no existence at all.

I have spoken at length with Benjamin – he will tell you about it.

Have you received my little essay 'Why do you really love your husband?'? You don't mention it, and I should be eager to hear from you.

I am just reading *The Old Curiosity Shop* by Dickens and being greatly moved – it is a book which ranks with the greatest: full of mysteries, compared with which those in Bloch's books are revealed as the latrine rumours from eternity, which they are.

In the latest *Fackel* there is a devastating polemic by Kraus against Willy Haas – you absolutely must read it.

The monodrama *La Voix humaine* by Cocteau is very beautiful – possibly something for Lili to translate.

In conclusion, two funny things. First: Baumann, my bookseller, told me that, because of your review (which I consider *magnificent*), Zarek's book has become a great success, that many people have been buying it and referring directly to your review, and that Zsolnay's representative spoke of your review with great gratitude. This does indeed go far beyond all that one might think possible. Second: Schoen has given a good definition of Margarete Susmann: she is, he says, a synthesis of Martin Buber and Fini Pfannes.

Good luck with the novel! How far have you got with it? I had started to compose again but have not had the peace to do so yet – and now the corrections have got in the way.

Very best wishes to you and Lili from your old

Teddie.

Original: typescript with handwritten corrections; Siegfried Kracauer papers, Deutsches Literaturarchiv, Marbach am Neckar.

thanks for the letter: not preserved.

the Kayser business: Germanist Rudolf Kayser (1889–1964) headed the editorial board of the *Neue Rundschau* from 1923 to the end of 1932. In 1933 he went into exile in the Netherlands and in 1935 to the USA, where he embarked on a university career. No intervention by Kracauer is documented among his papers, and it must have been effected verbally in view of his good relations with Kayser;

Kracauer was a frequent contributor to the *Neue Rundschau* from 1930 onwards.

Tillich has written to me: the correspondence with Paul Tillich is preserved among Adorno's papers only from 1953 onwards.

independent essays: this plan was not realized at this time as far as the *Neue Rundschau* was concerned.

write to him: no letter to Rudolf Kayser corresponding to this description survives.

Lectures … about modern music: documented in the GS: 'Zum Rundfunkkonzert vom 8. April 1931' (see Adorno, GS 20.2, pp. 793–6).

sent me Spuren: Ernst Bloch, *Spuren* (Berlin: Paul Cassirer, 1930); it came out in September of that year. Trans. Anthony A. Nassar as *Traces* (Stanford, CA: Stanford University Press, 2006).

Marcell Salzer-Buch: Marcell Salzer (1873–1930), reciter and author, published *Das lustige Salzer-Buch, heitere Lektüre- und Vortragsstücke* in 1911 (Hamburg: Anton J. Benjamin); further volumes and numerous reprints appeared in later years.

Reifenberg should write about it: Benno Reifenberg, 'Wie sieht unsere Zeitliteratur aus? Spuren: Zu dem ersten Band der Schriften von Ernst Bloch', *Frankfurter Zeitung*, 23 November 1930. Reifenberg approached the book by way of a monologue addressed to 'Friend Bloch', followed by seven 'roundabout ways to *Spuren*', whose subheadings are, among others, 'Tale', 'Forwards into the 19th century' and 'The disenchanter'.

Paris story … pauvreté *and* saleté: 'In the Rue Blondel lay a drunken woman who was picked up by the policeman. "*Je suis pauvre*", said the woman. "Well, you don't have to puke all over the street because of that!" roared the policeman. "*Que voulez-vous, monsieur, la pauvreté, c'est déjà moitié la saleté*", said the woman, and took a drink' (see Ernst Bloch, *Spuren*, Frankfurt am Main: Suhrkamp, 1969, p. 21).

The Old Curiosity Shop: Charles Dickens (1812–1870); on *The Old Curiosity Shop* (1840/41) see Adorno, 'Rede über den *Raritätenladen* von Charles Dickens' [Talk about Charles Dickens's *The Old Curiosity Shop*], *Frankfurter Zeitung*, 18 April 1931 (see Adorno, GS 11, pp. 515–22, 700).

Kraus against Willy Haas: Karl Kraus was commenting on the correspondence which he had carried on with Willy Haas since 15 February 1930, documented in the same volume (September 1930).

La Voix humaine: Jean Cocteau, *La Voix humaine*, Paris: Librairie Stock, 1930.

Baumann, my bookseller: the Frankfurt directory for 1930 includes a bookseller named Fritz Baumann with the address Oeder Weg 1.

review … Zarek's book: see letter no. 70, note.

Buber: Martin Buber (1878–1965), philosopher of religion and professor at the Johann Wolfgang Goethe-Universität (1924–33); he emigrated to Palestine.

Pfannes: Fini Pfannes, born Josefine Proper (1894–1967), a dietician, domestic science expert, advertising entrepreneur, and official in the Frauenverband, born in Romania; from 1920, she lived in Frankfurt am Main.

73 Kracauer to Adorno
[Berlin,] 21.12.1930

21 December 30.

Dear Teddie,

I could fill a letter with explanations about why I had not written a letter – but that would be tiring for us both. The fact is, however, that I have been living under great strain, and basically without any events that would tempt me to share them with you. Work for the paper, the city and the novel; as regards people, mainly Bloch and Benjamin – that's about all. I have had some scanty news about you, though – through Gretel, whom we met on one occasion, through Marcuse, about a radio discussion with Brecht, through reports about your radio talks, and not least through your articles themselves. I thought the review in the latest literary supplement very good; the conversation with Krenek was a little dry, which must have been occasioned by the shortage of space. I have no idea, though, how things stand with your habilitation. I take it that it will go through after Christmas?!

Yesterday I sent a package off to you. It contains Cocteau's *Opium* and a wallet, which I hope you will like. Why should we always give each other books? I have tried to suit your taste with a wallet of this kind. If you should already have the Cocteau, please return it and send me another request. I have specially reserved the right to exchange it.

As for more important matters, there is really only the performance of Brecht's didactic play *Die Maßnahme* to report. Yesterday evening there was a discussion of it here in the context of the International Tribune, chaired by Wittvogel. I was there for an hour to get a taste of the business. Objections were raised, and Brecht responded or had them noted by his secretary. This was only logical, as he takes the view that it is possible to alter the play, incorporate new parts, etc. All this is just so that you know. You will probably have heard that I had discussions with Brecht on two or three occasions. When the conversation is about theoretical matters, it feels like talking to a boy in the Upper Fourth. The craziest thing is that many people fall hook, line and sinker for this inverted romanticism, the brutality of which is only possible in a National Socialist country. In the case of Benjamin, I know of reasons which explain this; in others, not. Some time soon I shall be busying myself with Brecht on an article with reference to the Baden didactic play and *Die Maßnahme* and at the same time weaving Döblin's diary essays into it. My starting point is roughly as follows: that Brecht's things have no functional value but do perhaps have a poetic value.

Because of all this jobbing I live quite a secluded life. Benjamin and I had a few splendid conversations about which he will tell you. I am very excited about the Kraus essay after the few samples which he read to us. Bloch's *Spuren* is unfortunately doing very poorly; probably the book is also too expensive. In connection with this it occurs to me: Gretel K. told me that you are preparing a composition for radio to accompany a play by Cocteau. I was very glad about your return to musical creativity. When will the performance be? And another question: have you received Horkheimer's book from Dr Drill? I asked him on the basis of an exchange of letters with H. to give it to you. And how do matters stand as regards your trip to Berlin? We shall be staying here all the time, apart from going away for 10 to 14 days in January.

In the New Year I hope to be able to organize my work more economically. Then, too, I shall be able to write to you more easily and more often.

Original: typescript (carbon copy), fragment; Siegfried Kracauer papers, Deutsches Literaturarchiv, Marbach am Neckar. The location is deduced to be Berlin from the context.

Marcuse: Herbert Marcuse (1898–1979), philosopher and sociologist; his attempt to qualify as a lecturer under Martin Heidegger in 1932 was unsuccessful. A member of the Institute for Social Research, he went into exile in Switzerland in 1933 and the USA in 1934.

radio discussion with Brecht: not documented; the only possibility is Bertolt Brecht's participation in a conference held by Südwestdeutscher Rundfunk on 1 November 1930 at which Brecht spoke on 'radio as an instrument of communication' (see Werner Hecht, *Brecht-Chronik 1898–1956*, Frankfurt am Main: Suhrkamp, 2003, pp. 294f.).

your radio talks: 'Additional studio concerts of new music, at which Dr Wiesengrund-Adorno will give analytical introductory lectures, will offer works by Berg, Wiesengrund-Adorno, Zillig and Skalkottas, and the first performance of the jazz oratorio *H.M.S. Royal Oak*' (see 'Neues vom Frankfurter Sender' [News from the Frankfurt radio station], *Anbruch*, nos. 11/12, 1930).

review in the latest literary supplement: 'Was will die neue Musik' [What does new music mean?], *Frankfurter Zeitung*, 18 December 1930 – i.e. the review of Lotte Kallenbach-Greller, *Geistige und tonale Grundlagen der modernen Musik im Spiegel der Gegenwart und Vergangenheit*, Leipzig: Breitkopf & Haertel, 1930 (see Adorno, GS 19, pp. 346–8, 651).

conversation with Krenek: Ernst Křenek und Theodor W. Adorno, 'Arbeitsprobleme des Komponisten: Gespräch über Musik und soziale Situation' [The composer's working problems: a conversation about music and its social situation], *Frankfurter Zeitung*, 10 December 1930 (see Adorno, GS 19, pp. 433–9, 652).

Cocteau's Opium: Jean Cocteau, *Opium: Journal d'une desintoxication*, Paris: Stock, 1930.

performance of Brecht's didactic play: Bertolt Brecht, *Die Maßnahme* [The measure taken], first performed 13/14 December 1930 at the Haus der Berliner Philharmonie (director: Slatan Dudow). At the première Brecht paved the way for this 'discussion' by distributing questionnaires among the audience (see Brecht, W III, pp. 431–45).

Wittvogel: presumably Karl August Wittfogel (1896–1986), sinologist and author; he collaborated with the Institute for Social Research (1925–40) and emigrated to the USA in 1934.

with Brecht on an article: not realized in this form; Kracauer did review Brecht's *Versuche 8–10: Die Dreigroschenoper, Der Dreigroschenfilm, Der Dreigroschenprozeß* (Berlin: Gustav Kiepenheuer, 1932): 'Ein soziologisches Experiment? Zu Brechts Versuch "Der Dreigroschenprozeß"' [A sociological experiment? On Brecht's essay 'The Threepenny Trial'], *Frankfurter Zeitung*, 28 February 1932 (see Kracauer, W 5, no. 634).

weaving Döblin's diary essays into it: also not realized; for 1930 this might refer to 'Alfred Döblin, Vom alten zum neuen Naturalismus' [Alfred Döblin: from the old to the new naturalism], *Das Tagebuch*, 18 January 1930; 'Deutsche Frauentragödie in Italien' [German woman's tragedy in Italy], *Das Tagebuch*, 19 April 1930; 'Katastrophe in einer Linkskurve' [Catastrophe in a left turn], *Das Tagebuch*, 3 May 1930; 'Die besten Bücher des Jahres' [The best books of the year], *Das Tagebuch*, 13 December 1930 (see *Bibliographie Alfred Döblin*, ed. Louis Huguet, Berlin: Aufbau, 1972, pp. 111f.), or the next article on Döblin after this letter: 'Was soll Herr Hocke tun?' [What should Herr Hocke do?], *Frankfurter Zeitung*, 17 April 1931 (see Kracauer, W 5, No. 550) – i.e. the review of Döblin's *Wissen und Verändern! Offene Briefe an einen jungen Menschen* [Knowing and changing! Open letters to a young person], Berlin: S. Fischer, 1931.

Kraus essay: Walter Benjamin, 'Karl Kraus', *Frankfurter Zeitung*, 10 March 1931–18 March 1931 (in four instalments; see Benjamin, GS II.1, pp. 334–67, GS II.3, pp. 1078–130).

Spuren ... *also too expensive*: the cloth edition cost 9.50 marks.

a composition for radio: also under 'Neues vom Frankfurter Sender': 'Wiesengrund-Adorno has been commissioned by the broadcasting station to write a piece of music for the radio performance of Cocteau's *La Voix humaine*'; see *Anbruch*, nos. 11/12, 1930. The plan was not realized.

Dr Drill: Robert Drill (1870–?), editor of the *Frankfurter Zeitung*.

Horkheimer book: Max Horkheimer, *Anfänge der bürgerlichen Geschichtsphilosophie* (Stuttgart: W. Kohlhammer, 1930). Horkheimer wrote on the title page: 'With old contents but in new clothing from the publisher, these essays are sent with warmest greetings to S. Kracauer from M. Horkheimer' (Kracauer papers, Deutsches Literaturarchiv, Marbach).

exchange of letters with H.: Kracauer thanked Max Horkheimer for the copy with the dedication in a letter of 22 November 1930. He notified him that he would not be able to review it himself for lack of time and promised to search for a replacement among the members of the editorial board. Horkheimer replied on 24 November 1930 that he understood the situation but did not want a review 'from another pen'. In a letter of 1 December 1930, he suggested Adorno as a possible reviewer (all documents in the Kracauer papers, Deutsches Literaturarchiv Marbach).

74 Adorno to Kracauer
Frankfurt am Main, 2.1.1931

DR TH. WIESENGRUND-ADORNO
FRANKFURT A. M.-OBERRAD
SEEHEIMER STRASSE 19 TEL. SPESSART 62480

2 January 1931.

Dear Friedel, it is difficult to resume our correspondence after such a long silence; that is why I let the hurly-burly of the holidays pass by before answering your letter. I hope that you received my present – the graphic *chef d'oeuvre* of *surréalisme* – in good time. I was just about to send you Cocteau's *Opium* when I received it from you – that was why the Max Ernst was delayed. Thank you so much for the Cocteau and the very handsome wallet. It is all the more fitting not to give each other only books because, as a rule, we would send each other the same ones, which would produce a similar result as in the story of the toad which got eaten. The Cocteau is very interesting; sometimes, though, it plays on the edge of the occult and crosses questionably into it; often enough I have the feeling that even popes like Cocteau are highly fallible. The play for which I am writing a musical accompaniment is called *La Voix humaine* and is a kind of telephone ontology: very, very beautiful, with a psychological surface like *Les Enfants terribles* and very curious theological backgrounds.

To go on to external matters: the business of my habilitation is taking its slow but normal course. Tillich has received the work with great enthusiasm and understood it remarkably well; Schultz is championing it strongly (as is Horkheimer, naturally); Wertheimer doesn't really know what he wants, but there is no question that we shall be able to deal with him. Tillich declares that in any circumstances he will still push the habilitation through in this semester, and I too believe this, as it is not just a matter of goodwill but because I shall have to relieve him on many occasions – which, incidentally, is the greatest drawback of the habilitation, as I am afraid of being so extremely busy that it will be difficult to combine this with my own work – most of all because at present the subject of aesthetics is not represented in Frankfurt at all, and I am to be offered a lectureship in it; the *venia legendi* [permission to lecture] will, of course, be valid for philosophy with no restrictions. The whole business is, of course, a tiresome source of pressure until it is all signed and sealed. But one can get used even to that. Otherwise I am working on the Cocteau music (very strictly constructed) and a major critique (in pamphlet form) of Heidegger's *Sein und Zeit*. I originally thought of publishing it in the Ihering–Brecht–Benjamin journal *Krisis und Kritik*, but since Benjamin and Brecht have distanced themselves to a great extent from the journal project I have had second thoughts. What do you think about the journal plan? I should like to make my own attitude dependent on this to some extent. As far as Brecht is concerned, your argument – playing off the aesthetic against the utility value – seems right, and I should likewise have advocated this long ago, though perhaps arguing it differently. I have also defended it against Benjamin, who has succumbed to a quite peculiar fascination with Brecht's dull nature. Benjamin, moreover, gives me the impression of a deserter pushing to the front. With an infinite belief in culture at heart – far more than us (he calls himself a 'classicist') – he recognizes the breakdown of the organic and is now leaping straight into the opposite extreme – complete inhumanity. He wrote a frightful essay to this effect in *Uhu* about which I spoke my mind to him for the first time, quite openly and entirely recklessly; I believe, by the way, that it was the first time that I have done so with any success. By the way, our relationship has changed in so many ways, inasmuch as he is coming right out of his fox hole and offering criticism (and accepting some), which, despite a decline in politeness, makes dealing with him so much easier. On the Brecht phenomenon, of course, it needs to be said that, in spite of everything, in matters of the politics of art he represents one of the few assets. As I was arguing with Holl today about Herr Oboussier's scandalously stupid criticism of *Die Maßnahme* (whose music may be as stupid as it likes), Holl referred to you as a witness on Oboussier's behalf, which, I must say, greatly offended me. I genuinely believe that at this present moment, when the paper is becoming completely fascist, you should be especially careful about such matters and set your sights on avoiding any accord between the demands of the day and your own convictions which form the ironic subject of your new novel. I really am worried about your relationship with the paper. The dismissal of Feiler is far from being the end of the story; it is being rumoured that Rodenbach and Baberadt are also affected, that Dewall wants to give notice, Brentano has left, Kircher is the coming man, Benno Reifenberg, who is said to have been so unbourgeois, is crazy for war – these are anything but good auspices. Would it not be wise for you to put out feelers *in good time* (i.e. of your own accord) in other directions – at Mosse, perhaps? I see and hear a great deal about the atmosphere at the paper here, and in very intimate detail too; believe me, I don't want to make you nervous and have not succumbed to the general Jewish psychosis, but I regard the situation as critical – that of the paper in general, and yours in particular. Gretel has voiced the same opinion independently of me, purely on the basis of her Frankfurt impressions. Above all, do be careful of Kircher. Brentano, who has become somewhat attached to me and speaks frankly, has told me that Kircher hates you, and, even if Brentano himself is not a wholly irreproachable source, one should not simply shrug off something of that kind. I think, by the way, that Brentano has developed, and in this Frankfurt which has become a complete desert I can at least have a conversation with him (in contrast to Gubler). He is a terrible goy, of course, but with certain decent rebel qualities. A Saint-Loup-en-boche. I saw Soma Morgenstern briefly – still very nice, but he has retreated into his Jewishness as into a mighty fortress and finds *Hiob* so significant – an odd kind of enthusiast. I have not seen Ernst Bloch yet, although he is all afire in Ludwigshafen. I live a much more secluded life than last winter and am writing quite a lot. Incidentally, the *Neue Rundschau* never even replied to my letter. Your criticism of the dryness of my conversation with Křenek is quite right – but how else could one have gone about it without embarking on material aesthetic analyses or openly Marxist ones? I spoke to Gubler about Horkheimer's book; he agreed, but nothing has come of it. He is sure to have dawdled and messed it up, just like everything else. I should be very grateful if you would light a fire under him, as for understandable reasons this review is very important to me. You yourself can probably imagine my view of the book's importance.

I have given a talk on the radio about a novel by Dickens which seemed to me to have come off particularly well, and which I shall be glad to send you if you see any possibility of publishing it (*Zeitung* or *Rundschau*); I have only one copy, otherwise I could send it to you just like that.

In the present situation, would it not be better for you to return to Frankfurt for some time? Gubler will surely want to go into business on his own account; there is no relying on Kircher – so the situation in Berlin seems to me to be somewhat uncertain in economic terms too. But judging by the unanimous verdict of everyone except Heinz and Reifenberg, Gubler seems so incapable of organizing things here that it is possible that you may be urgently needed. Of course, I don't want to intrude in your business, and I am really not writing this to you out of egoism, especially as I myself would be glad to get away from Frankfurt. But I believe that I have a responsibility to discuss these things with you, as one may perhaps see things differently from outside and from a distance than when one is plugged into the daily business of the newspaper.

I have differing views about your last essays. I find many things magnificent, especially the polemics (the Flute Concert). Other things are too carelessly dashed off with your left hand for my taste – like the very thin piece about the Arcades and the essay which began with the words 'In a sophisticated bar which I visit from time to time …'. I assume that this has something to do with the fact that you have concentrated the bulk of your efforts on the novel, which I am very eager to read. This is quite right, I think – it is just that you should write the other things in as unencumbered a way as possible and not under pressure of demands which might compromise your own stuff. Might I see some of the novel?

As soon as I have got my habilitation, I am thinking of coming to Berlin for a few weeks – but I am tempted to suppose that before then you may turn up here sometime on newspaper business.

I was especially pleased with Lili's handwritten greeting – her first – and send her my warmest thanks.

I wish you both all the best as regards health. I was not too well for a while; I had a very painful attack of sinusitis, but now I am all right again. At the moment I have to write a summary of my Kierkegaard – a horribly incestuous business that is giving me more trouble than the whole book.

Do let me hear from you soon. It would be a pity if such gaps occurred between our letters again; little as letters on their own can do, they are still, after all, our one and only means of regular communication.

Very best wishes from your old

Teddie.

Original: typescript with stamped letterhead and handwritten corrections; Siegfried Kracauer papers, Deutsches Literaturarchiv, Marbach am Neckar.

graphic chef d'oeuvre *of* surréalisme: Max Ernst, *La Femme 100 têtes*, Paris: Carrefour, 1929; it was not found in the library which Kracauer left behind.

toad: no fable or similar story which fits the context has so far been discovered. Adorno varies the image at least twice in an unambiguous message which may suggest 'peasant wisdom': 'She embroiled him in the peasant's question about the toad he had eaten: why all the upset, if everything is meant to remain the way it has always been?' (see *Ad vocem Hindemith*, Adorno, GS 16, p. 245), and 'so the peasant's question about the toad he had eaten arises: why did all these things have to be tried out one after another?' (see *Quasi una fantasia*, Adorno, GS 16, pp. 539f. See also Adorno, *Quasi una Fantasia*, trans. Rodney Livingstone. London: Verso, 1992, p. 321).

Schultz: probably Franz Schultz (1877–1950), literary scholar; at the Johann Wolfgang Goethe-Universität since 1921/2.

Wertheimer: Max Wertheimer (1880–1943), psychologist and co-founder of Gestalt psychology; professor of psychology at the Johann Wolfgang Goethe-Universität (1929–33). In 1933 he went into exile in the USA and taught at the New School for Social Research in New York City.

Heidegger … Krisis und Kritik: Walter Benjamin added Adorno and Kracauer to his list of potential contributors to the projected journal he planned with Bertolt Brecht, *Krisis und Kritik* (see Benjamin, GS VI, pp. 619–21, 825–8). From the minutes of a planning meeting of 26 November 1930 preserved among Benjamin's papers, it emerges that Kracauer made the suggestion that Martin Heidegger should be covered by Adorno (the minutes are published in Erdmut Wizisla, *Benjamin und Brecht: Die Geschichte einer Freundschaft*, Frankfurt am Main: Suhrkamp, 2004). Whom Adorno invited to collaborate is not documented, any more than the article mentioned.

essay to this effect in Uhu: the November 1930 edition of *Uhu* published Walter Benjamin's 'Myslowitz–Braunschweig–Marseille: Die Geschichte eines Haschisch-Rausches' (see Benjamin, GS IV.2, pp. 729–37, 1075f.).

Oboussier's … criticism: Robert Oboussier (1900–1957), composer and music critic for the *Frankfurter Zeitung* in Berlin (1930–33); no review of *Die Maßnahme* is preserved in the archives of the Societäts-Verlag either.

Feiler: Arthur Feiler (1879–1942); from 1903 editor for economic affairs and from 1910 on the editorial board for politics of the *Frankfurter Zeitung*; in 1931, in the wake of organizational, personnel and political changes, he moved to a position which tended towards greater conservatism.

Rodenbach: Philip Rodenbach (?–1953); at the *Frankfurter Zeitung* from 1911 to 1943.

Baberadt: Karl Friedrich Baberadt (1880–1943); journalist.

Dewall: Wolf von Dewall (1882–1959), army officer; editor for international affairs and in 1932 Friedrich von Sieburg's successor as London correspondent of the *Frankfurter Zeitung*.

Kircher: Rudolf Kircher (1885–1954), lawyer; in 1912 he joined the *Frankfurter Zeitung* and in 1930 became political correspondent in the Berlin office. He represented the conservative line within the editorial board.

Mosse: Berlin newspaper press named after its founder, Rudolf Mosse (1843–1920), to which the *Berliner Tageblatt* and *Berliner Morgenpost*, among others, belonged.

Saint-Loup-en-boche: the image with which Bernard von Brentano is characterized by Adorno can be interpreted as a German version of the Marquis de Saint-Loup-en-Bray, nephew of the Duc de Guermantes in Marcel Proust's *A la recherche du temps perdu* (see the description of this figure in *In the Shadows of Young Girls in Flower* (trans. James Grieve, London: Penguin, 2004, pp. 308ff.)).

Hiob [Job]: Joseph Roth, *Hiob: Roman eines einfachen Mannes*, Berlin: Gustav Kiepenheuer, 1930.

I have not seen Ernst Bloch yet: Ernst Bloch left Frankfurt am Main for Ludwigshafen over the New Year.

polemics (the Flute Concert): 'Der bejubelte Fridericus Rex', *Frankfurter Zeitung*, 22 December 1930 (see Kracauer, W 6.2, pp. 430–4, 550) – i.e. the review of the film *Das Flötenkonzert von Sanssouci* (director: Gustav Ucicky), Germany, 1930.

piece about the Arcades: 'Abschied von der Lindenpassage', *Frankfurter Zeitung*, 21 December 1930 (see Kracauer, W 5, no. 524).

with the words 'In a sophisticated bar which I visit from time to time…': 'Der Klavierspieler' [The pianist], *Frankfurter Zeitung*, 1 December 1930 (see Kracauer, W 5, no. 518). Instead of 'zuweilen', Kracauer had written 'mitunter' for 'from time to time'.

Lili's handwritten greeting: not preserved in letter no. 73, which has survived as a carbon copy.

summary of my Kierkegaard: in the Theodor W. Adorno Archiv is a carbon copy of a 'self-review' of his writing on Kierkegaard which, until now, has been dated as 'c. 1932' (see letter no. 91).

75 Kracauer to Adorno
[Berlin,] 12.1.1931

12 January 31.

Dear Teddie,

Thank you most of all for the extraordinarily interesting work by Max Ernst, which I shall enjoy looking into frequently. I did not know it. I was absolutely enthralled by the pictures, though without understanding all of them – but that will come with time.

Thank you, too, for your news about the paper. It was very kind of you to write to me about this, even though, of course, I already have a close knowledge of all that has happened. Many sources of news send their streams to me here, and, believe you me, I know exactly which institutions and which individuals are involved – in Frankfurt and in Berlin. (What Brentano told you is not entirely accurate.) I am not coming to Frankfurt – at most for a day at a time, just passing through.

Things have not gone with the Horkheimer book as I had hoped. Gubler sent me an update as follows: 'Wiesengrund has informed me that you wish him to review H's book. Dr Drill has already assigned the book elsewhere after you turned the review down. He will be notifying W. of this.' This was although I had requested him to give you the book and to let me know about the reviewer. Please tell Horkheimer that matters did not go in accordance with my wishes despite my prompt efforts.

It is a pity that you didn't like my Arcades essay, which I myself think is good. Or, rather, it is *not* a pity – for why should we always be of one mind about everything, even the important things?

The journal edited by Brecht, etc., as I hear and believe, is not going to happen at all. I was actively present at a crucial session which, despite the presence of two secretaries who took everything down in shorthand, went on in such a dilettantish fashion that my non-appearance really would not have mattered at all.

I continue to be exceptionally overburdened with my many tasks, including talks with every possible kind of person – talks which will not least come in useful for future novels. I am intensely preoccupied with my novel. I have postponed sociological works and plans until further notice for lack of time.

I hope that your habilitation will soon be sorted out. Write to me soon. It is still more important that we should talk to each other here. I am looking forward very much to your coming.

Lili sends you her very best wishes.

Cordially as ever

Yours

Original: typescript (carbon copy) with handwritten corrections. Siegfried Kracauer papers, Deutsches Literaturarchiv, Marbach am Neckar; the location can be deduced as Berlin from the context.

update: internal memorandum to the editorial board of the *Frankfurter Zeitung*; the one quoted is not preserved among Kracauer's papers.

non-appearance: the equivalent of *ein Nichterscheinen*, the phrase used in the letter.

76 Adorno to Kracauer
[no address; before 20.1.1931]

Dear Friedel, the bearer of this card, Herr Plaut from Frankfurt, is a young *écrivain* who is studying in Berlin and will be looking you up. He will show you some of his pieces (I myself have read nothing of his), and I should be grateful if you would speak with him. In the meantime, you will have received a letter and manuscript from me. Kindest regards, Yours, Teddie.

Original: MS on the back of a visiting-card: Dr Theodor Wiesengrund-Adorno; Siegfried Kracauer papers, Deutsches Literaturarchiv, Marbach am Neckar; location from the context (see letter no. 77).

Plaut: Richard Plaut (1910–1998), son of Kracauer's doctor Theodor Plaut (1874–1938); studied in Frankfurt am Main with Paul Tillich, completing his studies in the field of German language and literature in exile in Switzerland in 1933. From 1938 onwards he lived in the USA, where the family name was changed to Plant; he was Klaus Mann's secretary and wrote for NBC among others until he was appointed to a professorship in German language and literature at City College, New York.

77 Adorno to Kracauer
Frankfurt am Main, 20.1.1931

DR TH. WIESENGRUND-ADORNO
FRANKFURT A. M.-OBERRAD
SEEHEIMER STRASSE 19 SPESSART 62480

20 January 1931.

Dear Friedel,

The little essay on the effects of your Zarek review which is enclosed was sent to me by my bookseller Baumann with a request that it be forwarded to you and offered to you for the *Frankfurter Zeitung*, where he would like to see it published without any mention of his name. I am fulfilling his request without concealing from you that I find the essay very poor and don't believe that you can publish it. I should like to stress this all the more because I gave that wretched Richard *Plaut*, who went to Berlin all by himself, a recommendation to you so that you might take a look at him and vouch for his complete lack of talent, while you, presumably for my sake, probably took great pains on his behalf – and now his drivel is in the paper. *Dixi et animam meam salvavi.*

Incidentally, I cannot conceal from you the fact that your last letter to me greatly offended me. First of all – forgive me – by its length. I took the time to write to you very thoroughly and at length, and, if you had seriously shown an interest in what I had to say, you too could have answered me at length. You must surely still be enough of a Marxist to know that working time in the abstract sense is a measure of all kinds of things, including intentional ones. Next, because of the arrogant tone in which you refer, or much rather do not refer, to my sentence about the newspaper – which, God knows, I wrote only in accordance with your views and from a distance, and not to give you instruction about any kind of facts – without finding so much as a single unambiguous word with which to state your position. The Gubler affair, in which an injustice was done not only to me but also to Horkheimer, is also part of this. Horkheimer had sent you his book at your own instigation for you to review it; at first you were willing to do so, but then you declined, and it was decided that it should not be reviewed at all. Then I got involved; Gubler or Drill or whoever it was messed things up through sheer sloppiness, and now there is the possibility that the book may fall into the hands of somebody who will tear it to pieces after you had originally declared your willingness to do something *in its favour*. My opinion is that you should at least have a look at the galley proofs. By the way, when I asked Herr Gubler, if I could not get the book, at least not to publish any review at all for those reasons, he became extraordinarily aggressive towards me, and I had to put up with being told some very unpleasant things by that ill-mannered little Switzer. All in all, he behaves to me with that same hostility which your friends generally display towards me, and he was rude about me to Ernst Bloch. Now this, of course, is not your fault, but this would be true to his character and, moreover, would give you the best of opportunities to display a solidarity which you do not value because it can be taken for granted.

Finally, I was also angered by the complacent manner in which you shrugged off my objective criticisms. If you regard as superfluous any disagreement about factual matters between people for whom person and matter are inseparable and take refuge in personal idiosyncrasies, then I have no idea what significance you assign to our correspondence in general. When I shall be coming to Berlin is quite uncertain, so it will not do for you to rely on a presence in which all will be well and until then treat things in a 'dilatory' fashion which will not bear it.

That is all I had to say to you today. The business of the habilitation is still not decided.

Give Lili my best best wishes.
Yours as ever,
Teddie.

Mind you, I would not wish to entangle you in an action involving Gubler, whom I can deal with by myself. It is solely a matter of your behaviour towards me.

Original: typescript with stamped letterhead and handwritten corrections; Siegfried Kracauer papers, Deutsches Literaturarchiv, Marbach am Neckar.

little essay on the effects of your Zarek review: not preserved; for the resonance of Kracauer's review, see letters no. 70 and 72.

within the newspaper: Richard Plaut wrote reviews for, among others, the *Frankfurter Zeitung*; some articles from 1930/31 are documented in Andreas Sternweiler, *Frankfurt, Basel, New York: Richard Plant*, Berlin: Rosa Winkel, 1996.

Dixi et animam meam salvavi (I have spoken and saved my soul): traditional concluding formula for speeches in ancient Rome.

78 Kracauer to Adorno
[no address], 23.1.1931

23 January 31.

Dear Teddie,

I am astonished at the offended tone of your letter and can only declare to you that you are wrong to feel injured.

It is unfair when you complain about the excessive brevity of my letter. Quite apart from the fact that quantity is not the main criterion, I had written you a longer letter only a short time before and naturally assumed that you would rather receive a shorter answer quickly than a more extensive one perhaps after several weeks – because in the end I must trust that you are aware of my excessive workload even without any explicit mention of it. Moreover, there was really no mistaking its cordiality and sympathy.

Nor can you call my tone arrogant. I do in fact think – and we have often talked about this in the past – that criticism of achievements, assuming that it takes place on our level, has its limits. You found the Arcades essay too thin, and I replied to you that I thought it was good. As you gave no further reason for your verdict, I had nothing to go by to explain my view of the situation. I also added then that I took no offence at such differences of opinion, and indeed I believe that, on condition that a shared mode of perception exists, they should and must be tolerated. You know very well that I have often criticized your articles, and that in doing so I was aware that this criticism was not the last word on the subject. Here I set myself apart from the interpreters *à tout prix* – you can imagine whom I mean. You think *that* is arrogant? It is reasonable.

As for the reviewing of Horkheimer's book, you have apparently been completely misinformed. When Horkheimer spoke with me in Berlin about his book, I explained at once in the course of our conversation that there was every prospect that I would not get to review the book, but that in any event I wanted to make sure of a good reviewer for it. I subsequently received a copy of his book and informed him yet again in writing of what I had already told him. I wrote to Dr Drill to this effect. Hardly had this happened than Horkheimer informed me that, if I did not review it, he would appreciate it if you did. I immediately passed on the information to Dr Drill and thought that that settled the matter. It was only much later that I had the message passed on to you from Gubler saying that, in the meantime, Dr Drill had assigned the book to someone else. I urgently request you to explain this to Herr Horkheimer – that I had put myself out for him to a quite exceptional degree, and that I am very anxious that he should acknowledge this and not spread reports about me which suggest otherwise. That would be misleading and unwelcome to me. Moreover, I will even go beyond my previous efforts and ask Herr Dr Drill about the reviewer. In a newspaper, other and even more important things do not always go as one wishes – you should know that. Herr Gubler, by the way, has to my knowledge nothing at all to do with this whole affair.

Finally, I don't understand your assertion that I comfortably and arrogantly shrugged off your information regarding the F. Z. On the contrary, I said how kind it was of you to write to me about it. I must at least intimate to you the fact that I know the state of affairs there very well, and I don't see anything high-handed in this statement of mine either.

Because of a salary cut of 100 marks per month I am still in a …

Original: typescript (carbon copy), fragment; Siegfried Kracauer papers, Deutsches Literaturarchiv, Marbach am Neckar.

to Dr Drill: in a letter of 26 January 1931 (Siegfried Kracauer papers, Deutsches Literaturarchiv, Marbach) Kracauer asked Robert Drill for information concerning the choice of a reviewer, expressed his regret that the book had not been reviewed by Adorno, and emphasized that Horkheimer deserved a positive review of his book.

79 Adorno to Kracauer
Königstein, 3.3.1931

Königstein, 3 March 1931.

Dear Friedel and dear Lili,

Please forgive my belated thanks for your kind telegram, which gave me great pleasure. I have been through a terribly stressful and, so to speak, enervating period in every respect, and to calm down a bit I have settled here for a few days, just at the very time where the seasons are colliding – a cosmic spectacle which is affecting me in a somewhat curious way. To recover from this in its turn, I am going to Berlin at the end of the week and hope to see you both very soon. So, *à bientôt*, and very best wishes from your

Teddie.

Original: typescript, postcard: Königstein in Taunus: Siegfried Kracauer archive, Deutsches Literaturarchiv, Marbach am Neckar.

telegram: not preserved.

enervating period: on 23 February the proceedings for Adorno's habilitation came to an end with the conferring of the *venia legendi* (permission to lecture: Universitätsarchiv Frankfurt am Main).

80 Kracauer to Adorno
[no address], 1.5.1931

1 May 31.

Dear Teddie,

I shall be thinking of you on the occasion of your inaugural lecture tomorrow. It is a remarkable thing – a beginning like this, with all its implications. I congratulate you on it in terms of content: I wish for you that you will make the best possible thing of this position, and always the right one. The potential for this still exists even under the present circumstances. I would be very glad to have an extensive discussion with you about how your functions might be organized in view of our shared interests in this field – but that will only be possible when we see each other again.

If you have written any interesting new essays, please send them to me.

I have plenty of projects, but they will have to lie fallow for another six months – at least, as long as I am working on my novel. In the meantime, I am trying a few experiments and producing by-products which will have to reveal their purpose only in the light of later work.

Lili too sends you her congratulations and warmest regards.

Your old

Original: typescript (carbon copy); Siegfried Kracauer papers, Deutsches Literaturarchiv, Marbach am Neckar.

your inaugural lecture tomorrow: the lecture took place on 8 May 1931 (see the date given on the invitation card in *Adorno in Frankfurt: Ein Kaleidoskop von Texten und Bildern*, ed. Wolfram Schütte (Frankfurt am Main: Suhrkamp, 2003), p. 113; 'Die Aktualität der Philosophie', Adorno, GS 1, pp. 325–44); no information survives as to whether it was originally planned for 2 May or if there is a mistake in the date written on the letter.

81 Adorno to Kracauer
Frankfurt am Main, 29.5.1931

DR THEODOR WIESENGRUND-ADORNO

PRIVATDOZENT AN DER
UNIVERSITÄT FRANKFURT A. M.

FRANKFURT A. M.-OBERRAD
19 SEEHEIMER STRASSE
SPESSART 62480

29 May 1931.

Dear Friedel,

This letter, planned a hundred times, has been postponed again and again. First of all, I must tell you that your last one, on the occasion of the inaugural lecture, gave me the greatest pleasure, and nobody could appreciate such a letter more than I of all people, as I am just as dependent nowadays on signs, gestures and demonstrations (on account of an unimaginable scepticism towards all that is merely internal) as I was in earlier days, whether grey or rosy – and my instincts in that direction were certainly not disappointed by your letter. I am able to appreciate this all the more as I am well aware that you yourself are not as sensitive about these matters as I am, and so the very fact that you wrote me those lines represents an act of self-abnegation on your part, or at the very least a very exact image of the type of person I am. And it is precisely against this background that the sign seems to me so clear and beautiful. Incidentally, your letter was the only agreeable thing to come out of the whole inaugural lecture. I am enclosing it for you, and all I will say on the matter is that I decided on the relatively programmatic form (which is not at all up my alley) for no other reason than that everyone kept wanting to hear in clear and concise words what my expectations of philosophy actually were. But when it came to the point, it wasn't to anybody's liking. Wertheimer had a convulsive fit of weeping from rage and excitement; Tillich was repelled by the form because of its definitive tone; Mannheim cursed; and Horkheimer (together with Leo, who has metamorphosed completely into one of his swarm of tsetse flies and satellites) thought it not Marxist enough. You can have no idea of the wrath – the flood of hatred, opposition and malice – that the lecture brought down on me. It would be too tedious to go into individual details, but not a single stage was lacking – from 'salon philosophy' and baseless arguments to abstruseness and complete craziness. (Leo found the whole thing 'inhuman'; he is planning to qualify as a lecturer.) None of this is at all surprising. I don't fit in. I have no wish to forge a 'science' or 'world view'; I want something that is fundamentally different – something which is entirely incompatible with academic categories and embitters people who basically want to enquire into the meaning of existence in Aristotelian or Hegelian terms. This was clear to me from the outset, and I believed that on this occasion I really ought to say what I think. But when everyone is against you all at once, even those you could count on in the past, then it really can cut you to the heart, no matter how strong you may feel. The feeling of utter intellectual isolation becomes all the more oppressive the more it reveals itself in the immanent confrontation with prevailing opinions. Now the waves have calmed down to some extent. I am working together with Horkheimer on a sketch of a theory of dialectics; Tillich has given in, but I am left with the prospect of a lengthy confrontation with Wertheimer and Riezler, from whom there came the 'fundamental and ontological' criticisms at the conclusion of my lecture. However, in practical terms the whole scandal has had *no* practical consequences, and none regarding the projected lectureship. The students have followed along nicely. In general, I get on very well with them – both in the introductory seminar, which I am conducting together with Tillich and which is attended by over 60 people, and in my own seminar on aesthetics, where I deal with Lukács's theory of the novel. If you are interested I could send you the notes. In the context of this seminar I am intending to discuss your work on the detective novel, which, despite all its modifications, certainly ought not to fall by the wayside. I enjoy working with the students; I certainly have the nicest and most talented ones that can be drummed up. Among them is Dolf Sternberger, who is coming on well and has something to be said for him, in contrast to the repulsive Günther Stern.

My health has not been all that good; I had a very unpleasant cough which hung on for a long time and is beginning to slacken off only now. In addition to that I am not sleeping as well as before, which is a great nuisance for my work. I am preparing a book of essays under the title *Philosophische Kritik* [Philosophical criticism]. It is going to contain a piece about Heidegger, one about psychoanalysis, one about the concept of *Gegebenheit* or 'givenness' in positivism, and one opposing the concept of a history of the mind [*Geistesgeschichte*], with a longish preface on philosophical criticism. There is a lot of material on the subject, but it is still quite impossible to predict how long it will take to get it into its final form.

Nothing has happened yet about Kierkegaard; I have heard nothing from Mannheim; Benjamin seems not to have embarked on anything, either – he talks only about financial matters, which is not altogether appropriate to our relationship, especially as things are really not as bad with him as he makes out. Have you had a read of the Kierkegaard? And what do you think? Here too the waves of stupidity are rising high, and I would be really grateful to hear something sensible about it for once, whether positive or negative. I would have sent you a better copy long ago, but it is impossible to winkle one out – this too must be numbered among the creature comforts of academia.

How did you like the Dickens? I have heard nothing previously about it from you, and I am somewhat anxious. I have just written a series of short pieces with a melancholy philosophical content which are to be called 'Words without Songs', and which I should like to send to the F. Z.

Of your things I especially liked the analysis of artistic photography (a pet hate of mine) and the essay about the movie fan/film star and an ophthalmic intervention – and also the one about Thiess, which might just have been rather more explicit in its conclusions, though the lack of that, of course, is explicable in view of the fact that it was written for the newspaper. You may perhaps be interested to know that it was that very essay which particularly displeased Heinz Simon, whom I met the following day at a party. On the other hand, though, the highly intelligent Albert Hahn spoke of your *Angestellten* with great enthusiasm.

How is your novel going? I expect it must be pressing towards a compact end now, which is borne out by the fact that you are writing less often for the newspaper than before. I am very excited about it. Perhaps I could see part of it sometime – as could Ernst Bloch, to whom, by the way, you might give a copy of my lecture, if you would. In the latest volume of *Scheinwerfer* there is a long essay of mine which might possibly interest you.

I had a very nice time with Gretel in Homburg, although both of us are seriously overworked. Before that we also had a very pleasant time with Grab, whom I particularly like, although he obviously had no great *succès* in our Berlin. What he writes is very variable and still very soft, but full of talent and genuine human experience – only it is still very *avant-guerre*; one cannot, after all, write *Recherche du temps perdu* all over again.

Gretel is sure to have informed you about the Carl Dreyfuss affair. I am convinced that it is by no means as voluntary as he pretends. Please don't exert yourself on his behalf, perhaps out of consideration for me. I myself am already doing enough for him and am by no means willing to regard the paper as a site for offloading material. There is a lot about his attitude that I don't like in the least, and I am cynical enough to ask where the quality in a man like Carl resides once he has – by an act of inexcusable irresponsibility – cut himself off from the only sphere in which he was actually of any account. I don't think much of the 'literary career' with which he is preoccupied. This is only for your information; I have no wish to do him any harm as regards the outside world but would only deter you from acts of solidarity which I fear could bear little fruit here.

Well, I have chattered on to you quite enough for now. I should be glad to have our correspondence up and running again. This is all the more necessary as I see absolutely no concrete prospect at all of coming to Berlin.

Please give Lili my warmest greetings.

Much love to you yourself from your faithful

Teddie.

Original: typescript with printed letterhead, handwritten additions and corrections: Siegfried Kracauer papers, Deutsches Literaturarchiv, Marbach am Neckar

inaugural lecture: Kracauer was informed about this by his aunt Hedwig Kracauer, who was in the audience, in a letter of 17 May 1931: 'On the Friday before Ascension Day we were at Teddie's inaugural public lecture, invited in the most formal terms. Such a large audience came streaming in that we had to migrate from lecture room Q to the main auditorium. … This time he really made an attempt to make his subject (which, of course, you know) as generally comprehensible as possible. I really understood it too, as long as I was sitting there, but I lack the points of comparison, and I couldn't judge whether he was being original or simply reproductive … All Teddie's friends and acquaintances were in the auditorium' (Kracauer papers, Deutsches Literaturarchiv, Marbach).

Mannheim: Karl Mannheim (1893–1947), sociologist; professor in Frankfurt am Main (1930–33), at the London School of Economics until 1945. On the sociological trend which he established, see Adorno, *Das Bewusstsein der Wissenssoziologie* (GS 10.1, pp. 31–46).

tsetse: appears as *tsetser* in the letter; probably a reference to the tsetse fly, the bite of which causes sleeping sickness.

a sketch of a theory of dialectics: this is the beginning, at least symbolically, of what was to become the *Dialektik der Aufklärung* [Dialectic of enlightenment]; the collaboration was not achieved until their period of exile in the USA.

Riezler: Kurt Riezler (1882–1955); diplomat, curator of the Johann Wolfgang Goethe-Universität (1928–33), exiled to the USA in 1938; taught at the New School for Social Research.

introductory seminar … seminar on aesthetics: the activities as assistant and university lecturer are announced in letter no. 58.

the notes: not preserved.

Sternberger: Dolf Sternberger (1907–1989), political scientist and journalist; his dissertation on Martin Heidegger is the subject of a report which Adorno prepared in 1932 for Paul Tillich (documented in Adorno/Horkheimer, *Briefwechsel* 1, pp. 546–51).

Günther Stern: Günther Anders (1902–1992), journalist and author; studied with Edmund Husserl and Martin Heidegger; in exile in France (1933) and the USA (1936). He planned to study for his habilitation with Paul Tillich at the Johann Wolfgang Goethe-Universität but attributed part of the responsibility for the failure of this plan to Adorno in a letter of 27 August 1963: 'When I came to Frankfurt long ago for my habilitation, I felt that your attitude towards my plan and the steps which you took to oppose it were monocratic' (see Adorno, *Bildmonographie*, p. 276).

a book of essays under the title Philosophische Kritik: the plan was never realized.

'Words without Songs': in *Frankfurter Zeitung*, 14 July 1931 (see Adorno, GS 20.2, pp. 537–43, 817).

analysis of artistic photography: 'The Kurfürstendamm is the modern *Siegesallee*. Instead of marble monuments of rulers standing with one leg extended, it is scattered with *photographs* of *prominent individuals* which represent something, or at any rate are meant to do so … the afternoon is the right time to saunter from photograph to photograph. Highly artistic photographs follow in succession at every step' ('Der Kurfürstendamm als Siegesallee', *Frankfurter Zeitung*, 22 May 1931; see Kracauer, W 5, no. 560).

film star: 'Rund um die Filmstars', *Frankfurter Zeitung*, 9 May 1931 (see Kracauer, W 6.2, pp. 504–7). The article ends: 'However, at the moment we are far away from the time when all movie fans will have their vision corrected.' Adorno's praise of Kracauer's critical essay 'über den gestochenen Filmstar' is a complex play on words using a double meaning of film star. It refers both to the idea of a movie idol (film star) and the cause of blurry vision (film) as well as to cataract surgery (den Star stechen) as their remedy. The translation suggests an affinity with Paul's report that something like scales fell from his eyes, and his sight was restored (Acts of the Apostles, 9: 18).

Thiess: 'Bemerkungen zu Frank Thieß' [Remarks on Frank Thiess], *Frankfurter Zeitung*, 3 May 1931 (see Kracauer, W 5, no. 555). Kracauer discussed the complete works to date of the author Frank Thiess (1890–1977), who after 1945 was regarded as a representative of 'internal emigration', in the series 'Wie erklären sich große Bucherfolge?' [How can best-sellers be explained?].

Hahn: Ludwig Albert Hahn (1889–1968), national economist and banker; professor at the Johann Wolfgang Goethe-Universität from 1928; exiled in 1933; worked at the New School for Social Research in New York.

In the latest volume of Scheinwerfer: the latest work of Adorno's at this time, which appeared in *Der Scheinwerfer: Blätter der Städtischen Bühnen Essen* was 'Gegen die neue Tonalität' (no. 16, May 1931; see Adorno, GS 18, pp. 98–107; GS 19, p. 641).

with Gretel in Homburg: not documented.

Before … with Grab: Hermann Grab sends his thanks in an undated letter, attributed to April/May 1931, for his stay in Frankfurt am Main (Theodor W. Adorno Archiv).

82 Kracauer to Adorno

[no address], 7.6.1931

7 June 31.

Dear Teddie,

You must forgive me for not having written to you until now, but I had so many additional tasks to carry out that I never even got round to business letters. I have had no free Sundays for a long time now.

Your inaugural lecture essentially is really a case of its own, something which might deserve a short dissertation. First of all, the content: I think the first part, the critical one, is excellent. It comprises in compressed form a criticism of present-day philosophy that could not easily be expressed in a more succinct and incisive way. The transition to materialism, however, fills me with a sense of unease. You are making use of a small back door which is not intrinsically materialist – I mean the image of the rebus. It may possibly explain the curious and, as I believe, very personal relationship between Benjamin's finesse with interpretation and his Marxism, which is no less curious but it stands in a skewed relationship to materialism itself. In my opinion, this is not the way to unveil dialectics. Quite apart from the fact that it would be better to emphasize the determining impulses of university philosophy on the one hand and of materialism on the other, instead of mediating them in this way. And then the conclusion! You defend the form of the essay, but in the final analysis the essay is a formal entity and its dimension is determined by its form. In any case, it is not so much a question of smallness as of the fact that every study in question takes up a given reality, pushes it on in dialectical terms, and thus changes it. *Das Kapital* was a work of this kind, and still corresponds to our requirements. My criticism already leads me to the essential discussion of the issues of principle mentioned above. It is probable, then, that you got caught up in this game of hide and seek because of the place in which you had to speak. You wanted to make a confessional declaration, and yet you could not. As a matter of fact, pledging allegiance to Marxism was simply not possible immediately after qualifying, and on this official occasion. It would also have been inopportune because you would have inevitably aroused the suspicion among the assistant professors that you were only speaking out clearly now, directly after your habilitation had gone through. I assume that you disguised matters in this way to avoid giving such an embarrassing impression of behaving unfairly. But in your place I should not even have gone so far as to make such statements. Instead, I should have presented some little genuinely dialectical examination rather than adhering to the programme, which was certainly not required of you, and would have broken this off precisely at the point where a natural reversal would be called for. By doing so you might have aroused more genuine and long-lasting disquiet among the professors than by the way you actually proceeded, as you would not have given affront by beating them over the head but would have penetrated into their brains, which was the only thing that mattered in this case. A *blague*, unless it was executed effectively, was not called for – and was, moreover, bad tactics. Tactically, all that is advisable immediately after entering the university is gradually to gain a position there for yourself and to work in the way that we intend on the basis of the weight which this position lends to your work. More than any other theory, Marxism requires tactical cleverness. Please do think carefully about your position, and the possibilities which it offers you, and suppress your quite understandable tendency to speak out as much as possible, as far as is objectively necessary. If you are not prepared to do so, you really should not have gone into the university.

I found your Dickens essay superbly written, but too markedly situated within Benjamin's purlieus as regards its atmosphere. You know that I can't rid myself of a slight distaste for Benjamin's own remarks on this subject. This in its turn transfers itself to works by you in which terms such as 'reconciliation' and 'salvation' play too great a part. But these criticisms, of course, apply only internally – just between us.

I won't write any more today. My novel is flourishing and almost half completed, and will perhaps require about another six months. Luckily I am making more progress with it than I was during my first days in Berlin. When it has reached a certain degree of completeness, of course you will receive it. Gretel hasn't given me your Kierkegaard yet. I am going to telephone her very soon.

Of course I want to read the seminar notes and your essay in *Scheinwerfer*.

I am glad to be allowed to keep the inaugural lecture – its dedication really delighted me. Its 'functional value' for me resides in its criticism of philosophy.

Warmest greetings to you,
Your old

Lili also sends you her very best wishes.

Original: typescript (carbon copy); Siegfried Kracauer papers, Deutsches Literaturarchiv, Marbach am Neckar.

the image of the rebus: 'Die Aktualität der Philosophie': the passage relating to 'seeking in the riddle the image of a meaning lying behind it' (see Adorno, GS 1, p. 335).

the form of the essay: 'For this reason the essay changed from a form of great philosophy to a lesser one of aesthetics, in whose appearance a concretion of interpretation took refuge which for a long time had no longer been available to philosophy as such in the major dimensions of its problems' (see Adorno, GS 1, pp. 343f., and also the continuation of this motif: 'Der Essay als Form', *Noten zur Literatur* I; see Adorno, GS 2, pp. 9–33).

the inaugural lecture – its dedication: not preserved among Kracauer's papers.

83 Adorno to Kracauer
Frankfurt am Main, 8.6.1931

THEODOR WIESENGRUND-ADORNO Frankfurt, 8 June 1931.

Dear Friedel,

Very quickly: yesterday I received a long letter from Ernst Bloch about my inaugural lecture to which I sent an exhaustive reply. As the tenor of his letter matched yours (introduction of materialism; I assume that conversations between the two of you were behind it), my answer to him is also the answer to yours in terms of its essential aspects. I have already asked him to show you the letter and would now like to ask you to read it very soon, as I believe I defended precisely those points which you attack. Chiefly, why the transition to materialism happened the way it did and was not accomplished by way of 'totality'. The idea behind the matter, though, is not such a tactical one as you perhaps assume. It is much more of an attempt to establish a new approach to materialism whose direction is, I think, the right one, although I am entirely clear in my mind about the flaws in its design. The business of the essay has a quite concrete background. It is an answer to criticisms by Wertheimer and Riezler of my Kierkegaard piece, which I reproduced word for word. It should, therefore, be understood as part of quite a definite situation. It goes without saying that I don't want to reduce his particular philosophy to the essay in any arbitrary way. I just believe that there is a principle couched within the essay which may be very profitably applied to philosophy on a larger scale.

I should be glad if you would take up the discussion at the point where my letter to Bloch left it. As long as your criticisms are of a nature relating to university *tactics*, I am inclined to concede them. On the other hand, I was required to provide nothing less than a programme, which made it impossible to avoid something like the lecture. What appalled people so much about it, by the way, was never quite made clear. Everyone said something different. The stupidest was Mannheim – he thought that I had gone over to the Viennese Positivists!!! Incidentally, nothing has happened yet about my Kierkegaard. I am beginning to feel uneasy about this. Gretel must finally give it to you.

Sohn-Rethel is here and wants someone to help him. However, I cannot see any real possibility, especially as I couldn't achieve any positive results at the Institute even for Benjamin. Leo is King of the Desert there, prowling around his territory. Sohn-Rethel, after a Heidegger episode about which he maintains a discreet silence, has become a scholar with pretensions to meticulous accuracy, which sits rather oddly with him. He is, however, a highly gifted person.

I am hoping to hear from you soon. Give Lili my warmest good wishes.

As always, your old

Teddie.

The essay 'Words without Songs' which I mentioned to you is finished and with the FZ, but as Gubler is away I am still without any information. It matters a lot to me. I find it difficult to gauge its objective scope, but actually I think it is the most specific thing that I have written up to now, and I feel that there is a lot of me in it. It would mean a lot to me, therefore, if you would write and tell me what you think of it. I take it as read that Gubler will publish it, as it is not difficult.

Original: typescript with printed letterhead and handwritten corrections: Siegfried Kracauer papers, Deutsches Literaturarchiv, Marbach am Neckar.

letter from Ernst Bloch ... answered: both letters have not been located to date.

84 Adorno to Kracauer

Frankfurt am Main, 19.7.1931

DR THEODOR WIESENGRUND-ADORNO

PRIVATDOZENT AN DER
UNIVERSITÄT FRANKFURT A. M.

FRANKFURT A. M.-OBERRAD
19 SEEHEIMER STRASSE
SPESSART 62480

19 July 1931.

Dear Friedel,

Whatever is the matter? I haven't heard a word from you for months – either in reply to my letter (the response to your criticism of the inaugural lecture) or to the long one to Ernst Bloch, which, as for its subject matter, was addressed to you as well, or independently of all this and directly – and am thrown back on Gubler and Carl Dreyfuss, who, moreover, contradict each other. Also, I have heard nothing about the Worte ohne Lieder [Words without songs]. After all this I am alarmed. As I am not aware of any guilt towards you, I must assume that you are ill – which is also consistent with Carl's information. Or is it the apartment which is making so much work for you? In any case, I should like to ask you for some news, even if only a few short words.

I am not well. I am in the midst of a rather depressed and not very productive period which is aggravated by the objective situation (which I view in *extremely* pessimistic terms). On top of this, there are all kinds of annoyances – the latest also with reference to Bloch and Benjamin, the first of whom is behaving like a synthesis of a washerwoman and Loyal Eckhardt, while the second (who has still not said anything directly) escapes into acting ambivalently. It is supposed to be something to do with the inaugural lecture's inadmissible dependences on Benjamin – as if his Kraus didn't have at least as much to do with my writings as the latter do with his. Perhaps you could take another look at the piece if you have time – little as all this deserves to be taken seriously, by the way. But, all the same, a word on the subject of my intellectual autonomy sent to the appropriate quarter (i.e. to Ernst, who is posing as the guardian of intellectual property) might be enough to put an end to things which are a nuisance at a time when one is not feeling entirely balanced.

My plans for the summer are still uncertain, more recently because of the emergency decree. What emerges from it should be Germany (Baden-Baden?). On the other hand, there is a fairly strong probability that I shall be in Berlin in September. I am also writing because I should like to know whether you will be there at that time, which of course is extremely important to me. In that case I can make arrangements according to the time of your presence or absence.

Do ask Benjamin (who should have finished with it) to give you the manuscript of my Kierkegaard piece in *large* writing. It is beginning to bother me that you still don't know it, and I should be glad if this could be arranged soon so that it will no longer merely relate to a private intellectual achievement of mine but to our shared philosophical past.

For a long time now I have read only little things of yours – mostly with considerable agreement, especially the magnificent Kurfürstendamm essay, and now also the one about the old Westend. I take it that this relates to the studies for the work on the physiognomies of major cities of which you spoke. I found the concluding essay on the 'best-sellers' less drastic than the essays themselves.

I should like to draw your attention to the works of Valéry Larbaud, whom I find very significant in parts. In a comparison, Cocteau won't stay the course in the long run.

Very best wishes to you and Lili. Do write soon to your

Teddie.

Original: typescript with printed letterhead and handwritten corrections; Siegfried Kracauer papers, Deutsches Literarturachiv, Marbach am Neckar.

Loyal Eckhardt: a reference to *Der treue Eckhart* (1854), a novel by Ludwig Bechstein (1854) or, more likely, to 'Der getreue Eckhart' (1799), a 'literary fairy-tale' by Ludwig Tieck.

his Kraus: see letter no. 73.

the inaugural lecture's inadmissible dependence on Benjamin: Walter Benjamin, in a letter to Adorno of 17 July 1931 (see Adorno/Benjamin, *Briefwechsel*, pp. 16–21), complained about the fact that, at the instigation of Ernst Bloch, he ought to have been named in connection with a passage in Adorno's inaugural lecture in which he saw an intellectual affinity with *Ursprung des deutschen Trauerspiels*. In the printed edition this was done in connection with the definition of the task of photography as serving to suspend 'those questions whose summing-up in succinct form is the task of science' (see Adorno, GS 1, p. 335).

emergency decree: with his decree of 14 July 1931, President Paul Hindenburg stopped payments by the credit institutions for two days after the collapse of the

Danat Bank had led to mass withdrawals; on 17 July there followed an emergency decree limiting the freedom of the press.

Kurfürstendamm essay: see letter no. 81, note.

about the old Westend: probably '3=6', *Frankfurter Zeitung*, 18 July 1931 (see Kracauer, W 5, no. 579), an article about the subdividing of living space in Berlin West.

on the 'best-sellers': 'Über Erfolgsbücher und ihr Publikum', *Frankfurter Zeitung*, 27 June 1931 (see Kracauer, W 5, no. 573).

Larbaud: Valéry Larbaud (1881–1957), author and translator; he translated, among other works, James Joyce's *Ulysses* into French; in Adorno's posthumous library he is represented by two translations of Samuel Butler.

85 Kracauer to Adorno

[Berlin,] 23.7.1931

23 July 31.

Dear Teddie,

I am not ill, but so stretched between major and minor pieces of work, and at the same time so much in need of a rest, that outside of my working hours I am suffering from enormous fatigue. This was why I have not written to you for all this time. This situation is being made still worse by the impossibility of making plans even a week in advance. We had planned to go away on holiday somewhere in France on 1 August, and in the meantime along comes the passport fee. Will it be suspended or not? If not, which I think more likely, we are still not sure whether we shall simply stay here or perhaps go away for part of August to get the rest that we so urgently need. Everything is uncertain, because even the move gets in the way of things. The provisional nature of the whole situation is draining me of all enthusiasm. Throw in the inevitable antics of the political know-alls which one is exposed to everywhere, and the measure is full. One day I should like to live in a time and a country where one can talk about sensible, comprehensible human affairs and make important arrangements six months in advance. What is to become of us in September is likewise not yet clear. In any event we shall be here for part of the month, as we are moving at that time, which is not exactly straightforward because of certain renovations. Of course Lili and I are looking forward to your possibly being here despite the inconveniences connected with the move. [(]From the beginning of October everything should be much easier.)

If I could have managed to write a proper letter I would have let you know immediately that mostly I agreed with your Words without Songs. Only the section about names in detective stories does not quite make sense to me. The piece is well written, too. One shouldn't expect, though, to get much out of this genre; it's the same with titbits. Why the motto from Brecht?

I don't see Bloch very often and have only spoken once to Benjamin since his return. The matter you mentioned, I believe, has to do with the concept of intentionless reality, but I was sure that you planned – if I remember rightly, it was in your letter to Bloch – to acknowledge Benjamin in the *published* version of the talk. Incidentally, my letter to you about obtaining the *venia legendi* was written without previous discussion with Bloch. I actually thought, as I also wrote to you, that an all-too-evident agreement with Benjamin was more markedly present in the Dickens essay, and precisely from an angle which isn't really to my taste in Benjamin's work either. I should take any possible strictures that may be expressed simply as a reason to expound what is germane to you even further beyond any possibility of confusion. Be it complaints or eulogies – very few people are worth the trouble. I should prefer to read your work on Kierkegaard, about which I am going to contact Benjamin, on holiday when I have collected my thoughts sufficiently. Of Larbaud's writings I know only his apologia in defence of Paris.

Now I have to write about the volume of Kafka's posthumous writings. It is very important, of course, but incomprehensible in places, and unfortunately of a monotonous nature which becomes boring over time. This may have something to do with the lack of sensuousness.

Well now, I have written to you, even if only sparsely. I wish the world had just a grain more sense (one can't rate it particularly highly); that would make corresponding so much easier.

Original: typescript (carbon copy), fragment; Siegfried Kracauer papers, Deutsches Literaturarchiv, Marbach am Neckar; the context suggests that it was written in Berlin.

passport fee: on 21 July 1931 the 'presidential decree of the imposition of a tax on foreign travel' came into force, starting on 30 July 1931; according to this decree, a tax of 100/150 Reichsmarks to leave the country was payable in advance at local passport offices or border crossings (see 'Die Gebühr für Auslandsreisen: Weitgehende Einschränkungen', *Frankfurter Zeitung*, 22 July 1931).

go away for part of August: The Kracauers spent the second half of August 1931 in north Germany (see *Marbacher Magazin* 47, p. 65).

as we are moving at that time: the new apartment was in Berlin-Charlottenburg at Sybelstrasse 35 (see *Marbacher Magazin* 47, p. 68).

your possibly being here: Adorno's visit to Berlin eventually took place in October 1931 (see ibid.).

names in detective stories: the fourth section of 'Worte ohne Lieder' (see Adorno, GS 20.2, pp. 539f.).

the motto from Brecht: 'Du hättest zu tun mit der Eisenbahn, und nicht zu tun mit der See. Bert Brecht' [You had some kind of job on the railway, and had nothing to do with the sea]; see Adorno, GS 20.2, p. 237; from Bertolt Brecht, 'Surabaja-Johnny'; see Brecht, W XIII, pp. 344–6, where it reads 'nichts zu tun').

apologia in defence of Paris: Valéry Larbaud, 'Lob von Paris: Übersetzung von Max Rychner', *Neue Schweizer Rundschau*, 1930. Kracauer reviewed this translation in *Frankfurter Zeitung*, 19 January 1930 (see Kracauer, W 5, no. 462).

volume of Kafka's posthumous writings: 'Zu Franz Kafkas nachgelassenen Schriften', *Frankfurter Zeitung*, 3 September 1931, 9 September 1931 (see Kracauer, W 5, no. 588) – i.e. the review of Kafka's *Beim Bau der Chinesischen Mauer: Ungedruckte Erzählungen und Prosa aus dem Nachlaß*, ed. Max Brod and Hans Joachim Schoeps, Berlin: Gustav Kiepenhauer, 1931.

86 Adorno to Kracauer
Berchtesgaden, 11.8.1931

Berchtesgaden, Grand Hotel.
11. VIII. 31. Dear Friedel, We have ended up here where it is rather beautiful, a quite decent transposition of a true high mountain landscape into a German environment, restorative even in the most appallingly bad weather. Are you still lurking in Berlin or already in the radiance of the West? My plans for Berlin in September are the same as before. A few days ago in Munich I couldn't help thinking a lot about 1924. Gretel sends warmest greetings. Much love to you both,
Your old Teddie.

Original: MS, postcard: Berchtesgaden from Reichenbach, Soleleitungssteg; Siegfried Kracauer papers, Deutsches Literaturarchiv, Marbach am Neckar.

thinking a lot about 1924: for their journey of that year, see letter no. 2.

87 Adorno to Kracauer
Ajaccio, 3.4.1932

Ajaccio (Corsica). 3 April 1932.

Dear Friedel, After ten days of the Riviera (Le Trayás in the Estérel mountains, between Cannes and St Raphaël) we grew tired of its dry tone, decided to go off in search of adventure, and have ended up in the land of my ancestors, in Corsica, a completely improbable area, like Provence at the bottom end, like the Engadin at the top, and like Capri around the edges. After a grand circular tour around the south of the island we have arrived at its tip, opposite Sardinia, which really exists and which we have seen, and reached Bonifacio, as attested by the map – a place whose invisibility, spectacular cliffs and location surpass even Positano itself. Now we are strolling about here. Warmest greetings to you and Lili, Yours, Teddie.

Original: MS, postcard: *Bonifacio* – Les Remparts – Entrée de la Ville; Siegfried Kracauer papers, Deutsches Literaturarchiv, Marbach am Neckar.

the land of my ancestors: Adorno means the home of his maternal grandfather, Jean François Calvelli; Adorno was travelling with Gretel Karplus.

88 Adorno to Kracauer
Frankfurt am Main, 21.11.1932

THEODOR WIESENGRUND-ADORNO

Frankfurt, 21 November 1932.

Dear Friedel,

Many thanks for your letter and your initiative regarding the little plan for Great Pan. I hope to be able to make use of your suggestions very soon; at the moment I am handicapped by certain negotiations with Kestenberg, which seem to me unlikely to lead to any results: as soon as things are clear I shall write to the publishers you recommended. The only one which should really be left out is Duncker and Humblot – i.e. because they will publish not only Bloch's book but also the book on white-collar workers by Carl Dreyfuss, and that is probably not the right place for me. In the meantime, I have sent you the second part of the work on music and am very keen to know what you think of it. There are, of course, still a few silly typographical errors in it which I must ask you to excuse. I read your latest reviews with great pleasure – 'Hähnchen', Seghers, Helbing and Naumann. I was especially taken with the Seghers review, and also with the attack on the educated, hence 'noble' fascists [*Edelfascisten*]. Your main argument here is one which I also used in my latest proseminar when a girl announced that she was not so sure about whether the world had a 'meaning', and the students began to express their displeasure over this reasonable doubt. I said, you see, that it was one of the primal phenomena of social repression not to hold society responsible for poor conditions of any kind but to blame those people who give them expression – the Enlightenment, in the case which you discuss, and so on. If people could be made aware of this distortion, much would be gained. I only have some doubts about a certain positive evaluation of the 'popular'and national [*volkhaft*] element in your critique. I am well aware that the pointers in this direction have their origins in tactical considerations; but I fear that others, too, will notice this – which devalues the tactics, so that it might be cleverer from the start to write cynically about things which nobody believes we would take seriously in a way that is commensurate with the one that is customary nowadays. But in the end that is really a question of tactics, and you will certainly have had your own experiences of it.

Benjamin has been here. He read me a lot of his new book *Berliner Kindheit um 1900* [A Berlin childhood around 1900]. I find it marvellous and entirely new – it also represents great progress against the One-Way Street as its archaic mythology is well and truly liquidated and the mythical is sought for only in that which is most timely to all ages – their modernity in its distinct variant. I am convinced that it will make a great impression on you, too. By the way, he has distanced himself from Brecht to an extreme degree – for practical reasons, as it seems to me, i.e. as Brecht's work with him produced no positive results. All in all, he makes a somewhat freer impression, and a very good one. Your critique of Seghers charmed him greatly, too. I hope that this will soon lead to friendly, cheerful, companionable conversations between the two Great Powers.

I am swamped with galley proofs of the Kierkegaard; it is an occupation which affords a certain narcissistic pleasure. Otherwise I have a lot of work to do for the course of Descartes lectures and the Simmel proseminar.

I enjoyed our meeting in Berlin very much. I have the feeling – if one may say such a thing – that a certain constraint has been dispelled which had existed in our constellation for years.

It is far from impossible that I may be in Berlin again at Christmas. Give Lili my very best wishes.

As ever, your old

Teddie.

Original: typescript with printed letterhead and handwritten corrections: Siegfried Kracauer papers, Deutsches Literaturarchiv, Marbach am Neckar.

your letter: not preserved.

the little plan for Great Pan: 'Great Pan is dead': the title of a planned collection of musical essays (see the reproduction of a manuscript of the table of contents, autumn 1934, in Adorno, *Bildmonographie*, p. 129).

negotiations with Kestenberg: probably Leo Kestenberg (1882–1962), pianist, teacher and writer on music; from 1918 music consultant at the Prussian Ministry of Sciences; exiled in Prague in 1933 and subsequently in Palestine. In 1929 he was one of Adorno's supporters in the choice of Weissmann's successor in Berlin (see letter no. 52 and also Adorno to Alban Berg, mid-June 1929, Adorno/Berg, *Correspondence*, p. 150).

Bloch's book: Ernst Bloch, *Erbschaft dieser Zeit*; pubd not by Duncker & Humblot but by Oprecht & Helbing, Zurich, in the autumn of 1934 (imprint: 1935).

the book about white-collar workers by Carl Dreyfuss: *Beruf und Ideologie der Angestellten*, Munich: Duncker & Humblot, 1933; a copy can be found in the library which Adorno left behind.

second part of the work on music: the second part of *Zur gesellschaftlichen Lage der Musik*, with the chapter heading 'Reproduktion, Konsum'; *Zeitschrift für Sozialforschung*, no. 3, 1932; the first part, 'Umriß, Produktion', had preceded it in nos. 1/2 (see Adorno, GS 18, pp. 729–77 and GS 19, p. 647).

'Hähnchen': 'Vivisektion der Zeit', *Frankfurter Zeitung*, 6 November 1932 (see Kracauer, W 5, no. 687) – i.e. the review of Erik Reger, *Das wachsame Hähnchen: Polemischer Roman* [The vigilant cockerel], Berlin: Ernst Rowohlt, 1932.

Seghers: 'Eine Märtyrer-Chronik von heute', *Frankfurter Zeitung*, 13 November 1932 (see Kracauer, W 5, no. 689) – i.e. the review of Anna Seghers, *Die Gefährten* [The companions], Berlin: Gustav Kiepenheuer, 1932.

Helbing and Neumann: 'Wunschträume der Gebildeten: Zu den Schriften von Lothar Helbing und Hans Naumann', *Frankfurter Zeitung*, 20 November 1932 (see Kracauer, W 5, no. 692) – i.e. the review of Lothar Helbing, *Der dritte Humanismus*, Berlin: Die Runde, 1931; Hans Naumann, *Deutsche Nation in Gefahr*, Stuttgart: J. B. Metzlersche, 1932.

Benjamin has been here: on 13 November 1932 (see Adorno/Benjamin, *Briefwechsel*, pp. 30f.).

Berliner Kindheit um 1900: Walter Benjamin, *Berliner Kindheit um neunzehnhundert* (see Benjamin, GS IV.1, pp. 235–304); it was published in book form by Suhrkamp only in late 1950 (see letter no. 149).

the course of Descartes lectures and the Simmel proseminar: Adorno's teaching commitments in the 1932/33 winter semester.

89 Adorno to Kracauer
Frankfurt am Main, 12.1.1933

DR THEODOR WIESENGRUND-ADORNO

PRIVATDOZENT AN DER
UNIVERSITÄT FRANKFURT A.M.

FRANKFURT A.M.-OBERRAD
19 SEEHEIMER STRASSE
SPESSART 62480

12 January 1933.

Dear Friedel,

Many thanks for your letter. I had worried that you might not be well because I had not heard from you for so long. I am all the happier now to hear that everything is all right. Your novel must be gradually nearing its end now, too – and your worries about the newspaper must be alleviated; first because I get the impression that the supplement is relying on you more than ever, and second because the radical change in the political situation is also sure to make itself felt in these matters. Just as a curiosity: Heinz Simon has gone to Rome lately to speak with Mussolini. He's in for a treat.

I am very glad that you find part two of my work convincing. I myself, on the other hand, am concerned that it contains a lot that reads like a sequence of theses, which in general was not quite what I intended.

However, in this attempt at a survey it was inevitable. By the way, the intention behind this piece of work was not merely to assist with orientation but to express ideas. I wanted not only to demonstrate the experience that in capitalism all roads are closed, and that everywhere one is, so to speak, running up against a glass wall, with reference to an example fairly remote from immediate social conditions, but really to develop it, i.e. by knocking on every single door that is closed there. And whether this intention which I wanted to express has been realized seems to me to be more important than anything else about the attempt. I am very pleased with your approach to *Wozzeck* and the Weill–Berg relationship. I don't have to tell you that I am entirely of your opinion. The only thing is that I don't believe that Weill is 'newer'. Rather, it's the old trick – that things which are further behind the times claim to be more progressive for the very reason that they are more readily accessible, and therefore more 'up to date'. Since *Die Bürgschaft*, too, it seems to me beyond question that Weill, who once had an (ambivalent) revolutionary function as a destructive Surrealist, has gone over to the line of positive reaction.

My Kierkegaard is coming out any day now, or must already have done so. I have arranged for your copy (which is also the one for the newspaper) to be sent directly to you so that no confusions may arise in Frankfurt as they did in the Horkheimer case. I would be grateful if you could let me know as quickly as possible whether you have received your copy, as otherwise I shall immediately send you one of my free copies, which should reach me today. As for the question of the review, I should like to say to you once again that it would be completely all right with me if, in the interests of purity of critical stance, you pointed out that the book is dedicated to you and bears witness to our shared work. I don't need to reiterate how eager I am to hear your opinion of it.

And now I must go on to discuss a particular matter. I have recently taken over the post of 'group consultant for philosophy' on the *Zeitschrift für Sozialforschung*, which means that I am officially in charge of the philosophical review section together with Horkheimer (and – which is important – without Leo having anything more than a nominal influence on matters, which will make things much easier, as otherwise Leo's bossiness would make everything impossible for me). The first and most important task of this kind that I have embarked upon is to acquire your services for the journal. Now, with the ill feeling that exists between you and Cronberg Central, this is not so simple. However, I have managed here to contrive for these matters to be liquidated, and I would be glad if I could achieve this with you as well – glad for the journal, which I should like to reshape into an organ for us and our views, and for which your collaboration would naturally be indispensable, but also glad for you, because it is at least a forum and may yet become even more of one in which you can say – and say openly – things which it would be difficult to say *à côté de chez Kircher*. The milieu will be a respectable one; Benjamin and Lukács are also on board; I am taking on the greater part of the philosophical reviews myself; I have thrown out the people who are not up to it, but on the other hand I want to attract gifted ones like Sternberger and Herbert Marcuse. Now, at this very moment a good opportunity is available to conclude a Pax Dei between you and the Institute. You see, a book by Herr Ernst Cassirer – the Goethe of our university – has come out which deals with the French Enlightenment, and does so in a disgraceful fashion: the Age of Enlightenment is treated with something like the lovingly superior understanding with which the thought of primitive ethnicities is discussed; it claims to be a study of 'Enlightenment modes of thought'. That in this context the Enlightenment is regarded in the old teleological schema only as a preparation for Kant who, according to the neo-Kantian cliché 'completes and transcends' it, can be understood tangentially. It is urgently necessary that this piece of hack writing, as representative as it is ghastly, should be despatched in as masterly and genuinely literary a manner as possible. Nobody can do this like you, and there is all the more reason for you to review the book, as you were the first of all of us to adopt a new approach to the problems of the Enlightenment. Even the Institute is highly delighted with the plan. We are only afraid of receiving a refusal from you, and for this reason I am first of all sounding you out 'unofficially' (the hyper-organization and overloading of such matters has not only been preserved in keeping with the Pollock tradition but built up and intensified still further by Leo – this is strictly *entre nous*). If you would like to take on this business, perhaps you could simply request the book from the editorial board, saying that it interests you and you would like to review it. You will then get it at once. Your critique could then have the maximum space of three printed pages in the review section (i.e. petit – you know the pages) – which is three times the normal amount – space for you to say all kinds of things. I would be all the more grateful to you for taking this on, as we could proceed from there and also make agreements about longer pieces of work. The matter is urgent, though, and it would be kind if you could let me know as quickly as possible, and most of all if you would write to the editorial board. And please excuse the formal mode of address; I am not responsible for it.

Give Lili my very best wishes and tell her that I am sorry not to have been able to show her the new plan for the organization of the journal drawn up by Pollock. She would have enjoyed it. It is so complicated that I still haven't understood it.

I hope you will soon make another appearance in Frankfurt. I believe it is two years since you were here last – and whether I shall be coming to Berlin in the next few months is quite uncertain, to say the least.

All the best from your old

Teddie.

Original: typescript with printed letterhead and handwritten correction; Siegfried Kracauer papers, Deutsches Literaturarchiv, Marbach am Neckar.

your letter: not preserved.

Heinz Simon has gone to Rome: no information is available about this journey.

Weill ... Bürgschaft: *Die Bürgschaft* [The guarantee] (1931), an opera by Kurt Weill, who wrote the libretto in collaboration with Caspar Neher; first performed on 10 March 1932 at the Städtische Oper, Berlin.

My Kierkegaard is coming out: according to Adorno's *Notiz* of January 1966, this happened on 30 January 1933 (see Adorno, GS 2, p. 261).

Cronberg Central: Max Horkheimer and Friedrich Pollock.

philosophical reviews: of the 32 reviews for the year 1933, six were by Adorno.

Benjamin and Lukács ... Sternberger and Herbert Marcuse: in 1933 Walter Benjamin and Georg Lukács contributed no reviews in the field of philosophy, Dolf Sternberger signed two, and Herbert Marcuse sixteen critiques.

a book by Herr Ernst Cassirer: Ernst Cassirer, *Die Philosophie der Aufklärung*, Tübingen: Mohr, 1932.

Lili ... Pollock: Lili Kracauer knew Friedrich Pollock through her work as a librarian at the Institute in the late 1920s (see letter no. 167).

90 Kracauer to Adorno
[no address], 21.1.1933

21 January 33.

Dear Teddie,

Many thanks for your letter. First of all, *Kierkegaard*; I was extraordinarily pleased with the copy and the printed dedication, which reads very well. I shall read the book as soon as I review it – I think in the first half of February (unless financial difficulties foil my plans). Now, in confidence, completely *entre nous*: I have already had a little correspondence with the editorial board about the book. The view from Frankfurt, where I had immediately earmarked the review for myself, was that this wouldn't do; a question of friendship was involved, and they would prefer to have it reviewed by another party, etc. The answer that I sent by return of post left nothing to be desired in terms of clarity. In a word: I delivered an ultimatum, insisting on having the book – and naturally they will fall in with this. At some point I shall make this correspondence available to you. When I have finished the review, I shall send you an offprint. I won't conceal my private opinion from you. Benjamin, to whom I spoke recently, expressed great approval. Your handwritten dedication, which he showed to me, touched him – something which I can't hold against him – and so you will soon be hearing from me about this. I am eager to read it and look forward to being able to write about this book of yours. (It will doubtless have reached your ears before mine that Benjamin wants to review it in the *Voss*).

As to your suggestion for the journal: I think it is a very good thing that you should gain some influence there. However, once again I must radically correct a misconception on your part and that of the Cronbergers (I have already done this face to face with you and in a letter to Horkheimer): it was anything but my fault that I didn't receive Horkheimer's book from the paper that time, although I took pains to ensure that I should in plenty of time. I had done what I could, and so Horkheimer has absolutely no scores to settle – a point which I ask him to consider. When things didn't work out with the paper, later on I tried yet again on my own initiative with the *Neue Rundschau*, where in spite of all my efforts the business likewise came to nothing. (They were gradually getting fed up with me.) The ill feeling is based on false assumptions; there is no cause for ill feeling, and for that reason I don't recognize the scores either. People like Horkheimer should be too grown up and experienced to sulk for no reason. The dialectical process always seems to be appropriate only for application to objects with which one has no personal connection. So – let bygones not be bygones! With specific reference to your enquiry, I am happy to collaborate on the journal. But this time you have hit precisely on a book that I would prefer not to review. Don't be cross; I can't get on with Cassirer's work – it doesn't excite me; and all that would come out of it would be cold eye-wash. (As it happens, I have the book in my hand.) Unfortunately, I know of no book that particularly tickles my fancy at present. So, instead, I shall make you a formal counter-proposal: select a topic for me – you do have a good enough idea of my specific angles, one can certainly say that – which could serve as a starting point for me to formulate something basic and representative (ideally even in the main section) – perhaps 10 to 20 pages. (Of course, it could be less – whatever is required.) Not so much about the book itself, but using the book as an opportunity. It could be about the technique of the novel, a political/sociological subject or a current phenomenon in the field of philosophy. I leave it to you (just not the Cassirer of all options – much as I would like to write something radical on the Enlightenment–fairy-tale–Marxism relationship). Of course I should then turn at once to the 'editorial board' officially, as is only fair. (I am not angry.) However, I must have some details from you in advance about the fee, which should not be too meagre – first as a general principle, and second because I rely on it urgently as an exploited jobbing labourer. I can only write about ideal subjects nowadays for material reasons. Well – you know how it is.

I have a factual criticism to make about a sentence in your letter. You said that you wanted to show how within capitalism one is 'always and everywhere running into a glass wall', that 'all roads are closed'. This proceeds from an 'either/or' and almost sounds as if it came from your Kierkegaard. Incidentally, it is precisely in this undialectical attitude that the hidden weakness of your dissertation lies. Utopia and the classless society should not be identified with each other like this without a murmur. (This might of course be done for polemical or emotional reasons – but not theoretically and purely in contemplation.)

Do you know what Weill is planning to do now? The film music for Fallada's trashy novel *Kleiner Mann – was nun?* He, Fallada, and Neher are announcing that they will be writing the screenplay for the film together. That was all we needed. Should Weill not have something better in mind than becoming a music-manufacturer who also turns successful novels published by Ullstein into films?

Warmest regards (from Lili too, of course)

Your old

Original: typescript (carbon copy); Siegfried Kracauer papers, Deutsches Literaturarchiv, Marbach am Neckar.

printed dedication: Adorno dedicated the book: 'To Siegfried Kracauer, my friend' (taken word for word from the first edition; see the variant in Adorno, GS 2, p. 8).

as soon as I review it: Kracauer's review, 'Der enthüllte Kierkegaard', was typeset by the *Frankfurter Zeitung* but not published (see Kracauer, W 5, no. 745).

the answer that I sent by return of post: not preserved.

your handwritten dedication: not preserved.

Benjamin … in the Voss: Benjamin informed Adorno of his plan on 14 January 1933 (see Adorno/Benjamin, *Briefwechsel*, pp. 34f.); 'Kierkegaard, *Das Ende des philosophischen Idealismus*', *Vossische Zeitung*, 2 April 1933 (see Benjamin, GS III, pp. 380–3, 660–2); the editors shortened his contribution by one section.

Weill … Kleiner Mann – was nun?: Kurt Weill informed Lotte Lenya in a letter of 9 January 1933 of the plan to collaborate with the Europa-Verleih on four films over the next two to three years. The ideal candidates to direct the filming of Hans Fallada's (1893–1947) novel *Kleiner Mann – was nun?* [Little man, what now?] (Berlin: Ernst Rowohlt, 1932) were Gustav Gründgens or Berthold Viertel. The plan came to nothing; Weill had nothing to do with the film, first shown on 3 August 1933 (director: Fritz Wendhausen), about whose inferior quality Lenya writes to Weill on 7 August 1933 (see *Sprich leise wenn du Liebe sagst: Der Briefwechsel Kurt Weill–Lotte Lenya*, ed. Lys Symonette and Kim H. Kowalke, Cologne: Kiepenheuer & Witsch, 1998, pp. 83, 105).

91 Adorno to Kracauer

Frankfurt am Main, 14.3.1933

Frankfurt, 14 March 1933.

Dear Friedel,

On the point of leaving for Berlin I received your letter and your Kierkegaard essay and am hastening to tell you in a few quick words how much I enjoyed them both, and how much I should like to thank you. The review is not only the finest evidence of our affinity that I could wish for – and I wish for that more than ever, as at present such evidence is doubly important. I also find it of quite extraordinary quality as a piece of writing. Nobody knows better than I how immense are the difficulties that my mentally quite excessive elaboration must create for any kind of commentary, especially one which has to take heed of being comprehensible, and I consider that you have mastered these difficulties in a truly superior fashion without in any way detracting from the content of the book. I myself would not have been capable of such an account (I am enclosing a card with a blurb that I wrote for Mohr, and which may serve to prove my helplessness to you). Above all it is astonishing how lucidly you have broken down the book's method of fitting ideas into one another into an uninterrupted sequence – a 'train of thought' understood as a form of presentation. But what pleases me most of all, naturally, is the fact that you really do have a positive opinion of the book. So much is invested in it that it may not be described as inadmissible narcissism if this makes me happy. We shall have to talk over the finer points in detail – and, of course, your criticisms, which naturally are extremely important to me. I can already tell you that I am very much inclined to acknowledge your reservations about the scope of the concept of the mythical and the way in which it is applied, and that I am endeavouring very energetically to come back to this point to make advances as far as these issues are concerned (incidentally, the second version of the book has already changed a lot in this respect compared with the first; the 'mythical content' section, which is linked to Kierkegaard's interpretation of Plato and aims to give concrete form to the concept of the mythical, is an entirely new addition). I am quite clear about the point that this is where the real problems lie, and if I am now, in Berlin, attempting to write a major piece taking issue with Klages (for the ZfS) this is being done, most of all, to come to grips with the mythical. I can't agree, however, to make any concessions in matters of reconciliation. This is a question of my most central experiences which I hope to explain progressively – but not to be able to 'prove'/demonstrate or 'leave out' anything. However, let's talk about that. You may possibly have been less than fair to the last chapter – do take another look at it, especially the passage about picture-sheets for children; it contains much that is of importance. Most of all, I should be keen to hear your criticisms regarding the language, to which I devoted a major proportion of my efforts.

I shall be away from Frankfurt until about 20 April, and shall use the holidays to work. Gretel is rather tied up, and so I shall be staying in Germany, although the South would have done me so much good after a very severe attack of the flu. I cannot promise, however, that I shall be in Berlin the whole time; we shall probably be going away somewhere for at least a fortnight (where??? – I have no idea yet; perhaps to the Baltic, or perhaps just to one of the Berlin lakes). My Berlin address is still uncertain. Perhaps you could write your plans on a postcard and send it to Gretel's address (Berlin N 20, Prinzenallee 60), so that we shall not miss each other, whatever happens. Then we shall talk about the *Zeitschrift für*

Sozialforschung and your collaboration. We shall not run short of other material either.

I hope that you are recovering a bit. How is *Genêt* coming along? How is Lili? Do drop me a line or two soon. And once again thank you – really, and very much indeed – for your critique.

Much love and very best wishes to you both from your old

Teddie.

Original: typescript with handwritten corrections; Siegfried Kracauer papers, Deutsches Literaturarchiv, Marbach am Neckar.

your letter: not preserved.

Kierkegaard essay: no evidence survives as to whether Adorno received a copy of the manuscript or an offprint of the typeset text from the *Frankfurter Zeitung*.

a card with a blurb that I wrote for Mohr: with a letter of 17 December 1932 Adorno sent a 'self-advertisement' to the Tübingen publisher J. C. B. Mohr, which might be identical with a typescript from his papers:

> On Wiesengrund-Adorno, *Kierkegaard*. The aim of the book is criticism and interpretation of the concept of the aesthetic in the context of the system of Kierkegaard's philosophy. On the one hand it rejects the assumption that Kierkegaard is a 'poet', and on the other his own verdict on the 'sphere of the aesthetic'. His doctrine that 'subjectivity is truth' is called into question. This leads to the main theses: Kierkegaard's 'inwardness' has its definite place in history and society. Its model is the bourgeois *intérieur* in which historical and 'mythical' features merge. His concept of existence has its origins in the idea of an 'objectless inwardness'. Through 'freedom' this interiority attempts in vain to posit transcendence out of itself. The whole of Kierkegaard's 'existence' reveals itself as despair in the sense of the 'sickness unto death'. In his doctrine of the stages Kierkegaard's idealistic foundation is merely covered by his theological purpose. The 'paradox' proves to be a mythical sacrifice, performed on the autonomous spirit itself. Beyond the deceptive theology of paradoxical existence Kierkegaard's actual elements of truth have migrated to precisely that realm of 'aesthetic' images which he repudiates. (Theodor W. Adorno Archiv).

your reservations … the concept of the mythical: 'which is present here in the form of criticism, and grants such a great latitude to the concept of the mythical which is undifferentiated in itself' (see 'Der enthüllte Kierkegaard', Kracauer, W 5, no. 745).

the 'mythical content' section: see 'Kierkegaard: Konstruktion des Ästhetischen' (Adorno, GS 2, pp. 78–84).

taking issue with Klages: Ludwig Klages, *Der Geist als Widersacher der Seele*, 3 vols, Leipzig: Johann Ambrosius Barth, 1929–32. Max Horkheimer mentions the plan of a comprehensive review by Adorno in his letter to Adorno of 30 June 1932 (see Adorno/Horkheimer, *Briefwechsel* I, pp. 13, 15f.); it was not realized.

picture-sheets: see 'Kierkegaard: Konstruktion des Ästhetischen' (Adorno, GS 2, p. 193).

to the Baltic: the holiday trip took them to Rügen (see Adorno, *Bildmonographie*, pp. 123f.).

How is Genêt *coming along?*: at the beginning of March 1933, Lili and Siegfried Kracauer arrived in Paris, the first stage of their exile; they had fled from Berlin on the night after the Reichstag fire, stopping in Frankfurt am Main on the way.

Genêt: the title of the French edition of *Ginster*, trans. Clara Malraux, Paris: Gallimard, 1933.

92 Adorno to Kracauer
Berlin, 10.4.1933

Berlin, 10 April 33.

Dear Friedel, It is a great pity that I missed you here, and I should be glad to hear from you soon. One more request: would it be possible to change the title of the Kierkegaard essay to 'A new look at Kierkegaard'? I'd be very grateful to you for this. All is going very well with me so far. I am working on Bachofen and Klages, aiming to write a more extensive study. Much love to you and Lili

Yours, Teddie.

Original: MS, postcard: Berlin. The new Jannowitz bridge; Siegfried Kracauer papers, Deutsches Literaturarchiv, Marbach am Neckar.

Bachofen: No work by Adorno on the Basel archaeologist, anthropologist and legal historian Johann Jacob Bachofen (1815–1887) has been found.

93 Adorno to Kracauer
Berlin, 15.4.1933

Berlin, 15 April 1933.

Dear Friedel,

Thank you for your letter, which moved me greatly. I at once informed my father, without, however, being able to tell you in advance whether he could assume the financial responsibility for the removal of your furniture, as he is financially stretched at present, as you yourself thought. I will report back to you as quickly as I can when there is any news. I had actually anticipated that your article about me would not be published; it is a curious and sad confirmation of my instinct. By the way, your boss's letter is just as hostile towards me as it is towards you – but that isn't important. I don't know of any other chance of publishing it, as a review of my book by Sternberger has already appeared in the journal which you suggest – and you would hardly want to abridge it for the F. Z. I am convinced that we cannot count on support from the Institute; it has already restricted its existing responsibilities, including, for example, those towards Carl, to an extreme degree and will certainly not be taking on new ones; it is better to entertain no illusions whatsoever about that. However, a letter from you would certainly have a better chance there than one from me. Moreover, my instinct as regards you is this: that you should come back to Germany. Everything is entirely calm and orderly here; I believe that conditions will become stable; your publishers are here; you can make an agreement with them here, and at the same time earn some extra money, which should not be difficult for the simple reason that there are so few people with an expert knowledge of film; besides, a hasty and expensive move does seem to me to be open to question (Gretel thinks the same). Of course, it is hard to advise you about this, but perhaps it is not unimportant to you to hear my assessment, as I am right in the thick of events here. I myself am staying in Berlin for the time being to finish my work, which, however, is progressing only with difficulty, as things are going extraordinarily badly with me in terms of my health; extreme insomnia associated with a gastric neurosis which makes eating an impossibility – or torture; you would hardly recognize me. I can't do anything about Lili's violin just now; it's a pity that you didn't write to me about it a week ago. I am writing in a somewhat harassed and nervy state – please don't be cross with me on that account. As soon as I can I shall write you a sensible letter, and naturally I shall keep you up to date about my father. Much love from your old

Teddie.

Original: typescript with handwritten corrections; Siegfried Kracauer papers, Deutsches Literaturarchiv, Marbach am Neckar. From 'By the way …' to 'events here', parts are underlined several times, presumably by Kracauer.

your letter: not preserved.

your boss's letter: it is not clear whether Adorno means Heinz Simon, the other directors of the publishing house, or Benno Reifenberg. No letter aimed at him and Adorno from those named is to be found among Kracauer's papers; however, on 6 April 1933 Kracauer wrote to Selmar Spier about a 'letter of dismissal' from Heinz Simon (any correspondence which may have been preserved between the Societäts-Verlag and the editors of the *Frankfurter Zeitung* is not available for consultation because of the current closure of the archives of both the publisher and the newspaper). Spier replied on 18 April 1933 with a more moderate interpretation of the letter and mentions the subject to which Adorno referred, the blocking of Kracauer's discussion of Adorno's postdoctoral thesis: 'I can completely understand that the paper is rejecting articles about Kierkegaard at the present time' (Siegfried Kracauer papers, Deutsches Literaturarchiv, Marbach).

a review of my book by Sternberger: under the title of the book in the philosophy review section of the *Zeitschrift für Sozialforschung*, 1933.

Lili's violin: Lili Kracauer had completed her musical education at the Konservatorium.

94 Adorno to Kracauer
Berlin, 26.4.1933

Berlin, 26 April 1933.

Dear Friedel, My father has been in touch with Selmar and will do something; Selmar will tell you about the details better than I can, as I was here all the time and didn't speak to him. Just this: he as well as Selmar is of the opinion that the exceptionally high cost of transporting your furniture from here is not worth it. *Gretel*, on the other hand, has announced that she is prepared to store your furniture in the rooms in her factory if you will take on the cost of transporting it from door to door, plus any necessary insurance. In explanation I should say that Gretel's former factory has gone into liquidation – she already has a new and more advantageous job – so that her space is available. Furthermore: do get in contact with Dr. *Moras*, editor of the *Europäische Revue*, about collaboration: Berlin, Wilhelmstrasse 37/38. He has asked after you most assiduously, and I am convinced that there is a possibility of placing articles there. The scope of the journal is very respectable, and I shall be writing regularly in it on musical matters. And finally: do you think it might be appropriate for me to get in touch with Anita Lothar on your behalf? I already suggested that to you at Christmas a year ago; at that time, you rejected it quite vigorously, but nowadays you may see the matter differently, and it goes without saying that I shall do all that I can provided (something which it is quite impossible for me to gauge from here) that you do not regard your situation vis-à-vis the newspaper as so far advanced and fixed that you consider any intervention pointless. For my part, I should not like to leave this stone unturned – it's just that I have been so much at sixes and sevens that I didn't stumble on it at once. As before, things are going far from well as regards my health; true, I can eat again, but to make up for that I am being plagued with unbearable headaches, and so I am not as able to work as I might have wished. For this reason, the Klages business is in abeyance, and also because I have decided to take the state examination for private music teachers, and preparing for this is imposing certain demands on me. I would be very glad to hear from you soon, especially as there has still been no reply to my last letter. Give Lili my very best wishes, and most of all, warmest regards to you yourself from your old

Teddie.

Original: typescript with handwritten corrections; Siegfried Kracauer papers, Deutsches Literaturarchiv, Marbach am Neckar.

Selmar: Selmar Spier; Kracauer interrupted his journey from Berlin to Paris briefly in Frankfurt am Main, where he also met Spier (see *Marbacher Magazin* 47, p. 70). In his function as a lawyer, Spier defended Kracauer's interests versus the 'Stelle für Devisenbewirtschaftung' [Office of Foreign Exchange Control] (Kracauer papers, Deutsches Literaturarchiv, Marbach); he intervened on Kracauer's behalf with Benno Reifenberg and Heinrich Simon, and, in case of need, he offered to store his furniture (see below) in his own apartment (Spier to Kracauer, 5 April 1933), Kracauer papers, Deutsches Literaturarchiv, Marbach).

your furniture: after his arrival in Paris, Kracauer learnt of the curtailment of his salary by the *Frankfurter Zeitung*; as the Berlin apartment could not be broken up at short notice, the question of the furniture caused an awkward financial situation because of the double rent. In September 1933 the household goods were brought to Paris by a removal firm (Kracauer to Benno Reifenberg, March to May 1933; Kracauer papers, Deutsches Literaturarchiv, Marbach; *Marbacher Magazin* 47, p. 77).

in the rooms in her factory: after the liquidation of her parents' firm in 1932, Gretel Karplus joined 'the firm of Georg Tengler, Berlin, Dresdenerstrasse as a junior partner on 1.1.1933 .... When my senior partner, Herr Tengler, died in 1934, I continued to run the firm single-handed with a staff of over 200 workers' (see a curriculum vitae composed by Gretel Adorno in Adorno, *Bildmonographie*, p. 114). She directed the business, which manufactured leather gloves, until going into exile in 1937.

Moras ... placing articles: for Joachim Moras, the *Europäische Revue*, and Adorno's and Kracauer's publications in it, see letter no. 49, note.

state examination for private music teachers: the attempt was connected with the anticipated termination of Adorno's university career through the application of §3, section 1, of the 'Law for the Restoration of the Professional Civil Service of 7 April 1933'; the enterprise probably came to nothing (see Gretel Adorno/Benjamin, *Correspondence*, pp. 30–1).

95 Kracauer to Adorno
Paris, 29.4.1933

Paris, 29 April 33.

Dear Teddie,

I received your second letter yesterday, and would like to catch up by thanking you for the first one now. First of all: after Selmar had given me the details of his conversation with your father yesterday I wrote to the latter at once to say how touched we were by his help ... As far as the storage of our things is concerned, we are very grateful to Gretel for her offer. However, in the meantime we have made other arrangements. At this stage we are not contemplating transporting the furniture to Paris, chiefly because of the high costs. I am very grateful to you for drawing my attention to Dr Moras. He always wanted to get in contact with me while I was still in Berlin, but we never managed to fix a date. I shall of course be writing to him. It is nice of you to offer to write to Anita L. The only thing is that I have the impression that this step would be pointless. I am dealing with the firm through Selmar, and at the moment that seems to me the only suitable way. Incidentally, I could write you whole treatises about the firm's behaviour, but can't write them just now. How did you express it so wittily that time? The ships are leaving the rats. Unfortunately, for the moment, I can't see any new ships appearing on the horizon. What was wrong with your stomach? That the cause of the matter is purely psychological is also clear from the fact that you are now suffering from headaches. In my opinion, this results from your pushing yourself too hard and not being lenient enough with yourself. To lock yourself away at this time for the sake of a treatise which is inevitably certain to remain esoteric for some years is nothing short of an attack on your nerves. The best thing would surely be for you to try to do nothing at all for a month so that you can get back to normal and be equipped to face any difficulties you may encounter. I am not usually in favour of sanatoria, but wouldn't you consider the compulsory routine associated with a stay in a sanatorium the best way of calming down? Gretel is sure to share my opinion, which is also Lili's. We are glad that Gretel has found a new job. Can you drop us a line about it? – and also about your plan regarding the music teacher examination? In the relevant circles here, too, projects and changes are the subject of endless discussion. Benje wrote me a postcard from Ibiza. I have heard nothing more from Ernst in Zurich since I had to tell him, to my regret, that things were going badly with us. He runs away from suffering. My days are spent in correspondence which is generally pointless. And instead I could write a great deal just now.

Warmest regards for now – from Lili too – to you and Gretel. Please write again soon; I shall reply quickly. The most important thing is for you to get your health right again.

Yours ...

Original: typescript (carbon copy); Siegfried Kracauer papers, Deutsches Literaturarchiv, Marbach am Neckar.

details of his conversation with your father: on 27 April 1933, Selmar Spier wrote to Kracauer that Oscar Wiesengrund had informed him by telephone that he was prepared to contribute three monthly payments of 50 Reichsmarks each, but that because of further responsibilities no more was possible at that time (Kracauer papers, Deutsches Literaturarchiv, Marbach).

I wrote to the latter at once: not preserved.

from Ibiza: Walter Benjamin wrote to Kracauer on 23 April 1933 (see Benjamin, *Gesammelte Briefe* IV, pp. 191f.).

had to tell him ... that things were going badly with us: not preserved among Bloch's or Kracauer's papers.

96 Adorno to Kracauer
Frankfurt am Main, 5.7.1935

Frankfurt, 5 July 1935.

Dear Friedel,

Allow me to thank you in the name of my parents for your lines, and allow me to do so also on my own behalf. Perhaps only you of all people can really take the measure of what I have lost – not merely the person to whom I owe most in regard to my development but, in addition, the one piece of nature to which I could hold fast – the one who nourished me in the most literal and deepest sense. I do not know how I am going to go on living without her – and, even worse, go on with this life at all. It is also impossible for me to console myself or come to terms with it. How ever could those children have consoled themselves when their cups had run dry. It is despair, then, that actually gives me the courage to write to you, transcending what keeps us apart, and to reach out to you. I am not unrealistic enough – and too old – to think that even a catastrophe like this – which indeed is a catastrophe for me alone – could sweep away what lies between us and wash away the bitterness – that bitterness which on my side might be summed up by the name of your friend Benno and which, I have no doubt, has names in your case, too. To accomplish that would require nothing less than for us to live together, and, all in all, I am still staring into life as if into the depths of a black cave. But at least that cruel silence which has prevailed between us for two years now shall not, as far as it depends on me, last any longer.

In May Agathe had her first, less serious stroke, in Amorbach, with speech impairments which, however, did get better. On the Tuesday after Pentecost there followed a second, which was very much more severe, and they wired me to come home. Agathe recognized me and was visibly glad, and over the last two weeks I was constantly with her, and I was also there when she died. In spite of the fact that her capacity to express herself was impaired and muddled – at the end she spoke German and French all mixed up – I don't believe that she was mentally confused, or at any rate only temporarily, and she even seemed to be becoming more lucid. Her death, then, was caused by a creeping inflammation of the lungs combined with a paralytic difficulty in swallowing. As far as could be ascertained, she was in no physical pain at all. When the inflammation attacked the whole of her lungs, she very quickly lost consciousness and never regained it; the end came about six hours later, while the doctors were still speaking in terms of days. She probably did not even know that she was going to die and believed me to the last when I told her that she would soon be better; she only seemed to doubt it once or twice, and so she died without fear. She bore the whole illness with perfect patience, without all the 'pagan' behaviour with which we so often reproached her – with resignation and without rebelling against nature. Oddly enough, by the way, she neither knew nor suspected that she had had a stroke.

In my childhood, when Agathe kept me out of going to school on the pretext of some mostly non-existent illness, she used to wish me good night with a curious saying: 'Tomorrow you'll sleep until a cow costs a penny.' During her genuine illness these words, which had comforted me more than I can say as a child, came into my mind, and I said them to her every night. This made her happy, and when I began to say them she would finish them herself. It was like that even on the Tuesday; on the Wednesday, when she died, she did not utter a word. That was the last thing that I ever heard her say, and now it seems to me as if a whole life would not be long enough to reflect on it.

Very few people were present at the funeral in consequence of strenuous attempts to dissuade them. I was able to prevent speeches; there was only music – a few pieces of which she was particularly fond. My connections with the *Frankfurter Zeitung* were still adequate to ensure an appropriate position for the announcement of her death.

Maria, who cared for Agathe with unimaginable self-sacrifice, is bearing up bravely. In the middle of July, she is going on holiday with Gretel and me; as we cannot imagine that she would be up to a long journey, we shall probably stay in Germany – perhaps the Black Forest. My father is in a terrible state.

Just this much about myself for now: in Oxford I am attached to Merton College as an advanced student (not, as rumour constantly has it, as a fellow or professor) and am writing a book on the theory of knowledge which has a considerable outer and perhaps also inner scope; for the time being it bears the title 'Phenomenological Antinomies', with the subtitle 'Prolegomena to dialectical logic'. I hope to use part of it (the analysis of categorical perception) as an English dissertation. In terms of success I should mention that I have been elected as a member of the highly exclusive Oxford Philosophical Society. The prospects for later on might not be too bad. But I am still here only on a temporary basis and my place of residence continues to be Frankfurt. I consider it out of the question that I should ever be able to express myself adequately as an author in English and have scarcely any ambitions in that direction. But what kind of worries are those!

Please let me have some serious news of you – about the novel, your work, your life and its fundamentals. Benjamin has sent me a summary of his *Arcades*; I owe him a detailed letter about it – please make it clear to him that it is quite impossible for me to write at present, so that he will not be angry. Please let Ernst know too about Agathe's death; I don't have his address. We had an argument about his latest book, but now peace reigns once more.

Thank you again for your words – all my thoughts are with you.

All my love to you and Lili

Your old Teddie.

Original: typescript with handwritten additions; Siegfried Kracauer papers, Deutsches Literaturarchiv, Marbach am Neckar.

your lines: not preserved.

cups had run dry: possibly an allusion to Psalm 23, reversing 'my cup runneth over'.

what I have lost: Agathe Calvelli-Adorno died on 26 June 1935.

bitterness … your friend Benno: exactly how Benno Reifenberg had offended Adorno and for what he, at least in part, blamed Kracauer, remains an open question.

curious saying: the answer to a jocular question, probably said here in the South Hessian dialect of Frankfurt: 'wann die Kuh en Batze gilt!', which perhaps implies 'an impossibly long time'.

announcement of her death: 'Our dear Agathe Calvelli-Adorno has passed away in her 67th year. What she gave us through the strength and depth of her engagement in a life full of goodness cannot be expressed in words. We keep faith with her. Frankfurt am Main, 1 July 1935. Her sorrowing family and friends. The cremation has already taken place quietly at the request of the deceased. No flowers or visits, by request' (*Frankfurter Zeitung*, 2 July 1935, in the 'Familien-Nachrichten' [family notices column]).

in Oxford: in April 1934, Adorno began his activities at Merton College; this was facilitated through the contacts of a brother of Oscar Wiesengrund, Bernard Robert Wiesengrund (anglicized to Bernard Robert Wingfield (1871–1935)), who was living in England, together with the aid organization Academic Assistance Council (see Adorno/Horkheimer, *Briefwechsel*, pp. 19f.n.).

'Phenomenological Antinomies': Adorno's Oxford works on Husserl were published in *Zur Metakritik der Erkenntnistheorie: Studien über Husserl und die phänomenologischen Antinomien*, Stuttgart: Kohlhammer, 1956 (see Adorno, GS 5, pp. 7–245, 385f.).

English dissertation: the plan was not realized.

Oxford Philosophical Society: three philosophical societies of this kind exist; the history of the oldest goes back to the seventeenth century.

about the novel: the manuscript of *Georg* was already finding readers, including Thomas Mann, who suggested the title *Gesellschaft* to Kracauer in a letter of 8 December 1934. Kracauer adopted Mann's recommendation for the time being, but not his offer of mediation with the Amsterdam exile publishing house Querido (see Kracauer, W 7, pp. 660f.); he signed a contract dated 25 January 1935 with European Press Limited, London, represented by E. Alexander, for the distribution of the novel in the 'English-language areas of England and the USA'. Kracauer's comments on the title: '*Gesellschaft* (a novel from the Republic of Germany). Note: I reserve the right to change this title, which is only *provisional*' (Siegfried Kracauer papers, Deutsches Literaturarchiv, Marbach).

a summary of his Arcades: the subject of Walter Benjamin's message to Adorno of 31 May 1935 (see Adorno/Benjamin, *Briefwechsel*, pp. 116–22) is documented ('Exposé. Paris. Die Hauptstadt des XIX. Jahrhunderts'; see Benjamin, GS V.2, pp. 1237–49).

a detailed letter: Adorno wrote this (dated 2–4 August 1935) in Hornberg, his holiday destination in the Black Forest (see Adorno/Benjamin, *Briefwechsel*, pp. 138–54).

his address: Ernst and Karola Bloch left Vienna in May 1935; at the time of this letter they were living in France.

argument about his latest book: Ernst Bloch, *Erbschaft dieser Zeit* (see letter no. 88). Of the correspondence concerning the dispute about the book, only Bloch's letters to Adorno survive (see Bloch, *Briefe* 2, pp. 423–37).

97 Kracauer to Adorno
Paris, 24.10.1936

Paris (17e) 24 October 1936
3, Avenue Mac-Mahon
(Tél: Etoile 36–61)

Dear Teddie,

I find your jazz article excellent and a true model of a sociological exegesis with empirical content. If the left had embarked on their analysis of the political situation with the same attention to practical content, we would probably have done better. The way in which the wealth of empirical experience is used as part of the interpretation, and the interpretation itself goes behind the manifestly sexual mechanism of jazz and reveals the real significance of the jazz subject – I liked all this very much. Good, too, was the derivation of the jazz subject from the eccentric – and the incorporation of the aleatory quality element which prevails in the selection of hits was also skilful. I could underline many passages as positive, but that takes us too far, and it seems more important to me that you should know that I approve of your methods. If I have any criticisms, they transcend the work. My reservations are aroused by the fact that the criteria which you employ in the interpretation are 100%. You speak of 'proper' society with the embarrassment into which we poor jazz subjects are all coerced, and you rightly assign jazz to the 'wrong' one. But, like the 'wrong' sort of society, jazz is also in your eyes – despite some minute exceptions – so 100% wrong that I can't see how anything right or 'proper' can be derived from it in dialectical terms. That would be justified only if you believed in a *total revolution*. Do you believe in that? You know that jazz has been heard and accepted in Russia, and I myself saw the Soviet film *Les Joyeux Garçons* here, in which jazz was played all the way through.

Conclusions? 1) Russia is a stage of the revolution: in that case you have shortchanged the transitional moments inherent in jazz.

2) Russia today is undergoing a counter-revolution: in that case, let anyone believe in total revolution; 3) Russia is catching up with various

things which it had left behind in its leap forwards; in that case, I ask only why of all things jazz and why with such fervour?

II.

The note from you which was forwarded to me lets me see that you have written to Horkheimer on my behalf. On this point I state explicitly: you did this without any instigation from me and without my knowledge. All that was discussed between us was that I was prepared to *talk* to Horkheimer, *when he is here*. After the diverse rejections which the Institute has dealt me, any initiative to establish contacts on my part is impossible. Completely impossible. So impossible that I would, and shall, pursue any other connection – only not this one. I never have and never shall knock on doors where I have been thrown out three or four times and treated in a way I find disgraceful. I shall go in only *through the front door, wide open*, and be received with full honours.

I earnestly request you not to write to me about this matter – unless the front door is opened. Lili gets far too upset about these things, and now more than ever I want to spare her any upsets. For this reason, I have not told her anything about your letter to Horkheimer, either. So, if you should write to me, don't allude to this business; *above all, not to your letter which was forwarded to me*. If you come in December, we can of course talk about it then.

My *Offenbach*, by the way, is not a work of interpretation but takes the form of a narrative, which of course leaves room for interpretation.

Lili sends you her warmest regards. Wishing you all the best

Yours, Friedel.

Important postscript:

Dear Teddie, as Lili feels so very unwell at present that I don't want to upset her under any circumstances, I have not *made any mention at all* to her of your two letters, which I *fortunately* received *on my own by the morning post* – something which goes entirely against the grain as far as I am concerned, and was very difficult for me.

For this reason, I request you most urgently – and I must be able to rely on you *in an absolutely rock-solid way* in this – *in no way* ever to refer *to your two letters and my replies to them* in future, either in any possible letter to me or subsequently in conversation. This *correspondence with me must be as if it had never been written or even existed* [i.e. with the exception of *my first* letter to you, about whose contents Lili knows – that I wrote to you about the jazz essay and told you that I would enter the Institute only by the front door].

In short, if you write to me (or speak to Lili in December), I implore you most fervently to do so *without any reference* to your two letters and this second one of mine. What you could write or say – naturally as a *completely new fact unknown to me* – might be that you had written to Horkheimer *on your own initiative* and that he had apparently recognized certain misunderstandings as just that and might be interested in one or the other piece of work by me. That *would be enough* – and perhaps also something about my comments on your jazz essay.

I should prefer it most of all if you would destroy *this note*, and naturally I beg you very, very strongly to treat this little conspiratorial intermezzo – a thoroughly embarrassing and unaccustomed one for me – with the very strictest discretion. (If Lili is up to the mark again, I shall of course tell her about it.) But please – if you should happen to write, don't *enquire about her* health *with any special concern*: it is essentially her nerves, and everything is curable. In any case, write in such a way that I can show her everything from now on; at this stage I should like to keep her up to date with things.

Yours, Friedel.

You *will* follow these instructions, won't you?

Original: MS; Theodor W. Adorno Archiv, Frankfurt am Main.

jazz essay: 'Über Jazz', *Zeitschrift für Sozialforschung* V, 1937 (see Adorno, GS 17, pp. 74–108, 347).

sexual mechanism … jazz subject: see ibid., pp. 94–100.

the eccentric: Kracauer writes 'aus *dem Exzentrik*' in the original.

Les Joyeux Garçons: a film by Gregori Alexandrov, USSR, 1934.

the note from you which was forwarded to me: not preserved.

written to Horkheimer: in his letter to Max Horkheimer of 12 October 1936, Adorno reported on his one-week stay in Paris at the beginning of the month, which had served to provide an opportunity for a conversation with Walter Benjamin to sound him out about his collaboration with the Institute. Adorno also met Kracauer, and in his letter suggested Kracauer's involvement in 'a study of propaganda' at the same time as he expressed understanding for the fact that resentments against Kracauer do exist (see Adorno/Horkheimer, *Briefwechsel* I, p. 185).

in December: Adorno spent the second week of December 1936 in Paris.

Offenbach: *Jacques Offenbach ou le Secret du Second Empire* was the subject of the publisher's contract which Kracauer signed with Éditions Bernard Grasset in April 1935. The book was issued by the Paris publisher in May 1937, a month after the German-language edition (*Jacques Offenbach und das Paris seiner Zeit*, Amsterdam: Allert de Lange; see Kracauer, W 8, esp. pp. 537–49).

both letters: not preserved.

98 Kracauer to Adorno
Paris, 9.11.1936

Paris (17e)
3, Avenue Mac-Mahon

9 November 1936

Dear Teddie

I know that I am in your debt, because I am only now acknowledging receipt of your essay on the Tales of Hoffmann, which, by the way, seems to me inferior to the jazz essay because it does not contain enough empirical evidence. The motif of the sketch is a fruitful one. It certainly corresponds, within the internal domain of music, to the emphatically positive accent which I, coming to it from outside, repeatedly grant to Offenbach's so-called superficiality. In the interpretation of the operettas as a whole we appear to be entirely in agreement about this, which makes me especially happy.

I would rather not return to my comment on the jazz essay, as this for me involves very loaded questions of attitude which, even in the form of a written outline, would include too many things that I cannot explain in a letter. I shall of course be happy to discuss it with you face to face if you wish. The words of Gide's which you quote, '*tout cela sera balayé*', are, by the way, extremely puerile. He has, I may remark in passing, come back with strong criticisms of Stalin and many things in Russia; those who parrot Soviet slogans, then, will once again have to put up with having their enthusiasm dampened.

Horkheimer's reply surprised me intensely after all that had preceded it. I shall answer you point for point about the passages relating to me in his letter and authorize you to reproduce my remarks in reply to him:

1) I was not invited several times by Leo, but only once – just after I emigrated – to collaborate with the Institute's *Zeitschrift*; not to collaborate in general or even simply to collaborate by commissioning an essay from me, but to provide a collective review article for the discussion section which was to cover the topic of German books (a highly distasteful one to me) with the instruction to write only twenty lines about each book and to obtain the books myself. For this, a fee was named which would have made the work a luxury which I could not afford. I naturally declined this unworthy offer with I forget what justification. Since that time I have *never again* been invited by the Institute through Leo to collaborate with it. True, Professor Lederer did write to me in the spring of this year, saying that he had spoken with Horkheimer about me,* and, according to the latter, means to have me know that I should get in touch with Leo about reviews, so as to make contact with the Institute – but as I had learnt in the meantime (as you recently

* Notabene this happened entirely without my knowledge and was very unpleasant for me.

confirmed to me) that the Institute had arrived at negative decisions about various initiatives regarding me, and moreover, as Horkheimer's suggestion looked desperately like a deliberate humiliation, I did not walk into the trap but wrote to Lederer that I did not consider this proposition a proposition at all, but would leave it to Horkheimer's discretion for once to *discuss matters directly* with me when he came to Paris again. All these embarrassing contacts, or rather non-contacts, aroused in me the irrefutable certainty that the Institute is filled with an animosity towards me that renders any relationship impossible.

2) I am glad to hear from you that H. appears to be in the process of revising his attitude towards me. I believe, incidentally, that I can distinctly remember that on the occasion when you were here you spoke to me not of a study of propaganda but of *publicity and advertising*. Well, *tant mieux* – for a project about propaganda and the problem of the masses today – *entre nous*! – has at any rate been part of my programme for a long time, and I made notes about this and arranged consultations as early as last summer.

3) a) About the first of the two *conditions* laid down for the execution of such a plan – that the project would have to fit in with the ideas of the Institute – I should say that I would naturally be prepared to discuss my theses in detail with Horkheimer, Pollock and you (with nobody else, though) and accept the results of the discussions. For my part, I would make it an indispensable condition that these discussions should be of a purely research-related character, would declare *nothing* taboo, and would refrain from any outbursts of dictatorial behaviour. I assume that this was also the view on the part of the Institute.

b) The second condition – that I must provide a summary – is legitimate per se. But you are completely mistaken in the assumption that in my situation I could allow myself the risk of a 'major outline'. Since, as we may conclude from your letter, Horkheimer has not yet made an unequivocal statement about whether he is thinking only of an article or of a research proposal, the preconditions are, first and foremost, far too vague a promise that would enable me to devote myself to a longer project and by doing so *neglect other enterprises*. That will not do. On the contrary, what should be done is as follows: you go on trying right up to your visit to Paris in December

α) to obtain a binding assurance from Horkheimer that he – assuming he agrees with what I am thinking – will allow the topic be treated as a research proposal whose organization I could imagine in the way which you mentioned in private. If this basis is provided, and if in addition I obtain a guarantee – I am also asking you to let me know about this *before*

β) your journey to Paris – that Horkheimer (always assuming a fair agreement) is thinking of a satisfactory financial agreement with me – there is no need to mention any figures as yet; it is a matter first and foremost of the *assurance in principle* of such an arrangement, about whose details I myself could correspond with H. on the basis of this assurance – I should immediately write an appropriate summary, discuss all the necessary details with you, etc., etc.

This should give a precise answer to your letter. Warmest regards,

Yours, Friedel.

Original: MS; Theodor W. Adorno Archiv, Frankfurt am Main.

essay on the Tales of Hoffmann: 'Hoffmanns Erzählungen in Offenbachs Motiven', in *Programmschrift der Städtischen Bühnen Düsseldorf*, VIII, 1932 (see Adorno, GS 17, pp. 42–6, 347).

motif of the sketch: 'Otherwise the law of the opera is itself that of the sketch' (see ibid., p. 43).

'tout cela sera balayé': roughly, 'All that will be swept away', the beginning of an extract from André Gide's *Les Nouvelles Nourritures*, Paris: Gallimard, 1935, p. 140. Max Horkheimer wrote to Adorno on 14 May 1926 of his wish to insert the quotation as a motto for an essay of his own (see Adorno/Horkheimer, *Briefwechsel* I, p. 142).

criticisms of Stalin: André Gide travelled through the USSR in the summer of 1936 at the invitation of the Soviet government. His report on the trip (André Gide, *Retour de l'U.R.S.S.*, Paris: Gallimard, 1936) did not meet his hosts' expectations. 'And I doubt whether in any other country today, even Hitler's Germany, this spirit is less free and more bowed, more anxious, more terrorized and subjugated' (see André Gide, *Reisen und Politik: Zurück aus Sowjetrußland*, ed. Raimund Theis and Peter Schnyder, Stuttgart: Deutsche Verlags-Anstalt, 1996, p. 79).

Horkheimer's reply: to Adorno's letter of 12 October 1936; Horkheimer wrote on 22 October 1936 (see Adorno/Horkheimer, *Briefwechsel* I, pp. 192–8).

I was not invited several times by Leo: the invitation mentioned by Kracauer to review for the *Zeitschrift* was issued by Leo Löwenthal in a letter to Kracauer of 19 December 1933; the field which Kracauer wished to cover, including 'French social novels', had already been assigned by the editorial board to Walter Benjamin according to Löwenthal's letter of 18 January 1934 (see Kracauer/Löwenthal, *Briefwechsel*, pp. 74–7): 'Zum gegenwärtigen gesellschaftlichen Standort des französischen Schriftstellers', *Zeitschrift für Sozialforschung*, no 1, 1934 (see Benjamin, GS II.2, pp. 776–803, GS II.3, pp. 1508–19).

Professor Lederer ... in the spring: Emil Lederer (1882–1939), sociologist and economist; professor in Heidelberg (1920) and Berlin (1931); went into exile in the USA. He conveyed Max Horkheimer's suggestion in a letter of 10 May 1936 (MS, Kracauer papers, Deutsches Literaturarchiv, Marbach).

a study ... of publicity: 'Publicity/Advertising and Propaganda' was the subject of Kracauer's planned project as designated in a letter to Max Horkheimer of 15 December 1936.

a summary: Kracauer composed this in December 1936 under the title 'Exposé: Masse und Propaganda (Eine Untersuchung über die fascistische Propaganda)'; the manuscript of this work has been lost (see the printed version of the summary in *Marbacher Magazin* 47, pp. 85–90; a successful reconstruction of the complex appears in Kracauer, W 2.2; on the change of title in the course of the work, see letter no. 120, note).

a binding assurance from Horkheimer: Max Horkheimer had already agreed to the plan for a study of propaganda by Kracauer in his letter to Adorno of 22 October 1936; on 14 November 1936 he expressed this in concrete terms, with recommendations for the forthcoming dialogue between Adorno and Kracauer (see Adorno/Horkheimer, *Briefwechsel* I, pp. 196, 213).

I myself could correspond with H.: Kracauer wrote to Max Horkheimer on 22 December 1936 (MS; Max Horkheimer papers, Archivzentrum der Universitätsbibliothek Johann Christian Senckenberg, Frankfurt am Main); among other things he pointed out that the essay could only be written on the basis of comprehensive studies of the relevant material (see the partial reprint in Adorno/Horkheimer, *Briefwechsel* I, pp. 265f., n.).

99 Kracauer to Adorno
Paris, 21.11.1936

Paris (17e)
3, Avenue Mac-Mahon

21 November 36

Dear Teddie,

My last letter to you (of 9 Nov) was the product of a severe depression and the confusion into which I was thrown, not least by Lili's state of health – but you will have noticed this. I am writing to you chiefly to tell you that I think back on that letter with anxiety.

Fortunately, Lili is feeling much better again – so I should like to recapitulate the main points of the letter to you once again after removing its pathological local colour. There is nothing further to add to the explanations about the past which I gave you at your request – and, as to the two conditions laid down by Horkheimer, I have accepted them with certain reservations to which I should not expect any form of objection – i.e. I am unreservedly prepared to act in accordance with the outcome of the discussions with Horkheimer, Pollock and yourself insofar as these are conducted in a free and impartial way – but that, in fact, goes without saying. In addition, of course, I am prepared to take into account the legitimate conditions applying to a summary which serves a specific purpose, so long as I know for certain beforehand that Horkheimer is not thinking merely of an essay but of a commission for a research project – the subject could not be tackled in any other way – and that, besides this, he is willing to guarantee an income sufficient to live on for the duration of the work. I would try to make such a financial arrangement easier for him – this is a *new addition* – by committing myself to matching the amount offered by contributing to the journal in some way. There should, in any case, be no lack whatsoever of goodwill on my part.

About the material itself, I would say, in addition, that the subject in question has greatly interested me for a long time from a particular point of view. I believe that I can contribute innovations and give the work a character which would make it at least as stimulating as were the *Angestellten* in their time. It might well be that the planned association could be useful to the Institute too. So, dear Teddie, that was what I wanted to say to you once more in summary (with a request for you to forward it if required) so that my position (which was naturally summed up in my last letter) may become entirely clear, and so that you may know precisely that I shall not be causing you any unreasonable difficulties and unexpected hitches in your mediation. On the contrary, I hope that you will be coming to Paris in December with the assurances I have requested, and I am convinced that when we talk things over face to face we shall reach the positive result which is so desirable.

With warmest regards,
Yours,
Friedel

NB. If you write to me, please keep to the instructions in my last letter. So don't allude to our correspondence (or at most to my first letter to you in which I explained that I could only come in by the 'front door'), but just write to me in quite general terms as follows: because of our conversation, and thanks to your actions, certain misunderstandings have been dispelled, and Horkheimer is now prepared to negotiate with me about a major project. That, in fact, is exactly how it is. Doubtless it will be even easier for you to couch your letter, when you write it, in terms that will wipe out any justified bitterness. Once you are here, this secrecy which I have been exercising out of hysterical anxiety and which has nothing whatsoever to do with the business – and, moreover, has only a purely private significance – will become unnecessary. *Tu comprends, n'est-ce pas …*

Yours, Fr.

Original: MS; Theodor W. Adorno Archiv, Frankfurt am Main.

100 Adorno to Kracauer
Oxford, 4.12.1936.

4 December 1936.

MERTON COLLEGE,
OXFORD.

Dear Friedel,

So – I'm coming to Paris to represent the Institute on Tuesday evening (for eight days) and look forward to discussing all the outstanding questions with you. Perhaps you could give me a call at the Littré on

Wednesday morning around 10–11 so that we can fix an appointment straight away.

Much love to Lili too,

Your old Teddie.

Original: MS with printed letterhead; Siegfried Kracauer papers, Deutsches Literaturarchiv, Marbach am Neckar.

with you: Adorno wrote 'with me'.

Littré: Hotel Le Littré, 9 rue Littré, Saint Germain des Prés.

101 Adorno to Kracauer
Oxford, 19.1.1937

MERTON COLLEGE

47 Banbury Road
19 January 1937.

Dear Friedel,

I am back in Oxford and would be extremely grateful if you could give me some news by return of post and let me know about the state of things – and, above all, if you would inform me about what has been happening to you in the five weeks of my absence; I will then write to you at length. Just this short letter for now as I am under a lot of pressure finishing off the Mannheim project.

In Frankfurt, Berlin and Brussels I found everything in good order and had no problems of any kind either.

I spoke to your aunt on the telephone.

I hope that the New Year has got off to a good start for the two of you. Absurd as it sounds, we had an especially nice time in Berlin.

Much love to you both,

Your old Teddie.

Original: MS with printed letterhead, card; Siegfried Kracauer papers, Deutsches Literaturarchiv, Marbach am Neckar.

Mannheim project: of the manuscripts leading to the printed version (*Das Bewußtsein der Wissenssoziologie*, published under the title 'Über Mannheims Wissenssoziologie', *Aufklärung*, 1953; see Adorno, GS 10.1, pp. 31–46, GS 10.2, p. 839), two versions dated 1937 have survived (Theodor W. Adorno Archiv); one consists of 37 pages, the other 21 (see letter no. 118, in which Adorno mentions a shorter variant). On a further work on Mannheim, 'Neue wertfreie Soziologie', see letter no. 106.

Brussels: possibly a visit to Gabriele and Paul Oppenheim, who lived in exile in Brussels, Gabriele Oppenheim's native city, until their emigration to the USA in 1939 (see Adorno/Horkheimer, *Briefwechsel* I, p. 80, note).

102 Adorno to Kracauer
Oxford, 27.1.1937

Oxford, 47 Banbury Road,
27 January 1937.

Dear Friedel,

I am somewhat surprised – and concerned – to have heard nothing at all from you. Didn't you receive my card with the little note? Or have you been laid low by the flu?

In the meantime, Horkheimer has sent me a carbon copy of his letter to you, with which I am entirely in agreement. I hope that this has brought matters to a positive conclusion and that you gave him a positive answer. The question of what you might live on for the duration of the project seems to me to be satisfactorily cleared up by the method of payment suggested by Horkheimer. I would be grateful if you could let me have a brief outline of your work (as you described it to Horkheimer, if I understood him correctly) as a guide, i.e. a carbon copy of the outline that is going to New York.

In addition, I should like to suggest that you should not lose sight of the plan which I instigated for a longer essay about architecture. As you know, I have a plan to put together Benjamin's work on film, mine on jazz, and possibly a few others for publication as a collective book on art and consumption in the monopolist phase, and I have proposed that Horkheimer take on the task of writing the introductory essay. The project is still quite vague, but in principle Horkheimer's attitude towards it is positive, and an essay on architecture would fit in well (quite apart from the possibility of prior publication in the *Zeitschrift*). If the business of the propaganda project works out (i.e. the Institute also agrees about its content), there might be a possibility of a second contract on the lines of the present one. But please take these initiatives as, first and foremost, private ones on my part. Horkheimer doesn't know anything yet about the architecture plan; I would just like you to think the matter over – especially if you believe that it might somehow be arranged around a common denominator that it could share with the theory of jazz.

Meanwhile I have been finishing a major piece of criticism (longer than the 'Jazz') in opposition to Mannheim's so-called generalizing sociology; and I am very pleased with it. Back to the Husserl book since yesterday.

I hope that I shall soon be coming to Paris again. However, plans for the whole of the spring are still somewhat unclear.

An exceedingly charming letter from Gubler came today.

Warmest regards, to Lili too,

Your old

Teddie.

Original: typescript with handwritten additions and corrections; Siegfried Kracauer papers, Deutsches Literaturarchiv, Marbach am Neckar.

Horkheimer sent me a carbon copy: this accompanied Max Horkheimer's letter to Adorno of 11 January 1937. In the letter addressed to Kracauer of 9 January 1937, Horkheimer confirmed the contract for an essay with an honorarium of 6,000 francs and left the question of the form of the work open, inasmuch as, in the case of the article's proving unsuitable for the *Zeitschrift*, he would consent to the inclusion of the work in the Institute's Archive (see Adorno/Horkheimer, *Briefwechsel* I, pp. 267–70).

that you have written: this was done on 28 January 1937: 'First of all, allow me to thank you for your kind offer. I am happy to accept this offer.' It may be assumed from the letter that Kracauer enclosed with it the requested summary (Kracauer to Max Horkheimer, 28 January 1937; Max Horkheimer papers, Archivzentrum der Universitätsbibliothek Johann Christian Senckenberg, Frankfurt am Main).

publication as a collective book: the volume *Massenkunst im Monopolkapitalismus* was abandoned for economic reasons; its contents were also to have included 'The detective novel / Neue Sachlichkeit / applied art / radio / illustrated papers (international) / film in a narrower sense' (Adorno to Walter Benjamin, 2 July 1937; see Adorno/Benjamin, *Briefwechsel*, pp. 258f.).

charming letter from Gubler: not preserved in the Theodor W. Adorno Archiv.

103 Adorno to Kracauer
Oxford, 1.2.1937

Oxford
47 Banbury Road
1 February 1937

Dear Friedel,

Many thanks for your letter. I cannot deny that the latest developments have taken a load off my mind – and I hope that I didn't misunderstand you by taking your 'prepared to concur with Horkheimer's offer' as an acceptance of this offer. I would be especially grateful if you would clear up this point at once, even if only by postcard. I should just like to add that it seems particularly important that, in order to avoid any possible clashes in the future, it is made clear to the Institute that the matter of the stipend will be dropped on your acceptance of the offer, as it would of course be a very sensitive matter for the Institute if a piece of work undertaken under contract to it suddenly appeared in another context, and possibly one with purposes completely contrary to ours. Well, as surely as I know that nothing of the kind is to be anticipated, do I consider it advisable at the same time, not least for reasons relating to the psychological climate, that things should be clearly understood from the outset. As far as that climate is concerned, by the way, as soon as Horkheimer is in Europe there will be (*rebus sic stantibus*) plenty of opportunities to deal with any lingering misunderstandings. It goes without saying that I shall contribute to this in every possible way.

As for the question of whether the work should be concerned with content or methodology, I really wouldn't worry too much about that and by no means place too much emphasis on it, as it seems to me that in this aspect we differ from bourgeois scholarship precisely in the fact that, rather than sharing the division by method and subject, we let both emerge dialectically one from the other (to use an expression which cannot be avoided).

I am immersed in my book again. This week Chapter VII will, I hope, be finished in rough draft – and then there is just one left, and after that the final version of the whole thing, of which the first three chapters have already been written up and the later ones will need to be pruned. Just now I am stopping at the section about phenomenology and Jugendstil, which I find especially interesting.

Much love, also to Lili,
Your old
Teddie.

Original: typescript with handwritten corrections; Siegfried Kracauer papers, Deutsches Literaturarchiv, Marbach am Neckar.

your letter: not preserved.

the matter of the stipend: in his letters to Max Horkheimer of 22 December 1936 and 28 January 1937, Kracauer referred to the fact that he had written a summary of his work on *Masse und Propaganda* for the purpose of applying for a research grant; see the abstract sent with the following letter by Kracauer in his letter to Max Horkheimer of 5 February 1937.

Chapter VII … section about phenomenology and Jugendstil: the chapter and sections of the 'Husserl book' differ significantly from the structure of *Zur Metakritik der Erkenntnistheorie*; the original manuscript is preserved in the Theodor W. Adorno Archiv.

104 Kracauer to Adorno
Paris, 6.2.1937

Paris (17e),
3, Avenue Mac-Mahon 6 February 1937

Dear Teddie,

I am sending herewith the copy of a letter which I sent to Horkheimer yesterday; I wrote it on receipt of yours. This letter of yours made me aware of the danger of a possible misunderstanding, and I share your view that absolute clarity must prevail. That was why I sent the letter to New York; its content is, I believe, so clear that it needs no further comment. There is just this one point: that now – in the interest of avoiding any remotely imaginable contaminations which I could not foresee – *en tout cas* I should prefer to change the subject. If Horkheimer, as I hope, agrees to my suggestion, the horizon will indeed be cloudless at last. In the two to three weeks which will elapse before his answer arrives I will still be completely occupied by the various Offenbach editions. The foreign-language ones have recently been joined by the German version, for which I have a whole lot of things to do as it has to be put together quickly. On receiving Horkheimer's letter I shall have progressed precisely to the point where I may be able to make a start on the work for the *Zeitschrift*.

Much love and kind regards to you, from Lili too, and very best wishes for your work.

Yours,

NB. You will receive the summary next week.

Original: typescript (carbon copy); Siegfried Kracauer papers, Deutsches Literaturarchiv, Marbach am Neckar.

copy of a letter which I sent to Horkheimer: quoted from the original, Kracauer to Max Horkheimer, 5 February 1937, typescript (Max Horkheimer papers, Archivzentrum der Universitätsbibliothek Johann Christian Senckenberg, Frankfurt am Main):

Dear Herr Horkheimer,

I recently received a letter from my friend Wiesengrund which was, however, written in ignorance of the wording of my letter which I wrote to you on 22 December 1936. In Wiesengrund's letter the following passage occurs:

'I should just like to add that it seems particularly important to me that, in order to avoid any possible clashes in the future, it be made clear to the Institute that the matter of the grant will be dropped at your acceptance of the offer, as it would of course be a very sensitive matter for the Institute if a piece of work undertaken under contract to it suddenly appeared in another context, and possibly one with purposes completely contrary to ours.'

The opinion which Wiesengrund expresses here is the reason that I am writing to you at once, to forestall any possible misunderstanding which might have slipped in despite the clarity of our correspondence.

May I recapitulate the passages relating to the decisive point?

a) In my letter of 22 December I informed you that I was applying for a grant for a major study precisely on this very subject of propaganda; that in pursuit of my efforts to obtain such a grant I had written a summary entitled *Masse und Propaganda*; and that should my endeavours be successful I would happily distil an essay for the *Zeitschrift* from the material to be collected with a view to the full-scale study which I was planning.

b) From your letter of 9 January I learnt to my satisfaction that you were offering me the material opportunity to collect the necessary documentation for the purpose of the essay. Your letter was silent about the question that I had raised about the grant, which led me to the unambiguous conclusion that you did not want either to entangle this question with that of the *Zeitschrift* essay or to broach it at all at present.

c) In my reply to your letter (dated 28 January), in which I thanked you for your offer and accepted it, I also thought, from what it said, that I should not refer to the matter of the grant any longer. I did, however, remind you once again, for the very purpose of avoiding any misunderstanding, that I had written the enclosed summary as a basis for an application for a grant which I had set in motion.

This was the course of our correspondence, from which I had no reason to suppose that you (as Wiesengrund assumes) were of the opinion that my acceptance of your offer for me to write the essay in question automatically entailed renouncing the application which I had initiated, by means of the summary which I sent to you, for an independent grant. It was all the more unhesitatingly that I upheld my application as Wiesengrund's other fears seem to me to be unfounded.

The matter of the grant stands as follows: I am endeavouring, for work in the fields mentioned in the summary, to obtain a major research contract which would guarantee me a secure living for approximately two years – i.e. that it would provide financial security for the probable duration of the work. It is still quite impossible to predict, for the time being, whether my efforts will actually be successful. But should they achieve their purpose – how could any conflicts arise from that? I did not know to what extent the ideas of the party which I was trying to interest in my summary, which was explicitly in keeping with my approach, could be opposed to those of the Institute, and I am equally unable to imagine that the essay which was planned and destined exclusively for the *Zeitschrift* would lose any of its value to the Institute if a book by me on the same subject, commissioned by that institution, should happen to be published at some time in the future.

But I do not want to prejudice your opinion by stating mine. In the end, I may be mistaken and, in fact, for reasons I fail to understand at this time, you do consider my writing the essay to be irreconcilable with proceeding with the application I mentioned. If this is the case, I should have – as you will understand – to withdraw the consent which I had given you in the interests of possibly obtaining a long-term grant and give up the essay for the *Zeitschrift.*

Understandably, I should be reluctant to find myself in such a dilemma. And to avoid it at all costs, and at the same time to ward off in advance any shadow of one of the complications which Wiesengrund fears, I should like to suggest to you not to restrict your offer to the topic of propaganda but should give me a certain *carte blanche*, which would allow me, in the course of the first few weeks after the beginning of our agreement, to outline another important topic, which I would, of course, assume the responsibility of writing up within the designated time-limit of four months. After going through several volumes of the *Zeitschrift* and some preliminary reflections, I have gained the impression that roughly with the following subjects surrounding the array of ideas in my summary we would be thinking along the same lines: a sociological evaluation of broadcasting; a study of democratic advertising or a historical/critical examination of the various theories about the masses, which would be of particular interest to me personally. I am expressing these views without any obligation and in anticipation of your own counter-statements in response to them.

If (as I hope) you agree with these suggestions of mine arising from Wiesengrund's concerns, I would, as already stated, provide you with a final detailed list of topics to choose from within a few weeks.

In anticipation of a reply at your earliest convenience, I remain,

Yours sincerely,

S. Kracauer.

Offenbach editions: as well as the French- and German-language editions, in May 1937 *Offenbach and the Paris of his Time* was published by Constable, London (see Kracauer, W 8, p. 539). In 1938, the English translation by Gwenda David and Eric Mosbacher was published by Alfred A. Knopf, New York, under the title *Orpheus in Paris: Offenbach and the Paris of his Time.* Also in the same year a Swedish edition came out (see Levin, no. VIIIg).

105 Adorno to Kracauer
Oxford, 11.2.1937

Oxford
47 Banbury Road
11 February 1937.

Dear Friedel,

I am very grateful to you for the clarity created by your letter, and especially by the one to Horkheimer, but I must confess that the outlines which become apparent through such clarity do cause me some concern. You will allow me – poor diplomat that I am – a certain degree of frankness in attempting to explain to you the reasons for my concern.

If nothing more were involved than an occasional essay with no strings attached, there would be no need to waste words on the matter. But this essay itself *is* – to use your words – part of a four-month 'research contract'. It seems to me irreconcilable with the sense of such a contract if the Institute were to gain the benefit only of a 'programmatic' essay while the actual results would be to the advantage of another party – and, now as before, one completely unknown to us.

There is a whole series of partial aspects which confirm this view of mine. First and foremost, the very fact that you don't mention this party by name, either to Horkheimer or to me. You believe that its intentions would certainly be reconcilable with those of the Institute. But should the Institute not have a say in the decision? And it cannot do so as long as we do not even know who and what is actually involved. Lucidity, however, would be all the more desirable in this case because you know very well that, with this project as a whole, I was pursuing further perspectives that were by no means delimited by those four months. Moreover, the fact that you did not say a single word about this plan for obtaining a grant and your own idea on the same subject when I unfolded the idea of the propaganda project in Paris in October, but only in a letter which you wrote to me here when I had already made an official approach to the Institute, makes me feel rather uneasy. Not that I had the slightest doubt about your presentation of the matter – but the delay in letting me know has dislocated the whole thing to some extent. But, finally – your suggestion of limiting yourself to methodology in the essay for the *Zeitschrift* now takes on another meaning. When I suggested a preliminary 'methodological' summary to you in December, you declined on the grounds that you could not manage this without substantial preparatory work. I conveyed this to Horkheimer, and this resulted in his offer in its present form. Now that you have a four-month research contract from the Institute and yet are still restricting yourself to 'methodology', that can only mean that you want to keep your material results in reserve for the other place while, at the same time, the Institute is contributing to funding the substantial preliminary work as well. I don't see, though, how I can justify this to the Institute.

Now, I know very well that all this is open to discussion, and in no way do I want to dwell on the details. One thing, however, appears to me to be out of the question: that the form which they constitute as a whole is not good for the psychological atmosphere. I had hoped that our collaboration – which to a very great extent would be one between you and me – would find its shape as a result of a practical association combined with personal solidarity. However, I cannot dismiss the impression that, for you, the Institute and our work represents just one card – and not one of any great value – in a pack of cards which you are holding carefully in your hand. Indeed, I cannot dispel the impression that you are not hugely tempted by the thought of this collaboration – that you would rather prefer other possibilities, or in any event prefer to remain open to them. But when Ginster rightly says that he would not wish to be the 'last mouse', you will not blame the most genuine humanism for not wanting to be the last bird in your hand, or, least of all, the flies that the Devil eats as a last resort. I have the greatest understanding for your financial situation and your wish to earn as much money as possible. But your collaboration with the Institute cannot consist of your selling your 'labour power as a commodity'. Rather, we presume that these things are kept in sight from the outset, with complete frankness and no reservations – and thus, first and foremost, that you should discuss this plan about the grant with us so that we can eventually come to an agreement. However, I am not enthusiastic about incorporating the Institute idea into a system of tactical considerations and calculated measures. But if *I* react like this, how will things go with those who are not so close to you. I don't think that the worldly wisdom you are developing in this situation will do much to help the cause.

Nor do I think that your alternative suggestions are very happy ones. The topic of broadcasting can be excluded because for the last three months we have already had a manuscript by Schoen, whom we cannot disregard as a specialist in this field – especially as his situation is truly desperate. On closer examination, the two other suggestions are parerga to the propaganda project – and parerga are the very thing I would wish to avoid.

I will make a suggestion. Try to get a clear and definite perspective on the grant business before beginning work on *Propaganda und Masse* – that is, of course, within the next three weeks. It has been up in the air for so long now that it should not be difficult to arrive at a decision. If you obtain the grant, then the Institute's suggestion becomes redundant – which naturally would not affect agreements about other pieces of work for us. If you don't get it, the offer from the Institute holds good, on condition that the Institute possesses exclusive rights to the work as a whole. I cannot advocate that the work should be done jointly for the Institute and for the mystery institution. This is conditional on Horkheimer's agreeing to my suggestion. I shall let him know.

When I shall be coming to Paris is quite uncertain. It depends partly on Horkheimer's trip to Europe and partly, to be frank, on the development of the situation with you.

Warmest regards, to Lili too, from your old

Teddie.

Original: typescript with handwritten additions and corrections; Siegfried Kracauer papers, Deutsches Literaturarchiv, Marbach am Neckar.

party … unknown to us: it remains unclear whether there actually was the prospect of a grant for a major piece of research on the 'propaganda' complex of ideas or whether this option was part of a strategy for negotiating with the Institute.

limiting yourself to methodology: Kracauer made this suggestion in his letter to Max Horkheimer of 28 January 1927 (see letter no. 102, note).

not wish to be the 'last mouse': 'An appeal was launched in the town to defend the Fatherland to the last man and mouse. Ginster did not want to be the last mouse at any price, and still less to creep out of his hole at all' (*Ginster*; see Kracauer, W 7, p. 236). Adorno's imagery includes a reference to the popular saying 'In der Not frißt der Teufel Fliegen' [Anything is allowed in a highly difficult situation], which, in turn, makes use of the epithet 'Herr der Fliegen' originally associated with the Aramaic ba'al-debaba (Beelzebub). See also the self-characterization of Mephistopheles in Goethe's *Faust*, lines 1516–17: 'Der Herr der Ratten und der Mäuse, Der Fliegen, Frösche, Wanzen, Läuse …' [The Lord of Rats and Lord of Mice, / Lord of the Flies, Frogs, Bugs, and Lice, …], in *Faust I & II*, ed. and trans. Stuart Atkins, Cambridge, MA: Suhrkamp/Insel, 1984.

topic of broadcasting … a manuscript by Schoen: Adorno informed Max Horkheimer in a letter of 26 October 1936 that he had received Ernst Schoen's study of broadcasting; this can almost certainly be identified as the typescript which survives among Schoen's papers, *Über die Funktion des Rundfunks in den Vereinigten Staaten, England und Deutschland* (see Adorno/Horkheimer, *Briefwechsel* I, pp. 173f., note 200).

Horkheimer's agreeing ... let him know: Adorno informed Horkheimer about the 'suggestion' by enclosing a carbon copy of this letter with his letter to Adorno of 12 February 1937 (see Adorno/Horkheimer, *Briefwechsel* I, pp. 283–5). Horkheimer thanked Adorno in a letter of 22 February for the latter's 'attitude of solidarity towards Kracauer', adding immediately afterwards: 'Just like you, I myself am constantly feeling yet again that the extension of our circle is probably completely impossible' (ibid., p. 296).

106 Adorno to Kracauer
Oxford, 28.2.1937

Oxford, 47 Banbury Road
28 February 1937

Dear Friedel,

The term is coming to an end; in all probability I shall be here only until the 14th, then in London for a few days and then in Germany (Frankfurt and Berlin, in any case; probably for two weeks in Baden-Baden). I am not thinking of coming to Paris, unless the course of day-to-day business at the Institute makes it necessary.

In this I am thinking, first and foremost, of what concerns you – and so I should like to ask you urgently as well as warmly to answer my letter as quickly as possible so that I may be able to report back to New York. In any case, it is too late to exchange letters with H.; everything would have to be done by telegram. I assume, though, that in the meantime you have got a clear picture of things, especially about the question of the grant – so please don't keep me waiting any longer. Otherwise it will hardly be possible to reach me before the end of April. This would possibly mean the loss of two months – for the Institute, but also for you.

Many thanks for the summary, which I have studied in depth. I will write to you in detail about it over the next two weeks. At present I quite simply don't have the time.

In the meantime, I am sure that you will have read the rough version of the manuscript of my work on Mannheim, and I should be very grateful if you would give me your views on it.

I am in the process of finishing the rough draft of my book (now already 420 typewritten pages like these). But I still have the whole task of the *Instrumentation* before me – turning a monstrous concept into a book of no more than 250–300 printed pages which will satisfy both the factual and linguistic demands of the subject in equal measure. I still shudder whenever I think of it.

I hope that you and Lili are hale and hearty, and that the Offenbach is doing well.

Warmest regards
Yours ever
Teddie.

Original: typescript; Siegfried Kracauer papers, Deutsches Literaturarchiv, Marbach am Neckar.

the rough version of the manuscript of my work on Mannheim: among Kracauer's papers there exists a version of 'Neue wertfreie Soziologie: Aus Anlass von Karl Mannheims *Mensch und Gesellschaft im Zeitalter des Umbaus*'; typescript (carbon copy) with a handwritten title under the pseudonym of Hektor Rottweiler; it differs in places from the version in the GS (see Adorno, GS 20.1, pp. 13–45).

107 Kracauer to Adorno
Paris, 5.3.1937

Paris (17e),
3, Avenue Mac-Mahon. 5 March 1937.

Dear Teddie,

I am only answering your letter of 11 February today (I have also received the one of 28 February) because I wanted to wait first of all for Horkheimer's reply to my letter of 5 February. It arrived yesterday. Herr Horkheimer has informed me that the propaganda topic seems to him to be the only possible one and that he will leave it to you to settle the questions which I touched on in the letter of 5 February mentioned above.

Without lingering over those observations in your first letter which you yourself say are all open to discussion – they actually impute motives and attitudes to me of which I know myself to be innocent – I shall come straight away to its practical core. The alternative which you set before me reads as follows: either the matter of the grant must be dropped or I must give up the essay for the Institute. In other words, you give me to understand in the name of the Institute that the offer of the four-month contract by the Institute cannot be reconciled with the fact that I am seeking a grant for a subject in this same area which would guarantee me a secure income to live on for one to two years and would likewise enable me, because of its duration, to undertake a project of far broader scope and, consequently, to develop other material.

Unfortunately, I have so far been unable to find anything out about the success of my application for the grant. Nevertheless, I have now made up my mind to accept the contract from the Institute under the conditions which you propose – i.e. that the study which I shall carry out under contract to the Institute over the four months envisaged for this on the subject of 'Mass and Propaganda' will be for the sole benefit of the Institute, and I shall not use it for any other purpose. It is in this sense that I understand the sentence in your letter: 'If you don't get it (i.e. the grant), the offer from the Institute holds good, on condition that the Institute possesses exclusive rights to the work as a whole.' It goes without saying that I retain the freedom to embark on possible research projects at a later date in the field in question.

Herr Horkheimer has asked me to let him know what terms I have agreed with you. Now that the obstacle has been removed which stood in the way of your offering the contract, please drop me a line which will allow me to inform Horkheimer that I shall make a start on the study on 1 April at the latest.

Warmest regards, from Lili too,
Yours
Friedel

NB. Benjamin, whom I shall be seeing again in the next few days, is going to take this opportunity of bringing me your Mannheim essay. Of course I shall be happy to write to you soon with my opinion of it.

Original: typescript; Theodor W. Adorno Archiv, Frankfurt am Main.

Horkheimer has informed me: in a letter of 23 February 1937 (see Kracauer papers, Deutsches Literaturarchiv Marbach).

108 Adorno to Kracauer
Oxford, 6.3.1937

Oxford
47 Banbury Road.
6 March 1937.

Dear Friedel,

Your letter has arrived at last; I was very pleased with it. I think that the sense of the agreement has now been unambiguously established, and there is no longer any obstacle to its taking effect.

Just one more thing: as you formulate it, 'In other words, you give me to understand in the name of the Institute that the offer of the four-month contract by the Institute cannot be reconciled with the fact that I am seeking a grant for a subject in this same area which would guarantee me a secure income to live on for one to two years and equally would enable me, because of its duration, to undertake a project of far wider scope and in consequence to develop other material.' If I understand the tone of this sentence correctly, it implies that my 'condition' expects you to sacrifice, as it were, a major opportunity for the sake of a modicum of security. Now, the meaning of my suggestion was precisely to avoid such a sacrifice – i.e.

to give you the opportunity to clarify the matter of the grant *first*, and, if it materialized, to give up the Institute idea in preference to that. This, it seems to you, was unsuccessful, and as a result that element of risk continues to be present. I cannot do away with it, as I cannot delete that so-called condition. Naturally, though, I should not want your accepting my suggestion to prejudice any subsequent chances you might have of obtaining that grant either. So do think again about whether you want to take on something which seems to you like a risky business. I couldn't assume the responsibility of depriving you of that prospect by pressing the point. In the end you must make the decision for yourself. Please be kind enough to let me know of it very soon. If it should happen to be a positive one – and as long as I have no need to expect any reproaches from you should the grant fall through – I shall give instructions at once for payment at the agreed rates to begin on 1 April.

When you go on to say that the 'motives and attitudes' which I aired in my long letter are not yours, nobody would be happier than I; you will have a very straightforward means of dispelling any confusion by discussing the matter of the grant openly with me, and also by telling me who the other party is. Please be assured that I am not suggesting this out of curiosity (and, of course, without its affecting our present agreement in any way) – but precisely because I am envisaging a collaboration lasting beyond these four months, such a clarification of the situation would be highly desirable for the whole atmosphere, and in your interest.

Perhaps, however, the opportunity may arise for us to have a talk about this. It is not out of the question that because of our agreement I may be coming to Paris around the 20th, after all. This partly depends on Pollock's trip to Europe. I may possibly send Horkheimer another message about Paris; for that very reason it would be especially important to me to have an answer from you as quickly as possible. If I were to come to Paris we would also have time to discuss your summary and the plans for the project in detail. Until now I have literally not been able to find the three hours that would have been necessary for a relatively thorough letter about the summary. I am up to my ears in work on finalizing the concept of the Husserl book – and next week is still looking very murky. Because of this I should be very glad if I could come to Paris.

About the Mannheim project, let me just add that the copy which you will receive is – also for reasons of lack of time – an uncorrected one. The definitive text contains countless changes, corrections, deletions and additions. The version in front of you is hardly more than a concept. Especially in matters of language I must ask your forbearance.

I am glad that at least this preliminary project is signed and sealed, and hope to have some information from you as quickly as possible.

Much love to you and Lili

Your old

Teddie.

If you should come to a positive decision, you can of course let Herr Horkheimer know that we have reached an agreement.

Original: typescript with handwritten corrections and postscript; Siegfried Kracauer papers, Deutsches Literaturarchiv, Marbach am Neckar.

Pollock's trip to Europe: Max Horkheimer informed Adorno in a letter of 12 March 1937 that Friedrich Pollock's journey had been postponed for at least a week because of illness, and for this reason Adorno should proceed with his *Dispositionen* independently (see Adorno/Horkheimer, *Briefwechsel* I, p. 318).

109 Kracauer to Adorno
Paris, 8.3.1937

Paris (17e),
3, Avenue Mac-Mahon 8 March 1937.

Dear Teddie,

Many thanks for your letter, which I answered immediately to the effect that the decision which I set out in my letter to you of March 5th still holds good. I shall write by the same post to Herr Horkheimer to tell him that we have come to an agreement and that I shall make a start on the study on April 1st.

If you should come to Paris, after all, we could also discuss the Mannheim essay (which I received yesterday evening) in person.

In haste – warmest greetings from Lili too,

Yours –

NB. It is very welcome news and means a lot to me that, as I gather from your letter, you want to give instructions for payment immediately at the agreed rates to commence on April 1st.

Original: typescript (carbon copy); Siegfried Kracauer papers, Deutsches Literaturarchiv, Marbach am Neckar.

write by the same post to Herr Horkheimer: in a letter of 8th April 1937, Max Horkheimer confirmed receipt of Kracauer's note and also ratified the agreement (Kracauer archive, Deutsches Literaturarchiv, Marbach).

110 Adorno to Kracauer
Oxford, 9.3.1937

9 March 1937

MERTON COLLEGE,
OXFORD.

Dear Friedel!

Everything is all right, then; I wrote to Geneva at once and sent a telegram to New York.

If or when I come to Paris depends on the reply. As I have business in London for a few days from Monday onwards, the middle of next week is the earliest that I could be there. If that materializes, I shall let you know in plenty of time. Then the two of us must set aside a whole day to discuss the plan.

Much love, to Lili too
Your old Teddie.

Original: MS with printed letterhead, card; Siegfried Kracauer papers, Deutsches Literaturarchiv, Marbach am Neckar.

wrote to Geneva: not preserved.

sent a telegram to New York: the telegram to Max Horkheimer of 10 March 1937 reads: 'KRACAUER ACCEPTS CONDITIONS STOP PLEASE WIRE WHETHER INSTITUTE EXPECTS ME PARIS MIDDLE NEXT WEEK CORDIALLY TEDDIE' (see Adorno/Horkheimer, *Briefwechsel* I, p. 317).

111 Adorno to Kracauer
London, 17.3.1937

ALBEMARLE COURT HOTEL
LEINSTER GARDENS. LANCASTER GATE. W2.

17 March 37.

Dear Friedel,

So I am leaving for Paris tomorrow, primarily to discuss the plans for the work and everything connected with it with you. It seems better to me to come *now* – i.e. before you have made a start – than to wait until the end of April.

Please be so kind as to call me early on Friday at the Littré (tel. Littré 6771) – between 10 and 11 would be best.

And I should very much like to reserve *Saturday* for us; I would be very grateful if you could arrange for us to have the whole day – i.e. so that you can have lunch with me too.

À bientôt – warmest greetings
Your old Teddie.

Original: MS with printed letterhead; Siegfried Kracauer papers, Deutsches Literaturarchiv, Marbach am Neckar.

the whole day: Adorno informed Max Horkheimer about the conversation in a letter of 23 March 1937 (see Adorno/Horkheimer, *Briefwechsel* I, pp. 326f.).

112 Adorno to Kracauer
Oxford, 13.5.1937

Oxford, 47 Banbury Road
13 May 1937

Dear Friedel,

Warmest thanks for sending the Offenbach, which greatly delighted me. I read the book at once, and very thoroughly. I should like nothing better than to be able to agree with it, just as I agreed with your *Ginster* in the end. But I can't; as I have criticisms which apply to much more than mere details, I feel that it is my duty to mention them to you. The decision to do so has not been easy at all for me, just as it will not be easy for you to listen to my criticisms. However, if our relationship still exists in the present and is not merely feeding on the past, I could not take on the responsibility of remaining silent at a moment like this. I would rather expose myself to the reproach of spurious profundity which is expressed with such insistence in your book than turn our relationship into a farce from which even you would have to withhold the legitimation which you concede to Offenbach's farce. If a matter which stands to reason, i.e. to criticize a friend, becomes so exceptionally difficult in this case, then the reason is not merely that we have for far too long been out of the habit of criticizing each other. I do also know that the book had its genesis in a period of acute distress and that one could easily reduce all the flaws to which I must raise objections to this predicament. But you yourself rejected the possibility of proceeding in this way by declaring explicitly to me that you would defend the book; and what has even greater weight – for even if you assumed a cynical attitude towards your text, it might well be distasteful to you to admit your cynicism, although I would feel this kind of cynicism to be honourable and not the opposite – is that the book betrays the fact in every word that it is not merely evidence that you have to earn a living but that it lays claim to a certain distinctness. This is clear enough even from the preface. My criticisms, then, are directed not so much against the fact that, as you put it in Paris, it dispenses with theory and retains a narrative/descriptive form of representation. I considered this approach entirely feasible, and also wholly justified by the situation. What I object to is precisely the theory, or rather the attitude that shows through it, and the fact that your style has been determined by such an attitude.

Let me begin with a few musical details which it may be useful to correct for the French and English editions. The double bass is called in German not *Kontrebass* but *Kontrabass*, and it is known solely by this name. The harp tremolos mentioned on page 37 are indeed technically possible and are even mentioned in Berlioz's *Treatise on Instrumentation*, but they represent a highly unusual and isolated orchestral effect which is very rarely used. It is out of the question that the boulevards of Louis Philippe's day resounded to such tremolos – you probably had the chirping or twangling of harps in your ears and lent it the name of tremolo – which is more musical, it is true, but factually inappropriate. The assertion that Offenbach 'placed the greatest emphasis on rhythm' (p. 217) is quite meaningless in musical terms and would require the most scrupulous exactitude to imply anything more than any random journalist's idea of 'rhythm that makes one tingle'. But, above all, on p. 233 you speak of the 'piccolo score'. Any amateur knows (as Lili, as a musician, would certainly confirm) that 'score' is exclusively the name given to the sum of all the parts resounding simultaneously to create a single entity consisting of systems of notes superimposed on one another; a *single* instrument never has a 'score' but only what it plays, i.e. its own 'part', and thus we speak of the 'piccolo part' or the 'voice of the piccolo'. The lordly declaration in the preface that the book abstains, 'faithful to its intention, from the intricacies of musical analysis and interpretation' is compromised to a very serious degree by such errors.

How, then, does this abstinence fare in the overall structure of the book? It claims to be a 'societal biography'. Surely this can only mean that Offenbach's work and its history are examined in the context of the social history of the period. But, if the period is indeed to be 'reconstructed' in the work, that can only be done when both genuinely absorb each other – i.e. in its musical character or, more precisely, through its technical analysis. Dispensing with it means nothing less than presenting analogies or vague relations in place of succinct definitions. Now I know, of course, how difficult it is to express a technological analysis in social terms. Nevertheless, in the case of Offenbach, the commensurate analytical approach has been, as it were, predecided. It would involve unfolding the dialectic between the composer's productive force and 'banality' in Offenbach's work, deciphering the boundary lines towards the banal and pursuing the technique of the sketch, on which you merely touch in passing, in scrupulous detail. None of this happens at all. The music is described in the most general terms and often in such a way as leaves one aghast – when comparisons are drawn with Mozart, which presupposes the most lumpen and conventional image of Mozart, or when you spin a web of such noncommittal metaphors as the one of the sylph over the music. Basically, what is said about the works relates merely to their texts.

Now you will say that it is precisely this renunciation that is central to the book's intention. But it seems to me to be a crucial point that it also applies to the social construct. As soon as the sphere of measurable technical communication is abandoned – you of all people, who are so strongly against dissolving productive forces into social conditions, should have been the last to abandon this – basically, nothing remains except the bourgeois truism that Offenbach had a knack of sensing what was in the air, had 'adapted' to the times and then influenced them in turn, and that kind of thing. The profoundly bourgeois character of this conception lies in the abstract quality of the opposition between the individual and society, as if the individual were autonomous and entered into an entirely external relationship with 'his time', of which he was independent to the profoundest extent. The task of a 'social biography', if I have to adopt an expression which is not at all to my taste, would have been to define the social character of Offenbach's music itself. Instead of this, it is confined to confirming a more or less pre-stabilized harmony between the monadological author and the given period. The oft-repeated assurance that the times were, at a particular date, 'not yet ripe for this or that', and that for this reason these things did not materialize, is the most drastic expression of the external and undialectical conception of the relationship. The preface sets itself up in opposition to the Ludwigs and Zweigs. I fear that they would have little to say against it and would be only too ready to concede that the personalities of which they write moved against a temporal background which could be fabricated just as you do that of the Second Empire; and they might promise to try again in future. However, it would not be a matter of 'depicting' the background; indeed, as long as one conceives the individual in such a monadological way as you do, any such attempt is probably likely to be misleading, and in the end you would be able to capture more of the social character by faithfully adhering to the monadological. The actual task which you have set yourself might have implied abrogating the dualism of the figure and its background. This, of course, would have meant demolishing, very much in your sense, the surface appearances which Offenbach maintained. As a stylistic analyst, you are the last person who should have missed how arbitrarily the different modes of perception have been slapped one on top of the other, despite their harmony. Just look, for example, at the clumsy bridging passages (on p. 178, for example) which link the parts relating to Offenbach and the social ones!

The dualism of figure and background continues to exist; nothing takes place other than that the background is painted in and padded out with anecdotes. However, this also means that the social analysis is conducted in as abstract a form (in the Hegelian sense) as the aesthetic one. What happens is the erection of an empty social framework that is filled with anecdotes which are probably more of a pleasure to narrate or write up than to read. But the fact that the social construct is not more than abstract, after all, can be determined in exemplary fashion and most precisely by looking into the way in which you handle the concept of 'reality' – which one would be more poorly abstract? – chiefly to make the term 'phantasmagoria' that Benjamin introduced into interpretation an accessible part of the critical vocabulary. I shall cite only a few extreme examples: 'but as the regime was based on the flight from reality' (p. 180): yes, but from *which* reality? Was there one beyond that of the prevailing economic system? Was the latter not represented most fittingly by the Second Empire? And, at the time of the great industrial boom, was not financial speculation an integral element in the constitution of the economy? If (p. 248) you contrast it (perhaps with a certain irony which you should have noted in the margin) with 'industry, which was close to the earth', the concept of reality against which phantasmagoria is measured appears to have been taken directly from the National Socialist body of ideas, to which you also come close when – *horribile dictu* – you speak of 'just reward' (p. 250), as if you had never had the least awareness of basic exploitation. The conformism of such a phrase is entirely equivalent to that in which the relationship between author and society is conceived, meaning the divertissement through anecdote as well as the style of speaking. I really should like to know what it means in social terms – that the bourgeoisie of the Second Empire 'baulked at reality'. Well, then – should it have led the proletarian class to struggle against itself, as when the Naumann Jews shouted 'Out with us'? You expect too much of the people. I fear that you expect nothing at all of them. And nothing at all of Offenbach, certainly. It is profoundly significant that the whole book, if one disregards the cheap triumph over the *Nymphes du Rhin*, does not contain a single trenchant word of criticism against him. To come up with another anecdote: in Worms the Jews called the usurers among them 'interest-monitors' – as if usury was an endearing little foible. (I know this because my own grandmother herself came from a highly respected family of usurers in Worms.) That is how you deal with Offenbach: his ephemeral quality becomes, by means of an unspeakably ramshackle and outdated paradox, the profundity of the superficial, and his repellent busy-bodying becomes an enchanting naivety – on one occasion with a deceptively narcissistic air (p. 152). You take Offenbach to be a representative of society, or at least half so – and does that mean that you agree with him? Are you then not on the side of that type of society? A part of ours, seen in the phantasmagorical mirror of his?

You are – and that is the reason that everything in this book, even the fruitful approaches, appears to be dogged by misfortune. I wish – not to weaken my criticisms by stating this – that you might be able to dismiss them as 'transcendent' (although you yourself recently defended the rights of transcendent criticism against me) without at the same time involving myself in theoretical expositions but instead giving you a couple of pieces of evidence – a very few out of a hundred possible examples. One cannot imagine what would have happened to an author to whom you might have quoted them in the *Frankfurter Zeitung* four years ago. The view of erotic matters is conformist; sexuality becomes the object of a humour which regards it with a lewd wink. Words like 'smooching' (p. 177) and 'little lady' (p. 284) occur, as if you appear to have completely liquidated all kinds of nervous reactions to banality. But what can one say about the truly intolerable affectation of piquancy with which you say of the skirts in the cancan that they whirled around to 'rise higher *and higher*'? (p. 54), or with which you praise the same dance for the 'charming lingerie'? That is an old boys' humour – nothing less than a genuinely positive attitude to sexuality; irony towards it resounds with the whole of bourgeois sexual repression, as in the sentence about Jérôme (p. 170) or the thoroughly silly anecdote (p. 258) or the particularly disputatious passage about venereal diseases (p. 367). No, it is actually the sexuality of 'juicy titbits' which appears in person (on p. 101). Then there is the fascination with the brilliance of society which can be sensed throughout; one needs only to hear the tone in which the expression 'man of the world' is used, or to read a sentence such as the following: 'His spirit, too, produced pearls, just like champagne bubbles: witty epigrams, which he tossed at friends and enemies like little balls' (p. 102), or similarly, at the top of p. 220, a particularly smashing passage. There is a diabolically unhappy love of show and *esprit* in all this – of show, perhaps, when (on p. 367) bugles greet the arrival of every guest with the mort, while, as is well known, the mort is blown only to *end* the hunt; of *esprit* in that kind of unspeakable paradox which is forcibly imposed from without on a simple and banal idea by the style of speaking used to express it: 'But Offenbach's most powerful London experience was beyond doubt – Paris' (p. 122). What a coup after that dash! Or likewise the sentence on p. 248 – pretentious and empty at the same time – and also perhaps 'fraud' (p. 254). We are not spared even the profound melancholy of the comedian; it is as if you wanted to unburden yourself of all the banalities which you have no longer trusted yourself to utter for the last twenty years. Even the anecdotes which you consider so important mostly hover on that borderline between *esprit* and the merely foolish of which I spoke in our conversation about scepticism. The one on p. 407 would have delighted Leonie Meyerhof. I shall break off here so as not to bore you, but if you regard these examples as *trouvailles* picked up by a malicious eye, I can show you others from every page. I have not even embarked on an analysis of the language in our sense of the term.

Please release me from any obligation to say that the book 'also has its good parts'. To say that would be a greater insult than the sharpest word of criticism. In your case, it goes without saying. In the later part of the book the quality visibly improves (I find this is particularly true from p. 347 onwards). But that is not the issue – and nor is the notion that I am criticizing you in order to tell you things that you may not have known. I am attacking you so as to defend you against yourself – against a resignation for which you are too good – and to appeal to your true ambition, in which my own found a teacher. I could not say anything to you against the book which you would not surely have known as well as I did – and I only wish to help you to be aware of it and not conceal it from yourself. In the book's weaknesses one can sense a terrible contempt for humanity and a worrying compulsion to destroy. Contempt for humanity: 'I write quite well enough for swine like you.' Compulsion to destroy: directed against language and everything that you yourself have ever discovered. I know that for a long time now you have been surrounding yourself with a layer of insulation, and that it is enormously difficult to get through to you properly. But if my letter shows you that what you forbid yourself to think or what you are doing to yourself is quite clear to someone who is standing here as a representative to speak not merely for the 'public' – who may like the book very much – but for you yourself, making no claim to say anything that you could not say to yourself, but claiming to say it as forcefully and as clearly as it needs to be said, then perhaps it will not miss its mark – and then I should be able to take responsibility for having offended you.

Yours ever, Teddie.

Original: typescript with handwritten additions and corrections: Siegfried Kracauer papers, Deutsches Literaturarchiv, Marbach am Neckar. First published version from the typescript (carbon copy), Theodor W. Adorno Archiv, Frankfurt am Main: Adorno, *Bildmonographie*, pp. 157–62.

sending the Offenbach: Adorno received the German edition published by Allert de Lange.

clear enough even from the preface: at the end of the first paragraph: 'It is not a personal biography of Jacques Offenbach. It is a social biography' (see Kracauer, W 8, p. 11).

harp tremolos: 'While around noon harp tremolos rang out on all sides' (see Kracauer, W 8, p. 36).

Berlioz's Treatise on Instrumentation: see the chapter 'The Harp' in Hector Berlioz, *Treatise on Instrumentation*, trans. Theodore Front, New York: Dover, 1991, pp. 137–44.

p. 217: see Kracauer, W 8, p. 170.

p. 233: see ibid., p. 181.

'reconstructed': 'in which the era of Napoleon III is reconstructed in particularly acute detail' (see ibid., p. 12).

pre-stabilized harmony: thus in the letter.

opposition to the Ludwigs and Zweigs: Emil Ludwig (1881–1948) made his mark on the genre of the fictionalized biography with works about Napoleon, Bismarck, Richard Wagner, Rembrandt and Michelangelo, among others; in 1936 he published *Die Kunst der Biographie* (Paris: Phénix). Stefan Zweig (1881–1942) published three fictionalized biographies in six years, about Joseph Fouché (1929), Marie Antoinette (1932) and Mary Queen of Scots (1935). In 1930 Kracauer took issue with the 'fashion for biography' in an article (see letter no. 64).

the term 'phantasmagoria': e.g. in his summary of the Arcades project, 'Paris, die Hauptstadt des XIX. Jahrhunderts' [Paris, the capital of the nineteenth century]; see Benjamin, GS V.1, pp. 54, 57).

p. 178: see Kracauer, W 8, p. 140.

flight from reality (p. 180): see ibid., p. 142.

'industry, which was close to the earth': see ibid., p. 192.

you speak of 'just reward' (p. 250): 'Instead of creating a reality in which work is justly rewarded' (see ibid., p. 194).

'baulked at reality': see ibid., p. 192.

Naumann Jews: Max Naumann (1875–1939), a lawyer, founded the Verband nationaldeutscher Juden (Union of Jewish German Nationalists) in 1921; it existed until 1935. The union's close association with the right-wing political spectrum in the Weimar Republic led to the adoption of anti-Semitic attitudes by its Jewish members.

my own grandmother: Caroline Mayer (1846–1894), born in Worms and married in 1868 to David Theodor Wiesengrund (1838–1920).

(p. 152): 'Intermezzo' (see Kracauer, W 8, p.120).

'smooching' (p. 177) and 'little lady' (p. 284): see ibid., pp. 140, 219.

'*rise higher and higher'? (p. 54)*: 'to rise high and still higher?' (see ibid., p. 49).

'charming lingerie': see ibid., p. 190.

sentence about Jérôme (p. 170): see ibid., p. 135.

silly anecdote (p. 258): see ibid., pp.199f.

passage about venereal diseases (p. 367): see ibid., p. 281.

sexuality of 'juicy titbits': see ibid., pp. 82f.

'His spirit, too, produced pearls … like little balls' (p. 102): see ibid., p. 83.

or similarly, at the top of p. 220: see ibid., p. 172 (the first third of the page).

But Offenbach's most powerful London experience was beyond doubt – Paris' (p. 122): see ibid., p. 98.

likewise the sentence on p. 248: 'The operetta could come into being because the society in which it originated was like something out of an operetta' (see ibid., p. 192).

'fraud' (p. 254): see ibid., p. 197 above.

The one on p. 407 would have delighted Leonie Meyerhof: see ibid., p. 313, first section. Leonie Meyerhof (1858–1933), pseudonym Leonie Hildeck; an author and critic, she also published in the *Frankfurter Zeitung*. In novels such as *Töchter der Zeit* [Daughters of the age] (Stuttgart: J. G. Cotta, 1903) she discussed the relationship between the sexes.

I find that this is particularly true from p. 347 onwards: see Kracauer, W 8, pp. 266f.

113 Kracauer to Adorno
Paris, 25.5.1937

Paris (17e), 3, Avenue Mac-Mahon / 25 May 1937

Dear Teddie,

From my knowledge of your outlook this was exactly the criticism that I expected from you. It may seem destructive to you, and it is certainly foolish – not, of course, where it touches on matters germane to the music itself, but on this point I have nothing more to say, in keeping with the basic assumptions of the book. These are as follows: that in the case of the operetta with which the book deals, it is not only the music that is the subject of debate but also the libretto – or, rather, the whole form which derives from the French vaudeville, and this derivation does not miss the mark. The expression 'flute score' slipped through inadvertently; as a result of the haste which was required with the German corrections, I regrettably forgot to weed out a Gallicism here. If the blowing of the mort generally signifies the end of the hunt, in the case you mention it was, according to a contemporary report, actually used to greet the guests – and so you should have berated the organizers of the event, not me, for this offence. … I call your criticism foolish because it partly misrepresents and partly overlooks the material content of my book on the basis of a fixed attitude, albeit one which is certainly familiar to me. The concept of reality is, in what I wrote, not a merely abstract one but a well-defined one with concrete boundaries – it signifies (this is made explicitly clear) the bourgeois republic which, after it had been abandoned in a fit of panic, as it were, in 1850/1851, fought its way back once again scarcely ten years later. However, even the Second Republic was already an excellent instrument of class rule in its time, and to represent the existing economic system adequately there would have been no need whatsoever for the Second Empire, as the Third Republic demonstrates more clearly than ever. It is plain from a historical analysis that the Second Empire was actually a farce with its origins in fear and flight. Thus in my writing 'reality' has the legitimate meaning of a historically inevitable republic, and from this approach, in its turn, there consequently derives the concept of phantasmagoria as applied to the Second Empire – a term which has its exact counterpart in social conditions and does not, as you insinuate, represent the adoption of a term coined by Benjamin (and one, by the way, completely unknown to me). If it were a matter of claims to priority, I should have a long-established title to the term 'phantasmagoria'. In a blind fury, as you wilfully confuse these two principal concepts, you also thrust aside the fact that I specifically classify financial speculation under the heading of reality, and you assert in the face of this fact that I characterize it as a component of phantasmagoria. If you have read the book in depth, an even more radical inhibition has prevented you from comprehending what you have read. I can only explain such blindness as the effect of uncontrolled reactions

which for their part may have originated from the fact that my depiction of the era does not derive from those categories which are familiar to you. Nothing, though, would have been more mistaken than to operate on the basis of these categories, as I can process material drawn from within the sphere of the bourgeoisie adequately and without distortion only by taking the bourgeois republic as my starting point – a methodical point of departure which never claims to be the last word on the subject or even conceals its Marxist basis. There is no path which leads from Marx's writings on the contemporary history of France to the distinctions demanded by my subject. The very fact that you believe that you can conclude from my approach (which is consciously rooted in the immanence of bourgeois society) that I am in agreement with the society in question just makes your foolishness completely obvious, and once more discredits your criticism retrospectively. Establishing these points simultaneously does away with the criticisms that you level at the way in which I include the element of the individual in my book. Rejecting a monadic quality does not mean abolishing any kind of specificity and/or interpreting it out of existence – least of all when objects are involved which immediately become blurred when one retreats too far. If interpretations of concrete material cross a certain threshold which cannot be uniformly defined, they cease to function, assume a subjectively arbitrary character, and attain at best the problematic charm of aesthetic curiosities. At the point where this threshold lies in my own case, the construction makes the transition into narrative. You take the objective form of narrative dictated by the material so little into account that your various pronouncements about the anecdotal, the treatment of the erotic and the alleged banality of my language become empty statements, devoid of all meaning. What you regard as banal is in actual fact an appropriate means of representing a factual world which came into being in such and such a way. Furthermore, in recording, to sum up, that the deliberate and total annihilation of my work has achieved no other result for you than a total disregard for its actual importance, I really do, unfortunately, make myself guilty of an act of banality – Voilà …
In our old spirit of cordiality, *quand même*,

Yours

Original: typescript (carbon copy); Siegfried Kracauer papers, Deutsches Literaturarchiv, Marbach am Neckar.

a long-established title to the term 'phantasmagoria': there are various examples of Kracauer's use of the term, including: 'You recognize a symbol of it in that glassy phantasmagoria, and lost in the boundlessness of a hollow space with no shore you dismiss all the occasions of bliss that you have possessed and will never possess again' ('Der verbotene Blick', *Frankfurter Zeitung*, 9 April 1925; see Kracauer, W 5, no. 237).

114 Adorno to Kracauer
Oxford, 27.5.1937

Oxford, 27 May 1937

Dear Friedel,

Let me first of all take up the *quand même* in your letter – which promises that we shall meet up in Paris in the coming week (I am planning to arrive on the 2nd) and have a friendly tussle. It goes without saying that, for me, there can be no thought of any other kind of tussling with you than that.

What, incidentally, troubles me about your letter is not that you defend yourself and strike back. Both reactions are natural, and you are entitled to do so. I am much more saddened by the fact that you don't actually allow my attack to get through to you – whereas its sole intention was to reach you and break through the layer of encrustation. And it does seem to me – even now, after your answer – that this is not a bad idea, and one which is fair and justified.

You fend me off by taking me for an orthodox thinker whose arguments can be counted in advance on the fingers of one hand, which devalues them – and then as the representative of an attitude of mind that is preoccupied with aesthetic curiosities. I shall not defend myself against these two accusations, although they do appear inconsistent in my eyes. I will only ask you whether by doing so you are not making the discussion with yourself all too easy and comfortable.

Because, first and foremost, in my criticisms it is certainly not Marxist orthodoxy that is in question, or any kind of theoretical fixations, but something far more elementary – i.e. literary quality as understood in a sense which I cannot imagine we do not both share. I have attempted to reduce the literary criticisms to the realm of social theory. If that doesn't suit you, then do take them *à la lettre*. In the book there are a thousand formulations which cannot be justified in the face of your – and *only* your – literary standards; I can show you plenty of these at random; I don't believe that you will seriously contradict me; the interpretation is a *cura posterior*. There are absolutely no prejudices involved in this. Do you seriously mean to regard me of all people as someone who mechanically gibbers off his materialism as an abracadabra? Or do my criticisms indicate to you that, living as I obviously do in a world of fixed ideas, I would not be able to cope with the novelty of your conception? Is it not, quite simply, much more the quality of commodification, the conventional, the merely customary, that I am attacking? Once again, I am not saying a word against a form which represents rather than interprets; here your defence completely misses the point. I am only saying something against the *mode* of representation. You say that operetta is not only music. Indeed, it is not. But does not one miss the very centre of social communication by simply 'leaving out' the music? Is one not, then, forced into all too close proximity with the kind of biography of heroes which equates the life with the work – even such an unheroic life as Offenbach's?

There is only one point which I want to go into at present. You say that the 'reality' which I incriminate is the republic which was supplanted by the empire. Well, then – is one form of government more 'real' than another? And, on the other hand, is the empire, in economic terms, not entirely in keeping with its own substance as a society? And can one even equate a form of constitution with reality and use it as a measure for the quality of illusoriness? Does that not, then, lead to an astonishingly naive approach to the interpretation of society?

If, however, I direct my attacks against erotic humour, stale witticism and, indeed, the use of 'blindly furious' language, does that really result from the fact that your interpretation of the era does not derive from categories which are familiar to me? I don't believe that you can justify this to yourself. Just leave me out of it, and don't bother yourself about whether I am a perverse 'mixed breed' – a cross between Lenin and Mallarmé – or not, and rather give some thought as to whether this piece of writing can hold its ground in accordance with the legitimate criteria for a writer which we – largely together – have developed over the last twenty years. I believe that my attack will be of far greater use then. Believe me – one really doesn't have to be a Mallarmé to be shocked or a Lenin to be furious. All that is actually needed is to know the critical categories which you yourself established and to bear *Ginster* in mind as a yardstick (not some kind of model in a specific instance). The immanence of bourgeois society and familiar categories, the threshold between representation and interpretation, the problem of individual monads and all that – well, I chose those terms because they seemed to me the easiest ones in which to make myself comprehensible to you. However, I have no need of them. Believe me – it is a question of something much simpler – the 'immanence' of your literary achievement. Everything else just follows on from that.

I hope that we shall be able to take things further in Paris on the basis of this. I am very keen to read the *Masse*, and I am looking forward to seeing you as much as ever – I'd rather have a tyrant than a 'don't you remember?' kind of friend. Gretel will also be in Paris.

Very, very best wishes to you and Lili
Your old
Teddie.

Original: typescript with handwritten corrections; Siegfried Kracauer papers, Deutsches Literaturarchiv, Marbach am Neckar.

115 Adorno to Kracauer

On board the *Normandie*, 4.7.1937

'Normandie'

FRENCH LINE — À BORD, LE 4 July 1937

Dear Friedel,

So as not to keep you waiting in vain, just these few words in haste on board.

The film project seems to be on a *favourable* footing. Schapiro is said to have expressed a positive opinion; Horkheimer and the others (– even, and precisely, Leo –) are doing all they can, but it wouldn't do either to rush things or to prejudice the final outcome just now. If you take my psychological advice into account, it is better not to 'press' Horkheimer, as you habitually put it. He really is making every effort – but pushing too hard in any way would be counter-productive.

As for the propaganda project, you should have received the authorization for a further payment of 2 x 1000 French francs.

About the essential relationship with the Institute: essays, reviews, etc., are extremely welcome. But there is *no* question whatsoever of a *permanent* appointment or a *long-term* research commission. H has not given way on this point, and I am telling you this in such brutal terms because I could not be responsible for leaving you with any illusions. The reason is *only*, *sérieusement*, that the budget is so overextended that there is no possibility of a new ongoing commitment. I am sure, however, that, if the propaganda project takes off, it will be possible to commission a new series of essays. (NB: my financial efforts on behalf of Benjamin and Sohn-Rethel met with *no* success, either.)

At the end of July, I shall be coming to P. for the Logical Positivists' Congress and the philosophers' congress in conjunction with it. Then we shall be able to talk in depth, and perhaps even be able to discuss the manuscript of your work *before* it goes to NY.

My address for the time being is:
Albemarle Court Hotel,
18 Leinster Gardens,
London, W.2.

My business has, in a modest way, come to a satisfactory conclusion. I have seen *nothing* of New York, and am proud of that. The journey was extremely pleasant.

Much love, *à bientôt*,
Your old Teddie.

Gretel will likely be coming to Paris.

Many greetings to Lili, if you tell her about this letter!

Original: manuscript with printed letterhead; Siegfried Kracauer papers, Deutsches Literaturarchiv, Marbach am Neckar.

On board the Normandie: Adorno was returning on the ship from his two-week stay in New York to prepare for his induction at the Institute there.

film project: Max Horkheimer included in his letter to Adorno of 4 May 1937 a message to Kracauer of 3 May 1937 in which he informed him about the plan of the Film Library of the Museum of Modern Art to conduct research, based on its comprehensive collection of German films, into 'the connection between social development in Germany and the art of film. I declared at once that I knew nobody who could perform such a task more expertly than you' (Horkheimer, GS 16, p. 137; see Adorno/Horkheimer, *Briefwechsel*, pp. 347–51). The funding of the enterprise remained uncertain for a long time; Kracauer did not begin his work for the Film Library until 1941.

Schapiro: Meyer Schapiro (1904–1996), Lithuanian by birth, art historian at Columbia University in New York. He was an intermediary in the film project and strongly supported Kracauer's escape to the USA. Traditional lore has it that their correspondence started on 28 January 1937 with Schapiro's request for a contribution to the *Marxist Quarterly* (Kracauer papers, Deutsches Literaturarchiv, Marbach).

payment: Max Horkheimer informed Kracauer about the increase of his honorarium for his work on 'Propaganda' by the stated amount in a letter of 18 June 1937 (Horkheimer papers, Archivzentrum der Universitätsbibliothek Johann Christian Senckenberg, Frankfurt am Main.)

efforts on behalf of Benjamin and Sohn-Rethel: on 2 July 1937, Adorno wrote to Benjamin that he was as little able to succeed with an increase in his stipend projected to start in November of 1937 as with procuring financial support for Alfred Sohn-Rethel. The reasons were 'the enormously burdened budget of the Institute' (see Adorno/Benjamin, *Briefwechsel*, pp. 256–62).

Logical Positivists' Congress: announced as 'Konferenz der internationalen Kongresse für Einheit der Wissenschaft', Paris, 29–31 July 1937 (see *Erkenntnis*, 7/1 (1937), pp. 63f.).

philosophers' congress: Adorno and Benjamin attended, in addition to the conference mentioned above, the ninth International Congress of Philosophy, on Descartes. The reports on these events, which they wrote together, have been published (see Adorno/Horkheimer, *Briefwechsel* I, pp. 560–79).

my things: the agreement stipulated 'the de facto administration of Institute business for the next 2 years'. His emigration to New York was to follow (see Adorno/Benjamin, *Briefwechsel*, p. 259).

116 Adorno to Kracauer

London, 12.7.1937

ALBEMARLE COURT HOTEL
LEINSTER GARDENS, LANCASTER GATE W.2.

12 July 1937.

Dear Friedel,

Many thanks for your card. I shall probably come to P. *this* week for the empiricists' congress and shall stay until after 6 August, so that we can discuss plenty of things – including your manuscript, before it goes to N.Y., which I think is very practical.

In *your* interests, I also think it would be sensible if you were able to publish an essay about the ZfS in one of the Swiss or Prague papers where you have contacts. Do think it over. Then we can also talk over the plans for the book.

Is Benjamin in Paris?

Gretel, unfortunately, will probably *not* be able to come on account of the need for a visa.

Much love, to Lili too
Your old
Teddie.

Original: manuscript with printed letterhead; Siegfried Kracauer papers, Deutsches Literaturarchiv, Marbach am Neckar.

your card: this has not been preserved.

essay about the ZfS in … Swiss … papers: Kracauer published articles in the *Neue Zürcher Zeitung* and the *National-Zeitung* from 1936/37 onwards. Instead of the article suggested here, there appeared one by Walter Benjamin, 'Zeitschrift für Sozialforschung', edited for the Institute for Social Research by Max Horkheimer (Paris: Félix Alcan), *Mass und Wert*, no. 5, 1938 (see 'Ein deutsches Institut freier Forschung', Benjamin, GS III, pp. 518–26, 681–96).

117 Adorno to Kracauer
London, 13.9.1937

21, PALACE COURT,
HYDE PARK. W. 2.
BAYSWATER 3738.

13 September 1937.

Dear Friedel,

This is just to tell you what will surely come as no great surprise to you: Gretel and I were married last Wednesday – in Oxford, where my friend Opie gave a lunch for us in the unbelievably beautiful Magdalen College. He and Max were the witnesses; apart from them only Maidon, Gretel's mother and my parents were present. It was so beautiful that the embarrassing and comical aspects of the ceremony were as good as forgotten, as well as our resistance to matrimony, tried and tested as it certainly is.

By the time you get this letter, Max will be back in Paris. It would be sensible to ring in good time (personal: at the Lutétia, around 10 am; or else in the rue d'Ulm) and make some arrangements; he is only in Europe for another ten days. You can imagine how everything is being crammed in. I would advise you to *show* him the text, which I am sure will have been completed in the meantime, but to *send* it to me first, before you *send* it to him, unless he is very insistent. Then I hope to be able to let you have the contract for that essay very soon; Max has just asked me to wait to do so until the propaganda project is finished. For the time being I should like to give you a choice between detective novels and applied art. It is still uncertain whether the planned book will materialize, but, if the worst comes to the worst, it will simply be published in the *Zeitschrift*. Meanwhile, the American film plan should also be ready for a decision.

It's possible that I may come over again to Paris for a day. A journey to the South is out of the question because of the horrible business of furnishing the flat and all the nonsense that goes with setting up a household of one's own. I'm completely overworked with all this and more than ready for a break – but it will probably amount to no more than having a good sleep here.

Do get Max to tell you about the plans for his book, which you should find extremely interesting.

I hope that you are both in good health and spirits. Have you noticed that in many places reviews of the Offenbach and the Berg book appear side by side? And have you received the latter? I would be very glad of your criticism, but must say at once that I can only assume responsibility for the parts signed by me. Gretel sends you her warmest regards. She is developing great energy in domestic and other matters, and I am very busy getting in her way, hindering her and generally making a nuisance of myself. In return, however, I have the satisfaction that she still doesn't know that, when people talk of 'my wife', they mean her.

Much love and very best wishes to you and Lili from
Your old
Teddie.

The address given here is valid for at least the next three weeks; I hardly believe that we shall be able to move into our apartment – situated in Holland Park and really quite decent by local standards; it even has central heating, although it is a little below ground – before mid-October. The parents have sensibly come to terms with the fact that we have emigrated for good. For all that, though, it is only now that we are undergoing in earnest the same experience that you did four and a half years ago – and, although it has lost its terrors in our case because of Max's solid support, it is still of such a kind that I have dreams about it.

Original: typescript with handwritten corrections and additions; Siegfried Kracauer papers, Deutsches Literaturarchiv, Marbach am Neckar.

last Wednesday: 8 September 1937.

Opie ... Magdalen College: Redvers Opie (1900–1984), national economist, working in Oxford since 1931. Magdalen College was founded in 1449 under the name of Magdalen Hall.

Gretel's mother: Emilie Karplus, née Cahn. No further information is available.

Max ... back in Paris: Max Horkheimer's journey to Europe lasted until late September 1937.

planned book: This is *Massenkunst im Monopolkapitalismus* (see letter no. 102).

Max ... plans for his book: it remains unclear which plans of Max Horkheimer's are in question.

Berg book: Willi Reich, *Alban Berg: Mit Bergs eigenen Schriften und Beiträgen von Theodor Wiesengrund Adorno und Ernst Křenek* [Alban Berg: with Berg's own writings and contributions by Theodor Adorno and Ernst Křenek], Vienna: Reichner, 1937 (see Adorno's information in the preface to *Alban Berg: Master of the Smallest Link*, Cambridge: Cambridge University Press, 1991). Reviews appearing simultaneously with Kracauer's book on Offenbach are not recorded.

118 Adorno to Kracauer
[London,] 3.12.1937

3 December 1937.

Dear Friedel,

The long break which has intervened in our correspondence – a break for which, according to conventional ideas, I am to blame – has its grounds solely in the somewhat complicated conditions of our life. I wanted to reply by return of post to your very dear letter on the occasion of our marriage, which reawakened so many old and genuine emotions, and was putting it off until we were able to move into our own apartment. That was delayed, first of all, by the difficulty of obtaining all the necessary papers and then by matters which impinged still further on our plans. The fact is that, all of a sudden, the possibility arose of moving to America in the near future through a foundation for the study of radio, for which a colleague at the Institute is making the arrangements. (The funding for the foundation comes from a completely different quarter.) This colleague urgently desires *me* to collaborate on the radio project, especially on questions relating to the sociology of music. Accepting this project means, above all, that I would be joining forces with Horkheimer, and that we could finally get to grips with the joint work which we had long been planning, and also, as part of my salary will be paid by this foundation, the lifting of a not inconsiderable burden from the Institute. This, however, is of great importance at the moment, as the Institute has been severely affected by the collapse of prices on Wall Street and faces the need to make cuts across the board, whereas this new collaboration with Princeton guarantees us a minimum standard of living – at least, for some time. In these circumstances we have accepted the American offer. A further pressing reason for this is Gretel's condition. Not only does she feel very depressed in the atmosphere of England (insofar as one can speak of such a thing, apart from the fog), which really is hard to bear, but she is also very far from well as regards her health, without being organically ill. We have therefore applied to the American consul for our immigration visa, and if all goes well we shall have the decisive interview with him in mid-December. Then for Gretel's sake we want at all costs to spend a couple of weeks in the South before we sail to America, and for this we have our eye on Dora Benjamin's inexpensive and highly praised guest-house in San Remo. For the time being, though, we continue to carry on our existence as 'one-room dwellers' – for over three months now, and I don't need to tell you what that means. We stopped the transport of our furniture in time, and we easily got rid of the lovely apartment to an eccentric old Irishman, who creates the impression of a white-slaver who has settled down in comfort and would do honour to any play by Wedekind. That's enough about us.

In spite of everything, giving up our abode in Europe is not easy for us, and at times it has depressed us as much as, conversely, that abode itself did. Now we are in a somewhat better mood on account of the prospect of moving, and even Gretel's stomach has joined the burgeoning optimism.

Without beating about the bush, let me come to what is worrying me most of all about leaving Europe: your situation. I have been completely out of the picture for about three months now and have heard nothing from New York either. It is a question of two things:

(1) the propaganda project, which has very likely been completed by now. You had announced to me that you were sending a carbon copy of at least the theoretical part, but so far this has not reached me. From your pessimistic tone I now fear that your inner and outer situation has deteriorated so much that it has not yet been possible for you to complete this, and this is causing me grave concern. For this reason, I would like to ask you, more than anything else, urgently and from the bottom of my heart, to let me have some news as soon as possible and, if circumstances permit, the manuscript too, so that I can put in my pennyworth in New York. But please don't take this as any kind of pressure – it is *exclusively* the thought of you and not of the project which made me decide to ask the question, and this question arises solely from my own initiative, without New York uttering a word about the whole complex of matters.

(2) the American film project. The negotiations were due to begin in autumn, but I have heard no more about it either. According to my information there is no longer any possible doubt that a new economic crisis is looming, even though not such a crazy one as that of 1930 – and such crisis situations have, first and foremost, the effect of creating a scarcity of all resources for intellectual matters. For this reason, it would be a very good thing to get the project signed and sealed *in good time.* I can't do anything about this, either from here or later on in New York, unless I have precise information from you about the state of affairs.

As to the question of the collective volume *Massenkunst im Monopolkapitalismus*, unfortunately all our controversies about this matter have ended with there no longer being any prospect of carrying out the plan. The motto is save, save, save; all costly projects of this kind must be put on a back burner, just like all other possible peripheral plans, in favour of a few major works, and I am in even less of a position to insist on this pet project of mine, as it has transpired that, for the time being, it is completely impossible to mobilize a sufficient number of properly qualified collaborators.

Just for now, let me report in addition that, to my great sorrow, the Husserl essay will not be coming out – at least in the immediate future; that I have prepared a new, shorter version of the Mannheim one, which will now be published and which I hope will delight you; and that the preliminary work on the Wagner is so far advanced that I am expecting to get the full text written in the next few weeks.

I hope in any case to see you before the journey across the big pond, which I cannot see happening before mid-January, but hope above all that a meeting on the other side of the big pond will follow very soon. Please do write to me about Lili's state of health too.

All our love to you both from Gretel and

Your old
Teddie.

Original: typescript with handwritten corrections and additions; Siegfried Kracauer papers, Deutsches Literaturarchiv, Marbach am Neckar.

your kind letter: not preserved.

moving to America: on 20 October 1937, Max Horkheimer informed Adorno by means of a telegram and a letter of explanation that Princeton University had received 'a fairly large fund for a radio study'. The sociologist Paul Felix Lazarsfeld (1901–1976) was working in Princeton on the research project 'The Essential Value of Radio to All Types of Listeners', supported by the Rockefeller Foundation. He suggested Adorno as a collaborator, which opened up the option of Adorno's moving to New York (see Adorno/Horkheimer, *Briefwechsel* I, pp. 440–2; Adorno, *Bildmonographie*, pp. 163–9).

collapse of prices on Wall Street: Max Horkheimer wrote to Adorno on 13 October 1937 about the dependence of the Institute on the financial markets: 'The slump which has been growing worse and worse since the end of August has hit the entire portfolio of almost all economic experts – including us. Our losses are very great, and from all the evidence they seem likely to increase still further. As our assets have been from the outset far too small for us to be able to live off the interest, the expenses have been defrayed from our profits. As in the years to come we can count on losses rather than profits, we cannot go on without severe cutbacks' (see Adorno/Horkheimer, *Briefwechsel* I, p. 422).

collaboration with Princeton: the radio project was to provide Adorno with financial security but make only limited claims on his time so that about half of his working capacity was at the disposal of the Institute.

the decisive interview ... mid-December: the conversation on 13 December ended with the granting of the entry visa.

Dora Benjamin: Dora Sophie Kellner ran the 'Villa Verde' guest-house in San Remo, where she provided accommodation for the Adornos from December 1937 to January 1938. Walter Benjamin took refuge there in exile from Paris.

Husserl essay: Adorno voiced his plan to Max Horkheimer for an essay stemming from the 'Husserl book' for the *Zeitschrift für Sozialforschung* in a letter of 28 February 1937 (see Adorno/Horkheimer, *Briefwechsel* I, p. 305); see 'Zur Philosophie Husserls' (Adorno, GS 20.1, pp. 46–118, GS 20.2, p. 812).

Mannheim: see letter no. 101.

preliminary work on the Wagner: this plan appears in the correspondence with Max Horkheimer on 7 August 1937 and in that with Walter Benjamin on 13 September 1937 (see Adorno/Horkheimer, *Briefwechsel* I, p. 392; Adorno/Benjamin, *Briefwechsel*, p. 273). For the partial publication of *Versuch über Wagner* entitled 'Fragmente über Wagner', *Zeitschrift für Sozialforschung*, nos. 1/2, 1939, see Adorno, GS 13, pp. 7–148, 497–508, 517–20.

119 Kracauer to Adorno
Paris, 10.12.1937

Paris (17e), 3, Av. Mac-Mahon / 10 Dec. 37

Dear Teddie,

News from you at last! You would certainly have heard from me in the meantime had I not been compelled to assume, on the evidence of your previous letter, that the two of you had long ago set up house in the new apartment, whose address, of course, I did not know. I had already asked Horkheimer about this address several weeks ago, and now it does not exist at all. And this has taken me to the news of your emigration – one of the reasons for it, Gretel's poor physical state, has worried Lili and me very much. You ask about Lili's state of health; at the moment all is going rather nicely. A year ago she found a particularly good doctor here who has been a great help in setting her nerves to rights again. Lili would suggest that Gretel should consult this doctor during your stay in Paris – that is, unless she has already made other arrangements. That might perhaps provide long-term support to sustain the recovery which she will have found in the South. Otherwise, as far as your move is concerned, you are both doubly and trebly right to seize this chance without hesitation. We are delighted for you, and the prospect of collaborating with Horkheimer is a splendid one for you, dear Teddie. In addition, there is nothing we wish more fervently than that the New York film project may become reality as soon as possible, and we would rather leave today than tomorrow. Your conjectures that speed is of the essence are mine too, of course, and for my part I have done absolutely everything that, in my view, could be done – not only because of the American crisis but also very much on account of my own existential crisis, which might be described as a total one. I recently received the first semi-official report on the state of affairs. According to this, the New York Museum is seriously interested in my coming and is at present busy with obtaining the necessary funds for the commission. Of course, nobody is concealing from me that raising the money for it will be more difficult because of the crisis. Keep your fingers crossed! Horkheimer, of course, is still managing things in the background. The prospect of meeting up with you and Gretel over there makes the move seem all the more tempting to us.

As for the propaganda project, the greater part of the work – the analytical section, which is complete in itself and runs to over a hundred pages – is finished and already in New York. Horkheimer, with whom I spent quite some time here and had a very satisfactory conversation, had already written to me on receiving the main part of this section, which had been sent off to him first, to say that he was delighted that our first collaboration was in the process of coming to fruition, and that he was thinking of publishing the whole thing in the *Zeitschrift* with the abridgements necessitated by reasons of space. Of course you would have received the 105 pages if only I had been in possession of your address. Now that you are announcing your arrival I would find it almost nicer if you were to read the work here and we could discuss it face to face at once. At present I am working on the two final sections, which deal with the development of totalitarian propaganda in accordance with an ideology of ideal types. Unfortunately, the wretched conditions in the outside world are making things difficult for me in every respect.

What a pity that your splendid essay on Husserl is being postponed.

Please tell Gretel that Lili and I are thinking of you and sending many good wishes. Warmest greetings to you and her from us both, in the hope of seeing you again soon and in happier circumstances

Yours, Friedel.

Original: manuscript; Theodor W. Adorno Archiv, Frankfurt am Main.

asked Horkheimer: in a letter to Max Horkheimer, 26 November 1937, manuscript; Max Horkheimer archive, Archivzentrum der Universitätsbibliothek Johann Christian Senckenberg, Frankfurt am Main.

a particularly good doctor: not identified.

120 Adorno to Kracauer
[New York,] 3.5.1938

3 May 1938.

Dear Friedel,

If I am writing back to you after such a long interval only today, the simple fact of this delay is perhaps a sufficient sign to you of the immense turbulence in which my first two months in America have passed. This does not mean just getting used to living and working here, in the somewhat vague sense which one usually associates with these notions, but also involves quite specific and extremely demanding tasks. At one point I had to write a memorandum in English developing the plan for the entire musical part of the radio project and explaining the main theoretical ideas, even at this early stage; this memorandum has turned into a small book of around 150 printed pages in its own right. (In the meantime, it has been decided that, within the context of the radio project, I shall write a longer book about music on the radio, which is to be brought out as an independent publication by Princeton University Press – a considerable success in terms of forging a career.) But in addition I had to press ahead to force the Wagner project to its conclusion, and even though it turned out in the end that there was no need for such a great hurry because of a necessary change to the *Zeitschrift*'s publication date, which delayed the publication of the parts of this project that were to come out first, I am still very glad to have got it all signed and sealed. It was finished yesterday – only the last chapter is waiting to be typed out. A text of about 100 of my big typed pages – and so quite an imposing manuscript, given my circumstances and the density of the text, and one which I cannot look at without a certain fatherly pride. I hope that you will get acquainted with this creation of mine very soon; it is, above all, an attempt to mediate between social and aesthetic/technical categories, but there are other points in it which should also interest you.

However, I am writing today not about my sacred texts but about yours – i.e. the propaganda project. As you will have heard from Herr Pollock, the next stages of the business are in my hands. These hands, before anything else, are now reaching out for more material, i.e. pages 106–136. Leo will already have written to you to say that these pages never arrived here; nor did Pollock bring them with him, and had nothing to report about them – so either they have gone missing, which is unlikely but not wholly out of the question as matters stand with the post here, or by some oversight you didn't send them and then thought they had been sent off. In any case I should be very grateful if you could let me have them – if possible, by return of post – at my private address: 45 Christopher Street, Apt. 11G, New York, N.Y. – as I should like to spend the little pause for breath from my own scribbling that I am expecting to have in the next few weeks on your work.

After this preamble there would be no sense in trying to conceal the spectre of cuts from you any longer. Like most spectres, this one too has its material basis – i.e. the Institute's austerity measures. In the present circumstances there can be as little question of publishing your work as a pamphlet as of my projected book about mass art in monopoly capitalism. At the same time, though, the scope of the *Zeitschrift* itself, which has indeed increased in volume over the last few years, must be reduced to its former scale. Under this *dura necessitas* my work and Benjamin's will suffer just as much as yours. However, while I hope to be able to excise a specific complex of ideas out of the Wagner to some extent as an independent entity (i.e. the derivation of the *Gesamtkunstwerk* from the nature of a commodity), it seems to me that no similar possibility exists in the case of your work, but that a publication of a work of this very kind in a journal would make sense only if it gives some idea of the multiplicity of motifs by summarizing the most trenchant passages of different chapters, which means, given our circumstances, to detach them from the current arrangement. At present I am in no position to formulate an exact estimate – but that is how it appears to me after a very careful reading. The main emphasis will then have to be placed on certain analyses of the content, for which I should like to cite primarily pages 53–57 as a model. I should like to emphasize arguments such as the mobilization of partial ideologies in fascism, much in the presentation of terror, the splendid method of reaching conclusions about fascism from the 'mirror reflex', and also the arguments about the constant reproduction of the masses though fascism and the critique of the contrast between the personality of the leader and the masses as mere illusion, and finally the evidence for the antinomies of propaganda. On the other hand, in this Reader's Digest version the 'framework' – theoretical bridging terms, more general introductions, etc. – would necessarily have to take a back seat. We also would prefer not to lay too much stress on the deduction from war – not because we may fail to recognize the importance of this phenomenon, but because this very argument would lead to an endless controversy about the relationship between economics and politics which we would rather not unleash precisely in a situation where the main theoretical interest is focused on quite different matters.

Since a detailed correspondence about the montage programme contained in these suggestions would necessarily extend over an unforeseeable period of time and would inevitably remain unsatisfactory and full of gaps precisely as regards considerations of the tactics for publication in the journal, I have made an attempt to create this kind of edited version. I hope that you will be convinced that I shall make my very best efforts on behalf of this project, and that I shall not adopt a fetishistic attitude towards it if it should prove that such a version would, in the end, do such violence to your text that we should have to abandon the idea of publishing it. In any case, an editorial note will indicate that it is only a matter of reproducing some of the most important motifs and not your text in its entirety. Nevertheless, I should like to let you know in good time about the forthcoming procedure.

By the way, I should now like to give you the following news: we met up with Schapiro, a charming, very decent person with a passionate interest in our work and an exceptional level of intelligence. He is very keen indeed to bring you over here, and, judging from a remark of his, a possibility of doing so does in fact exist. As I don't know about your commitments in other areas, or whether what he has in mind would provide you with an adequate means of making a living, I could not, of course, say anything positive to him. I would, however, strongly advise you to follow up the Schapiro business (that is, if the success of the Offenbach, which promises to be quite considerable here too, has not already relieved you of such problems). I should try to get over to America as soon as possible with his help. The reasons for this are:

(1) Things in Europe are looking darker all the time; the reports of the latest campaign of terror against the Jews have plunged us all into the deepest anxiety; at the same time Pollock reports a considerable increase in anti-Semitism in France. The fact that, according to our theory, a war on account of the Czechs is out of the question offers no protection from the consequences that will arise if our theory should turn out to be wrong after all – i.e. if capitalist solidarity disintegrates and the antagonism between England and Germany (France is an English colony) explodes.

(2) If you succeed in getting over here, I am convinced that, even if you have only a modest basis, you will soon find the means to earn an

additional income. I think that you know my defeatist attitude well enough not to regard such a hope as excessively sanguine. The defining impression which people in America have of *all* European countries is that of 'openness'. In particular, the precise timing of the publicity for your Offenbach (one simply cannot imagine anything better than a review like that in the *New York Times*) convinces me that this is the *most favourable* opportunity to make a start. In addition, there is the fact that living conditions over here, all foolish rumours to the contrary, are generally pleasant and free from aggravation, and that the city as collective individual and image should provide you with enough inspiration for you possibly to feel more at home here than in perfidious Paris. It really would need diabolically bad luck for you not to have every possible opportunity here. But don't wait too much longer – above all, not until the great stream of emigration from Austria gets under way. It would be a fine thing, and a good one too, if we were living in the same place again after eight years.

I was glad to hear from Pollock that he found you in such good order, and I hope that Lili too is well. Gretel is feeling really well here and recovered from England much better than on the Riviera; she has even grown a little plumper.

Somebody or other told me that you were writing a book about film for Allert de Lange – is that true? My next literary plans, apart from the radio book, are still undecided. In connection with the Wagner, I have been reading a great deal of Schopenhauer with considerable interest. I am thinking of writing something about the general regression in listening and the characteristics of fetishism in music. Please don't pay me back in my own coin, and do reply soon.

Much love to Lili and you from us both,

Your old
Teddie

Original: typescript with handwritten additions and corrections; Siegfried Kracauer papers, Deutsches Literaturarchiv, Marbach am Neckar.

months in America: Gretel and Theodor W. Adorno had sailed on the SS *Champlain* on 16 February 1938 with New York as their destination.

memorandum … a small book: see *Current of Music: Elements of a Radio Theory*, ed. Robert Hullot-Kentor, Frankfurt am Main: Suhrkamp, 2006. For the material which was already available in the spring of 1938 and Adorno's outline of the book, see the editor's preface, especially pp. 52–65.

heard from Herr Pollock: within a period of two weeks, Friedrich Pollock visited Geneva, Amsterdam, London and Paris on business connected with the Institute (see Max Horkheimer to Adolph Lowe, 4 May 1938, Horkheimer, GS 16, p. 444). At their meeting in Paris on 12 April 1938, Kracauer noted down keywords, including 'I. Prop. Project: 1) do you want to take conclusion with you 2) anonymous/pseudonymous (mother) 3) incidentally, Silone 4) publication … 5) English translation! II. Institute possibility 1) know financial difficulties – but 2) regular reports 3) new contract … III. Ask Hork. why film material … VI. We want to go to America … 1) Film Library 2) if grant too low, can Institute help or mediate? 3) In what form? … 4) Offenbach – New Y-Times 5) have heard that affidavit can be obtained even without relatives: can Institute help? V. Immigration visa: can Institute help with this?' (Kracauer papers, Deutsches Literaturarchiv Marbach).

page 106: the manuscript up to this point is the subject of a memorandum by Adorno dated 5 March: 'Memorandum on Siegfried Kracauer's study *Die totalitäre Propaganda Deutschlands und Italiens*, pp.1–106' (typescript, Max Horkheimer papers, Archivzentrum der Universitätsbibliothek Johann Christian Senckenberg). Adorno stated at the beginning 'that Kracauer is neither connected with us in any binding fashion by reason of his theoretical approach nor can be ranked in any way as a scholarly author by reason of his working methods.' The work was, he declares, 'neither of any intrinsic theoretical value nor sufficiently based on empirical material, but records – at times using formulations which are extremely useful in literary terms – specific experiences and observations which possess a validity beyond the author's position as an outsider.' An 'aversion to Marxist methods' in places derives, he suggests, from 'individualistic reservations'; where Kracauer 'has recourse to arguments of Horkheimer's, he twists them 'into their precise opposite in terms of meaning'. Adorno additionally suggested deleting the part of the study relating to Italy (and, as far as the material was concerned, attributed by him to Ignazio Silone) and rewriting the remainder. He gave a more positive verdict on a passage discussed later in the letter; at the end he emphasized: 'In this work Kracauer has obviously attempted, making a great and mighty effort which I value very highly, to work his way out of the sphere of commercial writing to which the book on Offenbach belongs.' (The memorandum is reproduced in its entirety with the reconstruction of the *Masse und Propaganda* study in Kracauer, W 2.2.)

Leo will already have written to you: not preserved in the Kracauer/Löwenthal correspondence.

dura: correction of a typing error; Adorno wrote '*dira*'.

a specific complex of ideas out of the Wagner: in the end chapters I, VI, IX and X were published (see letter no. 118, note).

pages 53–57: Adorno in his memorandum (see above): 'I see the advantages of the work in the quality of the observation, the literary experience of many of the expressions (we are not overly blessed with contributions of a high authorial quality) … Most of all, I should like to cite pages 53–57, which keep within the framework of mere phenomenology but must be considered truly exceptional in this context. The thesis about the mobility of partial ideologies within fascism, much in the description of terror, the method of drawing conclusions about fascism from the 'mirror reflex', i.e. the fascist presentation of non-fascist facts; moreover, the arguments about the constant reproduction of the mass through fascism and the critique of the contrast between the personality of the leader and the mass as a merely illusory counterpart (a criticism which, incidentally, could be made even more acute) – I find all this so illuminating and also so new that we ought to publish it.'

mirror reflex: In his posthumously published treatise *Totalitäre Propaganda*, Kracauer describes a 'frequently observed stratagem of fascistic propaganda' as betraying a mentality for which lies and truth are equally irrelevant and that accuses its political opponents 'precisely of those actions and machinations which are a perfect example of its own intents'. The metaphor that he uses is derived from the technique (*Spiegelreflex*) of creating a mirror-inverted image inside a single- (or double-) lens reflex camera (see Kracauer, W 2.2, pp. 70ff.)

latest campaign of terror against the Jews: the spread of anti-Semitic persecution after the annexation of Austria in March 1938; immediately before this letter was written, on 26 April 1938, an obligation was imposed to register all 'Jewish property' both inside and outside the country.

review like that in the New York Times: Katherine Woods, 'Offenbach and the Paris of his Time: The Musician's Biography Is a Dramatic Story, and the Background Is Admirably Rendered', *New York Times*, 27 March 1938 – i.e. the review of the American edition, *Orpheus in Paris: Offenbach and the Paris of his Time*, trans. Gwenda David and Eric Mosbacher, New York: Alfred A. Knopf, 1938.

a book about film for Allert de Lange: a contract was signed with Walter Landauer in the first half of February 1938 (see *Marbacher Magazin* 47, p. 92); in a document dated May 1939 the publisher Allert de Lange confirmed the agreement.

general regression: 'Über den Fetischcharakter in der Musik und die Regression des Hörens', *Zeitschrift für Sozialforschung*, 1938 (see Adorno, GS 14, pp. 14–50 and the Preface, pp. 9f.).

121 Kracauer to Adorno

(no address), 24.5.1938

to *Wiesengrund* 24 May 38.
on the *Normandie*
in NY on 30 May.

In a dismal state of mind, I can only confirm receipt of your letter and notify you of the despatch of pages 105–35. I shall come back later to suggestions for cuts.

I am surprised that you are in some sense advising me to come to New York soon. Doubtless you know that for many months I have been making desperate efforts to find a commission or any kind of opportunity there. In spite of the help of many friends, nothing has materialized yet.

For my own part, I would grasp at any straw. But nobody is holding one out to me – not even Schapiro, who has not been in direct communication with me for ages, so that I had to conclude that he has failed.

The success of my O in America, as in other countries, does not generate financial benefits for me.

Original: manuscript, written in shorthand, copy or draft; Siegfried Kracauer papers, Deutsches Literaturarchiv, Marbach am Neckar.

122 Adorno to Kracauer
Princeton, 2.6.1938

PRINCETON UNIVERSITY
PRINCETON NEW JERSEY
SCHOOL OF PUBLIC AND INTERNATIONAL AFFAIRS

OFFICE OF RADIO RESEARCH
203 ENO HALL

2 June 1938.

Dear Friedel,

I am replying to you very quickly because your letter disturbed me to an extraordinary degree – and I think that I may venture to take the responsibility for committing an indiscretion with the request that you, for your part, will not write or speak to anyone about the matter to which I allude with the exception of Leo, if he should happen to mention it in a letter of his own accord. You are mistaken if you think that Schapiro has failed you. On the contrary, as I *know* for a fact, he has made the greatest efforts on your behalf, and his plan only went awry because the Museum of Modern Art has no money whatsoever at the moment – which, by the way, I had already heard from a third party in Europe – but I did not want to write to you about this so as not to make you nervous. Now, though, a new possibility has come up through Schapiro. He is friends with a millionaire in Philadelphia who is said to be a connoisseur of some standing with a special interest in the nineteenth century. He directed this man's attention towards Offenbach, and he, although right-wing in his political views, is said to be most enthusiastic about the book. He and Schapiro are airing plans to fund a major project about film for you. This man is coming to Europe soon – in the next four weeks, I think – and will get in touch with you in Paris. Schapiro, nothing if not sanguine, is investing so much hope in the project that I see every reason to be confident. I assume that he is not writing to you about it until the project is further advanced. However, I think it best, *rebus sic stantibus*, to set this precaution aside for now.

I also let Horkheimer know about your letter today, and he was deeply moved. I shall talk to him at great length tomorrow. It need hardly be mentioned that there is no lack of goodwill on his part or insistence on mine. That is all for today – in great haste.

All our love to you and Lili from Gretel and

Your old Teddie.

Original: typescript with printed letterhead, handwritten additions and corrections; Siegfried Kracauer papers, Deutsches Literaturarchiv, Marbach am Neckar. Handwritten note by Kracauer: 'Arrived 10 June 1938'.

millionaire in Philadelphia: Henry McIlhenny (1910–1986), art collector and curator at the Philadelphia Museum of Arts (see *Marbacher Magazin* 47, p. 92).

123 Adorno to Kracauer
New York, 3.6.1938

New York City
45 Christopher Street
3 June 1938.

Dear Friedel,

Today I shall just confirm receipt of pages 107–135, which I received this morning. I received the *last* 40 pages, which you had F. P. bring along, from him immediately after his return here – so now there is a complete copy of your entire manuscript with us.

We are probably staying here until about 1 July, then, of course, Nova Scotia. M. H. is going west next week for three months.

All our love to you both,
from Gretel too. Your old

Teddie.

Original: manuscript; Siegfried Kracauer papers, Deutsches Literaturarchiv, Marbach am Neckar.

Handwritten note by Kracauer: 'Arrived 10 June 1938'.

which you had F. P. bring along: at his meeting with Friedrich Pollock in Paris on 12 April 1938 (see letter no. 120).

M. H. is going: Max Horkheimer announced his journey into the interior of America, planned for the summer of 1938, in these terms: 'In summer my wife and I are probably going west' (Horkheimer to Adolph Lowe, 4 May 1938; see Horkheimer, GS 16, p. 447).

124 Adorno to Kracauer
New York, 28.6.1938

New York, 28 June 1938

Dear Friedel,

This is just to let you know about the manuscript of the propaganda project in the version which I composed and then revised thoroughly yet again with Leo and Franz Neumann with an eye to the politics of publication.

I have already put you in the picture about the need for an abridged version and also about the fact that this abridged version should not be created merely by making deletions. I assume that you will feel as much as we do that I have tried to take account of the limited space available in the *Zeitschrift* without conferring on your work a fragmentary quality and that, because of this, I had to depart from the original layout as much as from the exact wording of the original text.

This new version has been read by a fair number of our members and seems to have met with a wholly positive reaction. Even Horkheimer, who looked through the MS in the haste of the last days before his departure for the west, seemed very much taken with it. Of course I can't anticipate an answer to the question of whether it will definitely be published now or not – first, because some members are not acquainted with the manuscript yet, and also because the question of publication depends on certain tactical considerations which are by and large independent of the question of the composition of the text itself. It goes without saying that I shall make every effort to get it published – all the more so because I myself, as you will readily recognize, have invested not only a lot of work in the text but also a great deal of enthusiasm and pleasure. In any case I would be very happy if you, for your part, would give the publication your *imprimatur*.

Gretel and I are going on holiday on Friday – on something of a mystery tour, to find a place to live somewhere in New England. It is not a holiday in the strict sense – i.e. I am hoping to make good use of the distance from the radio project to rewrite the Husserl for publication (an operation very similar to the one performed on your work) and then get the long-projected essay on the character of fetishism in music and the regression of hearing signed and sealed. This autumn Horkheimer and I are planning at long last to tackle our joint work on dialectics.

In the meantime, you should have heard from Schapiro and/or his friend. Please do keep me posted in any event about how matters stand with you. I might also advise you to let Pollock know about your situation. Horkheimer was of the opinion that he (i.e. Pollock) might possibly be able to manage something through an aid organization. However, as Pollock is immensely overburdened and I don't know whether Horkheimer has even been able to discuss the idea with him once more, perhaps it might be sensible for you to get in direct contact with him yourself.

I have no permanent address for the next six weeks. The surest way for you to reach me would still be at the Institute's address. From 15 August onwards we shall be in our new apartment: 290 Riverside Drive, New York, N.Y.

Much love to you and Lili, from Gretel too,

Your old
Teddie

Original: typescript with handwritten additions and corrections; Siegfried Kracauer papers, Deutsches Literaturarchiv, Marbach am Neckar. The underlinings are probably by Kracauer.

Neumann: Franz Neumann (1900–1954), lawyer; he met Max Horkheimer and Adorno in Frankfurt am Main in 1921. In 1933 he went into exile in England, and from 1936 to 1942 he was a member of the New School for Social Research in New York (see Adorno/Horkheimer, *Briefwechsel* I, p. 45, note).

joint work on dialectics: this was the realization of a plan from the time when Adorno was working to qualify as a lecturer (see letter 81).

Schapiro and/or his friend: Meyer Schapiro informed Kracauer in a letter of 31 March 1938 that he was in contact with Henry McIlhenny.

let Pollock know about your situation: this was done in a letter of 28 September 1938; Kracauer expressed his anxiety about the possible outbreak of war and asked for money to be wired to him. Pollock assured him on 4 October 1938 that help was available in case of an emergency (Kracauer papers, Deutsches Literaturarchiv, Marbach).

125 Adorno to Siegfried and Lili Kracauer
Bar Harbor, 5.8.1938

Bar Harbor (Maine)
5 August 38.

Dear Friedel and Lili,

We have taken refuge from the heat of New York in a very remote and quiet place in the extreme north-east of the States – by the sea, but with forests and mountains; it might almost be a landscape if only the traces of human hands were to be seen there rather than those of dynamite and automobiles. We are busy relaxing: I have carried out the surgery on Husserl – successfully, I hope. Ernst Bloch has been in America for a few weeks now. We shall be back in New York from the 15th; the address is 290 Riverside Drive. Do get in touch soon. Much love from both of us to both of you,

Your old
Teddie

Original: MS, picture postcard: Echo Lake from Beach Bluff, Acadia National Park, Mt Desert Island, Maine; Siegfried Kracauer papers, Deutsches Literaturarchiv, Marbach am Neckar.

Bloch: Ernst Bloch and his family arrived in New York on a Polish ship in July 1938.

126 Kracauer to Adorno
Paris, 20.8.1938

Paris (17e). 3, Avenue Mac-Mahon / 20 August 1938

Dear Teddie,

I wrote to the Institute on 26 July – asking them to let you know – that I had received your manuscript and would be writing to you about it much sooner. Please excuse me for not doing so until today – but I have been through weeks of turmoil which have not allowed me to get round to writing a letter, and, besides, I knew that you were on holiday.

Before I comment on your manuscript in detail, I should like to say in advance that I could only gather from your first long letter of 3 May that you had been planning a selection of especially important passages from my work in view of the limited space available. In that letter you wrote explicitly: 'In any case, an editorial note will indicate that it is only a matter of reproducing some of the most important motifs and not your text in its entirety.' Then, though, it was borne in upon me by your letter of 28 June that, in the manuscript which you had completed in the meantime, you had made the most drastic alterations – an announcement which caused me serious concern. However, I wanted to wait and see your manuscript first.

A reading of it, unfortunately, confirmed my concerns. I must inform you to my great regret that I *cannot* consent to the publication of this manuscript. Believe me, this is very painful for me, not only because of the repeated postponement of publication or partial publication of my work but also on account of the effort you have invested in it.

It seems to me that those structures within your manuscript which make it impossible for me to give my consent can in part be blamed on your intention to compress the main content of my work into a fifth of the space that it occupied in the original and, moreover, to present the version thus created as a self-contained entity. But this plan is – as I surely do not need to justify to you – problematic from the outset when applied to a genuine text like mine.

I shall attempt to demonstrate to you how ruinous I am convinced that it is in this case. You wrote to me on 3 May that, in your reworking, the 'framework' would necessarily have to be of secondary importance. I should certainly have had no objection to that. In fact, though, in your version it is not the 'framework' that stands aside but a considerable part of the essential content of my work. I took infinite care to separate the theoretical elements from the given realities, and to this end I maintained a specific middle distance from events, to which the use of closed categories such as that of the nihilistic will to power corresponds. Apart from the tactical appropriateness of such a procedure when applied to topical issues [current affairs] it was with the help of this that I succeeded (as I hope) in making the rise of fascism comprehensible and constructing the development of totalitarian propaganda from this. These insights, which are by no means a 'framework', all but disappear in your manuscript – probably because you prefer to capture fascism by means of a network of coordinates which may have some validity at a far greater distance from the phenomenon than the one which I consciously intended. This is explicit in your eliminating the closed categories which I employed and with them all the perceptions which arise from confrontation with the material at close quarters. In your text, fascism emerges as a finished product which can be 100% classified and categorized. You identify it from the first with counter-revolution, set its interests in diametrical opposition to those of the majority, and push aside the ambiguity of its relationship with capitalism. Characteristic of the dimension in which you operate is the trifling fact that Ortega y Gasset, who in my text is a 'thinker from the *grande bourgeoisie*', becomes a 'reactionary' in yours. I am not alleging, let it be known, that abbreviations of this kind are wrong, but they are too summary to have any weight and, above all, they completely leap over the level on which I move and where I acquire the insights that are indeed drawn from significant phenomena and correspond to them. The omission of this level in your text is entirely in accord with the way in which you arrange the motifs. While I employ an arrangement dictated by the challenges and difficulties of the material, yours treats its object as a matter which is already completely subsumed into categories, which can be elaborated without any consideration of the pre-existing form of the material. In my estimate, your arrangement is (in part) of a purely ornamental/cosmetic nature.

In short, I cannot back this manuscript for the very reason that features and content of decisive importance in my work are missing from it. In addition, there is a fundamental objection which is of equal gravity. I noted with the greatest amazement that you did not exactly take scrupulous care to preserve my original text in your version but, on the contrary, displace my text with a mass of your own additions. Over and over again, within a version abridged by four-fifths, it is you yourself who are speaking, without even identifying the additions as such. Some of them are, by the way, wholly contrary to the approach which my work adopts; in contrast to you, I renounced all the opportunities for linguistic analysis which offered themselves. And, not content with constantly intervening, in the process you capriciously change the direction of my text – that is, when you actually have recourse to it at all. There is scarcely a sentence of mine which is accurately reproduced; most of them have been plucked, gutted and changed beyond recognition. I must confess to you that never in my entire literary career have I set eyes on an edition which runs counter to every legitimate usage in this way – not to mention the fact that in my own personal practice I should never have played around with another author's text like that.

To tell the truth, you have not edited my manuscript but used it as the basis for a work of your own.

What gives this away is, not least, its style. Expressions such as these: 'propaganda as a flower in one's buttonhole ...', 'the beery bliss of amateur choral festivals ...', 'the sun-bathing director chauffeured by one of his employees ...', 'the dream of a newspaper-reader who plunges unresistingly from cliché to cliché ...', 'the professor registers ...' belong to a linguistic sphere which, however one may judge it, has so little in common with that of my work that I have deliberately avoided it altogether – not to mention the fact that, throughout the whole thing, the style peculiar to you riots all over the pitiable remnants of mine.

I believe that, with this, I have given you the reasons that I find myself faced with the regrettable necessity of being unable to assent to the publication of your version. What can be done to save my work for the *Zeitschrift*? After the failure of your attempt to compress a text distinguished by characteristics and the quality that are genuinely mine into a fifth of its volume but without bestowing on this extract, as you wrote to me on 28 June, 'the nature of a fragment' – though such an attempt, as was evident to me even when you announced it, was in any event bound to fail! – and in view of the calamitous lack of space, there is only one solution left which seemed to me from the outset to be the only fitting one: for the *Zeitschrift* to print a fragment of my work. Passages might be selected from all the chapters to be linked by brief editorial bridging texts which would be clearly denoted as such – or a separate extract of the requisite length might be published with a preliminary note stating that this represented a fragment taken from my work. In the interests of the *Zeitschrift* as well as my own I am definitely inclined towards the second and more profitable solution – that is, I suggest that the chapter on the masses, and if possible the final chapter, too, with its construction of the process of self-immolation of totalitarian propaganda, should be the ones to be published. A fragment of this kind would be a clear and honest matter; it would not only contain some explanations which are important in themselves but would also provide, over and beyond this, a real idea of my work.

To conclude, I must not forget one very important point. You signed your manuscript with my name – but unfortunately I cannot in any circumstances publish the fragment of my work which I have suggested under my name, but only under a pseudonym or without giving a name at all, for reasons which I explained to Herr Pollock on the occasion of his visit here in April. Herr Pollock considered these reasons entirely cogent and promised to see that things were done in accordance with my wishes.

I am writing to Horkheimer by the same post. So as not to have to repeat myself, I am enclosing a copy of this letter for him in the interests of simplicity.

Many thanks for your postcard from your summer holidays which arrived yesterday. We were very glad to learn from it that you and Gretel had a pleasant time on vacation.

Much love and best wishes from Lili and me to you both,

Yours,

NB. I must also thank you for your letter of 2 June. However, your news about the millionaire from Philadelphia whom Schapiro had interested in me would at that time not have required the discretion which you requested of me, as it had already been shared with me by various friends, including Leo.

Original: typescript (carbon copy); Siegfried Kracauer papers, Deutsches Literaturarchiv, Marbach am Neckar.

I wrote to the Institute on 26 July: not preserved in Kracauer's papers or in Max Horkheimer's.

Ortega y Gasset: José Ortega y Gasset (1883–1955), in his *The Revolt of the Masses* (New York: W. W. Norton, 1930), presented an analysis of fascism from an aristocratic perspective.

under a pseudonym: out of consideration for his mother, who was living in Germany (see letter no. 120, note).

I am writing to Horkheimer: the letter to Max Horkheimer of 20 August 1938 has been published (see Horkheimer, GS 16, pp. 458–64).

shared with me by … including Leo: in a letter from Leo Löwenthal to Kracauer of 3 May 1938 (see Kracauer/Löwenthal, *Briefwechsel*, pp. 86f.).

127 Adorno to Kracauer

New York, 12.9.1938

12 September 1938.

Dear Friedel,

I am sorry that you could not give your approval to the revised version of your propaganda project, and I assume that you have seen from Leo's letter that the regret about this is shared by the others. In this regret I feel that I am to some extent innocent of unjust stepfatherly feelings, as the work, apart from its practical intent, had no purpose other than that of being helpful to you. I was aware from the outset of the things about which you complain, especially the question of 'distance', and to the best of my knowledge I can only speak in their defence. The reproach implicit in phrases such as the one about the 'reworking which goes against all legitimate practice' seems to me to be unjustified. I did not wilfully meddle with your text but tried to reformulate it in keeping with the precise theoretical approach which underpins the *Zeitschrift*, and, although I am prepared to assume entire responsibility for the new version, I cannot regard this new version as my private business. I cannot help it; I believe that publication would have been to your definite advantage.

But I can understand your negative decision, and I respect it. The only wish that I might add would be that you would look at my text in sufficient depth to be able to arrive at a verdict about it which would acknowledge that the interventions which I performed were not arrogant or capricious.

We have moved into the new apartment – the first apartment of my own which I have had in my life – and are now in possession of my grand piano. We would both feel well and be happy were it not for the fact that the weight of anxiety which presses on us all nowadays makes a sense of individual wellbeing quite impossible even in the most elementary things. Among these anxieties I include, above all, those for the few people for whom one feels concern. I do not, however, count international politics among them, as I don't believe there will be a war any more than I did previously. If there is one, after all, it would indeed be a victory not only for crude violence but also one of empiricism over theory – and even my hatred of Hitler and his ilk can hardly make me disposed to wish for that. But that shouldn't be taken literally; seriously, I know very well that there is no longer any hope except for a catastrophe. Only I no longer have even that.

Much love to you and Lili, from Gretel too,

Your old
Teddie

Original: typescript; Siegfried Kracauer papers, Deutsches Literaturarchiv, Marbach am Neckar.

Leo's letter: on 9 September 1938 Leo Löwenthal wrote to Kracauer about the latter's refusal to give permission to publish the version produced by Adorno of *Masse und Propaganda*, saying that Max Horkheimer and the other members of the Institute were 'sincerely sorry' about the matter (see Kracauer/Löwenthal, *Briefwechsel*, pp. 90f.).

128 Adorno to Kracauer
[New York,] 1.11.1938

1 November 1938.

Dear Friedel,

I have the impression that you are maintaining a silence towards me which does not suggest a willingness to cooperate. But the questions involved are far too urgent for me to be able to play the offended auntie.

I don't know if you are aware that the whole Schapiro business was organized by him in cooperation with me – that we weighed every single step together with the utmost precision, and that among other things I composed that lively sketch for a biography of Kracauer which has obviously proved its worth. From the way the whole thing developed I was as optimistic as he was – and, indeed, your friend Krautheimer, too – and I still am. The crucial point about this is that the things which have been achieved up till now are to be considered merely as a *beginning*, and that I am firmly convinced that, if this beginning has been a success, it will turn out to be relatively easy for us to achieve still more. For this reason, I have taken a view from the outset that is also backed up by my own convictions – namely, that you will be capable without further ado, in spite of the language difficulty, of teaching in a small group and within the quite relaxed and informal context of a seminar. I can well see that a certain degree of awkwardness is part and parcel of this, but from what I know of the situation this really is no tragedy, and I believe that I can unreservedly recommend to you to go ahead. Of course nobody imagines that they could expect you to give lectures as your main professional activity – it's just for form's sake.

Far more serious, though, is the question of the visa. It is always a very unpromising situation if one has already exposed oneself to the possibility of a refusal, and it appears that particular difficulties exist in getting a visitor's visa if one has previously applied for an immigration visa. (That was how it turned out in the past, for example, in the case of Carl Dreyfuss's attempt to immigrate.) Now, however, I should like to advise you most urgently, in spite of this, not to let it discourage you, and to persevere with the matter – and especially in scrupulous agreement with whatever Schapiro suggests to you. I have every reason to assume that in the end we *shall* manage it, and it would be an immense pity to ruin our chances by throwing in the towel.

I am well aware that the money guaranteed to you up till now will be enough for the purposes of the visa but does not represent any real basis for a livelihood. You know how matters stand with the Institute at present – and so today I have launched another initiative through an acquaintance who has a certain influence with the Jewish aid committee. She says that they will be able to get something done there too in combination with the other two projects. This combination is the immediate reason for my letter. I think that it would be a good thing if you wrote directly and quickly to this lady, mentioning my name, describing your situation and adding a brief survey of your previous activities and your publications. (Your name, of course, is well known to her.) Her private address is: Miss Catherine Savard, c/o Miss von Minkus, 350 West 55th Street, New York City.

As well as the revised Husserl I have also written (under great pressure) a major piece of work, 'Über den Fetischcharakter in der Musik und die Regression des Hörens', which has gone to press in the last few days. You can hardly imagine what a burden I am carrying on my shoulders here.

Do get in touch, and give warmest greetings to Lili from both of us. As ever, your old

Teddie

Original: typescript with handwritten corrections and additions; Siegfried Kracauer papers, Deutsches Literaturarchiv, Marbach am Neckar.

A biography of Kracauer: see letter no. 134.

Krautheimer: Richard Krautheimer (1897–1994), art historian and friend of Kracauer, in exile in the USA since 1935; professor in art history at the Institute of Fine Arts, New York University (1952–71).

in spite of the language difficulty: Kracauer had a stammer; in addition, his knowledge of English was not yet up to his usual standard of expressing himself.

whatever Schapiro suggests to you: in addition to the long-drawn-out preparation of the film project, this included the acceptance of a post at the New York Evening School (Meyer Schapiro to Kracauer, 3 October 1938, Kracauer papers, Deutsches Literaturarchiv, Marbach).

Von Minkus: no information is available.

Catherine Savard: no correspondence which corresponds to this description survives among Kracauer's papers; no more exact information is available.

Lili: Adorno wrote 'Lily'.

129 Kracauer to Adorno
Paris, 17.11.1938

Paris (17e), 3, Avenue Mac-Mahon / 17 November 1938

Dear Teddie,

I should have already written in reply to your letter before last if this would have contributed to the discussion about your reworking of my propaganda manuscript. But, as I had the impression from your letter that our points of view regarding the adaptation of a text are fundamentally different, I will say no more on the subject. All that needs to be added – though it is self-evident, and something which you should never have had to doubt – is that my criticism of your version rested on a detailed study of your alterations and additions. Moreover, that I do not understand how you can call it 'in my interest' to publish a text to which, despite my strong willingness to tolerate acceptable compromises, I cannot take the responsibility of signing my name. As before, of course, my suggestion that you might publish a longish fragment of my work in the *Zeitschrift* still stands.

Enough on that matter. I shall go on now to your letter of 1 November and thank you most warmly, in Lili's name too, for your efforts in the YMHA business; I knew about them, it is true, but could only gauge their *full* extent from your report. I really am very glad of your endeavours in this direction. As we, like you, regard this business simply as a start, I shall of course write to the YMHA that I shall be delighted to accept the job – not, however, on the basis of a visitor's visa but on that of the immigration visa for which we had already applied before the YMHA business, and which now requires that we speed up the process of obtaining it. Only if we really are able to stay in the country will the job represent a start for me, in your sense and in mine. However, we had to put our names down for immigration at the beginning of October because at that time there was such a stampede on account of the political situation that had just arisen that they explained to us at the consulate that, by hesitating for too long, we would be throwing away the chance of immigrating for years to come. So when Schapiro offered me the prospect of the invitation from the YMHA, I gathered the necessary information at once and succeeded in finding out that we would be going about it the wrong way round if we were to break off the immigration process we had initiated and travelled over on a visitor's visa.

1) Once one has put in the request for immigration, obtaining a visitor's visa is, as you yourself write, bound up with specific difficulties which make all subsequent dealings very awkward.

2) Receipt of a visitor's visa – and this is especially important – results in immediate removal from the immigration list.

3) If the visitor's visa has expired, one has to leave the country immediately. In practical terms, the possibility of converting it into an immigration visa no longer exists.

4) As we should only be able to apply for an immigration visa after our return were we to come over on a visitor's visa, this would result in that very delay which is to be avoided at all costs, because it effectively renders any possibility of immigration illusory.

In view of all this, the only proper thing to do now in my situation is to work towards speeding up the immigration visa as much as possible. Leo, too, is of this opinion by reason of his exact knowledge of things. By the way, he and Golde (something for which we are incredibly grateful) have sent us a very carefully composed affidavit which represents a great step forward for us – but you will probably know about this, and also about the supplementary affidavit with which Franz Neumann has very kindly provided us.

I have, of course, written to Schapiro about all the arguments relating to the visa and also asked him – in addition to all the other things which he has already done for me in such a marvellous way – to facilitate the *acceleration* of the granting of the immigration visa. I have let him know what would be necessary for this; most of all it requires an affidavit from an *American* party with particularly solid financial resources.

Many thanks, too, for establishing the connection with Ms Savard. I shall get in contact with her in the way that you mention the moment that I know that the business has been set in motion on the basis which I have described.

Thank you once again – and warmest greetings to Gretel and yourself from both of us.

Yours

Original: typescript (carbon copy); Siegfried Kracauer papers, Deutsches Literaturarchiv, Marbach am Neckar.

YMHA business: Young Men's Hebrew Association; Meyer Schapiro wrote to Kracauer on 10 October 1938 about the option of giving 'seminars and lecture courses on modern art and culture' there for a fixed salary (Kracauer papers, Deutsches Literaturarchiv, Marbach).

Leo, too … by reason of his exact knowledge: in a letter of 17 November 1938, Kracauer confirmed to Leo Löwenthal the arrival of the latter's affidavit; Franz

Neumann's guarantee (see below) was also enclosed with Löwenthal's letter. In his letter of 1 November 1938, Löwenthal mentioned that he and Neumann had provided the 'declaration of sponsorship … for immigration purposes', as a visitor's visa could not be obtained after applying for an immigration visa (see Kracauer/Löwenthal, *Briefwechsel*, pp. 95f.). Löwenthal's affidavit says of Kracauer: 'That Dr Siegfried Kracauer, who is making application for himself and his wife for immigration visas, is one of the oldest friends of both of us. I, Dr Loewenthal, have a deep moral obligation towards Dr Kracauer. During my studies at the universities and during my subsequent scientific career he was my friend and adviser. I have the feeling that my scientific career would not have been as successful as it is without a constant personal contact with Dr Kracauer. I am also grateful to him because he rendered me financial aid at the beginning of my academic activity when I had to struggle hard. We, Leo Loewenthal and Gertrud Loewenthal, have constantly been in touch with Dr and Mrs Kracauer; even in times when we did not live in the same city, we corresponded and visited frequently. By reason of our friendship with Dr and Mrs Kracauer we feel the strong moral obligation to assist them in any possible way to become established in this country' (Max Horkheimer papers, Archivzentrum der Universitätsbibliothek Johann Christian Senckenberg, Frankfurt am Main).

the supplementary affidavit with which Franz Neumann has very kindly provided us: in a letter of 17 November 1938 (Kracauer papers, Deutsches Literaturarchiv, Marbach), Kracauer thanks Franz Neumann for the affidavit.

130 Adorno and Gretel Adorno to Kracauer
Princeton, 29.1.1939

PRINCETON UNIVERSITY
PRINCETON NEW JERSEY
–
SCHOOL OF PUBLIC AND INTERNATIONAL AFFAIRS

OFFICE OF RADIO RESEARCH
FIELDHEADQUARTERS
22 EAST 17 STREET
NEW YORK, N.Y.

TELEPHONE
ALGONQUIN 4-7949

29 January 1939

Dear Friedel,

I woke up early this morning with the thought that on 8 February you will be 50 years old – and I should not like to let the day go by without sending you every imaginable good wish – knowing very well how sceptical you are about such official dates, but also with a presentiment that you, just like me, take a secret pleasure in them (don't be afraid of any dialectical interpretation!). Among my wishes, the chief one is that you will soon get out of that unfriendly Europe and over here – for a barbarism which is already old is greatly preferable to its new variety. I have as little doubt as Schapiro that your affairs will go well once you are here. By the way, I gave a talk in Brooklyn recently as part of a series of lectures on aesthetic questions in radio which he is directing, and he was as charming on that occasion as in other matters.

As I have said before, we do *not* believe that there will be a war – i.e. fascist solidarity is even stronger (faced with the possibility of a collapse of the Central European system) than its imperialist counterparts – which, however, have already reached a point of acute crisis. For France I consequently foresee an extremely black future – to some extent along the lines of the fate of the Czechs. I should like to say, however, that my certainty is no longer *quite* as strong as it was during the September crisis – but I am afraid they'll get away with it. The confederates in London are too strong.

You know, of course, about all the calamities that have befallen my parents. I finally managed to get them an entry visa for Cuba – but my father suffered a severe attack of pneumonia which once again held up their emigration for weeks, and a new disaster could break out in Germany any day now.

How are things with your aunts in Frankfurt? Are there any chances of getting them out?

The diabolical thing about the situation is that, in all seriousness, the Germans could not survive a war, and what is keeping the others in check, and ultimately driving them towards catastrophe, is nothing but a fear of their own victory.

Do get in touch very soon. You will find some of my latest things in the *Zeitschrift*.

Much love to you and Lili

Your old Teddie

Warmest greetings and congratulations
and all the best to Lilli too
Yours, Gretel

Original: MS; Siegfried Kracauer papers, Deutsches Literaturarchiv, Marbach am Neckar.

in Brooklyn ... a series of lectures on aesthetic questions in radio: not preserved.

the calamities: Adorno described these events in his letter to Walter Benjamin of 1 February 1939: Oscar Wiesengrund suffered an eye injury during the pogrom of 9 November 1938; when their 'protective custody' ended, Adorno's parents were not immediately able to use the exit visa obtained for them by American contacts because of Oscar Wiesengrund's bout of pneumonia (see Adorno/Benjamin, *Briefwechsel*, p. 389).

your aunts: an expression equivalent to Adorno's 'mothers' (see letter no. 7). Kracauer's efforts in support of Hedwig and Rosette Kracauer's emigration came to nothing; both were deported in 1942.

in the Zeitschrift: 'Fragmente über Wagner: Über den Fetischcharakter in der Musik und die Regression des Hörens' (see letters no. 118 and 120, notes).

131 Adorno to Kracauer

[New York,] 6.3.1939

6 March 1939.

Dear Friedel,

By pure chance I discovered today that the Rockefeller Foundation is starting – or has already started – a major film research project which in a certain sense represents a counterpart to the radio project of which I am the musical director. The director of the film project is a man named Schlesinger – a name which inspires confidence – and he is said to be fair and decent. I at once let Schapiro know about this matter and told him that we must make every effort to involve you in this project. I should imagine that the people there will be able to get you a post similar to mine, i.e. of such a kind that you will officially or effectively be the *theoretical* director of the project.

So that you can understand this, I must give you the following facts: projects of this kind (apart from our own, I also have a close knowledge of the National Orchestral Survey, for example) are in general basically exercises in statistical stocktaking, working with questionnaires, interviews and similar media. Every year thousands of so-called research workers are spewed out of the universities and let loose on the country – all of them trained in a wholly schematic fashion and doing exactly the same thing. Their entire education is based on a strictly enforced ban on thinking. As a result, such projects are becoming more and more alike and more and more senseless, and awareness of this is beginning to spread. This means, however, that in enterprises of this kind theorists of our background are gaining, so to speak, in exchange value. With this in view you must, in my opinion, forge ahead with your application.

As I see it, you should write first of all to Schapiro about this matter, and likewise to Dr Paul F. Lazarsfeld, 801 Westend Avenue, New York City, whom I have to thank for this information. He will be lunching with Schlesinger in the next few days and has promised me that he will intervene on your behalf. Schapiro, on the other hand, knows the Schlesinger family and will try this approach. In the letter to Lazarsfeld it will be a good thing if you refer not merely to me but also to Horkheimer and Pollock, and present your past involvement with film in the most comprehensive terms possible. (He is a great believer in success.)

I think it entirely likely that they may be able to obtain something like a part-time post on the film project for you, which would then, in combination with the things which Schapiro has arranged for you, offer you and Lili the prospect of an existence free from material constraints.

At the same time, I should advise you to prepare – right now and with great care – an English summary of the plan for a study of the sociology of film that you can send off at once when you have heard something back from one of us (I shall probably send a telegram). An extraordinary amount inevitably depends on such a summary, which would be known in practice as a 'theoretical memorandum for the film project'. The two important stipulations for this piece of writing, which should be no shorter than ten and no longer than twenty typed pages, would be: first, that it should contain genuinely specific theoretical ideas about the sociology of film from which these people can see that your contribution will be something really new and illuminating (and so more than just pronouncements about the wish-fulfilment function of film and similar things which have made the rounds here).

In this memorandum I should feel it quite safe for you to include, so to speak as a speculation, some of your *important* ideas about the sociology of film. Second, the memorandum must be as detailed as possible and contain concrete suggestions – and indeed, if possible, in such a way as to create the impression that the empirical studies verify the theoretical arguments. I don't have to tell you how critically I regard the concept of verification, and I do believe that, when it is a serious matter, one can liberate oneself from such fetishistic concepts. *In the outline*, however, with an eye to the Americans, a reference should be made if at all possible to something of that kind. Projects of the type of the film project are usually subdivided into individual studies. It would certainly be sensible if you could take this into consideration in your memorandum and suggest a series of individual studies which are clearly distinct from one another (for example, a historical one, a psychological one with tests based on mass reactions to films, an analysis of specific films, etc.); I would say about six to eight studies, as precise as possible. The risk that is present in the case of such detailed suggestions is one which, in my opinion, has to be taken. I am reiterating to you from my own experience that even the primary suggestions must be so detailed and tempting that people will take the bait. Please ask Brill to send you the new volume of the journal – first and foremost because of the Horkheimer essay, but also because of my long one which at the same time may perhaps provide you with some inspiration in connection with the application of our categories to American experiences. If you wish, I shall be happy to send you more material about my radio study.

You know that as a general rule I am uncommonly pessimistic about everything of this kind – all the more reason, I believe, that you should take my advice, as in this case, for once, I am at last proving myself to be really hopeful. My optimism is also shared by Lazarsfeld.

I am dictating this in extreme haste. That's all for now – much love to you and Lili, also from Gretel

Your old
Teddie

Original: typescript with handwritten corrections; Siegfried Kracauer papers, Deutsches Literaturarchiv, Marbach am Neckar.

Schlesinger: no information is available.

let Schapiro know about this matter: not preserved among Adorno's papers; no further information is available.

National Orchestral Survey: the 1938/39 study included, among other things, an investigation of the economic situation of American symphony orchestras.

English summary of the plan for a study of the sociology of film: see *Ideenskizze zu meinem Buch über den Film* (Kracauer, W 3, pp. 807–10; see p. 872 for the English version); the effect of the summary is recorded: John E. Abbott, head of the New York Film Library, whom Kracauer got to know in 1938 during his stay in Paris (see Kracauer, W 3, p. 810, note), reacted to it on 19 June 1939 with the offer of a research post to work on this subject at his institution (see *Marbacher Magazin* 47, pp. 94f.).

Brill: Hans Klaus Brill, secretary of the Paris branch of the Institute.

Horkheimer essay: 'Die Juden in Europa', *Zeitschrift für Sozialforschung*, nos. 1/2, 1939 (see Horkheimer, GS 4, pp. 308–31).

132 Adorno to Kracauer
New York, 10.3.1939

New York, 10.III.1939

Dear Friedel,

Things are getting off to a promising start. Schlesinger himself is not the director, but he does have to make the decision about the grant – i.e. to appoint the director; nothing has happened yet, but the money is there – so your chances are good. L. has approached him, and he reacted well. At the same time Schapiro had a word with Abbott, who has some authority in the matter of your other business, and he, too, is acting in a positive manner. Schapiro had been afraid that the two plans might overlap; judging from A's reaction, there is nothing to fear. Abbott himself will speak to Schlesinger about you and is thoroughly optimistic. If needs be, we shall also mobilize Lynd. Because of this your memorandum is all the more important. Please get on with it at once with all the intense concentration you can muster and send a copy each to me, to Schapiro and to Lazarsfeld. The last says that it is of crucial importance.

If I am not mistaken, I have at last found a possible means of actually putting your situation to rights. Do write soon; all our love to you and Lili from us both

Your old

Teddie

Original: typescript with handwritten addition, postcard; Siegfried Kracauer papers, Deutsches Literaturarchiv, Marbach am Neckar; underlinings of uncertain origin.

10.III.1939: dated by Adorno as '10.II.'; the context and the postmark 'MAR 10' show this to be an error.

L.: probably Paul Lazarsfeld.

Lynd: Robert S. Lynd (1892–1970), sociologist at Columbia University.

send a copy each to me, to Schapiro and to Lazarsfeld: not preserved in the correspondence with Adorno and Meyer Schapiro; no further information is available.

133 Kracauer to Adorno
Paris, 24.3.1939

Paris (17e), 3, Avenue Mac-Mahon / 24 March 1939

Dear Teddie,

Your letter and your card arrived – remarkably, together – only after my letter to you of 16 March had gone and at the same time, unfortunately, so shortly before the departure of the boat train for the *Queen Mary* that I could no longer reply to you by return of post. I just had time enough to send a hasty word about the business to Schapiro by the *Queen Mary*.

First of all, thank you very much for having thought of me at once for the *Film Research Project* about which you learnt by chance, and at the same time for taking steps in this matter. As any possibilities which might exist would relate to my precise field of work, they are naturally of the greatest interest to me.

I must just tell you, however, what I have also told Schapiro: the business which I have already been guaranteed must take priority in all circumstances – and if it is pushed into the background to even the slightest degree or even foiled by the attempt to get onto the *Film Research Project*, I will give up that attempt at the outset.

Your reports and suggestions were all, of course, very important to me. I am going to write to Dr Lazarsfeld by the same mail-boat.

On the other hand, as for the memorandum of which you write, I believe that at the moment I should in principle desist from its composition. Objectively speaking, it would be a mistake to sketch out a programmatic summary – to a certain extent, into the blue – as, despite your close and detailed accounts, I cannot possibly judge its applicability to conditions in New York from here. I am much more inclined to think that such a memorandum will be feasible and sensible only once some kind of negotiations have been concluded both with the Film Library and with the *Film Research Project* on the basis of my demonstrable qualifications as a specialist – because only then, in my position as a collaborator, would I be able to obtain the knowledge of the project and all the relevant requirements which are indispensable for compiling a binding memorandum.

We have once more been living through some very unsettled weeks. Yet again, war seems to have been avoided for the time being.

With warmest regards from us both to you and Gretel

Your

Original: typescript (carbon copy; Siegfried Kracauer papers, Deutsches Literaturarchiv, Marbach am Neckar.

letter to you of 16 March: not preserved.

to send a hasty word about the business to Schapiro: a letter to Meyer Schapiro of 17 March 1939, which Kracauer mentions in a letter of 31 March, has not been preserved; in the preceding one (3 March 1939) he asked Schapiro to stop John Abbott's efforts regarding a visitor's visa so as not to jeopardize the awarding of a visa for immigration (Kracauer papers, Deutsches Literaturarchiv, Marbach).

write to Dr Lazarsfeld: in a letter of 24 March 1939, Kracauer mentioned to Paul Lazarsfeld that he was 'indisputably the first German film critic and sociologist of film' (Kracauer papers, Deutsches Literarturarchiv, Marbach).

134 Adorno to Kracauer

[New York,] 27.3.1939

27 March 1939.

Dear Friedel,

Many thanks for your lines. In the meantime, you will have received my letter and my card and seen that things are coming on well for you here – and the developments are even more positive: we managed things so that Abbott intervened directly with Schlesinger on your behalf about collaborating on the film project, and Schlesinger has, in principle, taken a positive attitude. I am convinced that if we all proceed with a certain degree of finesse you can be really 'settled' at last. The film project itself, of course, is just at the preparatory stage: the staff members will only be engaged over the summer, and the whole thing is scarcely likely to get off the ground before autumn. True, that does mean a certain delay, but, on the other hand, it also means an opportunity for thorough preparation. If you send me a first draft soon, I will write back to you about it in detail and possibly add a list of supplementary suggestions which I have thought up. (A collaboration between the film project and the radio project is by no means out of the question, and my suggestions are partly connected with that.)

One more request in connection with this: the need is constantly arising for me to write snappy biographies of you for presentation to various institutions. It would be very kind of you if you would check the last opus of this kind (which I am enclosing for you) for content as regards the 'poetry and truth' of it. In all of this, poetic imagination is the less important problem; what counts is not the truth but, rather, a glossy presentation. But more facts and dates would give the whole thing a more solidly dignified look, and if you supply these you would do our shared enterprise a great service. The outline which I am sending you is a rough draft and will not fall into the hands of any third party unless the wording has been revised by Meyer Schapiro.

It is hard to describe the kind of stuff that I have had to devote myself to over the last few months. However, Horkheimer and I are hoping to get back to something more sensible now. I am dictating in haste – this is simply the tribute that even my resistance has to pay to America.

Much love to you and Lili, from Gretel too

Your old Teddie

The problem is no longer how you will manage to earn an income here; it is, instead, just how you can enter the country fast enough! Also you must devote all your energies to this. At this very moment further interventions are being made in Washington in support of this. My parents, unfortunately, are still in Germany, but at the moment things are not going badly.

Curriculum vitae.

Siegfried Kracauer born 1889 in Frankfurt on the Main. Studied architecture and history of art in Munich and Berlin. Took his state examination ('Diplom Ingenieur') in architecture and his doctor's degree (with a thesis about wrought iron work in the Mark Brandenburg[)]. At the same time he took an early interest in philosophical questions particularly in cultural philosophy and sociology. These interests brought him into contact with Georg Simmel and Max Scheler with whom he remained in close relations throughout their lives. Shortly before the war he started his career as an architect. During that period he won several contests for public buildings and held different major jobs. In spite of his success in the practical field his theoretical interests became stronger and stronger. He contributed to philosophical and sociological publications in periodicals such as 'Logos' and 'Preussische Jahrbücher'. Consequently, he entered the editorial staff of the Frankfurter Zeitung in the early twenties. Here he determined for more than ten years the whole line of cultural

[18] politics of that influential paper by his articles on philosophical
[19] and sociological subjects. He became renowned particularly by his criticisms in the
[20] field of architecture and moving pictures. He achieved a close
[21] knowledge of the whole realm of the film by extensive research and
[22] practical collaboration with the industry and finally was regarded
[23] as the greatest authority of film criticism in Germany.
[24] His work at the Frankfurter Zeitung gave him sufficient time for
[25] book publications such as:
[26] 'Soziologie als Wissenschaft' (about the epistomological foundations
[27] of sociology) and 'Die Angestellten', an analysis of the German
[28] employee class which made sensation in Germany. 1926 he finished a

–2–

[1] book on the sociology of the detective story which he withhold from
[2] publication. Further he published pseudonomously the novel 'Ginster'
[3] which proved a great literary success in Germany and later was trans-
[4] lated into French.
[5] When Hitler came into power, K published in the Frankfurter Zeitung
[6] some biting satires against the new regime; especially one which
[7] denounced the fake about the Reichstagsfire. By these publications
[8] as well as by the book about the employees he drew the hatred of the
[9] Nazis upon himself but succeeded in escaping their revenge.
[10] He then settled in Paris where he wrote his famous book on Offenbach
[11] which became published in German, English and French. This work
[12] created a new type of biography treating its hero not as much
[13] as a private person but as an exponent of social trends. By analyzing
[14] the social back ground of so called 'light art' this book follows
[15] up the line of Kracauer's film analyses through an earlier period
[16] of the modern art of masses. After the accomplishment of the
[17] Offenbach book the International Institute for Social Research at
[18] Columbia University, New York, entrusted him with an extensive study
[19] on the methods of propaganda within the totalitarian countries
[20] which he finished 1938. At the same time he resumed his research
[21] on the sociology of moving pictures and is busy at present with a
[22] comprehensive theoretical study on that field.

Original: typescript with handwritten corrections, additions and postscript, with those in the curriculum vitae (in English) in another hand; Siegfried Kracauer papers, Deutsches Literaturarchiv, Marbach am Neckar.

[1]: handwritten numbering of the lines by Kracauer, who produced a typewritten copy with minimal deviations from the original; this is not included.

Simmel: Georg Simmel (1858–1918), philosopher and sociologist; he held an 'extraordinary [i.e. supernumerary] professorship' in Berlin, where Kracauer became a student of his in 1907, and in 1914 a professorship in Strasbourg. 'To have been one who revealed the truth as surely no thinker before him ever did; a pathfinder in the realm of the inner and outer life' (see *Georg Simmel*, Kracauer, W 9.2, p. 280).

Scheler: Max Scheler; he and Kracauer met in person for the first time in Frankfurt am Main in 1916.

135 Kracauer to Adorno
Paris, 7.4.1939

Paris (17e), 3, Avenue Mac-Mahon / 7 April 1939

Dear Teddie,

Many thanks for your news and the sketch of the *Biography.*

Today I have even less to add to my letter of 24 March, since, as you mention, the *Film Research Project* is still at a preparatory stage. For me the main thing is – as I wrote at once to Meyer Schapiro and to you – that the attempt to associate myself with the *Film Research Project* in no way affects the work guaranteed me at the *Film Library*.

Your admonition that I should devote all my energies to getting us to New York quickly enough coaxed an elegiac smile out of me. If it depended only on me alone ... But with every ship's mail I am waiting for certain documents with whose help it may be possible, after all, to speed things up.

Thanks also for the great pains that you have taken with the *Biography.* It is something very close to my heart that this sketch should not end up in the hands of strangers, as it contains various inaccuracies which I must correct. I shall send you these corrections, and also a few additions, by the next possible ship.

We are so sorry that your dear parents are still in Germany. Incidentally, things are just the same with my mother and my aunt, as the permit to reside here which they applied for is still outstanding at present.

All our love and best wishes for now from both of us to both of you

Yours

Original: typescript (carbon copy); Siegfried Kracauer papers, Deutsches Literaturarchiv, Frankfurt am Main.

136 Kracauer to Adorno

Paris, 13.4.1939

Paris (17e), 3, Avenue Mac-Mahon / 13 April 1939

Dear Teddie,

Here I am putting together for you the additions and corrections to the *Biography* written by you that I mentioned in my letter of 7 April.

May I ask you to take a look at all the dates relating to my curriculum vitae and bibliography on the enclosed sheets: *Curriculum vitae* and *List of publications*?

I shall now follow your sketch in detail:

Page 1 of your text:

Lines 1–2: addition: see my *curriculum vitae.*

Lines 3–4: It does not seem necessary to me to give the title of my thesis. As a general request, I ask you to allow my activities as an architect to slip into the background, where they actually belong, and for the additional reason that otherwise the question might arise of why I don't go back to architecture.

Line 7: 'with Georg Simmel and Max Scheler …' One might also add Husserl, who wrote to me in Paris just a short time before his death, saying that in my *Soziologie als Wissenschaft* I had developed ideas which occur in his own unpublished papers, and that my articles in the F.Z. had always been of great interest to him.

Lines 9–11: 'During … jobs'. For the reasons mentioned above, please leave this sentence out and instead simply add the following words: 'In spite of his success in this practical field …'

Line 16: '… Zeitung in 1921.'

Line 20: please leave out the words 'of architecture' – once again, for the reason already given.

Line 22: 'practical *contacts* with the industry' is correct – provided that the word 'contact' can be used in this way.

Page 2 of your text:

Lines 5–9: this section must be completely changed because of its inaccuracy. After Hitler's seizure of power, I did not write 'some biting satires' but only the article about the Reichstag fire. In addition, I did not (as your text gives the reader to understand) 'flee from the Nazis', but the *Frankfurter Zeitung*, foreseeing that it itself might be compromised by me, sent me to Paris to stand in for Sieburg, where I wrote a few more articles about film and literature. Then, after four weeks, the paper let me go once and for all. This is just to set you straight personally. In the text it is enough to state that the *Frankfurter Zeitung* dismissed me because of my political views and that my books were burnt in Germany.

Line 11: the editions in other countries should be mentioned here.
Line 22: the word 'work' is more exact than 'study'.

I am very sorry that the changes mean more things for you to do.

I urgently request you to send me a copy of the revised text.

All our love and best wishes to you and Gretel
from us both

Yours,
Friedel

Original: typescript (carbon copy): Siegfried Kracauer papers, Deutsches Literaturarchiv, Marbach am Neckar.

my curriculum vitae: not preserved with the corresponding additions.

Husserl ... wrote to me in Paris: Edmund Husserl (1859–1938), philosopher; professor in 1901 in Göttingen and from 1916 in Freiburg; the last letter from him which is preserved among Kracauer's papers dates from the year 1934.

article about the Reichstag fire: 'Rund um den Reichstag', *Frankfurter Zeitung*, 2 March 1933 (see Kracauer, W 5, no. 727).

Sieburg: Friedrich Sieburg (1893–1964), journalist, author and critic; correspondent for the *Frankfurter Zeitung*, among others, in London and Paris, where he was in the service of the German occupation. Co-editor of *Gegenwart*; literary editor of *Frankfurter Allgemeine Zeitung*.

LIST OF PUBLICATIONS

1) *Soziologie als Wissenschaft* (Dresden, Sibyllenverlag, 1925)
2) *Ginster*, novel (German edition: Berlin, S. Fischer, 1928;
   French edition: Paris, Gallimard, 1933)
3) *Die Angestellten: Aus dem neuesten Deutschland* (German edition:
   Frankfurt am Main, Frankfurter Societäts-Verlag, 1930; also a Czech edition)
4) Essays in *Logos*, *Neue Rundschau*, *Archiv für Sozialwissenschaften*, *Preussische Jahrbücher*, *Revue du Cinéma*, etc.
5) Articles in *Frankfurter Zeitung*
6) *Orpheus in Paris: Offenbach and the Paris of his Time*
   American edition: New York, Alfred A. Knopf, 1938
   German edition: Amsterdam, Allert de Lange, 1937
   French edition: Paris, Bernard Grasset, 1937
   English edition: London, Constable, 1937
   Swedish edition: Helsingfors, Soderstrom, 1938
   Polish edition: Warsaw, Przeworskiego, in press 1939
   Czech edition: Prague, Vilimek, was in press 1938
7) A manuscript *Totalitarian Propaganda*, International Institute for
   Social Research at Columbia University, New York, 1938
8) In preparation: a book on the history and sociology of motion pictures,
   which was a study for Allert de Lange, Amsterdam

Dr Siegfried Kracauer
Paris (17e)

3, Avenue Mac-Mahon

137 Kracauer to Adorno
Lisbon, 28 March 1941

Lisboá
c/o Wagons-Lits Cook

28 March 1941

Herrn Teddie Adorno

Dear Teddie,

This is just to let you know that we are hoping to sail on the *Niassa* on 15 April; if nothing comes up in the meantime, we shall be arriving in New York between 25 and 30 April. It is bad to arrive as we shall be doing – after eight years of an existence which isn't worthy of the name. I have grown older – also within myself. Now there comes this last stage, this last chance, which I must not lose, otherwise it will all be over. And, as for this last chance, I can only take it if I get a first one as soon as I reach New York – for I am arriving as a poor man, poorer than I have ever been, and so it is impossible to take the first steps relying on my own strength alone. Please read the letter to Pollock which I am sending at the same time as this one – talk to him, and consider what is to be done. I am looking forward so much to seeing you; the more time passes between now and then, the closer the Seeheimer Strasse feels to me; nothing can change that in the slightest.

Greetings to Gretel from us both and to you yourself from Lili and me. See you soon, Teddie – if all goes well, which nobody can say.

Yours, Friedel.

Original: MS (copy); Leo Löwenthal papers, Archivzentrum der Universitätsbibliothek Johann Christian Senckenberg, Frankfurt am Main.

Lisboá c/o Wagons-Lits Cook: not entirely legible in the original; given in accordance with what is written on the parallel letters (see below).

Herr Teddie Adorno: the letter, like another to Leo Löwenthal, was enclosed in one of the same date addressed to Friedrich Pollock.

eight years of an existence: on this subject he wrote to Max Horkheimer (11 June 1941): 'We have a very real need to thank you, too, from the bottom of our hearts for the great help which the Institute has granted us. Without this help we should hardly have been able to overcome the endless difficulties which the journey from France and the crossing have presented right up till now. ... at a certain point the thought of suicide was never far away. By the way, we spent a lot of time in Marseilles with Benjamin, and only a few days after him we crossed the mountains to Port-Bou, where, like him, we were turned back. It was the darkest time in eight dark years. Once I am even halfway to feeling calm again, I shall note down our experiences over the last two years under the title *Journey to America*. Either I shall succeed in putting Kafka in the shade, or I shall not have been capable of describing the events properly' (Max Horkheimer papers, Archivzentrum der Universitätsbibliothek Johann Christian Senckenberg, Frankfurt am Main).

138 Adorno to Kracauer
Los Angeles, 22.12.1942

429 WEST 117TH STREET
New York, NY.

316 So. Kenter Ave.
Brentwood Heights
Los Angeles, Calif.
22 December 1942.

Dear Friedel,

After we have once again continued a silence towards each other for an eternity, today I should like to send you both just our very best wishes for the New Year and tell you that we are well, that we have a nice little house and a little car, and above all that the past year has been devoted to very intensive work in partnership with Horkheimer, and that the coming one shall be much the same. I hope that you will soon get to see some of the many and varied results.

Apart from that, it has transpired that Eisler – who, as you know, was directing the Rockefeller film music project – and I are going to be writing a book together about film and music, for which we have a contract with the Oxford University Press. It is a sideline project, but one about which I feel extraordinarily passionate and which I can well imagine may be of some interest to you, too. I would be extraordinarily grateful if, as you have a detailed overview of the relevant film literature, you could let me have the titles of books about film music which have been published and possibly, in addition, important passages about film music from writings devoted purely to film as such, if that is possible for you without going to too much trouble. I am assuming that the literary material relevant to this highly specific problem will be very limited. As I don't know whether it will be possible to obtain the books given the bleak state of affairs prevailing in libraries here, I would be still more obliged to you if you could tell me whether any possibility exists of borrowing the material in question from the Film Library. This could, of course, be done easily in the name of the Institute.

Do get in touch and tell me how your work is going and, above all, whether you are managing to write the major book on film or are mainly occupied with individual studies of film material. I hope that Lili is well and that you continue to be comfortable in New York, but I have no doubt that sooner or later your path will bring you here, to the absolute end of the flight. Trust me when I tell you that it is extraordinarily beautiful in Hollywood (apart from Hollywood).

What is more, I believe that the defeat of Hitler, with all that this prospect involves, has become predictable.

Much love to you both, from Gretel too, and a thousand thanks in advance

Your old
Teddie

Original: typescript with printed letterhead and handwritten corrections; Siegfried Kracauer papers, Deutsches Literaturarchiv, Marbach am Neckar.

nice little house: the Adornos moved to California in November 1941; a photograph exists of the house in Brentwood (see Adorno, *Bildmonographie*, p. 179).

film music project: Hans Eisler directed the 'film music project' sponsored by the Rockefeller Foundation from 1940 to 1942.

book … about film and music: *Composing for the Films*, New York: Oxford University Press, 1947; the collaborative venture appeared (as did the first German-language edition: *Komposition für den Film*. Berlin: Henschel, 1949) with Hanns Eisler named as the sole author. On the occasion of the edition published by Rogner und Bernard (Munich, 1969) Adorno claimed his rights as author; on the political motivation for his previous reticence, see 'Zum Erstdruck der Originalfassung', Adorno, GS 15, pp. 144–6, Adorno's memorandum of 6 February 1969 in Adorno/Suhrkamp/Unseld, *Briefwechsel*, pp. 669–72, and also the afterword by Johannes C. Gall to the new edition which he edited (Frankfurt am Main: Suhrkamp, 2006).

139 Kracauer to Adorno

New York, 5.1.1943

56 West 75th Street
New York City

January 5, 1943

Dear Teddie,

We had already heard from Horkheimer to our great joy that you were both well and are glad to have this confirmed by you. We don't feel greatly attracted to Hollywood, and if it were up to us we should prefer to remain here in New York, but one never knows in the present circumstances how things will turn out. Your and Eisler's plan is naturally of great interest to me. By the way, we sent him a New Year's card too; please do ask him whether he received it, as I had mislaid his address and sent the card to an acquaintance whom I asked to forward it. The enclosed list was made by the librarian of the Film Library at my instigation. As the Film Music Notes mentioned at the end are published in Hollywood, it will be easy for you both to find further bibliographical details there. I myself am not an expert in this specialized area. The Film Library is strictly a reference library and does not send books out on loan – but the most important items must surely be available in Los Angeles. It is a pity that I have no time to send you important and relevant passages as you wished – but, if you really do need something of this kind, you can surely mobilize someone from the Institute here for this. I myself am under fearful pressure, as in a few months I have to submit the results of my work on the history of German film. Recently I have been writing a long paper about the Nazi war newsreels. I hope that this work will be published somewhere. My report about Nazi film propaganda, which was published in lithoprint by the Museum, aroused gratifying echoes in Washington and elsewhere. If things here continue with a new grant this coming year, I shall be very satisfied. I have already made really strong progress in writing in English; I have a passion for it. I am very keen to hear more about the results of your work with Horkheimer. We spent New Year's Eve with Meyer; it was a splendid beginning to the year – but of course you received our New Year's greetings. Lili is in rather good form, and, if we regret anything, it is only that we could not come to New York much earlier. Warmest good wishes to you both – Gretel and yourself,

Yours

Original: typescript (carbon copy); Siegfried Kracauer papers, Deutsches Literaturarchiv, Marbach am Neckar.

heard from Horkheimer to our great joy: not preserved in writing.

New Year's card: not preserved among Hanns Eisler's papers.

Film Music Notes: the official publication of the National Film Music Council, 1941–1950.

results of my work on the history of German film: these were necessary to authorize the continuation of funding for the project, which was provided from July 1943 by the John Simon Guggenheim Memorial Foundation (see *Marbacher Magazin* 47, p. 104).

Nazi war newsreels: a piece of work commissioned for the Experimental Division for the Study of War Time Communications, directed by Harold D. Lasswell: *The Conquest of Europe on the Screen: The Nazi Newsreel 1939–1940* (Washington, DC: Library of Congress, 1943), completed in May 1943 (see *Marbacher Magazin* 47, p. 104).

Nazi film propaganda: Kracauer finished the study supported by the Rockefeller Foundation, *Propaganda and the Nazi War Film* (New York: Museum of Modern Art Film Library, 1942) in June 1942 (see *Marbacher Magazin* 47, p. 103); the work was published as an appendix to the book *From Caligari to Hitler: A Psychological Study of the German Film* (Princeton, NJ: Princeton University Press, 1947); see Kracauer, S 2, pp. 321–95).

New Year's card: not preserved.

140 Adorno and Horkheimer to Kracauer
Pacific Palisades, 26.6.1943

13524 D'ESTE DRIVE
PACIFIC PALISADES, CALIF.

June 26, 1943.

Dr S. Kracauer
56 West 75th Street
New York City

Dear Dr Kracauer:

Don't ever think that I did not appreciate your letter of March 27th and your pamphlet on the Nazi newsreel. I read the good news of your fellowship with the greatest of pleasure and your study with interest and admiration. It is still your old style, sober as well as loaded with allusions; as a matter of fact, it withstands the translation into English much better than Teddie's or my own way of expression.

I should like to see your comment on American motion pictures. The comparison drawn on pages 18–20 is most inspiring. When I read it I was tempted to amend it by a lengthly discourse in social philosophy.

I hope to be in New York in fall. One of the things I am particularly looking forward to are some good gab feasts with you and Mrs Kracauer.

Affectionately yours,
Max Horkheimer

Dear Friedel,
Just warmest greetings to you both for now – in summer I shall be here in the East for a few weeks and very much hope to see you. Until then, much love from your old

Teddie

Thank you for the very interesting film memorandum!

Original: typescript (in English) with handwritten postscript by Adorno; Siegfried Kracauer papers, Deutsches Literaturarchiv, Marbach am Neckar.

141 Adorno to Kracauer
[Los Angeles,] 28.12.1944

28 December 1944.

Dear Friedel,

Thank you very much for your lovely New Year's card. We are very sorry to hear of Lili's illness, especially because (as you probably don't know) Gretel suffers from exactly the same thing. In November 1943, she had such a severe attack that she was bedridden for many weeks; she was then under constant treatment for more than six months and is now back in action, true, but still severely disabled, especially over the last few days. It is the only illness which is practically unknown in Europe but is cropping up unexpectedly all over the place here. Many doctors suggest cures involving traction and even operations on the spine; however, I would strongly advise against the latter, as I have just heard of a case in San Francisco where a lady subjected herself to such an operation and was crippled as a result. We can consider ourselves experts of long standing in relation to this kind of suffering, and it almost seems to me that, apart from heat treatment, muddling through is still the most advisable course – but in no circumstances should one get involved with invasive cures. There is a trend here to treat this illness not symptomatically but by looking at its origins, but as these are unknown it is to a great extent an opportunity for the orthopaedic and neurological racket.

Now that Horkheimer is in New York we are quite alone here, but at least before he left Horkheimer and I were able to get a large part of our work done and dusted. In my leisure time I have written a little book with Eisler, 'Composition for Film', which should interest you.

Together with a professor of psychology from Berkeley I am now directing a major research project about anti-Semitism (within the framework of the American Jewish Committee's grand plan), which gives me much pleasure. Alongside this I am writing as much of my own stuff as I can.

I'm very curious about your book. There is good reason to anticipate that I shall pop up in New York for a few weeks in February.

Much love to you and Lili from us both, and best wishes for the New Year – that finally, at least, the worst and most immediate anxieties may be silenced.

Your old

Teddie

Original: typescript; Siegfried Kracauer papers, Deutsches Literaturarchiv, Marbach am Neckar.

New Year's card: not preserved.

Lili's illness ... Gretel suffers from exactly the same thing: 'mechanical changes in the spine, making a vertebra press against the sciatic nerve and cause symptoms of sciatica' (see Adorno, *Letters to his Parents*, p. 160).

Horkheimer is in New York: Max Horkheimer was the director of the research department of the American Jewish Committee.

professor of psychology from Berkeley: Robert Nevitt Sanford (1909–1995); Adorno writes of their collaboration: 'The Berkeley study was organized in such a way that Sanford and I acted as directors and Frau Brunswik and Daniel Levinson as chief collaborators. From the outset, though, everything was done in perfect teamwork, with no hierarchical moments. The title "Authoritarian Personality", "credited" to us all equally, is an altogether accurate statement of this fact' (see Adorno, GS 9.2, p. 413).

Research project about anti-Semitism: in a memorandum of December 1944, Adorno sketched out the 'Research project on Social Discrimination, done jointly by the Institute of Social Research and the "Berkeley Public Opinion Study" of the University of California' (published in the appendix to Adorno/Horkheimer, *Briefwechsel* II, pp. 623–5); this relates to the 'caesura between the old anti-Semitism project and the new project, which resulted in the "Authoritarian Personality".'

your book: *From Caligari to Hitler*; see letter no. 139.

in New York for a few weeks in February: the visit lasted from the middle of February to the middle of March 1945 (see Adorno/Horkheimer, *Briefwechsel* III, p. 49).

142 Kracauer to Adorno

New York, 8.1.1945

56 West 75th Street
New York 23, N.Y.

Jan. 8, 1945

Dear Teddie,

We had no idea, of course, that Gretel is probably suffering from the same condition as Lili – and for such a long time, and so badly! As we know exactly what that means, we have the deepest sympathy with you, dear Gretel, and only hope that from now on things will go on improving all the time. In fact, we had put it down to the murderous New York climate – Lili caught the thing when she was sitting in the draught from a fan on one of those well-known hot, humid days – but it might also be that the trouble can be traced back *to sitting in a cramped position* on that day – and because of this we were amazed to hear that one is not safe from it even in California. It was very kind of you, dear Teddie, to write to us immediately about this at such length. Every detail, naturally, is important to us. What do you mean when you say that Gretel 'is now back in action, true, but still extremely disabled'? Do the attacks sometimes recur, and is she then in as much torment – even temporarily – as during those first bad times? Or have the pains abated generally, but still give her considerable trouble? And what bearing does the weather have on this? With Lili it is a matter of pronounced sacro-iliac pains which, however, do not, as they do in other cases, radiate from the spine itself. There are violent pains in the left leg which shift from place to place there, even though they are some distance from the sacro-iliac joint which is their actual point of origin. The doctor was able to establish this much with certainty; the only thing is that he cannot offer any effective help. He says that science is still very much in its infancy in this field. He also mentioned a traction cure, but we cannot make up our minds to go ahead with this, or even an operation – for the same reasons that you state. In November the illness was already much better, but then there came a relapse (probably because of an awkward movement) and we were back to square one. After that the doctor advised a belt which, when pulled tight, keeps the whole area under control. Does Gretel know about this belt? The belt certainly provides relief inasmuch as it restricts the range of movement, but it doesn't cure the problem, or only in a very indirect manner. She was getting on better in the belt, and then, quite a short time ago, there came another attack – not as bad as the previous relapse, but still very painful, with a slight change in the location of the pains. In addition, damp and cold aggravate matters every time. Have you heard of the so-called osteopaths? It is said that they are not infrequently able to realign slight displacements of the bones by manipulation with their fingers. We have heard of successes, but until now we have not been able to make up our minds to go ahead. In this, though, we are entirely of your opinion: as long as the malady is so little known, it is wiser not to subject oneself to any kind of operation or similar drastic measures. Most of the experts say that one has to have patience – there are nearly as many of them as there are football experts – and all will be well. That is quite right – it is just that life is short, and many months of it are going by like this in enforced inactivity and pain.

I heard from Horkheimer himself about your Berkeley research. We look forward to seeing you in February. The film music book interests me very much. All good wishes from both of us to both of you,

Yours,

Original: typescript (carbon copy) with a written addition whose reading is uncertain ('it might also be ... on that day'); Siegfried Kracauer papers, Deutsches Literaturarchiv, Marbach am Neckar.

143 Kracauer to Adorno
New York, 17.7.1946

56 West 75th Street
New York 23, N.Y.

July 17, 1946

Dear Teddie,

As we knew how seriously and hopelessly ill our dear Oscar was, we were not unprepared for the news of his death. It was a great sorrow to us, as it is no help at all to know that death can also be a release. We wanted to let you know at once that all our thoughts are with you and Gretel.

For me, another piece of the past has vanished – or, rather, the past takes on more and more of a domestic aspect and assumes a life of its own which increasingly supplants the life one has actually lived, until in the end everything becomes the past and nothing more. I am sure that you will be coming here, or may even be here already after all, but I don't know, and so it is better for me to write to you. I had not seen your loved ones here for a long, long time, and now it is too late for Oscar – but for the last year at least I was able to take only the most essential steps on account of the nervous pains in my back, which have still not quite gone. We have heard that you too have not been well for some time, but now they say that you are all right again, and Leo told me that Gretel is well too.

There are an infinite number of things that I might write, ask you, and tell you about, but I won't do so in this letter. The best thing of all would be if we could see each other once again.

Much love and best wishes from Lili and me to you both,

Your

Original: typescript (carbon copy); Siegfried Kracauer papers, Deutsches Literaturarchiv, Marbach am Neckar.

Oscar: Oscar Wiesengrund died on 8 July 1946 in New York from the after-effects of a stroke (see Adorno, *Letters to his Parents*, pp. 258–61).

144 Kracauer to Adorno
New York, 24.4.1947

56 West 75th Street
New York 23, N.Y.

April 24, 1947

Dear Teddie,

My book came out a few days ago; the significance of this, however, is lessened for me on account of the *excess costs* of my corrections, which are roughly the same as the *royalties* from the first edition – and, until further notice at any rate, the first edition is all there is going to be. I feel like Shaw, who at the end of a long conversation with Samuel Goldwyn said to the latter, *'Alas, there is one difference between us, Mr Goldwyn. You are interested in art and I am interested in money.'*

But that wasn't at all what I wanted to say. I just wanted to tell you how sorry I am that I can't mail you a copy – as I did to Horkheimer – but every copy that I have managed to obtain in addition to the few that I was allowed meant a battle with the publisher. And as I myself am going through a *period of recess* at the moment … In short, I ask you – please don't think that I had overlooked you. I just could not manage it. I hope that I shall soon be able to repair the omission. I am counting on your understanding.

Some time ago I read your Wagner essay in the *Kenyon Review* and found it altogether excellent. Really a *first-rate piece*. I shall bring it to the attention of as many people as possible.

A long article which I wrote about Sturges – 'Preston Sturges, or Laughter Betrayed' – will probably come out in the autumn, God willing. Everything is going slowly – the publishing as well as my writing business.

We very much hope that all is well with you and Gretel as regards health and in other ways too.

Warmest greetings from both of us to both of you,

Yours,

Original: typescript (carbon copy), Siegfried Kracauer papers, Deutsches Literaturarchiv, Marbach am Neckar.

Shaw, who at the end of a long conversation: a legendary story about George Bernard Shaw (1856–1950); see a variant in *Narr oder Weise: Anekdoten um Bernard Shaw* [Fool or sage: anecdotes about Bernard Shaw], ed. Ursula Michels-Wenz (Frankfurt am Main: Suhrkamp, 2000), p. 77.

'period of recess': this phrase is written in English, as are those words in this letter which the translator has italicized.

Wagner essay: 'Wagner, Nietzsche, and Hitler', *Kenyon Review*, 9/1 – i.e. the review of Ernest Newman, *Life of Richard Wagner*, Vol. IV, New York: Knopf, 1946 (see Adorno, GS 19, pp. 404–12, 652).

about Sturges: 'Preston Sturges, or Laughter Betrayed', *Films in Review*, February 1950. For the difference between the manuscript mentioned in the letter and the printed version, see Kracauer, W 6.3, pp. 441–51, 496–511.

145 Adorno to Kracauer

[New York, late 1948]

Dear Friedel,

Many thanks for your card. It really is a scandal like race defilement that one hears not a thing from one another – and the chances that I shall come to N.Y. in the near future are minimal – does Hollywood not tempt you in the least? I am, at any rate, glad to sense from your letter that your affairs are getting off to a better start.

The Berkeley book is being published by Harpers. You know, of course, that the big book by Max and myself has been published by Querido under the title *Dialektik der Aufklärung*. My *Philosophie der neuen Musik* has gone to press with my old publisher Mohr (Siebeck) in Tübingen, in the same series as the Kierkegaard. By the way, did you see 'Composing for the Films'? I withdrew my name at the last minute, but it is mostly my work. Here in the West they will hardly be able to accuse me of laziness! Do write to me sometime at greater length!

All our love to you and Lili

Your old Teddie.

Original: MS, Christmas card: It's time to trim the Christmas tree and wish you a season as bright as can be; signed separately 'Gretel and Teddie'; Siegfried Kracauer papers, Deutsches Literaturarchiv, Marbach am Neckar.

race defilement: Adorno uses the Nazi term 'Rassenschande', a dubious play on the phrase 'es ist eine Schande' [it's a (crying) shame].

The Berkeley book is being published by Harpers: *The Authoritarian Personality*, by T. W. Adorno, Else Frenkel-Brunswik, Daniel J. Levinson and R. Nevitt Sanford in collaboration with Betty Aron, Maria Herz Levinson and William Morrow, New York: Harper & Brothers, 1950 (Studies in Prejudice, ed. Max Horkheimer and Samuel H. Flowerman, Vol. I).

Dialektik der Aufklärung: a mimeographed edition of *Dialectic of Enlightenment* was published in 1944, edited by the Institute for Social Research, under the title *Philosophische Fragmente*; the addition of the preface by Adorno and Max Horkheimer for the book edition published by Querido, Amsterdam, is dated June 1947.

my old publisher Mohr: *Philosophie der neuen Musik*, Tübingen: J. C. B. Mohr (Paul Siebeck), 1949; *Kierkegaard: Konstruktion des Ästhetischen* had been published by the same firm in 1933.

146 Adorno to Kracauer

[no address], 7.2.1949

7. II. 1949

Dear Friedel,

Tomorrow is your birthday, and, if I am not seriously mistaken, it is your sixtieth. I wish you every imaginable happiness on this festive day. Random as these caesuras may be when measured against the grand scale of nature, they do have a strong symbolic force within that of the laws of mankind, and I am too deeply permeated by the way nature and social practice are intertwined to be able to take these dates lightly – as, by the way, I don't like any postponement of holidays to a day other than the one appertaining to them. The saying that one should celebrate feasts as they fall has a deeper sense than merely that of an invitation to *carpe diem*. Allow me, then, to join you in my thoughts and celebrate with you with all my heart, in loyal awareness of a friendship which has lasted thirty years.

Above all, there are two wishes which I have for you. The first is that a solution may be found for you which will finally relieve you of financial insecurity. The second is that you will manage to bring to fruition all that has been ripening within your intellectual being. I know of nobody for whom it would be more fitting for his decisive successes to occur after the age of sixty – not for nothing did you always say in the past that August was your favourite month – and it is the absence of anything forced in the works you produce, and the ability to entrust yourself to experience without any over-hasty pressure to finish something, that more than anything else gives me the hope that you will find that fulfilment of 'what you have always meant' to accomplish. I know only too well how much this fulfilment depends on that of the first wish, the provision of a financial footing in keeping with human dignity, without the anxiety about 'what will happen next' hovering behind it. But I believe that there is something in the rhythm of your life which will allow the inner and the outer elements to come together at last, and you yourself have indeed always been guided by that belief.

If I am speaking a little more solemnly than is really appropriate between the two of us, please forgive me – it is just the fault of the strong emotion that grips me when faced with this day, and the lack of that everyday empirical reality that might put the element of pathos in its proper place. So – I wish you all the best, much love and all that is splendid, right into the pianissimo of advanced age.

Warmest good wishes to you and Lili, from Gretel too,

Your old

Teddie

Original: typescript; Siegfried Kracauer papers, Deutsches Literaturarchiv, Marbach am Neckar.

Lili: Adorno wrote 'Lily'.

147 Kracauer to Adorno

[New York,] 12.2.1949

12 February 1949

Dear Teddie,

I was so touched by your letter. And it actually arrived on the day itself; I found it waiting at home in the evening. It was a great joy for me – and for Lili too. As if I had not been aware of it, I was struck again by the fact that ours is a friendship of thirty years and by the old pictures that we had sketched of ourselves and which contained so much truth. I thought of those days in Oberrad, of our reading Nietzsche, and of the many great and small things from those years in which we were both still very young – young enough, in any event, to know of the transient nature of things only in the same way that one knows about many things. I am really grateful to you for remembering, and for your words, which conjured up the life of the past encapsulated within them. It is so comforting to know that you know what we shared and that you store it up within yourself. It gives me a feeling of security – of not being lost – for the foreseeable future; and I know that it is like that for you too.

Whether I shall ever achieve what you regard as possible for me depends entirely on external circumstances, which are bad. However, perhaps a possibility will arise for me to realize one of my plans – a book about film aesthetics; an old plan, and, if it can be carried out, definitely my last book about film. In this book, too, film would be merely a pretext. I should like to show which aesthetic laws and which affinities for particular themes a medium develops that belongs to a time in which the scientific interest in the connections between the smallest elements more and more 'suspends' the individual force of those great ideas, which embrace the whole human being, and ever more strongly abolishes our receptivity to such ideas. Or to express it in film language: the aesthetic of the film belongs to an era in which the old 'long-shot' perspective, which in some way is believed to capture the absolute, is being replaced by the 'close-up' perspective, which sheds light on what is perhaps meant by the solitary independent detail – the fragment. During the months which we spent in Marseilles in fear and poverty I made lengthy notes about this. I should so much like to discuss these problems with you – you have the superior experience in these areas. If you should come to New York any time in the near future, you must certainly keep some time free for me.

I am very keen to read your book which Harpers is publishing. I read the Thomas Mann–Schoenberg polemic in the *Saturday Review of Literature*, in which your name is mentioned, with great interest. Schoenberg must be very embittered. I found his naive claim to greatness bizarre and Thomas Mann's dapper superiority embarrassing. Who could have foreseen twenty years ago that one day you would be slipping Thomas Mann something under the counter? Indeed, who could have told us *any* of this? It was as if your letter woke me from a dream – and I had feared that I would have to go on dreaming for the time being – well past my sixtieth birthday, and other birthdays too. That is what life demands of us.

I have not read the Mann novel, though I have read a few reviews. To conclude from these, I am surprised that nobody has made the following criticism: a character like that of the hero could never have achieved the breakthrough to atonal music. I am convinced that Thomas Mann has not grasped the implications of your contributions – but I am speaking without any knowledge of the book itself.

Lili has been with the USNA (United Service for New Americans), that well-known giant organization. Unfortunately, she has to do a lot of overtime at the moment. It is exhausting – too exhausting – and cuts into our private life. But the work is not unsatisfying because it is in a good cause, and we must be glad of that. I myself wrote a study last year for UNESCO

(Hadley Cantril and Otto Klineberg), which is now going to be published in *Public Opinion Quarterly*. Now I am going to do a short piece of work for Lowe – apart from that, all kinds of journalism. But I have not yet achieved the important thing – a job that will finally give me a modicum of security. If only your wish – the one which you quite rightly put first – might come true! It doesn't seem to me to be too much to ask, after all.

Give the Horkheimers our best regards. (Isn't it his birthday one of these days? I extend so many good wishes to him in his [your?] sense as much as in ours.) Your kind letter has stirred up much emotion in me. Lili sends you both a kind remembrance and most cordial greetings.

Yours,
Friedel

Original: typescript; Theodor W. Adorno Archiv, Frankfurt am Main.

a book about film aesthetics, an old plan: the further development of the 'Theory of Film' took off with the award of a 'grant for the planned book' from the Bollingen Foundation, as Kracauer wrote to Erwin Panofsky on 23 January 1949 (Kracauer/Panofsky, *Briefwechsel*, pp. 50f.).

spent in Marseilles … lengthy notes: see the *Marseiller Entwurf*, Kracauer, W 3, pp. 521–803.

your book which Harpers is publishing: *The Authoritarian Personality* (see letter no. 145).

the Thomas Mann–Schoenberg polemic: Arnold Schoenberg had been engaged since 1948 in a conflict with Thomas Mann, as he considered that Mann, to judge from the portrayal of the character of Adrian Leverkühn in the novel *Doktor Faustus*, had not paid sufficient attention to his rank as the creator of twelve-tone music. Mann sought to placate him with an afterword, which first appeared in a subsequent print run (of between 8,000 and 15,000 copies) of the German edition (Frankfurt am Main: Suhrkamp, 1948), in which he attributed the intellectual origins of the 'type of composition depicted in Chapter XXII' to Schoenberg. The latter took offence at the expression employed here about 'a contemporary composer and theorist', which caused him to write an open letter to the *Saturday Review of Literature*, printed in the 1 January 1949 edition, together with a reply by Thomas Mann (see the extensive presentation in Adorno/Mann, *Correspondence*, pp. 29–31).

study last year for UNESCO … in Public Opinion Quarterly: 'National Types as Hollywood Presents Them', *Public Opinion Quarterly*, 1, spring 1949. An offprint in the Theodor W. Adorno Archiv bears the handwritten dedication: 'To Teddie with warmest greetings / Friedel / June 1949'.

Cantril: Hadley Cantril (1906–1996), social psychologist at Princeton University and co-founder of the Office of Radio Research there; he was instrumental in directing the commission for the above-mentioned study towards Kracauer (see Kracauer/Panofsky, *Briefwechsel*, pp. 37, 42, notes).

Klineberg: Otto Klineberg (1899–1992), psychologist at Columbia University and Hadley Cantril's successor in the above-mentioned project.

work for Lowe: Adolf Lowe (1893–1995), sociologist and economist at the New School for Social Research; extracts from the work in question, *Analysis of Images*, are published in Kracauer, W 2.2.

Horkheimers ... birthday: on 14 February [1895].

148 Kracauer to Adorno
New York, 1.10.1950

56 West 75th Street
New York 23, N.Y.
October 1, 1950.

Dear Teddie,

I would have liked to write to you much earlier – soon after I received your reprint *Zur Philosophie Husserl's*, which I am very glad to have. It is a good piece of work and full of memories for me. But I had so much to do – occasional pieces that kept distracting me from my real work. And now I am actually glad that I have only got round to writing now, as I heard so much about you and Horkheimer from Leo a short time ago, nothing but splendid things, about which I can now speak in this letter. It will be a real letter of congratulation. The fact that you have been appointed to a professorship is indeed a great cause for congratulation. You should have had one long ago, but it is never too late. We certainly know what such a thing means – it is a great convenience in dealing with the world – one doesn't need to be constantly explaining one's position, one *has* it. But of course the great recognition which you are being given now means even more, or probably it comes in the wake of that same development which has also led to the consolidation of your position. Leo told me that your *Philosophie der neuen Musik* was a great success. I think all this is wonderful, including the satisfaction that your teaching and your students give you. And it seems to be beyond question that the Institute will be revived. It looks as if your harvest-time is coming at last, and that fills me with deep satisfaction because of the poetic justice which it implies, for I know hardly anyone who has worked for so long, and indefatigably so, without compromise as you have – and of course without financial worries, as I must add (with affectionate restraint).

My book is making only slow progress, partly because of numerous interruptions, partly because of its branching construction, which requires time. With every new paragraph I cannot simply go on, but like a puppy going for a long outing with its master (who I also am) I have to run back and forth, sniff around everywhere, and often follow scents which may possibly lead me on a false trail. The first chapter, a systematic historical analysis of the snapshot, will appear in the course of the winter (in a somewhat abridged version) in the *Magazine of Art*. And while we are on the subject of our own books – *From Caligari to Hitler* will soon be published in Italian. Finally, during our summer vacation in Stamford, N.Y., which lasted over five weeks, I did a report for Voice of America – an analysis of a sample of broadcasts into various countries – where qualitative finesse was most important, as it had been in your chapter of *Authoritarian Personality*. Perhaps I should do more of that kind of thing. I don't like burning the candle at both ends, but it may be necessary for practical reasons.

Over the last few weeks Lili and I have been sorting a lot of old papers which were still lying unsorted in two boxes from Paris. It was a real sensation: the past revisited, *le temps retrouvé*. I now possess a whole portfolio of your work, dear Teddie – printed essays and manuscripts. A copy of the *Detektivroman* has turned up again. I was no longer aware that I had written a complete book-length manuscript about Georg Simmel. I also found a fair copy of the novel, which I completed in 1935, which is set in a newspaper office under the Weimar Republic. At the time Thomas Mann found a home for the manuscript in Holland, but – for reasons which seemed valid to me then and were probably nothing of the kind – I withdrew it from publication. It is possible that we may not have heard the last of this matter. And then I found a fine collection of my best essays about streets in the *Frankfurter Zeitung* (Berlin, Paris, Marseilles, etc.), which were to have been published by Bruno Cassirer under the title *Strassenbuch* – Book of Streets. But then along came Hitler. Even nowadays such a slim volume wouldn't be a bad idea; the essays have kept their freshness, there could be drawings to accompany them, and a title like 'Streets in Old Europe' would perhaps be attractive to the reader. But the main thing is that this rummaging through the past, including a lot of correspondence, aroused in me an uncontrollable desire to write my memoirs – really in the grand style, I mean. But that would be a luxury that I may possibly never be able to afford.

All our love to you and Gretel from Lili and me. Please give Horkheimer our best wishes; I congratulate him no less than you. Warmest greetings to Frau Horkheimer from us both.

Yours, Friedel.

Would you send me a copy of your article about Benjamin in the *Neue Rundschau*?

Original: typescript; Theodor W. Adorno Archiv, Frankfurt am Main.

your reprint Zur Philosophie Husserl's: Kracauer mistook the condensed partial publication in *Archiv für Philosophie*, no. 4, 1949 (in which the printed date is given as 1950), pp. 339–78 (see Adorno, GS 20.1, pp. 46–118) for a reprint; in fact, this was the first publication, about whose previous failure Adorno had reported in December 1937 (see letter no. 118). An offprint or a copy of the page proof bears the handwritten dedication: 'To my dear Friedel in remembrance of old times / Teddie / Frankfurt, April 1950'.

appointed to a professorship: in September 1949 an invitation reached Adorno in Santa Monica from the dean of the Faculty of the Humanities at the Johann

Wolfgang Goethe-Universität, asking him to return to Frankfurt am Main, which he did in November 1949. On 23 November 1949 the faculty decided 'to apply to the Ministry of Culture ... on the basis of the Law on Reparations' for a non-regular supernumerary professorship for Adorno (see Schütte, *Adorno in Frankfurt*, p. 147, and also Adorno/Horkheimer, *Briefwechsel* III, pp. 352–6). The appointment was made in May 1950.

Philosophie der neuen Musik *was a great success*: inasmuch as the Tübingen publisher J. C. B. Mohr (Paul Siebeck) had accepted the manuscript in 1948 without seeing it (Adorno to Horkheimer, 3 May 1948; see Adorno/Horkheimer, *Briefwechsel* III, pp. 222f.) and published it the following year (see letter no. 145); the edition sold out within four years. In his address on Adorno's 60th birthday, Siegfried Unseld, who oversaw the volume's publication by Mohr, described the hurdles which the book had had to overcome in the face of 'a small, and perhaps also esoteric ... circle' (see Adorno/Suhrkamp/Unseld, *Briefwechsel*, pp. 698f.).

The first chapter ... will appear in the course of the winter ... in the Magazine of Art: it did so in 1951, in vol. 3, March, pp. 107–113 (see Kracauer, W 3, afterword and editor's note, p. 869), under the title 'The Photographic Approach' (in the afterword there is a reference to pp. 44–59 of the first chapter of *Theorie des Films*).

From Caligari to Hitler *will soon be published in Italian*: *Cinema Tedesco (Dal 'Gabinetto del Dott. Caligari' a Hitler) 1918–1933*, Milan: Arnoldo Mondadori, 1954 (see Levin no. Xg).

report for Voice of America: 'Voice Broadcasts to Russia, Poland, Germany and Italy (March 26–May 13, 1950): A Report' (Kracauer papers, Deutsches Literaturarchiv, Marbach).

your chapter of Authoritarian Personality: in the original edition this is 'Part IV' (see letter no. 145), pp. 603–783; see *Studien zum autoritären Charakter*, ed. Institut für Sozialforschung, Frankfurt am Main: Suhrkamp, 1973.

two boxes from Paris ... a whole portfolio of your work: including: 'Alban Bergs frühe Lieder' [Alban Berg's early songs], clipping from *Anbruch*, February 1929 (see Adorno, GS 18, pp. 465–8, GS 19, p. 645); 'Neue Tempi', cutting from *Pult und Taktstock*, no. 1, 1930 (see Adorno, GS 17, pp. 66–73, 347); 'Zur gesellschaftlichen Lage der Musik II: Reproduktion – Konsum, Fahnen' [On the social situation of music II: reproduction – consumption, page proofs], *Zeitschrift für Sozialforschung*, no. 3, 1932 (see Adorno, GS 18, pp. 752–77, GS 19, p. 647); [Hektor Rottweiler,] 'Über Jazz' ([On jazz]; offprint), *Zeitschrift für Sozialforschung*, no. 2, 1936 (see Adorno, GS 17, pp. 74–100); [Hektor Rottweiler,] 'Ensemble, für Detlef Holz [Walter Benjamin] geschrieben' [Ensemble, written for Detlef Holz [Walter Benjamin]], clipping from *23: Eine Wiener Musikzeitschrift*, 15 September 1937 (included in *Motive*; see Adorno, GS 16, pp. 259–83, 678); Kracauer papers, Deutsches Literaturarchiv, Marbach.

A copy of the Detektivroman *has turned up again*: see letter no. 14.

a complete book-length manuscript about Georg Simmel: *Georg Simmel: Zur Deutung des geistigen Lebens unserer Zeit* [Georg Simmel: on the interpretation of the intellectual life of our times; 1919] (see Kracauer, W 9.2, pp. 139–280, 286–91, published in full there for the first time following the publication of the first chapter in *Logos*, no. 3, 1920/21, and its inclusion in *Das Ornament der Masse*, Frankfurt am Main: Suhrkamp, 1963).

a copy of your article about Benjamin in the Neue Rundschau: 'Charakteristik Walter Benjamins' [Characterization of Walter Benjamin], *Die Neue Rundschau*, no. 4, 1950, pp. 571–84 (see Adorno, GS 10.1, pp. 238–53).

149 Adorno to Kracauer

Frankfurt am Main, 17.10.1950

123 Kettenhofweg
Frankfurt/Main

17 October 1950

Dear Friedel,

Please accept my warmest thanks for your letter of 1 October, which I found waiting on my return from Amorbach – old Amorbach, so dear to you too – where we spent a few days of extremely belated holiday and where so little has changed that for the first time I really did have something like a feeling of being at home, insofar as such a thing still exists at all or should exist.

It is kind of you to congratulate us on the development of things here – but you can believe me when I say that I am as little affected by the recognition as previously I was willing to adjust to the new situation. Everything is looking very good indeed, at the university as well as the Institute. The standard of the philosophy students is astonishing – at least as high as before Hitler, or so it seems to me, and I can now finally speak without inhibitions – that is, in my own naturally inhibited manner. The downside is there is such an endless burden of day-to-day tasks weighing on Max and me that for the time being there can be no thought of producing anything of my own. After that rather turbulent period of productivity that lies behind me, I was not annoyed about the one-year interruption with all the experiences that accompanied it, but now we are both suffering severely as a result.

The Benjamin essay will be published together with his own theses on the philosophy of history in the fourth issue of the *Neue Rundschau.* The *Berliner Kindheit*, with an afterword by me, is to be published in November by Suhrkamp, who are planning a two-volume edition of Benjamin's works. They are also bringing out my book of aphorisms, *Minima Moralia*, probably before Christmas.

I don't need to tell you that I am extremely keen to read your film book. You know, of course, that I have been spending a lot of time on related matters looking in from the periphery in *Composing for the Films*; incidentally, these have meanwhile been published in German in the Eastern Zone without my name appearing even in a footnote. By the way, do you know Benjamin's essay on photography? An authoritative theoretical book on film is of the greatest significance. I mean this indeed in the term's most heavily weighted sense and not merely in the usual sociological one, because it is here that are to be found the deepest levels of changes in experiencing, all the way into perception itself. I should be glad if there were an esoteric German version, but God knows whether the best of all possible worlds will leave you time for diversions of this kind. Yes, of course – carrying a load on both shoulders has gradually become a way of life by now.

If you could sacrifice a copy of your novel which has turned up again – which, of course, I never got to see – I should naturally be very glad.

Europe, after America, is salutary and instructive. Salutary as far as healing the traumas of emigration is concerned, and instructive because even things which were taken for granted before have now become strange and reveal unsuspected aspects whose extreme allegorical form, only in a manner of speaking, is to be found in the ruined cities. Faced with the immediate fact of it, one cannot entertain the idea that life still exists here. The very character of these cities is affected by the realization that untouched enclaves do still exist in them, but measured against the image of technological civilization they assume a somewhat grubby, obsolete and even tatty quality, and the life which remains hungers only to be nothing of the kind. Many things could simply not have been anticipated at all – for example, that all the little towns along the Rhine strike one nowadays as having been afflicted with a likeness to one another similar to that of Main Street townships over there. If you will, people in Europe are being more thoroughly de-romanticized than in America, but that should not serve as an apology for either one continent or the other. Only Paris is as irresistible as ever. Here we have a pretty apartment after a longish period of existing in furnished rooms, and the conditions of empirical existence are much more agreeable than could be imagined at a distance.

Very best wishes to you and Lili from us both

Yours, Teddie.

Original typescript; Siegfried Kracauer papers, Deutsches Literaturarchiv, Marbach am Neckar.

on my return from Amorbach … a feeling of being at home: the Adornos spent several weeks at this holiday resort in the Odenwald in September/October 1950.

theses on the philosophy of history: on the ten pages preceding 'Charakteristik Walter Benjamins', the journal published Walter Benjamin's 'Über den Begriff der Geschichte' (see Benjamin, GS 1.2, pp. 691–704).

Berliner Kindheit, *with an afterword by me*: 'Walter Benjamin, *Berliner Kindheit um neunzehnhundert*', autumn 1950; the author of the afterword remained anonymous (see Adorno, GS 20.1, pp. 170ff.).

a two-volume edition of Benjamin's works: since the autumn of 1950 Peter Suhrkamp had been preparing an edition of Benjamin, together with the Adornos, Gershom Scholem and the Suhrkamp reader Friedrich Podszus. The edition, published in 1955 under the title *Schriften* (see letter no. 159), had been held up by difficulties of many kinds; this is documented in Adorno/Suhrkamp/Unseld, *Briefwechsel* (see, in particular, pp. 82–114).

Minima Moralia: the volume appeared in bookshops on 1 March 1951.

Composing for the Films: see letter no. 138.

Benjamin's essay on photography: probably 'Kleine Geschichte der Photographie' (1931; see Benjamin, GS II.1, pp. 368–85). Eng. trans.: 'Small History of Photography (1931)', in Walter Benjamin, *On Photography*, ed. and trans. Esther Leslie, London: Reaktion Books, 2015.

150 Kracauer to Adorno
New York, 4.7.1951

56 West 75th Street
New York 23, N.Y.
July 4, 1951

Dear Teddie,

I have the worst possible conscience about having let week after week pass without thanking you for the *Minima Moralia*. My only excuse is that I have to do a major report for the Voice of America (at Leo's instigation), with a *deadline, ahead of me*. I am still not through with it, but if I were planning to wait until the work was finished everything would have faded too much from memory and receded too far into the past – so I would rather write to you today, even if only a word. It can't be much and I cannot go into anything in detail, but it is the best that I can do for now. One day you will come through New York, and then I should like to discuss the whole book with you at greater length.

First of all, I should like to tell you that I found your Benjamin essay really excellent. The way in which you analyse Benjamin's dialectic and tease it out – a dialectic which does not expand or never concludes and is constantly catching fire from the stuff of rubbish – gives a very profound insight into this unique and at the same time curiously mechanistic thought process. I was lent the volume of the *Neue Rundschau*; I wish I had it. Can you have a copy sent to me?

Your book filled me with the greatest admiration for the extraordinary power of thought that prevails throughout it, along with an incomparable and relentless intensity. Really, Teddie, as I read it I was fascinated throughout by the ability in your thinking to penetrate the matter of existence, and what especially impressed – and often convinced – me was this: that, when an interpretation seemed to me to be one-sided or appeared unsatisfactory for some other reason, shortly afterwards a passage would follow which revised or supplemented your initial approach, so that in the end it was just as if the phenomenon had been totally incorporated into the dialectical process. As you completed your train of thought, you yourself corrected many of the objections which I raised while I was reading. At times I felt that it was quite uncanny – as if you had looked over my shoulder or even right into me, smiled at my reservations, and held out to me the next link of the chain of thought which already anticipated what I wanted to say to you and most of the time even overtook it. In such instances I gladly admitted defeat and rejoiced at your enormous cleverness. In fact, in the whole of literature I hardly know a single work to equal yours in its comprehensive vision and energy in burning up – or whatever you call the process of interpretation in the light of utopia – both the smallest and the greatest facts. If I had time – but I am thoroughly exhausted by my work on the report, for the sake of which I had to break off my book altogether – I should give you evidence of this with reference to particular details. There are so many striking discoveries in the book – very concrete discoveries which produce a beneficial shock effect – that I should have liked to single them out one by one to share with you my delight at them. (At this minute I am thinking of your splendid comments on the business of scholarship here and now.) But if I were to begin I should not be able to stop. And that is exactly what I can't allow myself to do.

I should like to save what I might have to say in the way of criticism for discussion face to face – soon, I hope. Almost all of it relates to things which are integral to your development and immutable – perhaps with the exception of the fact that there remain a number of opinions in the case of which, I think, you have not succeeded in overcoming the impression that they are only 'opinions'. (I have noted down a couple of examples.) If I had seen the manuscript beforehand, I should have advised you to remove these residues. (On the other hand, I understand only too well the pleasure of holding an opinion.) Just to mention something of the 'immutable' kind for now: I should launch a polemic against your use of the term 'utopia' – i.e. the hidden criteria of evaluating what 'merely is', which come to the surface only rarely – even in passing. It seems legitimate to me that genuine utopian flashes of insight should in general remain hidden – but less so, on the other hand, that their content should be hidden, and the way in which they can be mobilized in opposition to the existing state of affairs. A second point is dialectic itself: it may seem to you almost to be a contradiction, but steeped as I am in the force of your dialectic, on the one hand, I am, on the other, convinced that it doesn't go far enough in its thorough examination of the present: it seems to me that you have not got to the heart of mass culture, to name only one example. Perhaps this derives from the fact that certain basic concepts from an earlier period of your thought which relate to the present have been blindly taken on board. Nor does your justification of your style, penetrating as it is, make sense to me. I am, however, naturally aware that every genuine work, once it has set out on its wanderings, is vulnerable to such criticism, which touches on its fundamental nature. Attack and defence are part of the very essence of things.

Leo told me about your topping-out ceremony, and from what I hear from other sources, too, it seems to me as if you and Horkheimer can derive great satisfaction from your work. I hope that Horkheimer's operation went well; do give him all our good wishes and tell him that he is very much in our thoughts – and much love to Gretel from Lili and me. Please give Frau Horkheimer and the Pollocks our warmest regards. I am very glad, dear Teddie, that I have now managed to say at least these few things to you about your work.

All good wishes and kind regards
from Lili and me,
Yours
Friedel

Original: typescript; Theodor W. Adorno Archiv, Frankfurt am Main. First published (apart from the last paragraph) in Adorno/Suhrkamp/Unseld, *Briefwechsel*, pp. 31–4.

report for the Voice of America: 'Voice of America Broadcasts to Bulgaria, Greece, Spain and Austria (Dec. 10, 1950 – Jan. 27, 1951): A Report' (Kracauer papers, Deutsches Literaturarchiv, Marbach).

comments on the business of scholarship: *Minima Moralia*, 'Gedankenfreiheit' (see Adorno, GS 4, pp. 76f.).

Leo told me about your topping-out ceremony: at the end of 1951 the Institute for Social Research moved into its premises on Senckenberg Park.

Horkheimer's operation: the threatened kidney-stone operation was not performed (see the following letter).

the Pollocks: Friedrich Pollock and Carlotta Weil.

151 Adorno to Kracauer

Frankfurt am Main, 19.7.1951

INSTITUT FÜR SOZIALFORSCHUNG
JOHANN WOLFGANG GOETHE-UNIVERSITÄT

FRANKFURT A. M. 19 July 1951
SENCKENBERG-ANLAGE 34
TELEFON 70091 ... NEBENSTELLE 39
POSTSCHECKKONTO
FRANKFURT (M) 148195

Herrn
Dr Siegfried Kracauer
56 West 75th Street
New York 23, N.Y.

Dear Friedel,

Many thanks for your letter. It gives me great joy that my book meant so much to you. After all, where should a piece of work set out like this find its target audience if not with you, who possess not only the necessary prerequisites in terms of specialist knowledge and experience but also, I might say, the historical ones to such a consummate degree. Incidentally, the book – to my most genuine astonishment – has been an extraordinary success, not only in the 'literary' world but also in the bookshops. The reason for this is difficult to determine; I am neither vain nor modest enough to attribute it to the subject in itself, and it must have something to do with a series of lucky conjunctions, such as the fact that the ground was well prepared, that people were fed up with Heideggery, and above all that a kind of vacuum existed in which the far from homely *Minima Moralia* could find a home. In any event, I am as famous as a dog that is all the colours of the rainbow, and, to borrow Goethe's words, that does help to ward off all kinds of pushing and shoving in a crowd.

About your criticism: what you say about the concept of 'opinion' affected me very deeply, as more than 14 years ago, when Bloch sent me his *Erbschaft dieser Zeit*, I mobilized the same category against him and then presented him with the very challenging claim that the task of philosophy was the 'liquidation of meaning'. How far I myself met this claim I cannot determine, but nevertheless I should like to plead in defence of this – that where mere opinion is involved, it should confess itself as such and thus be, to a certain extent, included in the absolution, while meditations which present themselves as having genuine claims to objectivity should to some extent be equal to this and establish a kind of 'criterion', rather like the Theory of the Novel 30 years ago. Have I succeeded in this, I wonder?

I readily concede that the pieces about mass culture don't offer anything like a complete theory of the subject; that was not what I intended at all. Don't forget that the theory of mass culture which Max and I developed jointly in *Dialektik der Aufklärung* is itself of a fragmentary nature in places; I hope that in the end we shall manage to complete this project. I would also concede the point that my comments on this subject do bear residual traces of the undialectical – it's just that, if dialectic here is equated with the slightest indulgence towards the object, I should turn stubborn. And, as regards language, I already am obstinate – if I have anything against the piece in linguistic terms, it is that it doesn't correspond purely enough to my own ideal of language rather than anything that concerns the principle of the thing.

I am sending you the volume of the *Neue Rundschau* with the Benjamin under separate cover, and also a little parergon to the Kierkegaard which may perhaps interest you. A major and very heavy piece of work is going to be published in the next number of the *Neue Rundschau*; it relates to Huxley, but in reality it deals essentially with the problem of utopia (*The Disenchanted Dream*); in the festschrift for Leopold von Wiese there will be an essay, *Kulturkritik und Gesellschaft*, which represents something like a piece of critical soul-searching on the part of a cultural critic. Both have their beginnings in the famous drawer from my émigré period; over here, since Benjamin, I haven't found the time to write anything of my own except for a little thing about Bach; the work at the Institute, together with my activities at the university (which are demanding a great deal of time and responsibility because of the doctoral theses in progress at present), make it completely impossible. But after the somewhat tumultuous period of productivity during the last few years in Los Angeles I feel as little irritation about the break as I do about my recent experiences in Europe.

Do write some time and tell me in greater detail about your own doings. How is the film book getting on? Is there going to be a German version too? I just cannot rid myself of my superstitious belief that we can express crucial things only in our own language, and I imagine that I have a certain right to this opinion, as it can hardly be put down to a sour-grapes theory on my part. Max, by the way, didn't have the operation; his kidney stone vanished into thin air, and he is quite all right again, apart from his immense and excessive workload, especially on account of being dean for the last two semesters.

Do get in touch again soon – and very best wishes to you and Lili, from Gretel too.

Your old

Teddie

Original: typescript with printed letterhead, handwritten additions and corrections; Siegfried Kracauer papers, Deutsches Literaturarchiv, Marbach am Neckar.

an extraordinary success: this includes the reactions of the press; the publisher sent out around 110 review copies of *Minima Moralia* in March/April 1951, and well over 90 proofs of reviews survive.

Goethe's words … pushing and shoving in a crowd: 'A title and a medal ward off many a push and shove in a crowd'; see Johann Wolfgang Goethe, *Briefe, Tagebücher und Gespräche von 1928 bis zu Goethes Tod*, Part I, ed. Horst Fleig, Frankfurt am Main: Deutscher Klassiker Verlag, 1993, p. 479.

The concept of 'opinion' … mobilized the same category against him: this occurred in a letter which has not survived, to which Ernst Bloch presumably replied in the first half of December 1934: 'That is more the doctrine of "opinion", and the accusation of undialectical carelessness which is associated with it … But I also feared that your curious "theory of opinion" is a personal one and is less concerned with philosophical than with psychological method. Why, what is "dogma which must always turn out to be the anticipated opinion" supposed to mean?' (see Bloch, *Briefe* 2, p. 426).

rather like the Theory of the Novel 30 years ago: Georg Lukács, *The Theory of the Novel: A Historico-Philosophical Essay on the Forms of Great Epic Literature*, trans. Anna Bostock; London, Merlin Press, [1920] 1978.

a little parergon to the Kierkegaard: the first enclosure, 'Kierkegaards Lehre von der Liebe', in *Zeitschrift für Religions- und Geistesgeschichte*, no. 1, 1951; in Kracauer's collection there is an offprint of the English version, 'On Kierkegaard's Doctrine of Love', *Studies in Philosophy and Social Science*, 8/413, 1939 (*Zeitschrift für Sozialforschung*, no. 3, 1939/40; see Adorno, GS 2; pp. 217–36, 265).

The Disenchanted Dream: below the title given in the letter in *Die Neue Rundschau*, no. 2, 1951, pp. 74–96 – i.e. 'Aldous Huxley und die Utopie' (see Adorno, GS 10.1, pp. 97–122).

festschrift for Leopold von Wiese: on the occasion of the 70th birthday of the sociologist (1876–1969) there appeared *Soziologische Forschung in unserer Zeit*, ed. Karl Gustav Specht, Cologne, Westdeutscher Verlag, 1951. *Kulturkritik und Gesellschaft* (see Adorno, GS 10.1, pp. 11–30) became the subtitle of *Prismen* in 1955. An offprint among Kracauer's papers bears a note in an unknown hand: 'With Professor Adorno's compliments'; Deutsches Literaturarchiv, Marbach.

little thing about Bach: 'Bach gegen seine Liebhaber verteidigt', *Merkur*, no. 6, 1951 (see Adorno, GS 10.1, pp. 138–51).

Lili: Adorno wrote 'Lily'.

152 Adorno to Kracauer
Frankfurt am Main, March 1952

WE SEND HEARTFELT THANKS TO ALL WHO HAVE EXPRESSED THEIR SYMPATHY ON THE DEATH OF MY DEAR MOTHER MARIA WIESENGRUND.

THEODOR W. ADORNO

FRANKFURT A.M., MARCH 1952

Dear Friedel,

A thousand thanks for your letter. Two years ago, I tried to bring my mother over here, where she would have been very comfortable, but she could no longer make up her mind to take this step and has now died in the country to which she emigrated, quite alone, at the age of almost eighty-seven. My mourning has a strong flavour of bitterness about it.

We received your New Year's greetings; as an immensely harassed creature, I must ask your forgiveness for not having thanked you and sent a reply.

Your book – that must be the one on the aesthetics of film? Is there an 'esoteric' German version? If that is the case, I have no doubt that it would easily find a publisher here. How are things between you and Germany in general? I could quite understand, of course, if you would prefer not to come over under any circumstances.

The Institute's work is developing well; I think that there will be a major project coming up in the next six months.

I hope to see you in the not too distant future. Much love to you and Lili, from Gretel too. Your

old Teddie.

Original: MS on a printed card expressing thanks; Siegfried Kracauer papers, Deutsches Literaturarchiv, Marbach am Neckar.

the death of my dear mother: Maria Wiesengrund died on 23 February 1952 in New York.

your letter: not preserved.

your New Year's greeting: not preserved.

come over: Kracauer visited post-war Germany for the first time in 1956 (see letter no. 161).

153 Adorno to Kracauer
Frankfurt am Main, 24.9.1953

INSTITUT FÜR SOZIALFORSCHUNG
AN DER
JOHANN WOLFGANG GOETHE-UNIVERSITÄT
T. W. Adorno

FRANKFURT A. M. 24.9.1953
SENCKENBERG-ANLAGE 26

Dear Friedel,

A thousand thanks for the telegram – I am eagerly awaiting your letter.

I came here straight from New York and haven't seen a soul. My haste to get away from Los Angeles and over here will give you some inkling of my precious inner life. At least in my time over there I got a whole lot of work out of the way – above all, a big chunk of the Husserl book which has been dragging on for years (this will, once again, be published in the *Archiv*) and an essay on Kafka, which I had likewise been brooding over for ten years and which will be in the *Neue Rundschau*. I am very keen to hear what you have to say about these things. Now, of course, my own production has ceased as my commitments at the Institute are greater than ever because of Pollock's absence, and my commitments at the university involve an increasing burden of responsibility.

I should like to tell you, though, how much I liked your essay in *Public Opinion Quarterly*. Is it available in German, and how are your aesthetics of film getting on? In the meantime, I have been working on a series of things about television, based on the qualitative analysis (or so they call it) of 34 scripts which I was able to get hold of from the Hacker Foundation. It is being published in English in the *Hollywood Quarterly*, and two long essays in German in *Rundfunk and Fernsehen* have also come out of this. Besides this I have written a longish study in English for the Hacker Foundation, called 'The Stars Down to Earth'. You can see that I haven't been lazing around, but in my life things have turned out in such a way that work is a pleasure and only the business side is a burden.

So do get in touch soon. Much love to you and Lili, from Gretel too,

Your old Teddie

Original: typescript with printed letterhead; Siegfried Kracauer papers, Deutsches Literaturarchiv, Marbach am Neckar.

the telegram: not preserved.

to get away from Los Angeles and over here: at the end of October 1952 the Adornos reluctantly embarked on the journey to Los Angeles, where Adorno was in charge of the research department of the Hacker Foundation until the end of July 1953; a by-product of their stay was the renewal of their American citizenship. The collaboration with Frederick Hacker (1914–1989), a psychiatrist from Austria, ended in discord. After obtaining new passports they returned as quickly as possible to Europe, embarking in New York on 19 July 1953 (see Adorno/Horkheimer, *Briefwechsel* IV, especially letters nos. 631–4).

a big chunk of the Husserl book: 'Kritik des logischen Absolutismus' [Critique of logical absolutism], *Archiv für Philosophie*, no. 2, 1954 (i.e. the first chapter of *Zur Metakritik der Erkenntnistheorie*; see Adorno, GS 5, pp. 48–95; possible variations have not been checked in full; the essays begin with the same words in both printed versions).

essay on Kafka: 'Aufzeichnungen zu Kafka', *Die Neue Rundschau*, no. 3, 1953 (see Adorno, GS 10.1, pp. 254–87, GS 10.2, p. 839). 'Notes on Kafka', in *Prisms*, trans. Samuel Weber and Shierry Weber, Cambridge, MA: MIT Press, 1981, pp. 243–71.

Pollock's absence: Friedrich Pollock was no longer working continuously at the Institute at this time.

your essay in Public Opinion Quarterly: 'The Challenge of Qualitative Content Analysis', *Public Opinion Quarterly*, winter 1952/53; a version translated into German by Karsten Witte was published in *Ästhetik und Kommunikation*, March 1972 (see Levin no. 2068).

working on … television: 'How to Look at Television', *Quarterly of Film, Radio and Television*, spring 1954; see Adorno's first note to 'Prolog zum Fernsehen', *Rundfunk und Fernsehen*, no. 2, 1953 (Adorno, GS 10.2, pp. 507–17, 841), according to which this work resulted from the American study, and, similarly, 'Fernsehen als Ideologie' [Television as ideology], *Rundfunk und Fernsehen*, no. 4, 1953 (see Adorno, GS, 10.2, pp. 518–32, 841).

The Stars Down to Earth: in *Jahrbuch für Amerikastudien*, ed. Walter Fischer, Vol. 2, Heidelberg, Carl Winter, 1957 (see Adorno, GS 9.2, pp. 11–120, 413).

154 Kracauer to Adorno

New York, 27.9.1953

56 West 75th Street
New York 23, N.Y.
September 27, 1953

Dear Teddie,

Shortly before your birthday it occurred to me – and this sudden recollection must have deep roots – that it was your fiftieth. Leo confirmed this, and the result was our telegrams. Unfortunately, I wasn't able to write to you as soon as I wanted. In the meantime, you will have got over the shock of this caesura – for it *is* a shock, even more than the same event ten years later when one has learnt, so to speak, to take the process of chronological ageing on board. And for you, at least, the shock must surely be considerably mitigated by your now having a position which, in the eyes of the outside world, is secure and highly regarded. (Leo told me about your appointment as *professor extraordinarius*.) I was deeply touched – in a pleasant way, as between friends – by the fact that you, who are in my eyes such an intimate and purely private being, have become an objective phenomenon receiving external recognition. By the way, you will be able to derive some satisfaction from the fact that you are advancing along a path that has already been marked out by your achievements.

Many thanks for the copy of your study 'How to Look at Television'. This paper was also of interest to me because it goes into an area that I have to become involved with for practical purposes. Reading it, I was aware that this piece of work is one of those that are not authentically yours and thus calls for legitimate compromises on your part. (Otherwise there would be no explanation for various arguments which occur in it.) The association with the Hacker Foundation would also have imposed certain restrictions on you. Within this context there are various things which I find excellent, such as the historical references at the beginning. As you have since parted company with Hacker, as I have heard, I shall say no more about it except that I consider your practical suggestion at the end – to make the audience more 'stereotype-conscious' – unrealistic. Incidentally, the themes in television and film seem to differ from one another; it is not typical for film to make intellectuals into figures of fun. I was surprised that on several occasions you referred to the Wolfenstein–Leites book. Did you ever have a chance to look at my review of the book in P.O.Q.? It occurs to me that the only reason I didn't send you my P.O.Q. paper, 'The Challenge of Qualitative Content Analysis', was that I knew you would get it one way or another. I wish I could write at length to you about your Wagner study, which I am so delighted to have, but sadly – sadly – I don't have time for these things, which are nevertheless the most important. Why is it only possible for us to see each other so rarely? It would make so many things much easier. I myself have just resumed work on my book, which I had to interrupt for almost a year because of the big research project which I was carrying out for Leo in connection with the Bureau. I hope that I can go on with it, even in the event of a new assignment, for which I must also hope.

Once again, many good wishes to you, dear Teddie, from Lili and me, and warmest greetings from both of us to you and dear Gretel, Yours,

Friedel

Original: typescript with handwritten corrections; Theodor W. Adorno Archiv, Frankfurt am Main.

our telegrams: the birthday telegram which Leo Löwenthal may be assumed to have sent has not survived either.

appointment as professor extraordinarius: this occurred in the autumn of 1953.

association with the Hacker Institute: see the brief description in 'Wissenschaftliche Erfahrungen in Amerika', Adorno, GS 10.2, pp. 702–38, esp. pp. 732ff. 'Scientific Experiences of a European Scholar in America', in *Critical Models: Interventions and Catchwords*, trans. Henry W. Pickford, New York: Columbia University Press, c. 1998, pp. 215–44.

'How to Look at Television': preserved among Kracauer's papers (Deutsches Literaturarchiv, Marbach).

the Wolfenstein–Leites book … my review: Martha Wolfenstein and Nathan Leites, *Movies: A Psychological Study*, Glencoe, IL: Free Press, 1950; the review appears under the title of the book in *Public Opinion Quarterly*, 3, fall 1950 (see Kracauer, W 6.3, no. 801).

about your Wagner study: a belated reaction to *Versuch über Wagner*; the book had been published by Suhrkamp on 19 September 1952.

155 Kracauer to Adorno
New York, 28.8.1954

56 West 75th Street
New York 23, N.Y.
August 28, 1954

Dear Teddie,

I had been meaning for months to thank you for the German edition of your television papers – which of course I already knew in the original – and the Kafka essay with the kind personal dedication, but because of a load of scheduled projects in connection with the Columbia Bureau I have simply had to abandon my private correspondence. And when I had more or less finished, in the second half of July, I felt so run down that I attempted to make up for the overexertion of the last few months by several weeks of doing absolutely nothing in Lake Minnewaska, where we shall be until Labor Day. Now I am back on form again.

Your Kafka essay must surely be among your best works. I was delighted with various things in it: your rejection of the concept of the symbol in aesthetics, so overrated nowadays (in film the anti-symbolic nature of the intended meaning cannot be too strongly emphasized); your insistence on taking Kafka literally; your leitmotif of Kafka's understanding the 'system' from its refuse (like someone going through the rubbish and putting together beautiful shapes from discarded rags and splinters all by himself) – a topic which, I believe, I have addressed repeatedly in my own essays about Kafka in the *Frankfurter Zeitung*; the passage about Kafka and Expressionism and his intention throughout of allowing power to admit its own guilt. The Cooper quotation is a real find, and the marvellous Lessing parable works well in this context. One more thing has just occurred to me on the subject of Kafka and rubbish – that Benjamin once said something similar about me: in his great critique of the *Angestellten* he compared me to a rag-picker who comes along in the early morning and sifts through the rubbish. Not everything impressed me to the same degree. The attempt to uncover connections between Kafka and Freud seems to tend towards superficiality; in addition, one of the examples of this which you provide – the figure of the 'third door-keeper' – seems to me to be too far-fetched. In addition, your various references to the political and social situation are, in my opinion, not only problematic in themselves but are scarcely adequate to express Kafka's relationship to his times, even in a merely formulaic way – but these things are probably unavoidable.

Leo told me that the two of you are now going to be editing the *Zeitschrift* again; that is wonderful. I also know about the other things which are up in the air – I am thinking of Horkheimer – in general outline – so everything is making progress. I can imagine that you are as overworked as ever and perhaps even more so, with so many burdens on your shoulders – but, on the other hand, the influence which you exert there cannot be underestimated; that must surely be a satisfaction to you.

I myself shall be picking up my work on the film book again after having had to let it lie fallow for two years. I hope to be able to finish the book in one go. Parts of it have already been published here and in Italy. Minor interruptions are of course inevitable – most of all because of my ongoing activities in the Bureau. Among other things I have now written a long essay which culminates in an analysis of the connections between empirical research and basic theory. It may develop into a major project. I have also directed another project.

Lili is very well and doing a lot of work. We are glad to hear the same of Gretel. It has occurred to me that it will soon be your birthday – so I shall let this letter end with warmest good wishes from both of us for your work and your health – and much love and kind regards from both of us to dear Gretel.

Your old
Friedel

Original: typescript; Theodor W. Adorno Archiv, Frankfurt am Main.

Kafka essay with the kind personal dedication: the handwritten dedication reads: 'To my dear Friedel / from his incorrigible Teddie / Christmas 1953' (Kracauer papers, Deutsches Literaturarchiv, Marbach am Neckar).

anti-symbolic nature … taking Kafka literally: 'Every sentence represents a literal statement, and every one means … Kafka's prose maintains solidarity with the condemned too in striving to emulate allegory rather than symbol' (see Adorno, GS 10.1, p. 255).

refuse: 'but at the same time the image of that kind of history with which children who have to cope with the refuse of the historical world are wholly preoccupied, the "children's image of modernity", the hope bequeathed to them that some day history may yet be possible again' (see Adorno, GS 10.1, p. 270).

Kafka and Expressionism: chapters 7 and 8 (see Adorno, GS 10.1, pp. 274–83).

The Cooper quotation: 'the true Golden Age of literature cannot emerge until works are as precise in their thrust as a ship's log – as pithy in their content as a report from the watch' (see Adorno, GS 10.1, p. 255); Adorno's source has not been preserved.

essays … in the Frankfurter Zeitung: see letter no. 85.

Lessing parable: see Adorno, GS 10.1, pp. 281f.; Gotthold Ephraim Lessing, *Eine Parabel*, in *Werke 1778–1780*, Frankfurt am Main: Deutscher Klassiker Verlag, 1993, pp. 41–4.

Benjamin … compared me to a rag-picker: 'So in the end this author rightly stands before us as a loner. A malcontent, not a leader. Not a founder: a spoilsport. And if we try to imagine him all alone before us in the solitary nature of his occupation and his endeavours, what we see is a rag-picker, early in the grey light of dawn, poking with his stick at the rags of speech and shreds of language, surly and stubborn, and a little the worse for drink, to throw them into his cart, not without occasionally setting one or another of these faded scraps of calico – "humanity", "intimacy", "profundity" – fluttering mockingly in the morning breeze. A rag-picker, early – in the dawn of the day of revolution' (Walter Benjamin, 'Ein Außenseiter macht sich bemerkbar'; see letter no. 57, note.)

figure of the 'third door-keeper': 'In *The Trial* a high official says, "Even I can no longer bear so much as to look at the third door-keeper"' (see Adorno, GS 10.1, p. 261); 'This is countered by arguing that he may have been appointed by a voice calling from the interior, and that anyhow he cannot have been far inside, since the sight of the third door-keeper is more than he can endure' (see Franz Kafka, *The Trial*, trans. Willa Muir and Edwin Muir, London: Penguin, 1953, p. 235).

Parts of it … published here and in Italy: for these advance publications of extracts from *Theory of Film*, see Kracauer, W 3, pp. 869f.

long essay: 'The Social Research Center on the Campus' (Kracauer papers, Deutsches Literaturarchiv, Marbach).

156 Kracauer to Adorno

New York, 20.2.1955

56 West 75th Street
New York 23, N.Y.
February 20, 1955

Dear Teddie,

Today, may I ask you for some information? I was recently asked by a music publisher here whom I know, and towards whom I feel a certain obligation, whether I could tell him anything about the significance of the

Swiss philosopher of music (or whatever he is) Hans Kayser. Kayser is said to have links with the Pythagorean tradition and to have written a series of works which are highly regarded in Europe – among others, *Der hörende Mensch*, *Harmonia Plantarum* and, recently, a *Lehrbuch der Harmonik* (Occident Verlag, Zurich, 1950). Judging from the details which I have received, Kayser's philosophy seems to be a mathematical mish-mash with the principles of 'measure' and 'value' at its centre. Apparently someone approached the publisher desiring to introduce Herr Kayser to the public here. I promised to ask you for information about him. Do you know anything about the man? If so, I should be very grateful for a few details about his general direction, his approach and something of his significance, and also any response that he may have encountered. Really, just a few keywords would be enough. Would it be possible for you to send them to me soon? I know how overworked you are – which, I also assume, must be the reason why you have never answered my August letter with the birthday wishes at the end – but the wishes still retain their force for all that. Before Leo left, he told me about your splendid Proust essay; I should like to have a copy.

Warmest greetings to you and dear
Gretel from us both,

Yours,
Friedel

Original: typescript; Theodor W. Adorno Archiv, Frankfurt am Main.

Swiss philosopher of music: Hans Kayser (1916–1964), composer and musicologist; he was active in Berlin until 1933, then returned to Switzerland.

'measure' and 'value': thus in the letter [*'Mass' und 'Wert'*]; central concepts in the harmonics developed by Hans Kayser. *Mass und Wert* was the title of a cultural journal edited by Thomas Mann and Konrad Falke in Zurich between 1937 and 1940.

your splendid Proust essay: 'Im Schatten junger Mädchenblüte', originally a lecture (Hessischer Rundfunk, August 1954) in which Adorno advertised the publication by Suhrkamp of Volume 2 of the edition of Proust in the German translation by Eva Rechel-Mertens (see Adorno, GS 11, pp. 670–5). 'On Proust', in *Notes to Literature*, Vol. 2, ed. Rolf Tiedemann, trans. Shierry Weber Nicholsen, New York: Columbia University Press, 1992, pp. 312–17.

157 Adorno to Kracauer
Frankfurt am Main, 23.2.1955

INSTITUT FÜR SOZIALFORSCHUNG AN DER JOHANN WOLFGANG GOETHE-UNIVERSITÄT
T. W. Adorno

FRANKFURT A. M. 23.2.1955
SENCKENBERG-ANLAGE 26

Dear Friedel,

I don't know Hans Kayser – either the name or what he wrote; that wouldn't mean anything in itself, except that at least he isn't among the better-known European musicologists. But from your information one must fear the worst – one of those books that offer us plus signs and integers, on the one hand, and, on the other, as far as they can, the ancient Babylonians – in general with the intention of deriving from this some kind of aesthetic categories that are devoid of history and thus always completely meaningless. To the question of whether there is any need to publish such stuff somewhere or other, I should reply with a resounding negative; but I know the world well enough to be aware that precisely this kind of thing, especially when based on paranoia, finds readers everywhere. If the matter is important to you, I can make further enquiries (already in progress).

I feel an enormous guilt towards you for not having answered your last letter – please don't be cross with me about that. Just at that precise time things were going very badly with me health-wise – blood pressure much too low, with acute symptoms of exhaustion which plagued me especially during those bleak holiday weeks in Locarno. In the meantime, however, an energetic doctor has patched me up again, and I have survived the very demanding semester well. The Institute's first two major publications are in the process of coming out now, and quite an imposing volume of essays of mine (all previously published) as well – to which I have given the name *Prismen* [Prisms], which is meant to convey that in the book the material itself is seen through the medium of intellectual imagery and dissected into its components. Of course you will receive it as soon as it arrives. On the other hand, all that remains to be done on my book on the theory of knowledge is the final writing up of one very difficult chapter and the introduction; God only knows when I shall get around to it.

How are your things going – especially the *Theory of Film*? Are you writing it in German first, and are you considering publishing it in Germany? You know how obstinate I am on this point, despite all that has happened – which, however, should not seduce us into inflicting on ourselves yet again what Hitler had, of course, already inflicted on us.

Incidentally, the Institute is growing, blooming and flourishing. Wouldn't the two of you like to pay it a visit?

Much love to you and Lili from us both,
Your old
Teddie

Original: typescript with printed letterhead and handwritten additions; Siegfried Kracauer papers, Deutsches Literarturarchiv, Marbach am Neckar.

holiday weeks in Locarno: at least during the period between 29 August and 15 September 1954, the Adornos stayed at the Hotel Reber au Lac, Locarno (see Adorno/Horkheimer, *Briefwechsel* IV, p. 284; Adorno/Suhrkamp/Unseld, *Briefwechsel*, p. 140).

The Institute's first two major publications: *Frankfurter Beiträge zur Soziologie*, ed. Theodor W. Adorno and Walter Dirks, Frankfurt am Main: Europäische Verlagsanstalt, 1955, Vol. 1: *Sociologica: Aufsätze*; Vol. 2: *Gruppenexperiment: Ein Studienbericht*.

quite an imposing volume of essays: *Prisms*, trans. Samuel Weber and Shierry Weber, Cambridge, MA: MIT Press, [c. 1967] 1981.

158 Kracauer to Adorno

Lake Minnewaska, 27.8.1955

LAKE MINNEWASKA MOUNTAIN HOUSES
GEORGE H. SMILEY & SON, INC.
LAKE MINNEWASKA, ULSTER CO., N.Y. August 27, 1955

New address: 498 Westend Avenue, New York 24, N.Y.

Dear Teddie,

When I look at the date of your last letter, I note, *hélas*, how far behind I am with a letter to you. Many thanks yet again for your prompt information about Hans Kayser. It is really dreadful that, because of sheer pressure of work and preoccupations – often quite unimportant ones – we so rarely get round to doing what might be of much greater concern to us – in this case, writing a letter to you. We were so glad to hear – Lili and I – that your low blood pressure – probably resulting from overwork – was only a passing phenomenon – but nevertheless you ought to watch yourself. I myself noticed for the first time in the course of the last year that I had a kidney: a small kidney-stone – harmless but painful beyond belief.

In the meantime, I have carefully studied all the three shorter things that you have had sent to me. I shall probably quote in my book the sentence in your Proust lecture which says that Proust opens up the tiniest elements of reality as force-fields. The outline of the general interpretation of the work at the end does seem to me to be correct on the whole, but not precise enough. The terms 'happiness' and 'truth' feel to me as if they were slightly off-kilter; in any case I should have preferred it if, in this construction, you had employed the relationship of the name to reality which is so important in Proust's work. In the *Carmen* essay I find your interpretation, with the identification of banality and fate, quite magnificent; I am referring to the core of the work – the scene with the cards. Am I right in suspecting that the words of Thomas Mann's Adrian Leverkühn which you quote bear the stamp of your influence? What a splendid death Thomas Mann died! Some works of his may endure: *Buddenbrooks*, perhaps *The Magic Mountain*, and some short stories. Definitely not the essays, which are all style and too little thought. But in the end, though, the figure itself will endure – it was influential and one may even say significant at the intermediate levels – provided that time itself doesn't in the end destroy everything on such a level. Your *Musikalische Warenanalysen* unfortunately arrived in a mutilated condition; pages 5 and 8 are missing. To tell the truth I can't really get on with this article, for reasons which would take me too far away from the subject to explain here. As for the reactions of the masses to the cinema, Hofmannsthal once added a few very good observations on this subject – even (which is unusual for him) with a sociological slant. Is the dividing-line between the conscious and the unconscious among the masses really more tenuous today than in the past? Here I should have liked more history than construction, or, better still, more construction in terms of history. In your letter you promised me your *Prismen*, but it hasn't arrived. Can you still have the book sent to me? I should like to have it. I read somewhere that you were going to publish two volumes of sociological texts in partnership with Dirks (whom I knew quite well in Frankfurt). May I put my name down for a copy now? How you get all this done – quite apart from the Institute, the lectures, etc. – is a mystery to me.

I myself am doing a lot of work on my book. At the moment I am still busy with plotting the organization which provides a complete guideline right throughout, with all the arguments and references in the right order – a method which I have never employed before. I resorted to it because, in a theoretical work of this kind, it would otherwise be too difficult to sustain the main concept from the beginning to the end. After that, the writing will be relatively easy. I am under contract to the Oxford Press – in England the book will probably be published by Routledge & Kegan Paul and in Italy by Mondadori. Of course I am also counting on a German publisher. There can be no thought of completing it before 1957; I do have other things to do, after all. As I am sure you know, I am working in collaboration with the Columbia Bureau.

And what else is there? Every time that I hear of your great successes in Germany, I am delighted, and I am proud of you. Many hearty congratulations from us both on your birthday – and, most of all, best wishes for good health; all the rest will surely not be lacking, in any case – and all our good wishes to you and dear Gretel from Lili and me.

Yours, Friedel

As you see from the above address, just before the holidays we finally found a new apartment which is highly satisfactory.

Original: typescript with printed letterhead; Theodor W. Adorno Archiv, Frankfurt am Main.

in my book ... force-fields: 'Proust was preoccupied with splitting the atom in an intellectual sense and attempted to open up tiny elements of reality as force-fields, in which all the power of life comes shooting together' ('Im Schatten junger Mädchenblüte'; see Adorno, GS 11, p. 674); for Kracauer's indirect adoption of this motif, see Kracauer, W 3, p. 98.

The terms 'happiness' and 'truth': 'But while he will not be content with anything less than complete happiness, his need for happiness becomes one with that for truth which is not narrowed or restricted by any convention' ('Im Schatten junger Mädchenblüte'; see Adorno, GS 11, p. 674).

Carmen *essay*: 'Fantasia sopra Carmen', *Die Neue Rundschau*, no. 3, 1955 (see Adorno, GS 16, pp. 298–308, 678).

The words of ... Adrian Leverkühn which you quote: 'The sounds of French Impressionism, extended to the point of caricature, bourgeois salon music, Tchaikovsky, Music Hall, the syncopations and rhythmic somersaults of jazz – it all whirls around with the glitter of a circus act: but it moves above the basic language of the main part of the orchestra which asserts the intellectual standing of the work, grave, obscure and difficult, with radical rigour' (see Adorno, *Quasi una Fantasia*, trans. Rodney Livingstone, London: Verso, 1992, p. 56; Adorno, GS 16, p. 300); also Thomas Mann, *Doctor Faustus*, trans. John E. Woods, New York: Alfred A. Knopf, 1997, p. 395. 'Fantasia sopra Carmen' bears the printed dedication: 'For Thomas Mann on his eightieth birthday, in warmest admiration'.

Musikalische Warenanalysen: in *Die Neue Rundschau*, no. 1, 1955, pp. 59–70 (see Adorno, GS 16, pp. 284–97).

reactions of the masses to the cinema ... Hofmannsthal once added a few very good observations on this subject: 'What people seek in the cinema ... what all working people seek in the cinema is a substitute for dreams. They want to fill their imagination with images, powerful images ... for such images are what life owes them' (see Hugo von Hofmannsthal, 'Der Ersatz für die Träume' [Substitute for dreams], in *Gesammelte Werke*, Prose IV, ed. Herbert Steiner, Frankfurt am Main: S. Fischer, 1955, pp. 44–50, quotation, pp. 44f.).

Dirks: Walter Dirks (1901–1991), journalist, editor of the supplement to the *Frankfurter Zeitung* (1935–1943), co-founder of the *Frankfurter Hefte* and radio editor.

Oxford Press: *Theory of Film: The Redemption of Physical Reality*, New York: Oxford University Press, 1960.

In England ... in Italy: *Nature of Film: The Redemption of Physical Reality*, London: Dennis Dobson, 1961; *Film: ritorno alla realità fisica*, Milan, 1962 (Levin nos. XVa, XVf).

Columbia Bureau: from 1952, Kracauer was director of research at the Bureau of Applied Social Research at Columbia University.

159 Adorno to Kracauer

Frankfurt am Main, 1.9.1955

INSTITUT FÜR SOZIALFORSCHUNG
AN DER
JOHANN WOLFGANG GOETHE-UNIVERSITÄT

FRANKFURT A. M. 1.9.1955
SENCKENBERG-ANLAGE 26

T. W. Adorno

Dear Friedel,

Many thanks for your letter and good wishes. I am much better now as regards health, and I was also able to convalesce properly during the holidays, which we spent in Sils Maria.

The little piece about Proust which I sent you is quite lightweight – an improvised lecture – and without any claim to being an interpretation that does justice to Proust. I shouldn't dare to contemplate anything like that at all at the moment. However, the piece about *Carmen*, over which I exerted myself to an insane degree, is all the more serious for that, and I am especially pleased that you liked it. You are quite right in your assumption that the passage from *Doctor Faustus* to which you refer had its origins with me; the whole thing is quite cryptic and contains, among other things, the little secret that it begins its interpretation at the very point in *Carmen* – the third act – where Thomas Mann's description in the famous gramophone record chapter of *The Magic Mountain* breaks off. By the way, I had a most remarkable experience with him. Just a few days before his death I received a letter from him in Sils Maria – handwritten, and addressed by hand – in which he invited us to Kilchberg and also alluded in a way which no one could have imagined to his own illness and his own death. The letter contained the sentence: 'instead of me you will now find Hermann Hesse up there' – and together with this I also received the news of his death. It upset me far more than I should ever have believed possible; I was greatly attached to him.

If you have received a mutilated copy of the *Musikalische Warenanalysen*, I can well understand that the book doesn't convey much to you. Incidentally, it was written as far back as 1939, and those in the know will find it difficult to overlook something anachronistic in its tone. If you are amazed by the sheer scope of what I have published over the last few years, by far the major part of it was written during my émigré period, and then still more in America in 1952–53, a period which I spent over there with little pleasure, but which did give me enough time to write a series of things of my own. Here, at present, I can scarcely manage to formulate my own stuff. I can get you the first two volumes of the Institute's new series of texts, for which Dirks and I are named as joint editors, as long as I can be certain that you will publicize it in a newspaper or journal. Please be kind enough to do so and let me have the details very soon. The volume *Gruppenexperiment* should be of great interest to you, and the *Sociologica* too contains a series of essays from which you should get something, such as a long one by Pollock about automation, the excerpts from the book on Freud by Marcuse, the report on the de-Nazification study by the Institute, a series of unpublished fragments by Benjamin, and my own essay (drafted while I was still in America) on the relationship between psychology and sociology, which, it is true, I regarded as a mere draft rather than as anything definitive. As for *Prismen*, I shall see whether I can get a copy released for you; Suhrkamp is at present extremely reluctant to distribute free copies to authors. In a few weeks, by the way, it is publishing the two-volume edition of Benjamin's writings, with a new introduction by me.

I don't need to tell you how eagerly I am awaiting your film book. Don't mistake me for Cato the Elder if I keep on constantly reminding you that it is only in German that it is possible for us to express the crucial things which people like us have to say. We can in any event write like other people in English, but like ourselves only in German – and, as regards the film book, you really have done your utmost.

In Sils Maria we met Erich Itor Kahn and his wife, and from him I heard for the first time that you were both good friends of theirs. I was delighted to hear this; he is a charming person and an exceptionally serious musician of the highest standard imaginable. Your ears and Lili's must have been burning. Much love to you both, from Gretel too,

Your old

Teddie

Original: typescript; Siegfried Kracauer papers, Deutsches Literaturarchiv, Marbach am Neckar.

holidays ... in Sils Maria: the Adornos spent August 1955 at the Hotel Waldhaus.

gramophone record chapter: see the *Carmen* sequence in Thomas Mann, *The Magic Mountain*, trans. H. T. Lowe-Porter, Harmondsworth: Penguin, 1960, pp. 646–9.

before his death ... a letter from him: Thomas Mann died on 12 August 1955. On 30 July he wrote his last letter to Adorno from the Kantonsspital in Zurich; the sentence paraphrased here reads: 'You will find the Hesses in the Waldhaus, but not me' (See Adorno/Mann, *Correspondence*, p. 115) Hermann and Ninon Hesse were staying at the Waldhaus at approximately the same time as Adorno (see Adorno/Suhrkamp/Unseld, *Briefwechsel*, pp. 185f.).

a long one by Pollock: Friedrich Pollock, 'Automation in USA: Betrachtungen zur "zweiten industriellen Revolution"' [Automation in the USA: reflections on the 'second Industrial Revolution'], in *Sociologica*, pp. 77–156; see also letter no. 157 as the basis for the next four notes.

from the book on Freud by Marcuse: Herbert Marcuse, 'Trieblehre und Freiheit' [The doctrine of urges and freedom], in *Sociologica*, pp. 47–66. See also the English translation of Marcuse's book: *Eros and Civilization: A Philosophical Inquiry into Freud* (London: Abacus, 1972).

report on the de-Nazification study: Walter Dirks, 'Folgen der Entnazifizierung: Ihre Auswirkung in kleinen und mittleren Gemeinden der drei westlichen Zonen' [Consequences of de-Nazification: its effects on small and medium-sized communities in the three Western zones], in *Sociologica*, pp. 445–70.

fragments by Benjamin: Walter Benjamin, 'Zentralpark', in *Sociologica*, pp. 431–44 (see Benjamin, GS 1.2, pp. 55–690).

my own ... essay: 'Zum Verhältnis von Soziologie und Psychologie' [On the relationship between sociology and psychology], in *Sociologica*, pp. 11–45 (see Adorno, GS 8, pp. 42–85).

the two-volume edition of Benjamin's writings: Walter Benjamin, *Schriften*, ed. T. W. Adorno and Gretel Adorno, 2 vols, was published by Suhrkamp on 4 October 1955 (see letter no. 149).

a new introduction by me: see Adorno, GS 11, pp. 567–82.

Cato the Elder: Marcus Porcius Cato (234–149 BCE), Roman statesman; throughout his speeches there recurs his call for the destruction of Carthage: 'Ceterum censeo Cartaginem esse delendam' [In addition I give it as my opinion that Carthage should be destroyed].

Kahn and his wife: Erich Itor Kahn (1905–1956), composer and pianist; from 1928 to 1933 he occupied a leading position at the Frankfurt radio broadcasting station. In 1930 he married Frida Rabinowitz; in 1933 they went into exile in France and in 1941 to the USA.

160 Kracauer to Adorno

New York, 5.9.1955

498 Westend Avenue
New York 24, N.Y.
September 5, 1955

Dear Teddie,

It was kind of you to write to me at once. I am replying immediately because you will want to have details quickly concerning the Institute's series of publications. Unfortunately, as things stand here it is impossible to guarantee a review of the two volumes in advance, gladly as I would do so. (Previously, in Germany it would have been somewhat different, but even there I was not always able to do as I wished.) And so I will really understand if you are unable to send me the books. As they are of interest to me, I shall certainly be getting hold of them at some time or another – and I can already guarantee that one day I shall be writing to you about them. Very many thanks for your efforts to get a copy of the *Prismen* – though you did actually promise me this book once before.

A few more words in reply to your letter. As far as the *Musikalische Warenanalysen* are concerned, I don't believe that the two missing pages would have changed my opinion about them significantly. In any case, I received the important closing passage in its entirety. Moreover, my reaction to the essay had little to do with its anachronistic tone, which had not escaped my notice.

I know exactly what you mean when you tell me that we can express the crucial points only in German. What you say is certainly true of particular fields of literature – poetry, the novel, and (very tentatively) even the essay. (I no longer really feel drawn to the essay, despite making an attempt to give verbal expression to my present mistrust of this form.) But your Catonic dictum definitely does not apply to works which involve thought and theory – and here I mean one's own most personal thoughts and most personal theory. How splendid it would be to have a discussion face to face with you about this one day! My ideal of style is for language to disappear into the subject as the Chinese painter does into his picture; in this I am aware that the painter and the picture, the thinker and the subject, are one – up to a point.

I was glad that you met up with Hermann Hesse. Hesse liked several of my writings very much, including my *Ginster*, about which he wrote many splendid things. I have several good letters from him. Actually, did you know that we were planning to come to Europe for three months this year? We already had the tickets and everything – but in April I decided to call off the journey because I felt that I couldn't interrupt my work for so long. Everything depends on continuity at present. We should have been so glad to see you!

All good wishes and love to you and dear Gretel
from Lili and me,

Yours, Friedel.

Original: typescript; Theodor W. Adorno Archiv, Frankfurt am Main.

Hesse liked several of my writings very much, including my Ginster: favourable mentions are documented, e.g. in the Basel *National-Zeitung* of 18 January 1929 or in the *Kölnische Zeitung* of 26 March 1929; see Hermann Hesse, *Sämtliche Werke* 19, pp. 113 and 116.

I have several good letters from him: among Kracauer's papers there is a postcard from Hesse from the year 1939 and also a letter dating from 1947.

161 Kracauer to Adorno
New York, 3.6.1956

498 Westend Avenue
New York 24, N.Y.
June 3, 1956

Dear Teddie,

Just a line to tell you that we shall be coming to Europe this year – at last.

If all goes according to plan, we are hoping to be in Frankfurt on 24 or 25 July, probably for two to three days. From there we shall initially go to Switzerland.

I don't need to tell you how much we look forward to seeing you and Gretel in Frankfurt.

Very best wishes from both of us
to both of you,
Yours

Original: typescript (carbon copy); Siegfried Kracauer papers, Deutsches Literaturarchiv, Marbach am Neckar.

in Frankfurt on 24 or 25 July: the Kracauers travelled through Germany, Switzerland, Italy and France between 16 July and October with financial support from the Bollingen Foundation. On 28 October 1956, Kracauer wrote about their stay in Frankfurt to Leo Löwenthal: 'Incidentally, the meeting with Suhrkamp was an unforgettable experience. He is a truly exceptional man – one of the few whom we have had the privilege of meeting. The Nazis imprisoned him in a concentration camp, and he is now a very sick man. We spent an evening with Horkheimer and had lunch at the Teddies' after Gretel had given us a guided tour of the Institute. It did us good to see her again' (see Kracauer/Löwenthal, *Briefwechsel*, pp. 182–4). The meeting with the publisher marked the beginning of Kracauer's gradual involvement with Suhrkamp Verlag. In the correspondence with Peter Suhrkamp, plans for publications occur as early as the 1960s; in a letter of 15 June 1957, Kracauer announces that he has forwarded *Ginster*, for which Rowohlt had not taken up the option, to Suhrkamp. Included with the letter is a 'list' of essays, some of which would be published in *Das Ornament der Masse* and *Strassen in Berlin und anderswo* [Streets in Berlin and elsewhere]. The reason for the suspension of these plans seems to have been Peter Suhrkamp's poor state of health. There is no information about how much of this previous history was known to Siegfried Unseld (1924–2002) when Kracauer resumed contact in 1962 (see letter no. 189). Unseld joined Suhrkamp in 1952 and from 1958 was a co-signatory on an equal footing with Peter Suhrkamp. After Suhrkamp's death on 31 March 1959, Unseld managed the firm until the end of his life (Archives of the Peter Suhrkamp Stiftung at the Johann Wolfgang Goethe-Universität/Kracauer papers, Deutsches Literaturarchiv, Marbach).

162 Adorno to Kracauer
Frankfurt am Main, 6.6.1956

PROF. DR. THEODOR W. ADORNO

FRANKFURT AM MAIN 6.6. 1956
KETTENHOFWEG 123

Herr Dr Siegfried Kracauer
498 Westend Avenue
New York 24, N.Y.

Dear Friedel,

Many thanks for your letter. I don't need to tell you how glad I am that the two of you are coming. However, a massive shock will probably await you here – and at the end of July, I hope, the indescribable rat race which this semester has meant for me will at last be over – especially the exams, with which I have been completely overburdened this time. For the whole of August, we shall also be in Switzerland (back in September), and then we shall have much more peace and quiet. Perhaps you will both return here at that time.

In the meantime, I have finished my Husserl book and in addition a little volume of essays on music titled *Dissonanzen*. Besides these there is a kind of introduction to sociology in the form of lectures which is being published as a collective project by the Institute, but for which I did most of the work. As you see, nobody can as yet have any reason to accuse me of laziness, although I should much prefer it if they could.

Much love to you and Lili, from Gretel too,

Your old
Teddie

Original: typescript with printed letterhead; Siegfried Kracauer papers, Deutsches Literaturarchiv, Marbach am Neckar.

for the whole of August, we shall also be in Switzerland: on 2 August 1956, Adorno wrote to Max Horkheimer about their arrival in Sils Maria and on 2 September 1956 about breaking the journey in Basel (see Adorno/Horkheimer, *Briefwechsel* IV, pp. 360f.).

my Husserl book: *Against Epistemology: A Metacritique – Studies in Husserl and the Phenomenological Antinomies*, trans. Willis Domingo. Oxford: Blackwell, 1982.

a little volume of essays on music: *Dissonanzen: Musik in der verwalteten Welt*. Göttingen: Vandenhoeck & Ruprecht, 1956 (see Adorno, GS 14, pp. 7–167).

introduction to sociology in the form of lectures: *Soziologische Exkurse: Nach Vorträgen und Diskussionen*, Frankfurt am Main: Europäische Verlagsanstalt, 1956; there is no indication of the author or editor. Adorno and Max Horkheimer write in the preface: 'The authorship of the book is the shared responsibility of the Institute for Social Research as a whole' (see ibid., p.7).

163 Kracauer to Adorno
New York, 16.12.1956

498 Westend Avenue,
New York 24, N.Y.
December 16, 1956

Dear Teddie,

It was so good to see you and Gretel again, and that, more than anything else, is what we wanted to say to you today. The splendid thing was that, from beginning to end, we were back again in the middle of our old familiar territory. By the way, Proust did indeed exaggerate the corrosive influence of chronological time considerably; the possibilities for restoration in that same realm of time are enormous. In the meantime – in fact, on the journey – I read with strong approval what you write about psychology – especially psychologism – in *Sociologica*. It goes right to the root of the matter – perhaps even too far. Discussion at some intermediate levels might have been desirable. I myself have always wanted to try my hand at putting an end to the tendency of psychology to encroach; perhaps I shall yet find an occasion to do so. I am very, very sorry that I have not yet got around to reading your *Prismen*. I have a considerable workload, and I do have the book to write as well. I am making progress with it and am quite satisfied, even if things are going much too slowly. (A course on this subject will be held starting at the beginning of February, based on a very extensive synopsis – sponsored by the Museum of Modern Art together with the Extension Division of Columbia University.) We wanted to send you a Caligari, but we had no luck with it: Princeton University Press has sold all the copies and is still considering when (and if) a new edition should go to press. In the meantime, I have been left with only two copies, which I need. I shall get other people to hunt for copies, and as soon as I get hold of any I shall send you one. You have indeed produced a whole lot of things! We were impressed by your name over there, by the Institute, by Gretel inside it – and by everything. A happy New Year to both of you – let's hope that the year won't fall apart with a bang – and, not least, good health!

Yours,
Lili and Friedel.

Original: typescript, card: Virgin and Child in a Crescent, woodcut by Albrecht Dürer, German, 1471–1528. Metropolitan Museum of Art; Theodor W. Adorno Archiv, Frankfurt am Main.

to see you and Gretel again: see letter no. 161, note.

what you write about psychology … in Sociologica: Adorno gives his views about the 'prevailing psychologism of Freudian orthodoxy' and 'psychologism of any kind whose default approach to the individual is ideology' (see letter no. 157; see 'Zum Verhältnis von Soziologie und Psychologie' [On the relationship between sociology and psychology], Adorno, GS 8, pp. 52, 56).

the book to write: his *Theory of Film*.

A course ... will be held: on the 123-page synopsis and the film seminar at Columbia University, see Kracauer, W 3, p. 860.

Caligari ... sold all the copies: the second edition came out in 1959 (see Levin, no. X).

164 Kracauer to Adorno
Wilmington, Vermont, 17.8.1957

THE CRAFTS INN
WILMINGTON, VERMONT

August 17, 1957

Dear Teddie,

Just a word to thank you for your analysis of the Los Angeles astrology column – as excellent as it is prudent. We both read it with great pleasure. I especially enjoyed the dissection of the contradictions in the biphasic procedure – a twist which you have brilliantly analysed right down to its fundamental principles. In short, it is a content analysis after my own heart. How you can achieve this with all your multifaceted activities (about which I know) without sacrificing any degree of intensity is a riddle to me. We are here in Vermont for a fair part of the summer, and I am doing a lot of work on my book. About half of it is finished, which is not a bad beginning. We have dreams of coming to Europe next year and seeing you both again. Leo told us that he had read such a fine analysis you wrote of a poem. Do send me a copy if you still have any. Were you in Sils Maria again?

Warmest regards from Lili and me to you and dear Gretel. We still think very often of those happy hours which we spent with you.

Yours,
Friedel

Original: typescript with printed letterhead; Theodor W. Adorno Archiv, Frankfurt am Main.

analysis of the Los Angeles astrology column: 'The Stars Down to Earth' appeared in *Jahrbuch für Amerikastudien* in 1957 (see letter no. 153, note).

such a fine analysis: 'Rede über Lyrik und Gesellschaft' [Talk on lyric poetry and society], *Akzente*, no. 1, 1957; in this Adorno compared Eduard Mörike's 'Auf einer Wanderung' [On a walking tour] and Stefan George's 'Im Windes-Weben' [In the murmuring wind]. An English translation of the poem by Mörike can be found in *Poems by Eduard Mörike*, trans. Norah K. Cruickshank and Gilbert F. Cunningham, London: Methuen, 1959, and one of the poem by George in *The Penguin Book of Lieder*, ed. and trans. S. S. Prawer, Harmondsworth: Penguin, 1974, p. 164.

165 Adorno to Kracauer
Sils Maria, 24.8.1957

Sils Maria, Waldhaus, 24 VIII 57

Dear Friedel, many thanks for your letter; I am very glad that you both liked the astrology; it was my main project when I was directing the Hacker Foundation in 1953 – written over there. I should be happy to send you 'Lyrik und Gesellschaft', together with the Hegel critique which has come out in the meantime. We are recovering resolutely, hence well, and are sorry that we have to go back next week. Hoping to see you soon! Much love to you both – from Gretel too,

Your old Teddie

Original: MS, postcard: Sils in Engadin with the Silsersee and Fextal, looking towards Piz Corvatsch; Siegfried Kracauer papers, Deutsches Literaturarchiv, Marbach am Neckar.

I should be happy to send you 'Lyrik und Gesellschaft': an offprint among Kracauer's papers bears the handwritten dedication: 'For Friedel with warmest regards / Teddie'.

the Hegel critique which has come out in the meantime: 'Aspekte der Hegelschen Philosophie' [Aspects of Hegel's philosophy], published on 16 April 1957.

166 Kracauer to Adorno
New York, 22.4.1958

498 Westend Avenue,
New York 24, N.Y.
April 22, 1958.

Dear Teddie:

I am writing to you today for a practical reason. But first: I would like to let you know that I have a very guilty conscience as far as you are concerned: I never thanked you for your essay 'Soziologie und empirische Forschung', with its kind personal dedication. My excuse is not even that I am terribly overworked, but something different; I am so completely in agreement with you on all the fundamental points that I almost regarded the essay, in its critical passages, as an expression of my own views, and I assimilated it, so to speak. And that was that. But even when one agrees, one should not, of course, remain silent ... By the way, I too have been writing a paper in the last few weeks which applies roughly this same sort of criticism to research methods here in a more specific way. It goes by the name 'On the Relation of Analysis to the Situational Factors in Case Studies' and will serve as the starting point for a seminar.

And here is the practical reason: Lili needs, for purposes of reparations, an *official confirmation* that she was employed by the Institute in the years from *1924 to 1930 as a librarian.* Could you please send us this official confirmation – by return of post, if possible? At that time, of course, we were not yet married, and her maiden name was *Elisabeth Ehrenreich.* One more thing: Lili can no longer remember whether the employees were insured under the Reichsversicherung insurance scheme. We would also be grateful to you for information about this.

Many thanks indeed in advance. We hope that you and dear Gretel are very well, and that you too have nothing to complain about as far as your health goes. Lili had an attack of flu which hung on for some time, but is quite well again now.

Warmest regards from both of us
to both of you,
Your old
Friedel

Original: typescript; Theodor W. Adorno Archiv, Frankfurt am Main.

'Soziologie und empirische Forschung', with its kind personal dedication: in *Wesen und Wirklichkeit des Menschen: Festschrift für Helmuth Plessner*, ed. Klaus Ziegler, Göttingen: Vandenhoeck & Ruprecht, 1957, pp. 245–60 (see Adorno, GS 8, pp. 196–216, GS 9.2, p. 407); the handwritten dedication reads: 'To my dear Friedel / warmest regards, Teddie / January 1958' (Siegfried Kracauer papers, Deutsches Literaturarchiv, Marbach).

'On the Relation of Analysis to the Situational Factors in Case Studies': Kracauer papers, Deutsches Literaturarchiv, Marbach; the text is published in Kracauer, W 2.2.

Lili … was employed by the Institute … as a librarian: see letter no. 37, note.

167 Adorno to Kracauer

Frankfurt am Main, 8.5.1958

PROF. DR. THEODOR W. ADORNO

FRANKFURT AM MAIN 8 MAY 1958
KETTENHOFWEG 123

Dear Friedel,

Many thanks for your letter of 22 April. The reason for my answering it only now is that Gretel and I took a few days off for a holiday in Burgundy with a friend, and that immediately after our return I had business in Berlin. This is also the reason that I didn't send the official confirmation for Lili myself but left it to Rosenberg, a member of the administrative board, on the basis of a conversation which he had with Pollock, who worked with Lili at that time, and who is therefore more competent to provide it. As I had no opportunity to see Pollock beforehand, I made these arrangements as I didn't want to delay the business in any way. If you should need additional confirmation from me, then please write to me at once.

I am very glad that my little piece about sociology and empirical research appealed to you. It does indeed testify to the general intellectual regression that one is nowadays forced to put such things into words in view of the prevailing way of thinking in administrative terms. A new little book of mine is coming out in the next few days – a series of essays, *Noten zur Literatur*. 'New', of course, is a euphemism, inasmuch as the pieces which it contains have almost all appeared before. Only two contributions are new in print, 'The Essay as Form', a discussion of the genre's fundamental principles, and a previously unpublished fragment on 'Epic Naivety'.

How are you getting on with your film aesthetics? When can we look forward to the publication of the full text?

And what are your plans apart from these?

All is well with us, aside from the chronic condition of being overburdened, from which one has, to some degree, to steal one's own work.

Much love, from Gretel too,

Your old Teddie

Original: typescript with printed letterhead; Siegfried Kracauer papers, Deutsches Literaturarchiv, Marbach am Neckar.

holiday in Burgundy: Strasbourg, Ronchamp and Dijon are mentioned as stages on the journey on a postcard to Max and Maidon Horkheimer of 28 April 1958. Their companion signed herself Tanja Winterfeldt; no further information is available.

business in Berlin: Adorno was taking part in a discussion forum organized by Kulturkreis Berlin on the theme 'Leisure – Opportunity or Danger?'; at this venue he spoke on 'Kultur and Culture' (see 'Freizeit – Chance oder Gefahr?', *Der Tag*, 5/6 May 1958).

Rosenberg, a member of the administrative board: Albert Rosenberg (1894–1978) joined the Institute shortly after it was founded and became the head of its administrative board.

Pollock … more competent: see the following letter.

Noten zur Literatur: published on 16 May 1958 (see Adorno, GS 11, pp. 7–126).

168 Kracauer to Adorno
New York, 13.5.1958

498 Westend Avenue,
New York 24, N.Y.
May 13, 1958

Dear Teddie,

I was half-waiting for a personal line from you to send you our thanks for the prompt confirmation for Lili, and now it has actually arrived. It was very kind and perspicacious of you to see that the matter was quickly settled in this way; many thanks from us both for this. I am enclosing a word of thanks for Dr Pollock; as we don't know his address, please would you have this forwarded via the Institute? Thank you.

Your excursion to Burgundy must have been delightful. I take it that you enjoyed the wine there. Many congratulations on your forthcoming collection *Noten zur Literatur*. I am keen to read the essay 'Essay als Form'; I have some ideas of my own about the essay as a form, based on our own situation. By the way, Leo recently sent me a good article of his – a longish review of a book about international communications research.

I have had to interrupt work on my book for two months, alas – first of all there was the paper for the Bureau, about which I wrote to you, and, second, I had a few chores to get out of the way. But now I am free again and can, God willing, remain so until the end. Close to 330 pages of typescript, about two-thirds of the total, are now in their final form. The book is being eagerly awaited; the American, English, Italian and German editions are all signed and sealed, and a few authors are already mentioning it in their books. That, of course, sounds like more than it actually is – but I mention this only as a curiosity.

Dear Teddie, we shall be coming to Europe again this summer. I have a small commission, which unfortunately will not take us to Frankfurt. (In the unlikely event that we should be able to make a brief stop there – this would be around the end of July – I should of course write to you.) But how glad we should be to see you and dear Gretel! We are staying in Switzerland for a few weeks for a rest (and in my case to work), which will be from 1–21 August – possibly in Klosters again. If the two of you were also in Switzerland around this time, we should certainly be able to arrange something; that would be wonderful.

In the meantime, all the best and warmest regards from both of us to both of you,

Yours,
Friedel

Original: typescript; Theodor W. Adorno Archiv, Frankfurt am Main.

a word of thanks for Dr Pollock: Kracauer to Friedrich Pollock, 13 May 1958: 'Dear Dr Pollock, my wife and I would like to thank you very much indeed for making it possible for the Institute to send my wife immediate confirmation of her employment there. We appreciate it greatly, indeed. We hope that you are very well. With warmest greetings from us both, yours …' Handwritten addition: 'Enclosed, in envelope, letter to Teddie of May 13' (Kracauer papers, Deutsche Literaturarchiv, Marbach).

international communications research: this may refer to two studies by Löwenthal on this subject; see Löwenthal, 'Veröffentlichungen', nos. 50 and 60.

coming to Europe again this summer: the journey, funded by the American Philosophical Society, was for the purpose, among other things, of consulting film archives in London and Paris; in addition, Kracauer visited Venice as a guest of honour at the Biennale (see Kracauer, W 3, p. 862).

169 Kracauer to Adorno

Klosters, Switzerland, 6.8.1958

GRAND HOTEL VEREINA
KLOSTERS
Switzerland

6 August 1958

Dear Teddie,

Just a line to let you know that we are here in Switzerland. We even had an unexpected stopover for a couple of hours in Frankfurt on 25 July, but I didn't try to get hold of you in such a last-minute way as I know how overburdened you are, especially in these last days of the semester. Very many thanks for *Noten zur Literatur*, with the kind dedication inside. I could only read parts of it in New York, considering how strained I have been recently. But I did read, for example, the essay about Eichendorff and a few pages of it absolutely delighted me; I do believe that they are among the best things you have ever achieved. I don't agree with the essay about the essay, but this is a long story. (In your place, by the way, I should have left out the words about Heine; they are not on the same level as the ones about Eichendorff, for example.) Where might you be now? If in Switzerland, shall we perhaps be seeing you? That would be wonderful. We are staying here until the 21st.

Love from Lili and me
for you and Gretel,
Your Friedel

Original: MS with printed letterhead; Theodor W. Adorno Archiv, Frankfurt am Main.

Noten zur Literatur, *with the kind dedication inside*: the dedication reads 'To my dear Friedel: warmest regards, Teddie / 22 May 1958' (Kracauer papers, Deutsches Literaturarchiv, Marbach).

essay about Eichendorff: 'Zum Gedächtnis Eichendorffs, vor *Noten zur Literatur*', lecture, Westdeutscher Rundfunk, November 1957, published in *Akzente*, no. 1, 1958 (see Adorno, GS 11, pp. 69–94, 698).

words about Heine: 'Die Wunde Heine, before *Noten zur Literatur*', lecture, Westdeutscher Rundfunk, February 1956, published in *Texte und Zeichen*, no. 3, 1956 (see Adorno, GS 11, pp. 95–100, 698).

170 Adorno to Kracauer
Frankfurt am Main, 5.9.1958

PROF. DR. THEODOR W. ADORNO

FRANKFURT AM MAIN 5 SEPTEMBER 1958
KETTENHOFWEG 123

Dear Friedel,

Many thanks for your letter of 6 August, which I found here yesterday on returning from my holidays. What a pity that you only wrote so late. Otherwise we could easily have met – we were in Sils Maria again, at the Waldhaus. But I didn't have any mail forwarded so that I could relax properly, and so your letter was lying unopened on the desk. Let us hope that it will work out next time.

A volume of essays such as this one is a funny business. You especially like the Eichendorff – this was the very piece with which I didn't feel quite comfortable because of a certain general enthusiasm which it arouses. It needs only someone like me to be fond of something, and immediately there is such an outburst of joy over the notion that criticism does, after all, know its limits. Horkheimer considers the Heine which you dislike so much the best thing in the book, and I too am strongly attached to this piece. Of course, what would interest me most of all would be to hear what you have to say about the long article on the essay. True, it can be appreciated as it deserves only when set in the context of the *Metakritik der Erkenntnistheorie*, which of course you know. How are your film aesthetics going? I am quite extraordinarily curious about them.

Much love to you and Lili, from Gretel too,

Your old

Teddie

Original: typescript with printed letterhead; Siegfried Kracauer papers, Deutsches Literaturarchiv, Marbach am Neckar.

article on the essay … in the context of the Metakritik der Erkenntnistheorie: on the internal connection between 'Der Essay als Form' (see Adorno, GS 11, pp. 9–33) and *Zur Metakritik der Erkenntnistheorie*, see the 'Editorial Afterword' in the latter: 'Above all, he [Adorno] used to refer to the introduction as the piece of work which, next to the essay "Der Essay als Form", ... came closest to containing a programme of his philosophy' (see Adorno, GS 5, p. 386).

171 Adorno to Kracauer

Frankfurt am Main, 3.2.1959

PROF. DR. THEODOR W. ADORNO

FRANKFURT AM MAIN 3 FEBRUARY 1959
KETTENHOFWEG 123

Dear Friedel,

If my memory, which still serves me tolerably well, has not failed me shamefully this time, the 8th, i.e. Sunday, is your 70th birthday – last summer it was forty years since we became acquainted at Rosie Stern's, when the First World War was still going on; and even though, partly for reasons of distance, we have got out of the habit of sending each other birthday congratulations, this date is still, *tant bien que mal*, such a solemn one that you must surely allow me to send you every possible good wish from the bottom of my heart – aside from the obvious one: that you will get your great works all done and dusted, the first of which, of course, is the aesthetics of film; I am not the only one who is looking forward to this with great curiosity. Egoistically, I should like to add the further wish that you should produce the German version yourself; first, because (as I was forced to realize on the occasion of the 'Stars Down to Earth' piece) translations of English texts into German done by us can only result in torment, but also because I cannot shake off the belief that one can express oneself in earnest and with full responsibility only in a language which comes with all the associations from one's childhood, no matter how deeply buried.

There is little to report here apart from the fact that I have more work to do than I could wish, especially during the semester when Max is on leave. Of the things for which I had a firm commitment, I have finished the major version of the Hegel lecture which I gave in French at the Sorbonne. I expect you have seen the polemic against Lukács in *Monat*. A collection of writings about music – all of which have been around for a long time now – is being published by Suhrkamp in the spring; there is, of course, unpublished material in it too, especially a very extensive text about criteria in new music. My entire energy is being absorbed by the Institute – above all by the completion of a major political investigation of students, but also by a report on the state of sociology in Germany. I am hoping somehow or other to manage to get my breath back for ten days or a fortnight during the spring. In August we shall certainly be back in the Engadin, and then I have two engagements in Italy in the autumn.

Do get in touch, especially to tell us how you celebrated your birthday, and, once again, all the very best and *ad multos annos*.

Gretel joins me heartily in sending her best wishes. All our love to you and Lili

from your old

Teddie

During the Hegel congress Ernst B. and I were able to make things up without too much trouble.

Original: typescript with printed letterhead, handwritten additions and corrections; Siegfried Kracauer papers, Deutsches Literaturarchiv, Marbach am Neckar.

Stern: Rosie Stern (1876–1953), teacher, exiled to England. It was at her house, according to Adorno's account, that his first meeting with Kracauer occurred: 'I was in the lower sixth when I got to know him at the end of the First World War. A friend of my parents, Rosie Stern, a secondary-school teacher at the Philanthropin, to whose teaching staff Kracauer's uncle (the historiographer of the Frankfurt Jews) belonged, had invited us both. As our hostess surely intended, this led to an intense association between us' (*Der wunderliche Realist*; see Adorno, GS 11, p. 388).

the major version of the Hegel lecture: 'Erfahrungsgehalt', *Archiv für Philosophie*, nos. 1/2, 1959 (see Adorno, GS 5, pp. 295–325).

in French at the Sorbonne: on 24 November 1958, Adorno gave a lecture on Hegel in Paris; the French translation was made by Gertrud Straulino (see the postcard from Paris to Max Horkheimer of 22 November 1958; Adorno/Horkheimer, *Briefwechsel* IV, p. 525).

polemic against Lukács in Monat: 'Erpreßte Versöhnung: Zu Georg Lukács: "Wider den mißverstandenen Realismus"', *Der Monat*, November 1958 (see Adorno, GS 11, pp. 251–80, 698).

A collection of writings about music: *Klangfiguren: Musikalische Schriften I* was published on 16 May 1959 (see Adorno, GS 16, pp. 7–248).

investigation of students: Jürgen Habermas, Ludwig von Friedeburg, Christoph Oehler and Friedrich Weltz, *Student und Politik: Eine soziologische Untersuchung zum politischen Bewußtsein Frankfurter Studenten*, Neuwied: Luchterhand, 1961.

report on the state of sociology in Germany: 'Zum gegenwärtige Stand der deutschen Soziologie', *Kölner Zeitschrift für Soziologie und Sozialpsychologie*, no. 2, 1959, pp. 257–80 (see Adorno, GS 8, pp. 500–31, GS 9.2, p. 409).

engagements in Italy: Adorno gave the above-mentioned lecture, 'On the Present State of German Sociology', at the fourth world congress of the International Sociological Association in Milan and Stresa in the second week of September 1959.

During the Hegel congress Ernst B. and I: in 1942, during their exile in America, the estrangement between Adorno and Ernst Bloch, originating from political as well as philosophical differences of opinion, had come to a head as a result of an appeal published by Adorno for donations in support of Bloch without the latter's consent (see Adorno, GS 20.1, pp. 190–3 and GS 20.2, p. 813, and also Bloch, *Briefe* 2, pp. 443–7). On the events during the Deutsche Hegel-Gesellschaft conference on 25/26

October 1928 at the Johann Wolfgang Goethe-Universität, Adorno wrote to Peter Suhrkamp on 10 November 1958: 'This reconciliation was in fact achieved – or, rather, there was actually no need for any such thing; the "heart-to-heart" which both of us had envisaged never took place, but instead, as we were sitting alone together one afternoon, the two of us were in a state of such complete understanding with each other that such a formal act would have seemed ridiculous. I am very glad about this' (see Adorno/Suhrkamp/Unseld, *Briefwechsel*, p. 298).

172 Kracauer to Adorno
New York, 15.2.1959

498 Westend Avenue
New York 24, N.Y.
February 15, 1959

Dear Teddie,

It was so good to hear from you, and I thank you from the bottom of my heart for your kind thoughts and wishes – even if the chronological reason for them was an ominous one. To anticipate your question about how we celebrated the day: not at all – quite deliberately, not at all. I had taken the necessary pains to ensure that nothing got into the papers, and so it remained a purely private affair. I worked just as I would on any other Sunday – that is, as far as this was possible, as I am still left with a little fatigue after a virus infection which condemned me to stay at home and do nothing for the whole of January. It was awful, and detective novels are so poor nowadays. But now I am ready for anything again, and even Lili (a few days after the doctor) has signed me off as fit. Did you know, by the way, that antibiotics are ineffective in fighting viruses, but for this reason have the effect of making the viruses even stronger? Is it really true that there is a limit to how high trees can grow? We don't see it, though.

I admire your energy and its magnificent results again and again. Do let me have the Hegel essay if it has come out. I shall order the issue of *Monat* with your critique of Lukács. I read Lukács's article about European literature with very little pleasure. This man (we liked him as a person), who said unforgettable things about chronological time and Flaubert, is a traitor to literature and to his past (or his possible future as well). At the very least, he should not have needed to betray the paradoxical nature of his situation under communism so completely. It is a pity that you merely made a brief remark about your meeting with Ernst Bl. Something of the old affection always wells up in us whenever we think of him.

On our last trip to Europe we learnt to love London. (There was also a reception in my honour there, and all kinds of other things.) And then there were the rambles through the labyrinth of Venice; I was there as a guest of the Biennale, in connection with my book. I had better not start talking about Paris. Once we were back here in the apartment, it was difficult at first for me to give up the nomadic life, going from hotel to hotel like that. Of the 16 chapters of my book, there are only two more left for me to write, but the last is perhaps the most difficult. The title will probably be *Theory of Film: The Redemption of Physical Reality.* Unless too many other things get in the way, the book might be published next spring. Among my further plans is a collection of thoughts about history. About writing in German, you are right – up to a point, as I once wrote to you. I entirely agree with what you say about translations: one which was recently made of the first chapter – the one about photography – was such a disgrace that I refused to approve it. But where can one find the time to translate one's own writings? If we should come to Europe this year – unlikely, but perhaps business with the publishers might offer a faint possibility – we shall certainly count on seeing the two of you.

Please thank dear Gretel for her good wishes too –
and warmest regards from both of us to both of you.

Yours,
Friedel

Original: typescript; Theodor W. Adorno Archiv, Frankfurt am Main.

chronological time and Flaubert: for example, Georg Lukács, *Die Theorie des Romans*, Darmstadt: Hermann Luchterhand, 1971, pp. 110–12.

Venice: see letter no. 168.

thoughts about history: these thoughts led to *Geschichte – Vor den letzten Dingen* [History: before the last things, published posthumously, 1965], Kracauer, W 4.

173 Kracauer to Adorno
New York, 24.3.1960

498 Westend Avenue
New York 24, N.Y.
March 24, 1960

Dear Teddie,

I should like to thank you for the three offprints with your kind dedication – at the same time repaying your silence with action which speaks volumes, as you never even confirmed receipt of a paperback volume which went off to you a year ago with a pre-publication excerpt from my new book. I was impressed with your Hegel essay, which appears to me to be an admirable feat of interpretation. There is much that might be said about it, and about your oeuvre as a whole – but I can't do so in writing. We ought to have another long talk together. If all goes well, Lili and I shall be in Europe for a little over three months this year. However, as I am not travelling for pleasure I am tied to a fixed route, which unfortunately will not take me to Frankfurt. But we shall be recuperating in Switzerland for much of August – possibly in Klosters again, as it is at just the right altitude. What do you say to a rendezvous in Switzerland? By the way, my book is finished at last; it is coming out in the autumn.

Warmest greetings from Lili and me
to you and dear Gretel,

Yours,
Friedel

Original: typescript; Theodor W. Adorno Archiv, Frankfurt am Main.

three offprints with your kind dedication: two offprints by Adorno of uncertain date are preserved among Kracauer's papers; the first was probably sent as early as late December 1959: 'Zur Schlußszene des Faust', *Akzente*, no. 6, 1959 (see Adorno, GS 11, pp. 129–38); the handwritten dedication reads: 'To my dear Friedel from his old Teddie / Frankfurt, Christmas 1959'. The handwritten dedication of the second, 'Erfahrungsgehalte der Hegelschen Philosophie' (see letter no. 171) reads: 'To my dear Friedel from his old Teddie / Frankfurt, January 1960' (Deutsches Literaturarchiv, Marbach).

paperback volume … with a pre-publication excerpt from my new book: 'The Spectator', in *Film: Book I: The Audience and the Filmmaker*, ed. Robert Hughes, New York: Grove Press, 1959 (see *Theorie des Films*, chapter 9: 'Der Zuschauer', Kracauer, W 3, pp. 253–75, 870).

174 Adorno to Kracauer
Frankfurt am Main, 7.4.1960

PROF. DR. THEODOR W. ADORNO

FRANKFURT AM MAIN 7 April 1960
KETTENHOFWEG 123

Dear Friedel,

Many thanks for your letter.

Just for form's sake – or, rather, just so that you shouldn't think I have become *verkaffert* and lost my wits in my old age – I should like to let you know that I never received the item you mentioned sending in your letter. Otherwise, of course, I should have thanked you for it.

I am taking this opportunity to ask a favour. Suhrkamp Verlag would like to publish a volume of Benjamin's letters. I don't know whether you still have any material, but I would like to ask whether you would be prepared, if that is the case, to make them available for this purpose. This would be important as very few of Benjamin's letters have been preserved; apart from those in the possession of Scholem, Hofmannsthal's heirs, and Florens Christian Rang, as well as a man in Palestine by the name of Werner

Kraft, there are only – though these are more or less complete – the ones which Gretel and I received. Any addition to this material would therefore be most welcome – it is, of course, possible to undertake the whole business only if the circle of recipients is not too small. Scholem and I shall take on the task of editing the letters together. Many thanks in advance.

I myself am putting the finishing touches to my little book about Gustav Mahler, which over the course of many decades has now crystallized after all. It will be published by Suhrkamp in the autumn. Heartiest congratulations on finishing yours! I don't have to tell you how eager I am to see it. Will it be published in German – and in a version made by you yourself? For my part I think this is important, though of course I know that our views differ somewhat with regard to this complex of ideas.

Our plans for the summer are still somewhat uncertain on account of my state of health, which is still not without its problems; although I am much better and have really got my strength back after a few weeks on Lake Constance, I still have a slight tendency to attacks of vertigo and am not sure whether I can trust myself to such a high altitude – on the other hand, though, I never feel so well as I do up in the mountains. In any case, we must continue to correspond about this; it would be too idiotic to miss each other.

Much love to you and Lili, from Gretel too – from

Your old

Teddie

Original: typescript with printed letterhead: Siegfried Kracauer papers, Deutsches Literaturarchiv, Marbach am Neckar.

verkaffert: Yiddish word for 'being a dunce', an oaf.

a volume of Benjamin's letters: the beginning of Adorno's preparation of this edition is documented in a memorandum in his files dating from 15 February 1960; Adorno was passing on Gershom Scholem's question about whether Suhrkamp Verlag would bear the cost of duplicating Benjamin's letters, which met with an affirmative reply. On 29 February 1960, Adorno wrote to Siegfried Unseld: 'Today I have dictated quite a large number of letters to various people who may have material in their possession' (See Adorno/Suhrkamp/Unseld, *Briefwechsel*, p. 331). Walter Benjamin, *Briefe*, ed. Gershom Scholem and Theodor W. Adorno, was published in two volumes on 7 November 1966; *The Correspondence of Walter Benjamin, 1910–1940*, trans. Manfred R. Jacobson and Evelyn M. Jacobson, Chicago: University of Chicago Press, 1994.

Hofmannsthal: Hugo von Hofmannsthal (1874–1929); it was in *Neue deutsche Beiträge*, which he edited, that Walter Benjamin's *Goethes Wahlverwandtschaften* appeared in April 1924/January 1925 (see Benjamin, GS 1.1, pp. 123–201, GS 1.3, p. 840).

Rang: Florens Christian Rang (1864–1924), theologian and administrator; he and Walter Benjamin were friends from about 1918 onwards.

Kraft: Werner Kraft (1896–1991), author and acquaintance of Walter Benjamin's from 1915 onwards; a librarian until 1933, when he emigrated to Palestine.

my little book about Gustav Mahler: *Mahler: Eine musikalische Physiognomik*, published on 6 September 1960 as vol. 61 of the Bibliothek Suhrkamp. *Mahler: A Musical Physiognomy*, trans. Edmund Jephcott, Chicago: University of Chicago Press, 1992.

175 Kracauer to Adorno
New York, 30.4.1960

498 Westend Avenue,
New York 24, N.Y.
April 30, 1960

Dear Teddie,

We were very worried to hear that the state of your health has become a problem. In my opinion, all this is a result of the fact that you are overworking. This is also supported by your recovering within a few weeks on Lake Constance. You probably ought to slow down a bit and delegate everything which is not absolutely necessary to others.

It is a pity that the requested offprint never reached you – but the best thing now would be to wait for the book itself. If all goes smoothly, it should be published in October.

About our rendezvous: if you happened to be in Switzerland in August, even though at a lower altitude, we could certainly arrange something there. We are planning to take a break there for a few weeks – roughly between 1 and 22 August – so, if the two of you are going to be in that little country again, do write to me in good time so that we can take steps. Some other dates of interest: from 20 to 25 July we are in Munich; from about 15 September to 10 October in Paris. I have things to do everywhere, and the hustle and bustle will be enormous. But that suits me perfectly – it is the best way to recover from writing the book and to work – in my head, I mean – on the new ideas that I am anticipating. Background noise expedites my imagination.

Unfortunately, I have no Benjamin letters for you. There are probably some very old ones lying around somewhere – I don't know where – and they would certainly not be of any significance. The lack of correspondence arises from the fact that during our émigré years in Paris – and then up to the end in the South – we were together without interruption.

We are highly excited about your Mahler and are already looking forward to reading it. I can almost believe that I know what will be in it.

Much love to you and dear Gretel
from Lili and me,

Yours,
Friedel

Original: typescript; Theodor W. Adorno Archiv, Frankfurt am Main.

in Munich … in Paris: the first stop on the journey was London, from 6 to 20 July 1960 (see *Marbacher Magazin* 47, p. 127).

not … of any significance: Kracauer's mistake was revealed when his papers were indexed; the result was: Walter Benjamin, *Briefe an Siegfried Kracauer: Mit vier Briefen von Siegfried Kracauer an Walter Benjamin*, ed. Theodor W. Adorno Archiv, Marbach am Neckar, 1987; *The Correspondence of Walter Benjamin, 1910–1940*, ed. Gershom Scholem and Theodor W. Adorno, trans. Manfred R. Jacobson and Evelyn M. Jacobson, Chicago: University of Chicago Press, 1994.

176 Adorno to Kracauer

Frankfurt am Main, 12.7.1960

PROF. DR. THEODOR W. ADORNO

FRANKFURT AM MAIN 12 July 1960
KETTENHOFWEG 123

Dear Friedel,

Many thanks for your lines.

As far as our summer plans are concerned, we are intending to go to Sils Maria again. However, because last year I was very unwell there – I was suffering from agonizing headaches and tiresome circulatory problems – we don't know whether we shall be able to stay up there. It is very peculiar; on the one hand I never recuperate anywhere as well as I do there, but on the other I am not quite certain whether I can still tolerate the high altitude so well – last year I returned in a state which was a curious mixture of recovery and illness. If things were to go wrong again we should have to break off our stay early, and should make the decision relatively quickly. On the other hand, I very much hope that that will not be necessary. In any case, please do us the favour of getting in touch with us at the Waldhaus (we will be there from 1 August). It would be wonderful if you and Lili could arrange to visit us there once again.

Our days in Vienna were splendid and varied, but very tiring, and now I am once again feeling very exhausted. The Mahler book is already past the first galley-proofs stage.

See you very soon, I hope – all our love to you both, from Gretel too,

Your old

Teddie

Original: typescript with printed letterhead; Siegfried Kracauer papers, Deutsches Literaturarchiv, Marbach am Neckar.

you and Lili could arrange to visit us: the meeting, which Kracauer documented by taking notes of their conversation (see letter no. 180, note), took place in the resort of Bergün in the canton of Graubünden (Grisons).

Our days in Vienna: on the occasion of Gustav Mahler's 100th birthday on 7 July 1960, Adorno gave a celebratory lecture in Vienna (see Hans Wollschläger, *Moments musicaux: Tage mit TWA* [Moments musicaux: days with TWA], Göttingen: Wallstein, 2005, p. 19). Published under the title 'Gustav Mahler: Zur Feier des hundertsten Geburtstags' [Gustav Mahler: in celebration of the centenary of his birth], *Neue Zürcher Zeitung*, 2 July 1960; 'Mahler: Centenary Address, Vienna 1960', in *Quasi una fantasia: Essays on Modern Music*, trans. Rodney Livingstone, London: Verso, 1992, pp. 81–110.

177 Adorno to Kracauer
[no address], 30.9.1960

30 September 1960

Dear Friedel,

May I remind you once again today about the *unpublished* manuscript of your old book on Simmel (i.e. not about the Logos essay, which is available here)? You really would be doing me a great favour if you could send it to me as quickly as possible. I can guarantee that the copy will be treated with scrupulous care.

I hope that you have both returned safely from your Greek trip, which I envy you a little. You should have found the Mahler waiting for you there; today I am sending you, *separatim*, a little piece which was my contribution to the Viennese European Dialogue in June. It is composed with special pointedness considering the Phaeacian traditionalism of the Viennese.

Much love to you and Lili, from Gretel too,

Your old

Original: typescript (carbon copy); Theodor W. Adorno Archiv, Frankfurt am Main.

unpublished *manuscript of your old book about Simmel*: see letter no. 148. The publication in *Logos: Internationale Zeitschrift für Philosophie der Kultur*, 1920/21, under the title 'Georg Simmel', was not a separate essay but the first chapter of the 'old book' (see Kracauer, W 9.2, pp. 143–76, 304).

your Greek trip: in the first half of September 1960, as a further stage of his journey through Europe, Kracauer took part in the fourth international congress on aesthetics in Athens (see *Marbacher Magazin* 47, p. 117).

my contribution to the Viennese European Dialogue: 'Musik und Tradition' [Music and tradition], originally a lecture for Norddeutscher Rundfunk, broadcast on 16 February 1960; delivered in Vienna on 23 June 1960, published, in, among others, *Europa-Gespräch 1960: Die Funktion der Kunst in der modernen Gesellschaft*, ed. Amt für Kultur, Volksbildung und Schulverwaltung der Stadt Wien, Vienna, [1960]; included in the third edition of *Dissonanzen* in 1963 under the title 'Tradition' (see Adorno, GS 14, pp. 127–42).

178 Kracauer to Adorno
New York, 16.10.1960

498 Westend Avenue,
New York 24, N.Y.
October 16, 1960

Dear Teddie,

On our return a few days ago we found your *Metakritik* ... and the *Mahler* – and yesterday your article 'Musik und Tradition' arrived. Many thanks for all these and the kind dedications. Please bear with me – I have to deal with the backlog before I have time for my own things. But you will hear from me, even though it may take some time.

We are still thinking often of our meeting with you and Gretel in the Hotel Sonnenheim amid pouring rain. It was good to have a proper talk once again. Don't you think so too? I had been wishing for this so much.

I shall send you my *Theory of Film* and the mimeographed article about Bureau methods very soon. In the meantime, my ideas about history have continued to ripen, but nothing has been committed to paper yet.

Please allow these signs of life to suffice for now. Very best wishes to you both from Lili and me,

Yours,
Friedel

Original: typescript; Theodor W. Adorno Archiv, Frankfurt am Main.

Many thanks for all these and the kind dedications: on the *Metakritik der Erkenntnistheorie*, see letter no. 265; the handwritten dedication in *Mahler: Eine musikalische Physiognomik* reads: 'Hoping, dear Friedel, that you will not be able to imagine in advance all that is in this little book / Your old Teddie / Frankfurt, September 1960'; in *Musik und Tradition*: 'For Friedel from his old Teddie / Frankfurt, September 1960' (Kracauer papers, Deutsches Literaturarchiv, Marbach am Neckar).

in the Hotel Snnenheim: Kracauer took notes [in English; the errors are Kracauer's own] on the conversation of 12 August 1960 in Bergün, Hotel Sonnenheim (see letter no. 176):

Talk with Teddie.

(1) *Concept of Utopia*:

I argued that he uses this concept in a purely formal way, as a borderline concept (*Grenzbegriff*) which at the end invariably emerges like *a Deus ex Machina.* In my opinion, I told him, Utopian thought makes sense only if it assumes the form of a vision or intuition with some sort of definite content of a sort. T. was inclined to admit the justice of my argument. He says – of course, he would – that he will deal with the concept of Utopia in future, more systematic and elaborate works. His intention is then to show that the concept of Utopia is a *vanishing* concept when he besieged; it vanishes if you want to spell it out.

(2) *Dialectics vs. Ontology*:

Teddie is presently making notes for a course on this theme. The Ontology will have nothing to laugh, he says. To be more precise, he rejects any ontological stipulations in favor of an infinite dialectics which penetrates all concrete things and entities, and, taking its clue from what they may reveal, works its way through them in a process which has no goal outside the movement itself and no direction that could be stated in terms other than those immanent in that movement. I told Teddie that many of his articles concocted this way made me just dizzy; that I had often the feeling that other interpretations might be as conclusive than his, or even more so; that his whole dialectics seemed inseparable from a certain arbitrariness to me; and that, in sum, my dizziness was presumably caused by the complete absence of content and direction in these series of material evaluations. I traced thus my dizziness to the fact that he seemingly deals in substances without, however, actually being attached to any substance. Hence the arbitrariness, the lack of orientation. I related this argument against his dialectics to my statement on the formality, the emptiness of his Utopian concept: indeed, if the movement, he unchains gravitated toward an Utopian goal, it still remains unoriented throughout because the term 'Utopia' as used by him, is nothing but a conceptual stopgap.

Teddie's response showed that he was struck (though he is a skilled enough debater not to show it). My objections, said he, reveal that I still cling to obsolete, ontological habits of thought in requesting that something fixed must be given, postulated or desired. No sooner does one fall into this common error than the consequence is a ready-made 'system' starting from the vision or postulate and passing above the concrete material of things and entities instead of *through* them. And he insisted that, contrary to ontological bias, the truth, as revealed through this immanent processing of concretions, is always 'hovering' (*schwebend*). As for my reproach of dizziness, arbitrariness, etc., he declares that there is after all a definite outlook in his writing which, of course, is accessible only to those absorbing his production in its entirety. He demands, in fact, that the student should understand each meaning from the contexts of what he, Teddie, has written (and will write in the future.) Then, Teddie, seems to believe, the student cannot but experience the substance behind it all and get the sense of direction I am missing. (I could have answered him, but did not so, that, since his dialectics consists of an unending sequence of concrete moments and each moment is supposed to be interpreted in depth, the sum total of these moments is unattainable. Which means that the reader familiar with all of Teddie's writings will feel exactly as insecure and dizzy as one who has read only part of Teddie's output. The emphasis lying on the movement from moment to moment, more samples of the same may increase the impression of the movement punctuated by 'hovering' truths, but are extremely unlikely to endow it with the substance it deliberately negates as sheer movement.)

Instead of bringing in this pertinent argument, which did not occur to me at the moment, I resumed my objections from an entirely different angle. I compared Teddie's dialectics with a film made up exclusively of close-ups. Such a film is of course imaginable, I said; but the close-ups of which it consists would be completely undefined and, hence, puzzling rather than revealing, were they not every now and then, interrupted by 'establishing' shots relating them to the reality with which we are confronted after all and thus defining, however tentatively, their approximate position. Otherwise expressed, the radical immanence of dialectical process will not do; some ontological fixations are needed to imbue it with significance and direction. I spoke of '*ontologischen Würfen*' within this context and remarked that Hegel's dialectics moved toward, or implied, an ontological end. This was a bit careless of me, for Teddie knowing my liefelong aversion to Hegel, immediately exploited the situation by saying that Hegel never committed the sin of orienting the dialectical process toward anything allegedly 'Objective' outside that process. But even though for Teddy Hegel is an infallible authority, it was quite obvious that my new attack came unexpected to him; all the more so since I supplemented it by the observation that a really meaningful dialectics would have to bring into play some ontological vision also. There upon he admitted that ontological elements might indeed be needed – – but only in the form of hypostasized elements, not as eternal truths. Well, I replied, no one has spoken of eternal truths; rather, what is required is a dialectics between the endless, purely immanent movement – – Teddie's procedure – – and an ontological stipulation outside it, a 'Schau' which, itself, may, or should not assume a definite character.

Exploring further my advantage, I cited *Benjamin* against Teddie. Does not Benjamin, I continued, time and again feel himself bound by visions of partial ontological truths? And does he not orient his penetrations of concrete entities toward these Messianic visions which are rich in content, as indeed Utopian ideas should be in order to carry meaning? Here I had Teddie trapped. True, he tamely criticized Benjamin for not being the perfect dialectician à la Hegel and Teddie himself (who involves the Hegel of his making as a sort of protective cover and shield), but on the other hand he could not well deny Benjamin's strength as an autonomous thinker and try to undermine his position. I emphasized all this by drawing a graph illustrating his, Benjamin's and my own way of thinking.

Both Benjamin and I coinciding in not accepting immanent dialectics. I subtly implied that we are engaged in terms of substances. We think under a sort of ontological compunction, Utopian or not, whereas Teddie is, indeed, free-hovering and does not feel any such compunction.

At this point, I believe, Teddie was at the end of his rope. I am sure, however, he will not admit this to himself but immediately manage to believe that all my thoughts are in reality his own, annex these thoughts, which he already considers his property, to his 'system' and pass them off as the natural outgrowth of the latter. As Benjamin said: he grabs everything he is told, digests it and its consequence and then takes over.

(3) Ideology and Sociology

The formality and possessiveness of Teddie's mind flagrantly show in the way he relates the ideological to the sociological dimension. In all his articles or books he invariably traces the aesthetic or conceptual characteristics of some entity – – a poem, a philosophical viewpoint, or the like – – to the social situation from which that entity (historically) arises, but does so in a manner which unmistakingly reveals his complete unconcern for the material nature of society, past or present, and for the means of improving our social condition. His sociological concepts are much too wide to be able to characterize any social reality; they are just leftovers, never revised, from his Marxist past. This applies in particular to his term 'bürgerlich' which he constantly uses. Ontological thinking, ideology-formation, etc. – – all this he lays to the 'bürgerliche' Warengesellschaft, which he makes also responsible for the 'Verdinglichung' of specific values, abstractness in our approach to the world, unjustified relativism, and the loss of substance in general. I asked him to define his concept of 'bürgerlich'. He said it goes beyond Capitalism proper, covering the 'Tauschgesellschaft' with its exchange of goods. It goes without saying that, on some other occasion, he declared that Aristotle's Politeia with its emphasis on Moderation and the middle way etc. resulted from *bourgeois* mentality. (!) What are the counter-concepts, I further asked. The feudal society, the primitive horde, and so, he answered. Whereupon I gave him to understand that his concept of 'bürgerlich' is much too wide to define the social forces which may account for this or that intellectual or artistic phenomenon.

Incidentally, when discussing the relations between ideological events and social developments, I pointed out that it would be an urgent task for research to find out how the intellectual and social life of a given period are actually connected with each other. What are the channels, if any, that lead from a work of art to the social circumstances under which it was created? What counts now, is to prove or disprove the widespread tacid assumption of the unity of any historical period. Without realizing that he proceeds from this assumption, Teddie contended that he was in complete agreement with me and had already dealt with the issue, I raised, in one of his essays. To repeat it, he grabs every thing. In order to prove him how alienated he is from all substances, intellectual or social, he pretends to penetrate and set moving, I told him: You curse the 'bürgerliche Gesellschaft', reject Communism, frown down on the Social Democracy, etc.: what do you suggest should be done in terms of social changes, other institutions? His (pitiable) answer was: I know and say, what is bad; is this not enough? In sum, all that exists, exists only to be devoured in the dialectic process which Teddie keeps going on and on because of his lack of substance, of vision. To him, dialectics is a means of maintaining his superiority over all imaginable opinions, viewpoints, trends, happenings, by dissolving, condemning or again rescuing them, as he pleases. Thus he establishes himself as the master and controller of a world he has never absorbed. For had he absorbed at least segments of it, his dialectics would come to a stop, somewhere. As matters stand, it reflects, viewed sociologically, a world voided of beliefs and attachments.

article about Bureau methods: the only mimeograph to be found among the papers is 'On the Relation of Analysis to the Situational Factors on Case Studies' (1958). No further information is available.

179 Adorno to Kracauer

Frankfurt am Main, 11.11.1960

PROF. DR. THEODOR W. ADORNO

FRANKFURT AM MAIN 11 November 1960
KETTENHOFWEG 123

Dear Friedel,

This is just to thank you at once, as a temporary measure, for the film book and for the piece of work for the 'Bureau'. I must ask you too for a little patience until I can write something sensible about the book. The next few months will mean an unusual degree of overexertion, even for me.

Apart from the university and the Institute, where a major new project has started up, I not only have to finish the second volume of the *Noten zur Literatur* – all that is outstanding is the third and final version of the text about Beckett and also that of the minor, loose marginal notes on Balzac – but I must also extract three talks on ontology and dialectics from my current lectures and condense them, as I have to deliver them in March at the Collège de France; these, combined with an essay (tentatively) titled 'Notes on Hegel's Logic', because it is still to be written, and the *Aspekte* and *Erfahrungsgehalte*, with which you are already familiar, are meant to represent something like a new introduction to dialectics, perhaps under the paradoxical name of 'Dialectical Meditations'. If I tell you that, in addition, I still have to write two pieces for the book *Der getreue Korrepetitor: Schriften zur musikalischen Praxis*, you will perhaps think I am insane; but you will in any case understand that my receptive faculties, which are somewhat limited no matter what, will, to some degree, be in a state of submersion for the next few months. Incidentally, the programme is perhaps not quite so crazy after all, as all the things which I have mentioned involve ideas which have to a great extent long been sketched out, and which I just have to get done and dusted now – and the urgency of these plans, in their turn, is connected with the fact that I have, as they say, to clear my desk to make space for my own proper work, about which I have the distinct feeling that it is still something to be accomplished; I regard everything that I have done until now, even including my somewhat tumultuous output over the last few years, as finger-exercises. God alone knows whether I shall manage to get on to the symphonies after the études, but, if not, it will not be for lack of trying.

Let me, then, merely tell you for now that your book leaves a splendid impression, purely as regards its external form, and let me offer you my heartiest congratulations on the success that the very fact of its visual appearance represents.

In October I took a few weeks' late holiday in Styria by myself, in an utterly remarkable social environment, and in a world which really has retained some of the warmth and the aura of happiness that southern Germany used to have in my earliest youth, forty or fifty years ago. There I was able to recharge myself to some extent with the energy which now I really do need. Next spring, by the way, I have been invited, after Paris, to do a lecture tour of Italy, which I can cover in intellectual terms by using material I already have to hand (it is only the translations which are still causing me concern) and which I am looking forward to very much; this time Gretel will join me for everything. Then, starting with the summer semester, I shall reduce all my external commitments to a minimum in order to be able to approach the really grand designs.

Of course I should be very glad if you didn't pay me back in my own coin and would let me know your reaction to the Mahler – especially to the method applied there – in the not too distant future. By the same post I am sending you an unassuming little text, reflecting on certain ideas which occurred to me during a cursory reading of your book and which coincide with my reflections as much as they differ from them. This may well be exactly what defines the sphere of the dialogue which our writings generate of their own accord before we ourselves actually attain it as individuals.

With love and best wishes to you and Lili, from Gretel too,

Your old

Teddie

May I once again remind you of my request to send me your work on Simmel (the long, unpublished one, not the essay)? You would be doing me – or, rather, the doctoral candidate – a very great favour. Many thanks.

Original: typescript with printed letterhead; Siegfried Kracauer papers, Deutsches Literaturarchiv, Marbach am Neckar.

a major new project: *Grenzen des Lohnanreizes* [Limits of pay incentives], hectographed research reports, 2 vols, 1962.

the second volume of Noten zur Literatur: *Noten zur Literatur II*, published on 1 September 1961 as vol. 71 of the Bibliothek Suhrkamp.

text about Beckett: 'Versuch, das Endspiel zu verstehen' (see Adorno, GS 11, pp. 281–321); on 27 February 1961, Adorno initiated Suhrkamp Verlag's seventh publisher's evening; Samuel Beckett was present.

marginal notes on Balzac: 'Balzac-Lektüre' (see Adorno, GS 11, pp. 139–57).

three talks on ontology and dialectics: Adorno gave these on 15, 18 and 21 March 1961 at the Collège de France. The Frankfurt lectures on the same theme are documented (see *Ontologie und Dialektik*, ed. Rolf Tiedemann, pp. 7–341); on the significance of the Paris lectures for the development of his 'negative dialectics', see the *Nachbemerkungen des Herausgebers* (ibid., pp. 419–31). Adorno recorded the stay in Paris and the 'tour in Italy' which followed it (see below) in a travel diary (see Adorno, *Bildmonographie*, pp. 252–73).

'Dialectical Meditations': the title occurs in a letter from Siegfried Unseld to Adorno of 30 November 1959, in which Unseld summarizes plans for publications which they had discussed together. In this, Adorno sketched out a complex of ideas and writings from which he separated, among other things, *Ontologie und Dialektik*, his studies of Hegel, and *Jargon der Eigentlichkeit*. From 1963 at the latest, *Dialektische Meditationen* is used in place of *Negative Dialektik*, whose last chapter was given the title 'Meditationen zur Metaphysik' (see Adorno/Suhrkamp/Unseld, *Briefwechsel*, pp. 322–4, and also a memorandum dated 16 December 1963 (ibid., pp. 480–2).

Der getreue Korrepetitor: this book was among Suhrkamp Verlag's planned publications; after several years of preparatory work this title was discontinued there; Adorno published the volume, probably as a compliment to Rudolf Hirsch, in 1963 with S. Fischer Verlag, Frankfurt am Main (see letter no. 190; see Adorno, GS 15, pp. 157–402).

late holiday in Styria: on 14 October 1960, Adorno wrote to Max Horkeimer from Graz about the 'promise of happiness' which radiated from the city, 'as it did from south German towns in our youth' (see Adorno/Horkheimer, *Briefwechsel* IV, p. 635).

tour of Italy: the trip, including the stay in Paris, lasted from 13 March until 17 April 1960; it was sponsored by the Deutsche Forschungsgemeinschaft (see Adorno, *Ontologie und Dialektik*, p. 427; English translation, Theodor W. Adorno, *Ontology and Dialectics*, trans. Nick Walker, Cambridge: Polity, 2018).

an unassuming little text: this refers to an offprint, 'Kunst ohne Leitbilder', *Neue deutsche Hefte*, no. 75, October 1960 (see 'Ohne Leitbild', Adorno, GS 10.1, pp. 291–301), with a handwritten dedication: 'To my dear Friedel with warmest regards, Teddie / Frankfurt, November 1960'; Kracauer noted its arrival: 'Rec: No. 28, 1960' (Kracauer papers, Deutsches Literaturarchiv, Marbach).

the doctoral candidate: in letter no. 84 Adorno mentions a female student on whose behalf he requests the work on Simmel; her identity cannot be established with any certainty.

180 Kracauer to Adorno
New York, 11.12.1960

498 Westend Avenue
New York 24, N.Y.
December 11, 1960

Dear Teddie,

Many thanks for your kind letter and the various enclosures. I was impressed by your superabundant work schedule – but I am sure that you will soon get it all done. I myself am under considerable pressure because of external responsibilities and preparations for formulating some thoughts about history. In spite of this, I found the time to read your Mahler – that is, fragments of it – as I simply could not follow the technical explications and analyses of the music; and your stylistic intentions are of a kind which offers no crutches to a musical layman such as myself. Pity – the technical sections are the most important thing, or ought to be. In what I did read I found, as you hoped, something that I could never have foreseen. Your interpretation of Mahler's romanticism, of his 'banality', of his anticipation of what was to come by drawing on what was available from the past, of his protest against the splitting of music into a higher and a lower sphere – all these insights seem to me to be convincing and significant – not to mention the fact that they are brilliantly constructed. In spite of this, in the new Mahler there is enough of what can be expected: the matrix from which the specific aesthetic analyses originate, and against which they are set, remains unchanged. We discussed this matrix itself – your principal ideas with their radical anti-ontological dialectic – at length in our conversation in Bergün, which I shall never forget, and so as far as your basic approach is concerned I shall confine myself to a reference to Bergün. But I congratulate you on this book, which is certainly magnificent as an interpretation of music. (By the way, the fact that the tone of it is sometimes Bloch-like, with its many references to wayfaring lads, outcasts and children, is probably due to the material.) I shall study your meta-criticism, which interests me greatly, and the offprints as soon as I can get around to them.

I am surprised that you regard the 'splendid' edition, as you call it, of my book on film as a success. When might you have begun to draw conclusions about the fate of a book from its appearance?

It may amuse you to hear that, just in these last few weeks, I have been occupying myself with Hegel: I have been analysing the introduction to his philosophy of history for my own particular purposes. As – *hélas* – it cannot be otherwise, my results deviate considerably from yours (which, of course, does not diminish my personal appreciation of your empirical facts).

So as not to come entirely with empty hands (when yours, in contrast, are always so full), I am enclosing a piece of prose which appeared last June in a festschrift for Friedrich T. Gubler on his sixtieth birthday.

All good wishes to you and Gretel for the New Year – and may you have a lovely time in Paris and Italy that will bring you both much happiness.

With warmest regards from Lili and me,

Yours,

Friedel

Original: typescript; Theodor W. Adorno Archiv, Frankfurt am Main.

formulating some thoughts on history: Kracauer wrote to Leo Löwenthal on 29 October 1960 that on his recent trip to Europe he had 'been meditating a lot on history' (see Kracauer/Löwenthal, *Briefwechsel*, p. 231).

at length in our conversation in Bergün: see letter no. 178.

the introduction to his philosophy of history: in *History*, Kracauer examines Georg Wilhelm Friedrich Hegel on several occasions; a direct quotation comes from the *'Vorrede' zu den Grundlinien der Philosophie des Rechts* (see Kracauer, W 4, p. 218).

A piece of prose … in a festschrift for Friedrich T. Gubler: 'Die Zeitung', in *Freundesgabe für Friedrich T. Gubler zum sechzigsten Geburtstag am 1. Juli 1960, überreicht von der Buchdruckerei Winterthur AG*, 1960 – i.e. a passage from the fourth chapter of *Georg* (see Kracauer, W 7, pp. 299–305, 634). An offprint among Adorno's papers bears the handwritten dedication 'For dear Teddie in greeting and remembrance / Friedel Dec. 1960'.

181 Kracauer to Adorno
New York, 23.5.1962

498 Westend Avenue
New York 24, N.Y.
May 23, 1962

Dear Teddie,

Just this brief word to let you know that Lili and I shall be coming to Frankfurt on 18 July and staying there until the 21st (address: Frankfurter Hof). Will you be in Frankfurt around this time? We should be very happy if we could see you and Gretel. At the same time, I should like to thank you and Horkheimer (please tell him so) for *Sociologica II*, which contains also much that is unfamiliar to me. More about that, I hope, in Frankfurt. Revising the German translation of my *Theory of Film* in detail has stolen several months of my life. As well as this, I am busy with the lengthy preparations for my book about history – which, by the way, is also going to be published by Oxford University Press. Before I forget: our warmest congratulations on the magnificent article about you in the Times Literary Supplement.

Warmest regards from us both
to dear Gretel and yourself,
Yours,
Friedel

Original: typescript; Theodor W. Adorno Archiv, Frankfurt am Main.

to Frankfurt on 18 July: further stops on the trip to Europe from early July to late August were London, Munich and Switzerland (see *Marbacher Magazin* 47, p. 119).

Sociologica II: with the title of their volume of 'speeches and lectures', Adorno and Max Horkheimer created a link to *Sociologica*, the festschrift for Horkheimer's sixtieth birthday, dating from 1955 (see letter no. 157). The sequel was published in 1962 by the Europäische Verlagsanstalt, Frankfurt am Main, as vol. 10 of the Frankfurter Beiträge zur Soziologie.

German translation of my Theory of Film: Friedrich Walter and Ruth Zellschan were preparing their translation into German for the edition planned by Rowohlt Verlag; the translation, revised by Kracauer, was finally published in 1964 by Suhrkamp, following Siegfried Unseld's decision in March 1963 to accept the book for publication (see letter no. 211).

magnificent article about you: 'Intelligence and Servitude', *Times Literary Supplement*, 16 February 1962 – i.e. a review of *Noten zur Literatur.*

182 Adorno to Kracauer
Frankfurt am Main, 4.6.1962

PROF. DR. THEODOR W. ADORNO

FRANKFURT AM MAIN 4 June 1962
KETTENHOFWEG 123

Dear Friedel,

Many thanks for your letter. We shall be here for the whole of July, and I am very much looking forward to seeing you. It is just rather a pity that your visit happens to coincide with the last weeks of the semester, in which, because of countless examinations and other densely scheduled commitments, things usually proceed at such a hectic pace that the embarrassing question of what they call 'time management' intervenes. In September we would have much more ease, but you both have your fixed plans.

I am sorry that you lost so much time over the German edition of the film book, but I cannot suppress a narcissistic sense of triumph at having predicted this vexation. I myself had a similar experience only last year. My work 'The Stars Down to Earth', of which you know the English original, is now, as you may perhaps have seen, available in German in the volume of essays by Max and me. There was already an older translation by Frau von Eckardt with which I was not very satisfied, and so I had a second one made by my highly gifted student Schweppenhäuser [he has written an *extraordinary* postdoctoral thesis on Kierkegaard and Hegel, a revision of the whole controversy!]. But even this was so far from what those like us require of a German text, both factually and linguistically, that I completely rewrote it from beginning to end – it cost me six weeks' work, time in which I could have made a start on something more productive. The comparison between the English and the German texts should be very instructive, especially because the difference between the objective desiderata here and there becomes apparent – perhaps you might take another look at it. By the way, I find myself repeatedly confirmed in the opinion that, rather than make a translation, it is easier in the case of our work to find completely new formulations on the same subjects in the two languages. As an experienced administrator (God help me) I know – and not only from this – that attempts to save time in most cases lead to time being lost.

A female student of mine – not lacking in talent – is just finishing a dissertation on the sociology of film which suffers from certain journalistic leanings. If you come over, I ought perhaps to put this young (if not very attractive) lady on to you. Incidentally, she hasn't succeeded in getting hold of an English copy of your new book on film here, and I do not lend my own copy. You know that another student of mine, a Frau A. (a refugee from the Eastern Zone) has written a diploma thesis on your sociological oeuvre; at the very least it should provide a really thorough survey which will prepare the ground for a later and more intellectually substantial study of your work. You can have a look at her too, if you like.

Ceterum censeo that the most important thing for the German aspect of your output would be for *Ginster* to be published – and, moreover, under your own name. A few people who understand what is what, and to whom I have given the book, were quite extraordinarily impressed; I have no doubt that the novel would achieve an outstanding effect, and there is no need to be bothered for a second about the idiotic notion that its subject matter lies too far back in the past.

I myself am nurturing a whole series of projects side by side – as I am very tenacious and have been pursuing most of my plans since my youth, a lot of things are finally coming to fruition; however – something which is monstrously unfair – I seem to have a reputation among malicious types as someone who writes a lot with great facility, whereas in fact I make it as difficult for myself as I actually find it. At the moment I am putting the finishing touches to the treatises on musical practice, *Der getreue Korrepetitor*, which is to be published by Fischer next year with a gramophone record to accompany it. Still this year, Suhrkamp wants to bring out the lectures on the sociology of music which I gave here last semester and which have been written up in their entirety as a single text and edited – a really comprehensive manuscript. Perhaps it also gives you pleasure to hear that this autumn the good old Kierkegaard book is being reissued with an additional supplement; moreover, it is now being translated into Italian.

Until very soon, then, much love to you both, from Gretel too,

Your old

Teddie

We shall be in Vienna over the Whitsun holidays at the Hotel Erzherzog Rainer.

Original: typescript with printed letterhead, handwritten additions, corrections and postscript; Siegfried Kracauer papers, Deutsches Literaturarchiv, Marbach am Neckar.

'The Stars Down to Earth' … now … available in German: 'Aberglaube aus zweiter Hand' [Second-hand superstition], in *Sociologica* II (see the preceding letter; see Adorno, GS 8, pp. 147–76, GS 9.2, pp. 405f.).

Frau von Eckardt: the translator is cited at the end of the essay in *Psyche*, January 1959, as 'Marianne von Eckard, Heidelberg'.

highly gifted student Schweppenhäuser: Hermann Schweppenhäuser (1928–2015), philosopher, assistant to Adorno at the Institut für Philosophie; he wrote a post-doctoral thesis entitled *Kierkegaards Angriff auf die Spekulation* [Kierkegaard's attack on speculation] (Frankfurt am Main: Suhrkamp, 1967) and in 1962 was appointed to a professorship at the Pädagogische Hochschule Lüneburg. He is cited in the publication with the words 'German version after a translation by Hermann Schweppenhäuser'.

[he has written ...]: handwritten addition not in the original letter.

lectures on the sociology of music: *Einleitung in die Musiksoziologie: Zwölf theoretische Vorlesungen* was published on 16 November 1962; *Introduction to the Sociology of Music: Twelve Theoretical Lectures*, New York: Continuum, [1967] 1989.

the good old Kierkegaard book: *Kierkegaard: Konstruktion des Ästhetischen, mit einer Beilage. Neu, um die Beilage erweiterte Ausgabe* was published on 13 October 1962. *Kierkegaard: Construction of the Aesthetic*, ed. and trans. Robert Hullot-Kentor, Minneapolis: University of Minnesota Press, c. 1989.

translated into Italian: an enquiry was made by an Italian publisher early in 1960, and a licence granted in 1983.

Vienna ... Hotel Erzherzog Rainer: on the Wiedener Hauptstraße in the fourth district.

183 Kracauer to Adorno
New York, 7.6.1962

498 Westend Avenue
New York 24, N.Y.
June 7, 1962

Dear Teddie,

Excuse the air-letter, but today I must be brief and should like to thank you right away for your kind letter. We are looking forward to seeing you again. In order that we can both arrange things in good order, I should like to make the following request, which will help both of us to arrange things properly: we shall be coming in from Hamburg (God willing – it depends on the flight) on Wednesday 18 July, arriving at the Hotel Frankfurter Hof in the early afternoon (so that, in principle, even the evening of that day would be possible) and go on to Munich on Saturday 21 July. May I suggest that you should leave a message at the Frankfurter Hof for me to find when we arrive on 18 July to let us know when the two of you would be free to see us? Please make a note of this. Then I could arrange the other things I have to do around this – time is short, after all. I know very well how overburdened you yourself are. (By the way, will Horkheimer be available over this period?) You write that you would have more free time in September. I don't think that I can make it then, but if another possibility were to come up in early September I should of course write to Frankfurt to let you know.

I shall be happy to see the student who is working on the sociology of film – but for this she would need to read my *Theory of Film* – and that brings me to Frau A., of whom I know through direct communication with her. She has corresponded with me about her work, and I sent her some material and answered her questions to the best of my ability. She wrote to me at the beginning of this year to say that she had managed to obtain *Theory of Film* (and my other books) with no difficulty. This should also be possible for the sociology of film girl. What seems best to me is for her to get in touch with Frau A. about this. In the meantime, I myself have written to Frau A. to say that I shall be coming to Frankfurt and should like to see her.

I am glad to hear what you wrote to me about the latest reactions to *Ginster*. Some people here who were reading the book for the first time reacted in a similar way. (The love letter which Alban Berg wrote to me about *Ginster* is one of my greatest treasures.) I entirely share your views about publishing it – under my own name, of course. Well, in spite of all you say, the quantity of your publications is very impressive indeed. We will talk later on about the translation problem and many other matters. I shall probably give you the *Preliminary Statement* about my book on history when I am in Frankfurt.

Warmest regards to both of you from both of us, and *à bientôt*,
Yours,
Friedel

Wonderful that the Kierkegaard is coming out again!

Original: typescript with handwritten postscript; Theodor W. Adorno Archiv, Frankfurt am Main.

the love letter which Alban Berg wrote to me about Ginster: Alban Berg to Kracauer, 31 December 1928: 'I could not have had a better end to this year, dear Herr Kracauer, than with reading your *Ginster*. I had to postpone it – initially because of an urgent piece of work, then because of illness. Now, though, that I have read – or, rather, devoured – this book, I cannot find the right words to express my glowing enthusiasm for it. Indeed, this book is not only a literary masterpiece but also a *document humain* in the truest sense of the word, hence a wholly successful synthesis of the two – something which has always seemed to me to be the ideal condition of a work of art, but something which I think has been achieved only in the rarest instances. *You* have achieved this in *Ginster* – and for this I can only thank you from an overflowing heart, both as a human being and as an artist! With most sincere greetings to you as a colleague, I remain, Yours, Alban Berg' (Kracauer papers, Deutsches Literaturarchiv, Marbach).

Preliminary Statement: see letter no. 205.

184 Adorno to Kracauer

Frankfurt am Main, 22.6.1962

PROF. DR. THEODOR W. ADORNO

FRANKFURT AM MAIN 22 June 1962
KETTENHOFWEG 123

Dear Friedel,

Many thanks for your letter – it was forwarded to me in Vienna, where we spent the Whitsun holidays, unfortunately overshadowed in a rather painful way by an accident which Gretel suffered – as a result of a fall in the Wachau she sprained both ankles so badly that she had to stay in bed for two weeks; in spite of that it was a rich and remarkable time.

Because of my timetable it transpires that the 19th is definitely out and the 18th probably so (examinations and a faculty meeting). The evening of the 20th (Friday) looks like much the best prospect, and I should be grateful if the two of you could reserve it and come to us for supper. Before that I really ought to put my students Frau A. and Frau B. on to you, if that would not be too much of an imposition; if you would rather have some peace, please let me know immediately, and I shall then keep both of them – the thick-set one and the athletic one – well away from you. By the way, I shall tell Frau B. to get in touch with Frau A. about the *Theory of Film.* Incidentally, would it be possible for you to bring along a copy of your old work on Simmel for a third – and in every respect more rewarding – student?

I thought that Rowohlt wanted to publish *Ginster.* Since we talked about it, a few years have gone by and I haven't heard any more about it. By its nature the book would, of course, be most suitable for Suhrkamp, and if you like I can put a word in there at any time. I am just putting the finishing touches to the lectures on the sociology of music, which Suhrkamp wants to bring out as a kind of treatise.

Do drop us a line soon about the Friday.

Much love to you and Lili from us both,

Your old

Teddie

Original: typescript with printed letterhead and handwritten addition; Siegfried Kracauer papers, Deutsches Literaturarchiv, Marbach am Neckar.

185 Kracauer to Adorno
New York, 26.6.1962

498 Westend Avenue
New York 24, N.Y.
June 26, 1962

Dear Teddie,

Just a brief word to let you know that the evening of Friday 20 July will suit us very well indeed for dinner with you. *We look forward* – we are already looking forward to spending time with you and talking. I shall probably ring you beforehand about the time and such. I shall make an appointment with Frau A. Quite separately from this, I should very much like to come to the Institute on Thursday or Friday and see what is going on there. Could that be arranged? And couldn't I simply see Frau B. there? In addition, I have to see an old friend in Frankfurt whose health is not good (Selmar Spier). Perhaps an appointment with Horkheimer might also be possible. If anything relating to this happens to occur to you, please leave a note for me at the Frankfurter Hof, where we shall be arriving from Hamburg during the afternoon of 18 July. I have already tried to track down the work on Simmel for you but did not find it. It must be buried somewhere or other. I shall have another look, but the chances of finding it are minimal. In its place, though, I am bringing you something old which is sure to amuse you; it is all ready and waiting.

We were concerned about poor Gretel's (fortunately minor) accident; we hope that she is back on her feet and in good order.

We shall discuss everything else – the greater part – face to face. See you very soon – and warmest greetings to you both.

Yours,

Original: typescript; Siegfried Kracauer papers, Deutsches Literaturarchiv, Marbach am Neckar.

ring you beforehand: Kracauer uses a Berlin dialect expression here.

Selmar Spier: see letter no. 49. In the year before his last meeting with Kracauer, Selmar Spier published *Vor 1914: Erinnerungen an Frankfurt, geschrieben in Israel* (Frankfurt am Main: Kramer, 1961). The publication was instigated by the mayor of Frankfurt, Walter Leiske (1889–1971), as Spier mentions in the preface (p. 7). In a note he draws the following portrait of Kracauer (pp. 123f.): 'Dr Siegfried Kracauer, born in Frankfurt, nephew of the historian Isidor Kracauer; after completing his studies (architecture, philosophy, sociology) he became an editor on the *Frankfurter Zeitung* (1920–33) in Frankfurt and Berlin. In 1933 he was forced to emigrate. He now lives in New York as an author and consultant to academic institutions. Kr. was among the first to observe the metamorphosis of civilization in its traditional form into a mass society and described the phenomena associated with this process in the feuilleton of the *Frankfurter Zeitung* under the editorship of Benno Reifenberg. A list of his books and other writings can be found in the

1959 reprint by the Verlag für Demoskopie (Bonn) of his study *Die Angestellten*, dedicated to Reifenberg, which appeared in the F.Z. and attracted considerable attention. Oxford University Press is scheduled to publish a new work by Kracauer (who nowadays writes in English), *Theory of Film – The Redemption of Physical Reality*.'

186 Kracauer to Adorno

Kandersteg, 22.8.1962

HOTEL SCHWEIZERHOF
KANDERSTEG

August 22, 1962

Dear Teddie,

We should like to thank you both once again for the lovely evening at your place, which we look back on with great pleasure. We take the fact that dear Gretel held up until the end, although she was not feeling at all well, as a sign that she enjoyed it too. We hope that she will make a good recovery in Sils.

I was delighted with your critique of Brecht in *Zur Dialektik des Engagements*. It is striking – and it comes at exactly the right time, while Brecht is in vogue – i.e. is starting to be misunderstood in all quarters. My criticism of the pre-war Brecht took the same direction. Incidentally, he seems to have been attracted to rustic wisdom at a very early stage. Once (I think it was in 1931), when a big party of us were sitting together until late into the night in the Café Kurfürstendamm after the première of Dovzhenko's *Earth*, a vehement discussion broke out between Brecht and myself about this film, which mythologizes peasant life in such a way as to put it beyond any kind of dialectic. I said something to this effect, while Brecht earnestly defended the close-ups of the apples gleaming in the sunlight and the villagers' faces glowing with a warmth from within. If I remember rightly, Bloch sided with me then. (It occurs to me that wisdom doesn't have to be rustic; the genuine kind has its own intrinsic dialectic.)

It is kind of you to be prepared to talk to Unseld (Suhrkamp Verlag) about my *Ginster* and my Collected Essays. (In parenthesis, Bloch is willing to do something similar.) I am firmly convinced that both these books could be of some significance in Germany today. In the meantime, I have been brooding a lot over my project concerning history, but it is not yet rounded – or, rather, angular – enough. Some day I should like to have a long conversation with Enzensberger, whose *Einzelheiten* I have been reading. It's worth taking the trouble – but he still has a lot to learn (and some things to unlearn).

From 28 August we shall be in Zurich (Hotel Eicher, Claridenstraße) for another 5 to 6 days (at least). Then from 10 September we shall be in Paris, probably until the very end of the month (Grand Hotel du Louvre, Place du Théâtre Français, Paris 1er).

Warmest regards and best wishes to you both from Lili and me,

Friedel

Please give the Glücks our best wishes if you happen to see them. I still remember him well and should be delighted to see him again.

Original: MS with printed letterhead; Theodor W. Adorno Archiv, Frankfurt am Main.

Your critique of Brecht in Zur Dialektik des Engagements: in *Die Neue Rundschau*, no. 1, 1962; broadcast in March 1962 as a radio talk with the title 'Engagement und künstlerische Autonomie' (see Adorno, GS 11, pp. 409–30, 699). According to Adorno, Brecht fails to understand 'the essential nature of capitalism to which the parable addresses itself ... On the opposite side, a political naivety corresponds to this which only helps the victim of Brecht's attack to grin at the thought that you would have nothing to fear from such foolish enemies' (ibid., p. 417); 'Brecht's sound' turns itself into 'the echo of archaic social circumstances which are irretrievably gone' (ibid., p. 422).

Dovzhenko's Earth: in his film *Earth* (*Zemlya*, 1930), the Soviet director and author Aleksandr Dovzhenko (1894–1956) dramatized the conflict between a Ukrainian village collective and the owners of large estates. Kracauer's review was published on 24 July 1930 in the *Frankfurter Zeitung* ('Die Filmprüfstelle gegen einen Russenfilm'; see Kracauer, W 6.2, pp. 384–7). His criticism of the idealization of a rustic idyll set in the heart of nature reads: 'The same nature which Russia is assaulting at both an economic and a social level here creeps back into the house by a back door and is welcomed with the highest honours. Is religious faith suppressed, only to be replaced by a heavy-handed mythology? Indeed, the funeral procession with its songs and the apple-bough distantly recalls a troop of Happy Wanderers who, in their jolly sing-song, gushing enthusiasm for nature, harbour delusions of freedom and yet are more inhibited than many of those of an Orthodox persuasion' (p. 385).

Bloch sided with me then: Ernst Bloch welcomed Kracauer's review of *Earth* on the day after its appearance in the *Frankfurter Zeitung* (see Ernst Bloch to Kracauer, 25 July 1930, in Bloch, *Briefe* I, p. 341).

Enzensberger ... Einzelheiten: Hans Magnus Enzensberger (b. 1929), author; his book *Einzelheiten* was published on 28 June 1962. According to Enzensberger, the conversation which Kracauer wished to have with him did not come about.

Glücks: Gustav Glück (1902–1973), a banker from Vienna, who, in the 1920s, belonged to Walter Benjamin's circle of friends and in 1937/38 emigrated to Argentina via London. He and his wife, Elisabeth, returned to Europe; they lived in Frankfurt am Main until 1968, and subsequently in Vienna.

187 Adorno to Kracauer
Sils Maria, 26.8.1962

Sils Maria, Waldhaus, 26.VIII.1962

Dear Friedel,

I thank you for much for your letter. The Suhrkamp business I shall address immediately on my return next week. A pity that we won't see each other any more, but it is more complicated to get here from the Bernese Oberland than from Paris to New York. We had the most glorious weather the whole time; Gretel is much better – or was, until a relapse yesterday – and I am being lazy and am in high spirits, which will possibly be good for my work, too. I hope that you two have also had a relaxing time. Gretel sends her very best wishes! Much love, Your old

Teddie

You shall have the new edition of the Kierkegaard as soon as it comes out!

Original: MS, postcard: the 'Nietzsche-Haus' in Sils Maria; Siegfried Kracauer papers, Deutsches Literaturarchiv, Marbach am Neckar.

188 Adorno to Kracauer
Frankfurt am Main, 4.9.1962

PROF. DR. THEODOR W. ADORNO

FRANKFURT AM MAIN 4 September 1962
KETTENHOFWEG 123

Dear Friedel,

On my return here I spoke to Unseld straight away. The response was rather favourable – to my surprise, even more positive as regards the plans for the book of essays than in relation to *Ginster* – but even there I am rather more inclined to see things in a rosy hue, as I emphasized not only its quality but, above all – and this aspect is crucial for publishers nowadays – the fact that the book had not become dated after more than thirty years. I am therefore writing to you on the instructions of Dr Unseld, as it were, to ask you to get in contact with him about both projects – if possible, by return of post. The address is: Dr Siegfried Unseld, Suhrkamp Verlag, Frankfurt am Main, Untermainkai 13. The only thing which caused him to hesitate was the concern that, with these individual publications, he might jeopardize your plans for a collected edition, as you were involved in negotiations with other publishers about this. Referring to our conversation here, I tried to dispel these concerns, but it would be a good thing if, one more time, you too could drop Unseld a line about this. My own feeling is that it is easier, rather than more difficult, to approach plans for this kind of collected edition if the individual items are already available and have made a considerable impression.

For the book of essays, I was bold enough to suggest the title *Das Ornament der Masse*, after an old and memorable essay of yours. This title could, I think, do the book a great service; whether it is actually suitable for it depends, of course, on the choice of the essays.

Much love and best wishes, to Lili too, and also from Gretel, from

Your old

Teddie

Original: typescript with printed letterhead; Siegfried Kracauer papers, Deutsches Literaturarchiv, Marbach am Neckar.

an old and memorable essay of yours: 'Das Ornament der Masse', *Frankfurter Zeitung*, 9/10 June 1927 (see Kracauer, W 5, no. 358).

189 Kracauer to Adorno

Paris, 11.9.1962

LE GRAND HOTEL DU LOUVRE
PLACE DU THÉÂTRE FRANÇAIS
PARIS – 1er

September 11, 1962

Dear Teddie:

On our arrival from Zurich last night I found your kind letter waiting here – something which made us both very happy. To think that, in spite of all your many preoccupations and occupations, you spoke to Unseld straight away – and the considerable tact with which you did so! That is wonderful – and I mean it. Thank you *de tout coeur*. (The expression of emotions nowadays calls for Volapük, it seems.) By the way, many thanks too for the greetings from Sils. I should just like to add that your idea for the title, *Das Ornament der Masse*, is simply magnificent. The title would cover much of the very varied content.

On your advice I have written to Dr Unseld – entirely in accordance with the suggestions in your letter. I wrote that, if he writes and gives his approval, I shall send him the material for the volume of essays and *Ginster* as quickly as possible – both within easy reach. I *did not* send him the following information, as I am sharing it with you in confidence, or for careful use *à discrétion*: Herr Ledig-Rowohlt telephoned me abruptly in Zurich to say that, on second thoughts, he was considering a withdrawal from his contract with Oxford University Press for the German edition of my *Theory of Film*. How things will turn out is still up in the air. But there is now a strong possibility – which I would really welcome – that the German edition of this work, which is so important to me, will become free again – and, what is more, together with the German translation which I thoroughly corrected with so much torment, and which Rowohlt Verlag would naturally have to surrender to me in the case of a dissolution of our contract. With regard to this possibility, but without mentioning it, I have also written to Dr Unseld to say that we shall be staying in Europe (i.e. Paris) until around 28 September, and that, because of this, an opportunity for a face-to-face conversation may yet come about.

Oh, these tiresome affairs ... I am spending a lot of time poring over the organization of my new book, drafting plans, etc. I am pursuing a few really major ideas but can't quite get a grip on them yet; my ineptitude is nothing short of colossal. One of these has to do with the 'Dialectic of Progress' about which – so I read – you will soon be speaking. Do let me have the text. By the way, is my ancient review of your Kierkegaard still of topical interest to you? I have been doing a bit of work on Heidegger recently; what a magnificent instrument he has created for such a ridiculous entity as the creative force! Here in Paris I shall be seeing a whole string of people (or, in some cases, I *have* to see them) and working on the plans for the book.

Warmest regards and best wishes
from both of us to both of you,
Yours,

Friedel

Original: MS with printed letterhead: Theodor W. Adorno Archiv, Frankfurt am Main.

Volapük: an artificial language developed by Johann Martin Schleyer (1831–1912).

to Dr Unseld: Kracauer also wrote this letter, as mentioned above, on 11 September 1962:

> Dear Dr Unseld:
> On arriving in Paris last night I found a letter waiting for me from my friend Professor Adorno, in which he informed me that he had spoken to you about the plan for an edition of my collected essays and my *Ginster*. He wrote that you were interested in both projects, and that I should get in contact with you as soon as possible about this.
> I am doing so now, and with great pleasure. In fact, should you wish to publish the volume of essays and *Ginster*, I would for the time being postpone the idea of a complete edition, of which you were not in favour in the past. At least, as far as I am concerned this idea would be no obstacle.
> What would be the best way to proceed now? If you wish, I could put *Ginster* and the material for the volume of essays at your disposal very quickly – what is needed for both books is in Europe. About this material, I should add that its arrangement, etc., is altogether provisional. (By the way, I think that the title which Professor Adorno has suggested to you for the volume of essays, *Das Ornament der Masse*, is quite excellent.)
> Please write to me at your earliest convenience so that, should you agree, I can see about having the documents sent at once. For this reason, I am placing a certain degree

of emphasis on speed, as before our return to New York we (my wife and I) shall be in Paris, where I have various things to do, until about 28 September. This may even provide an opportunity for us to have a conversation in person. Such a thing would seem to me to be highly desirable for more reasons than one – always assuming, of course, that you are interested.

In the meantime, I remain,

Yours faithfully,

Siegfried Kracauer.

P.S. Allow me also to mention that Ernst Bloch, with whom we spent three days recently in Munich, would like to talk to you about my works – *Ginster*, the essays and prose pieces.

Dialectic of Progress: see the following letter.

my ancient review of your Kierkegaard: 'Der enthüllte Kierkegaard' [Kierkegaard revealed] (see letter no. 90).

190 Adorno to Kracauer
Frankfurt am Main, 12.9.1962

PROF. DR. THEODOR W. ADORNO

FRANKFURT AM MAIN 12 September 1962
KETTENHOFWEG 123

Dear Friedel,

Many thanks for your letter. I hope that everything will proceed as we would wish. I think that the idea of coming over here and dealing directly with Unseld is a very good one. I am only afraid that the next two weeks will be awkward. The big book fair takes place here at the end of September, and, from my experience, all the publishers in the world are so overburdened in the weeks before this circus that they scarcely have a free moment. It may happen, then, that Unseld, who is busy, in addition, with major projects of every possible kind, will not be able to free up any date at all, or that a conversation might take place when he is pressed for time – not the most desirable situation. My advice would be to ring him up (telephone number: 2 10 76 or 2 35 06) and arrange something with him for *after* the book fair if possible. I think that postponing your return for a few days would not do too much harm in view of the importance of the matter in question here. I myself am here until 4 October, have a television recording in Baden-Baden on the 5th, and in all probability will be going on to France (Alsace and Burgundy) for a few days immediately after that. It would be nice, then, if you could arrange things so that you could be here *before* the 4th, although of course you should not make your negotiations with Unseld dependent on my timetable. If I were you, I would under no circumstances raise the matter of the film book – nor would I mention anything about Herr Ledig's (most peculiar) behaviour or include the book as part of the negotiations at present. Such a refusal – one that any author, of course, may experience at any stage – is not an ideal starting point for negotiations, and on the other hand I would not overburden my dealings with Unseld with suggestions which are far too extensive in scope. Once the book of essays and *Ginster* are there, the business of the *Theory of Film* will fall into place by itself – of that I have no doubt whatsoever. By its nature the book (which does, admittedly, require a certain amount of expenditure on its external appearance) would be just the thing for Fischer – where, of course, my own *Getreue Korrepetitor* is being published (it has already gone to press). It's just that things have become so complicated there because of the fact that my friend Hirsch has just stepped down as director of the firm, and the production plans for next spring, too, have obviously become so restricted that I would rather not initiate any negotiations there at the moment. If the film theory plan should, at a somewhat later stage, run up against any difficulties with Suhrkamp contrary to expectations (Unseld has a certain resistance to very expensive books – understandable after his experiences with the all too pretentious *Dreigroschenbuch*), I could envisage a few other possibilities offering themselves. But it is, of course, much too soon to talk about that.

The piece of work on progress – which, by the way, will quite definitely be included in my new book – exists, for the time being, only in my head – though with some degree of clarity. It will be committed to paper in October – and then I shall be delighted to send you a carbon copy straight away.

Warmest greetings and much love to you both, from Gretel (who is still limping) too,

Your old

Teddie

Original: typescript with handwritten corrections; Siegfried Kracauer papers, Deutsches Literaturarchiv, Marbach am Neckar.

big book fair: The Frankfurt Book Fair lasted from 20 to 25 September 1962; the Peace Prize of the Deutscher Buchhandel was awarded to Paul Tillich.

a television recording in Baden-Baden on the 5th: on 5 October 1962, Südwestfunk Baden-Baden advertised a discussion on the topic of 'Public Relations – Information oder verkappte Werbung?' [Public relations – information or advertising in disguise?]; besides Adorno the participants were Dieter Göbel (moderator), Albert Oeckel (union official) and Carl Wingenroth (Lufthansa); the programme was broadcast on 8 October 1962 by ZDF [Zweites deutsches Fernsehen] (Theodor W. Adorno Archiv).

my friend Hirsch: Rudolf Hirsch (1905–1996), reader and director of the firm, retired from S. Fischer Verlag on 1 October 1962.

the all too pretentious Dreigroschenbuch: *Bertolt Brechts Dreigroschenbuch: Texte, Materialien, Dokumente*, ed. Siegfried Unseld, was published in 1960 in a de luxe edition (with illustrations, in a slipcase, and with a gramophone record included). The print run of a special edition as 'Suhrkamp Hausbuch [book of the year] 1960' ran to 40,000 copies. Together with Bertolt Brecht's writings and the work by John Gay which inspired them, the volume contained texts about the *Dreigroschenoper*, including a passage by Adorno from the *Frankfurter Opern- und Konzertkritik* of December 1928 entitled 'Zur Frankfurter Aufführung der "Dreigroschenoper"' and 'Zur Dreigroschenoper' (see Adorno, GS 19, pp. 137f., and GS 18, pp. 535–40), and also Kracauer's 'Der Prozeß um die Dreigroschenoper: Einige nachträgliche Randbemerkungen' (see Kracauer, W 6.2, pp. 418–23).

The piece of work on progress … in my new book: the material here pertaining to the complex of ideas in the *Dialektische Meditationen* became the paper 'Dialektik des Fortschritts', which Adorno presented at the seventh Deutscher Kongress für Philosophie in Münster on 22 October 1962. It was published in *Argumentationen: Festschrift für Josef König*, ed. Harald Delius and Günther Patzig, Göttingen: Vandenhoeck & Ruprecht, 1964, and finally under the title 'Fortschritt' in *Stichworte* (1969; see Adorno, GS 210.2, pp. 617–38, 841).

191 Kracauer to Adorno

Paris, 16.9.1962

LE GRAND HOTEL DU LOUVRE
PLACE DU THÉÂTRE FRANÇAIS
PARIS – 1er

Sept. 16, 1962

Dear Teddie,

Thank you very much for your kind and most considerate letter. In the meantime, Dr Unseld has sent me a very friendly reply relating to his conversation with you. Because of the book fair, which is not over for him even when it comes to an end, he cannot as yet put himself on standby for a personal meeting. There would be little sense in it for either party as long as he has not had a look at my material. He expects the items, which I will send him, by the end of September. In the meantime, he has already obtained *Ginster*. For precisely those compelling reasons which you cite, I have not said anything to him about the *Filmtheorie* and shall not do so in the future.

The difficulty with this book, by the way, has arisen from the fact that the necessary changes to many film titles and the scrupulous German editing of the apparatus – notes, bibliography, index – will result in extra costs, of which Herr Ledig claims he has only now become aware. He says that he simply cannot absorb them – but, if I would like a paperback edition without all these frills, it would still be all right with him. This, though, is obviously no more than a rearguard action on his part. I shall only send him a definite answer from New York. The business with Rowohlt has left us completely cold; one way or another, the book will certainly be coming out in Germany. And didn't you promise me an essay about it? I don't need to tell you that I am already excited about it.

We shall definitely not be flying back before 28 September – perhaps not until 1 or 2 October. Unfortunately, I am urgently needed in New York, where in the first two weeks I shall have to work through a fair-sized backlog. (If anything should come of the business with Unseld, I could perhaps come over for a few days if absolutely necessary – but this is a fantasy.)

Have a lovely time, both of you, in Alsace or Burgundy. We were actually planning to go there too, but then preferred to stay in Zurich because of the chance to brood over history. I must measure out my sightseeing in careful doses.

Write back soon. All our good wishes to our poor, still limping Gretel – and warmest greetings to you both from Lili and me,

Yours,

Friedel

Original: manuscript with printed letterhead; Theodor W. Adorno Archiv, Frankfurt am Main.

Dr Unseld has sent me a very friendly reply: in a letter of 13 September 1962, Siegfried Unseld expressed his interest in a collection of essays and a new edition of *Ginster*, about which he wrote to Kracauer: 'I have already ordered *Ginster* from the library here. The book has a certain history of its own for me, as it was in Suhrkamp's private library in Königstein. I took it on my visits to the invalid, during which there were increasingly long breaks which I could use for reading; Suhrkamp, however, never gave it to me to take home. I should like to read it again now in connection with your request' (Archiv der Peter Suhrkamp Stiftung an der Johann Wolfgang Goethe-Universität).

192 Adorno to Kracauer
Frankfurt am Main, 4.10.1962

PROF. DR. THEODOR W. ADORNO

FRANKFURT AM MAIN 4 October 1962
KETTENHOFWEG 123

Dear Friedel,

Many thanks for your letter. I would have answered long ago, as I had hoped to talk to Unseld before now, but I am not seeing him until tomorrow; then I am going away for a week, and so I would at least prefer not to let an inappropriate break intervene.

By the way, as far as the film book is concerned, the difficulties – the picture section and the increase in costs – should also have a positive side, i.e. making the book a possibility for so-called art publishers. Perhaps I may soon be able to have something more concrete to write to you about this.

Meanwhile I have been making quite good progress with my great work, although it has got completely out of hand and, to a great extent, still represents a draft which still needs organizing and is also very extensive in its scope. But at least I shall not be without something to work *on.* Two of the books on music, the *Einleitung in die Musiksoziologie* (the texts of the lectures which I gave here) and the *Getreue Korrepetitor*, have gone to press in the meantime. However, in the case of the latter, because of copyright difficulties I had to do without the gramophone record, which would have been very useful.

I hope that you both had a good flight. Max also flew over yesterday. Will you be seeing him, I wonder? Incidentally, I don't think that I told you that Horkheimer and I, for increasingly serious reasons, have completely broken with Leo Löwenthal. It is always better if people know such things.

Warmest greetings to you both, from Gretel too,

Your old Teddie

Original: typescript; Siegfried Kracauer papers, Deutsches Literaturarchiv, Marbach am Neckar.

I am not seeing him until tomorrow: at their meeting on 4 October 1962, Adorno and Siegfried Unseld established the timetable for Adorno's forthcoming publications (see the memorandum in Adorno/Suhrkamp/Unseld, *Briefwechsel*, pp. 428f.).

because of copyright difficulties I had to do without the gramophone record: the official statement about the abandonment of the gramophone record contains the words: 'Gramophone records are only helpful when they unambiguously realize the ideas behind an analysis of an interpretation … Recordings of this nature, either of the works analysed or the conductor's interpretations cited, are extremely rare … While ordinary recordings may suffice for the most rudimentary kind of orientation, they are more likely to cause confusion when one examines subtler questions'; there follows a list of 'authentic recordings' (*Der getreue Korrepetitor*, note; see Adorno, GS 15, p. 402).

Max also flew over yesterday: Max Horkheimer wrote to Adorno on 6 October 1962 about the New York 'business' in which he had become involved, and on 20 October about his journey back to Zurich (see Adorno/Horkheimer, *Briefwechsel* IV, pp. 694, 697f.).

Horkheimer and I … have completely broken with Leo Löwenthal: the relationship between Leo Löwenthal and the representatives of the Institut für Sozialforschung who had returned to Frankfurt am Main was hampered by disagreements regarding Löwenthal's pension claims; these did not amount to a 'complete break'.

193 Kracauer to Adorno

New York, 12.10.1962

498 Westend Avenue
New York 24, N.Y.
October 12, 1962

Dear Teddie,

It was good to have your nice letter so soon after our return. (The flight was as usual, apart from an unforeseen stop in Montreal which delayed us by an hour and a half.) Unfortunately, we haven't heard anything from Horkheimer. He did tell us, though, when we talked in Frankfurt about his stay here, that his days in New York would all be full to overflowing with business matters. We hope that the two of you had a lovely time in Baden-Baden and afterwards. What is this great new work of yours actually about? I don't remember your talking to me about it. By the way, in Paris I read – quite by chance – your little article in *Frankfurter Allgemeine* in memory of Maria Proelss. A good article. I quite often met up with her and Hanni Rocco, with whom she lived. She was as impetuous and emotional as Rocco was fragile. I liked her, although we were not kindred spirits. Thanks for the three books from the Institute which I found waiting for me here. Since then I have read the one by Alfred Schmidt on the concept of nature in Marx's work and got a lot out of it (including material for my work). It is a really excellent study of the source material, with a restraint in the presentation which I esteem very highly. His exposition of his findings about the idea of utopia in Marx's writings is extraordinarily interesting – to me, at any rate.

I have still not sent a reply to Rowohlt. To put your kind allusion to this business on the right footing: what would create the costs which (he says) cannot be borne is not so much the illustrations as the extra research for a German edition which would be beyond reproach in scholarly terms. The following tasks would need to be carried out: (1) a search for the German trade titles of films marketed commercially in Germany; (2) the insertion of the original text of quotations from works in German, which would of course have to be located; (3) the finding of authorized German translations of such works in other languages (e.g. Proust, E. M. Forster) from which quotations are taken, and the insertion of these to correspond with the German edition; (4) a corresponding revision of the bibliography. (The German index presents no problem as long as it is confined to an index of names and titles.) Before I received Rowohlt's conditional refusal, the plan had been to have the editing of the film titles and everything pertaining to them done as an extra task by an employee of the publishers; Frau A. had already stated that she was prepared to undertake the actual literary research for an appropriate fee. Rowohlt reckons the total increase in the expenses which this would cause him at DM 10,000 (which is probably an overestimate). If I decide to do the necessary research myself, Rowohlt would undoubtedly publish the book – in a big paperback edition, of which a small proportion might be in hardback. But, as my life is becoming more and more of a race against time (and I have already lost valuable time over the corrections to the translation), I can scarcely force myself to make this decision (quite apart from the fact that I am opposed to Rowohlt's solution of a paperback edition) – so it will probably result in the book being up for grabs again.

Please excuse these boring details, which I am sharing with you only because you appear to see an opportunity with an art publisher. I think that an art publisher would be an excellent idea. Whether this possibility is feasible or not, a new publisher would in any case be cheaper, because he would have received the revised translation (which lacks only the notes at present). (Ledig claims that he has paid DM 3,500 for the translation; it goes without saying, we should note in passing, that one cannot expect to receive a proper version for so little.) There is still the question of research for some other publisher. I could give a bit of help with this without wasting too much time, so that the additional sum could probably be kept well below the DM 10,000 that Rowohlt calculated for this purpose. The whole business is really causing me heartache because it is completely out of my hands, and my thoughts and ideas are focused on very different matters. I have always been a cruel stepfather to my 'children'. However, I am prepared to acknowledge my responsibilities towards them (even if only for financial reasons).

Warmest greetings to you both from Lili and me,

Yours,

Friedel

Dr Unseld's decision will probably take longer to arrive, which of course is connected with the nature of the matter.

Original: typescript; Theodor W. Adorno Archiv, Frankfurt am Main.

Your little article … in memory of Maria Proelss: Adorno's obituary of the pianist appeared in the 28 September 1982 edition (see letter no. 4).

Hanni Rocco: see letter no. 8.

three books from the Institute: presumably further numbers of the *Frankfurter Beiträge zur Soziologie*.

Schmidt: Alfred Schmidt (1931–2012), philosopher and sociologist; he graduated from the Johann Wolfgang Goethe-Universität in 1960 (see below), and from 1972 was Jürgen Habermas's successor there in the chair formerly occupied by Max Horkheimer; he retired in 1999. Adorno and Max Horkheimer provided a 'preface' to his dissertation *Der Begriff der Natur in der Lehre von Marx*, Frankfurt am Main: Europäische Verlagsanstalt, 1962, pp. 7f. Kracauer frequently quotes from this work in his *History*.

194 Adorno to Kracauer
Frankfurt am Main, 22.10.1962

PROF. DR. THEODOR W. ADORNO

FRANKFURT AM MAIN 22 October 1962
KETTENHOFWEG 123

Dear Friedel,

Many thanks for your letter.

Just a few words for now on the subject of your book. Last Wednesday I was in Mannheim for a discussion on questions relating to film, in connection with the Modern Film Week there. You may perhaps not know that I am a close friend of the theorist and producer Axel Kluge, who has just published a most remarkable book. Through him I got to know Eno Patalas, with whom, until then, I had only corresponded. I am sure that his name is familiar to you; I think that he once had some dealings with you about a pre-publication excerpt from your book. He belongs to the by no means limited number of those who, without having formally studied with me, regard themselves as students of mine. He is now publishing a series of books, and incidentally he had already been informed that there were certain problems with Rowohlt about the publication of your book. He would, of course, have a burning interest in it. I think it would be very wise – and, take my word for it, you would have nothing to lose in the slightest by doing so – for you to get in touch with him straight away about the matter. The address is: 8 Munich 13, Mittermayrstrasse 10. It would, of course, be important for the German translation really to represent a text *by you*, and you would also have to be absolutely clear about the alleged extra costs to be incurred, as everyone is worried about expenses. By the way, my instinct tells me that a major part of the work required could certainly be done by you yourself – if there really is any, and this is not just an excuse. In any case I should follow this up, as it would be good if your works could be published in an intellectual/humane context from the outset. Everything that is decent in German film nowadays is more and more closely connected with the Oberhausen Group, and I don't blame them for not being able to say exactly what they want – they know exactly what they *don't* want, and Spinoza is right in saying that the false is an indication of the true.

I am going to Münster today for the philosophers' congress. There is indeed such a thing; I recall your old essay on congresses – but I must go, because I myself have to say my piece there (on the concept of progress, and therefore something to do with the philosophy of history, which should interest you). It fits into the context of my book on dialectics. You will soon get to see it – and, before that, the sociology of music, of which I am just reading the page proofs.

In the meantime, a new book by Ernst Bloch has just come out, *Verfremdungen*, which once again includes everything – even the truth; but it is devalued by the very fact that it *does* include absolutely everything. It is like an illustrated guide to philosophy.

Much love to you both, from Gretel too – who, unfortunately, is recovering only very slowly –

from your old

Teddie

Original: typescript; Siegfried Kracauer papers, Deutsches Literaturarchiv, Marbach am Neckar.

22 October 1962: this appears as '1952' in the letter (a typing error).

in Mannheim for a discussion on questions relating to film: the participants on 17 October 1962 at the International Film Week were Richard Erny, Alexander Kluge, Edgar Reitz, Joseph Rovan, Haro Senft and Hans-Rolf Strobel (see Adorno/Horkheimer, *Briefwechsel* IV, p. 267, note).

Kluge ... a most remarkable book: Alexander Kluge (b. 1932), jurist, film director and producer, author and media expert; for Adorno's recommendation, see *Lebensläufe*, Stuttgart: Henry Goverts, 1962.

Patalas: Enno Patalas (1929–2018), film expert, critic and curator. He published the two volumes of *Spectaculum: Texte moderner Filme* with Suhrkamp in 1961 and 1964.

Oberhausen Group: in the 'Oberhausener Manifest' of 28 February 1962 the rising generation of film-makers in the Federal Republic of Germany proclaimed: 'The old film is dead. We believe in the new one' (see *Geschichte des deutschen Films*, ed. Wolfgang Jacobsen, Anton Kaes and Hans Helmut Prinzler, 2nd edn, Stuttgart: Carl Ernst Poeschel, 2004, p. 218). Alexander Kluge acted as head of the 'Oberhausen Group'.

Spinoza is right in saying that the false is an indication of the true: 'est enim verum index sui et falsi' / 'For the true is its own touchstone and that of the false' (Spinoza to Albert Burgh, early in 1676; see *Spinoza: The Letters*, trans. Samuel Shirley, Indianapolis: Hacket, c1995.

about congresses: 'Der Kongreß', *Frankfurter Zeitung*, 29 July 1925 (see Kracauer, W no. 249; see letter no. 190).

a new book by Ernst Bloch: Ernst Bloch's *Verfremdungen* I was published on 7 September 1962.

195 Kracauer to Adorno
New York, 27.10.1962

498 Westend Avenue
New York 24, N.Y.
October 27, 1962

Dear Teddie,

I find it very touching – and I mean it, really, as one would inevitably add here – that, in the midst of your many activities and your travelling to and fro, you have taken the time to write so promptly and, what is more, about the tiresome business of the book. Who is your friend Axel Kluge? I have never heard of him, *hélas.* You know that I am very keen to read your Münster lecture *Dialektik des Fortschritts* – for reasons which you know. (I myself have a whole series of notes on the concept of progress, parts of which I shall be using for my book on history.)

As to the film book – I mean *Theory of Film*. It seems as if there is a kind of telepathic sympathy operating between us: about a week before your letter arrived I had made up my mind to carry out the necessary 'research' for the German edition myself. This means a major sacrifice of time on my part, but I can see no other way out. I have already made a start on it – and fortunately it turns out that you were quite right: the sacrifice of time, as is already clear, will be far less great than I had feared. As for the quotations from German books and German translations of important works in other languages (e.g. Proust or E. M. Forster) I shall probably have to call on a student in Germany for help – in return for a fee, naturally. Perhaps Frau A. may be prepared to do this; if not, may I ask you for the address of a willing student? (By the way, the German works quoted also include *Komponieren für den Film*.)

Oxford Press will now deal with Herr Ledig-Rowohlt about the consequences arising for him from my taking over the research. I almost wish that the negotiations would break down and he would have to give me back the manuscript which I corrected. (I made the corrections as well as I could, so that the German text really can stand as the authorized one now.) Oxford Press already knows of a German and a Swiss publishing house that are interested in the book. This very day I received a letter from Frau A. telling me of interest on the part of a certain Luchterhand Verlag. (The world is obviously teeming with publishers – as many as the stars in the sky.) And you have written to me about Herr Patalas – many thanks. I know Patalas and Ulrich Gregor from the 1958 Venice Biennale, where we had many conversations with one another. In principle, I should be quite content with him. But first the Rowohlt affair has to be settled one way or another.

Because of the 'research' – if research it can be called! – I can't, of course, get on with my own work. I am like a fish out of water. And, with all the explanations arising from your kind intervention in my literary fate, I haven't even got around to writing the most important thing: that Lili and I are very worried that dear Gretel has been struggling for so long with that sad business of hers. What is the explanation? We should be glad of more detailed information about it. For the time being, we send our most fervent wishes for the speedy (and altogether undialectic) progress of her recovery – and warmest greetings to both of you from both of us.

Yours,

Friedel

If you see the Glücks, please give them our regards. Horkheimer, unfortunately, has not been in contact.

Original: typescript with handwritten postscript; Theodor W. Adorno Archiv, Frankfurt am Main.

Komponieren für den Film: Kracauer quotes from *Komponieren für den Film* in six places.

Gregor: Ulrich Gregor (b. 1932), film historian; with Enno Patalas he wrote *Geschichte des Films*, Gütersloh: S. Mohn, 1962.

1958 Venice Biennale: see letter no. 168.

196 Adorno to Kracauer
Frankfurt am Main, 31.10.1962

PROF. DR. THEODOR W. ADORNO

FRANKFURT AM MAIN 31 October 1962
KETTENHOFWEG 123

Dear Friedel,

This is just to tell you that yesterday, at my instigation, you were elected as a corresponding member of the Deutsche Gesellschaft für Soziologie. I would have preferred it had they made you an honorary member on account of your work; the only reason why this was not possible was because the institution of honorary membership of the DGS simply does not exist. However, the letter which Stammer, the president of the society, is writing to you will no doubt be everything that is right and proper.

In the meantime, a man from Luchterhand has also been in contact with me about the *Filmtheorie*. I have asked him to get in touch with you directly, mentioning my name. So, as you see, things are moving on all sides.

Warmest greetings to both of you, from Gretel too,

Your old

Teddie

I have just received your letter, the contents of which partly overlap with my own words. Axel Kluge is a young and enormously gifted person, comparable in a certain way with Enzensberger. A jurist by training, he gave up the prospect of a brilliant career (at the age of just 27 he could have become a government representative on the senate of a great university) to devote himself to his literary works and especially those on film. He is the real theorist within the so-called Oberhausen film group and has had exceptional success with *Lebensläufe*, a most remarkable prose work. The title of the book he is working on at present may perhaps betray to you the secret of what manner of man he is: *Anwesenheitsliste bei einer Beerdigung* [List of those present at a burial].

Warmest greetings

Original: typescript; Siegfried Kracauer papers, Deutsches Literaturarchiv, Marbach am Neckar.

Stammer: Otto Stammer (1900–1978), sociologist; Kracauer conveyed his acceptance of the election in a letter of 28 November 1962 (Kracauer papers, Deutsches Literaturarchiv, Marbach).

a jurist by training: Alexander Kluge gained his doctorate in 1956 with a thesis on autonomy in the universities; he was legal adviser to the Institute for Social Research.

Anwesenheitsliste bei einer Beerdigung: the title appears in the new edition: Alexander Kluge, *Lebensläufe: Anwesenheitsliste bei einer Beerdigung*; Neubearbeitung der *Lebensläufe* mit wesentlichen Änderungen [Curricula vitae: list of those present at a burial: new edition of *Curricula vitae* with significant changes], Frankfurt am Main: Suhrkamp, 1974.

a man from Luchterhand: Frank Benseler (b. 1929), jurist, sociologist and publisher's reader for sociology at Luchterhand Verlag from 1962 onwards and its reader in chief from 1967; appointed in 1972 to the chair in philosophy at the Gesamthochschule Paderborn. The initiative is documented: Deutsches Literaturarchiv, Marbach, A: Luchterhand Verlag / Benseler / unrealized projects.

197 Kracauer to Adorno

New York, 4.11.1962

498 Westend Avenue
New York 24, N.Y.
November 4, 1962

Dear Teddie,

Just a brief word of thanks for now for the honour which you spontaneously arranged. It is precious to me because it comes from you. I am, in fact, quite unaccustomed to such things; but one can't help being pleased with it – just a bit. (Recently the Hamburger Gesellschaft für Filmkunde elected me as a member – something to mention in this context.)

It was meet and right of you to advise Luchterhand to get in touch with me. Before that we must await the outcome of Herr Ledig's new negotiations with the Oxford Press in London – for which I gave precise instructions. I hope to have completed my own 'research' for the German edition in 8–10 days; I worked like mad on it, driven by an urge to get back to my book on history. There may be a very small remnant which can only be carried out in Germany. Perhaps Frau A. will do this. If she has no time, I might ask you, in due course, for the name of a student.

How was the conference in Münster? Once again: your *Dialektik des Fortschritts* is important to me. (I can roughly piece together Karl Löwith's views on progress from what I know of him.)

I know something about the Oberhausen group – though not Axel Kluge – partly from Amos Vogel, who comes over every year as one of the judges for the prize.

I am delighted, dear Teddie, that our correspondence is blossoming (and, God knows, not because of the book).

You haven't written anything at all about Gretel. We hope that she is fully mobile once more.

Warmest greetings to you both from Lili and your

Friedel

Original: typescript; Theodor W. Adorno Archiv, Frankfurt am Main.

Hamburger Gesellschaft für Filmkunde: the Hamburg Society for Film Studies was founded in 1952.

Karl Löwith's views on progress: the philosopher Karl Löwith (1897–1973) gave the second keynote paper alongside Adorno (see 'Das Verhängnis des Fortschritts', in *Die Philosophie und die Frage nach dem Fortschritt*, ed. Helmut Kuhn and Franz Wiedemann, Munich: Anton Pustet, 1964, pp. 15–29). Kracauer would have been familiar with the chapter entitled 'Fortschritt' in *Weltgeschichte und Heilsgeschehen*; the book was first published in 1949 by the University of Chicago Press (during his exile in America, Löwith taught at the New School for Social Research).

Vogel: Amos Vogel (1921–2012), an expert in film studies from Vienna who went into exile in the USA in 1939; he founded the film club Cinema 16 in New York.

198 Adorno to Kracauer
Frankfurt am Main, 15.11.1962

PROF. DR. THEODOR W. ADORNO

FRANKFURT AM MAIN 15 November 1962
KETTENHOFWEG 123

Dear Friedel,

I am sending you herewith (under separate cover) my work on progress, in a third version which has been substantially altered in response to the criticism of the Münster version. Before the piece is finally published – as a chapter of my *Dialektische Meditationen*, which has made considerable progress in the meantime – I shall certainly be making some further changes, but I think that it can already stand as it is. As, in the insane pressure of the beginning of the semester, I couldn't even glance through the text again, I ask you to excuse any typing errors and, where they affect the meaning in some way, to hazard a guess at the right one. And please be so kind as to send the manuscript back to me at your earliest convenience – the reason being that I still don't regard it as the final version.

Has anything happened in the meantime about the affair of your book? Have you heard from Patalas, or from Luchterhand? Frau A. will certainly seek out for you the things that can only be found here; I can understand that you would like to let her have the fun of doing so, although Fräulein B. is much more intelligent and capable – but I myself harbour a certain grudge against Frau A. in my heart of hearts for not making the work about you anything remotely like what it might have been. … I just give her great credit for having had the idea at all. Perhaps someone will come along to perform in a sublime fashion the task which she carried out in such a pedestrian way.

You will be receiving the *Musiksoziologie* in the next few days. I am very much tied up with the corrections to the *Getreue Korrepetitor*, but am nevertheless making very good progress with the chapter on the philosophy of language in the dialectics book.

Much love to you and Lili – also from Gretel, who really is feeling much better now.

Your old
Teddie

Original: typescript with printed letterhead; Siegfried Kracauer papers, Deutsches Literaturarchiv, Marbach am Neckar.

chapter on the philosophy of language: i.e. *Jargon der Eigentlichkeit*.

199 Kracauer to Adorno
New York, 27.11.1962

498 Westend Avenue
New York 24, N.Y.
November 27, 1962

Dear Teddie,

Many thanks for your kind letter and the two items which you sent. I have studied your manuscript on progress with great care. I am constantly amazed at the intellectual energy and subtlety with which you track down the fallacies of the philosophy of identity – not to speak of those of philosophy – in all their hiding places, and, as you are equally at home in the realm of aesthetics in a way that hardly anyone else is, you can fully include the aesthetic dimension. (The passage about progress in art is good.) Perhaps one of your main tasks is to carry out the abolition of philosophy by philosophical means. (In this connection, by the way, the end of philosophy in Hellenism and then under the Empire is of interest – and also the transition at that time from pure thought to (moral and religious) practice. Naturally the analogy should not be overburdened.) You have gone through and unambiguously pinned down all the antinomies involved in the *idea* of progress. I was delighted with your rehabilitation of Kant against Hegel. I don't know whether you can house-train Kant and make him ontologically quite fit for polite society; it is precisely his vacillations in this respect which strike me as especially profound. It might possibly be in accordance with your intentions not to cast out the ontological element so radically but to save it as a 'false representation' or 'disguise' in a double sense. What you say about decadence is very fine. I could go on like this for ages, but then something that should go on to become a dialogue in practice would remain a monologue. Just one more thing: my own ideas on this subject run – as it goes without saying – along the same lines but originate more from immersion in the empirical substance of history, and therefore take on a different colour. I should go in depth into something which, understandably, you could only hint at in the context of your own work – the unfathomable paradox (or dialectic) of the concept of time, i.e. chronological time. One thing is firmly established: I have taken from your work a great deal of importance for myself.

I am delighted with the resurrected book on Kierkegaard and the kindly reference in it to the 'distinguished visitor'. I shall have to postpone reading the supplement on love – oh, Agathe! Because of nothing but hindrances up till now I have only just got around to the history book, which is bad. First of all, I had to tackle the work for the German edition of the film book, and then over the last ten days I have had to compose a statement 'About the State of the Humanities in this Country'. (By the way, have you seen my statement 'Concerning History'? It doesn't, however, have anything to do with the content of the book in the making.) Now I am hoping to be able to stick with my own things again. We learnt recently that my old friend Selmar Spier had died in Israel. He went right back to my student days in Munich. We are glad that we saw him one last time in Frankfurt – the evening before our visit to the two of you.

Here follow a few more practical matters:

Deutsche Soziologische Gesellschaft: the letter from Professor Stammer which you announced has not yet arrived.

Suhrkamp Verlag: no news yet from Dr Unseld – and yet the publication of my Collected Prose (and my *Ginster*) is one of my most profound desires. If you should happen to have a good opportunity to put out feelers to Dr Unseld, that would, I think, be no bad thing. (But perhaps you may have already done so?)

Frau A.: she wrote to me just yesterday, saying that she will be glad to undertake the few things that need seeking out, and that you had already discussed the matter with her. Thank you. I shall send her the material, then. It mostly involves quotes from the German edition of Proust and the book by you and Eisler, *Komposition für den Film*. Both should certainly be easy for her to obtain. Yes, her thesis could have been more profound, but frankly, as regards profundity, the student (Frau B.) didn't entirely convince me either. One has to take what one can get. If there were someone who could better express what I meant and continue to mean – and what I myself am perhaps only just beginning to understand now, when it is almost too late – it would be a great joy, for me at any rate.

Luchterhand Verlag: Dr Frank Benseler, who edits the *Soziologische Texte* there, has written to me, saying that he is very interested in my *Theory of Film* (and my book on history). I thanked him and asked him to have patience until we have had a definite reply from Rowohlt. Here, then, is a possibility in the Rowohlt affair willy-nilly. What kind of publisher is this? Would you recommend them? Frau A. had already written to me to say that they were interested in me there – especially a Professor Maus of Marburg. (I am not making any agreements in advance about my unwritten book on history.)

Patalas: heard nothing from him.

We were really happy to hear that Gretel is finally back on form again. We have been so sorry for her with this stubborn disability. As you wish, I shall return your manuscript in the next few days as printed matter, air mail.

Warmest greetings from both of us to both of you,

Yours,

Friedel

Original: typescript; Theodor W. Adorno Archiv, Frankfurt am Main.

progress in art: see *Fortschritt* (Adorno, GS 10.2, pp. 632–5).

rehabilitation of Kant against Hegel: see ibid., pp. 623–5.

about decadence: see ibid., pp. 625–7.

the kindly reference in it to the 'distinguished visitor': the copy of the 1962 edition of *Kierkegaard* preserved among Kracauer's effects bears the handwritten dedication: 'To the distinguished visitor, his old Friedel, from his old Teddie / Frankfurt, October 1962'.

supplement on love … Agathe: the first supplement, *Kierkegaards Lehre von der Liebe* [Kierkegaard's doctrine of love], bears the dedication 'In memory of Agathe Calvelli-Adorno' (see Adorno, GS 2, p. 217).

'About the State of the Humanities': ten pages, Kracauer papers, Deutsches Literaturarchiv, Marbach am Neckar.

'Concerning History': see letter no. 205.

Professor Maus: Heinz Maus (1911–1978) began his studies in 1932 in Frankfurt am Main with Max Horkheimer, among others, and was appointed to the chair of sociology at Marburg in 1959. He was the joint editor of Luchterhand's *Soziologische Texte*.

200 Adorno to Kracauer
Frankfurt am Main, 7.12.1962

PROF. DR. THEODOR W. ADORNO

FRANKFURT AM MAIN 7 December 1962
KETTENHOFWEG 123

Dear Friedel,

Many thanks for your letter of 27 November and the message that, in the meantime, the matter of your nomination as a corresponding member of the Deutsche Gesellschaft für Soziologie has turned out well.

I am glad that you like the work about progress; it will only achieve its true significance in the book, on which I am working just now with the greatest energy. I am well over the hump with it, although producing the final text, which has to be submitted in about a year, is still going to create an insane amount of work, as I am ploughing right through everything all over again.

I too saw Selmar Spier here; he joined us once at the philosophical seminar, and we shared many memories of old times.

When I spoke to Unseld, I heard that in the meantime he had written to you at length and in a positive way. The plan of publishing two books of essays by you, a long one with a heavy load of information and an ostensibly lighter one, makes very good sense to me. I see the situation with Suhrkamp as so positive in general that I would accept the present suggestion by Unseld in any event, even if no final arrangements have yet been made about *Ginster*; its intrinsic quality ensures that those will follow later. I am viewing the matter of the *Ginster* business in such a rosy light because Martin Walser, who has considerable influence in the firm, is championing it as much as I am. By the way, the man who is working on your material, a Herr Michel, belongs to the circle of my closest students; he is an excellent man, and he too will be a strong advocate for it. I believe that you can have every confidence about this whole matter.

What you say about Fräulein B. is, God knows, justified, but I would think that she does have more intellectual energy and spontaneity than Frau A., who seems to me like the unquiet ghost of ponderousness.

Did you know, incidentally, that Hanns Eisler died recently?

Luchterhand Verlag is an excellent academic publishing house; right now we are in the process of launching a new series of texts with them which is to consist of older texts on sociology and, above all, on early socialism. Gottfried Salomon is involved in this, which cannot be helped; but I have sufficient control over things for him not to be able to make too much mischief. I think that you would have much less trouble with Luchterhand Verlag than with Rowohlt. I shall be seeing Benseler here on the 19th; if you give me details before then, I can also discuss your things with him. Maus is likewise a former student of mine – he is now a professor at Marburg, neither very strong nor very reliable, but that needn't bother you; I was very favourably impressed by Benseler. Perhaps in this matter you may be able to get round the point that Maus is printing his name in the book as its editor, which would not be exactly fair in the circumstances. You would just have to consider whether Rowohlt is not much more advantageous in financial terms; naturally a big literary publisher is much stronger in terms of capital than a specifically academic one.

I haven't heard anything from Patalas, but it would be easy for me to intervene with him through mutual friends. In the meantime, I have been dipping into the history of film by him and Gregor; it is deplorable. But that is part and parcel of the subject; there is something silly about writing a history of the culture industry, which, as the dross of intellectual history, derives its very nature from the basic principle that it is always the same thing in new packaging. Patalas means extremely well, but he is not a very strong thinker.

Your Offenbach is being advertised as a translation under the new title *Pariser Leben*. Is this right, and is it different in any way from the old version? List Verlag could quite easily send me a copy.

Gretel is quite all right again, and extremely active – busy at present with the technical revision of my *Prismen*, which is being published in a new edition, as a paperback, in a print run of 40,000 copies. The forty thousand guaranteed subscribers will have a treat in store for them. I hope you have received the *Einleitung in die Musiksoziologie*. Perhaps you could confirm this? Meanwhile I too have finished the corrections to the *Getreue Korrepetitor*, which I completed as far back as the summer of 1961.

Much love to you and Lili, from Gretel too,

Your old Teddie.

Original: typescript; Siegfried Kracauer papers, Deutsches Literaturarchiv, Marbach am Neckar.

the message: not preserved.

Walser: Martin Walser (b. 1927) made his debut in 1955 with the volume of short stories *Ein Flugzeug über dem Haus*; like Hans Magnus Enzensberger and Uwe Johnson, he was one of the authors whom Siegfried Unseld involved in strategic planning.

Michel: Karl Markus Michel (1929–2000) worked from 1955 to 1958 at the Institute for Social Research; from 1962 to 1974 he was a reader for Suhrkamp.

Hanns Eisler died recently: on 6 September 1962 in Berlin.

Luchterhand Verlag … a new series of texts: the plan came to nothing (see letter no. 208).

Your Offenbach: *Pariser Leben, Jacques Offenbach und seine Zeit: Eine Gesellschaftsbiographie*, Munich: Paul List, 1962. The book contained, in a translation by Wolfgang Weyrauch, the preface by the French historian Daniel Halévy with which the French edition, *Jacques Offenbach, ou Le Secret du Second Empire*, had been published by Grasset in 1937 (see the text and details about the circumstances in the appendix to Kracauer, W 8, pp. 503–8, 551f.).

Prismen *… in a print run of 40,000 copies*: Siegfried Unseld informed Adorno in a letter of 6 November 1962 of a corresponding offer from the Deutsche Taschenbuchverlag; Adorno gave his consent on 8 November (see Adorno/Suhrkamp/Unseld, *Briefwechsel*, pp. 432f.).

201 Kracauer to Adorno
New York, 10.12.1962

498 Westend Avenue
New York 24, N.Y.
December 10, 1962

Dear Teddie,

I am answering your letter by return of post (though in some haste) so that you will receive it before seeing Benseler. First of all: going back to the topic of Luchterhand Verlag, it [is] welcome news to me to hear that it is a good firm which might publish an honourable edition of my *Theory of Film*. Presently, the negotiations between the Oxford Press in London and Ledig are still in progress. I am fatalistic about this; if Rowohlt does want the book after all, it is o.k. with me; if not, Luchterhand is there in reserve. I am glad to hear that their programme will include a collection of early socialist texts. I am extremely interested in the debate between Marx and the early socialists – a debate which is generally distorted in literature influenced by Marxism – just like the debate, we might say, between Origen and Celsus and between Catholics and Protestants in the

Renaissance; those are exceptional periods of history. I make the point in my statement 'Concerning History', which contains quite a long interpretation of Erasmus. You didn't write and tell me whether you know it. I should be delighted to send it to you. To return once again to my book: I have written to Dr Benseler about the situation with the publishers. Whatever else you may want to say to him on the subject is all right with me.

Truth be told, I am not really interested in Patalas. No surprise that his history of film is so bad that it is almost a work of art. How can anyone even attempt such a thing (unless for financial reasons)? I once said to Sadoul in Paris that he would have the shock of his life if he ever got beyond the year 1925 in his great history of film. Patalas *does* mean well in his film reviews; it is just that he isn't exactly sensitive to the finer points.

Yes, Dr Unseld has written to me and sent me suggestions, asking at the same time for my agreement in principle, as he would like to publish the bigger volume of essays as early as the spring of 1963. I accepted at once. I was delighted – and I am aware how much I owe to your intervention in this matter. If possible, Lili was even happier; an old and very sincere wish which was dear to her heart has come true with the publication of these pieces. I have promptly made a suggestion about the choice and order of the items in the volume, which, in accordance with your brilliant idea, is to be called *Das Ornament der Masse*. The fact that in further discussions I can count on a man like Michel who has a solid understanding of the subject is a great relief to me. What you write about the chances for *Ginster* gives me hope. Dr Unseld wrote to me that the book was still going the rounds – so for the time being I am imagining, in my daydreams, that he really will take it.

I am writing by the same post to Paul List Verlag, asking them to send you my *Offenbach* immediately. The word 'translation' probably refers to Weyrauch's translation of the introduction by Daniel Halévy, which has now been incorporated into the German edition. The edition is an unaltered reprint of the 1937 Allert de Lange edition.

Many thanks for the Axel Kluge *Lebensläufe*. I have already dipped into it. The book is magnificent in a certain way. I haven't read it all yet, but I was struck by the stylistic as well as the factual consistency with which Kluge depicts the *Lebensläufe* so that one can actually grasp the fact that the *Lebensläufe* are not just careers or the characters just characters. It is the old *Neue Sachlichkeit* – new factuality – but crasser and more terrible, true to the circumstances. Benjamin might also have said about this book what he said of *Ginster*: it could only have been written in Germany. (Although – I don't know – something like this is also possible in France nowadays, only it sounds different there.) Kluge and Enzensberger – who is in Norway, I know – are two young people whom I should like to know. Once again, the old Platonic Eros is awakening here.

Frau A., to whom I sent my few desiderata, has written to me saying that she was getting to work on them straight away. As for the Eisler book, I directed her to you as the last resort. I did read about Eisler's death.

Once again, what a lot of things you are working on, in spite of your many duties! I wish the paperback edition of your *Prismen* a guaranteed success. We were most delighted to hear that Gretel is so well again that she is working flat out on it. (By the way, I am still receiving royalties from the pocketbook edition of my *Caligari*.) In the meantime, I have organized my book on history properly and will probably write an outline of my thought processes – as a kind of rehearsal – before I plunge into it.

I am toying with the idea of coming to Frankfurt again next year – but this is just a pipe-dream. (A face-to-face interview with Dr Unseld is certainly important, among other things.)

Warmest greetings to both of you from Lili and me,

Yours,

Friedel

Original: typescript; Theodor W. Adorno Archiv, Frankfurt am Main.

Origen and Celsus: The Greek theologian Origen (c. 185–253/54) presented a consistent account of Christian doctrine; the Greek philosopher Celsus raised objections to Christianity with his *alēthēs logos* in 179 AD.

Sadoul: Georges Sadoul (1904–1967), French film critic and historian; in his *Theory of Film*, Kracauer occasionally examines this critic's various writings.

Unseld has written to me: in his letter of 3 December 1962, Siegfried Unseld mentioned, going beyond *Das Ornament der Masse*, 'a parallel with Benjamin's *Berliner Kindheit*', a 'summary of works associated with Berlin' (Archiv der Peter Suhrkamp Stiftung an der Johann Wolfgang Goethe-Universität).

I have promptly made a suggestion: on 7 December 1992, Kracauer sketched out the following 'schema' for *Das Ornament der Masse*:

Introduction: Natural Geometry
Boy and Bull
Two Surfaces (not in Herr Michel's selection)
Analysis of a Town Plan
For completely irrational reasons, I could imagine that these three little pieces would make a good beginning on account of their atmosphere. Because of their geometrical character, they would harmonize with the word 'Ornament' in the main title.
Exterior and interior objects
Photography
Travel and Dance
The Ornament of the Mass
On Friendship
Here I miss the articles 'Those in Waiting' and 'Productive Conversation'. I feel that using them would be good for the inner balance of the whole thing.
Works
Georg Simmel
The Bible in German (must be retained)
Catholicism and Relativism

(Max Scheler)
Franz Kafka
(On the Writings of Walter Benjamin)
(The Crisis in Science)
Sociological
The Group as Vector of Ideas
On Best-Sellers and their Readership
The Challenge of Qualitative Content Analysis
Film
The Little Shop-Girls Go to the Cinema (= Film and Society)
Film, 1928 (= Contemporary Film and its Audience)
Cult of Distraction
National Types as Hollywood Presents Them
German Cultural Policy, 1930–1933
A Sociological Experiment? (On *The Threepenny Opera*)
Revolt of the Middle Classes
(Show of forms or politics?)
Biography as a Neo-Bourgeois Art Form
Conclusion: On the Subject of History
History: Ideas for an as yet Unwritten Book
I am sending you this possible, unpublished, closing article (title: *Concerning History*) by the same post by air mail. It contains preliminary ideas about my new book, under contract with the Oxford Press.
(Archiv der Peter Suhrkamp Stiftung an der Johann Wolfgang Goethe-Universität)

Weyrauch's translation: see the previous letter (note).

it could only have been written in Germany: for *Ginster*, Kracauer contemplated the subtitle 'Novel from the German Republic' (see Kracauer, W 7, p. 658).

two young people whom I should like to know: for the meeting with Kluge, see letter no. 265.

pocketbook edition: the first edition of *From Caligari to Hitler*, published by Princeton University Press, 1947, was followed by the first pocketbook edition, published by Noonday Press, New York, in 1959; later paperback editions were also published in their turn by Princeton University Press.

202 Kracauer to Adorno

New York, 12.12.1962

498 Westend Avenue
New York 24, N.Y.
December 12, 1962

Dear Teddie,

Just a word about the confirmation which you requested – to say that your Sociology of Music with its kind inscription (thanks for that) has arrived here in good order. It will be a while before I can get around to reading it. Incidentally, I have a terrible cold at present and, accordingly, am feeling very low.

Allow me to take this opportunity (these lines, I mean, not the cold) to send you and Gretel our warmest good wishes for the New Year; in any event, wishes always come in handy.

Kindest regards,
Yours,

Original: typescript (carbon copy); Siegfried Kracauer papers, Deutsches Literaturarchiv, Marbach am Neckar.

Sociology of Music ... kind inscription: Adorno provided Kracauer's copy of his *Einleitung in die Musiksoziologie* with the handwritten dedication: 'To my dear Friedel – a little by-product from his Teddie / Frankfurt, December 1962' (Kracauer papers, Deutsches Literaturarchiv, Marbach).

203 Adorno to Kracauer
Frankfurt am Main, 14.12.1962

PROF. DR. THEODOR W. ADORNO

FRANKFURT AM MAIN 14 December 1962
KETTENHOFWEG 123

Dear Friedel,

Many thanks for your letter.

I am delighted that the business with Unseld is working out and very optimistic with regard to *Ginster*. Of course I shall follow this up – only it is a bit difficult to get hold of Unseld, who is engaged in some kind of mammoth negotiations connected with the movement towards consolidation in German publishing which was unleashed by what was ostensibly a purely private conflict within Fischer Verlag.

At the same time, I am writing to Benseler once again and confirming our appointment for the 19th; I shall not fail to mention your film book, but without putting you under any kind of obligation. By the way, I am not entirely happy about the Offenbach coming out *before* the other books for reasons which will be obvious to you – but there is nothing else to be done about this now. In any case, my thanks for the book in advance. Incidentally, have you seen Silbermann's Offenbach book? Among other things, he has discovered Offenbach's mistress (Bouffar), who also, of course, features in your book and must have been enchanting. Not everyone makes things so difficult for his biographers in such matters as Offenbach.

Did you actually receive *Einleitung in die Musiksoziologie*? You don't say anything about it. Of course I have a fervent interest in the *Statements Concerning History*; I don't know it, and neither do I know where it stands. Your words of confirmation have just arrived – many thanks!

I shall pass your words on to Axel; he is sure to be very pleased with them.

I am definitely counting on your coming to Europe in the course of the next year; perhaps you can arrange things this time so that we can meet in Frankfurt, where there would certainly be every possible kind of interesting thing for you to see and hear.

Otherwise there is nothing new to report from us except a mass of work; I am shuddering at the task of turning my grand design into a well-organized text. This time I have entirely let myself go in the direction where my reflections drove me; perhaps this anarchy was not without results, but now – old *constructeur* that I am – I am having to pay the full price for it.

Much love to you both, from Gretel too,

Your old

Teddie

Original: typescript with printed letterhead and handwritten additions; Siegfried Kracauer papers, Deutsches Literaturarchiv, Marbach am Neckar. Handwritten note by Kracauer: 'Dec. 18: HIST Statement + long hand note' (see letter no. 205).

mammoth negotiations … the movement towards consolidation in German publishing: Siegfried Unseld reacted to the intention of Gottfried Bermann Fischer (1897–1995), the publisher at S. Fischer, to retire from its everyday business for reasons of age with the offer of a takeover of S. Fischer Verlag by the Suhrkamp Verlag shareholders; the plan did not meet with unanimous approval on the part of the Fischer family, which in 1963 disposed of it to Georg von Holtzbrinck (1900–1983). Jutta von Hesler (1906–2004), the daughter of Anton Kippenberg (1874–1950) and senior partner at Insel Verlag, also planned to sell, in response to which the Suhrkamp shareholders took over Insel Verlag in February 1963 with effect from 1 January of that year.

Silbermann's Offenbach book: Alphons Silbermann (1908–2000), a sociologist, accepted an appointment at the University of Cologne in 1958, bringing an end to his exile which had lasted since 1935. In 1960 he published *Das imaginäre Tagebuch des Herrn Jacques Offenbach* with the publishing house Bote & Bock.

Bouffar: The French singer Zulma Bouffar and Jacques Offenbach were united in an artistic and erotic partnership which had its origins in 1863 in a visit by Offenbach to a concert by Bouffar, with which the description of the relationship begins in Kracauer's book (see Kracauer, W 8, p. 235).

204 Adorno to Kracauer
Frankfurt am Main, 19.12.1962

PROF. DR. THEODOR W. ADORNO

FRANKFURT AM MAIN 19 December 1962
KETTENHOFWEG 123

Dear Friedel,

Good news today – I hope just in time for Christmas, and just briefly.

Yesterday I had the opportunity to talk at some length to Unseld again about *Ginster*. From the outcome of the conversation I no longer have any reason whatsoever to doubt that he is going to publish the book. The only condition he imposes is that I should publicize the book, as I am, so to speak, responsible for its reissue – perhaps through a notice included in a radio programme or something similar. Of course I shall be delighted to do so.

I didn't want to keep the good news from you a second longer and am passing it on to you – always allowing for the possibility that something may yet intervene, as is always possible until contracts have been signed. Perhaps this business will amuse Lili, too. What Unseld expects of me is actually an explanation of how the reissuing of this book after such a long time is justified. In other words, I am to answer the question of its topicality. This is – even viewed objectively – a most attractive task.

It is possible, though not entirely certain, that I shall be in Munich for a few days in the first week of January. Please let me know if I should talk to Patalas or someone else from the Oberhausen Group about the *Theory of Film*. By the way, you may have seen that a vehement and less than fair attack on Axel Kluge has appeared in *Die Zeit*. I am sure that he would welcome a few friendly words of support from you. The address is: Dr Alexander Kluge, 8 Munich, Bauerstrasse 21.

I hope that the two of you will have a very happy Christmas – we wish you both all the best for it, and for the New Year.

Warmest greetings to you both, from Gretel too,

Your old
Teddie

Original: typescript with printed letterhead; Siegfried Kracauer papers, Deutsches Literaturarchiv, Marbach am Neckar.

on Axel Kluge: Marcel Reich-Ranicki, 'Ein neuer Name: Alexander Kluge. Erfundene Tatsachenberichte und verlorene Maßstäbe' [Invented documentaries and lost standards], *Die Zeit*, 14 December 1962.

205 Adorno to Kracauer
Frankfurt am Main, 21.12.1962

PROF. DR. THEODOR W. ADORNO

FRANKFURT AM MAIN 21 December 1962
KETTENHOFWEG 123

Dear Friedel,

In haste: I forgot to request that you not mention anything to Unseld about any of the things that I have written to you until you have heard from him directly. It is, after all, a justified if narcissistic gratification which he has the right to expect – that of feeling himself to be the bearer of good news and that his pleasure will not be spoilt by you having known about it in advance. Besides, I have behaved a bit indiscreetly towards him, strictly speaking, albeit in good conscience. I am sure, though, that you won't have to wait much longer.

Thank you for the 'Statement'. I shall read it over the holidays.

All good wishes,
Yours,
Teddie

Original: typescript with printed letterhead; Siegfried Kracauer papers, Deutsches Literaturarchiv, Marbach am Neckar. Handwritten note by Kracauer: 'Answered by long-hand air letter, Dec. 27. 1962'; the reply has not been preserved.

heard from him directly: in a letter which Siegfried Unseld wrote to Kracauer on 18 December 1962, the day of his conversation with Adorno about *Ginster*, the decision to publish the novel was not mentioned (Archiv der Peter Suhrkamp Stiftung an der Johann Wolfgang Goethe-Universität).

Thank you for the 'Statement': 'Concerning History: A Preliminary Statement'; the copy bears the handwritten dedication: 'For Teddie, this little excursion into other areas, / Friedel, / December, 1962'; no accompanying letter has survived (Theodor W. Adorno Archiv).

206 Kracauer to Adorno
New York, 23.12.1962

498 Westend Avenue
New York 24, N.Y.
December 23, 1962

Dear Teddie,

Your letter with the news for the holidays arrived just now – and so just in time for Christmas, as you will see from the date. Your sentence saying that it might well amuse Lili is an (English) understatement. I have to tell you from Lili that she is absolutely delighted and full of gratitude for your extraordinarily kind intervention. The same, of course, goes for me too. I am especially impressed by the fact that you are willing to advertise *Ginster* in person in the interests of its being published – and this when you are so terribly pressed for time! I couldn't imagine a finer proof of friendship. Like you, I remain sceptical until I have something written down in black and white. But I believe that, in this case, there is a real hope that, thanks to your intervention, the miracle may happen.

I should be happy to write to Kluge. As we don't get to see any German newspapers apart from the dreary *Aufbau*, I haven't heard anything about the attack on him. If you should be going to Munich, please don't say anything about my film book to Patalas and the people from the Oberhausen Group except in general terms. The whole thing is still up in the air. But please give Patalas my regards, and also Lili's.

To keep you in the picture about the film book, the latest state of affairs is this – a very tricky situation for me: Herr Ledig-Rowohlt wrote to me recently saying that in spite of my taking over all the necessary 'research', he could bring out the book only as a paperback – something which runs counter to our original agreement, which was confirmed last summer in Hamburg. At the same time, he is trying to do his utmost to palm me off onto Luchterhand Verlag, which contacted him directly about the book. Herr Ledig's letter actually enclosed a copy of a letter to him from Luchterhand Verlag, written to him at the instigation of Herr Reifferscheid (the owner of the publishing house, I presume). But what does Herr Reifferscheid want? He declares to Herr Ledig that he would only be able to publish my film book not as an individual work but solely 'within the framework of an independent Kracauer programme comprising several volumes' (his own words). This is a notion, however, to which I in turn cannot agree, inasmuch as many of the very items in which Luchterhand Verlag is interested are with Dr Unseld at present. Moreover, Luchterhand Verlag has not yet come to me in person with its new idea – and so the film book is back in no man's land again. I have written to Herr Ledig asking him to be patient and wait for a more definite reply, and I keep waiting. I also thought it only right and fair to inform Dr Unseld about this situation in general in my letter of yesterday. Don't worry: I haven't offered him the film book. I just feel that he ought to know how matters stand with it – all the more so as in his last letter to me he expressed his general interest in me as an author.

So much for practical matters. This is about the extent of what I can write to you today, *hélas*. Are you too in a state of being rapidly inundated by correspondence – on such topics, I mean?

In any event, we both wish you and Gretel all the best for the New Year, especially as regards health. Lili has a profound belief in the power of wishes, and that should tell you that ours carry weight.

Warmest greetings from Lili and me,

Yours,

Friedel

Original: typescript; Theodor W. Adorno Archiv, Frankfurt am Main.

I should be happy to write to Kluge: he did so on 24 December 1962 (Kracauer papers, Deutsches Literaturarchiv, Marbach).

Aufbau: *Aufbau: Nachrichtenblatt des German-Jewish Club*, New York, was published from 1934 to 2003, then from 2005 in Zurich; the periodical represented a constant in the journalistic accompaniment to Jewish life far beyond the USA.

Reifferscheid: Eduard Reifferscheid (1899–1992), publisher; part-owner and director of Luchterhand Verlag from 1936 onwards.

Dr Unseld … I haven't offered him the film book: the decision not to offer *Theory of Film* to Siegfried Unseld reads as follows in Kracauer's letter to him of 23 December 1962: 'Please don't be alarmed; I am not offering you the book. In the present circumstances, I think it only fair to keep you informed about this situation. Perhaps I should also add that I myself regard *Theory of Film: The Redemption of Physical Reality* as one of my major works; it does indeed deal with film, but also is concerned with aesthetics in general and flows into a philosophy of our times. Professor Adorno, who knows the book, can tell you about this' (Archiv der Peter Suhrkamp Stiftung an der Johann Wolfgang Goethe-Universität).

207 Kracauer to Adorno
New York, 15.2.1963

498 Westend Avenue
New York 24, N.Y.
February 15, 1963

Dear Teddie,

I haven't heard anything from you for a long time – which is something of a breach of our new convention.

I am writing to you today to let you know of a decision which I hope will please you: I should like to dedicate my volume of essays to you – i.e. the words '*Für Theodor W. Adorno*' should appear at the beginning. I had in fact intended that to be a surprise for you, and the publisher was also prepared to say nothing about it to you beforehand – but, on second thoughts, I do think it is better that you should know about it. In spite of this, it may still come as something of a surprise to you when the dedication actually appears in print.

Dr Unseld had dinner with us the evening before last, and we spent some pleasant hours together. We arranged that I should write to you myself about the dedication – something which has now been done. He brought me some news which came in part as news to me (Herr Michel had already written to me about it) – that *Ginster* would be published in August, three months after the volume of essays. (I said nothing, of course, about your kind prior notice of this event.) The book about streets is to come out in 1964. He has a strong interest in my book on history.

All that remains now is the matter in which, if you will, you might exert some slight pressure. I apprised Dr Unseld of the complicated situation in which *Theory of Film* finds itself as regards the publishers. (You know, of course – the one with Rowohlt and Luchterhand.) The result was that he wants to think about whether he should not take over the book himself. He took an English copy along for the journey home and agreed with me that I should not write to Rowohlt and Luchterhand until further notice, which keeps this whole business up in the air for the time being. I believe that to achieve a positive outcome it would be important for you to present the book to him as a contribution to aesthetics in general, and as a basically philosophical statement. (There is also a point here from the publisher's perspective: the book has a good chance of being a standard work for a long time.) For me personally the German edition from Suhrkamp would be a desirable solution – that way I should have some kind of roof over my head.

Incidentally, we did of course take *le tour d'horizon*, sauntering through mutual territory – your ears must have been burning. As Unseld will not be in Frankfurt in July, we were wondering whether we ought not to come over until September. Would that be all right with you? How are the plans going for your visits in general? We must have some further correspondence about this.

Warmest greetings from both of us to both of you,

Yours,

Friedel

Original: typescript; Theodor W. Adorno Archiv, Frankfurt am Main.

Für Theodor W. Adorno: the plan was carried out.

Dr Unseld had dinner with us: Siegfried Unseld visited New York from 5 to 16 February 1963 on the occasion of the premières of Max Frisch's *Andorra* and *Biedermann und die Brandstifter* [The fire bugs] (on 9 and 11 February); over dinner Kracauer and Unseld discussed, in addition to the publications already in preparation, the possible adoption of his *Theory of Film*, Suhrkamp's taking up the option to *History* from Oxford University Press, and also the possible publication of *Georg* (Siegfried Unseld Archiv, Frankfurt am Main).

book about streets: see letter no. 148; *Straßen in Berlin und anderswo* was published by Suhrkamp on 25 May 1964.

Unseld will not be in Frankfurt in July: Siegfried Unseld spent his holidays in July 1963 in Brittany.

208 Adorno to Kracauer

Frankfurt am Main, 20.2.1963

PROF. DR. THEODOR W. ADORNO

FRANKFURT AM MAIN 20 February 1963
KETTENHOFWEG 123

Dear Friedel,

Many thanks for your letter. I ask you most cordially to excuse my silence. You can simply have no idea what the last two months have been like here. I had succumbed to the delusion that I could put all my energy into my own things in tandem with working on the entire administrative business of the university and the Institute, going beyond the limits of my strength – and inevitably the most pressing and most rewarding matters themselves had to suffer because of this – and, moreover, without getting as far as I had wanted. I had to interrupt work on the final version of the major text on the *Jargon der Eigentlichkeit* [Jargon of authenticity] somewhere in the middle to tackle the writing up of the essay 'Skoteinos, or How to Read Hegel', which is intended for the new edition of *Aspekte*, which, together with the Skoteinos and the *Erfahrungsgehalt* [Experiential contents] are also to become a short book. I have not yet finished dictating the Hegel, or finished putting the *Jargon der Eigentlichkeit* in order. I shall try, though, to take advantage of the next two months, in which at least the university is at rest. Because of the opportune date of Shrovetide, I shall have my last lectures and seminars as early as tomorrow. The *Eingriffe* is already complete in page proof; the *Getreue Korrepetitor* is in the middle of that stage.

You have given me great pleasure with the dedication, and I thank you for it with all my heart. It was especially kind of you to tell me now, and this doesn't detract in the least from the brightness of the surprise. The form of the dedication is simple and dignified too. However, it gives me just as much pleasure, believe me, that *Ginster* is now being reissued at last.

I think that the idea of taking the film book to Suhrkamp is a very fortunate one. I have spoken to Unseld twice today on the telephone. He is going away yet again for a few days, to Winterthur and Vienna; we have fixed a meeting for the end of next week, and I will then take the matter up very vigorously. I would advise you against Luchterhand. Young Dr Benseler is a pompous little snob, who, after we had reached a firm agreement about our series of texts, broke off the whole business, which had already reached an advanced stage, allegedly because of a veto by his superior, Herr Reifferscheid. I think that it would be better not to have any dealings with such unreliable people – all the more so because there is a strong element of financial pettiness involved here. In addition, I am annoyed because they are publishing a sort of complete edition of Lukács, in the preface to which he blackens my name in the most ridiculous and servile fashion by calling me a nihilist. Of course that should not influence you, but I have a feeling that the climate is not favourable. I would not venture to decide, naturally, how far old Gottfried Salomon, who was in charge of the negotiations, and who has remained identical with the non-identity of his youth, is to blame for the failure of the Institute's plans with Luchterhand.

You don't write anything at all about Lili; I hope with all my heart that she is restored and that the American saying 'no news is good news' is proving true. If the two of you were to come over here in September, it would be a good time, as I shall most probably be here and under a bit less pressure, whereas the university is carrying on throughout the whole of July, and in August we shall be trotting off to Sils Maria again.

Give all our good wishes to Lili, with much love to yourself – from Gretel too – and, once again, a thousand thanks from

Your old

Teddie

Original: typescript with printed letterhead and handwritten corrections; Siegfried Kracauer papers, Deutsches Literaturarchiv, Marbach am Neckar.

Jargon der Eigentlichkeit: *Jargon der Eigentlichkeit: Zur deutschen Ideologie*, published on 23 October 1964 (see Adorno, GS 6, pp. 413–526).

Skoteinos … also to become a short book: *Drei Studien zu Hegel: Aspekte. Erfahrungsgehalt. Skoteinos oder Wie zu lesen sei*, published 23 September 1963 (see Adorno, GS 5, pp. 247–381).

Eingriffe: *Eingriffe: Neun kritische Modelle* was published in the inaugural series of edition suhrkamp, of which twenty volumes came out on 2 May 1963. With edition suhrkamp Siegfried Unseld created the publisher's most influential series; Adorno commented on it in a letter to Unseld of 9 May 1963: 'It is especially dear to my heart that things of mine are being published in edition suhrkamp. The form of this series of publications appeals greatly to me. It combines an unpretentious exterior with the strict and stringent demands of the content. This combination lends the whole enterprise a subdued dignity. It is ordered in such a way that it is entirely suited to the readership which authors like myself would wish' (see Adorno/Suhrkamp/Unseld, *Briefwechsel*, p. 446).

to Winterthur and Vienna: from 21 to 24 February 1963 Siegfried Unseld visited the publisher's limited partners in Winterthur – Peter Reinhart (1907–1988) and Balthasar Reinhart (1916–2005) – as well as booksellers and theatres in Vienna.

our series of texts: see letter no. 200.

Lukács … a nihilist: 'A considerable part of the leading German intelligentsia, including Adorno, has moved into the "Grand Hotel Abyss"', as Georg Lukács stated in his 1962 preface to *Die Theorie des Romans* (Frankfurt am Main: Luchterhand, 1971, p. 16).

209 Kracauer to Adorno
New York, 24.2.1963

498 Westend Avenue
New York 24, N.Y.
Feb. 24, 1963

Dear Teddie,

How good to hear from you again! I am glad that you are pleased with the dedication and can still let it be a surprise to you. By the way, do you know that my article about your book *Der enthüllte Kierkegaard* will be published in this volume – now, thirty years after it was not able to appear in the *Frankfurter Zeitung*? What a triumph over time, and over that paper! 'Die Hotelhalle', a chapter from the study about the detective novel, also appears in this same volume; Herr Michel requested it, and quite pressingly.

What you write to me about your work and your achievements over the last few months makes me feel as if I were looking up into the starry skies: new stars are constantly appearing. I have great admiration for your energy and for the multiplicity of your topics – but please don't overstretch your bow. *Hélas*, you too are growing older – at least in a physiological sense. By the way, what about *Scotlinos*? I wish you would give my cultural deficiencies a bit of help. The time before last you wrote to me about your *Dialektische Meditationen*. I assume, though, that they won't fall too far short.

Lili was very touched by your intervention and thanks both of you cordially. There is nothing but good news to report of her – what a piece of good fortune. Apart from a few extreme movements which are not going properly and still need some time, the bone near her shoulder has healed miraculously, thanks to her good constitution and a solicitous old orthopaedist from Vienna who calls himself an 'Austrian by training'. In fact, we have very nearly resumed our normal way of life again. We are already looking forward now to seeing you both again and will try to arrange it for the end of September in Frankfurt, or, when all is said and done, as early as August in Switzerland – say, Zurich? In any event, if all goes well we shall be somewhere in Switzerland in August too, for purposes of work and relaxation.

I am glad, and very grateful, that you are going to talk with Dr Unseld about *Theory of Film*. From what he wrote to me just now I almost have the impression that things are beginning to come to fruition there but still need one good push. (Your news confirms my instinct that Luchterhand is completely out of the question.) The book really does belong with the old circle of friends gathered around Unseld.

I have started to write a chapter from my book on history in advance – the one about the historical concept of time – for a specific purpose. I am going at it with real passion – a sign that I still do feel quite young after all.

So long, dear Teddie. Much love to you and Gretel from the almost repaired Lili and me,

Yours,

Friedel

Original: typescript; Theodor W. Adorno Archiv, Frankfurt am Main.

Der enthüllte Kierkegaard: see letter no. 90.

'Die Hotelhalle': see letter no. 12.

What about Scotlinos?: Adorno corrected a typing error in 'Skoteinos' by hand; Kracauer read the correction, 'e', as 'l'.

the bone near her shoulder: Lili Kracauer suffered a fracture to her right arm just below the shoulder in a fall on the stairs (see Kracauer to Leo Löwenthal, 18 February 1963, Kracauer/Löwenthal, *Briefwechsel*, p. 243).

a chapter from my book on history: this would become Kracauer's contribution to a festschrift on the occasion of Adorno's 60th birthday (see letter no. 219).

210 Adorno to Kracauer
Frankfurt am Main, 5.3.1963

PROF. DR. THEODOR W. ADORNO

FRANKFURT AM MAIN 5 March 1963
KETTENHOFWEG 123

Dear Friedel,

Just a few words for today – and thank you for your letter of 24 February.

I had a long conversation with Unseld about the *Theory of Film*; I think that he will publish the book, but would just – quite naturally – like to see the German version first. I myself am hardly less curious about this; it always goes against the grain when I have to read something by you, or any of my own work, in English.

I was especially glad to hear that 'Hotelhalle' will be published in *Ornament der Masse*.

As for my own work: I had to break off the *Dialektische Meditationen* because of the third Hegel study, as this, together with the *Aspekte* and the *Erfahrungsgehalte*, is to replace the old *Aspekte* volume. I think, though, that that will soon be behind me and I shall shortly be back to the main business, as Goethe used to say.

Gretel and I are only going to take about ten days' holiday, in Baden-Baden, and in April I have to go to Berlin to deliver a little speech which carries a relatively high level of responsibility to a group of bigwigs.

I am delighted to hear that Lili is quite well again.

September here would be ideal – better than Zurich, where we shall barely spend any time at all.

I am keeping my fingers crossed for your history book.

Much love to you and Lili, from Gretel too,
Your old
Teddie

Original: typescript with printed letterhead; Siegfried Kracauer papers, Deutsches Literaturarchiv, Marbach am Neckar.

the main business: Johann Wolfgang von Goethe's code-word for his work on the second part of *Faust*, e.g. in his diary entry for 1/2 July 1831: 'Kept myself to myself, to get on with the main business' (see Johann Wolfgang von Goethe, *Briefe, Tagebücher und Gespräche*, Part II, Vol. II, ed. Horst Fleig, Frankfurt am Main: Deutscher Klassiker Verlag, 1993, p. 423).

in April I have to go to Berlin: see letter no. 212.

211 Kracauer to Adorno
New York, 26.3.1963

498 Westend Avenue
New York 24, N.Y.
March 26, 1963

Dear Teddie,

Just a brief word for now. Thank you for talking to Unseld about *Theory of Film*. He let me know just now that he has definitely decided to accept it. It means a lot to me that this book has now found its way home, so to speak. I shall go through the German version in detail once again (in October). The manuscript is not yet available at the moment – so this too has come to a good conclusion.

At your request and Unseld's, 'Der enthüllte Kierkegaard' will unfortunately have to be left out of the volume of essays once again. It seems that the poor essay is never to be granted a permanent home; something always gets in the way.

A question about the holidays: when and where shall we be seeing each other? July isn't good for you, and, as Unseld is away, we shall not be coming to Frankfurt at all in July as far as I can see. From the end of July to the end of August we shall in all probability be in Interlaken to relax and work on the history book. In the first half of September I shall probably have various commitments, partly of a professional nature (but that is not yet entirely certain). Frankfurt immediately after the middle of September would suit us well, before I have to go to Paris. But that is the time of the book fair and Frankfurt is bursting at the seams. As far as

Unseld is concerned, I am certain that he will have no time to spare for me. And I have to be back at the beginning of October at the latest, so I have no idea how it will work out. Do write to me, though, in any case about your plans and possibilities. For example, when will the two of you be back from Sils, and when are you going there?

How was Baden-Baden? Or are you there right now? We wish you a big time in Berlin in April. What is the event at which you are speaking?

Warmest regards to you and dear Gretel from Lili,
who is now completely restored, so to speak, and from

Your
Friedel.

Original: typescript with handwritten addition; Theodor W. Adorno Archiv, Frankfurt am Main. The underlinings and abbreviations are in another hand.

definitely decided to accept it: Siegfried Unseld made the acceptance of the *Theorie des Films* conditional on a revision of the translation by Kracauer; in a letter of 21 March 1963 he informed him of the 'positive decision' (Archiv der Peter Suhrkamp Stiftung an der Johann Wolfgang Goethe-Universität).

'Der enthüllte Kierkegaard' will unfortunately have to be left out of the volume of essays yet again: on 5 March 1963 Siegfried Unseld wrote to Kracauer: 'Adorno is delighted with the dedication; we have just added it to the book. However, a problem has arisen for both of us (i.e. Adorno and myself) in connection with this dedication. If the book is dedicated to Adorno, it seems to us inappropriate for your review of the Kierkegaard book to be included' (Archiv der Peter Suhrkamp Stiftung an der Johann Wolfgang Goethe-Universität).

a big time in Berlin: in English in the original.

212 Adorno to Kracauer
Frankfurt am Main, 10.4.1963

PROF. DR. THEODOR W. ADORNO

FRANKFURT AM MAIN 10 April 1963
KETTENHOFWEG 123

Dear Friedel,

Just a few words for now.

We spent ten days in Baden-Baden – a very short time, but we recovered tolerably well – only all hell has broken loose now because I have committed the folly of taking on more commitments than I can actually manage. Such as a definitely interesting one in Munich about the sociological problems of television, though this went off quite well. Next week I have to go to Berlin for the so-called Berliner Begegnungen, or Berlin Encounters, where I have to give the main lecture along with Auden and

Madariaga – about Schoenberg's *Moses und Aron.* This is also the final piece in the second volume of the so-called *Musikalische Schriften*; there is a complete rough draft and I should have it ready in the finished version tomorrow or the day after. The *Skoteinos* (that is Greek, meaning 'the dark one' and is the epithet of Heraclitus: the title of the essay is 'How to Read Hegel') is also finished in every important respect; there are just a few additions to put into the right places. And the last additions to the second volume of the *Musikalische Schriften* have also been corrected. I would therefore finally be free for the main business if the Hölderlin piece were not still weighing very heavily on me; I simply could not get out of this, and it is about nothing less than basic questions regarding the interpretation of the late hymns, but I hope that I will manage to get that done too. Otherwise, in lesser matters there is just the basis for a discussion in a radio conversation on the occasion of Kierkegaard's 150th birthday, *Darf Kierkegaard siegen?* [Should Kierkegaard be victorious?]; the formulation is my own, and you can imagine what sort of thing is taking place there.

À propos Kierkegaard: the main reason that we would rather not include your review in the *Ornament* – Unseld and I had the same reaction – is the dedication of the book, which is indeed much stronger; there are also imponderable factors about which we can talk sometime; in any case, I ask cordially for your understanding. I am certain that this text too will come to light again one day.

I am very glad that Unseld has made a firm commitment about the aesthetics of film. My unsolicited advice is this: go through the German text as thoroughly as possible. The difference between an American publication and a German one is very great indeed for people like us; our presumptive readers here approach our works with the highest standards in every respect, and it is extremely important that these expectations are satisfied, both in the density of the thought and in the thoroughness of the presentation. What translator or re-translator would have so much as an inkling of this? For my part I am firmly resolved never again in future to re-translate any of my American pieces but to dictate the items in question again, quite freely, if I want to publish them here. That was what I did with the *Gewürdigte Musik* and also with the *Radio-Theorie*, the opening and closing pieces of the *Getreue Korrepetitor*, which is being published by Fischer in May. Please don't think me hysterical or idiosyncratic in these matters, but believe me when I say that I have a very good overview of the literary situation here.

Our plans look as if we shall be leaving here on 27 July and staying up in Sils Maria again until the beginning of September, provided that I live until then, which at my current pace of work is more a question of metaphysics, i.e. election by grace, than a physical one. As the end of July is generally taken up with examinations and faculty meetings, it would in any case be better for us to meet in September in Frankfurt – you would get more out of me then, when I have had a certain amount of rest, as in

Sils Maria I am not going to touch anything at all – or write notes at the very most.

In June, by the way, I shall be in Vienna for a few days – invited to the Europe Dialogue, but in reality more for pleasure.

I will send you the *Eingriffe* as soon as it is published – in about four weeks.

I am glad that Lili has recovered so quickly – Gretel is very well too, and has managed to steer me through the perils of these immensely taxing months like a good pilot.

Much love from both of us to both of you,

Your faithful old

Teddie

Original: typescript with printed letterhead, handwritten additions and corrections; Siegfried Kracauer papers, Deutsches Literaturarchiv, Marbach am Neckar.

sociological problems of television: this was, according to the title of Adorno's lecture on 7 April 1963, the question 'Can the Public Will?' (see Adorno, GS 20.1, pp. 342–7), and following the reply to this the discussion led by Joachim Kaiser of a further question: 'What You Will – a Fiction?'.

Berliner Begegnungen: on 21 April 1963, Adorno gave the lecture 'Sakrales Fragment: Über Schönbergs Moses und Aron' there (Theodor W. Adorno Archiv; see the essay version: Adorno, GS 16, pp. 454–75; 'Sacred Fragment: Schoenberg's *Moses und Aron*', in *Quasi una Fantasia: Essays on Modern Music*, trans. Rodney Livingstone, London: Verso, 1992, pp. 225–48).

along with Auden: the poet W. H. Auden (1907–1973) took part in a discussion about Arnold Schoenberg's opera on 23 April 1963 (Theodor W. Adorno Archiv).

Madariaga: Salvador de Madariaga y Rojo (1886–1978), an author, diplomat and literary scholar from La Coruña; in 1936 he went into exile in England and became a professor at Oxford.

last additions to the second volume of the Musikalische Schriften: *Quasi una fantasia: Musikalische Schriften* II, published on 22 November 1963; the volume contains, after 'Sacred Fragment', the essays 'Music and New Music' and 'Vers une musique informelle' (see Adorno, GS 16, pp. 249–540).

Hölderlin piece: Adorno used his contribution to the annual meeting of the Hölderlin-Gesellschaft in Berlin, 7–9 June 1963, on the occasion of the 120th anniversary of Hölderlin's death, as a critique of Martin Heidegger's *Erläuterungen* [Explications] *zu Hölderlins Dichtung* (2nd edn, Frankfurt am Main: Vittorio Klostermann, 1951): *Parataxis: Zur späten Lyrik Hölderlins* (about its first publication, see letter no. 236; see Adorno, GS 11, pp. 447–91). In his report on the conference ('Der Dichter des Empedokles', *Der Tagesspiegel*, 11 June 1963), Joachim Günther writes about Adorno's performance and the reactions within the festive gathering: 'He denounced the phrases taken from the jargon of the decision between being and time in which the poet in the end "becomes the one cast out": "What Hölderlin keeps silent about is not what Heidegger extrapolates." The stridency of this polemic … found no opponent in the discussion who may have been able to formulate more than personal displeasure and distancing from Adorno's "truths". Hence, "Heidegger's "defeat" in the halls of the Academy and at the conference of the Society to both of which he belongs, remained unalloyed' (see the quotes from Adorno's paper in GS 11, pp. 452f., 455).

basis for a discussion in a radio conversation: Adorno presented 'Darf Kierkegaard siegen?' on 3 May 1963 on Hessischer Rundfunk; the actual broadcast took place through the Westdeutsche Rundfunk in mid-May (Theodor W. Adorno Archiv; on its first publication, see letter no. 215 and Adorno, GS 2, pp. 239–59).

opening and closing pieces of of the Getreue Korrepetitor: these are 'Die gewürdigte Musik' and 'Über die musikalische Verwendung des Radios' (see Adorno, GS 15, pp. 163–87 and 369–401). Adorno points out in his preface that the basic concepts of his 'radio theory' originated in the USA; see *Current of Music: Elements of a Radio Theory*, ed. Robert Hullot-Kentor, Frankfurt am Main: Suhrkamp, 2006 (see letter no. 120).

In Vienna … invited to the Europe Dialogue: on 11/12 June 1963, Adorno spoke about 'Laienkunst – Organisierte Banausie?' [Laypeople's art – organized philistinism?]; other participants included Robert Jungk, Arnold Gehlen and Eugen Kogon (see the documentation: *Licht und Irrlicht: Europa-Gespräch 1963*, ed. Amt für Kultur, Volksbildung und Schulverwaltung der Stadt Wien; Adorno's contribution pp. 54–71).

213 Kracauer to Adorno
New York, 7.6.1963

498 Westend Avenue
New York 24, N.Y.
June 7, 1963

Dear Teddie,

Forgive me for not responding to your letter from April in some detail, as I really should, and for thanking you only in passing for the *Eingriffe* and its kind remembrance. Just don't overdo things with all the articles, interviews and meetings. But we trust dear Gretel to see that you don't. This is just *en passant*, as now I want to go straight on to the reason for this letter: the days in Frankfurt. We had planned – and are still planning – to be in Frankfurt for the period from *14 to 18 September* – that would be all right for you and Gretel, and it would suit Dr Unseld too. So far, so good. But now it transpires that the city of Frankfurt will be completely jam-packed at this time because of the international automobile exhibition. I wrote in March (and later) to all kinds of hotels in Frankfurt and even telephoned the local offices of the new Pan-Amerika Hotel in Frankfurt the day before yesterday: everything sold out to the last man. The hotels, without exception, treated me with pitying condescension. In a desperate state of mind,

I wrote about three weeks ago to Markus Michel of the publishing house, imploring him to act as a go-between if he were in a position to do so. He was so kind; he telegraphed and wrote to me that he had reserved a room for us at the Hotel Antoinette, Wolfgangstrasse 20 – a nice name. But, sceptic that I am – when I was travelling by train as a child I always thought it possible that the engine-driver could go wrong – I wrote at once myself (air mail, special delivery, with two international reply coupons enclosed) to Hotel Antoinette, asking them for immediate confirmation of the reservation, and saying that I would be happy to pay a deposit. No answer. Still no answer. Four days ago I sent a reply-paid telegram to the Antoinette, once again requesting confirmation of Michel's reservation. No reply. So the day before yesterday I wrote to Michel himself – it is a shame that I should have to bother him about such a thing – told him about the mystery just as I am telling you now, and asked him whether he could clarify it. I am sure to hear from him very soon – but I think that I shouldn't wait any longer to give you a report on this situation. It is time that you both knew that we planned to come and when, and that it may well be that a higher (or should I say lower?) power may prevent us from coming. If it really is not possible – I am still hoping, though, that it will be – we would have to try to meet in Switzerland – provided that you can manage that. We are in Interlaken from 25 July to around 2 September (Grand-Hotel Beau-Rivage), where I want to work on the book; then for about eight days in Zurich (Hotel Neues Schloss, Stockerstrasse 17). Once again, forgive me for talking only about immediate practicalities, but this is just so pressing, and, not least, I myself am right in the midst of a whirlwind of business.

Warmest greetings to you both for now from both of us,

Yours,

Friedel

Original: typescript; Theodor W. Adorno Archiv, Frankfurt am Main.

its kind remembrance: Adorno's handwritten dedication in the *Eingriffe* reads: 'For Friedel, kindest regards! / Teddie / Frankfurt, May 1963' (Kracauer papers, Deutsches Literaturarchiv, Marbach).

I wrote about three weeks ago: in the matter of the hotel, Kracauer turned to Karl Markus Michel, who left a reply in the form of a handwritten draft of a telegram, attached to the letter; the reservation was valid from 14 to 18 September 1963 (Archiv der Peter Suhrkamp Stiftung an der Johann Wolfgang Goethe-Universität).

214 Kracauer to Adorno
New York, 26.6.1963

498 Westend Avenue
New York 24, N.Y.
June 26, 1963

Dear Teddie,

Just a hasty word today to let you both know about the collapse of our Frankfurt project (14–18 Sept.). It was kind of you to get your Fräulein Olbrich on the case, and at first I believed that she had succeeded, as she wrote to me that, at her instigation, Hotel Antoinette had been prepared to reserve a room for us if I paid for three days in excess – i.e. from 12–19 September. Sheer extortion, all because of the Motor Show. I replied to Fräulein Olbrich by return of post that, for reasons of *force majeure*, I would nevertheless be willing to take the room, and that she should see to it that the Antoinette sent me an immediate confirmation of the reservation from 12–19 September and write to me straight away about the final result of this business. A few days later I received a telegram from the Antoinette gangsters (paid for by me a long time before in New York) to the effect that they had reserved a room for the period from the 12th to the *22nd* of September. That was the limit. I am no sucker, after all. So I wrote to this gang, saying that I would forego the reservation; I was not inclined to pay for a room for 11 days that I would be using for 4. Incidentally, I have heard no more from your Fräulein Olbrich since your first letter which I mentioned above, in spite of my request that she herself should write to me again – and so Frankfurt is out.

Shall we really not be able to see each other, then? We should be very sorry. In any case, let us give you our addresses in Switzerland:

25 July to 2 Sept.: Grandhotel Beau-Rivage, Interlaken. Tel: (036) 2.22.21

3 September to c. 13 Sept.: Hotel Neues Schloss, Stockerstrasse 17, Zurich. Tel: (051) 27.16.30

Perhaps you could give us a ring in Interlaken, or so. Dr Unseld has been informed. As we have to see each other and have a talk, he will perhaps be coming to Switzerland. It is well nigh incredible that things should have turned out so negatively as regards Frankfurt – a real disaster. I am unhappy about it, believe me.

Warmest greetings to you both from Lili and me. We are flying to Amsterdam at the end of next week.

Yours,
Friedel

Original: typescript; Theodor W. Adorno Archiv, Frankfurt am Main.

Fräulein Olbrich: Elfriede Olbrich (1923–2006), Adorno's secretary since 1956. She was responsible for a handwritten note on the letter: 'Michel has written to S. K. – there is *nothing* to be done.'

Amsterdam: before the stay in Switzerland the stopping places on the journey from 5 July onwards were Holland and Belgium (see *Marbacher Magazin* 47, p. 120).

215 Adorno to Kracauer
Frankfurt am Main, 9.7.1963

PROF. DR. THEODOR W. ADORNO

FRANKFURT AM MAIN 9 July 1963
KETTENHOFWEG 123

Dear Friedel,

Just a few lines today in reply to your letter of 26 June.

Hotel Antoinette is obviously nothing but a gang of crooks. I don't understand the fact that after you booked so far in advance they couldn't reserve something for you in good time because of that idiotic motor show. The idea has now occurred to me whether the two of you might stay, as you did some time ago, with the Blochs, the Unselds or in the publishing house's new guest-room. I would rather not be put up like this either, but it would surely be no more unpleasant than in such a beastly boarding-house. Unseld, it is true, is on holiday at present, but we could at least drop a hint about this. He probably has not written or said anything about this for the sole reason that he didn't have the courage to do so.

A meeting in Switzerland would be difficult at this time because in my state I must practise absolute intellectual asceticism and lead the life of an illiterate, so to speak. Nothing else will do – but meeting up with an illiterate would not be exactly productive. You will get incomparably more out of me in Frankfurt. But for this very reason, I think, it is important not to let oneself be terrorized by this situation with the hotel.

Yesterday I finished the second version of the *Jargon der Eigentlichkeit*; it is far from being the last one, but it is, so to speak, half-time for Heracles in the Augean stables. An extract from it – about the first 25 pages – is likely to be published in the *Neue Rundschau*.

In the meantime, I have given a major lecture here under the auspices of the faculty to mark Kierkegaard's 150th birthday. It should be published in September; of course, you will receive it.

Otherwise I am dreadfully tired and having headaches, but in spite of that am in quite good spirits and not letting up in my efforts to finish my big book; I am now dictating all kinds of additions in order to take a bit of a break from editing the long chapter, and I often find that there is more substance in this material than in the first dictated versions of the texts themselves. I am a classic case of *esprit de l'escalier*; the trick lies in organizing this to such a degree that it can still be applied to the subject matter itself.

Much love,
Your old
Teddie

Original: typescript with printed letterhead; Siegfried Kracauer papers, Deutsches Literaturarchiv, Marbach am Neckar.

with the Blochs, the Unselds or in the publishing house's new guest-room: Siegfried Unseld moved into his house at Klettenbergstrasse 35 in 1959; it served as accommodation for authors on a visit to Frankfurt, for which Ernst and Karola Bloch established a tradition with their one-week stay in March 1960. The publishing firm was housed in Grüneburgweg 69 from April 1963 to November 1968.

an extract from it … in the Neue Rundschau: 'Sections of the first parts, published in *Neue Rundschau* 1963 (issue. 3), have been incorporated into the text'; see *Jargon der Eigentlichkeit*, note (Adorno, GS 6, p. 526).

Kierkegaard … should be published in September: 'Darf Kierkegaard siegen?' (see letter no. 212), *Neue deutsche Hefte*, no. 95, 1963.

216 Adorno to Kracauer
Frankfurt am Main, 22.7.1963

PROF. DR. THEODOR W. ADORNO

FRANKFURT AM MAIN 22 July 1963
KETTENHOFWEG 123

Dear Friedel,

In the midst of the last few weeks, which were somewhat chaotic and overflowing with academic annoyances – both are much the same thing – the *Ornament der Masse* with its dedication was a real breath of fresh air. I thank you from the bottom of my heart. You can imagine how the volume – which in its outward appearance is so very similar to two of my own books – moved me, how much of old memories it has stirred up. I have not, of course, managed to read it systematically yet, but at least I did use no less than an unexpected free weekend for casual reading. To judge from my first impression – which will hardly surprise you – the genuinely philosophical texts – the ones most loaded with meaning – have proved the best at standing the test of time; this is only an apparent contradiction to the thesis about the temporal core of truth. It is lamentable that the book on Simmel and the one on the detective novel are not available *in toto*, and most of all that they were not published at the time when they originated. I especially liked the piece against Buber, which is as topical nowadays as it was then; it is sure to annoy the old man, which he richly deserves, given his admiration for Heidegger. Perhaps this work, sharply as it delineates the phenomenon discussed, does not as yet fully pinpoint its specific form; what is going on there has a lot to do with rehashed neo-romanticism, but at the same time already with that sphere which I have christened *Jargon der Eigentlichkeit* [Jargon of authenticity], and whose matadors are Jaspers and none other than Heidegger. But the gruesome difference between it and neo-romanticism was less easy to anticipate in those days than the relatively innocent affinity. In the next volume of *Neue Rundschau* they are going to publish, under the title 'Jargon der Eigentlichkeit', the beginning of the chapter of that name from my book on dialectics; it may perhaps arouse similar memories in you to the ones that your work did in me.

The writings criticizing the culture industry have naturally retained every kind of validity by virtue of their substance, as it is part of this whole sphere that everything is ceaselessly changing, and yet nothing is. Your articles, nevertheless, have a certain element of innocence compared with the craftiness with which the culture industry has since learnt to leaven the mush that it feeds to people long enough until those people have forgotten that it is mush they are being fed, and in the face of the increasing integration of society in which no proletarian is aware any longer that he is one. But the very fact that your essays make such historical changes discernible is in itself something very fruitful.

What remains fundamentally a matter of controversy between us is the question of the angle from which to approach criticism. Yours is, consistently, transcendent; mine is immanent. But that can only be settled face to face, and certainly not while my head is exhausted to death.

Gretel has sent you the invitation for 11 September. I wonder whether the two of you will be here?

For all that, I have at last finished the corrections to my two books and can once again concentrate on the main business, provided that I succeed in recovering. I should like to take not even a notebook with me to Sils Maria, where we are going on Saturday. Once again I sound to myself like a scratched gramophone record. The most difficult thing for me is to have to talk incessantly to people about every possible kind of more or less administrative business.

Much love to you both, from Gretel too, and once again, a thousand thanks.

Your old
Teddie

Original: typescript with printed letterhead; Siegfried Kracauer papers, Deutsches Literaturarchiv, Marbach am Neckar.

Ornament der Masse *with its dedication*: *Das Ornament der Masse*, published on 8 July 1963; for the printed dedication, see letter no. 207.

in outward appearance is so very similar to two of my own books: Willy Fleckhaus (1925–1983), who was responsible for the publisher's covers and advertising material from 1959, was commissioned to design the format and binding of *Das Ornament der Masse*, using graphics by Josef Albers and the design guidelines for a small series in which Adorno's *Kierkegaard: Konstruktion des Ästhetischen* and an edition of *Minima Moralia* had appeared.

the book on Simmel and the one on the detective novel: from this complex the volume contains the chapters 'Georg Simmel' (see letters nos. 148 and 177) and 'Die Hotelhalle' (for the difference between this version and the chapter 'Hotelhalle' in the *Detektiv-Roman*, see the references in Kracauer, W 1, pp. 313–15).

the piece against Buber: 'Die Bibel auf Deutsch' (see letter no. 31).

whose matadors are Jaspers and none other than Heidegger: the philosopher Karl Jaspers (1883–1969) and Martin Heidegger appear together in *Jargon der Eigentlichkeit* and elsewhere: 'All experts in jargon, from Jaspers on down, unite in praise of positivity. Only the perspicacious Heidegger avoids a too candid affirmation for its own sake and indirectly complies with this imperative by his tone of obsequious authenticity' (see Adorno, GS 6, p. 427; *The Jargon of Authenticity*, trans. Knut Tarnowski and Frederic Will, London. Routledge & Kegan Paul, 1973, p. 22).

the invitation for 11 September: a copy of the printed invitation card with the names added by hand for the celebration of Adorno's 60th birthday is preserved among Max Horkheimer's papers: 'Theodor W. Adorno and Gretel Adorno have the honour … to invite […] to a dinner on Wednesday, 11 September 1963 at 7.30 p.m. at the Frankfurter Gesellschaft für Handel und Industrie, Siesmayerstrasse 12. R.S.V.P.' (see Adorno/Horkheimer, *Briefwechsel* IV, pp. 713f.).

217 Kracauer to Adorno
Interlaken, 3.8.1963

August 3, 1963
GRAND-HOTEL
BEAU-RIVAGE INTERLAKEN

Dear Teddie,

All your July news was forwarded to us in Europe. I was delighted with your last letter of 22 July – on that day we had just arrived in Milan. It is good that you accept the arguments in my volume of essays to such a great extent. In more than one sense it really belongs to you – or, rather, to us. I could say a lot in response to your comments, confirming here and adding there, but you are right – it only makes sense to discuss all this and also our various other controversial positions face to face. (Not even a typewriter – which I don't have here – would do.) We may not reach an agreement, but to arrive at a point where we could go no further and simply tolerate one another. Once again, what you say about *Ornament der Masse* increases the value of the book for me; and nothing better could have happened to me than that, thanks to your advocacy, it is appearing in the company of old friends. I am keen to hear the reactions, if any. Incidentally, *Ginster* is coming out on 12 August; we deleted the last chapter (in Marseilles). *Theory of Film* and the little book of articles about streets will follow. We read about your official Kierkegaard lecture in *Frankfurter Allgemeine*; the report was not at all bad and full of awe. I am awfully curious about *Jargon der Eigentlichkeit*; here Buber too would have his place in the lower regions. (One thing impresses me about Buber: his zest of life [*sic*], which probably, however, is connected with his greed for prizes and honours. One could derive the whole of today's culture industry from his – and Tillich's – reputation; on this point, by the way, my views differ slightly from yours.)

Dear Teddie, we did, of course, also receive the invitation from you and Gretel to the grand dinner on 11 September. How glad we should have been to come – and I should certainly have drunk a toast to you. But right from the outset we had not planned to be in Frankfurt on your birthday. Splendid as it would have been for us to be witnesses to the honours paid to you on your sixtieth birthday, we are convinced that on such a tumultuous occasion we would not be able to talk to you in private, and that means missing out on the most important thing. Hence our idea, which you already know, of being in Frankfurt from 14 to 18 Sept. But, as you also know, it seems that this idea is not feasible because the whole of Frankfurt is blocked by the automobile fair from the 11th or 12th of Sept. onwards. This is a bitter disappointment, and it is hard for me to get used to the idea that because of external circumstances we shall probably not be able to see each other. I should have liked to make an appearance at the publishers, too. Dr Unseld knows about the situation. I think I shall be hearing from him in the next few days when he is back from his holidays. Perhaps – though I am pessimistic – there may still be a solution; he too, I assume, sets great store by a meeting.

Just have a good rest, dear Teddie, and do nothing – really. I myself shall be trying to get some work done on my history book here. But I haven't managed it so far. It is so terribly difficult, as the ideas are new – new even to me – and I am still so very tired after this whole year.

With all good wishes to you and Gretel
for a wonderful time over the coming weeks, and
warmest greetings from Lili and me,

Your Friedel

P.S. We are staying here until 2 Sept.

3–13 Sept.: Hotel Neues Schloss, Stockerstrasse 17, Zurich.

Frankfurt should come next, but will not.

18 Sept. until the end of the month: Grand Hotel du Louvre, Place du Théâtre Français, *Paris* 1er.

Original: MS with printed letterhead; Theodor W. Adorno Archiv, Frankfurt am Main.

Ginster *is coming out on 12 August; we deleted the last chapter (in Marseilles)*: the novel was published on 19 August 1963. Kracauer himself gives the reason for dispensing with chapter XI in a letter to the reader Walter Boehlich (1921–2005):

> am very grateful to you for sharing with me your reaction to the final chapter of *Ginster*. The fact that this is the reaction of all of you made a strong impression on me, as you know far better than I do how what was written in the past suits the present time from which you are speaking. In response to this I had another look at the last two chapters, and I am inclined to concede that in a certain sense you are right. The novel does perhaps really come to an end with the penultimate chapter, where, moreover, one reads at the very end 'What kind of war is coming now? he pondered in bed' (p. 342). And, as the final chapter doesn't round things off but adds something which today is (apparently) beside the point, I can well understand that you would prefer to liquidate it in the interests of giving the book the effect of a rounded conclusion.

Kracauer annouced his decision in a letter of 2 May 1963 to Boehlich: 'So I have definitely made up my mind to follow your advice and *cashier* the final chapter' (Archiv der Peter Suhrkamp Stiftung an der Johann Wolfgang Goethe-Universität).

Kierkegaard lecture ... in Frankfurter Allgemeine: on 28 June Adorno delivered the lecture in celebration of the 150th anniversary of Kierkegaard's birth (see letters nos. 212 and 215) at the Johann Wolfgang Goethe-Universität. Kracauer read Helmut Scheffel's 'Darf Kierkegaard siegen? Ein Vortrag von Theodor Adorno', *Frankfurter Allgemeine Zeitung*, 8 July 1963.

218 Adorno to Kracauer
Frankfurt am Main, 4.9.1963

PROF. DR. THEODOR W. ADORNO

FRANKFURT AM MAIN 4 September 1963
KETTENHOFWEG 123

Dear Friedel,

Many thanks for both your messages, together with a plea for you to forgive my silence; I was in such a wretched state that even writing a card meant an immense effort. All in all, I have made a good recovery, though admittedly today – one day after our return – I feel limp, and as if I had been hit over the head – but I think that will go away. I hope the two of you have had a really good relaxing time.

By the way, you must not fail to make contact in Zurich with the very nice and highly gifted Dr Peter Szondi, a young friend of mine. His address is Zurich 7/44, Dunantstrasse 3.

Unseld is still away travelling; I am trying, naturally, to get hold of him as quickly as possible. It would be too idiotic if we were to miss each other.

Ginster must have already come out; the fact that you have left out the last chapter seems wise to me and, most of all, beneficial to the book itself.

In the meantime, I have read all of the page proofs of the Hegel and a major part of those of the new and very voluminous book on music. Otherwise, however, I have been practising the utmost asceticism in intellectual matters during the holidays. What lies before me still looks at present like the magnetic mountain. Keep your fingers crossed for me to get it done.

And, once again: let's hope that it may still work out after all.

Much love to you both, from Gretel too,

Your old

Teddie

Original: typescript with printed letterhead; Siegfried Kracauer papers, Deutsches Literaturarchiv, Marbach am Neckar.

in Zurich … Szondi: Peter Szondi (1929–1971), a literary scholar from Budapest; together with his family, he escaped deportation by fleeing to Switzerland. Szondi wrote his doctoral thesis, *Theorie des modernen Dramas* (Frankfurt am Main: Suhrkamp, 1956) under Emil Staiger; in 1965 he accepted an appointment at the Freie Universität Berlin after the failure of Adorno's attempt to secure him for the Johann Wolfgang Goethe-Universität (see letter no. 244). Shortly before the move to take up a professorship in Zurich as Paul de Man's successor, Szondi took his own life. The meeting instigated by Adorno did take place (see letter no. 231).

Unseld is still away travelling: Siegfried Unseld was travelling in Denmark and Norway from 29 August to 3 September 1963; his central purpose was a visit to Hans Magnus Enzensberger in Tjöme.

magnetic mountain: the subject of a legend, according to which ships which approached the mountain too closely were smashed to pieces on it (see Gustav Schwabe, *Die deutschen Volksbücher*, Part 3, Frankfurt am Main: Insel, 1978, pp. 36f.).

219 Adorno to Kracauer

Frankfurt am Main, 20.9.1963

PROF. DR. THEODOR W. ADORNO

FRANKFURT AM MAIN 20 September 1963
KETTENHOFWEG 123

Dear Friedel,

The fact that we didn't see each other after all has truly added a bitter drop of wormwood to the recent festive days. I missed you both terribly, and you would have enjoyed it so much too. Everything went off in the most dignified fashion, with official honours and the Goethe medal, and yet in such a way that it wasn't at all embarrassing, although of course I did feel embarrassed. Strange how these things do in the end give one a lot of pleasure; perhaps it is less immodest to admit it than to conceal it in a supercilious fashion. I need not tell you that all this couldn't get me to identify with the current state of affairs.

In the meantime, I have once again been working at full throttle on the big book. The Hegel has come out in the last few days; you will receive a copy as soon as possible, and also the fragment about the *Jargon der Eigentlichkeit* from the Rundschau (which begins with a memory that you and I share) and the Kierkegaard lecture.

For the time being, please accept my most heartfelt thanks for the contribution on the philosophy of history. Of course, I haven't been able to study it in all the hurly-burly, but just to look through it. It may perhaps interest you to learn that I have known Jauss (whom you quote) very well for years from our time in Heidelberg, and that I wanted to get him the chair in Romance Studies here, which only failed to come off because he had received an offer from Giessen shortly before and could not be wrested away from there on account of the three-year clause. His book about Proust is (at least among the existing German publications about him) the only one from which I have learnt anything.

Much love again to both of you, from Gretel too – and hoping to see you soon,

As ever,
Your old
Teddie

Original: typescript with printed letterhead; Siegfried Kracauer papers, Deutsches Literaturarchiv, Marbach am Neckar.

a memory that you and I share: 'In the early 1920s a number of people active in philosophy, sociology, and even theology were planning a gathering … To his slight annoyance, a friend who was at that time attracted by this circle, was not invited. He was – they intimated – not authentic enough. For he hesitated before Kierkegaard's leap, suspecting that religion which is conjured up out of autonomous thinking would subordinate itself in consequence to the latter, and would negate itself as the absolute which, after all, in terms of its own conceptual nature, it wants to be' (*Jargon der Eigentlichkeit*; see Adorno, GS 6, p. 415; see letter no. 221; *The Jargon of Authenticity*, trans. Knut Tarnowski and Frederic Will, London: Routledge & Kegan Paul, 1973, pp. 1–2).

contribution on the philosophy of history: 'Time and History', in *Zeugnisse: Theodor Adorno zum sechzigsten Geburtstag*, ed. Max Horkheimer, Frankfurt am Main: Europäische Verlagsanstalt, 1963, pp. 50–64 – i.e. the sixth chapter of *Geschichte – Vor den letzten Dingen* (see Kracauer, W 4, pp. 154–80).

Jauss (whom you quote): Hans Robert Jauss (1921–1997), authority on Romance languages and literature; Kracauer cited Jauss's dissertation *Zeit und Erinnerung in Marcel Prousts 'À la recherche du temps perdu'*, Heidelberg: Karl Winter, 1955.

220 Adorno to Kracauer
Lucca, 18.10.1963

Lucca
18 October 1963

Dear Friedel,

As I planned, I have flown to Tuscany for a late holiday and have had some splendid days – and there is something even finer in prospect. Before I left I reached an agreement with the head of the Abendstudio at Radio Frankfurt for a major programme about you to be broadcast on 8 February 1964, your 75th birthday. I would be *most* grateful to you now for information about the German edition of your aesthetics of film. When and where is it going to be published? Could I have the page proofs of it *in good time* for my broadcast? Or, possibly, the typescript? Please let me know so that I can tailor my (one-hour) piece of work around it. It is already planned; I want to dip my brush deep into the paint-pot. I shall be back in Frankfurt at the end of the month.

Much love to you and Lili, Your old Teddie.

Original: MS, postcard: Lucca – Facciata di S. Michele sec. XI–XIV; Siegfried Kracauer papers, Deutsches Literaturarchiv, Marbach am Neckar.

head of the Abendstudio at Radio Frankfurt: Hans Heinz Holz (1927–2011), a philosopher; PhD from Leipzig (external candidate); professor at Marburg in 1973. He worked at the Frankfurt radio station from 1964 to 1973.

221 Kracauer to Adorno
New York, 25.10.1963

498 Westend Avenue
New York 24, N.Y.
October 25, 1963

Dear Teddie,

Your kind card from Lucca (which I know only from Heine) delighted me both for its view and for its content. Were you on your own this time? You more than deserved a nice late holiday.

You can imagine what I think of your plan to make a long radio programme about me. It is a great gift that you are making me by doing this. I am overjoyed, and that is almost an understatement.

But there is something about it that has – quite literally – profoundly terrified me – the fact that the broadcast is to take place on the occasion of my 75th birthday. Dear Teddie, I fervently implore you – and I mean it – not to allude to my age by as much as a single word in your broadcast. As far as I am concerned, this is a matter which is deeply rooted and highly personal. Call it an idiosyncrasy – but, the older I become, the more everything in me struggles against making a display of my chronological age. Of course, I know about the dates, which are becoming more and more ominous – but, as long as they don't come marching to meet me in an official procession, at least they don't assume the nature of an indelible inscription which everyone, myself included, cannot help continually seeing. Luckily I can overlook the chronological embarrassment, and that is of infinite importance for the progress of my work and my entire internal economy. My way of existence would be literally on the line if the dates were to be flushed out and attack me from outside. That was why I was so terrified by the chronological reference in the Lucca card. How deep this goes with me is also indicated by the fact that I have suppressed my date of birth in all the Who's Whos. My 70th was to have been the occasion for an article here; I put a stop to it in good time, and was glad that I did.

So, dear Teddie, do not mention the figure, and don't make it the occasion. As far as I can judge, the present publication of my things is occasion enough. If I remember rightly, you promised Unseld to speak about *Ginster* and told me yourself that you wanted to write about the aesthetics of film. So I assume that the broadcast would appear to be justified even without any reference to a specific date. Indeed, it would then place greater emphasis on the products themselves and the continuity between them.

Things will probably be easy for you as regards the German manuscript of the film book. On our return at the beginning of October I sent to Suhrkamp Verlag the German translation, which I had revised for a second time in the first half of the year, and Dr Unseld has already confirmed receipt. I hope that you will be able to get the manuscript from him for a short time. The book is to come out in the spring, as I gather from a letter from Michel.

I still have to thank you for your September letter which was forwarded to me in Paris. I can understand only too well your rejoicing at the honours in spite of all your nonconformity.This legitimate ambivalence could be the subject of an essay – a genuine symptom of the *condition humaine*.

Jargon der Eigentlichkeit and the Kierkegaard speech have arrived. Many thanks. You will understand that after just three weeks here I have still not found the proper leisure to read the pieces as they deserve. I have just read the beginning of *Jargon* where you describe what happened to me, at the hands of 'those who have religion', in the age of 'those who wait'. Can you still remember their names? Was it Herrigel et al.?

Much love and warmest greetings to you and dear Gretel from Lili and myself,

Yours,

Friedel

Original: typescript; Theodorn W. Adorno Archiv, Frankfurt am Main.

Lucca (which I know only from Heine): see letter no. 1, note.

to speak about Ginster: this happened in the 'radio programme'; Adorno declared that *Ginster* was, for him, Kracauer's 'most significant achievement' (see Adorno, GS 11, p. 401).

Unseld has already confirmed receipt: on 11 October 1963, Kracauer wrote to Siegfried Unseld that he had 'completely revised' the manuscript 'yet again' and was sending it 'by the same post'. Unseld confirmed the arrival of the package on 15 October 1963 (Archiv der Peter Suhrkamp Stiftung an der Johann Wolfgang Goethe-Universität).

The book is to come out in the spring: as Karl Markus Michel wrote to Kracauer in a letter of 26 August 1963, in which he considered it unlikely that there would be 'problems of which we are unaware' with the manuscript of *Theorie des Films*. In fact, it took Michel two weeks to edit the translation (Michel to Kracauer, 8 November 1963, Archiv der Peter Suhrkamp Stiftung an der Johann Wolfgang Goethe-Universität).

nonconformity: in English in the original.

what happened to me: the constellation mentioned at the beginning of *Jargon der Eigentlichkeit* (see letter no. 219).

222 Adorno to Kracauer

Frankfurt am Main, 28.10.1963

PROF. DR. THEODOR W. ADORNO

FRANKFURT AM MAIN 28 October 1963
KETTENHOFWEG 123

Dear Friedel,

Sometimes the post travels with amazing speed. Yesterday evening I returned by plane from Tuscany and I found your letter waiting for me this morning.

It goes without saying that I shall take your wishes into account and not mention your 75th birthday in my talk by so much as a single word. However, I cannot guarantee that Hessischer Rundfunk will not say something about the date, as when I let the matter slip to Abendstudio there the head of it told me that they knew the date, and had, at any rate, invited me to give a talk to mark the occasion. I don't believe that the precise wording of such an announcement will become common knowledge in America, but I will try to prevent anyone talking about it. If I should not succeed and they will only broadcast my talk on condition that they say something about the date, I shall leave it to you to decide whether I should give the talk in spite of that. I should be very sorry if you were to veto it, but everyone has the right to their own idiosyncrasies. Of course it would make formulating this issue more *difficult* if I can't say where the original idea came from – but *quand même*!

The circle of which I spoke at the beginning of *Jargon der Eigentlichkeit* included Buber, Rosenzweig, Rosenstock and also Herrigel (later on the last of these, out of a sheer need for concretion, became a vehemently outspoken Nazi). By the way, the gentlemen were immediately recognized from my lecture; Scholem was especially delighted because the portrait of Buber seemed to him to be such a success.

As for the Filmästhetik, I shall get in touch with Suhrkamp immediately about it. It would be a great relief for me personally if I were able to see the corrections to the page proofs, or at least the galley proofs, and not the typescript, simply for the sake of my overstrained eyes; but if there is no other way I shall be content even with the typescript. Perhaps you could step in once again to see to this.

Now things of every possible kind are piling up in front of me, but at least I have completely finished my dictation of the rough draft, and I shall in any event be able to get on top of editing and shaping the material to some extent during the semester. I am back on top form once again.

Much love to you and Lili, from Gretel too,

Your old

Teddie

Original: typescript with printed letterhead and handwritten additions; Siegfried Kracauer papers, Deutsches Literaturarchiv, Marbach am Neckar.

Rosenstock: Eugen Rosenstock (1888–1973) legal historian and sociologist; he co-founded the Akademie für Arbeit in Frankfurt am Main in 1921 and went into exile in the USA in 1933.

Scholem: Gershom Scholem was on a visit to Frankfurt am Main in October 1963 (see Adorno/ Suhrkamp/Unseld, *Briefwechsel*, p. 456, note).

the portrait of Buber: 'Since Martin Buber split off the Kierkegaardian concept of the existential from the latter's Christology …' (see Adorno, GS 6, pp. 423f.).

223 Adorno to Kracauer

Frankfurt am Main, 29.10.1963

PROF. DR. THEODOR W. ADORNO

FRANKFURT AM MAIN 29 October 1963
KETTENHOFWEG 123

Dear Friedel,

Good news: I have just spoken to the director of the Abendstudio at Frankfurter Rundfunk (a former student of Ernst Bloch's, by the way) and he is entirely in agreement about omitting any reference to the date, let alone your age. People will, of course, be able to work it out approximately from certain details about you, which I simply do have to include; it is precisely our early years that I want to discuss. But, if I understand you correctly, the sole focus of your idiosyncrasy is the identification of the date. The radio station has also promised to leave out any other reference to the date, no matter how it is couched. I think, then, that you can be entirely reassured on this point, and I would just be grateful if you could confirm it explicitly once more to me – because after all we want to be able to enjoy this business, not to let it send you into a panic.

Much love to you and Lili, from Gretel too,

Yours ever,

Teddie

Have you actually received the *Drei Studien zu Hegel*?

Original: typescript with printed letterhead and handwritten postscript; Siegfried Kracauer papers, Deutsches Literaturarchiv, Marbach am Neckar.

224 Kracauer to Adorno
New York, 31.10.1963

498 Westend Avenue
New York 24, N.Y.
October 31, 1963

Dear Teddie,

Many cordial thanks for your two letters, which arrived here at the same time. It is good of you to take into account my 'idiosyncrasy' – an unsatisfactory term, but one which will suffice between us – but of course I never doubted it for an instant. And it really reassures me to know that Hessischer Rundfunk is – surely thanks to your insistence – in agreement with the suppression of any allusion to the date and my age. (If that were not the case, I should – albeit with a heavy heart – have asked you not to give the lecture.) The promise which was given to you there to omit any other possible reference to my age does a great deal to reassure me.

There is just one point which still needs a brief mention. You write that it is inevitable that people might be able to work out my approximate age from certain details relating to me which you would have to include when discussing our early years. Dear Teddie, I think that you underestimate your own presentation skills. I am convinced that you are able to evoke those early years, and above all the affairs of that time and later on, in such a way that nobody will feel any urge to engage in chronological calculations and yet, at the same time, to bring all the important points into sharp focus. Of course I concede that this makes their formulation more difficult

– but, although it is only with the most extreme reluctance that I suggest anything more than you are already doing in any case, I do beseech you most fervently, dear Teddie, to select the emphasis, etc., in such a way that my age does not become apparent. I just wanted to get this off my chest so that everything was clear. I am sure that you will fulfil my request. And so now I really am quite reassured – and terribly keen to hear everything that you might say. (Incidentally, as no dates are being mentioned, your lecture is not tied to any set day.) I shall of course be happy to write to Suhrkamp Verlag about your – our – concern. (I am expecting a letter from them any day now about procedures in connection with the film book.) By the way, the manuscript is quite readable.

No – your Hegel piece has not arrived yet. I myself am at present still doing the reading for my history book – mostly stupid stuff, but one has to be able to anticipate the objections from this quarter – i.e. the majority.

Warmest greetings to you and dear Gretel from Lili and me; we are delighted to hear that the post-cure stay in Tuscany was a success.

Yours,
Friedel

Original: typescript; Theodor W. Adorno Archiv, Frankfurt am Main.

a letter from them ... in connection with the film book: Karl Markus Michel discussed mainly editorial details in a letter of over four pages of 8 November 1963 (Archiv der Peter Suhrkamp Stiftung an der Johann Wolfgang Goethe-Universität).

225 Adorno to Kracauer

Frankfurt am Main, 5.11.1963

PROF. DR. THEODOR W. ADORNO

FRANKFURT AM MAIN 5 November 1963
KETTENHOFWEG 123

Dear Friedel,

Many thanks for your letter. Everything is all right, then – and it goes without saying that I shall proceed as carefully as is humanly possible in formulating my text in the way which you indicate. Of course, though, we should not deceive ourselves; people follow everything relating to those like us with an immense, libidinously obsessive curiosity, and, if someone or other in Germany discovers your date of birth and announces it with a loud drum roll, it would come as no surprise to me. I shall not be mentioning it to any outsiders and shall allow my skill as an author with which you endow me to prevail, taking pains at least not to fall short of Proust who, as Jauss has so charmingly pointed out, in his novel on the subject of time avoided giving any tangible definitions of time in categories of *temps espace*.

There is just one more thing that I should like to discuss with you – the question of the title. As I see it, there is a choice of two titles: *Der intellektuelle Schwejk* [The intellectual Švejk) or *Der wunderliche Realist* [The curious realist] – both with the subtitle *Über S. K.* [On S. K.]. The first title would have the advantage of being derived from an expression which you yourself coined and which would *ipso facto* place the relationship to the figure of Ginster into the centre. I myself should prefer the second, as it gives central importance to the conception which will provide the basis of my lecture. If this is agreeable to you I should be delighted; if you prefer the first option, I should be happy to fall in with you about this.

I shall see to whatever is necessary in the matter of the Hegel.

Much love to you and Lili from us both,

Your old

Teddie

I have been – as I forgot to write to you – elected president of the Deutsche Gesellschaft für Soziologie.

About the expression 'idiosyncrasy': it was you yourself who suggested the term. If something quite different should be involved, I should be all the more grateful for enlightenment – though of course with regard to *genuine* reasons – as my own 'innervations' concerning this whole complex of associations are fundamentally different from yours. I tend to emphasize my own age as drastically as possible to dispel any appearance of trying to attach myself to youth; in intellectual matters I set no store by this term even as a *young* person, and still less today as an *old* one; and one cannot evade age. It would be worth discussing all this one day just for the sake of the matter.

Kindest regards!

Original: typescript with printed letterhead, handwritten corrections and postscript; Siegfried Kracauer papers, Deutsches Literaturarchiv, Marbach am Neckar.

As Jauss has so charmingly pointed out: see letter no. 219.

Der intellektuelle Schwejk: see letter no. 251.

president of the Deutsche Gesellschaft für Soziologie: Adorno held this office until 1967 as Otto Stammer's successor.

226 Kracauer to Adorno
New York, 8.11.1963

498 Westend Avenue
New York 24, N.Y.
November 8, 1963

Dear Teddie,

Many thanks for your understanding and your willingness to overlook the chronological factor – à la Proust. I am now completely reassured.

I too prefer the second title which you have chosen – *Der wunderliche Realist* – to the Švejk alternative; it seems to me to be more comprehensive. So let it remain as you yourself prefer – as was only to be expected. I am very curious about the content to which you are going to apply the term 'curious' – but I shall deny myself the pleasure of anticipating anything.

I called the expression 'idiosyncrasy' unsatisfactory because it usually covers an aversion of a physiological or psychological nature for which no further reason can be found. In my case it entails more of an old and deeply rooted need to live extra-territorially – as regards the intellectual climate as well as chronological time. That is why New York suits me, as it makes this extra-territorial existence possible – and that is why I seek to escape chronological labelling. It is not as if I were concerned with appearing young or younger; it is merely the aversion to being torn away from chronological anonymity by the fixing of the date and the inevitable connotations of such fixing. But, as I have already written to you, this really is a purely personal attitude, and as such it can, of course, be called an idiosyncrasy even so – provided the term is understood in a sufficiently broad sense. Your own, different attitude to this set of problems appears entirely obvious to me and – no need to say so – seems to me at least as well justified as my own. The question of legitimacy does not arise here at all. I entirely agree with you that at some time we should discuss everything that may lie at the root of this in objective terms. (I deeply regretted not being able to see you this summer.)

We think it is marvellous – even though it is also one more commitment – that you have been elected president of the Deutsche Gesellschaft für Soziologie. (I received the notification of the sociologists' conference at the end of April in Heidelberg and contemplated it nostalgically.) All our congratulations!

A few days ago – in a seminar at Columbia – Horkheimer suddenly popped up, having come straight from Frankfurt. It was a great surprise, and a very pleasant one.

Warmest greetings from both of us to both of you,

Yours,

Friedel

Original: typescript; Theodor W. Adorno Archiv, Frankfurt am Main.

Heidelberg ... nostalgically: see letter no. 3.

Horkheimer suddenly popped up: Adorno wrote to Max Horkheimer in New York on 11 November 1963 about Kracauer's brief note; the exact dates of Horkheimer's trip have not been determined.

227 Adorno to Kracauer
Frankfurt am Main, 14.11.1963

PROF. DR. THEODOR W. ADORNO

FRANKFURT AM MAIN 14 November 1963
KETTENHOFWEG 123

Dear Friedel,

So we are agreed – there is just one small point remaining to be settled – i.e. that I should write the piece. Keep your fingers crossed for it to come off; I can always manage such things only as a kind of *coup de main*. However, the conditions for this have become rather more favourable, as with Unseld's agreement I have made a slight change to my publication plans, which were threatening to strangle me. I have completely removed the *Jargon der Eigentlichkeit* (in the longer version) from the complex of the book on dialectics; it will still come out next year, but the book not until the year after. This is a load off my mind.

By the same post I am sending you the *Prismen* which, as far as I know, you don't have; it is the first of my books to come out in a mass edition as a paperback – I believe 25,000 copies were printed. God only knows who is supposed to read it, but, since the *Eingriffe* (have you got that, by the way?) has now gone into 18,000 copies, I consider anything possible.

Please be kind enough to let me know whether the publisher, who gave me a firm promise to do so, has finally sent you the Hegel. I would be glad, too, to hear about your reaction to the other things, most of all the fragment of the *Jargon*.

Much love to you and Lili, from Gretel too,

Your old

Teddie

I still have *not* received the manuscript of the film book.

Original: typescript with handwritten corrections and postscript; Siegfried Kracauer papers, Deutsches Literaturarchiv, Marbach am Neckar.

completely removed ... the book on dialectics: see letters nos. 179 and 208.

Eingriffe ... *has now gone into 18,000 copies*: the second impression (11,000–17,000 copies) was prepared in July 1963, and the third (18,000–25,000) became available in August 1964.

228 Kracauer to Adorno
New York, 22.11.1963

498 Westend Avenue
New York 24, N.Y.
November 22, 1963

Dear Teddie,

Your Hegel has not arrived yet. About your *Jargon* article: the attack on the 'authentics' with Heidegger at their head and that foolish Jaspers in the rear could not have come off better and more strikingly. I believe that the article is among your most incisive pieces. It is effective because you show – and show with such exuberance – how much Heidegger has in common with the lower kind of scum. One can see from your locutions the fun you had with them, and that is as it should be. Some of them enchanted me – for example, the 'Ascension of the Word' and even 'Man/the human being is the ideology of dehumanization'. (The Ascension sounds like an attack on Buber.) (By the way, the concept of 'man'/human being is questionable even in the writings of Marx himself; while at first more or less meaningful, his use of the concept tends more and more in the direction of a stereotyped border-line concept). Reading *Jargon*, it struck me that – at least in parts of your work – you are among the truly great *moralistes*. Of the few things that I read in *Eingriffe*, I especially liked 'Philosophy and Teachers' – not only because of the accurate observations in it but most of all because here, to cut a long story short, the ideological and the sociological elements arrive at a complete congruence. That doesn't seem to me to be always the case in your works – not even in *Jargon* – a problem exists here, *en tout cas*, that we ought also to discuss one day. I haven't got round to the Kierkegaard lecture at present. I have the *Prismen* in the original edition. To return to the 'authentics': will this German species never stop replenishing itself? Even I have had my difficulties – and my fun – with Buber et al. Michel wrote to tell me that the German manuscript of the film book was going to press, so you are sure to be able to have a look at the galley proofs. Until now you have only mentioned my contribution to your festschrift *en passant* – but perhaps you will be referring to it in your lecture?

Warmest greetings from us both to dear Gretel and yourself,

Yours,
Friedel

Original: typescript; Theodor W. Adorno Archiv, Frankfurt am Main.

'Ascension of the Word'/ ... the ideology of dehumanization: direct quotations (see Adorno, GS 6, pp. 420, 452).

'Philosophy and Teachers': before *Eingriffe*, in *Neue Sammlung*, March–April 1962 (see Adorno, GS 10.2, pp. 474–94, 840).

My contribution to your festschrift: see letter no. 219.

229 Kracauer to Adorno
New York, 6.12.1963

498 Westend Avenue
New York 24, N.Y.
December 6, 1963.

Dear Teddie,

This is just a practical interpolation, but I am taking the opportunity to thank you most cordially for the pocket edition of your *Prismen* with the challenging dedication. Actually, the subject in question does not involve your field at all, but perhaps you can set it in motion even so. I am worried about the delay in receiving the offprints of 'Time and History', my contribution to your festschrift. I was promised them as far back as several weeks ago. On 8 November I wrote to Tiedemann, who has always replied promptly in the past, and enquired when the offprints would go off to the 30 addresses which I had given him and when the remaining 70 would be sent to me. I said that he really ought to let me know. No reply. So on 24 November I asked Schweppenhäuser in Lüneburg (it *would* be Lüneburg of all places) for the same information. No reply. Whatever is the matter with these two young people? It would be important for me to get the information soon so that I know where I stand. I am reluctant to bother you with such a trifle, but I see no other way out of this – and of course you too would need to see to the necessary arrangements. In any event, my most sincere gratitude in advance.

Much love to Gretel and yourself from us both,

Yours,

Original: typescript (carbon copy); Siegfried Kracauer papers, Deutsches Literaturarchiv, Marbach am Neckar.

pocket edition of your Prismen *with the challenging dedication*: Adorno added his handwritten dedication to the title above the text of the blurb of the dtv edition (see letter no. 200): 'You, dear Friedel, and not the man who wrote the blurb, must give your opinion [of this book]! / Your old Teddie / Frankfurt, 14. XI. 63'.

230 Adorno to Kracauer

Frankfurt am Main, 17.12.1963

PROF. DR. THEODOR W. ADORNO

FRANKFURT AM MAIN 17 December 1963
KETTENHOFWEG 123

Dear Friedel,

Please forgive me for your not having heard from me until today. You – free man that you are – can scarcely have any idea of what a burden these past few weeks have been. However, this strain did have its bright side; I have made far better progress with my major work than I dared to hope while I was still in Italy, and because of this the realization of the lecture about you has now also come within reach.

To prevent any misunderstanding, however, I must tell you that your exact date of birth – like that of all of us émigrés – is given in the book by Sternfeld and Tiedemann (*not* our Tiedemann!) entitled *Deutsche Exilliteratur von 1933 bis 1945*. Given all that most curious interest which exists in Germany in teasing out every imaginable kind of intellectual activity that occurred in the years before 1933 – an inclination which is probably connected with a profound unconscious knowledge of the futility of the culture which was resurrected after Hitler – we must reckon with the possibility that someone or other will find this out and publicize it. I myself have maintained absolute silence and asked the only person with whom I discussed the matter before I wrote to you, Herr Holz of Abendstudio, likewise for the strictest discretion, which he will unquestionably exercise. So, if something connected with the date *should* become public knowledge after all, please don't blame me.

The business of the offprint of that extraordinarily important essay which you dedicated to me on my birthday has since been settled, as I have ascertained, in the way that you wished – including the matter of the copies which will go to you, as well as those going to the addresses which you specified.

Your praise of my piece on teachers and philosophy from the *Eingriffe* almost makes me blush. It really *is* something very modest, taken down at my dictation in one single afternoon for a specific and pressing occasion and then edited only as much as was necessary to prepare it for the press. Incidentally, we really ought to have a fundamental conversation one of these days about the concept of the concrete and specific. My view is that, within the medium of philosophy, it means something quite different from the inclusion of immediate observations and experiences – but I can't help myself being seriously corrupted by Hegel. Have you had a look at my little book?

Your agreement about the *Jargon der Eigentlichkeit* delighted me all the more as amid all the immense difficulties of the long version such an incitement immediately transforms itself into a motor. Granted, I didn't entirely understand what you write there about the relationship to 'ideology' in the simple sense that I don't know exactly what you mean by this suggestion. I should like to think that in making it you were thinking of the desideratum of a transparent relationship between our own theoretical positions and physiognomic observations. On this point I think that I can reassure you, as the task of the long version of *Jargon* is indeed to deduce this and its untruthfulness from an untrue philosophy, and to this extent to transform its criticism into a genuinely philosophical one. For this very reason the text was originally intended for inclusion in the great book on dialectic; the fact that it has now become independent of this book has made many things much easier for me, without the relationship itself being severed; the connection between my various writings is just becoming closer and closer and, I hope, also more explicit.

A propos ideology: I would urge you to eliminate from the German edition of the aesthetics of film what appears in the American one about 'loss of ideology'. In Germany this argument has been thoroughly worked to death [*durchexerziert*], as they say here, for more than ten years now, and, what is more, by the very people with whom we have nothing in common theoretically, such as Schelsky – in the sense of a flattening and enlarging the strict concept of ideology into a broad 'total' one of the Pareto and Mannheim variety. If absolutely everything constitutes ideology, one can easily talk of the loss of ideology; moreover, empirical studies (for example, one undertaken by the Institute) have disproved their concept. The Institute's study, contrary to all expectations, revealed drastic ideological differences between workers and members of the bourgeoisie. I know that you have nothing in common with the thinking that is associated with the doctrine of loss of ideology in Germany, but you of all people will certainly not view your writings outside the constellation in which they appear and will take the greatest care in those places where misunderstandings could become dangerous. No offence meant. Incidentally, I haven't set eyes on the German film book yet; what I should really like would be a page-proof copy because of my terribly overstrained eyes. If you could make the necessary arrangements, I should be grateful; I don't want to keep dinning my request into Unseld's ears.

You will know, of course, that there was a brilliant and, what is more, a very perceptive review of *Ornament* in *Die Zeit*; I hear in the university bookshop here that both your books are selling very well. I hope that this is true in general.

The Christmas holidays begin at the end of the week, and lectures don't start again until 7 January. Although in the next few weeks I shall have to work most intensively on *Jargon*, which I should like to have finished at least in rough draft by then – and then all that will be left is what among film people is called the 'fine cut' – it really is almost a difference affecting the whole project, whether one is occupied with autonomous or heteronomous work, to say nothing of the countless examinations which I have had to conduct, and which, however, I do take seriously as a matter of conscience.

We, Gretel and I, wish you and Lili a splendid and very happy New Year and, above all, that you may get on well with your book on the philosophy of history. When I next write to you I very much hope to be able to give you some concrete news about the text which relates to you in a double sense.

Much love as always,
Yours,
Teddie

Original: typescript with printed letterhead, handwritten additions and corrections; Siegfried Kracauer papers, Deutsches Literaturarchiv, Marbach am Neckar.

Sternfeld and Tiedemann: Wilhelm Sternfeld (1888–1973), an expert on German literature, and Eva Tiedemann (1918–2000), a librarian, published their *Bio-Bibliographie* (as the subtitle calls it) *deutsche Exilliteratur von 1933 bis 1945* with Lambert Schneider, Heidelberg. In the first edition, current addresses were given as well as dates of birth and death, as in Kracauer's entry: 'Born 8.2.1889 in Frankfurt a.M.; Dr. Ing.; Exile: 1933 France, 1941 USA. Address: 489 Westend Avenue, New York 24, N.Y.' (p. 183).

our Tiedemann: Rolf Tiedemann (1932–2018) gained his doctorate with the thesis 'Studien zur Philosophie Walter Benjamins' [Studies in the philosophy of Walter Benjamin: with a preface by Adorno; see Adorno, GS 20.1, pp. 178–82], Frankfurt am Main: Europäische Verlagsanstalt, 1965; editor of both Adorno's and Walter Benjamin's complete writings and director (1985–2000) of the Theodor W. Adorno Archiv.

loss of ideology: on this Adorno wrote with regard to Martin Heidegger: 'But his operation once again becomes ideology because of his claim that he recovers the meaning of Dasein. This happens after the fashion of today's talk about the loss of ideology – talk which beats down ideology but means the truth' (see Adorno, GS 6, p. 515; *The Jargon of Authenticity*, trans. Knut Tarnowski and Frederic Will, London: Routledge & Kegan Paul, 1973, p. 153). Adorno found fault, above all, with passages in the Epilog to the *Theorie des Film*, where, for example, the question arises of whether 'ideological unity' has been 'irretrievably lost' (see Kracauer, W 3, p. 454).

Schelsky: Helmut Schelsky (1912–1984), sociologist; assistant to Arnold Gehlen (1938–40) and member of the SA and NSDAP; director (1949) of the Hamburger Akademie für Gemeinwirtschaft, with which the Institute for Social Research collaborated. He was appointed to a professorship in Hamburg in 1953 and later to others in Münster and Bielefeld (see Adorno/Horkheimer, *Briefwechsel* IV, note, p. 33).

the Pareto and Mannheim variety: Vilfredo Pareto (1848–1923), an economist and sociologist from Paris who grew up in Italy; in 1894 he was appointed to a professorship in Lausanne. Adorno on Pareto and Karl Mannheim (see letter no. 81): 'The later sociology of knowledge, especially that of Pareto and Mannheim, prided itself on its scientifically purified terminology and dogma-free enlightened nature by replacing this concept of ideology with another which it called "total" (not by mere chance) and which accorded all too well with blind, total domination' (see 'Meinung Wahn Gesellschaft' [Opinion, delusion, society], Adorno, GS 10.2, p. 285).

empirical studies (for example, one conducted by the Institute): the recognition of the continuing existence of ideological differences cannot be attributed beyond doubt to any particular individual study.

a very perceptive review of Ornament: Reinhard Baumgart, 'Ein Philosoph, der ins Kino ging: Späte Bekanntschaft mit Siegfried Kracauer' [A philosopher who went to the cinema: late acquaintance with Siegfried Kracauer], *Die Zeit*, 11 October 1963, beginning: 'The name of Siegfried Kracauer also has its place in the splendid utopian map of the stars of the 1920s.' Among other things, Baumgart especially singled out Kracauer's 'flair for ferreting out circumstantial evidence in the everyday world' as one who deciphered 'the essence and the historical trend of the age from its dust and tinsel', whose 'force and acuteness as a journalist' had been lost in the present day, and whose essays were received by today's readers 'like a novelty'.

231 Kracauer to Adorno
New York, 23.12.1963

498 Westend Avenue
New York 24, N.Y.
December 23, 1963

Dear Teddie,

It is snowing outside – very Christmassy, and afterwards we are left with its slush. Many thanks for your long and kind letter. I can well imagine your burdens, as I myself am not at all the free man that you claim I am. The only good thing is that my regular job leaves me a nice amount of free time. By the way, I am continually amazed at the way you are able to nurture your own work so single-mindedly despite all your many duties and distractions. The fact that a lot of people know my date of birth and are unflinchingly denouncing it abroad is probably my own fault; once, years ago, I provided it for inclusion in one of the many Who's Whos, and Rowohlt may also know about it. But the less any knowledge of it gets around, the better. I value your discretion enormously on the occasion of the planned event; I am also grateful to Herr Holz. This in any event diminishes the possibility of some unauthorized person exploiting my birth – in public, I mean.

The despatch of the offprints of my article seems to be working; in any case, someone here has already confirmed receipt of it. Thanks for your help. My 70 copies, which are to be sent directly to me by the publisher, have not yet arrived, but perhaps they may have been shipped as a small parcel, which takes longer.

I cannot comprehend how you could dictate your essay on teachers and philosophy in one afternoon; I should have needed at least a week for something like that. You will be interested to hear that Peter Szondi, with whom I met up in Zurich, also particularly liked this essay. We can probably arrive at an agreement – or at least a truce – about the concept of the concrete/specific. I know exactly where your objections are coming from, but you will see from my book on history (God knows when) that I use the term 'concrete' in a manner that is well grounded. I have only just been able to take a look at your Skoteinos piece. In it I came across a passage which I very much like – the one where you speak of the necessity of freely associating. The fact that I like it so much probably has also something to do with my interest in the concrete. In my letter written at the end of November I used the term 'ideology' not in the Marxist sense but in the English one: ideology = idea, conceptual construction. What I meant was that the conceptual construction of sociological reality – or speculation about this reality, as it results from empirical observation and close analysis – does not always and sufficiently make the close contact with the very reality at which, after all, it is aimed. The exact correspondence between idea and reality – or the 'construction in material terms', as I called it in the *Angestellten* – seems to me to have been achieved with a marvellous degree of success in your essay on teachers and philosophy. Others may think otherwise – but I myself always feel especially pleased when I read things where the idea doesn't overshoot its material facts by too much and the latter are permitted to raise their stubborn head. There is, as you know, a fair bit of Sancho Panza in me, and Kant, with his hesitation and wariness of ontological residues, is quite simply closer to me than Hegel – that's just the way it is. I'm glad that you are taking *Jargon der Eigentlichkeit* out of your dialectic book. The *Jargon* essay is complete in itself – a piece of work which goes deep into its topic.

Your advice to eliminate the passage on the 'loss of ideology' in my book on film is understandable from the situation in Germany as you describe it. But don't be annoyed if I don't follow your (genuinely good) advice; the book – above all, the final chapter – must stay as it is. I believe that this chapter would literally fall apart if I took anything out. I am downright superstitious about this kind of thing. I simply cannot lay another finger on it. Once again, don't be annoyed – and, despite this, do give me further advice. I shall write to Unseld today to let him know that you would like to see the page proofs of the book, but I fear that they won't arrive in time. Just a few days ago Unseld told me that he had suddenly had to decide to bring the book out no earlier than this autumn; the negotiations with the Oxford Press in London and Rowohlt have still not been wholly concluded; furthermore, the production costs are so high that he is being forced to consider a paperback edition to be able to recover his expenses. Michel had written to me to say that the book should already have gone to press, but perhaps now it will not be printed until later. However, I shall, of course, let Unseld know of your wishes even so. Why don't you simply use the American edition for your broadcast lecture? After all, everything is there in precise detail.

Your message about the good review of *Ornament* in *Die Zeit* was the first I had heard of it. I was delighted, and also to hear about its being sold in the university bookshop. Incidentally, Weyrauch has sent me his essay about *Ginster* in the *Deutsche Zeitung* of 15 December – a long article, genuinely profound in places, with a few minor flaws – nothing of any real importance. Should I really become a success at this stage? If I were Ginster, I should say that, in hindsight, I am full of admiration for myself.

Dear Teddie, we wish you and our good Gretel a year full of health, satisfying work and a few major pieces of luck. Cordial greetings from Lili and me!

Yours,

Friedel

When did the review of *Ornament* appear in *Die Zeit*?

Original: typescript with handwritten corrections and postscript; Theodor W. Adorno Archiv, Frankfurt am Main.

my regular job: ongoing since 1956 as a consultant to the Bollingen Foundation; his journeys to Europe were also undertaken for this purpose.

Szondi, with whom I met up in Zurich: see letter no. 218.

Skoteinos piece … necessity of freely associating: see Adorno, GS 5, pp. 372ff.

construction in material terms … in the Angestellten: not precisely formulated there but included in the preface as 'material for consideration' (see Kracauer, W 1, p. 213); on 25 May 1930, Kracauer described his working principle for *Angestellten* as 'material dialectics' (see letter no. 61). Adorno took up Kracauer's term 'material' in one of his dedications (see letter no. 265).

write to Unseld today: in his Christmas letter to Unseld of the same day Kracauer asked Unseld to send a copy of the page proofs to Adorno. The *Theorie des Films* had in the meantime been postponed for technical and legal reasons from the spring programme to the autumn of 1964 (Siegfried Unseld to Kracauer, 12 December 1963, Archiv der Peter Suhrkamp Stiftung an der Johann Wolfgang Goethe-Universität).

Weyrauch … essay about Ginster: Wolfgang Weyrauch, 'Kracauer, Ginster, David', *Deutsche Zeitung*, 14/15 December 1963.

232 Adorno to Kracauer

Frankfurt am Main, 10.1.1964

PROF. DR. THEODOR W. ADORNO

FRANKFURT AM MAIN 10 January 1964
KETTENHOFWEG 123

Dear Friedel,

Just a few words today in reply to your letter of 23 December.

My talk about you is to be broadcast on 7 February; there were the usual difficulties about the time available. However, I managed to push through my request and shall have a whole hour at my disposal. I am getting on quite well with the text itself and am already on the second version. The difficulties of realizing it as I visualize it are very great. It is precisely our extraordinary closeness that gets in the way of finding the specific word; one is so steeped in the subject that one feels that it is actually already present and thus runs the risk of remaining too general in one's approach. But I fancy that I do have a certain facility: the energy, as my own critic, of forcing drafts to become what they rightfully should be – and you can easily imagine that this energy is not going to run out this time.

I am over the worst with my 'problem child', the *Jargon der Eigentlichkeit*, thanks above all to Gretel. As you might imagine, because of this and the lecture about you, I didn't exactly have a lazy Christmas. In spite of that, I did have a nice relaxing time and have come back refreshed, to some degree, for the second half of the winter semester, which, from all my experience, is the most taxing time.

My piece of work about you will also, of course, be published as soon as it has been broadcast. I don't know where as yet, but it will be sure to be somewhere more than appropriate for it.

We were at Unseld's on New Year's Eve and Unseld came to us the following day. It was very nice, but there was no opportunity to discuss the typescript of your work with him. It is remarkable, by the way, that Michel, who is such a friendly and pleasant person, voiced something very similar to my suggestion (but quite independently of me) concerning the last chapter of your book. You may say that it was no coincidence, precisely because he is a student of mine; I think, though, that there are reasons to think this over at some length.

I can't tell you this minute for certain in which number of *Die Zeit* the essay about you appeared; the Suhrkamps will have to do that. Don't they send you the reviews regularly on specific dates?

A little book of mine is coming out in the 'edition suhrkamp' in February: *Moments musicaux* – short musical essays which don't appear in my other books, going back to 1928; I think it will be quite attractive, precisely because of the distance from many of them.

There is one more thing that will perhaps interest you. After I had finished the rough draft of the essay about you, I was going to summon Frau A. to encourage her to convert her diploma dissertation, which, as you know, rather disappointed me, into a doctoral thesis, which really does satisfy all the desiderata; my text could quite well provide the framework for it. However, she has fled back into the Soviet Zone, from which she had escaped – for love, it is said. *Au fond* she will feel more comfortable there than with us; she has, surely enough, retained all-too-strong marks of a heteronomous consciousness. On the other hand, I feel sorry for her, as the idea of working on you was a good one and well intentioned.

Much love to you and Lili, from Gretel too,

Yours ever,

Teddie

In the matter of the text about you, it appears that the period of one hour is very little. It was simpler with the essays on Bloch and Lukács – actually, do you have Volume II of the *Noten*, which contains the final versions? – because in both cases I could take a specific book as my starting point. That is impossible in your case; I have to provide both a sketch of your overall development *and* a portrait – and within the set limitations that compels me towards the thetic, where my first task should be developing everything.

You once wrote that you didn't entirely agree with my attitude towards the culture industry. Perhaps you could write, when you have the time and inclination, to tell me where you see the difference. This also, of course, enters into my text.

Kindest regards!

Original: typescript with printed letterhead, handwritten corrections and postscript; Siegfried Kracauer papers, Deutsches Literaturarchiv, Marbach am Neckar.

Moments musicaux: volume 54 of edition suhrkamp, published on 27 January 1964.

essays on Bloch and Lukács: 'Blochs Spuren: Zur neuen erweiterten Ausgabe 1959', *Neue deutsche Hefte*, April 1960; 'Erpreßte Versöhnung: Zu Georg Lukács: "Wider den mißverstandenen Realismus"', *Der Monat*, November 1958 (see Adorno, GS 11, pp. 233–80, 698). Both essays also reprinted in *Noten zur Literatur II* (1961).

Attitude towards the culture industry: see letter no. 217.

233 Kracauer to Adorno
New York, 16.1.1964

498 Westend Avenue
New York 24, N.Y.
January 16, 1964

Dear Teddie,

I was just about to write a few lines to you today when your kind letter arrived – so I shall go straight to its contents. At the risk of repeating myself, I must say to you once again that your powers as a thinker and as a writer arouse my admiration more and more; next to you I feel like a snail which, moreover, often withdraws completely into its house. I am awfully excited about everything that I am going to be learning about myself from you, and I am very much aware that your soundings and findings of my intentions will be of considerable importance. For me, it is exciting that you are now involved in, so to speak, taking soundings and conducting a survey of my own terrain. What I hope to gain from this – and also from conversations afterwards – is that the thinking of both of us – that thinking in general – will profit from it.

It is of course inevitable that, as you write in the postscript, you cannot avoid a few references regarding my 'development as a whole'. The subject matter demands this – I can see that. Oh, this tiresome biographical stuff! But I am sure you will have the dosage properly measured out – if I know anything at all, it is that. This takes me to Reinhard Baumgart's review of the *Ornament* in *Die Zeit*. You are right – the review is very good, and it is painstakingly written. Baumgart knows something, and he weighs his words – but in one respect his article is not as full of understanding as I had imagined it would be to judge from your letter. (I received the review only a few days ago from the people at Suhrkamp.) Baumgart makes too much use of my connection with the F. Z., it seems to me. That leads him to emphasize my journalistic side – to overemphasize it, I should say – and to drag Tucholsky and Jacobsohn into the discussion – as if I were to be comprehended when seen as coming from this direction. His being mesmerized by my job on the newspaper is no doubt also to blame for his taking it into his head that I can be defined as predominantly a 'stimulator and transmitter of ideas'. That really does not do me justice. But aside from these distortions (albeit serious ones), one really could not wish for a better review. (I wish that Baumgart had slipped in a word to plug my *Ginster* and the *Angestellten*. Do you remember what Benjamin once wrote about the *Angestellten*? I was groping around like a rag-picker in the early morning – he meant the morning of the Revolution, *hélas.*)

Yes – the last chapter of the film book. Unseld also wrote to me about your (and Michel's) concerns. Meanwhile, I have written to him, after careful consideration, to say that the chapter must be kept as it is – exactly in the same way as I also wrote to you. I am aware of the fact that perhaps in Germany the passage about the loss of ideology does not sound the same as it would elsewhere, and that in Germany the allusion to the concrete could be misinterpreted in a reactionary sense. But I cannot dispense with this chapter, to which my whole theory of film is directed and for whose sake it was written, because of such potential consequences and misunderstandings – which will be cleared up on careful reading and over the course of time. The ideas in it are profound and original, however one judges them – and, besides, they also provide a starting point for my theory of history. That, unfortunately, doesn't sound exactly modest, but what will one not do to justify oneself? And in other instances I am always more inclined to give way, or to do so readily.

About your attitude to the culture industry: what I meant by that would be best developed in a conversation. Of course I didn't mean your attitude itself; that is, and remains, entirely legitimate. I was thinking more of different aspects of the content – and one idea that came out of that was that it might perhaps be good if you were once again to carry out an empirical examination of one of the new developments within the culture industry – e.g. the travel racket – and elaborate it. The inevitable quantitative growth of the culture industry is probably also leading it to assume new qualities. I myself have made various observations about this – following on from my *Wunderlicher Realismus* [Curious realism]. But, as I was saying, we should talk about that and more fundamental matters soon. That above all is my wish for 1964: that this summer we may have some proper conversations.

The following item may amuse you. A short time ago I took part (at Columbia) in a discussion about the new German hermeneutics, especially in the writings of Heidegger and Gadamer – following a paper given by an American theologian who spends a lot of time in Germany and of course has great reverence for Heidegger. I said some rather rude things. But that is not the point. The point is that, after this experience of profound chit-chat about and around Heidegger, I am only now capable of fully appreciating the necessity and the whole beauty of your *Jargon der Eigentlichkeit*. If there were any justice – but when will there be? – this essay ought to initiate a 'turn' [*Kehre*] – a genuine turn. Through Werner Marx I have gained some knowledge of Heidegger's later development, which is as revealing as it is abominable. In this context two expressions occurred to me which would almost have fitted into your *Jargon*. One could call things that function as things [*Dinge die sich dingen*], and so gather together *das Geviert* [the fourfold] (oh, God!), 'meeting-places'. Among these things functioning as things Heidegger also seems to number the pitcher and the bridge. But: 'the pitcher will go over the bridge until it breaks'. Forgive the puns. By the way, Haag's review of *Fundamentalontologie* is brilliant – and the conclusion, with the quotation from the Hitler era, fits into it marvellously. From my point of view, it would perhaps have been even more effective – I mean, strategically more incisive – if Haag had first of all acknowledged *Sein und Zeit* as an original achievement. I myself prefer to proceed along Socratic lines. But perhaps that would be out of place in Germany. Give Haag our regards.

It was so kind of you to be willing to hand me over to Frau A. for her doctoral thesis. Now we can understand why we never heard another word from her. If someone returns to the Eastern Zone, he – or she – must have compelling reasons for doing so, or believe this to be the case. Actually, Erika looked more Western. Well, with every day it becomes more difficult for me to understand things – and indeed many people. She won't be able to write about me very well in the Eastern Zone. What a pity; a doctoral thesis about me would have been a real delight. (Why do dissertations always have to be only about Tillich?)

I have your *Noten, 2*: they are waiting for me to read them. I shall soon be writing to you about them. A request: let me know the day and hour and the exact name of the radio station where you are giving the lecture about me. Perhaps there may be some possibility of hearing you over here; I shall try to winkle out the information.

Much love and warmest greetings from us both to you and dear Gretel,

Yours,

Friedel

Original: typescript; Theodor W. Adorno Archiv, Frankfurt am Main.

Tucholsky and Jacobsohn: Kracauer wrote 'Jakobsohn'. Kurt Tucholsky attracted Kracauer's criticism after an appearance in Frankfurt am Main (see letter no. 69.); for Siegfried Jacobsohn, see letter no. 50. Reinhard Baumgart located Kracauer in this milieu in his review of *Das Ornament der Masse*: 'One would suppose the position and rank of this author to be somewhere between Tucholsky and Benjamin, between Jacobsohn and Adorno' (see letter no. 230).

what Benjamin once wrote about die Angestellten: see letters nos. 57 and 155.

Unseld also wrote to me … concerns: Siegfried Unseld reported on their shared criticisms in a letter of 2 January 1964: 'On New Year's Day I was with the Adornos … I mentioned to Adorno the great respect which I have for your book as an achievement but also shared with him certain concerns of mine regarding the epilogue. To my surprise, Adorno told me that he too had already corresponded with you about this … Now, the three of us (Adorno, Michel and I) have arrived at these concerns quite independently of one another. I am putting this to you yet again and would still like to ask you to consider whether we should not omit this section.' Kracauer replied on 7 January 1964: 'in the matter of the epilogue I am immodest enough to believe that all three of you are wrong. … The sequence of ideas in the epilogue is very logical and, as I believe, of great importance. I have no doubt that it will emerge in clear relief and will prevail. In any case, it is the goal and core of the work; if it were omitted the book would fall apart. In short, here I stand, etc. – and so the epilogue should stand too' (Archiv der Peter Suhrkamp Stiftung an der Johann Wolfgang Goethe-Universität).

travel racket: on the term 'racket' as a whole: 'The relationship of the individual towards the racket, be it business, profession or party, be it before or after admission to it – the gestures of the leader [*Führer*] before the masses, the lover before the object of his affections – assumes peculiarly masochistic features' (*Dialektik der Aufklärung*; see Adorno, GS 3, p. 176).

Gadamer: Hans-Georg Gadamer (1900–2002), philosopher; he obtained the *venia legendi* at the University of Marburg in 1929. After various professorships he taught at Frankfurt am Main (1947–9) and then in Heidelberg; his seminal work is *Wahrheit und Methode: Grundzüge einer philosophischen Hermeneutik*, 1960; *Truth and Method*, trans. Joel Weinsheimer and Donald G. Marshall, New York: Continuum, 2004.

Kehre: Martin Heidegger, *Die Technik und die Kehre*, Pfullingen: Neske, 1962.

Marx ... Geviert: Werner Marx (1910–1994), legal scholar and philosopher, 1933 exiled in the Netherlands, 1934 in England and 1938 in the USA; studied in New York City with Karl Löwith and others and taught at the New School for Social Research. In 1964 he returned to Germany, appointed to the former professorship of Husserl and Heidegger in Freiburg. Kracauer is referring to Marx, *Heidegger und die Tradition*, Stuttgart: Kohlhammer, 1961, where we read, for example: 'By contrast, the "worlding" [*das Welten*] gathers the "Geviert" [the fourfold], which, being "of itself at one" [*einig*] is an "*Einfalt*" [simplicity; singularity; one unit].' On 'Ding', 'Geviert' and 'Krug' in Heidegger, see Marx, 'Das Ding', in *Bremer und Freiburger Vorträge*, ed. Petra Jaeger, Frankfurt am Main: Vittorio Klostermann, 1994, pp. 5–21. Kracauer's pun plays on the popular saying: 'Der Krug geht so lange zum Brunnen, bis er bricht' [The pitcher goes to the well until it breaks]. In Heidegger's later thinking, the motif of the 'fourfold' is introduced for the first time in his Bremen Lectures (1949) in reference to the thing as a gathering of earth, sky, mortals and divinities.

Haag's review: Karl Heinz Haag (1929–2011), philosopher. Kracauer praises his Frankfurt *Habilitationsschrift: Kritik der neueren Ontologie*, Stuttgart: Kohlhammer, 1960. The quotation to which Kracauer alludes comes from an address by Heidegger of 11 November 1933, when he said: 'The German people have been called by the *Führer* to choose; but the *Führer* asks for nothing from the people, he rather offers the people their most immediate opportunity to make the highest free decision. This ultimate decision extends to the most extreme boundary of our people's existence ... It consists of that primal demand of all *being* to retain and salvage its own essence.' Haag's comment: 'By propagating "a subservient form of thinking", fundamental ontology as "essential thinking" does not, as it claims, concern itself with the liberation of individuals from their "enslavement by the impersonal one" but is intent on the destruction of any kind of subjectivity ... Objectively, it serves the negation of humaneness' (see ibid., pp. 82f., 95.)

Your Noten, 2: in Kracauer's papers, with a handwritten dedication: 'For Friedel, in memory of the old days, sincerely / Teddie / Frankfurt, 7 September 1961' (Deutsches Literaturarchiv, Marbach).

234 Adorno to Kracauer
Frankfurt am Main, 3.2.1964

PROF. DR. THEODOR W. ADORNO

FRANKFURT AM MAIN 3 February 1964
KETTENHOFWEG 123

Dear Friedel,

I should like to respect your taboo by not saying in these lines what ought to be said, but I should like them to reach you in good time, and you to know: *j'y pense*. That includes everything else.

My presentation, of course, ran over its allotted time – by seven minutes – but, as Herr Holz is making the cuts himself and is sure to proceed with extreme caution, I am not worried. What is more, perfectionist that I am, I have completely rewritten the whole thing yet again, and only now does it correspond to some degree to how I envisaged it. It was – believe you me – a very difficult task. I should have preferred you (one idiosyncrasy against another idiosyncrasy) to become acquainted with the text only after it has been printed – nice and clean and, so to speak, authentic – and I ask for your forbearance in this. I am still not clear about where it is to appear. I should prefer the *Merkur*, but I don't know whether my final version will exceed the space available there; still, I shall do all I can to terrorize the editor in chief with the help of Axel Kluge, who has a lot of influence there. If things really don't work out to publish it there, I would of course have other possibilities.

The talk will be broadcast, as Fräulein Olbrich has already written to you, on the so-called Second Programme of Hessischer Rundfunk on 7 February at 10 p.m. German time. But if you should actually manage to pick up the lecture via a short-wave receiver, I must ask you to regard it in fact as a kind of concept. In any case, the density of literary style which I inevitably expect of myself in a text like this is neither appropriate nor possible to reproduce in a broadcast version.

I am enclosing for you a really rather silly essay from the *Allgemeine Wochenzeitung der Juden in Deutschland*. It fulfils my prophecy that it would be impossible to keep the date a secret. You will be as little surprised as I was that everything is just the same in such a journal as it used to be in the *Stadtblatt* of the *Frankfurter Zeitung*.

Celebrate in secret, but well!

On that note, all the best to you both, from Gretel too,

Your old Teddie

Original: typescript with printed letterhead and handwritten corrections; Siegfried Kracauer papers, Deutsches Literaturarchiv, Marbach am Neckar.

Merkur ... *editor in chief*: Hans Paeschke (1911–1991), critic, editor and publisher; editor of the *Neue Rundschau* (1939–44); co-founder of the *Merkur* (joint editor with Joachim Moras until 1961).

Fräulein Olbrich has already written to you: in a letter of 20 January 1964 (Kracauer papers, Deutsches Literaturarchiv, Marbach).

essay from the Allgemeine Wochenzeitung der Juden: Ernst L. Siebenborn, 'Ein Jubiläum und eine Neuerscheinung' [A jubilee and a new publication], *Allgemeine Wochenzeitung der Juden in Deutschland*, 24 January 1964. Two paragraphs of the article cover Kracauer's biography, the broadcast of Adorno's lecture on the eve of his birthday, and the deportation of Hedwig and Rosette Kracauer.

235 Kracauer to Adorno

New York, 7.2.1964

498 Westend Avenue
New York 24, N.Y.
February 7, 1964

Dear Teddie,

Your kind lines did say what they didn't say; I was touched that you remembered.

About the Jewish newspaper, we can only hope that it doesn't get around too much. I read only the first few sentences – then Lili took it away from me.

I shall not be able to hear your broadcast today – it will be from 5 to 6 p.m. here; I thought so from the beginning. To say that I am keen to read your text would be an understatement. But, if I understand anything, it is this – that you would prefer me to read it only in the definitive printed version – and so I am glad to wait until your thoughts have been put in exactly the order in which they had occurred to you. I can well imagine that it must have been difficult to find an appropriate shape for this peculiar, intractable material.

Thanks for your *Bibliographische Grillen*. I do have a foible for this genre. You have succeeded in crossing the boundary between private preferences and proceeding to general profundity; many *Grillen* really do sing like crickets chirping! (For the titles of books to appear horizontally on the spines, one has to write the thick kind of them; to the best of my belief, I succeeded only with *Theory of Film*.)

I saw from the invitation to the Deutsche Soziologentag which was sent to me recently that you will speak about Theodor Heuss. Probably this is connected with your election as president? I had a long talk with Raymond Aron last September in Paris. Merton, whose participation had been announced, seems not to be coming. I am surprised that Löwith is missing; I found his study of Weber quite insightful.

It would be of some importance to me to know now approximately when and how we might see each other this summer. For our part, I know only that it would be possible around the middle of July, but that is so awkward for you. In August we shall be in Switzerland again – perhaps in Interlaken. In Switzerland, then? Then it would also be possible before we return home, towards the end of September – but that is usually the time of the book fair in Frankfurt, or some congress or other, and we found out last year what *that* means. I am saying this really casually; it is almost an act of sacrilege to make plans so far in advance, but the travel agencies force one to do so. Do drop me a line about this.

And – while you are writing – can you give me a hint, even by just a keyword, about how you have captured my 'intelligible self'? Frankly, I am tormented by curiosity.

I shall fulfil your kind wish for tomorrow. I have declined all invitations. Lili and I may possibly go to a major Toulouse-Lautrec exhibition here. That would be very appropriate. Other than that, I shall be working, as always.

Warmest greetings to Gretel and yourself from Lili and me,

Yours,

Friedel

Original: typescript with handwritten corrections; Theodor W. Adorno Archiv, Frankfurt am Main.

Bibliographische Grillen: an expanded version of a gloss from 1959, published in *Akzente*, no. 6, 1963 (see Adorno, GS 11, pp. 345–57, 699); the copy bears the handwritten dedication 'To my dear Friedel / Most cordially, Teddie / January 1964' (Kracauer papers, Deutsches Literaturarchiv, Marbach). Kracauer's reaction is a pun on 'Grille' (whim/fancy and cricket, the insect).

titles of books to appear horizontally on the spines: 'An old aversion to books whose titles are printed along the length of their spines. On any of human worth, the title should be placed horizontally' (see Adorno, GS 11, p. 353).

Deutsche Soziologentag … about Theodor Heuss: Kracauer marked the details in question on the printed invitation to the 15th Deutsche Soziologentag [conference of German sociologists] in Heidelberg (28–30 April 1964); on 29 April, '20.00: Prof. Dr. Theodor Adorno: words in memory of Theodor Heuss' (Kracauer papers, Deutsches Literaturarchiv, Marbach). Theodor Heuss had died on 12 December 1963; the obituary was published under the title 'Gedenkrede auf Theodor Heuss', *Die Welt*, 9 May 1963 (see Adorno, GS 20.2, pp. 708–12).

Raymond Aron: In his plenary address on the inaugural evening of the conference (see Adorno, GS 20.2, p. 703), Adorno extended a personal welcome to the French philosopher and sociologist (1905–1983), as well as to Leopold von Wiese, Herbert Marcuse and Talcott Parsons.

Merton: Robert K. Merton (1910–2003), sociologist, at Columbia University from 1941 onwards; director of the Bureau for Applied Social Research (1942–71) (see Adorno/Horkheimer, *Briefwechsel* II, p. 355, note).

Löwith is missing … his study of Weber: *Max Weber und die Soziologie heute* [Max Weber and sociology today] was the theme of the conference (on the occasion of Weber's 100th birthday on 21 April 1964). Karl Löwith's 'Max Weber und Karl Marx' was published in *Archiv für Sozialwissenschaft und Sozialpolitik*, no. 67,

1932; 'Max Weber und seine Nachfolger' [Max Weber and his successors] in *Mass und Wert*, no. 3, 1939/40); and also, more recently, 'Die Entzauberung der Welt durch Wissenschaft' [The disenchantment of the world through science] in *Merkur*, no. 196, 1964 (for all this information, see Karl Löwith, *Hegel und die Aufhebung der Philosophie im 19. Jahrhundert – Max Weber*, Stuttgart: J. B. Metzlersche Verlagsbuchhandlung, 1988).

Toulouse-Lautrec exhibition: at the Wildenstein Art Gallery (689 Fifth Avenue, New York), 7 February–14 March 1964.

236 Adorno to Kracauer

Frankfurt am Main, 13.2.1964

PROF. DR. THEODOR W. ADORNO

FRANKFURT AM MAIN 13 February 1964
KETTENHOFWEG 123

Dear Friedel,

Many thanks for your letter of 7 February. I hope that the two of you had a really good time on the 8th; we were thinking of you often. I couldn't hear the talk myself; the Faculty of Sociology had organized a fancy-dress party for the evening where I had to make an *acte de présence* at that exact time, although I didn't feel at all like doing so. But everyone who heard it, including Reifenberg and Gretel, appeared to be greatly moved by it. Reifenberg wrote me a really touching letter afterwards. The cuts seemed to have been made with such care that even Gretel didn't notice them. Now let us wait and see how, when and where the final version will appear; I expect to hear this very soon.

You were absolutely right in guessing that I spoke about Heuss at the sociologists' conference solely in connection with my election as president. I simply wanted to say a few words in memory of him; I knew him quite well – he was a humane man, although I harboured no illusions about his intellectual qualities. The preliminary announcement had turned this, as is so often the case, into something much too pretentious. Now I am trying to cut it down to its appropriate size. I should like to confine myself to saying that, for once, the Germans had a head of state who was a civilian through and through but who could also hold a fountain-pen and was still popular in spite of this – and thus to speak purely in the sense of political pedagogics, in which, of course, it is impossible to avoid a few words about his relationship to Max Weber, about whom he wrote a book which he gave me as a gift not so long ago.

As for our plans for the summer: we shall be here for the whole of July. If you were to come sometime in the second half of July, something could be arranged with no trouble and no pressure, in spite of the exams; this should be merely a question of making plans in good time. For the whole of August and the first few days of September we shall be, as always, up in Sils Maria. Then from 5 to 10 September I shall be in Salzburg, where I am giving the main paper at the Hegel congress – this time it is a heavily loaded piece of work even for me, sketched out a long time ago, on the connection between dialectical logic and music. This will be at the same time the missing link between my philosophical and musical activities. It is no longer possible for me to refuse – but perhaps you might feel like coming to Salzburg. It's pretty enough there. I am staying at the Österreichische Hof, a charming hotel where I used to stay in my youth before Hitler. You – or both of you – would just have to make your reservations in good time.

I am now putting the finishing touches to the *Jargon der Eigentlichkeit*. I have finished it in general terms but still have to resolve a couple of awkward questions about some finer points, and above all a couple of additions to write, which are weighing me down. In spite of this, I think I am over the worst.

In the meantime, I have had a little book sent to you – a collection of essays on music, most of them from my youth, which have not been reprinted elsewhere; perhaps a number of these might interest you, such as the piece about the Tales of Hoffmann (p. 32). In a few days the work on Hölderlin, which of course you will also receive straight away, should be available; I really rolled up my sleeves for that. Even though I have not been losing sight of the big book for a moment, and over the last few months, ostensibly to round things off, I have been covering the most important part of it. The end is in sight for this piece of work, too.

I have survived the semester quite well. In March Gretel and I are going to Baden-Baden again for a fortnight to recover.

Loving regards to you and Lili from both of us,

Ever your old

Teddie

In the last few days I have had to read something by Erich Auerbach – with utter horror. He is practically everything I hate in an academic. And not even his positive knowledge is adequate – about Leibniz he writes sentences which betray a truly legendary lack of education.

Original: typescript with printed letterhead, handwritten corrections and postscript; Siegfried Kracauer papers, Deutsches Literaturarchiv, Marbach am Neckar.

a fancy-dress party: Adorno's participation in events of this kind is documented by an undated photograph from that time; it shows him in costume (see Adorno, *Bildmonographie*, p. 236).

Reifenberg ... a really touching letter: Benno Reifenberg to Adorno, 9 Febrary 1964. Adorno cites Reifenberg in his letter of thanks of 13 February 1964: 'seldom has a letter given me so much pleasure as yours; the locution about the relationship between justice and friendship conveys in truly Tacitean terms the idea which I had in mind.' In addition, he recommended that Reifenberg should get in touch with Kracauer (Theodor W. Adorno Archiv).

I should like to confine myself ...: 'Max Weber genuinely meant something to him. Not long before he fell ill he sent me another piece of work about him ... Above all, Heuss very likely was the first German head of state in living memory to be a civilian through and through' (*Worte zum Gedenken anTheodor Heuss*; see Adorno, GS 20.2, pp. 709f.).

Hegel congress ... to refuse: a three-page manuscript, 'Musik und dialektische Logik', provides evidence of this plan (Theodor W. Adorno Archiv). The *Frankfurter Allgemeine Zeitung* reported on 11 September 1964, under the title 'Hegel-Forscher tagen in Salzburg' [Hegel scholars meet in Salzburg], of withdrawals which actually took place and wrote about Adorno's retraction: 'Theodor W. Adorno had written to the president of the society, Dr Beyer from Munich, that he would appreciate having the fact recorded that his declining the invitation was solely for reasons of health (overwork; strict orders from his doctor). Adorno requested that this letter should be read out, not because he believed that his personal state of health was an object of public interest but to prevent speculation about other possible reasons. In a telegram, which was also read out, he emphasized this yet again, also stating that on account of his state of overexertion he would also have been unable to write a paper.'

Österreichischer Hof: the hotel, situated in the centre of Salzburg, was built in the 1860s; Adorno mentions it in the 75th item in his *Minima Moralia*, titled *Kalte Herberge*: 'Who would not prefer the Blauer Stern in Prague or the Österreichischer Hof in Salzburg, even if he had to cross the hall to the bathroom and he was no longer woken in the small hours by the infallible central heating? The closer one gets to the sphere of immediate physical existence, the more questionable does progress become – a Pyrrhic victory for fetishized production' (see Adorno, GS 4, p. 133).

about the Tales of Hoffmann: 'Hoffmanns Erzählungen in Offenbachs Motiven' [The tales of Hoffmann in Offenbach's motifs], in *Programmschrift der Städtischen Bühnen Düsseldorf*, 1932, now published as the fifth item in *Moments Musicaux* (see Adorno, GS 17, pp. 42–6, 347).

the work on Hölderlin: 'Parataxis: Zur späten Lyrik Hölderlins'; the Berlin lecture of June 1963 (see letter no. 212) appeared in an expanded version in *Neue Rundschau*, no. 1, 1964,; an offprint among Kracauer's papers bears the handwritten dedication: 'For Friedel / cordially, Teddie / Frankfurt, 26 March 1964' (Deutsches Literaturarchiv, Marbach).

Auerbach: Erich Auerbach (1892–1957), specialist in Romance literature; he went into exile in Turkey in 1936 and emigrated to the USA in 1947.

237 Kracauer to Adorno
New York, 3.3.1964

498 Westend Avenue
New York 24, N.Y.
March 3, 1964

Dear Teddie,

Just a very quick word today to thank you at once from the bottom of my heart for your *Moments Musicaux*, with its kind dedication and the memories it evoked, which arrived here yesterday. At the same time, I should also like to let you know straight away that, everything going well, we should like to come to Frankfurt for a few days around 15 July. We are looking forward to seeing you both again. As Unseld has written to me to say that this time he will be in Frankfurt in July, these two things would fit together very well. Let us hope that this time no congress or fair will get in the way as it did last year. I shall know about that very soon. Salzburg, unfortunately, will not be possible for us.

I must also thank you for your last kind letter. Have a lovely holiday in Baden-Baden! Don't be cross on account of this short message just for now. More next time.

With much love from us both to dear Gretel and yourself,
Yours ...

Original: typescript (carbon copy); Siegfried Kracauer papers, Deutsches Literaturarchiv, Marbach am Neckar.

dedication and the memories it evoked: the handwritten dedication reads: 'To my dear Friedel, from old times – there is a little piece about Offenbach in here too – / Warmest greetings from Yours / Teddie / Frankfurt, 5 February 1964' (Siegfried Kracauer papers, Deutsches Literaturarchiv, Marbach).

a few days: in the letter, 'a day'.

Unseld has written to me to say that this time he will be in Frankfurt in July: in his letter of 14 February 1964, Siegfried Unseld continued the discussion of the German version of the subtitle of the *Theorie des Films*, for which Adorno, at his meeting with Unseld on New Year's day 1964, had suggested 'Erlösung' instead of the previously chosen term 'Rettung' for 'Redemption' (Unseld to Kracauer, 2 January 1964), which corresponds to the closing frame of *Der wunderliche Realist*: 'Properly speaking, it should be translated as "The redemption of physical reality" – that is how curious [*wunderlich*] his realism is' (see Adorno, GS 11, p. 408). Kracauer countered with 'Errettung' on 11 February 1964, Unseld pleaded for 'Rettung' [rescue] in a letter of 14 February, and Kracauer won with 'Theorie des Films: Die Errettung der äußeren Wirklichkeit' [Theory of the film: the redemption of external reality] (Archiv der Peter Suhrkamp Stiftung an der Johann Wolfgang Goethe-Universität).

238 Adorno to Kracauer
Frankfurt am Main, 9.3.1964

PROF. DR. THEODOR W. ADORNO

FRANKFURT AM MAIN 9 March 1964
KETTENHOFWEG 123

Dear Friedel,

Just this word of thanks for now.

In the meantime, I have heard indirectly that *Merkur* has accepted *The Curious Realist*, as well as the condition which creates an added difficulty – that not a comma in it can be changed; however, the official confirmation has not yet arrived. At the same time, though, another very important journal has applied to me for permission to publish it, so there is no danger that the piece will not be published or not in a way that reflects its character sufficiently well.

I am pretty well worn out now and very glad to be going to Baden-Baden. Splendid that you are going to be here around 15 July; it is important that you let me know your exact timetable as soon as possible so that I can make arrangements accordingly.

Did you, by the way, hear from Reifenberg?

I met up with Ernst Bloch a few days ago at Unseld's, and everything was thoroughly nice and peaceful.

Much love to you and Lili, from Gretel too,

Your old
Teddie

Original: typescript with printed letterhead; Siegfried Kracauer papers, Deutsches Literaturarchiv, Marbach am Neckar.

a few days ago at Unseld's: on 29 February 1964 in Klettenbergstrasse.

239 Kracauer to Adorno
New York, 18.3.1964

498 Westend Avenue
New York 24, N.Y.
March 18, 1964

Dear Teddie,

As you want to know my timetable as soon as possible, I am writing to you immediately after receiving positive news from the Frankfurter Hof, which only confirmed my reservation for 15–20 July today. Before that (providing that all goes well) we shall be in London for a week, where I have various people to see. Unless (contrary to my expectations) I am detained there for another day, we shall be arriving in Frankfurt on 15 July (a short flight). The days which I should have completely at my disposal, then, would be from the 16th to the 19th inclusive. I have to see Unseld, of course, and pay his publishing company a visit. (My little book about streets is to be published in the edition suhrkamp series in July.) More later about further details, if any.

Thanks for your letter. I hope that in the meantime you have received confirmation that the *Curious Realist* will appear in *Merkur*. Who knows – I may yet set eyes on the piece in Europe. It would be an understatement to say that I am eager to read your interpretation. Your meeting with Bloch seems to have been very pleasant – that is a good thing. I wish we could see him this time. Our extended meeting in Munich two years ago was wonderful.

Have a good rest in Baden-Baden. You have more than earned the fortnight's holiday.

Warmest greetings and thoughts from both of us to Gretel and yourself,

Yours,
Friedel

P.S. In answer to your question: I have heard nothing from Reifenberg.

Original: typescript; Theodor W. Adorno Archiv, Frankfurt am Main.

edition suhrkamp: Kracauer wrote: éditions Suhrkamp.

meeting in Munich two years ago: for the meeting with Ernst Bloch when passing through Munich (21–4 July 1962), see letter no. 189, note.

240 Adorno to Kracauer
Frankfurt am Main, 26.3.1964

PROF. DR. THEODOR W. ADORNO

FRANKFURT AM MAIN 26 March 1964
KETTENHOFWEG 123

Dear Friedel,

Yesterday we came back from Baden-Baden, where I received your lines before leaving. I am glad to know the exact dates. As the Tuesdays and Thursdays are out for me because of the lectures and seminars, it would be best for us to set our sights on 17 or 18 July, and you could perhaps arrange your business with Unseld for the 16th. For me the evening of the 17th is perhaps the safest. But please don't think that I have turned into old Fürstenberg.

The day before yesterday I had a conversation with Bloch on Südwestfunk, in Baden-Baden, which I think is of great documentary value. We thought a lot about you, and he would be very glad if he could see you two again.

In the meantime, what I half anticipated has happened: Paeschke from *Merkur* wrote me a long letter in which he explained that the *Curious Realist* was too long for *Merkur*. I would have to shorten it by about a third, but of course he didn't want to insist on such an imposition. On reading that, I gave the piece to Joachim Günther for *Neue deutsche Hefte* – he positively begged me for it and wanted not only to publish the text in its entire and complete form but, what is more, in the jubilee edition – Volume 100. For many reasons *Merkur* might have been preferable, but to change so much as a single word of this text would have been completely and utterly impossible for me. As this jubilee volume will come out in July, I shall probably be able to give you this piece directly at that time.

At the same time Herr Günther asked me to let you know that he would welcome you at any time as a contributor to the journal. The address is: Berlin-Lankwitz, Kindelbergweg 7. The standard is very respectable, the general outlook of the periodical is somewhat conservative, but not inflexible, and is certainly open to influence by people like us. If you have anything available, I could, with a clear conscience, advise you to submit it.

We have had a really good rest, and I am now returning to my great text, with which I can obviously come to grips only with a certain number of breaks in between. I hatched out another item in Baden-Baden, but it is still too soon to talk about it.

At the same time as this I am sending you the Hölderlin, not without the modest hope that you may like it better than *Philosophie und Lehrer*.

Much love to you both, from Gretel too,

Yours ever,

Teddie

Original: typescript with printed letterhead and handwritten corrections; Siegfried Kracauer papers, Deutsches Literaturarchiv, Marbach am Neckar.

old Fürstenberg: not identified.

a conversation with Bloch on Südwestfunk: Adorno and Bloch had a radio debate on 24 March 1964 in Baden-Baden with Horst Krüger as moderator, entitled 'Etwas fehlt ... Über die Widersprüche der utopischen Sehnsucht' [Something is missing ... on the contradictions of utopian longing] (in *Gespräche mit Ernst Bloch*, ed. Rainer Traub and Harald Wieser, Frankfurt am Main: Suhrkamp, 1975, pp. 58–77), broadcast on 6 June 1964; Adorno's keywords for the discussion bear the title 'Möglichkeiten der Utopie heute' [Possibilities of Utopia today] (Theodor W. Adorno Archiv).

to Joachim Günther for Neue deutsche Hefte: *Der wunderliche Realist* did not appear until no. 101, September/October 1964, pp. 17–39.

if you have anything available: Kracauer did not do anything about the offer of publication.

241 Kracauer to Adorno
New York, 1.4.1964

498 Westend Avenue
New York 24, N.Y.
April 1, 1964

Dear Teddie,

We were delighted to hear that you have both had a good rest in Baden-Baden. That is especially important. Good that I know your dates for Frankfurt before corresponding with Unseld about this. Perhaps I could even come to your lecture or seminar on the 16th, but that remains to be seen. (Incidentally, I would be interested in meeting some of the young people, such as Alfred Schmidt and Schweppenhäuser.) The main thing is that we talk with each other.

I too should have been very happy with *Merkur*, but what isn't to be, isn't to be, and, as you yourself are happy with *Neue deutsche Hefte*, so, of course, am I. In the meantime, Joachim Günther has written to me of his own accord, enclosing an article of his about the *Ornament der Masse*, which appeared on 22 March in a Berlin newspaper. It is interesting that the younger critics constantly recall the affinity between you, me, Benjamin and Bloch. For them we constitute a group which is set off against the background of the times. This should be fine by us, I think. I find it enthralling and curious to learn how we, who know each other from the *inside*, appear to the outside world. (Please, don't press the word 'know'.)

Let me note that Günther, too, takes my work for the feuilleton as his starting point – however, he then quickly rates my writings very highly and makes them stand out from their times. Even the word 'journalism' is used, even though it serves only as a springboard. I would wish that these words and references didn't keep recurring in connection with my things, which were conceived and written for the papers as little as, say, Benjamin's newspaper articles. Which reminds me – is there a possibility that Herr Günther might provide your text with an introduction? If so, would you be able to mention to him that he should not allude to my age in it? That would be kind of you. I have just been reading the galley proofs for the little book on streets, which is to be published in June – only just about, though, because the publisher was in a hurry to have them sent back. Besides this, I have at this juncture reached a particularly difficult point in the planning of my book. Your Hölderlin will probably arrive within the next few days; you have made me curious.

Warmest greetings to you both from Lili and me,

Yours,

Friedel

Original: typescript; Theodor W. Adorno Archiv, Frankfurt am Main.

the young people: a brief meeting with Alfred Schmidt took place in Frankfurt am Main, but the plans for a debate with him and Hermann Schweppenhäuser were never realized.

Joachim Günther has written to me: from Joachim Günther's letter of 28 March 1964, it follows that he had obtained Kracauer's address from Adorno (Kracauer papers, Deutsches Literaturarchiv, Marbach); the review ends: 'His intellectual return as a revenant from that era is a literary event which has more weight than ninety-five per cent of so-called new publications' (see 'Der dialektische Feuilletonismus des Siegfried Kracauer: Zu dem Essayband *Das Ornament der Masse*', *Der Tagesspiegel*, 22 March 1964).

242 Adorno to Kracauer
Frankfurt am Main, 6.4.1964

PROF. DR. THEODOR W. ADORNO

FRANKFURT AM MAIN 6 April 1964
KETTENHOFWEG 123

Dear Friedel,

Many thanks for your letter.

You need not have any worries about Günther; I made it explicitly clear to him that any reference to your age and your date of birth must be omitted.

Meanwhile I am once again immersed in my great book – so deeply that I have a certain amount of difficulty in doing the most pressing thing, the preparation for my lecture 'Elements of a Philosophical Theory of Society'.

In the meantime, you will no doubt have received the Hölderlin.

Warmest greetings to both of you from both of us,

Yours,

Teddie

Original: typescript; Siegfried Kracauer papers, Deutsches Literaturarchiv, Marbach am Neckar.

my lecture: 'Elemente einer philosophische Gesellschaftstheorie' [Elements of a philosophical theory of society], summer semester 1964, Tuesday and Thursday, 4–5 p.m. (see *Philosophical Elements of a Theory of Society*, ed. Tobias ten Brink and Marc Phillip Nogueira, trans. Wieland Hoban, Cambridge: Polity, 2019).

243 Kracauer to Adorno
New York, 25.4.1964

498 Westend Avenue
New York 24, N.Y.
April 25, 1964

Dear Teddie,

Just a line of thanks for your Hölderlin article, which arrived a few days ago. I think it is absolutely splendid. Your attack on Heidegger's language and the primitive nature of his criticism of aesthetic imagery did me good. Your theory of interpretation is illuminating and entirely in keeping with my views, most of all in the fact that it limits the poet's thought to a share in the object to be interpreted. As practitioners we both know, of course, from our own experience about the compulsion exerted by the image in the process of its genesis. The immanent formal analysis is ingenious and enlightening; I think of the ways that you penetrate the examples of parataxis and untangle sentences such as the one in which you say that Hölderlin understands, as it were, how to make words condemned to abstraction reverberate (note 2, p. 33). From the interpretation of contents I single out one point which seems to me to hit the mark – that the word 'thanks' [*Dank*, gratitude] signifies a turning or counter-movement against fate. Whether your interpretation that the intentions of the hymns as characterized by their convergence with the concept of utopia represents their 'truth content' is one of those problems which we shall perhaps have an opportunity to discuss. One more secondary remark: would it not perhaps have been tactically fitting to draw attention to the difference between your concept of reconciliation with nature and Heidegger's in his interpretation of Hölderlin? However, you, being at the appropriate place, will be better able to judge this. (In this context I am reminded of Schmidt's explication of Marx's concept of nature; if he is in Frankfurt, I should very much like to see him.) You see, I have read the piece very carefully; not the least detail that gives me pleasure is its exquisite precision. P.S. How long were you working on it?

You will probably still be in Heidelberg when my letter arrives. Things must be going along fast and furiously there. I hope that you haven't tired yourself out. That's all for now.

Much love to dear Gretel and yourself from us both,

Yours,

Friedel

Original: typescript with handwritten addition; Theodor W. Adorno Archiv, Frankfurt am Main.

thanks for your Hölderlin article: 'Parataxis: Zur späten Lyrik Hölderlins' [Parataxis: on Hölderlin's late poetry]; an offprint among Kracauer's papers bears the handwritten dedication: 'For Friedel / cordially, Teddie / Frankfurt, 26 March 1964'.

note 2, p. 33: this is note 65 according to the continuous numbering of the notes to each essay in *Noten zur Literatur III* (see Adorno, GS 11, p.473).

'thanks' … fate: 'Und trifft daran ein Schicksaal, aber Dank': Friedrich Hölderlin, 'Friedensfeier', line 58 (see the complex quotation in Adorno, GS 11, p. 451). English translation in *Friedrich Hölderlin: Poems and Fragments*, trans. Michael Hamburger, London: Anvil Press Poetry, 1994.

'truth content': Adorno employs this term [*Wahrheitsgehalt*] throughout in 'Parataxis'.

244 Adorno to Kracauer

Frankfurt am Main, 12.5.1964

PROF. DR. THEODOR W. ADORNO

FRANKFURT AM MAIN 12 May 1964
KETTENHOFWEG 123

Dear Friedel,

I am delighted that you like the Hölderlin; it is producing quite a considerable effect, and what is more, remarkably, even in the closest circle around Heidegger. I had an enthusiastic letter from Szilasi and very kind comments from Löwith and Gadamer.

The difference between the reconciliation with nature as I mean it and what Heidegger means should become fairly clear from the text – but I may be mistaken. As far as the utopian interpretation of 'Friedensfeier' is concerned, it may perhaps interest you that Peter Szondi, who at this moment is devoting himself to this poem with particular intensity (following an initiative of mine, he is going to be giving a lecture about it at the university in a few weeks), appears to have reached a very similar conclusion quite independently of me.

Your question about how long I worked on the piece is very difficult to answer. The whole thing was written in fits and starts. The conception occurred in the course of a few days last spring in Wertheim am Main which were quite simply unforgettable for me and happy beyond all imagining. First, I dictated the whole thing from my notes, partly at one sitting, as I generally do in order not to get bogged down by becoming too deeply immersed in the details. I then singled out the Berlin lecture which I gave last June and edited it carefully, and then in the autumn I produced the final text, using the material left out of the lecture and including numerous changes and additions. All in all, the whole business would not have taken more than six months; the manuscript went to the *Rundschau* at the beginning of September. I was, however, constantly interrupted by multi-layered projects such as the first version of the text on natural history.

Meanwhile I have been interrupted yet again in my work on the dialectics book, or have let myself be interrupted by the anniversary essay on Richard Strauss. However, even this piece is finished now, and I am plunging with all my energy, and more wildly than before, into the main business. The Strauss should probably be appearing in *Neue Rundschau* once again.

Perhaps you may not know that Gottfried Salomon has died since I last wrote. Fundamentally, he remained much the same as ever right up to the end – rather more good-tempered than before; a certain friendliness and innocence in his nature which may have been linked to his clownishness became increasingly marked. Certainly he was one of those people whose worst times were far behind them, and I have long since forgiven him certain dirty tricks that he played on me in the past. I couldn't even go to the funeral as I had to preside at the Heidelberg sociologists' conference. It is a strange feeling that a person with whom one could do any kind of thing except take him seriously has finally been transformed into some kind of serious being by reason of his death. The potential within him was, in spite of everything, much greater than what he was able to make real. If he had devoted himself altogether to his flair – his real genius – for books, he would probably have become the greatest antiquarian in the history of the world. Instead, he became an average academic sociologist, whose respect for the great names which intoxicated him deprived him of the capacity for thought.

Warmest greetings to you and Lili, from Gretel too,

Your old

Teddie

Radio Bremen also wants to broadcast the lecture about you.

Original: typescript with printed letterhead, handwritten corrections and postscript; Siegfried Kracauer papers, Deutsches Literaturarchiv, Frankfurt am Main.

enthusiastic letter from Szilasi: Wilhelm Szilasi (1889–1966), a philosopher from Budapest and successor to Martin Heidegger in the chair at Freiburg after the latter's suspension. He wrote the letter in question on 8 May 1964 (Theodor W. Adorno Archiv).

comments from Löwith and Gadamer: nothing survives in writing.

Peter Szondi … a lecture: in a letter of 12 February 1964, Adorno informed Peter Szondi of 'an invitation from our German department here to give a lecture either within the context of its seminar or the humanities faculty' (see Peter Szondi, *Briefe*, ed. Christoph König and Thomas Sparr, Frankfurt am Main: Suhrkamp, 1993; p. 145, note 1). The invitation was connected with Adorno's unsuccessful attempt to get Szondi an appointment at Frankfurt; it was issued in his name and those of the German experts Paul Stöcklein and Hans Otto Burger. Szondi gave his lecture, 'Er selbst, der Fürst des Fests: Über Hölderlins "Friedensfeier"' ['He himself, the prince of the feast: on Hölderlin's '"Friedensfeier"'], on 27 May 1964 (see ibid., p. 151, note 5). Adorno had 'Parataxis: Zur späten Lyrik Hölderlins' published with the prefatory note 'Peter Szondi gewidmet' [Dedicated to Peter Szondi] (see Adorno, GS 11, p. 447).

anniversary essay on Richard Strauss: 'Richard Strauss: Zum hundertsten Geburtstag: 11 Juni 1964' [Richard Strauss: on his 100th birthday, 11 June 1964], *Neue Rundschau*, no. 4, 1964 (see Adorno, GS 16, pp. 565–606, 679).

Gottfried Salomon has died: on 26 April 1964 in Frankfurt am Main.

preside at the Heidelberg sociologists' conference: see letter no. 235.

245 Kracauer to Adorno
New York, 15.6.1964

498 Westend Avenue
New York 24, N.Y.
June 15, 1964

Dear Teddie,

I was actually intending to drop you a line just before our departure – for London, on 7 July – but now there is a reason to do so before then. Hans Jonas, who recently gave a really excellent anti-Heidegger lecture, *Heidegger and Theology*, at Drew University [in Madison, New Jersey] has been invited by the faculties of theology (and, I believe, those of philosophy) at Göttingen, Heidelberg and Tübingen to repeat his lecture there. Should you wish to invite him, he asked me to tell you, in case I happened to be writing to you, that he would be free to give a lecture in Frankfurt on Tuesday 23 July (but that is in fact a Thursday, I see) and perhaps also on Wednesday 15 July. His address is 9 Meadow Lane, New Rochelle, N.Y. He is flying to Germany at the beginning of July. Perhaps it would have been better for him to write to you himself, but he knows that we are friends. I am well disposed towards Jonas, and I should be delighted if something could be arranged. I am, however, only the go-between. If all goes well, we shall be arriving in Frankfurt around 3 p.m. on 15 July and, I think, should be at the Frankfurter Hof by 5 at the latest. Perhaps we could speak on the telephone that same day? You wrote that you would be free on the 17th. I shall be seeing Unseld on the 16th. I look forward to meeting up with you, dear Teddie. We will be leaving for Zurich on the 21st. (Shall I have a chance to see something of the Institute and the university?)

I am under terrific pressure just now. Hence these dreadfully skimpy lines.

Much love to you and dear Gretel from Lili and me.

Yours,
Friedel

Original: typescript; Theodor W. Adorno Archiv, Frankfurt am Main.

Jonas ... a really excellent anti-Heidegger lecture: Hans Jonas (1903–1993) published the written version, 'Heidegger und die Theologie', in *Evangelische Theologie*, no. 24, 1964. Among Kracauer's papers there is a copy of the English version (Deutsches Literaturarchiv, Marbach).

I shall be seeing Unseld on the 16th: the appointment was agreed on in the letters exchanged by Kracauer and Siegfried Unseld in May 1964. In a letter of 9 July 1964, Unseld sent an invitation to the Adornos; Unseld gave a dinner in his house in Klettenbergstrasse (see Adorno/Suhrkamp/Unseld, *Briefwechsel*, pp. 490, 492). According to an entry in Kracauer's travel diary he met Adorno again on 17 July 1964 (Kracauer papers, Deutsches Literaturarchiv, Marbach).

246 Adorno to Kracauer
Frankfurt am Main, 18.6.1964

PROF. DR. THEODOR W. ADORNO

FRANKFURT AM MAIN 18 June 1964
KETTENHOFWEG 123

Dear Friedel,

Thanks for your letter.

I know Jonas and have a great regard for him too; I once invited him to give a lecture but the whole thing fell apart at the last moment – because of his schedule, I think. Now, it is terribly difficult to arrange something so quickly. The invitation has to come from the Dept. of Philosophy. My one colleague there, Liebrucks, cannot be reached; my other, Habermas (a highly talented student of mine, whom, to my great delight, I was able to get appointed to Horkheimer's chair), is in Heidelberg. I cannot let the invitation go out over the heads of both of them on my own initiative. I almost fear, therefore, that it will be too late – a pity that such good people always make up their minds so late. But if it does work out, after all, I would send a telegram to Jonas, if possible suggesting a definite date; moreover, the dates which he proposes are not good, as Tuesday and Thursday are the days of my major engagements – right through until the evenings – and out of egoism I try to keep Wednesday evenings free. I am in a downright wretched state of health (heart!) and can get through this miserable term only by dint of extreme dietary measures. You must prepare to meet a very much reduced Teddie this time – but that shouldn't stop us.

The timetable remains as stated. You will certainly be able to see a good number of things at the Institute; the university is awkward, because my lecture and seminar days are Tuesday and Thursday, and you, as far as I can foresee, will not be available then, unless you happened to be free to attend the main philosophy seminar (on problems of Kant's *Kritik der praktischen Vernunft*), which lasts from 6 to 8. But of course I wouldn't want to jeopardize your arrangements with Unseld, as they are of pressing importance to you.

To my astonishment, my projects have made good progress despite the most severe obstacles one might imagine. The text about Strauss, which I have tinkered with more than I can say, went to press today, but besides that I have dictated the major sketch on freedom and determinism (with the subtitle *Paraphrasen zu Kant*) right through to the end in a rough draft. It is thoroughly chaotic (just what the Viennese dialect would call a *Sauhaufen* [let's call it a 'dog's breakfast']) and still has to go through as many mills as the *Jargon der Eigentlichkeit* had to in its time. But it does at least include all my important motifs, and, if I am still alive, I shall get it done. Of the big book, all that remains to be done are the arguments (sketched out) on metaphysics and its general introduction. There are quite simply not enough fingers to cross in every respect.

Much love, to Lili too, also from Gretel,

Yours ever, Teddie

Liebrucks agrees. We hope that the business will work out; I shall send Jonas a telegram tomorrow.

Original: typescript with printed letterhead and handwritten corrections; Siegfried Kracauer papers, Deutsches Literaturarchiv, Marbach am Neckar.

Liebrucks: Bruno Liebrucks (1911–1986), philosopher; appointed to a chair at the Johann Wolfgang Goethe-Universität in 1959.

Habermas: Jürgen Habermas (b. 1929), philosopher and sociologist; he received his doctorate in Bonn in 1954, was an assistant at the Institute for Social Research from 1956 to 1969, qualified as a lecturer in 1961 in Marburg, and then held, among other posts, a professorship in philosophy at Heidelberg. In 1964 he was appointed to the Johann Wolfgang Goethe-Universität; from 1971 to 1981 he was director of the Max-Planck-Institut, Starnberg; in 1975 he returned to Frankfurt am Main as a *Honorarprofessor*, and was professor of philosophy there once more from 1983 onwards.

sketch on freedom and determinism: on the connection with the lectures given in the winter semester 1964/65, *Zur Lehre von der Geschichte und von der Freiheit* [On the doctrine of history and of freedom] (ed. Rolf Tiedemann, Frankfurt am Main: Suhrkamp, 2001) and the chapter 'Freiheit: Zur Metakritik der praktischen Vernunft' [Freedom: on the metacritique of practical reason] (*Negative Dialektik*; see Adorno, GS 6, pp. 211–94; *Negative Dialectics*, trans. E. B. Ashton, London: Routledge, 1973); see Rolf Tiedemann's notes on the lectures (GS 6, pp. 377–462); *Lectures on Negative Dialectics: Fragments of a Lecture Course 1965/1966*, ed. Rolf Tiedemann, trans. Rodney Livingstone, Cambridge: Polity, 2008.

I shall send a telegram to Jonas: Hans Jonas sent his thanks for the invitation to Frankfurt in a letter of 20 June 1964, regretting that he could not accept it because of a scheduling conflict (Theodor W. Adorno Archiv).

247 Kracauer to Adorno

New York, 15.10.1964

498 Westend Avenue
New York 24, N.Y.
October 15, 1964

Dear Teddie,

However briefly, I should like at least to thank you very much today for your article about me, which I found waiting for me here on my return at the beginning of October. It caught me at the most inopportune moment, inasmuch as I am still fully occupied; a heavy backlog has to be cleared, external commitments must be met before I can get on with my own work. (Perhaps this unfortunate chronological constellation is the result of the fact that the pages that you wrote to me so long ago arrived so late.) In any event, at present I am under such pressure that I cannot attend to your text in this letter and respond to it as it deserves and as I should wish. On the other hand, it is impossible for me just to confirm to you that I have received it; that would also be unthinkable in both practical and human terms. It goes without saying that I have read the article with the greatest interest, and while reading it I was moved by the thought that you had undertaken the task of giving the public a portrait of me which weaves together a knowledge born of long-standing personal closeness – a most private knowledge – and a distanced interpretation that follows your own conceptions (as well as uses it in the interest of the present interpretation) – and now it is lying before me in black and white. As I became absorbed in this sensitive material, I became more and more aware that much of what you say comes from the early days of our relationship; the old affinities and antagonisms are all there. It seems to me as if your article also derives from a need to put things which you felt, or were half aware of, at that time into a valid form at last, and by doing so to demarcate our types of thinking (dreadful expression) objectively from one another. Be this as it may, from your construction of the figure of myself – that is, of my relationship to the truth – your own became clearer to me; your view of me allowed me to see you more distinctly. Perhaps it would be an appropriate reciprocal gift to put this image of you into its mandatory form one day … (While we are on the subject: I deeply regretted that at our last meeting in the Operncafé we couldn't talk to each other undisturbed. I personally had wished for conversations that would have delved right down to the basics. That didn't happen.) Just this much for now about my reactions to the content of your portrait – that the whole tenor of it pleased me very much; that I was delighted with some of the remarks drawn from the private sphere (for example, those about the beginning of our friendship); and that several theoretical clarifications which established my position seem to me to be truly convincing and enlightening and, not least, help me to achieve a greater degree of self-objectivization. You will not have been expecting me to agree with your interpretations in every particular. By and large, the more they refer to the long period in which we had drifted apart – that is, the period which began just before I emigrated – the more I was affected by your conception of my attitude and, in part, of the writings I produced as a construction, which does indeed come from some distance and stems from your own mental premises rather than doing justice to the material at hand. From this, too, I believe that I may conclude that your commentary can at least in part be traced back to the old original affirmations and rejections. (But perhaps something of the value of your work lies in the fact that, from such natural and unforced experiences, it seeks to define two different if not unrelated ways of defining the truth – both of topical interest.)

Please write and tell me when you are preparing your article for publication in book form. I would then like to draw your attention to a few factual inaccuracies and things which I was unable to verify.

Warmest greetings and much love from both of us to both of you,

Yours,

Friedel.

Original: typescript; Theodor W. Adorno Archiv, Frankfurt am Main; underlinings by an unknown hand.

thank you … for your article about me: the offprint of *Der wunderliche Realist* (or an extract taken from the journal) among Kracauer's effects bears the handwritten dedication: 'To my dear Friedel / as a belated gift / for a date not to be mentioned / from his Teddie / Frankfurt, / 21 September 1964' (Deutsches Literaturarchiv Marbach).

248 Adorno to Kracauer
Frankfurt am Main, 28.10.1964

PROF. DR. THEODOR W. ADORNO

FRANKFURT AM MAIN 28 October 1964
KETTENHOFWEG 123

Dear Friedel,

Yesterday I arrived back from Vienna, where your letter of 15 October was forwarded to me.

I am very glad that my piece pleased you *in toto*; it was conceived in a truly euphoric state during the flight to Milan and then the train journey to Lucca last year, and I should be happy if something of this élan had been preserved in the structure of the whole. It is not my place to make judgements about its success – of course, lacking, as I do, the distance this requires. Just this much: in the parts relating to your work since the 'turn' [*Kehre*] (the word comes from Heidegger), I don't think that I have transgressed against the principle of immanent criticism which I regard as even more binding than you do, if possible. Only, even this principle is not to be taken too rigidly; one can only know something from within if one is at the same time outside it – this too is a piece of dialectic and non-identical thinking which is surely no more alien to you than it is to me. In short, I could not simply accept the premises of those works but had to measure them against what we have in common, and that is of course much more than the mere biographical fact of youth, however strongly convinced I may be that one undergoes all one's defining experiences in youth, and that later life is essentially an attempt to recapture one's own youth. If you recall our controversy about your Offenbach, you may clearly remember that I was not exactly lacking in support for the immanent criticism which you failed to perceive, and that my so-called standpoint had no need to bear on the matter from outside. It seemed to me that it would be more accurate, more humane and also worthier of our friendship, instead, to create a variation on a phrase coined by Hofmannsthal to explain properly that with which I did not agree, rather than simply 'criticizing' it, as one says. It is in this light, I think, that you should read the parts about those periods. However, the whole thing was written for the sake of the last few pages, and also constructed with these in mind, and I should be grateful if you would concentrate on these – from page 37 onwards. How you react to these would be the most important thing to me – without, of course, my wanting to press you to say anything about that.

I myself am not aware of having reproduced any facts incorrectly; in general, I still have a pretty good memory, and it is at times something like a reservoir of strength for me. If I should actually have committed any gross errors in factual matters, please let me know, and I shall see about correcting them. You will understand, though, that in this I must confine myself to the purely factual and not the intellectual aspects; I neither can nor wish to tamper with or change any points of emphasis. The text is conceived in such a way that that would immediately unbalance it – so let it stay as it is. One cannot, after all, direct the *Fata* of one's own *Libelli* – the image of oneself which they convey. I freely renounce any attempt to do that in my own case, and for this reason it is only right if we behave in the same way towards each other.

The impact of the publication has been quite considerable – not only on the public in the broadest sense – the organs of the press expressly referred to the essay – but also on the few people by whom I really set much store, and above all on Max, Rudolf Hirsch and Unseld. The extraordinarily intelligent Hans Kudszus in Berlin (at present the best critic of philosophy in Germany) let me know how much the piece had moved him. I really am quite glad about this, despite all the contempt I have of the public – this was, after all, an attempt to set up a monument at last to the figure which the two of us constitute, and monuments don't come about in a dead silence.

Vienna was extraordinarily lively and colourful and really refreshed me quite a bit. I had every possible kind of public duty to carry out, including giving the lecture on the *Jargon der Eigentlichkeit* in the famous Redoutensaal, and it was so packed that three hundred people had to be turned away. I don't give myself any airs on account of that; but it is interesting that, when one goes out of one's way so steadfastly to avoid any kind of effect as I do, one achieves a certain effect precisely by doing so; that many people obviously gain confidence in someone because they can be quite sure that he is not trying to pull the wool over their eyes or to sell himself. Even in the case of effects, then, there are these productive contradictions – but I know that I am being too dialectical for you.

Just one more thing: I was as sad as you were that I couldn't spend our last evening alone with you. That this was not possible was the work of a *force majeure* which I pointed out to you; it truly was not my fault. On the other hand, the things in question were of such importance to me that I could not possibly have arranged matters in any other way. I ask you most fervently for your understanding. I am hoping in real earnest that next time we shall indeed manage to discuss what you call 'the basics', although in the not too distant future you will be reading in the *Negative Dialektik* why I dispute the concept of the basic or fundamental. The chances in favour of this will be all the better if we don't see each other towards the end of the semester, when everything piles up enormously, and it would be best of all if we could meet quite alone in a third location. That, of course, presupposes a certain amount of planning.

I am now returning to the *Negative Dialektik* with all my energy; there is not so much more to write of the text itself, apart from the introduction – mainly additions; but the real task will be integrating the whole thing into a single entity. I shall be receiving the first advance copy of the *Jargon* in book form; it goes without saying that you will receive the little book as soon as the author's copies are available. The essay which was previously published has been entirely dispersed throughout it; the whole thing has changed beyond recognition, and I would be glad if you would read it with close attention to detail, also considering the form, which is, to a considerable extent, new – a text of 140 pages, broken down into sections but still delivered as if in a single breath, with no rough caesurae imposed from without. The third volume of *Noten zur Literatur*, which also includes the *Curious Realist*, has already gone to press and will come out in February.

Warmest greetings and much love to you and Lili, from Gretel too,

Yours,

Teddie

Original: typescript with printed letterhead and handwritten corrections; Siegfried Kracauer papers, Deutsches Literaturarchiv, Marbach am Neckar.

'turn' (the word comes from Heidegger): see letter no. 233.

from page 37 onwards: see Adorno, GS 11, pp. 407f.

Kudszus in Berlin: Hans Kudszus (1901–1977), author and critic; he published predominantly in *Tagesspiegel.*

lecture … in the famous Redoutensaal: Adorno spoke on 23 October 1964 in the Redouten-Saal of the Vienna Hofburg; this event was organized by the Österreichische Gesellschaft für Literatur; on 26 October, he gave a lecture to the Österreichische Gesellschaft für Musik in the Palais Palffy entitled 'Über einige Schwierigkeiten des Komponierens heute' [On some difficulties of composing today] (see the version *Schwierigkeiten, I: Beim Komponieren*; Adorno, GS 17, pp. 253–73).

third volume of Noten zur Literatur*: Noten zur Literatur III* was published by Suhrkamp on 2 February 1965.

249 Kracauer to Adorno
New York, 3.11.1964

498 Westend Avenue
New York 24, N.Y.
November 3, 1964

Dear Teddie,

That you would approve of your article and keep it unchanged was no more than I would have expected. I shall certainly not disturb its balance either. I am only concerned with letting you know about factual inaccuracies, as already stated. As the article has already gone to press for inclusion in the book, I shall hasten to do this.

p. 11: You write that my mother's sister had a great influence on me. That is not true – she never did.

pp. 23, 32: My most political years, you say, were those in Berlin – the ones which roughly coincided with my 'socio-critical phase'. This is not true either. In reality, especially important pronouncements, my intellectual endeavours and my practical efforts in this area belong to the time *before* Berlin.

p. 33: According to you, I took as little notice as possible of the objective reasons why my position at the F. Z. in Berlin had become precarious. My extensive correspondence from this period (which still survives) can prove the exact opposite to you.

pp. 32, 33: in the course of your attempts to characterize adaptation to existing circumstances as the cause of my success and my success as the effect of adaptation, you say that my 'visible success' began in those days before the Berlin period when I vowed to myself that I would be happy (?), came to terms with the world, and gave myself airs (a gesture which could not be less like me). You appear to need this in order to be able to suggest later that my 'surprising' success in America was also a consequence of such conformist behaviour. (That the suggestion of conformity is not wholly accurate is something which the reader can fortunately conclude from what you say about my opposition to the prevailing brand of American sociology.) The approach which your argument adopts is inaccurate. In fact, there is no causal connection between my success and the event, if any, which you call my 'vow of happiness'. My series of socio-critical essays, and most of all my *Angestellten*, did indeed enjoy very visible success – productions which certainly do not provide evidence of adaptation. I personally consider *Ginster* my greatest success, because it earned me a letter from Alban Berg which was a genuine declaration of love. *En passant*, if external success were an infallible sign of adaptation, the success which you are enjoying at present would have to betray that to the highest possible degree.

p. 33: Probably you are not fully acquainted with my unpublished novel. At the end the hero is dismissed from the newspaper because of his radical left-wing position, which gives the lie to all his previous non-conformist declarations of agreement. Because of this, however, the novel loses its usefulness for your argument.

There follow three possible factual errors:

p. 31: I was not aware that I was quoting Ringelnatz when I say in *Ginster* that broom [*Ginster*] flowers on railway embankments. Internal evidence, however, contradicts this.

p. 33: I can't remember receiving you in our hotel in Paris. As far as I recall, we met in the Deux Magots. (By the way, I cannot fathom what you mean by the expression that I received you 'like Stauffacher on his home ground'.)

p. 36: Have I ever used the saying 'Envy is ...' to characterize Heidegger's language? I can't remember. It seems to me, by the way, that this characterization is rather inadequate.

While we are on the subject, I should of course try at the same time to implement that passage from my previous letter in which I gave notice of my critical attitude to parts of your interpretation – but that would make my letter too long, so I shall content myself with picking out a few points where my reading differs from yours and merely naming them – just for the record. I don't believe that I failed to take pains to extrapolate the general from the extremely particular; I believe much more that it was always one of my main problems to find out how this could be done (as evidenced by passages in my book on sociology, the *Angestellten* and the *Theory of Film*). My book on history will reach its climax in an attempt to find an explicit solution to this problem. Then, too, I am surprised that you rank my *Caligari*, which contains important technical analyses (especially the new kind applied to the polyphonic Nazi film propaganda), on a level with *Offenbach*. This, I suppose, is done in the interests of your theory of adaptation. The result is that your commentary goes awry; it doesn't apply to the substantive points of the book. Finally, at the utopian end of your essay you confront my relationship to things, and my constant listening to them, with my scepticism regarding the possibility of change of the *condition humaine* in a way which I don't accept because it exaggerates my scepticism. For this, see my *Theory of Film*. (In the book about history I shall have something to say about the pull towards the utopian element.)

Warmest greetings and love
from both of us to both of you,

Yours,
Friedel

Original: typescript with handwritten corrections: Theodor W. Adorno Archiv, Frankfurt am Main.

p. 11: written over this by hand, presumably by Adorno, is '19'; see *Der wunderliche Realist* (Adorno, GS 11, p. 390).

pp. 23, 32: 'The most political years' became 'in the political Berlin years' (see ibid., p. 393); for the second quotation, see ibid., p. 402.

p. 33: the sentence about the position becoming 'precarious' was deleted.

pp. 32, 33: 'visible success' and 'covert readiness to adapt' became 'successful adaptation' (see ibid., p. 403).

a letter from Alban Berg: see letter no. 183.

quoting Ringelnatz: Adorno wrote then 'as he once said like Ringelnatz' (see Adorno, GS 11, p. 401). The passage in *Ginster* reads: 'He was glad that broom ran alongside the tracks which were vanishing straight ahead. He too would have liked most of all to have flowered on both sides of the embankment' (see Kracauer, W 7, p. 221). Adorno was referring to the poem 'Ich habe Dich so lieb' [I love you so much], or, more precisely, to the lines 'On the slopes by the railway / Glows the yellow broom so bright' (see Joachim Ringelnatz, *Gedichte* 1, ed. Walter Pape, Zurich: Diogenes, 1994, p. 261, and also vol. 2, p. 426). Joachim Ringelnatz (1883–1934) published it in his volume *Allerdings*, which was published in June 1928 by Ernst Rowohlt. The pre-publication serialization of *Ginster* began on 8 April 1928 (see Kracauer, W 7, p. 627). By coincidence, Ringelnatz's poems were published with the annotation 'Ginster gewidmet' [Dedicated to Ginster], but this Ginster 'is the merchant Edmund Kretschmer (1891–1931), for whose Munich firm Ringelnatz … wrote advertisements in verse' (see Ringelnatz, *Gedichte* 2, p. 426).

Stauffacher on his home ground: Werner Stauffacher's gesture, *Wilhelm Tell*, Act I, scene ii: 'But stay, until mine hostess comes – you are / My guest in Schwyz' (see Friedrich Schiller, *Dramen* IV, ed. Matthias Luserke, Frankfurt am Main, Deutscher Klassiker Verlag, 1996, p. 395.

'Envy is …': 'die Eifersucht ist eine Leidenschaft, die mit Eifer sucht, was Leiden schafft' [Envy's a passion, it is plain / Which seeks with zeal what causes pain] (see Adorno, GS 11, p. 405).

250 Adorno to Kracauer
Frankfurt am Main, 13.11.1964

PROF. DR. THEODOR W. ADORNO

FRANKFURT AM MAIN 13 November 1964
KETTENHOFWEG 123

Dear Friedel,

Your letter arrived at almost exactly the same time as the corrections to my book. I would like to see which of your suggestions remain to be acted upon. However, first of all it seems right to me to respond to individual points which you make.

p. 11. (I think this actually refers to p. 19). Not only was it my opinion that your Aunt Hedwig exerted a great influence on you but, long before our correspondence about the essay, Benno Reifenberg also confirmed that to me and backed it up with specific recollections. I should have liked to give this lady, who was murdered, the honour of mentioning her in this context. I also remember in the most specific detail remarks of yours in which you called her a woman of significance. Do you really not want to grant her this favour?

pp. 23/32. I had already restricted the sentence about your time in Berlin by using the expression 'roughly' and the fact that I put so much emphasis on the suite about the little shop-girls adequately expresses what was taking place. However, if it matters so much to you, I shall see about changing the passage slightly.

p. 33. I shall follow your suggestion.

pp. 32/33. This really does involve something of central importance. The fact that from a particular point in time you changed your whole attitude as I describe it in the essay was so central an experience to me that I cannot possibly deviate from this. The expression to which you object – that you made a vow to be happy – is a quotation from Stefan George; in my opinion it describes that change so accurately that I should not like to dispense with it. By the way, I am not implying that success as such is a function of adaptation; I don't think that there is a single sentence in the whole text to suggest that. There is also success through non-adaptation. I don't believe that anyone would get the idea that I of all people grudged you your success; my criticism is directed solely at certain aspects of an attitude which I discovered before it became crystallized also in your writings at the time of your emigration. It was actually you yourself who had played down the success of *Ginster* to me; no matter whether it was a major work or a minor success, the book has held its own in a remarkable way. Aside from that, I regard it as dating from *before* the 'turn'.

p. 33. I am grateful to you for bringing this to my notice, and will change this passage.

Now to the alleged factual errors:

p. 31. Fräulein Olbrich, my dear and faithful secretary, brought the lines by Ringelnatz to my attention one day when I quoted your comment about broom flowering on the railway embankment. I assume that you unconsciously recalled this. Otherwise the coincidence would be too fantastic. I think we ought to leave things as they stand.

p. 33. I can still see before my eyes the way you received me in your hotel – I think it was called the Madison – and your air of being at home in a situation in which neither of us could know any longer whether he might survive made an indelible impression on me. I believe that if I were to change this an important nuance would be lost.

p. 36. I can remember your application of the proverb to Heidegger with the utmost, absolute clarity. It made an impression on me as a genuinely illuminating piece of wit, and I would feel that it was a great shame if we had to sacrifice it. I can't imagine that you would want to be considerate on behalf of Herr Heidegger's feelings. By the way, how did your *rencontre* go with Henrich, etc.?

I didn't deal with *Caligari* in detail for the simple reason that I share old Plato's conviction that one should only write about things of which one actually has a solid understanding – as in this case I don't about film technique. I had to confine myself to something of which I do have a broad view – the general trend as a whole. It is obvious that you genuinely misunderstood the conclusion of my work, on which I place the greatest possible value, and that makes me sad. It would be good if you would just take a very close look at these pages sometime.

The tenor of your second letter deviates considerably from that of the first; I'm not quite sure why. Does my work not contain so much – and such new material – about you that it should not in every detail carry you away across the alternatives of pro and contra with playful ease? It almost seems to me as if the actual reason for the divergences between us is an increasingly strong tendency that you have been developing in your old age to direct the reception of your work and the image of yourself and to intervene everywhere, while I, conversely, am more convinced the older I get that nothing can be so fatal to an effect as taking matters into one's own hands instead of simply letting them take their course. A significant literary activity will survive, after all, only through criticism of one's oeuvre and not through a kind of positivity which might devalue its object through an obsequious attitude towards it. In the final analysis I behaved no differently towards Schoenberg from the way I did in the essay about you, and I absolutely cannot express myself in any way other than thinking as I do. You once said to me in a critical way when I was still a sixth-former or a very young student that, to use a word of Mörike's, you thought there was too much 'veryness' about me; that made a great impression on me at the time. Nowadays it almost seems to me as if I had followed your instruction better than you yourself. But it really is up to you rather than me to think that over.

You will receive the *Jargon der Eigentlichkeit* direct from the publisher; I would be grateful for a word of confirmation and also, of course, for criticism. The third volume of the *Noten* in which *The Curious Realist* is also included now, as well as the contribution on Karl Kraus, is coming out in February. In the meantime, my great book is making better progress than I could ever have hoped, although problems are constantly piling up in front of me. But some day or other my work on it will have to come to an end.

Much love and best wishes to you both, from Gretel too,

Yours ever,

Teddie

Original: typescript with printed letterhead, handwritten additions and corrections; Siegfried Kracauer papers, Deutsches Literaturarchiv, Marbach am Neckar.

which of your suggestions remain to be acted upon: see the preceding letter (note).

that you made a vow to be happy: see Adorno, GS 11, p. 402. Adorno paraphrases a line from the third verse of Stefan George's 'Es lacht in dem steigenden Jahr dir': 'So let us conceal what we miss, then, / And vow to be happy again, / Though no more be granted but this, then: / A round to be gone by us twain'; Stefan George, *Poems*, trans. Carol North Valhope and Ernst Morwitz, London: Kegan Paul, 1944 (see letter no. 1).

rencontre ... with Henrich: Dieter Henrich (b. 1927), philosopher; studied with Hans-Georg Gadamer, among others, in Heidelberg; professorships in Berlin, Heidelberg and Munich. The meeting refers to the colloquium 'Immanente Äesthetik – Ästhetik der Reflexion' [Immanent aesthetic – aesthetic of reflection], organized by the research group 'Poetik und Hermeneutik' in which Kracauer took part in September 1964 in Cologne (see *Marbacher Magazin* 47, p. 121).

to use a word of Mörike's ... too much 'veryness': see Eduard Mörike, 'An Longus', in *Sämtliche Werke*, ed. Herbert G. Göpfert, Munich: Carl Hanser, 1981, pp. 167–170, including the lines: 'Now, this kind gentleman, I thought, must be / Just what my Longus calls 'a very man'; / The lady too was *very* – highly so.'

contribution on Karl Kraus: 'Sittlichkeit und Kriminalität: Zum elften Band der Werke von Karl Kraus' [Morality and criminality: on the eleventh volume of the works of Karl Kraus], developed from a notice in *Der Spiegel*, 5 August 1964 (see Adorno, GS 11, pp. 367–87, 699).

251 Kracauer to Adorno
New York, 21.11.1964

498 Westend Avenue
New York 24, N.Y.
November 21, 1964

Dear Teddie,

My last letter doesn't deviate in any respect from the previous one but just provides the corrections, etc., about which I alerted you there (which leaves the positive things said in it entirely untouched). In the interests of settling this business once and for all I shall briefly answer the main points in your letter in sequence.

p. 19: the fact that my aunt Hedwig was a woman of importance in her own way does not include the assumption that she influenced me. Once again, she did not. And should I, who always think of her and of my dear mother with a feeling of heartache, not be the most credible source of information in this matter?

pp. 23, 32: It should not have escaped the notice of someone with such a grasp of the finer points of the language as you that your unjustified assertion that my political years were the ones spent in Berlin is not eliminated or even decisively limited by your addition of the words 'by and large' and the allusion which you include elsewhere to the 'little shop-girls'.

pp. 32–33: What I object to here, in a truly unambiguous way, is simply and solely your statement, in contradiction of the facts, that I had enjoyed 'visible success' from that day (before the Berlin period) when, as you put it, I came to be on better terms with the world, etc. (p. 33). By saying this, you are in fact stating as a fact that at least *my* visible success was a result of my so-called adaptation to the world. With what you say – that success as such would not have to be like this – you are kicking at an open door; I said so myself in my last letter. But no matter. My disclaimer refers purely to the demonstrably false causal connection that you establish between my success and my 'vow of happiness', *not* to your adaptation theory. I do, however, consider it – with good reason – to be a distortion of reality – of *my* reality – but you see me just the way you see me.

p. 31: About Ringelnatz: the coincidence is by no means too fantastic, but it can be explained simply by the fact that the presence of broom on railway embankments is a fairly well-known phenomenon. Your comment about this, incidentally, stirred up a memory within me of how, even before writing the novel, on the journey home from Paris, in Lorraine I saw these plants blooming on the left and right of the train tracks. We were travelling through a sea of yellow; I was greatly struck by this.

p. 33: That you received the impression in that hotel in Paris that I felt at home in the midst of malevolent chaos seems to me like an almost incredible misinterpretation of my state of mind and situation at that time. (It would be easy to prove this.) I assume that your impression of me was derived from the opinion of me that you had brought to the meeting; and, by using this impression to illustrate that opinion, you cover up with a single stroke my more than Kierkegaardian trembling at that time and in all those years. But here, too, all that is involved in the final analysis is a personal perception. If you need the colour, I have nothing against dyeing!

An alert: I subsequently came across an inaccuracy (of no importance in itself) which was not mentioned in my last letter. It wasn't I who called Ginster an 'intellectual Švejk' (p. 31), but Roth did so in a conversation with Benjamin. I found this in a note by Benjamin relating to this subject.

As you yourself in your writings on music rightly emphasize the importance of technical factors for interpretation, I was understandably startled to discover that in your commentary on *Caligari* you fail even to mention my technical analyses – which you merely needed to acknowledge. In connection with my original interpretations of the links between social, political and psychological processes, these analyses constitute the substance of the book. Your commentary passes over all this to confine itself to its 'general tendency'. What has become of the 'splitting of the atom', then?

When I am correcting your factual errors, this certainly does not mean that I have been trying to 'control' the public image of myself. Apart from a reply to Buber/Rosenzweig's pronouncement directed against my article on their translation of the Bible which was necessary for reasons connected with the newspaper, I have never in my entire life reacted to criticism of me, even when it got the facts wrong. In this I am less like a steersman than a blind passenger. Only because you are my friend am I deviating from my habitual reserve and playing the pilot to guard you against running onto the cliffs of false information.

May I suggest that with this we bring our discussion of your article to an end?

Warmest greetings from us both to dear Gretel and yourself,

Yours,
Friedel

Original: typescript; Theodor W. Adorno Archiv, Frankfurt am Main.

It wasn't I who called Ginster an 'intellectual Švejk' (p.31): 'Kracauer called Ginster an intellectual Švejk' (see Adorno, GS 11, p. 401). The expression attributed to Joseph Roth occurred in a letter from Walter Benjamin to Kracauer of 16 July 1927: 'I happened to run into Roth. He made me very eager to read your wartime memoirs and told me that you were writing the intellectual Švejk' (see Benjamin, *Gesammelte Briefe* III, p. 272).

splitting the atom: 'Geistige Atomzertrümmerung', a self-quotation by Adorno which occurs in *The Curious Realist* (see Adorno, GS 11, p. 394). He used this term in 1954 in a notice announcing a new translation of Marcel Proust's *À l'ombre des jeunes filles en fleurs* (see letter no. 158).

reply to Buber/Rosenzweig: see letter no. 31.

252 Adorno to Kracauer

Frankfurt am Main, 5.2.1965

PROF. DR. THEODOR W. ADORNO

FRANKFURT AM MAIN 5 February 1965
KETTENHOFWEG 123

Dear Friedel,

I don't know, to be sure, how far the taboo extends, but I don't think it can do any harm if I send you my deeply heartfelt good wishes for 8 February, and Gretel's too.

The third volume of the *Noten*, which contains the *Realist*, is finished – the final corrections done, the pages are made up, and it is now going to press. I have taken your desiderata into account – sometimes with Solomon-like solutions that might coax a smile out of you. As for our discussion about the whole business, I agree that it should come to an end, although, as I was the injured party, I do feel that it should be up to me to bring matters to such a conclusion. Anyway, I could imagine that, once we see each other on our own and are not under any pressure, we shall be talking this matter over once again.

In the meantime, I have been busy reading your film book with sustained concentration. I would gladly participate in a radio discussion with someone about it, but it is not easy to find somebody with whom this could be done *inter pares*, now that Kluge has opted out – and carrying on such a discussion with so-called film journalists would hardly be possible owing to the difference in the level of competence. Even with this book I am vacillating between being greatly impressed and having serious reservations – but that too might best be kept for our discussion. I was delighted by the Perseus theory – Perseus being my favourite myth, anyway – and, likewise, I had long ago seized the idea of perseverance, of holding one's own, while facing a horrifying image. The only question here is whether quantity doesn't turn into quality. It seems to me that the whole body of facts which the word 'Auschwitz' represents quite simply can no longer be contained in images, and even such an extraordinary work as Schoenberg's *A Survivor from Warsaw* has, I feel, something profoundly inappropriate about it. You will find my theories about this in the essay on engagement, which I assume you don't know as yet, and which likewise appears in the third volume of the *Noten*.

There is just one point about the film book which I should like to mention to you straight away. Throughout the book you discuss film solely in the sense of its immanent possibilities, premises and desiderata and criticize those intellectuals who refuse to take film seriously by stating that they misjudge its specific qualities and measure it against traditional art (the question of whether something is 'art' is in any case one which I don't regard as profitable; all my life I have constantly been hearing people ask the silly question, 'Is that still music?', and I believe that anyone who applies this argument to film is behaving in a very similar fashion). But as far as I can see there is no mention at all in your book – or only a peripheral one – of the point against which resistance on the part of serious people is directed – i.e. that, being more directly harnessed into the commercial system than any other form of expression, it has never managed to unfold the potential of its immanent system of distinct laws at all – that it is only an entity 'for other things' [*Für anderes*] and not 'in itself [*An sich*] – while you treat it as if it were the latter. But by doing this, you must admit, you shift the perspective substantially, and that should be added to the book as an N.B. of some considerable force.

Ernst Bloch spoke here some weeks ago, in an overflowing Auditorium Maximum, with enormous success; I had to introduce him. For the first time, though, it appeared to me that he really had aged a lot – not merely physically but also mentally – in that he seemed like a gramophone record of himself. It is precisely in the case of a person for whom everything is marked by the sign of vitality that this vitality acquires something of a rather sad quality when, as vividness, it becomes a mask.

The *Jargon of Authenticity* has already sold out, and a second impression is being printed. I can't deny my pleasure at the fact that my allegedly esoteric and inaccessible stuff is obviously making its effects felt. But apparently no direct proportion prevails between the authority of texts and their popularity, after all. You did receive the book, didn't you? I would be keen to hear your reaction.

Next week Gretel and I are going to Montagnola for a few days to visit Horkheimer, whose health is not at all good (I really am worried about him), but who has made a good recovery after experiencing tremendous circulatory symptoms. At the beginning of March, I shall be in Paris for ten days, using a few lectures as a pretext. Up to now I have been surviving the semester quite well (astonishingly for me) and hope to be able to hold out for the last three weeks as well. Then, in April, Gretel and I shall be going to Baden-Baden for a holiday between semesters. My great book is quite finished in rough draft, and major parts of it have advanced even beyond that stage, but there is still an unimaginable mass of work to do. Once that is behind me, I shall offer a cockerel to Aesculapius.

Warmest regards to you both, from Gretel too,

Your old

Teddie

Original: typescript with printed letterhead and handwritten corrections; Siegfried Kracauer papers, Deutsches Literaturarchiv, Marbach am Neckar.

the Perseus theory: 'When Athene instigated Perseus to slay the monster, she warned him never to look at the face itself but only at its reflection in the polished shield she had given him. Following her advice Perseus cut off Medusa's head … The moral of the myth is, of course, that we do not, and cannot, see actual horrors and cannot even see them because they paralyse us with blinding fear … The film screen is Athene's polished shield' (See *Theorie des Films*, 'Das Haupt der Medusa' (see Kracauer, W 3, pp. 467f.); *The Theory of Film: The Redemption of Physical Reality*, Oxford: Oxford University Press, 1960, p. 305).

Perseus being my favourite myth: Adorno inserted this motif in his second 'Musikalische Warenanalyse': 'The musical fetish comes into its own … Its magic is broken like that of the Medusa when Perseus confronts her with her own reflection' (*Quasi una Fantasia: Essays on Modern Music*, trans. Rodney Livingstone, London: Verso, 1992, 'Commodity Music Analysed', pp. 37–52; see Adorno, GS 16, p. 294).

Schoenberg's A Survivor from Warsaw *… something profoundly inappropriate*: Adorno on Arnold Schoenberg's op. 46 (1947), in 'Engagement' (*Die Neue Rundschau*, no. 1, 1964; see Adorno, GS 11, pp. 409–30, 699): 'But even the *Survivor from Warsaw* remains trapped in the aporia to which he – an autonomous depiction of heteronomy intensified to the point of hell – delivers himself without reserve … But when it is transformed into an image, despite all the hardness and impossibility of reconciliation, it is as if the shame felt in front of the victims were vitiated. Something is concocted from these victims, works of art, thrown as fodder to the world which murdered them' (see Adorno, GS 11, p. 423).

Ernst Bloch spoke here … I had to introduce him: Ernst Bloch spoke on 18 January 1965 at the Johann Wolfgang Goethe-Universität on 'Positivismus, Idealismus, Materialismus'; Adorno's salutation, 'Ernst Bloch zur Einführung' [Introducing Ernst Bloch], is printed in *Frankfurter Adorno Blätter*, 8 vols, ed. Rolf Tiedemann, Munich, 1992–2003, vol. III, pp.144f.

lectures as a pretext: among these, on 5 March 1965, was 'Über einige Schwierigkeiten beim Komponieren heute' [On some difficulties in composing today] at the Deutsches Haus of the Cité Internationale (see Adorno, GS 17, pp. 253–73) (Theodor W. Adorno Archiv).

253 Kracauer to Adorno

New York, 3.3.1965

498 Westend Avenue
New York 24, N.Y.
March 3, 1965

Dear Teddie,

First of all, very many thanks for your kind birthday wishes.

You are returning once again to our correspondence about your article and speaking now of 'desiderata' which I am supposed to have stipulated – but that is a complete distortion of the contents of my letters. In fact, I not only did not mention any 'desiderata' in them; I explicitly said that I did not want to bring up any. All that I did was to correct factual inaccuracies.

In addition to this I made some criticism of your adaptation theory, but always with the express proviso that it was your business to interpret, and I would not think of interfering with it.

Your preliminary comments on my film book naturally interested me very much. On the subject of Auschwitz: when the war in Germany was over, Eisenhower commissioned the making of documentary films about concentration camps. There was something entirely legitimate about this. It may be that films on this subject – factual films, I mean – are more legitimate than works of art. I am, God knows, no lover of definitions of 'art' or similar general concepts. In the film book, however, I had, for methodological reasons, to try to get a handle on the term 'art' one way or another, for that was the only way that it was possible for me to tease out the qualities which are peculiar to film. Moreover, this was in the service of a strategic/polemical interest. These peculiarities of the medium have been brought about over and over again throughout its history – regardless of economic and social kinds of resistance. I did not, therefore, invent them – although, naturally, construction is involved – but found them in existing material and analysed them in depth and detail. Therefore, it is hardly correct when you say that film has not managed at all to develop its immanent potential. It has done this, and continues to do so at various and sundry occasions. [And would do so even more if there were not so many would-be artists, men of letters (e.g. Resnais or, before him, Cocteau) and well-intentioned intellectuals who misuse film for their (allegedly) higher purposes.] I consciously distanced myself from sociological considerations, with which I should have been on home ground. Above all because social conditions nowadays are in such a state of flux that new definitions are needed to make them comprehensible. This is not something which I could undertake at the same time. My main task was to present the essential nature of photographic media as they have evolved relatively independently of political and economic systems everywhere – at any rate in their initial forms. By the way, the publishers have sent me a broadcast review of my book done by Theodor Kotulla which I found very clever and perceptive.

You ask about your *Jargon der Eigentlichkeit* in book form. You know that I rated the journal article very highly. I am less keen on the expanded version. Not that I didn't agree in principle with your criticism of Heidegger – above all, I subscribe to the idea that having to die is a scandal rather than an existential matter – but you are just a little bit too right about the man – and expanding it puts too much emphasis on jargon in its turn.

I am under great pressure just now. The time in Paris will, I hope, do you good.

Warmest greetings from both of us to both of you,

Yours,

Friedel

Original: typescript; Theodor W. Adorno Archiv, Frankfurt am Main.

Eisenhower commissioned the making of documentary films about concentration camps: General Dwight D. Eisenhower (1890–1969) had the liberation of the concentration camps documented even during the Allied advance in Germany, e.g: 'Nooit vergeten! [Never forget!] Original films made on the orders of General Dwight D. Eisenhower during the liberation of the concentration camps: Leipzig, Penig, Breendonck, Hannover, Arnstadt, Dachau, Mauthausen and Bergen-Belsen', 1945, in English with Dutch subtitles.

factual films: see the corresponding chapter of *Theorie des Films* (Kracauer, W 3, pp. 306–37), especially the passage about the portrayal of 'real horrors' (ibid., pp. 467f.).

[…]: the double parentheses are Kracauer's.

Resnais: Kracauer wrote 'Renais'; Alain Resnais (1922–2014), director. He achieved great success with *Hiroshima, mon amour* (1959; book by Marguerite Duras).

Kotulla: Kracauer wrote 'Katulla'; Theodor Kotulla (1928–2001), director and critic. He reviewed *Theorie des Films* for Hessische Rundfunk; the broadcast went out on 10 January 1965.

that having to die is a scandal rather than an existential matter: see the last part of *Jargon der Eigentlichkeit* (Adorno, GS, pp. 500ff.).

254 Adorno to Kracauer
Frankfurt am Main, 17.3.1965

PROF. DR. THEODOR W. ADORNO

FRANKFURT AM MAIN 17 March 1965
KETTENHOFWEG 123

Dear Friedel,

On my return from Paris I found your letter of 3 March waiting for me. I had in fact somewhat overestimated my strength. Rich and stimulating as the days were – and they flattered my vanity, too, as my French held out astonishingly well, and I even discovered praise for this in a sophisticated magazine – they were at the same time equally stressful, above all because I was relentlessly forced to adapt to the most diverse types of people. I am feeling truly battered and am looking forward to Baden-Baden, where we are going on 1 April for two weeks (address as always: Brenners Parkhotel). In the meantime, I am rushing around doing stuff for the Institute and dictating away at my book in a desperate fashion.

By now you must surely have received the third volume of the *Noten zur Literatur*; I should be grateful for a word of confirmation, just for the sake of order – and also because of the open letter to Horkheimer.

I have not yet found a compatible partner for a radio discussion of your book on film. Who and what is Kotulla, and is he worth considering? By the way, I continue to believe that, especially in the case of film, it is not possible to separate the economic, social and aesthetic aspects, simply because every film is bound up with the commercialization of capital on account of the production costs in a way that no intellectual entity has ever been before. It is paradoxical that I of all people, who am otherwise so much opposed to any kind of cheap sociologism in aesthetics, in this case believe more than you that it is necessary to emphasize the sociological aspect. As far as the role of intellectuals in film is concerned, that is certainly not such a simple matter, either. You are indeed right about Cocteau – if he caused only half as much mischief in film as he did in music (a field where, to my horror, in Paris I was still able to register traces of that even now), that would have been enough; he belongs through and through to those intellectuals who achieved the most heinous ideological effects by using intellectual means to champion the inferior, from music hall to high-class cinematographic kitsch. Things ought to be different with other intellectuals in films, and it almost seems to me that, without an appropriate dose of inoculated reflection and without a certain salutary exercise of terror against the mighty producers, film is completely done for. If I had to write a book about film, it would definitely be a picture-book which would consist exclusively of the mug shots of producers, perhaps adorned with typical comments. Perhaps we can agree on the formula that, precisely on account of that unholy alliance, film has realized its own potential only intermittently, I would say, in flashes and for odd moments. I can hardly ever see a film without having a feeling for a few moments of 'that is how it should be, that would be possible' – and then immediately afterwards one of fury that the wool is being pulled over our eyes by the calculation of the racket. In any case, it is not obvious to me that it would be possible to perform an operation to separate something like purely immanent technical laws of film from their socio-economic entanglements. In this case, just as everywhere else, the relationship between the productive forces and the conditions of production is much too reciprocal.

About *Jargon der Eigentlichkeit* I should only like to say that the book by no means represents an expanded version but was conceived as such from the outset, and that the essay in the *Rundschau* represented something only like an advance publication of parts of the draft, which of course have changed considerably. It is impossible to be proved right often enough against Heidegger, considering the effect which he produces; moreover, my argumentation leads directly to my most personal ideas in the new book on dialectics. As far as the phenomenon of jargon itself is concerned, one cannot possibly take its appeal in Germany too seriously; it is indeed the predominant form of present-day German ideology – believe you me.

Warmest greetings to you and Lili, from Gretel too,

Your old

Teddie

Original: typescript with printed letterhead, handwritten additions and corrections; Siegfried Kracauer papers, Deutsches Literaturarchiv, Marbach am Neckar.

praise … in a sophisticated magazine: no information survives.

open letter to Horkheimer: 'Offener Brief an Max Horkheimer', *Die Zeit*, 12 February 1965 (see Adorno, GS 20.1, pp. 155–63; GS 20.2, p. 812); Adorno's congratulations on Horkheimer's 70th birthday on 14 February 1965.

Kotulla: as in the preceding letter, Adorno wrote 'Katulla'.

255 Kracauer to Adorno
New York, 27.3.1965

498 Westend Avenue
New York 24, N.Y.
March 27, 1965

Dear Teddie,

All I can do today is fulfil your wish straight away and confirm receipt of both the Horkheimer article and *Noten zur Literatur III*. You wanted me to do this at once, and I am doing so at once, with my thanks. The reason for my taciturnity is that I have succumbed to one of those long-lasting kinds of influenza which are going the rounds here at present and have the bad habit of indiscriminately afflicting other organs – e.g. the stomach as well. I seem to be over it now, but am still tired.

Warmest greetings from both of us to both of you,

Yours,

Original: typescript (carbon copy); Siegfried Kracauer papers, Deutsches Literaturarchiv, Marbach am Neckar.

Horkheimer article: the copy among Kracauer's papers bears the handwritten dedication 'Most cordially! Teddie, February 1965' (Deutsches Literaturarchiv, Marbach).

Noten zur Literatur III: in the library which Kracauer left behind there is a copy of the second edition (see letter no. 264).

256 Kracauer to Adorno
New York, 23.4.1965

498 Westend Avenue
New York 24, N.Y.
April 23, 1965

Dear Teddie,

First of all, I should like to thank you very much indeed for having proposed me for the Entretiens de Monaco. Professor Chevalier mentioned this in his letter of invitation to me. The theme of the colloquium is of enormous interest to me – precisely because, in my first chapter (about the connections between history and science), I dealt with this and nothing else. Unfortunately, I had to decline the invitation for this year, as it came too late to change plans which do not depend on me alone.

I am still a bit tired after the flu and, moreover, so much swamped with chores that I would rather not go into practical details – but perhaps we shall soon have an opportunity to see each other. This is another reason for my writing to you now. If all goes well, we want to come to Frankfurt on 9 July after a few days in Berlin and stay there up to and including the 15th. I know that this is a bad time for you, and if I could have organized things differently I should certainly have done so – but it will work out somehow or other. It is still a long way off, and we can of course make more detailed plans later. There is just one wish of ours which I should like to mention now – that one day you and Gretel should be our guests at the Frankfurter Hof.

We greatly enjoyed the visits of Szondi and Habermas.

Warmest greetings and love from both of us to both of you,

Yours,
Friedel

Original: typescript; Theodor W. Adorno Archiv, Frankfurt am Main.

Entretiens de Monaco … Chevalier: no information survives.

come to Frankfurt: as part of the trip to Germany, France and Switzerland from mid-July to early October 1965.

Szondi and Habermas: the visits took place independently of each other; Jürgen Habermas was received in Kracauer's apartment at the beginning of April 1965. No information survives about the meeting with Szondi, who was also in the USA in the spring of 1965.

257 Adorno to Kracauer
Frankfurt am Main, 27.4.1965

PROF. DR. THEODOR W. ADORNO

FRANKFURT AM MAIN 27 April 1965
KETTENHOFWEG 123

Dear Friedel,

Many thanks for your letter of 23 April.

The trouble with July is not so much the regular business of lectures and seminars as the faculty and committee meetings and the examinations which, in my experience, come crashing down on me at that time. You can imagine what I think of functions of that kind, but I cannot escape them because, as I have more than once had occasion to realize, it is precisely in those meetings from which one absents oneself that the mischief (which one would want to prevent at all costs) is done. But we will manage something one way or another. Perhaps you might also enjoy attending my advanced philosophy seminar some time (Thursdays from 6 to 8). This time my topic is Kant's doctrine of ideas.

I hope that you are recovering from your flu; I know how stubborn the after-effects sometimes are, and I would tell you to take it easy if I didn't know only too well how little notice people like us take of such advice, no matter how well meant it may be.

You are sure to have heard something about the intellectual situation here, and also about us, from Szondi and Habermas.

You must surely have read Patalas's review of *Filmtheorie* in *Frankfurter Allgemeine Zeitung*. It made a great impression on me; there is something dignified about it, at once critical and respectful, which, as you know, is a very rare combination. I have invited him to participate in a radio discussion with me about your book; I had been procrastinating about this chiefly for lack of a partner whom I would have considered equal to the task. Now I have confidence in him. I have not yet had an answer from him, though. Young authors naturally feel a certain sense of inhibition about stepping in front of the microphone with old dogs like me. Incidentally, in a certain sense, Patalas, without ever having formally studied with me, can still be regarded as a student of mine. Most of all I should like to have a thorough discussion with you before long about the relationship between aesthetic and sociological categories, something which kept coming into my mind while studying your book. I had begun, a good while ago, to dictate a series of more or less disconnected ideas about film but was constantly interrupted in this, and at present it is only with the greatest difficulty that I can get to grips with anything but my big book. I should finally have finished dictating the rough draft within the next fortnight, but that is when the real torture is only just beginning. To quote myself: if I am ever born again, I shall be a playboy.

In the meantime, I have also sent in my contribution to the Bloch festschrift, 'Henkel, Krug und frühe Erfahrung' [Handle, jug and early experience] – a school essay comparing texts by Simmel and Bloch with reference to a related subject. Unseld told me that you had also made a contribution; I am very keen to see it. By the way, Bloch's 80th birthday is on 8 July – just one day before you arrive here. It is terrible that essays of yours such as 'Sie sporten' (especially topical at present), the one 'On Congresses', 'Falscher Untergang der Regenschirme' and others of this kind were not published in *Ornament der Masse*. No doubt you have enough such material to make an 'edition suhrkamp' volume out of it. Suggested title: *Caprichos* (like the series by Goya). Of course I haven't said anything to Unseld yet about the idea; I wanted to wait for your reaction.

Fritz Lang is here on a visit to us at present. I saw a new production of the *Threepenny Opera*; incredible how dusty and dated it has become. One might arrive at the reactionary conclusion that the works that last are not those written for the moment, as one might have thought at times forty years ago. I can't get beyond the homespun piece of wisdom which declares that the better something is cooked, and the more pungent spices one adds, the more people there will be who will want to eat it – even *post festum*. And in the *Threepenny Opera*, to stay with the metaphor, much of what they cook with is obviously water. I have serious doubts whether much of Brecht will actually survive anyway.

We were in Baden-Baden for the first half of April and had a really good relaxing time; now, however, I am already shuddering at the thought of the semester, and even more at the thought of all the inevitable annoyances.

Warmest greetings to you and Lili, from Gretel too,

Your old

Teddie

Original: typescript with printed letterhead and handwritten corrections; Siegfried Kracauer papers, Deutsches Literaturarchiv, Marbach am Neckar.

Patalas's review of Filmtheorie: Enno Patalas, 'Der Philosoph vor der Leinwand: Siegfried Kracauers "Theorie des Films"' [The philosopher in front of the screen: Siegfried Kracauer's *Theory of Film*], *Frankfurter Allgemeine Zeitung*, 10 April 1965.

a radio discussion: from the evidence which survives, this did not materialize.

disconnected ideas about film ... playboy: the assumption that this refers to remarks connected with *Filmtransparente* (published in part in *Die Zeit*, 18 November 1966; see Adorno, GS 10.1, pp. 353–61; 10.2, p. 840) is supported by the gloss there on the word 'playboy': 'While one's intention is always hostile to the playboy, *la dolce vita* and wild parties, the opportunity to observe them probably affords greater enjoyment than the over-hasty verdict levelled against them' (ibid., p. 356).

my contribution to the Bloch festschrift: *Ernst Bloch zu ehren: Beiträge zu seinem Werk* [In honour of Ernst Bloch: contributions on his work], ed. Siegfried Unseld, was published for Bloch's 80th birthday and included contributions by twenty authors: Adorno's was 'Henkel, Krug und frühe Erfahrung' (see Adorno, GS 11, pp. 556–66), and Kracauer's 'Zwei Deutungen in zwei Sprachen' [Two interpretations in two languages] (see Kracauer, W 5, no. 775). Adorno had instigated Kracauer's involvement in a letter to Siegfried Unseld of 16 October 1964 (see Adorno/Suhrkamp/Unseld, *Briefwechsel*, p. 507); he was invited to collaborate in a letter by Karl Markus Michel on 19 October 1964 (Archiv der Peter Suhrkamp Stiftung an der Johann Wolfgang Goethe-Universität).

essays of yours: 'Sie sporten' [They play sports], *Frankfurter Zeitung*, 13 January 1927 (see Kracauer, W 5, no. 330); 'Der Kongreß' [The congress], *Frankfurter Zeitung*, 29 July 1925 (see Kracauer, W 5, no. 249); 'Falscher Untergang der Regenschirme' [False decline of umbrellas] (see letter no. 52).

Caprichos: Francisco José Goya's (1746–1828) series of 80 etchings was published in 1799.

Lang: Fritz Lang (1890–1976), Viennese director, film producer and scriptwriter; he went into exile in France in 1933 and the USA in 1934, and belonged to the circle of Adorno's close friends in California.

new production of the Threepenny Opera: Harry Buckwitz produced this at the Schauspiel Frankfurt; the première was on 9 April 1965.

258 Kracauer to Adorno
New York, 8.5.1965

498 Westend Avenue
New York 24, N.Y.
May 8, 1965

Dear Teddie,

Many thanks for your letter. The outbreaks of flu were especially savage this year, and a certain fatigue is still hanging on. (The fight against the viruses forces the latter to desperate counter-measures and to manoeuvres intended to distract, so that all kinds of other organs are affected.)

As soon as we are in Frankfurt we shall be able to work something out. I too have various commitments there, especially during the first few days – over the weekend. Provided that everything goes according to plan, we shall be installed in the Frankfurter Hof on Friday 9 July, around 4 or 5 in the afternoon. Perhaps we can talk on the telephone then. I repeat, this time we should like to have both of you with us at the hotel one evening. Let us leave this to improvisation, for which, *hélas*, there is so little room nowadays. I was born under a pretty lucky star in this respect.

We shall soon be given an opportunity to read our contributions to the Bloch festschrift; the publisher wrote to tell me that the book is to come out at the end of this month. I have heard here that there is also a sermon on hope by Tillich in it. From what source am I supposed to know

Patalas's critique? I don't read German newspapers. I did arrange, though, to have the article sent to me. Kotulla would certainly have been a more suitable partner for the radio discussion, only I don't know his address. (I even mentioned one of his essays in my film book.) Does it absolutely have to be someone from this field? The book is essentially a philosophy concerned with material things. If my name came up when you two were talking to Fritz Lang, you are sure to have noticed that he is very angry with me because of certain things which I said about him in the *Caligari* book. At the same time, though, I did say plenty of good things about him as well. He was a great talent (only not great enough for all the lovely kitsch in his films). I would never have thought that I should have to defend Brecht against you. A year ago I read his *Galilei* and was strongly impressed. There seem to be no rules about the ability of works to endure. Even a rapid success can become a long-term one. A lot of mistakes occur here because matters are decided not only by authenticity but also by the manner of incalculable misunderstandings.

I am thoroughly overburdened just now. Warmest greetings and much love from both of us to both of you,

Yours,
Friedel

Original: typescript; Theodor W. Adorno Archiv, Frankfurt am Main.

the book is to come out at the end of this month: according to Helene Ritzerfeld in a letter of 12 April 1965; the actual date on which it was delivered was his birthday on 8 July 1965 (Archiv der Peter Suhrkamp Stiftung an der Johann Wolfgang Goethe-Universität).

A sermon on hope by Tillich: Paul Tillich, 'Das Recht auf Hoffnung' [The right to hope], in *Bloch zu ehren*, pp. 265–76 (see letter no. 257). The sermon in question is one which Tillich had preached in English in San Francisco (see ibid., p. 265).

mentioned … in my film book: which happened with this addition to the bibliography: Theodor Kotulla, 'Die Antwort des Mönchs: Bemerkungen zu Federico Fellini' [Theodor Kotulla, 'The Monk's Reply: remarks on Federico Fellini'], in *F-Film 58* no. 2, 1958, pp. 139–59) (see Kracauer, W 3, p. 484).

Fritz Lang … he is very angry with me: the reason for his taking umbrage might lie in Kracauer's comment on *Die Nibelungen*: 'In short, Lang declared that this film was a national document ideal for the purpose of advertising German culture throughout the world. This entire declaration of his reads like an anticipation of Goebbels's propaganda' (see Kracauer, S 2, p. 100).

259 Kracauer to Adorno
New York, 11.5.1965

498 Westend Avenue
New York 24, N.Y.
May 11, 1965

Dear Teddie,

To add just a brief word regarding the Patalas review, which reached me yesterday. I am surprised that you were impressed by it. Patalas doesn't even seem to have read my book properly. Otherwise he could not allege that I think that film affirms external reality by seeking to represent and unmask it. Even the passage from the preface to the book which he himself quotes, where I talk about the 'quivering world above in the dirty puddle', should have taught him to know better. And if I quote Marcel's words about 'the earth, our dwelling-place', I certainly do not mean to suggest that therefore the earth is a hospitable habitat. On the contrary. In many places, and especially in the section 'Confrontations' in the final chapter, I expressly emphasize the fact that it is an important function of film to unmask evil ideologies through the penetrating and, as far as possible, undistorted portrayal of reality. Patalas is simply following today's anti-realistic fashion – a danger of which Kotulla had already warned us in his critique of broadcasting. That Patalas fashionably praises 'art' – art used like this is a thoroughly reactionary motif – is a consequence of the fact that he is objecting to me with Resnais' aphorism which claims that it is better to watch a film with one's eyes closed rather than with one's ears covered. But this maxim shows only that Resnais simply has no idea about anything (just as little as Cocteau). His Marienbad film was in fact exactly what a literary *blague* should not be – a monstrous example of boredom. Although Patalas is always writing about film, he appears to understand nothing about film, either. If it were otherwise, he would at least have had to appreciate my analysis of the relationships between image and sound as a discovery. But this only in parentheses. I am writing to you about this so that you will be able to counter him with a correct version of my concept of filmic reality, the way it really is, should you happen to have a discussion with him – but perhaps he may decline. In that case, I would have a try with Kotulla. I shall send you a Xerox of his critique of broadcasting – perhaps as early as the day after tomorrow. He spoke on Hessischer Rundfunk as part of Dr Frisé's series on 10 January. You will certainly be able to find out his address there.

In haste – warmest greetings,
Yours,
Friedel

Original: typescript; Theodor W. Adorno Archiv, Frankfurt am Main.

'quivering world above in the dirty puddle': word-for-word self-quotation (see *Theorie des Films*, Kracauer, W 3, p. 21).

Marcel's words: Gabriel Marcel (1889–1973), philosopher and dramatist; Kracauer refers to 'this earth which is our dwelling-place' in the preface as well as in the section 'Moments of everyday life' (the supporting reference also occurs there; see ibid., pp. 20, 467).

'Confrontations': see ibid., pp. 469–72.

Marienbad film: *L'Année dernière à Marienbad*, 1961.

260 Kracauer to Adorno

New York, 23.6.1965

498 Westend Avenue
New York 10024, N.Y.
June 23, 1965

Dear Teddie,

The time of our departure – on 2 July for Berlin – is coming perceptibly closer, and before it there is still an insane amount to do. I would like to write to you about our meeting up in Frankfurt, something which, of course, we are definitely counting on, in spite of your being so overburdened at this time. (You did write that something could surely be worked out.) The best days for me would be *Tuesday 13 and Wednesday 14 July*. On the 15th Dr Unseld will be putting himself at my disposal (which, however, doesn't exclude various possibilities for us). And, finally, there would also be a chance before the 13th – how about Saturday the 10th? But I can make precise arrangements only in *Frankfurt itself*. We shall, if all goes well, be at the Frankfurter Hof on Friday the 9th, from 5 at the latest. Could you give me a ring there? Or shall we telephone each other early on Saturday – around breakfast time, I mean? Or do you want to leave a message for me at the hotel? I repeat that the two of you must be our guests this time – and I mean it.

Am I mistaken in assuming that you will be attending the reception in Tübingen on 8 July? I bitterly regret having to decline. I am detained up to the very last minute in Berlin (address: Savoy Hotel) by meetings which are connected with my job and can no longer be rearranged.

In the meantime, warmest greetings and much love to you and dear Gretel from us both,

Yours,
Friedel

Original: typescript with handwritten corrections; Theodor W. Adorno Archiv, Frankfurt am Main.

reception in Tübingen: Suhrkamp Verlag had issued an invitation for 8 July 1965 in celebration of Ernst Bloch's 80th birthday (to an academic celebration in the Uhland-Saal of the university; see 'Honneurs für Ernst Bloch', *Schwäbisches Tagblatt*, 9 July 1965). In a letter of 10 June 1965, Kracauer informed Siegfried Unseld that he was unable to accept the invitation because of commitments in Berlin, 'partly concerning the affairs of the Foundation' (Archiv der Peter Suhrkamp Stiftung an der Johann Wolfgang Goethe-Universität).

261 Lili and Siegfried Kracauer to Adorno
[no address given; before 21.12.1965]

CHRISTMAS GREETINGS

Dear Teddie,

Just these few lines for now to let you know that we continue to exist. I came home from Paris with a severe attack of bronchitis, then Lili followed with flu, and we have been back to normal only for a couple of weeks now. I must add that I found your *Krug* article in the Bloch festschrift excellent. Wishing you and Gretel a good start to the New Year and all the best in it,

Warmest greetings and wishes to you both,

Yours,
Lili and Friedel

Original: MS, Christmas card: Christmas Greetings, Three Angels, Detail from an engraving, Virgin surrounded by Musical Angels (after Martin de Vos) by Jan Sadeler I, Flemish, 1550–about 1600, Metropolitan Museum of Art; Theodor W. Adorno Archiv, Frankfurt am Main; dated by the context.

from Paris: the last stop on the 1965 trip to Europe, from which Kracauer returned to New York at the beginning of October.

262 Adorno to Kracauer
Frankfurt am Main, 21.12.1965

PROF. DR. THEODOR W. ADORNO

FRANKFURT AM MAIN 21 December 1965
KETTENHOFWEG 123

Dear Friedel,

Your kind wishes, which we reciprocate most warmly, crossed with something which I have sent you: my lexicon article about the concept of society. It is a short piece of work whose scope was precisely prescribed for me beforehand and which I could have polished off standing on just one leg. That was the very thing that stimulated me, and perhaps it has certain features of a 'declaration of intention' which I do not find unwelcome.

I was delighted that you liked my capriole about Bloch. For me the most important thing about it is the concluding point, in which something is mentioned which seems to me really relevant to Bloch – i.e. that the actual quality which people like us have responded to in him does not feature 'with so many words' in his texts and yet has developed from these. By the way, in my piece there is a typo which completely distorts what I meant, and which you might perhaps correct: on p. 15 of the book (line 3), *nicht* should be added after *Objekt*.

We too have had all kinds of health worries; Gretel had a stomach ulcer which, however, has completely healed after thorough treatment, and a polyp in the throat (fortunately equally harmless) which had to be surgically removed. This all went well – only, under the effects of the anaesthetic, gastritis has set in again, which is giving her all kinds of problems at present but which also seems to be in retreat now. We urgently need the few days of rest over the Christmas holidays – I do too, in my thoroughly overworked state. My book, though, is progressing so well that, if nothing unforeseen happens, it will be finished by the date we envisaged, at the beginning of May. I am applying for a leave of absence from teaching for the coming summer and winter semesters; the faculty has already agreed, and I am very glad to be rid of the most pressing obligations – the commitments to give regular lectures and seminars – for a while.

I hope that, in the meantime, you two have both fully recovered and are out and about again.

How are your travel plans for next year looking? And how are you getting on with your book?

Recently I gave a guest lecture in Giessen and saw a lot of Jauss and Heselhaus; your ears must have been burning. And in Royaumont I heard from Taubes that you had shown him an old picture in which I could be seen with my good old Wölfchen. I was glad to know that you had kept it.

All good wishes to you both for the holidays, and much love from Gretel and

Your old Teddie

Original: typescript; Siegfried Kracauer papers, Deutsches Literaturarchiv, Marbach am Neckar.

concept of society: published in the *Evangelisches Staatslexikon*, ed. Hermann Kunst et al., Stuttgart: Kreuz, 1966 (see 'Gesellschaft', Adorno, GS 8, pp. 9–19, 9.2, p. 404).

concluding point: 'It [the text] contains far more than it contains, and not merely in the vague sense of associations potentially ensuing from it. It unambiguously communicates what it refuses to communicate in plain language. That is Bloch in a nutshell' (see Adorno, GS 11, p. 566).

on p. 15 of the book (line 3): the faulty sentence in the festschrift reads 'Through immersion into the incommensurable nature of the object he guards himself against discovering what to the human mind would be hidden about the object itself and what he does [not] already know about the object in any case' (see Adorno, GS 11, p. 561).

guest lecture in Giessen: on 3 December 1965, Adorno delivered his lecture 'Society' at the Justus-Liebig-Universität.

Heselhaus: Clemens Heselhaus (1912–2000), literary expert and professor at Giessen from 1961 onwards.

In Royaumont I learnt from Taubes: Jacob Taubes (1923–1987), philosopher and historian of religion; he was joint editor, together with Hans Blumenberg, Jürgen Habermas and Dieter Henrich, of the series Theorie, published by Suhrkamp Verlag from the autumn of 1966 onwards. From 10 to 13 December 1965, Adorno was in Royaumont at the invitation of the French sociologist and philosopher Lucien Goldmann (1913–1979); he took part in a colloquium organized by Goldmann, 'Psychoanalyse et sociologie comme methode d'interpretation et d'explication de la creation culturelle'.

an old picture ... with my good old Wölfchen: such a photograph shows the adolescent 'Adorno with Wolf the sheepdog' (see Adorno, *Bildmonographie*, p. 40).

263 Kracauer to Adorno

New York, 12.5.1966

498 Westend Avenue
New York 10024, N.Y.
May 12, 1966

Dear Teddie,

May I assume that by now you have finished your Negative Dialectics? In any event, much of it is sure to have been completed, while I, *hélas*, am making only very slow progress. The road from conceiving the idea to writing it down by way of developing it properly seems to me as vast a distance as that to the nearest village. Actually, though, I did not want to write about that but just to let you both know that we will be arriving in Frankfurt on Sunday 3 July and are thinking of staying there for about a week (until the 10th). I know that this is a difficult time for you, but with the best will in the world I can't organize things any other way. I imagine that you will appreciate knowing the dates as early as this. Will it be possible to fit them into your programme? And when would be best? Please let me know about your schedule if possible – however approximately – so that I too can see to my own needs adequately. There is, of course, the publisher and possibly various additional things (among them, the Stadtarchiv on account of the new edition of my uncle's history of the Jews in Frankfurt). We are staying at the Frankfurter Hof again and look forward to seeing you both. Thanks also for your two articles, the one about society and the one about music and painting for the Kahnweiler festschrift. Let us discuss them face to face. In extenuation I can only say that I have been under pressure for months and still have an awful lot to get out of the way by the end of June, a not too distant future. It would be nice if the two of you could keep an evening free to have dinner with us at the Frankfurter Hof.

I am adding an extra word to dear Gretel (with a request).

Warmest greetings from Lili and me,
Yours,
Friedel

May 12, 1966

Dear Gretel,

First of all, we very much hope that things have been going really well for you in terms of your health over the winter months. The reason for my adding these lines to the letter to Teddie (naturally meant for you too) has to do with an enquiry and a request. I really don't feel comfortable about bothering you with this; please don't hold it against me. But, as it involves some old business relating to the Institute, Lili and I thought that you might be the best-informed person, or would at any rate know where the best place to get information would be. In a word, could you find out by some means or other whether employees of the Institute for Social Research (including Lili) were covered by social insurance in the years 1924–1930? Someone here recently asked Lili in the context of possible claims for compensation. If there is any possibility at all of obtaining this information, we would be infinitely grateful if you could let us know. And all our good wishes, and warmest greetings from us both,
Yours,

Original: typescript; Theodor W. Adorno Archiv, Frankfurt am Main; the enclosure from a typescript (carbon copy); Siegfried Kracauer papers, Deutsches Literaturarchiv, Marbach am Neckar. The letter bears a handwritten note by Adorno: 'TWA is in Vienna and will reply immediately upon his return', which Elfriede Olbrich wrote to Kracauer on 17 May 1966. The letter to Gretel Adorno: typescript (carbon copy); Kracauer papers, Deutsches Literaturarchiv, Marbach am Neckar.

to the nearest village: see Franz Kafka, 'Das nächste Dorf', in *Prosa zu Lebzeiten*, Frankfurt am Main: S. Fischer, 1994, p. 280.

arriving in Frankfurt: this was preceded by a meeting with Siegfried Unseld on 29 April 1966 in New York (Unseld travelled between 20 April and 4 May 1966 to New York and Princeton, where Gruppe 47 was meeting), for which Kracauer prepared with a handwritten sketch:

Unseld, Apr. 29, 1966

1. How was it here? Yersterday [*sic*] evening, etc. / 2. Tour d'horizon: Michel,

Boehlich, etc. / $ / saw Dahrendorf, Preise[n]danz / Teddie – letters. /

Bloch / Blumenberg, Jauß. / 3. *Lindau … Monaco.* / (paper)

4. Business / *Summerplan* / My letters unanswered / *Fra: July 3 thru 10:*

What about my books? / Want: Benjamin – *Kursbuch /previews* of my book. / 5. *Detektivroman* / 6. *Novel* / 7. *Sociology als Wissenschaft*

8. *Offenbach*: Buchgemeinschaften / Schweiz, Darmstadt / 9. *Caligari*: /show Pamphlet. Nazi film get from Rowohlt / new Princeton paperback

10. *Th. of Film*: show paperback at top of selling. / 11. *Hist book*: Begin translation (ask Jauß).

new edition of … history of the Jews in Frankfurt: Isidor Kracauer, *Geschichte der Juden in Frankfurt a. M. (1150–1824)*, 2 vols, Frankfurt am Main: Kauffmann, 1925–7. An undated draft of a contract between Kracauer and the publisher Dr Max Gehlen, Bad Homburg, exists (Kracauer papers, Deutsches Literaturarchiv, Marbach); the new edition did not materialize.

about music and painting: 'Über einige Relationen zwischen Musik und Malerei'; the work bears the dedication 'For Daniel-Henry Kahnweiler on his 80th birthday in respectful friendship'; see Adorno, GS 16, pp. 628–42. Kahnweiler (1884–1979), who paved the way for Cubism with his Paris gallery, was honoured with the festschrift *Pour Daniel-Henry Kahnweiler*, which was published in 1965 by Le Temps, Paris, and Gerd Hatje, Stuttgart.

extra word … (with a request): Kracauer repeated his request in a letter to Gretel Adorno of 28 May 1966; her replies to the effect that no documents had survived in the Institute are dated 1 and 15 June 1966 (Kracauer papers, Deutsches Literaturarchiv, Marbach).

264 Adorno to Kracauer
Frankfurt am Main, 23.5.1966

PROF. DR. THEODOR W. ADORNO

FRANKFURT AM MAIN 23 May 1966
KETTENHOFWEG 123

Dear Friedel,

Returning from an uncommonly rich and stimulating but also immensely taxing week in Vienna, I should like to thank you straight away for your letter. Our plans will cause no problems whatsoever, as I have taken a leave of absence for two semesters from my lecturing and seminar activities (all the administrative stuff, of course, is still going on), and thus am rather more flexible than before; however, we are going on holiday earlier, i.e. on 15 July. But we are certain to be here in the week from the 3rd to the 10th, and it all looks very favourable; there is no schedule this time, unless they foist more exams onto me (which would still leave me free in the evenings), and it is possible that I may have to do a bit of tinkering with the last parts of the manuscript of my book.

No, it still isn't completely finished, although five big sections of it – over 300 pages – have gone to press. One more section is still in need of one continuous workthrough, which may well be referred to as a 'fine cut', and there are still all kinds of serious work to be done on the middle section, about which I am not yet entirely certain whether it will be divided into two chapters, as now, or compressed into a single long one. But I can safely say that the worst is behind me, although in such matters (and actually, only in these) I am too superstitious to rejoice before the last page has been despatched. Something encouraging has come up about the piece on which I have been working for about seven years. In spite of the truly anarchic and sometimes chaotic method of production, you see, quite a simple structure – in three parts – has crystallized out of this all by itself, almost without my having to do anything at all. The first part is a critique of ontology and the derivation of the concept of dialectics as I conceive of it; the second develops the idea of a negative dialectic and some of its categories, and the third provides three models of an applied negative dialectics: one about freedom ('On the metacritique of practical reason'), one about the philosophy of history ('World spirit and natural history' – which, of course, is centred on a highly specific aspect which is of crucial importance for me), and, in conclusion, 'Meditations on Metaphysics'. I presented some extracts from the last during a lecture in Vienna to very considerable effect. Keep your fingers crossed, as I am doing for you, without letting these reciprocal activities prevent us from finishing off our own things.

Meanwhile, the second edition of the third volume of the *Noten* has been published. In the essay about you one sentence had ended up in a place which made no sense; now it is back where it belongs, and because of this I have sent you yet another copy of the book, which must have arrived in its final form (insofar as such a thing is possible for me). Perhaps, though, you will also read the other texts in it which (as far as I am aware) you don't yet know. All these things are gradually starting to converge, and I am hoping (just a little) that they will lend support to one other.

We are quite well. Gretel and I survived our trip to Czechoslovakia as well as I did mine to Vienna.

We look forward very much to seeing you both.

Much love, from Gretel too,

Your old
Teddie

Original: typescript; Siegfried Kracauer papers, Deutsches Literaturarchiv, Marbach am Neckar.

week in Vienna: on 17 May 1966, Adorno gave a reading from his *Negative Dialektik* in the Zentralsparkasse building; on 18 May he gave the lecture 'Funktionalismus heute' [Functionalism today] at the Österreichische Gesellschaft für Literatur (see Adorno, GS 10.1, pp. 375–95).

second edition of the third volume of the Noten: a copy with a handwritten dedication survives among Kracauer's papers: 'To my dear Friedel / xxx always from his Teddie / Frankfurt, May 1966' (Deutsches Literaturarchiv, Marbach).

In the essay about you: the misplaced sentence: 'Für das Unselige hat einmal ein Angepaßter triumphierend den Satz gebraucht, es gäbe keinen geistigen Transfer' [For things accursed there is no mental/intellectual transfer, as a well-adjusted person once triumphantly put it] occurred in the first edition of the *Noten zur Literatur III* on p. 105 (see Adorno, GS 2, p. 406), between 'psychologischen Mechanismus gehorchten' und 'Ein Korrektiv wäre gewesen'.

our trip to Czechoslovakia: in the last week of April 1966, Adorno accepted various invitations to give lectures in Czechoslovakia, including one on 'Sociology and Empirical Research' at Charles University in Prague and another on 'The Formal Principles of Contemporary Music' in Brno (Theodor W. Adorno Archiv).

265 Adorno to Kracauer

Frankfurt am Main, 28.9.1966

Prof. Dr. Theodor W. Adorno

Frankfurt am Main 28 September 1966
Kettenhofweg 123

Dear Friedel,

Today I am sending you two little books of mine, posted as printed matter.

The first is the Kierkegaard, augmented by a second supplement (my lecture of 1963 on the occasion of his 150th birthday). You will surely be glad that the book dedicated to you has now already gone into a third edition – and if I have anything to do with it, the last one. The two appendices – one dating from around 1940, the second from three years ago – should convey a fair idea of what has happened to my own thinking in all those years – expressed in concrete form on the same subject.

The other book is the *Metakritik der Erkenntnistheorie*, which I cannot imagine that I didn't send you as soon as it came out; some idiotic mistake must have occurred. The book is, in Doderer's words, to be understood as a 'ramp' leading up to *Negative Dialektik*, and I should be especially glad if you would read it carefully; as I see it, it is one of the most seriously overburdened things that I have ever written, loaded with meaning. Individual points, such as, above all, the treatment of categorical apperception, are too one-sidedly critical and not dialectical enough; I compensate for this in *Negative Dialektik*. For a full understanding of the latter, though, the *Metakritik* has to be almost completely indispensable.

Negative Dialektik has been made up and is in the last stage of production – the revision of the page proofs. If all goes well, it should be ready in four to six weeks. It goes without saying that you will then receive a copy at once.

Our holidays were not exactly a great success. First of all – obviously as a result of lowered resistance through complete overwork – I developed a case of furunculosis which up in Sils exploded in a frightful abscess on my elbow, requiring an operation. Scarcely had I recovered to some extent than Gretel suffered a painful recurrence of her gastritis, which confined her to bed for a fortnight and set her back badly. Fortunately, it is nothing serious, and by now she has quite recovered from her cure.

I myself am still not in top condition by any means. In a few days I shall be going to Italy for three and a half weeks – officially to give a few lectures, but really to renew myself once more in the South. Here, in any case, is my Rome address from 14–24 October: Hotel Quirinale, Via Nazionale 7. Gretel would prefer not to expose herself to the stress of the journey just yet and can follow her diet properly only here, and so I am embarking on this adventure (which once again will take me to Palermo) on my own.

Meanwhile you will probably have read that Axel Kluge had an extraordinary success with his film at the Biennale in Venice. His uncommonly talented sister, a physician by profession, played the lead and became famous overnight. The subject of the film is the story of a girl whom Eva Oertel – whom you will remember from the evening with Axel – took under her wing when she was working in a prison as a probation officer or whatever they call it. Incidentally, I have since seen a quite extraordinary avant-garde film by Mauricio Kagel, *Antithèse*, which was shown during the Kranichstein holiday courses for new music, where I was giving a lecture. It really is a crying shame that you didn't see it.

I hope that you had more luck with your rest cure than we did, and that you are both back in New York in good order.

Much love to you both, from Gretel too,

Your old

Teddie

Original: typescript; Siegfried Kracauer papers, Deutsches Literaturarchiv, Marbach am Neckar.

Kierkegaard ... a third edition: this refers to the third edition; the copy bears the handwritten dedication: 'To my dear Friedel, after so many years, from his old Teddie. / Frankfurt, September 1966' (Kracauer papers, Deutsches Literaturarchiv, Marbach).

Metakritik der Erkenntnistheorie: *Zur Metakritik der Erkenntnistheorie* was published in 1956 by Kohlhammer in Stuttgart; see letter no. 162. The copy preserved among Kracauer's papers bears the handwritten dedication: 'I wonder, dear Friedel / if this book goes deep enough / into its subject –? / Warmest regards, Yours, Teddie / Frankfurt, September 1966' (Deutsches Literaturarchiv, Marbach).

in Doderer's words, to be understood as a 'ramp': the novelist Heimito von Doderer (1896–1966) interconnected two of his novels which had their genesis at the same time, *Die Strudelhofstiege* and *Die Dämonen*, by means of their characters and other devices, which caused the publisher Biederstein Verlag in Munich, on the publication of *Die Strudelhofstiege*, to advertise the novel as a 'ramp' leading to *Die Dämonen* (1956) (see Dietrich Weber, *Heimito von Doderer: Studien zu seinem Romanwerk*, Munich: C. H. Beck'sche Verlagsbuchhandlung, 1963, pp. 77 and 276. No information is available as to whether the publisher was referring to a quotation from Doderer).

categorical apperception: the title of a column in *Zur Metakritik der Erkenntnistheorie* (see Adorno, GS 5, p. 203).

to Italy … to give a few lectures: among these were 'Gesellschaft' in Milan (5 October) and Rome (14 October); 'Problem der Vermittlung' (see the twelfth lecture of *Einleitung in die Musiksoziologie*, Adorno, GS 14, pp. 394–421) in Naples (7 October), Palermo (10 October) and Rome (17 October); and also 'Grundzüge einer Soziologie des musikalischen Hörens' (see the first lecture, Adorno, GS 14, pp. 178–98) in Palermo on 11 October 1966 (Theodor W. Adorno Archiv).

Axel Kluge … an extraordinary success: Alexander Kluge was awarded the Silver Lion for his feature film *Abschied von gestern* [Farewell to yesterday] after its première at the Venice Film Festival on 5 September 1966.

uncommonly talented sister: Alexandra Kluge (1937–2017), physician and actress; in *Abschied von gestern* she played the female lead with extraordinary success.

Oertel: Eva Oertel (b. 1937), actress.

back in New York in good order: The Kracauers were in Europe from July to the beginning of October; according to Kracauer's calendar, it was in Frankfurt am Main where they met with Adorno and Siegfried Unseld on 3 July 1966 (Deutsches Literaturarchiv, Marbach).

266 Adorno to Kracauer
Naples, 7.10.1966

7 October 1966

Dear Friedel,

Back here for the first time since 1929, I am greatly moved when I remember how we were here in 1925 and stayed at the Vesuvio. Since then many things have changed enormously; the triumph of cleanliness and order is unstoppable. But even more it is borne in upon me how life is literally rushing by – it feels as if those days here in Capri and Positano were yesterday, everything is so clearly before my eyes – I also still know my way around the city perfectly – and in the meantime one has grown old without knowing how this happened. However, may one not *really* be that person! Very best wishes, to Lili too,

Yours,
Teddie

Original: MS, postcard: Naples, panorama; Siegfried Kracauer papers, Deutsches Literaturarchiv, Marbach am Neckar.

how we were here in 1925: see letter no. 28.

267 Kracauer to Adorno
New York, 23.10.1966

498 Westend Avenue
New York 10024, N.Y.
October 23, 1966

Dear Teddie,

I am able to thank you only today for your letter from Frankfurt and your kind card from Naples – so full of memories – because I had barely returned when I caught a cold which left me pretty well crippled until a few days ago. The mishap that hit you both in Sils was really not pleasant. We hope most fervently that Italy has refreshed you in every respect; we are only sorry that Gretel couldn't be with you.

The two little books that you planned to send me at the end of September are probably still on their way – and so I am looking forward to the book on dialectics. Of course I shall read it all, but I must ask you to be very, very patient. I still have a good three chapters of my history book left to write – probably the most difficult ones. (The further one emerges from the tunnel, the more difficult the writing becomes – not least because of the overlaps which threaten to occur.) In addition, there is, in connection with this, a lot of obligatory reading to be done. (Nor should we forget my job.) And so, at present, I have little time left for many things that I should like to do. Hence my plea for patience.

Our own holidays went well; I think that we had a really relaxing time in Switzerland. We especially enjoyed the last three weeks in Rome to an extraordinary degree. We looked in depth both at well-known sights and at others as yet unknown, had interesting conversations, went for plenty of strolls and *lived* in the true sense; what was more, in the afternoons the hotel bar proved to be a stimulating place to work.

I happened to see a few reviews of Kluge's film, but I shall have to see it myself to form an opinion. If it comes to New York, I shall be sure not to miss it. It's the same with films as it is with summer holiday places: in both cases you can't get anywhere without inspecting them for yourself.

Please be content for now with this sign of life. Many good wishes to dear Gretel – and warmest greetings to you both from Lili and me.

Yours,
Friedel

Original: typescript; Theodor W. Adorno Archiv, Frankfurt am Main.

a really relaxing time in Switzerland: on 11 July 1966 the Kracauers travelled to Zurich, and from there on 21 July to Vevey. From 2 to 3 September they made another stop in Zurich; on 4 September they arrived in Lindau and on the 12th in Rome (again by way of Zurich). They returned to New York on 4 October 1966 (Kracauer's calendar; Kracauer papers, Deutsches Literaturarchiv, Marbach).

268 Adorno to Kracauer
Frankfurt am Main, 29.10.1966

29 October 1966

Dear Friedel,

Many thanks for your letter.

It goes without saying that I can completely understand that you have to postpone reading my things. By the way, I never intended that you should read the whole Kierkegaard, which of course you know well, yet again; you should just take a look at the two supplements, as they show how my attitudes towards this subject have changed over a period of almost forty years – and also how they have remained the same. I should just be grateful if you could send a word to confirm the arrival of what I have sent; one is never sure if such things actually get there.

I have come back from Italy safe and sound, without as yet being able to say whether the exertion outweighed the relaxation or vice versa. The journey was indescribably successful; it really might have gone to my head if I were not, to a certain degree, fortified against effects of this kind. Now I am once again immersed in work. Friedeburg has taken up his post as co-director of the Institute; I am very happy about this.

I hope that you have completely recovered from your cold and are making good progress with your things. Gretel and I are well. The *Negative Dialektik* should be coming out next week, as Unseld told me earlier.

All good wishes

as ever

yours

Original: typescript (carbon copy); Theodor W. Adorno Archiv, Frankfurt am Main.

Friedeburg: Ludwig von Friedeburg (1924–2010), sociologist; at the Institute for Social Research from 1955 onwards; at the Freie Universität Berlin (1962–6) after qualifying as a lecturer. In 1966 he returned to Frankfurt am Main, where he was minister of culture for Hesse (1970–74) and held various leading posts at the Institute until 2001.

completely recovered from your cold: the opposite was the case; Kracauer died on 26 November 1966.

should be coming out next week: *Negative Dialektik* was published one day before Kracauer's death. 'At the same time the thought that death is quite simply the last thing is unthinkable' (see *Negative Dialektik*, Adorno, GS 6, p. 364; *Negative Dialectics*, trans. E. B. Ashton, London: Routledge, 1973).

Illustrations

1 Opernplatz, Frankfurt am Main

'Profound as my reaction was when I made Benjamin's acquaintance ... at a rendezvous in the former Café Westend in the Opernplatz in Frankfurt, together with my friend Kracauer, who had arranged the meeting.'

Adorno, *Erinnerungen*, GS 20.1, p. 173.

2 Kracauer and Adorno: trip to the Dolomites, 1924

'After all, someone really ought to try to erect a monument here to the figure which we make together.'

Adorno to Kracauer, 28 October 1964.

3 *Adorno, before 1923*

4 *Kracauer, around 1918*

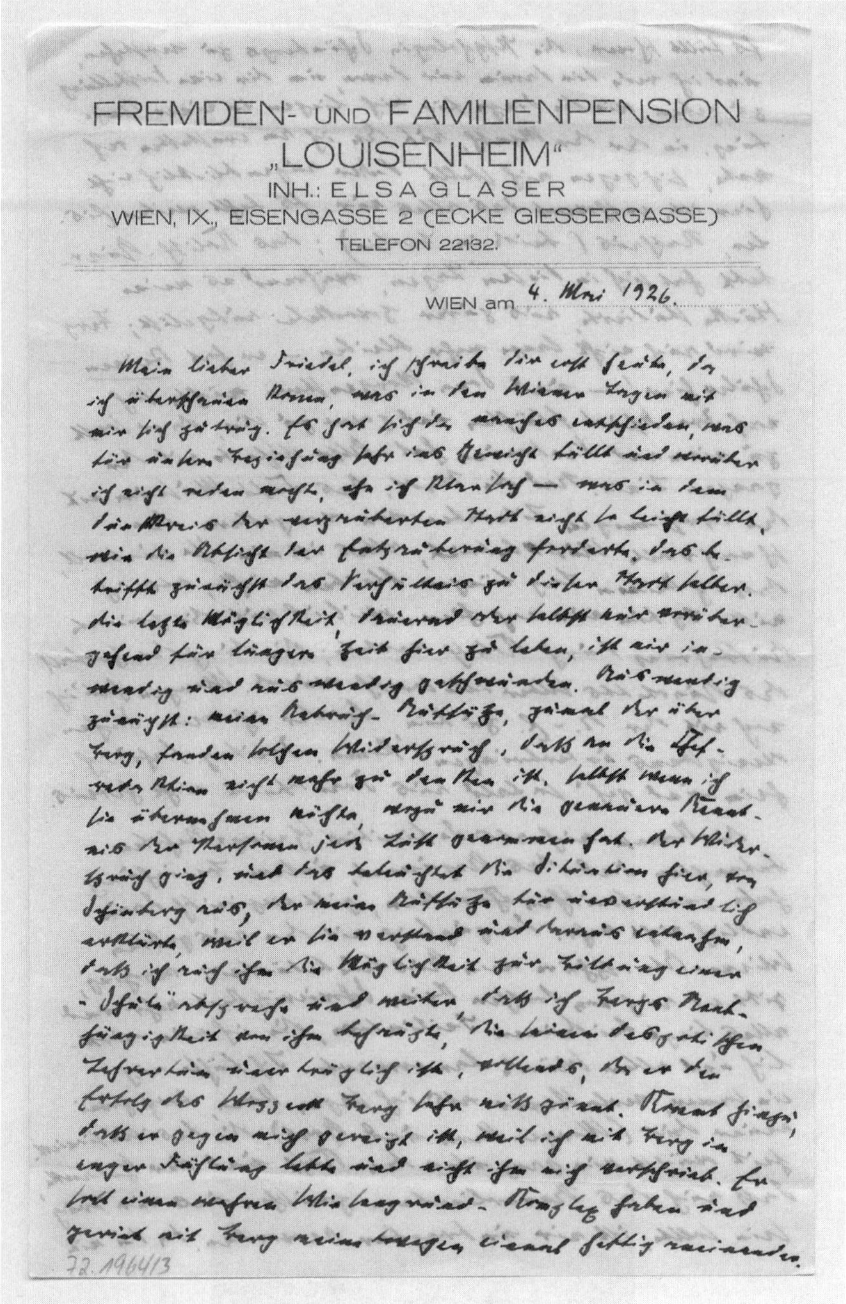
FREMDEN- UND FAMILIENPENSION
„LOUISENHEIM"
INH.: ELSA GLASER
WIEN, IX., EISENGASSE 2 (ECKE GIESSERGASSE)
TELEFON 22132.

WIEN am 4. Mai 1926.

5 *Adorno to Kracauer, 4 May 1926*

6 *Adorno, Vier Gedichte von Stefan George für Singstimme und Klaver, op. 1. Es lacht in dem steigenden jahr dir, 1925*

'So let us conceal what we miss, then, / And vow to be happy again, / Though no more be granted but this, then: / A round to be gone by us twain.'

Stefan George, *Poems*, trans. Carol North Valhope and Ernst Morwitz, London: Kegan Paul, 1944; see letter no. 1.

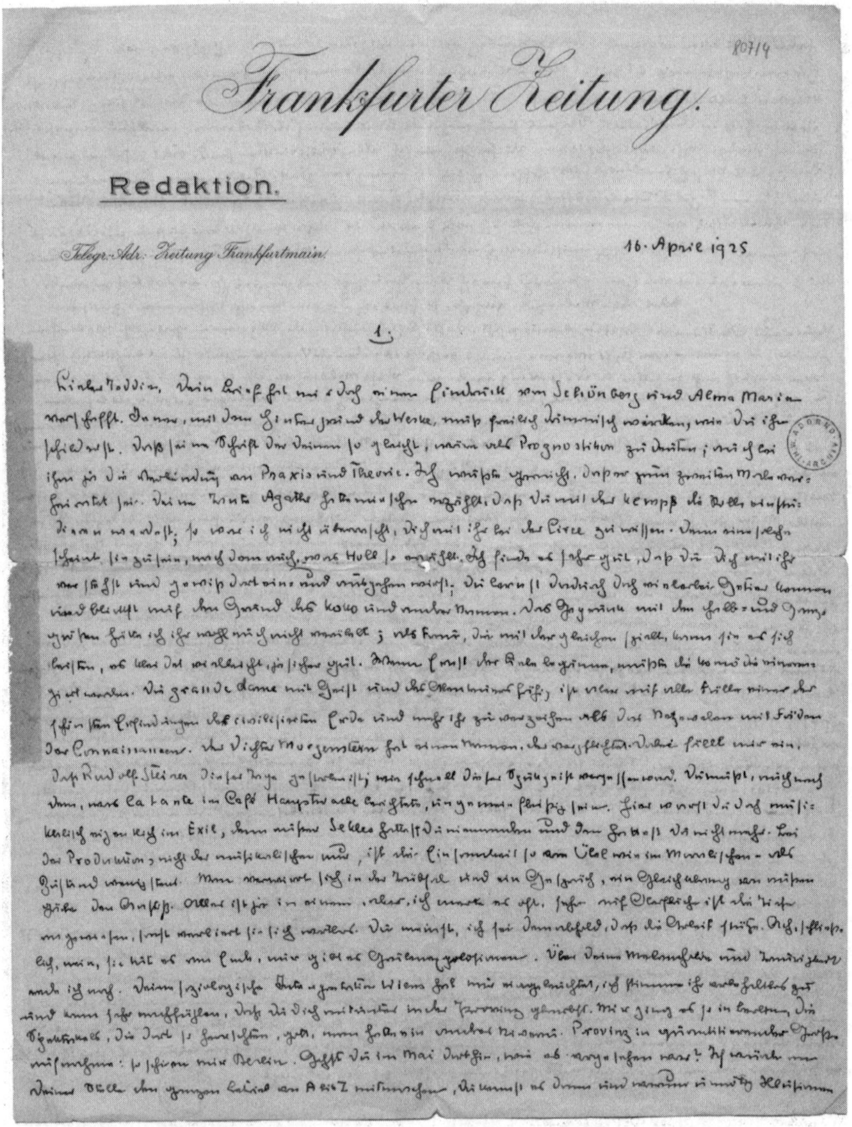
Frankfurter Zeitung.

Redaktion.

Telegr.-Adr. Zeitung Frankfurtmain

16. April 1925

1.

7 *Kracauer to Adorno, 16 April 1925*

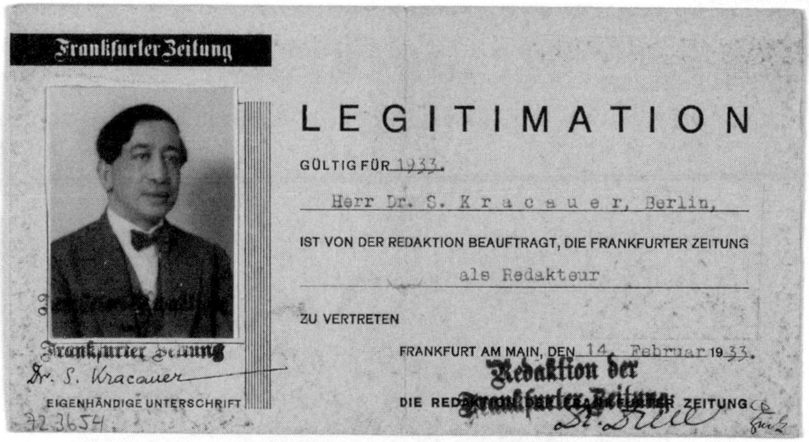

8 *Kracauer's 'legitimation' (press pass), Frankfurter Zeitung, 14 February 1933*

'In the middle the Reichstag stands starkly forlorn. From all four sides one has the same view of its cupola, which now soars somewhat bleakly into the air … Its glass surfaces are mostly burnt out … An endless procession of people winds around the isolated building … which holds all eyes in thrall with the magic power of a symbol under attack. Their gaze passes through this symbol down into the abyss opened up by its destruction.'

Kracauer, 'Rund um den Reichstag', *Frankfurter Zeitung*, 2 March 1933.

9 *Kracauer's reader's pass, Bibliothèque nationale, Paris*

10 Adorno to Kracauer, 6 February 1929, postcard: Berne, Kindlifresserbrunnen

'Here you have an image of Walter Benjamin just as you interpreted him.'

Adorno on the above postcard.

'This too is the very reason why Benjamin feels that he must have no respect for immediacy, tear down the façade and smash shapes into pieces. It is quite consistent with his outlook that he scarcely ever tackles images and phenomena in their heyday … For him, living entities are as confused as a dream; they become clearer as they decay.'

Kracauer, 'Zu den Schriften Walter Benjamins', *Frankfurter Zeitung*, 15 July 1928.

11 Walter Benjamin, Berliner Kindheit um neunzehnhundert [Berlin Childhood around 1900], 1950

12 Theodor W. Adorno, Minima Moralia, 1951

13 Ernst Bloch, Das Prinzip Hoffnung *[The Principle of Hope], 1959*

14 Siegfried Kracauer, Das Ornament der Masse *[The Mass Ornament], 1963*

'It is interesting that the younger critics constantly recall the affinity between you, me, Benjamin and Bloch. For them we constitute a group which is set off against the background of the times.'

Kracauer to Adorno, 1 April 1964.

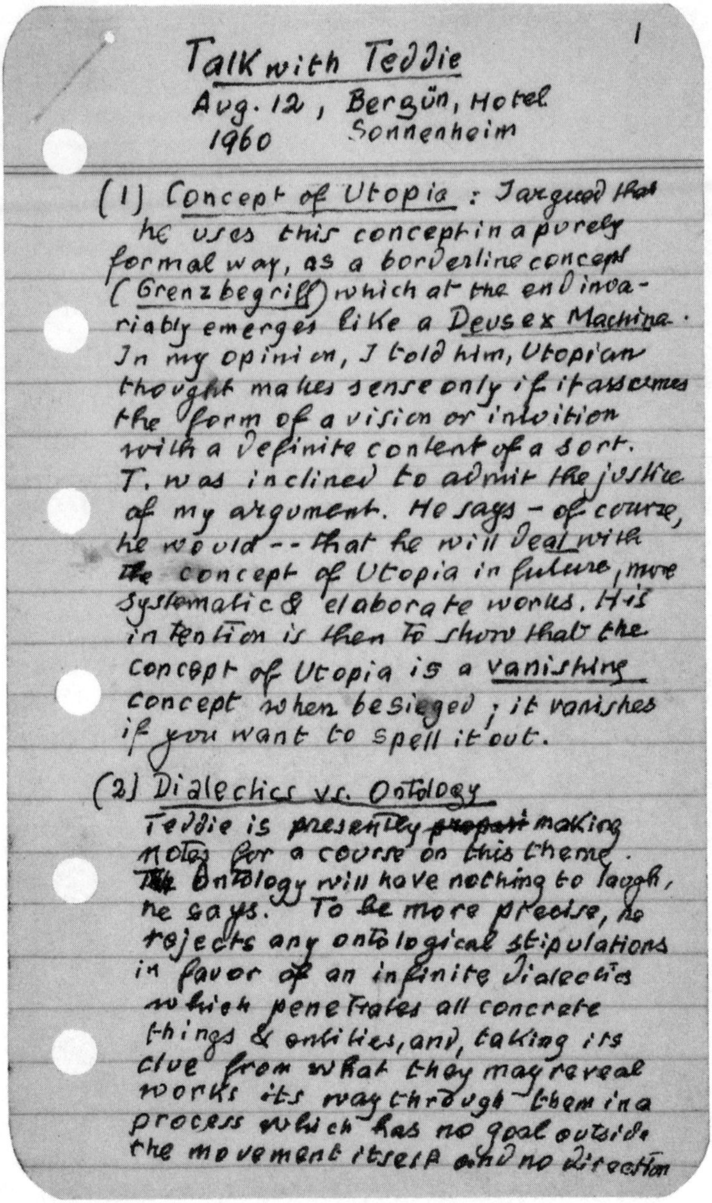

Talk with Teddie 1

Aug. 12, Bergün, Hotel
1960 Sonnenheim

(1) Concept of Utopia: I argued that he uses this concept in a purely formal way, as a borderline concept (Grenzbegriff) which at the end invariably emerges like a Deus ex Machina. In my opinion, I told him, Utopian thought makes sense only if it assumes the form of a vision or intuition with a definite content of a sort. T. was inclined to admit the justice of my argument. He says – of course, he would – that he will deal with the concept of Utopia in future, more systematic & elaborate works. His intention is then to show that the concept of Utopia is a vanishing concept when besieged; it vanishes if you want to spell it out.

(2) Dialectics vs. Ontology
Teddie is presently ~~propert~~ making notes for a course on this theme. ~~The~~ Ontology will have nothing to laugh, he says. To be more precise, he rejects any ontological stipulations in favor of an infinite dialectics which penetrates all concrete things & entities, and, taking its clue from what they may reveal works its way through them in a process which has no goal outside the movement itself and no direction

15 Kracauer, Talk with Teddie, handwritten draft, sheet 1, 12 August 1960

'We discussed this … at length in a conversation in Bergün that I shall never forget.'

Kracauer to Adorno, 11 December 1960.

16 Adorno to Kracauer, 7 October 1966, picture postcard: Naples, panorama

'In Naples we met with Benjamin shortly before our return, and engaged in a philosophical battle with him in which we were able to control the field, albeit not without finding it most necessary to regroup our forces.'

Adorno to Alban Berg, 15 October 1925.

'I am greatly moved when I remember how we were here in 1925 and stayed at the Vesuvio. Since then many things have changed enormously; the triumph of cleanliness and order is unstoppable. But even more it is borne upon me how life is literally rushing by – it feels as if the days here in Capri and Positano were yesterday, everything is so clearly before my eyes ... and in the meantime one has grown old without knowing how this happened. However, may one not *really* be that person!'

Adorno on the above postcard.

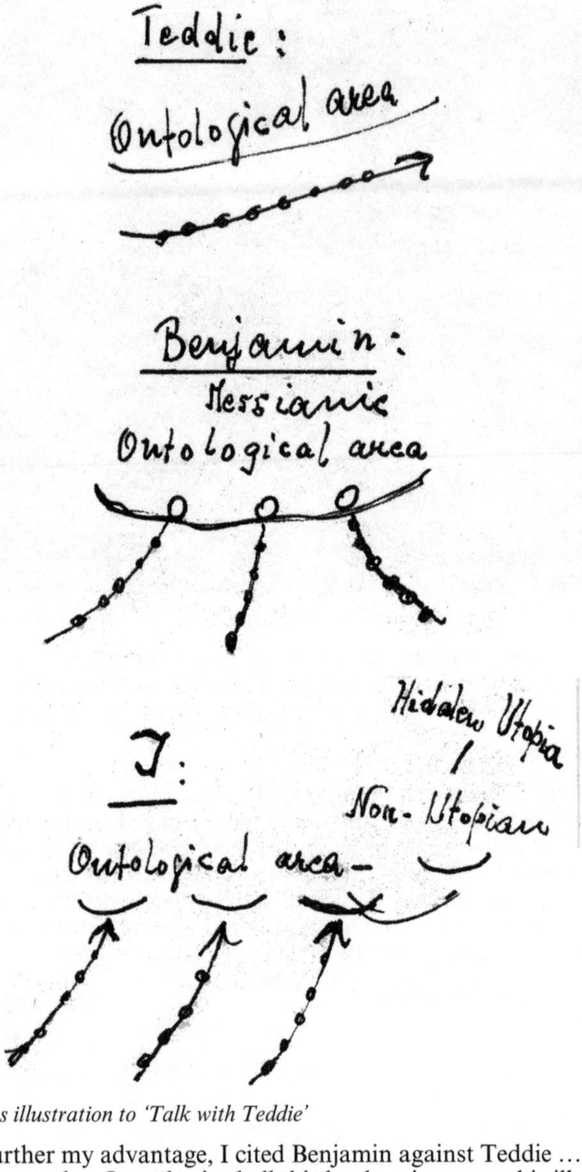

17 Kracauer's illustration to 'Talk with Teddie'

'Exploring further my advantage, I cited Benjamin against Teddie … Here I had Teddie trapped … I emphasized all this by drawing a graphic illustrating his, Benjamin's and my own way of thinking.'

Kracauer, Talk with Teddie, 12 August 1960.

Editorial Note

The documents which make up the correspondence between Theodor W. Adorno and Siegfried Kracauer are to be found in the Theodor W. Adorno Archiv, Frankfurt am Main, and the Kracauer papers in the Deutsches Literaturarchiv, Marbach am Neckar; one letter comes from the Leo Löwenthal papers in the Archivzentrum der Universitätsbibliothek Johann Christian Senckenberg, Frankfurt am Main.

Significant numbers of Kracauer's letters are lost; no information about the reason for this survives. If carbon copies or drafts of letters have survived, these have been included as equivalents; in one case we decided against this, as the draft bears the note 'not mailed' and was replaced by Kracauer with an almost identical letter, and in another case two drafts sketched out one day apart were combined.

The letters are reproduced, pursuant to the status of their extent at copy deadline, in their entirety, unabridged and, in the diplomatic sense, faithfully. In one case, protection of third parties' personal rights necessitated the omission of half a sentence, indicated by ellipses in square brackets; in addition, two personal names of third parties were encrypted. Ellipses in the text of a letter do not indicate an omission made by the editor but were made by the writer of the letter. Umlauts and the use of ss for *ß* have been standardized. Obvious typing errors have been unobtrusively corrected; on the other hand, orthographic peculiarities have been retained. Editorial additions in cases of lost pieces of text or missing endings are indicated by square brackets, and crossings-out missed by the author after correction of the text by parentheses; otherwise, conjectural readings are given in the notes. The transcription of Adorno's handwriting was carried out by Christoph Gödde and Henri Lonitz; that of Kracauer's handwriting was provided in the first version by Elisabeth Matthias, after which Ingrid Belke took over the final editing and Sabine Biebl resolved individual questions. Alois Schmidmeier contributed to the deciphering of a stenographic draft and a similar note by Kracauer. Readings which are open to question are indicated. This collaboration notwithstanding, responsibility for the compilation of the text rests with the editor.

As a new edition of Kracauer's feuilletons has been published as part of the edition of the complete works of Siegfried Kracauer, the relevant articles are indicated by the date on which they appeared in the *Frankfurter Zeitung*, together with their numbers in Kracauer, *Werke* 5.

The notes serve to enhance the readability of the letters and in certain instances to facilitate a reconstruction of their context; they are intended less to represent a critical commentary than to initiate a dialogue with research-based literature. In the case of quotations in the notes, omissions are indicated by ellipses.

The following editions are indicated with abbreviations in quotations:

Gretel Adorno and Walter Benjamin, *Correspondence, 1930–1940*, ed. Henri Lonitz and Christoph Gödde, trans. Wieland Hoban, Cambridge: Polity, 2008 [Gretel Adorno/Benjamin, *Correspondence*].

Theodor W. Adorno, *Gesammelte Schriften*, ed. Rolf Tiedemann with Gretel Adorno, Susan Buck-Morss and Klaus Schultz, 20 vols, Frankfurt am Main, 1970–1986 [Adorno GS, 1–20].

Theodor W. Adorno, *Kindheit in Amorbach: Bilder und Erinnerungen*, ed., with biographical research, by Reinhard Pabst. Frankfurt am Main, 2003 [Adorno/Pabst, *Amorbach*].

Theodor W. Adorno, *Kompositionen*, Vols. 1–2, ed. Heinz-Klaus Metzger and Rainer Riehn. Munich, 1980 [Adorno, *Kompositionen* 1, 2].

Theodor W. Adorno, *Kompositionen*, Vol. 3: *Kompositionen aus dem Nachlaß*, ed. Maria Luisa López-Vito and Ulrich Krämer, Munich, 2007 [Adorno, *Kompositionen* 3].

Theodor W. Adorno, *Letters to his Parents, 1939–1951*, ed. Christoph Gödde and Henri Lonitz, trans. Wieland Hoban, Cambridge: Polity, 2006 [Adorno, *Letters to his Parents*].

Adorno: Eine Bildmonographie, ed. Theodor W. Adorno Archiv, Frankfurt am Main, 2003 [Adorno, *Bildmonographie*].

Adorno in Frankfurt, ed. Wolfram Schütte, Frankfurt am Main, 2003 [Schütte, *Adorno in Frankfurt*].

Theodor W. Adorno and Walter Benjamin, *Briefwechsel 1928–1940*, ed. Henri Lonitz. 2nd edn, Frankfurt am Main, 1995 [Adorno/Benjamin, *Briefwechsel*].

Theodor W. Adorno and Alban Berg, *Correspondence 1925–1935*, ed. Henri Lonitz, trans. Wieland Hoban, Cambridge: Polity, 2005 [Adorno/Berg, *Correspondence*].

Theodor W. Adorno and Max Horkheimer, *Briefwechsel 1927–1969*, ed. Christoph Gödde and Henri Lonitz, 4 vols, Frankfurt am Main, 2003–6 [Adorno/Horkheimer, *Briefwechsel* 1–4].

Theodor W. Adorno and Ernst Krenek, *Briefwechsel*, ed. Wolfgang Rogge, Frankfurt am Main, 1974 [Adorno/Krenek, *Briefwechsel*].

Theodor W. Adorno and Thomas Mann, *Correspondence 1943–1955*, ed. Christoph Gödde and Thomas Sprecher, trans. Nicholas Walker, Cambridge: Polity, 2006 [Adorno/Mann *Correspondence*].

Theodor W. Adorno and Alfred Sohn-Rethel, *Briefwechsel 1936–1969*, ed. Christoph Gödde, Munich, 1991 [Adorno/Sohn-Rethel, *Briefwechsel*].

'So müßte ich ein Engel und kein Autor sein': Adorno und seine Frankfurter Verleger: Der Briefwechsel mit Peter Suhrkamp und Siegfried Unseld, ed. Wolfgang Schopf, Frankfurt am Main, 2003 [Adorno/Suhrkamp/Unseld, *Briefwechsel*].

Walter Benjamin, *Gesammelte Briefe*, ed. Christoph Gödde and Henri Lonitz, 6 vols, Frankfurt am Main, 1995–2000 [Benjamin, *Gesammelte Briefe* I–VI].

Walter Benjamin, *Gesammelte Schriften*, ed. Rolf Tiedemann and Hermann Schweppenhäuser, with the assistance of Theodor W. Adorno and Gershom Scholem, 7 vols, Frankfurt am Main, 1991 [Benjamin, GS, I–VII].

Ernst Bloch, *Briefe 1903–1975*, ed. Karola Bloch, Jan Robert Bloch, Anne

Frommann, Hanna Gekle, Inge Jens, Martin Korol, Inka Mülder, Arno Münster, Uwe Opolka and Burghart Schmidt, 2 vols, Frankfurt am Main, 1985 [Bloch, *Briefe* 1–2].

Bertolt Brecht, *Werke*, ed. Werner Hecht, Jan Knopf, Werner Mittenzwei and Klaus-Detlef Müller, 30 vols, Berlin, 2000 [Brecht, W I–XXX].

Notker Hammerstein, *Die Johann Wolfgang Goethe-Universität Frankfurt am Main, von der Stiftungsuniversität zur staatlichen Hochschule*, Frankfurt am Main, 1989 [Hammerstein].

Hermann Hesse, *Sämtliche Werke*, ed. Volker Michels, Vols 1–20, Frankfurt am Main, 2000–7 [Hesse, *Sämtliche Werke* {1–20}].

Max Horkheimer, *Gesammelte Schriften*, ed. Alfred Schmidt and Gunzelin Schmid Noerr, 19 vols, Frankfurt am Main, 1988–96 [Horkheimer, GS 1–19].

Siegfried Kracauer, *Schriften*, ed. Karsten Witte, 7 vols, Frankfurt am Main, 1971–90 [Kracauer, S 1–7].

Siegfried Kracauer, *Werke*, ed. Inka Mülder-Bach and Ingrid Belke, 9 vols, Frankfurt am Main, 2004–12 [Kracauer, W 1–9].

Siegfried Kracauer and Erwin Panofsky, *Briefwechsel 1941–1966*, with an appendix: 'Siegfried Kracauer "under the Spell of the Living Warburg Tradition"', ed. Volker Breidecker, Berlin, 1996 [Kracauer/Panofsky, *Briefwechsel*].

Siegfried Kracauer 1889–1996, ed. Ingrid Belke and Irina Renz, *Marbacher Magazin* 47, 1988 [*Marbacher Magazin* 47].

Thomas Levin, *Siegfried Kracauer: Eine Bibliographie seiner Schriften*, Marbach am Neckar, 1989 [Levin {no.}].

Leo Löwenthal and Siegfried Kracauer, *In steter Freundschaft: Leo Löwenthal/Siegfried Kracauer, Briefwechsel 1921–1966*, ed. Peter-Erwin Jansen and Christian Schmidt, Lüneburg, 2003 [Kracauer/Löwenthal, *Briefwechsel*].

Gershom Scholem, *Walter Benjamin – die Geschichte einer Freundschaft*, Frankfurt am Main, 1975 [Scholem, *Freundschaft*].

Alessandra Sorbello Staub, 'Verzeichnis der Veröffentlichungen Leo Löwenthals', in *Das Utopische soll Funken schlagen: Zum hundertsten Geburtstag von Leo Löwenthal*, ed. Peter-Erwin Jansen, Frankfurt am Main, 2000, pp. 182–97 [Löwenthal, 'Veröffentlichungen'].

This edition was made by the Archiv der Peter Suhrkamp Stiftung an der Johann Wolfgang Goethe-Universität in collaboration with the Theodor W. Adorno Archiv, the editors of the complete edition of the works of Siegfried Kracauer, and the Walter Benjamin Archiv. It could not have been realized without the cooperation of Ingrid Belke, Christoph Gödde, Henri Lonitz, Inka Mülder-Bach and Michael Schwarz.

Additional thanks are due to the following for information and assistance: Dorothee Aders, Frank Benseler, Sabine Biebl, Clemens Birnbaum, Volker Breidecker, Ulrich von Bülow, Michael Crone, Anna Czajka, Hildegard Dieke, Hans Peter Dieterich, Hans Magnus Enzensberger, Gunilla Eschenbach, Frank Estelmann, Eberhard Fahlke, Heidrun Fink, Roman Fischer, Ludwig von Friedeburg, Dana Giesecke, Jürgen Habermas, Volker Harms-Ziegler, Rachel Heuberger, Mathias Jehn, Wolfgang Jeske, Thomas Kemme, Alexander Kluge, Dorit Krusche, Reinhard Laube, Christian Lunzer, Willi Luth, Michael Maaser, Wolfgang Maderthaner, Ursula Marx, Elisabeth Matthias, Sabine Melius, Miklós Mesterhazi, Christoph Michel, Olaf Müller, Stefan Müller-Doohm, Michael Orou, Reinhard Pabst, Tobias Picard, Dorothea Rein, Gerhard Richter, Stephen Roeper, Alois Schmidmeier, Gunzelin Schmid Noerr, Alfred Schmidt, Ingolf Schulte, Roswitha Schure, Wolfram Schütte, Gudrun Schwarz, Hermann Schweppenhäuser, Bernd Schwibs, Joachim Seng, Nancy Shawcross, Heinz Steinert, Petra Uhlmann, Johannes Wachten, Ian Wallace, Karlheinz Weigand, Erdmut Wizisla and Friedrich Wolfzettel.

Index

Page numbers in *italics* indicate notes.